CW01159688

ISLAND HOPPING IN TASMANIA'S ROARING FORTIES

By the same author:
Instructions to Young Ornithologists. IV. Sea Birds
A Naturalist in New Zealand
Sub-Antarctic Sanctuary: Summertime on Macquarie Island
Town Bred: Country Nurtured
Islands of the Trade Winds
The Garth Countryside
Sand Dunes
Rivers
Limestone Downs
Coastal Downs
Sea Cliffs
The Natural History of Gower
Swansea Bay's Green Mantle

Island Hopping In Tasmania's Roaring Forties

Mary E. Gillham

Mary E. Gillham

ARTHUR H. STOCKWELL LTD.
Elms Court   Ilfracombe   Devon
Established 1898

© *Mary E. Gillham, 2000*
First published in Great Britain, 2000
All rights reserved.
*No part of this publication may be reproduced
or transmitted in any form or by any means,
electronic or mechanical, including photocopy,
recording, or any information storage and
retrieval system, without permission
in writing from the copyright holder.*

*British Library Cataloguing-in-Publication Data.
A catalogue record for this book is available
from the British Library.*

Wrapper Illustration — Nesting Crested Terns,
Pigface and granite. The Furneaux Group

ISBN 0 7223 3296-3
*Printed in Great Britain by
Arthur H. Stockwell Ltd.
Elms Court   Ilfracombe
Devon*

ISLAND HOPPING IN TASMANIA'S ROARING FORTIES

SYNOPSIS

This is the story of an English naturalist who spent three summers on the Bass Strait and other small islands around Tasmania helping with research into the viability of the Mutton Bird Industry and its relationship with grazing, burning and other forms of land management.

It is an anecdotal account of adventures on small boats and small planes and an extended tour on the lighthouse relief ship, SS *"Cape York"*, long since replaced by helicopter servicing.

Encounters with wildlife, both on and offshore, are described, with emphasis on the sea birds and especially the mutton birds (short-tailed shearwaters) and the stalwart characters who spend part of each summer roughing it on the islands to harvest them — for meat, fat, oil and feathers.

The main research base was a two-roomed hut on a two-acre island off Flinders Island, the largest of the Furneaux Group in Eastern Bass Strait. Two final chapters deal with a similar community to that of Flinders — of ex-soldier settlers, farmers, fishermen and birders — on King Island in the Western strait.

Other islands visited range north across Bass Strait along the coast of Victoria and around the east, south and west coasts of Tasmania — terrain very different from the often forested interior described by most travellers to this beautiful temperate Island State.

Most of the action takes place during 1958-1960, but the main regions have been re-visited in the late 1980s and early 1990s and changes recorded.

MARY E. GILLHAM

ACKNOWLEDGMENTS

This work was made possible by generous research grants from CSIRO and the Tasmanian Fauna Board and the good offices of the late Dr Dominic Serventy, director of scientific work on the mutton bird project.

I am greatly indebted to these and to all those islanders, farmers and fishermen, who offered help and hospitality in the field — also to my fellow scientists, particularly Bill Mollison, who shared the day-to-day tasks. There are too many to name them all, but special mention must be made of Leila Barrett, Derek Smith, Atholl Dart and Tom Langley on Flinders Island, Max McGarvie on King Island and Karl Jaeger in the Hunter Group. Warm memories remain of Captain Heriot and the crew of SS "*Cape York*" and the lighthouse keepers and their wives who welcomed us to their remote strongholds.

I have drawn freely on the published work of Irynej Skira who has made a painstaking study of mutton birds during the years following my sojourn on the islands and produced a considered assessment of their current status.

CONTENTS

Chapter
1. **Flinders Island, an Introduction**
    1. I meet the Islanders. — 23
    2. Blackboys, Wombats and Possums — 31
    3. The seamier side of Island Life — 39
2. **Flinders Island: Birds, Lagoons and Mountains**
    1. Some new angles on the Mutton Bird — 45
    2. South-eastern Lagoons — 51
    3. Exploring the Strzelecki Mountains — 59
3. **Flinders Island: Seafarers, Farmers and Naturalists**
    1. Of Ships and Straitsmen — 65
    2. Wresting a Living from the Land — 73
    3. Naturalists at large — 81
4. **Flinders Island Updated**
    1. Old Acquaintance, new Sanctuary — 89
    2. Settlement Point and Wybalena Historic Site — 97
    3. Trousers Point and the South — 105
5. **Flinders Island: Filling in More Gaps**
    1. West Coast Tour — 113
    2. Spewings of the Tide in the North and East — 119
    3. Franklin Sound and some Islands revisited — 127
6. **Stock Raising Islands Across Franklin Sound**
    1. Cape Barren Island — 135
    2. Vansittart and Puncheon Islands — 141
    3. Tin Kettle and Woody Islands — 149
7. **Fisher Island: Home From Home**
    1. Shearwaters, Oystercatchers and Herons — 157
    2. Visiting Birds and absent Boats — 165
    3. Sea Life and Fishermen — 173
8. **Fisher Island and the Happy Hermit**
    1. Life on the Home Front, human, avian and floral — 181
    2. Our resident Mutton Birds — 191
    3. Life between the Tides — 199
9. **Going to the Dogs**
    1. Rookery Fires on Little and Great Dog Islands — 207
    2. Birders' Huts, Geese and other Wildlife — 215
    3. I join Great Dog Island Bird Harvesters — 223
10. **More of the Rookery Islands in Franklin Sound**
    1. The Economics of the Bird Harvest — 231
    2. On and around the Dog Islands — 237
    3. Little Green Island: a Rookery reprieved — 243

11. The Babel Group and Cat Island Gannetry
1. Success at last — 251
2. All Go on Babel Island — 257
3. Cat Island Gannets — 265

12. Cat Island's Other Wildlife
1. Snakes, Skinks, Gulls and Terns — 275
2. Fur Seals and Shearwaters — 281
3. Penguins and matters Marine — 289

13. Lesser Sea Bird Islands in the Sound
1. White-faced Storm Petrel Colonies — 297
2. Shag and Tern Colonies — 305
3. Billy Goat or Scotts Reefs — 311

14. Big Black Tiger Snakes
1. February Visit to Big Green and Mount Chappell Islands — 317
2. With Eric Worrell in pursuit of Reptiles — 327
3. Catching Snakes on Mount Chappell Island — 335

15. Final Fling on the Furneaux Group and Beyond
1. Living with Poisonous Snakes — 343
2. Goose Island Lighthouse Renovations — 351
3. To Deal Island and the Kent Group — 359

16. More Islands in Eastern Bass Strait
1. Aboard SS *"Cape York"* to the Glennie Group — 367
2. Citadel Island, Wilsons Promontory and the Ansers — 375
3. Gabo and Cliffy Islands — 381

17. South with *"Cape York"* Through the Tasman Sea
1. Swan Island, Eddystone Point and Cape Forestier — 389
2. Tasman Island and the South — 397
3. Loading and off-loading Livestock, Bruny Island — 405

18. Landings by Sea and Air on Some Western Isles
1. Maatsuyker in the De Witt Group — 411
2. By 'Tiger Moth' to Trefoil Island in the Hunter Group — 419
3. Trefoil Island's Mutton-birders and Steep Island — 425

19. Airborne Visits to More North-Western Isles
1. Hunter Island and the Stack — 431
2. Three Hummock, Sandy and Stony Petrel Islands and Walker Island — 437
3. Robbins Island — 443

20. King Island in Midwinter
1. Land Settlement Scheme and northern Mutton Birds — 447
2. Skinner's Graveyard and Yellow Rock Lagoon — 455
3. Eroding Dunes and Limey Concretions — 461

21. King Island in Midsummer
1. Northern Farmlands — 467
2. East Coast Mammals, Minerals and Penguin Parade — 475
3. Southern Calcified Forest and Kelp Harvest at Currie — 483

Appendix Lists — 491

TEXT ILLUSTRATIONS

Chapter
Fig.   1. Map of Islands around Tasmania
       2. Map of Islands of the Furneaux Group, East Bass Strait
1.1.   3. Manuka or Broom Tea-tree *Leptospermum scoparium*
       4. Eastern Water Rat *Hydromys chrysogaster*
       5. Grass-leaved Trigger Plant *Stylidium graminifolium* and Broom Spurge *Amperea xiphoclada*
1.2.   6. Grass Tree or Blackboy *Xanthorrhoea australis*
       7. Wombat *Vombatus ursinus*
       8. Mammal Tracks, Wallaby, Wombat and Echidna
1.3.   9. Ring-tail Possum *Pseudocheirus peregrinus*
      10. Bennets Wallaby *Wallabia rufogrisea*
      11. Creeping Monkey Flower *Mimulus repens* and a white button daisy *Nablonium (Ammobium) calyceratum*
2.1. 12. Lady Barron Store in 1958
      13. Prickly Moses, *Acacia verticillata*
      14. Insectivorous Sundew *Drosera peltata* and parasitic Dodder-laurel *Cassytha glabella*
2.2. 15. Swamp Isotome *I. fluviatilis* and yellow water buttons *Cotula coronopifolia*
      16. Short Purple Iris *Pattersonia fragilis*
      17. Small Poranthera *P. microphylla* and Hairy Centrolepis *C. strigosa*
2.3. 18. Veined Bristle Fern *Polyphlebium venosum* and Austral Filmy Fern *Hymenophyllum australe*
      19. Yellow-throated Honey-eater *Lichenostomus flavicollis* and Sassafras *Atherospermum moschatum*
      20. Mountain Pepper *Tasmannia lanceolata* and Striated Rock Orchid *Dendrobium striolatum*
3.1. 21. Pacific Gull *Larus pacificus* and old Sailing Ship
      22. Wilsons Storm Petrels *Oceanites oceanicus* commonly seen at sea
      23. White-backed Magpie *Gymnorhina tibicen*
3.2. 24. Swamp Honey Myrtle *Melaleuca squamea*
      25. Love Creeper *Comesperma volubile*
      26. South African Boxthorn *Lycium ferocissimum*
3.3. 27. Brush-tail Possum *Trichosurus vulpecula*
      28. Swamp Club Moss *Selaginella uliginosa*
      29. Common Flat Pea *Platylobium obtusangulum*
4.1. 30. Wind-trimmed Coast Beard Heath *Leucopogon parviflorus*
      31. Cape Barren Geese *Cereops novae-hollandiae*
      32. Forty Spotted Pardelote *Pardalotus quadragintus* and Manna Gum *Eucalyptus viminalis*

4.2.	33.	Bladder Pea *Gompholobium hugelii*
	34.	Tasmanian Thornbill *Acanthiza ewingii* and Scented Paperbark *Melaleuca squarrosa*
	35.	Eastern Spinebill *Acanthorhynchos tenuirostris* and Yellow Dogwood *Pomaderris elliptica*
4.3	36.	A Wild Pea *Dillwynia glaberrima*
	37.	Starry-leaved Daisy Bush *Olearia stellulata* and blunt-leaved Heath *Epacris obtusifolia*
	38.	Water Milfoil *Myriophyllum salsugineum*
5.1.	39.	White Butterfly Iris *Diplarrena moraea* and Large Leek Lily *Bulbine bulbosa*
	40.	Stinkwood *Ziera arborescens*
	41.	Swamp Heath *Sprengelia incarnata*
5.2.	42.	Cunjevoi Sea Squirts *Pyura stolonifera*, Pencil Urchin *?Phyllocanthus irregularis*, Mermaid's Glove Sponge *Haliclona* and a Holothurian *Paracaudinia*
	43.	Cuttlefish Eggs *Sepiatheuthis australis*
	44.	Cup Sponge *Phyllospongia* and Finger Sponge *Chalinopsilla*
5.3.	45.	Sea Dragon *Phyllopteryx taeniolatus*, Green Algal Ball *Codium mamillosum*, Sponge *Sycon* and Sipunculid *Phascolosoma noduliferum*
	46.	Portugese Man-of-War *Physalia physalis*
	47.	Encrusting Moss-animals *Densipora corrugata* and Corallite *Pleisiastrea versipora*
6.1.	48.	Echidna *Tachyglossus setosus*
	49.	White *Kunzea ambigua*
	50.	Grey-backed Silver-eyes *Zosterops lateralis* and Drooping She-oke *Allocasuarina verticillata*
6.2.	51.	Pink Bindweed *Convolvulus erubescens*
	52.	Four Grasses, *Deyeuxia quadriseta, Paspalum dilatatum, Echinopogon ovatus* and *Lolium multiflorum*
	53.	White-fronted Chat *Ephthianura albifrons* and 'Couch' Grass *Cynodon dactylon*
6.3.	54.	Rough-beaked Mussels *Hormomya erosa*, Flame Dog Cockles *Glycymerus flammeus* and Buffalo Grass *Stenotaphrum secundatum*
	55.	Yorkshire Fog *Holcus lanatus*, Great Brome *Bromus diandrus* and Marram Grass *Ammophila arenaria*
	56.	Yellow Wood-sorrel *Oxalis corniculata* and Australian Salt Grass *Distichlis distichophylla*
7.1.	57.	Short-tailed Shearwater *Puffinus tenuirostris* and egg
	58.	Sooty Oystercatchers *Haematopus fuliginosus* displaying
	59.	Silver Gulls *Larus novaehollandiae* displaying aggressively
7.2.	60.	Pied Oystercatchers *Haematopus longirostris*
	61.	Drake Musk Duck *Biziura lobata*
	62.	Chestnut-breasted Shelduck or Mountain Duck *Tadorna tadornoides*
7.3.	63.	Crayfish or Spiny Rock Lobster *Jasus lalandii*

	64.	Flounder *Pleuronectes* and Cuttlefish *Sepia* 'bone'
	65.	Painted Lady *Phasianella*, Keyhole Limpet *Amblichilepas* and Orange-edged Limpet *Cellana*
8.1.	66.	Fruits and Crop Pellets of Taupata or New Zealand Mirror Plant *Coprosma repens*
	67.	Wind-scorched Taupata *Coprosma repens*
	68.	Germinating Strap-weed Seedlings *Posidonia australis*
8.2.	69.	Development of Short-tailed Shearwater Chick *Puffinus tenuirostris*
	70.	"The Thing"
	71.	Shearwaters *Puffinus tenuirostris* taking off at dawn
8.3.	72.	Funnel-shaped *Thorecta* and Fingered *Peyssonellia* Sponges
	73.	Black-faced Cormorants *Leucocarbo fuscescens*
	74.	Black's Glasswort *Sarcocornia blackiana* and Beaded Glasswort *Sarcocornia quinqueflora*
9.1.	75.	Erosion after Fire, leaving inadequate soil for burrowing
	76.	Stools of Silver Tussock *Poa poiformis* after fire and erosion
	77.	Pelicans *Pelecanus conspicillatus*
9.2.	78.	Birders' Hut with brick chimney on Little Dog Island
	79.	A Skink *Leiolopisma* and Stunted Pigface *Disphyma crassifolium*
	80.	A Mountain Dragon Lizard *Amphibolurus diemensis*
9.3.	81.	Bench Mark on Big Hill, Great Dog: View to NW of Little Dog
	82.	Try Pots in which Mutton Birds were formerly melted for their fat
	83.	Mutton-birder Carries Chicks through Rookery
10.1.	84.	Squeezing Oil and Gurrie from Mutton Bird Chicks outside hatch
	85.	Diagram of typical Processing Shed
	86.	Boiler for scalding Mutton Birds
10.2.	87.	Boxes of fresh Mutton Birds going off by sea
	88.	Rare White Mutton Bird Chick, fifth in succession in the same burrow
	89.	Large Black Cormorants *Phalacrocorax carbo*
10.3.	90.	Cormorant Chicks, early stages of development
	91.	Bower Spinach *Tetragonia implexicoma*
	92.	Old Man's Beard *Clematis aristata*
11.1.	93.	Map of the Babel Group
	94.	Aboriginal rowing water tank into Babel Island
	95.	Cormorants in flight
11.2.	96.	Leafy Pepper-cress *Lepidium foliosum*, Coast Candles *Stackhousia spathulata* and Sea Celery *Apium prostratum*
	97.	Pigface *Disphyma crassifolim ssp clavellatum*: three forms in relation to exposure
	98.	Gannets *Morus (Sula) serrator*: mutual preening
11.3.	99.	Gannets: Scissoring display and sleeping
	100.	Gannets: Development of Chick
	101.	Gannets coming in to land
12.1.	102.	Leek Lily *Bulbine semibarbata*
	103.	Feet modified for swimming: Cormorant, Penguin, Tern

          104. Feeding chicks of Gull and Shearwater
12.2. 105. Australian Fur Seal *Arctocephalus pusillus*
          106. Australian Fur Seal harem
          107. Short-tailed Shearwaters *Puffinus tenuirostris* in flight
12.3. 108. Pied Oystercatchers *Haematopus longirostris*
          109. Little Blue Penguins *Eudyptula minor*: Half Trumpet and Full Trumpet display
          110. Awkward Gait due to backward displacement of legs: Penguin and Shearwater
13.1. 111. Map of White-faced Storm Petrel Colonies in Franklin Sound
          112. White-faced Storm Petrels *Pelagodroma marina*
          113. Silver Gulls *Larus novaehollandiae*
13.2. 114. Silver Gulls flying over Nesting Colony
          115. Crested Terns *Sterna bergii*
          116. Kidney Weed *Dichondra repens*
13.3. 117. Sea Wrack *Halophila australis*
          118. Abalone Shell, Brown Seaweed *Phyllospora comosa* and Sea Urchin test
          119. Turtle Grass *Amphibolis antarctica*
14.1. 120. Blue-tongue Lizard *Tiliqua nigrolutea* with flowering Pigface *Disphyma crassifolium*
          121. Freehand sketch of Mount Chappell Island
          122. Austral Storksbill *Pelargonium australe*
14.2. 123. Pale Rush *Juncus pallidus* and Spiny Mat Rush *Lomandra longifolia*
          124. Barilla, Grey or Coast Saltbush *Atriplex cinerea*
          125. Seaberry Saltbush *Rhagodia candolleana*
14.3. 126. Mutton Bird Chick and Black Tiger Snake *Notechis scutatus*
          127. Black Tiger Snake *Notechis scutatus serventii*
          128. Tiger Snake basking: Sea Celery *Apium prostratum*
15.1. 129. Superb Blue Wren *Malurus cyaneus* and Native 'Fuchsia' *Correa reflexa*
          130. Prickly Broom Heath *Monotoca scoparia* and Blunt-leaved Heath *Epacris obtusifolia*
          131. Boobialla *Myoporum insulare* flowers
15.2. 132. Boobialla *Myoporum insulare* fruits
          133. Goose Island Lighthouse
          134. Climbing Lignum *Muehlenbeckia adpressa*
15.3. 135. Starry and Coast Daisy Bushes *Olearia stellulata* and *O. axillaris*
          136. Coast Twin-leaf *Zygophyllum billardieri*
          137. Deal Island Lighthouse
16.1. 138. Sketch Map of the Glennies and Ansers off Wilsons Promontory
          139. Cape Barren Geese *Cereopsis novaehollandiae* on Dannevig Island with SS "*Cape York*" and Citadel Island
          140. Fairy Prions *Pachyptila turtur*
16.2. 141. Cape Barren Geese *(Cereopsis)* in flight: SS "*Cape York*" and the Ansers

         142. Sooty Oystercatcher *Haematopus fuliginosus* and Sea Rocket *Cakile edentula*
         143. Tattered Coastal Paperbarks *Melaleuca ericifola*
16.3. 144. Automatic Lighthouse on Citadel Island, view north
         145. Dusky Coral Pea *Kennedya rubicunda*
         146. White-fronted Tern *Sterna striata*
17.1. 147. Swan Island Lighthouse
         148. Wedding Bush *Ricinocarpos pinifolia*
         149. Spotted Sun Orchid *Thelymitra ixioides* and Blue *Dampiera stricta*
17.2. 150. Map of South-east Tasmania
         151. Winged Spyridium *Spyridium vexilliferum* and Swampweed *Selliera radicans*
         152. White Correa *Correa alba* and Coast Pink Berry *Cyathodes abietina*
17.3. 153. Cape Bruny Lighthouse
         154. Flame Robin *Petroica phoenicea* and Seaberry Saltbush *Rhagodia candolleana*
         155. Potoroo or Long-nosed Kangaroo Rat *Potorous tridactylus*
18.1. 156. Brush-tail Possum *Trichosurus vulpecula*
         157. Red-bellied Pademelon *Thylogale billardierii* and Austral Seablite *Suaeda australis*
         158. Marsupial Mouse *Antechinus minimus* and Subterranean Clover *Trifolium subterraneum*
18.2. 159. Masked Lapwing or Spur-winged Plover *(Vanellus miles)*
         160. Map of North-western Islands: the Hunter Group
         161. Mutton Bird *Puffinus tenuirostris* and Swamp Paperbark *Melaleuca ericifolia*
18.3. 162. Sea Bird Beaks: Pelican, Gannet, Gull, Shearwater
         163. Black or Grey Duck *Anas superciliosa*
         164. Ross's Noonflower or Karkalla *Carpobrotus rossii*
19.1. 165. Silver Banksia *Banksia marginata*
         166. Variable Groundsel *Senecio pinnatifolius* and Rough Fireweed *Senecio hispidulus*
         167. Nankeen Kestrel *Falco cenchroides* and Shiny Cassinia *Cassinia longifolia*
19.2. 168. Green Rosella *Platycercus caledonicus* and Sweet Wattle *Acacia suaveolens*
         169. Grey Fantail *Rhipidura fuliginosa* and Common Heath *Epacris impressa*
         170. Beautiful Firetail Finch *Emblema bella* and Juniper Wattle *Acacia ulicifolia*
19.3. 171. Blackwood *Acacia melanoxylon*
         172. White-faced Herons *Ardea novaehollandiae*
         173. Silver Gulls *Larus novaehollandiae*
20.1. 174. Map of King Island
         175. Large Black and Black-faced Cormorants *Phalacrocorax carbo* and *Leucoarbo fuscescens*

    176. Coast Wattle *Acacia longifolia var. sophorae*
20.2. 177. Stinkwood *Ziera arborescens*
    178. Black Currawong *Strepera fuliginosus* and Box *Alyxia buxifolia*
    179. Coast Tea-tree *Leptospermum laevigatum*
20.3. 180. Brush Bronzewing Pigeon *Phaps elegans* and Running Postman *Kennedya prostrata*
    181. Hoary-headed Grebe *Poliocephalus poliocephalus*
    182. Red-capped Plover or Dotterel *Charadrius ruficapillus* and Slender Twine-rush *Leptocarpus tenax*
21.1. 183. Flax Lily *Dianella revoluta*, Coast Swainson Pea *Swainsonia lessertifolia* and Spotted Sun Orchid *Thelymitra ixioides*
    184. Brown Quail *Coternix ypsilophorus* and Tassel Rope-rush *Hypolaena fastigiata*
    185. Wickham Lighthouse, King Island
21.2. 186. Sea Elephant Bull *Mirounga leonina*
    187. Diving Petrels *Pelecanoides urinatrix* and Hairy Pennywort *Hydrocotyle hirta*
    188. Little Blue Penguin *Eudyptula minor* moulting among Pigface *Disphyma crassifolium*
21.3. 189. Metre-high Calcified Concretions on King Island Dunes
    190. Currie Lighthouse, King Island
    191. White-bellied Sea Eagle *Haliaeetus leucogaster*

LIST OF COLOUR PLATES
Illustrated section set between pp 256–257

I	1.	Land cleared for polled Hereford cattle. Whitemark, Flinders Island, 1960
	2. & 3.	Unloading roan and brindle cattle from the deck of *"Prion"* 1959
II	4.	Loading superphosphate for aerial top dressing. Flinders Island
	5.	*Kunzea ambigua* on Big Dog Island
	6.	Grass Tree fruiting spikes damaged by Yellow-tailed Black Cockatoos
III	7.	Yacca Gum crusher, Lady Barron. The Grass Tree material from Cape Barren Island
	8.	Grass Tree leaf bases from which resin is extracted
	9.	Yacca Gum exuded from Grass Tree in bushfire
IV	10.	Derek Smith with newly-caught Wombat, 1958
	11.	Brush-tail Possum: a Tasmanian 'black' from Mount Wellington
	12.	Echidna or Spiny Ant-eater
	13.	Pademelon or Rufous Wallaby Joey whose dam has been shot

V	14.	Trousers Point. South-west Flinders Island, 1958
	15.	Granite Peak above Dock, North-west Flinders Island, 1995
	16.	Castle Rock, Marshalls Bay, dwarfs beach walkers alongside, 1995
VI	17.	Mutton Bird or Short-tailed Shearwater and egg in nesting burrow
	18.	Adult Mutton Bird in the hand. Note tubular nostrils
VII	19.	Eric Worrell (squatting), Dom Serventy and Tas Drysdale ring a Mutton Bird chick on Fisher Island
	20.	Silver Gulls wait for breakfast outside the Fisher Island research hut
VIII	21	The author with "Half Safe" on the Fisher Island slip. Reef Island and Strzelecki Peaks beyond
	22.	Blue Penguin chick and Austral Storksbill on Scotts Reef
	23.	The author after rowing to Big Dog Island, 1959
IX	24.	A Cape Barren Islander prepares for the bird harvest on Chappell Island
	25	Bill Riddle carries Mutton Bird chicks in on Big Dog Island
X	26.	Paper Nautilus shells
	27.	Collection of sponges from Fisher Island
	28.	Marine treasures, Fisher Island
XI	29.	Crested Terns rise from Tuck's Reef
	30	Tuck's little boat off a Crested Tern colony in Franklin Sound
XII	31.	Crested Terns with fish
	32.	Cape Barren Goose
	33.	Remnant of the Gannetry on Cat Island, 1958
XIII	34.	Eric Worrell bags a black Tiger Snake among Chappell Island Barilla
	35.	Painting Goose Island lighthouse
	36.	Ross's Noon Flower
XIV	37.	Doleritic Columnar Basalt, Tasman Island, South-east Tasmania
	38.	Coast Cheeseberry or Pink berry on Tasman Island summit
	39.	Exhausted cow after swimming to Bruny Island from SS *"Cape York"*
XV	40.	Maatsuyker Island lighthouse and Brownie, off South-west Tasmania
	41.	Maatsuyker Island, South-west Tasmania. Temperate rainforest vegetation
XVI	42.	Corner of Steep Head Island, North-west Tasmania, viewed from 'Tiger Moth'
	43.	Calcareous concretions exposed by erosion on King Island dunes, North-west Tasmania

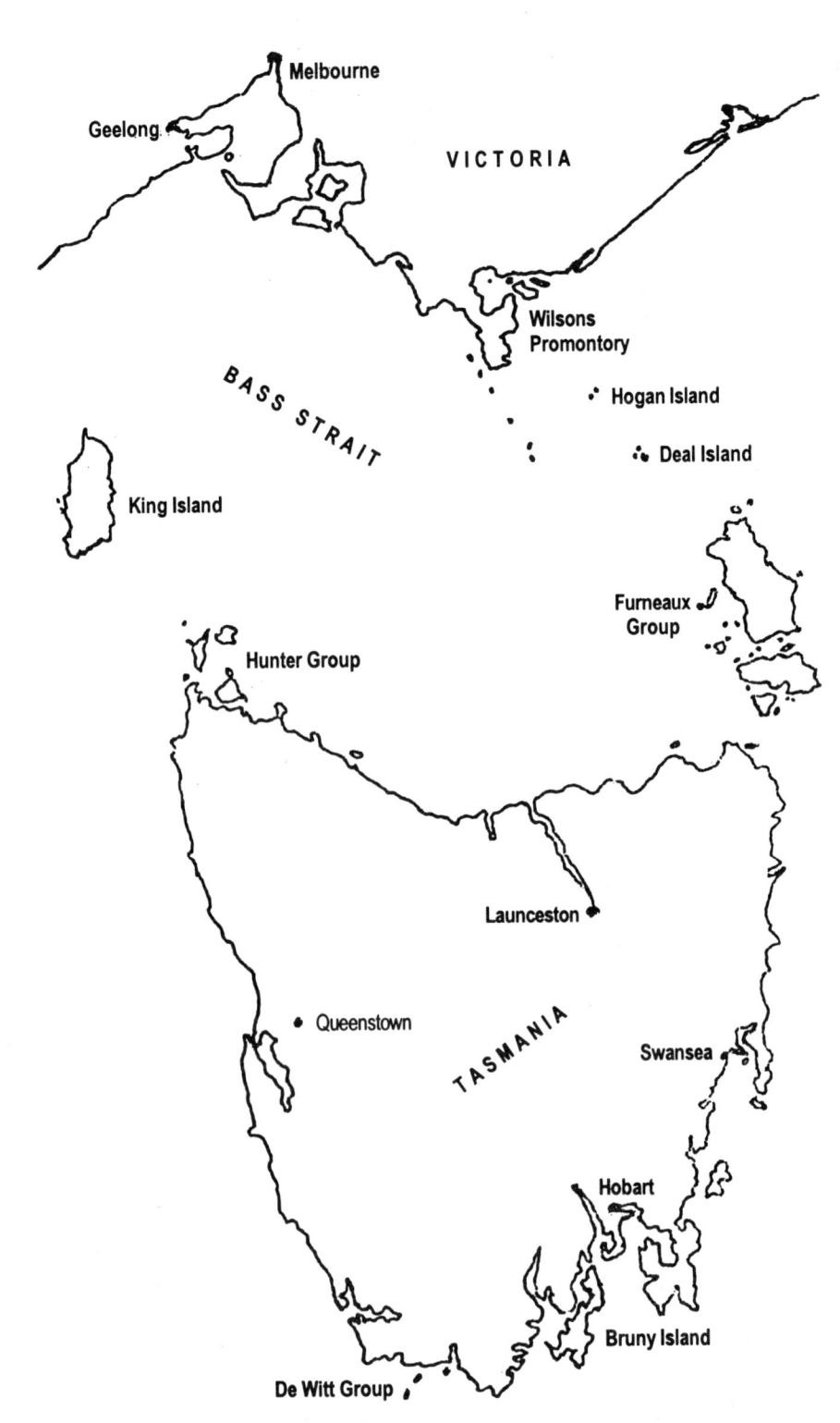

1 Map of Islands around Tasmania

2 Map of Islands of the Furneaux Group, East Bass Strait

Introduction

Remarkable environments support remarkable wildlife, which provide unusual livelihoods for humans. The scattered, wave-lashed islands of Bass Strait and other scraps of land around Australia's only island state is such an environment.

In the early years the people lived by sealing, in later years by fishing and cattle raising. In between the mainstay of many was mutton birds (short-tailed shearwaters) leading to a way of life almost unique to the Bass Strait islanders and New Zealand Maoris.

Bird harvesting has continued into modern times, unlike the cull taken by Scottish islanders of long ago, who scoured their cliffs for gannets and puffins to tide them over long hungry winters. Products of Tasmanian harvests appear in poultry and fish shops in Launceston, Hobart and Melbourne still, although dwindling in the 1990s. This tale is set in the period of the islands' history when the trade was in full swing.

The region appeared on the world's maps only two hundred years ago and the strong element of Scottish seafarers among the pioneering white settlers probably needed little persuasion to join the natives in eking out a living with the local wildfowl.

They were followed by a steady influx of Britishers, seeking a different way of life from the over-crowded, over-tamed one of home, in a climate resembling the one they had left behind. They merged with indigenous Aboriginals and white Australians drifting down from the states to the north — to form an independent, self-reliant breed whose destiny was closely bound up with the sea.

The founding fathers were hardy, rough-mannered sealers, who took Aboriginal wives and produced a tough sea-going breed known as the Straitsmen. Aboriginal blood is thinly distributed now, but Cape Barren Island in the main eastern archipelago of the Furneaux Group became the home of most of the remnants of the ill-fated Tasmanian Blacks.

Sea elephants were exterminated or retreated south to sub-antarctic islands: fur seals suffered a fate almost as final but are now moving back. Short-tailed shearwaters were present in such vast numbers and are so long lived that huge harvests of young birds taken over the years did little more than dent the population figures. Carcases were salted down for long-term sustenance with a surplus for export, along with the cash crops of oil and feathers.

Other harvests came from the sea, crayfish probably the most important. There was a wealth of wallabies and marine life to bait the cray pots but gannets and penguins were easier to come by. The gannets were wiped out as breeders: the penguins, nesting in the sanctuary of underground burrows, withstood the onslaught better.

Utilisation of the land for agriculture got off to a bad start, with livestock dying of mineral deficiencies and poisonous plants. These difficulties have been largely overcome by modern science, the successful rearing of cattle and sheep altering the composition of the grassland and texture of the soil in which the mutton birds excavate their nest holes. Burning, practised as a management tool, ensures young grass for the animals and easier access to the bird burrows.

The author was here during the three summers of 1958-60, as part of a team to help sort out the pros and cons of pastoral farming and bird harvesting, drawing on experience gained on Manx shearwater islands around Britain and sooty shearwater islands around New Zealand.

Her main Furneaux Group base was a small hut on Fisher Island with a rowing boat link to the settlement on nearby Flinders Island. Most usual mode of transport from island to island was the little mail boat or local fishing craft. A prolonged voyage on the lighthouse relief vessel took her to more outlying islands in and beyond Bass Strait. In the North-west friendly locals took her island hopping in a small plane and trundled her around in four-wheel drive vehicles. Subsequent shorter visits in the 1980s and 1990s have enabled her to update her findings.

Now, in the nineties, mutton-birding has lost favour with many, if not on conservation and humane grounds, because of the labour involved. Some of the islands have been designated as wildlife sanctuaries, others were passed over to the Aboriginals as part of the re-allocation of Crown Lands in the mid-1990s. Bird harvests — part of the local traditional culture — are still taken on some of these. For the rest there is public assistance or less arduous ways of earning a living.

The 1995 returns of the Tasmanian Parks and Wildlife Service (Successor of the old Fauna Board) which controls the industry, gives the current shearwater population as twenty-three million birds breeding in Tasmania and migrating annually across the Pacific Ocean to arctic waters off Alaska.

A mere seven per cent of the offspring are taken from the nests each year during commercial harvesting, with an estimated extra one hundred thousand taken non-commercially (under licence) for family consumption. This is well below the estimated sustainable yield of thirty-seven per cent. More significant is the natural high mortality of juveniles during their first year at sea. Survivors are sufficiently long-lived for the population level to be in no danger from the annual take.

Rather does it owe its equilibrium to what seems at first glance to be a catastrophic slaughter. Had the rookeries not been maintained through the years for the annual gathering of chicks — leaving unharmed the adult 'geese' which lay the golden eggs — the islands might have been turned over to grazing and the massed nesting burrows destroyed.

Man-made disaster, if it strikes, is likely to be from more widespread pollution. A worrying fact coming to light in 1997 is the disappearance of ninety per cent of the world's sooty shearwaters, which are the mainstay of the New Zealand mutton bird industry. American scientists have estimated that four million "sooties" disappeared between 1987 and 1994 as a result, it is thought, of a 0.5 degree Celsius rise in sea temperature, reducing plankton levels by seventy per cent: the first instance of massive losses due to global warming. Hopefully such far-ranging creatures may be able to catch up with the plankton in its migration to more amenable waters.

An important element of the human population, the lighthouse keepers, has gone with the automation of the lights. Necessary servicing is now carried out by the few in helicopters, instead of the many on the relief ship. Coastal shipping generally has dwindled in favour of air freight. Now that life would be so much safer and more comfortable for coast watchers and seafarers, with radio contact and all mod cons, there are few left to enjoy it.

As in outlying communities the world over, the specialist, self-sufficient way of outback life is giving way to tourism. The scenery, coastal and mountain, is superb, the climate absolutely right except for rather too many winds, but these are less icy that those assailing the equally beautiful and much visited islands of Britain's Atlantic fringes.

Conservation measures are helping the wildlife to re-establish: even the odd gannet is returning to fraternise with the painted concrete decoy birds, although none are nesting yet. The story told here — of *Island Hopping in Tasmania's Roaring Forties* — is that of an outsider looking in on a unique way of life that is fast passing into history.

Today's visitors can experience the beauty and diversity of wildlife without having to witness its exploitation. Smart tourist launches have removed the need to hitch a ride in whatever craft is going in an appropriate direction and all the comforts of civilised living can be enjoyed between voyages. The romance of the idyllic seascapes, flowery heathlands and scrub-covered mountainsides is undiminished and provides a refreshing change from the uncomfortable heat and dust of so much of the mainland.

MARY E. GILLHAM   Cardiff, 1997

Chapter One

FLINDERS ISLAND: AN INTRODUCTION

1. I MEET THE ISLANDERS

It had been a wonderful year in New Zealand. I had arrived there from Britain in December 1957 in time for Christmas on the beach, instead of huddled round the yule log. Sea bird islands, the love of my life since I had launched out on those of South-west Wales during my student days, were there in plenty. My bread and butter were in Massey University at Palmerston North, then an Agricultural College, where I was filling in for a year while one of the staff enjoyed sabbatical leave, but this left me plenty of time to explore.

I had been lured to scraps of sea-girt land from the Bay of Islands in the North to Stewart Island a thousand miles to the South. There were tern colonies in Hauraki Gulf and tuataras of ancient reptilian lineage on the islands of Cook Strait. Gannets thronged on Cape Kidnappers and more special royal albatrosses and yellow-eyed penguins on the mainland near Dunedin.

The highlight, however, was to sail among the bushed islands of the far South watching the tremendous flights of mutton birds or sooty shearwaters rafting on the sea surface and to botanise in their nesting colonies. Now, here I was again, a year later, in Australia, about to explore the haunts of those other mutton birds, the short-tailed or slender-billed shearwaters of Bass Strait.

I reached the continent just in time for another sort of summery Christmas on the wheatlands of the Murray Valley near Echuca, travelled south in the New Year to where I was to earn my keep for the next twelve months filling in at Melbourne University, and then boarded a plane for Tasmania in readiness for my debut to another archipelago of islands.

It was 6th January 1958 and I had been in Launceston for several days waiting for a seat on the little aircraft that plied to and from the Furneaux Group. Still very new to Australia, I was revelling in the different way of life and enjoying sight-seeing around this corner of Tasmania. Nevertheless, I was jubilant when the go-ahead came from the airport. This was it: the culmination of months of planning.

Much has been written about how the 'Roaring Forties' manifest themselves at sea level in Bass Strait. They spared some of their energy today for a frolic at 6,000 feet, adding spice to my entry to the promised land. As dark mountains faded through sun-scorched grassland to the open sea, we started to hiccough, so that the remnants of the partly drowned land materialising below seemed to be jigging around on the dark surface of the strait.

The lesser islands were pale blobs of yellow tussock grass patterned with sombre scrub. They lay on an indigo spread coloured by submerged sea-grass beds, but this background changed abruptly to translucent turquoise where the white sand of shoals and beaches neared the sea surface. Granite bastions of Cape Barren Island loomed, impregnable, to our right and the sun-bleached dome of Mount Chappell Island below. Then we were bumping in over the grassy airstrip at Whitemark, there being no surfaced runways in those early days.

The little plane spewed out her load, took on another and was away within minutes, allowing the one-man airport staff to return home for lunch. My destination was the research hut on Fisher Island, which lay beyond the island's other village of Lady Barron, and the driver of the dilapidated airport bus suggested that I hitch a lift on the 3 p.m. mail van.

Whitemark is now a thriving little town with bank, police station, hospital, agricultural and aviation headquarters, several shops, including a pizza takeaway and many houses. In 1958 it seemed to consist of about half a dozen buildings clustered around a dusty crossroads. One of these was an attractive, balconied, colonial-style hotel, the Flinder's Island Interstate, where I enjoyed my last roast meal for many weeks.

I kept my rendezvous with the mail man, whose vehicle bulged with goods piled around an old lady and two children who also needed a lift. The problem of squeezing in another was solved by the arrival of Tom Langley, the Lady Barron storekeeper, who bundled me and my luggage into his truck. Like most islanders, he was a man of many parts, farmer as well as storekeeper and taxi driver, and as we headed south, he explained about the War Service Land Settlement Scheme which had been launched by the Agricultural Bank of Tasmania a few years before. Most land was still under scrub, but clearing had begun on the more amenable lowland soils.

Big machines imported for the job were lumbering across the land like malevolent dinosaurs, sweeping away all in their path — regardless of the persistent ferocity of gales. The soldier-settlers who moved in to farm had therefore to set about planting shelter belts and hedges to protect their crops and stock. Those crops were almost exclusively pasture grasses and clovers, with much of the swampier land having to be drained before these would thrive, even when using strawberry clover instead of the more usual white or subterranean.

Heavy doses of superphosphate were being applied, and lime on the more acid soils. Deficiencies in copper, cobalt and selenium had also to be rectified, as on so many of Southern Australia's maritime grasslands, to forestall the so prevalent 'coast disease' of livestock.

Farm animals at that time were mostly beef cattle, with few sheep or milch cows, and most farmers were said to use powdered milk, although a creamery was to come into being later on. Dairying never got off the ground here, however, as it did on King Island at the other end of Bass Strait where the rains were more reliable, the grass greener and the production of butter and cheese a valuable money-spinner. Flinders lay in the rain shadow of Tasmania when water from the Indian Ocean was brought by south-westerlies rather than westerlies and the land was more prone to summer drought.

Swamp harriers cruised over the newly-drained swamps, wondering, perhaps, where lunch had gone, and the broad rump of a wombat disappeared into roadside tea-tree scrub. Coiled up in a capacious pothole was one of Bass Strait's black tiger snakes, the first of many that I was to encounter during my travels around the outer isles.

At Lady Barron I was led into the store from the rear and displayed to the locals, who converged on Monday, Wednesday and Friday to collect their mail and freshly-baked bread. They had been expecting me and every new face in so small a community creates a diversion. Many handshakes later, Jerry Addaway took me down through the fringing trees to show me my new island home. The dinghy was not on the granite slope which served as a slip, so we decided that the current residents must be ashore somewhere.

I had phoned the local officer-of-the-law, Trooper Lew Bailey, on arrival and he had waved and shouted to attract the islanders' attention to come and get me. This they were combining with a leg-stretch and the collection of stores, and so it was that I was whisked away to my first session in that little island paradise that was to be my home for many weeks during the next three years.

* * * * * *

On that initial crossing the 'seas between' were unbelievably calm, but it was not always like that and we needed to come and go quite often for stores. My diary for 10th January records a different state of affairs. The sun still shone from a cloudless vault, but the wind was more than brisk — the sort of day that had earned itself the title of 'island weather' during my prolonged stays on islands of Britain's Atlantic fringes in past years.

We needed bread and meat, so I joined Eric and Dell Lindgren, young West Australian teachers helping with the research project during their summer hols, for a trip ashore. I rowed on the way in, with a roaring forty behind, and we careered across like a ballistic missile, gyrating steadily to leeward until we reached the tricky bit of negotiating the half-submerged piles of the old jetty. We steered through the upstanding ones of the new without splintering anything, but had to work hard to swing the clumsy wooden boat round to the jetty steps.

Normally the landing was on the low rocky platform to windward, but we spared her the inevitable pounding there today. "Half Safe", as she was so aptly called, had suffered a bruising the night before, when hungry waves had lifted her off the slip and banged her playfully against the granite alongside until the tide retreated, leaving her listing on slightly frayed timbers.

Folk at the store were worried as to how we might get back. Seventy-four-year-old Tuck Robinson, who delivered mail and stores to Cape Barren Island and was a legend in his own lifetime, said he would tow us back. Lew Bailey said we would never make it. Derek Smith, baker and naturalist, hailing from a long line of vets, said "Wait till the tide turns at sunset, you might have a chance then."

These good-hearted islanders knew we were going to have a bash at it when we'd got our goods, so they waited around to see if they would be needed.

With Eric at the oars, Dell and I handled our way under the jetty into the full blast. He strained hard and we moved steadily sideways, even moreso when I took the stroke oar in the bow to help out, in fact hindering because I could not pull as hard as he. Although fairly wet, we were in no danger and could picture ourselves landing up on a pleasant sandy beach a couple of miles to leeward. We needed to go athwart the wind but headed into it with the idea of coming ashore to windward and towing the boat on to give the necessary leeway when we finally took off. It didn't work. The shoreline that side, although fairly level, was rock strewn. We were swept back under the jetty again, ducking low as a wave lifted us through.

Tuck's boat was aground by then and he had passed his self-imposed responsibility on to Bill Barrett, a ruddy-faced man in a well-salted digger hat. In twenty minutes our rescuer had rustled up a crewman and come round in his twenty-foot powered launch. We and the stores — much of the sugar now dissolved in the bilge water — went aboard, with "Half Safe" made fast astern. He left us on the leeward side of our island and we eased her round the rocks to the slip, hauling her well up to prevent a repeat of the previous night.

It wasn't much better when Eric and I went over on the 18th January, to keep tryst with Derek Smith, who had promised us a 'kangaroo hunt', although Bennets Wallabies *(Wallabia rufogrisea)* were the nearest one could get to 'roos here. We bolted down our crayfish lunch (we had our own crayfish pot a little offshore) and did not run with the wind this time but rowed athwart it to beach the boat where we would get a good start on the return trip. Creeping round in a westward arc, we were sheltered by Reef Island and a series of lesser reefs now above water, but we had a long walk through the shallows at the end. Derek met us on the beach.

"I didn't expect you. How are you going to get back?"

A good question. He helped haul and anchor, then brightened.

"I suppose you could sleep in the baker's dough bowl if you get marooned."

He went off to rustle up a vehicle, leaving his two dachshunds digging hysterically in the sand, each pretending the other was some tantalisingly desirable prey. When the two excavations met below ground, they slunk off, simulating unconcern.

It was these two who would leap out of Derek's boat when they spotted a water rat swimming past, and chase it round in circles, although they had little idea what to do with it when they caught up. Brought up on mental images of "Ratty" and "Moley" in their willowy river, I was surprised to see water rats in the sea. These were dinkum natives, *Hydromys chrysogaster*, although non-marsupials.

Long and lean, like robust ferrets, they had orange tums and black upper parts, swimming gracefully, like little otters, by day as well as night, and were comparatively easy to catch in nets. They put me in mind of the unrelated mink as they scavenged along the island shores and explored bird burrows in search of eggs or chicks. Seeking out gobies and other small fish and prawns in shoreline pools, they also made short work of prising the abundant mussels off the rocks. Their freshwater counterparts — a common sight along inland waterways, ate yabbies, and snails as well as fish fry.

To keep them warm and dry they wore dense under-fur protected by long guard hairs, so were persecuted by fur trappers in the early days. Around 40,000 pelts were exported in a single year when the fur trade was at its height.

The dachshund bitch, I learned later, was a motherly soul and would nurse anything according to her master. She had reared young wallabies and brooded a box of day-old chicks deserted by the hen-in-charge. The brush-tail possum joey which she had adopted would ride around on her withers, despite her unfamiliar shape. Indeed, the youngster was not fussy, riding on Derek's sinewy shoulder too, when opportunity offered.

The only four-wheel drive vehicle available was earmarked to take a load of children to the 'cinema' at Whitemark, so we set off on foot for the first of many treks to the local viewpoint of Vinegar Hill. Thirteen-year-old Lynette Smith, the oldest of Derek's six, came with us and was fascinated by the showy pink flowers of the grass-leaved trigger plant *(Stylidium graminifolium)* when we demonstrated the trigger mechanism by which it exchanges pollen with its insect visitors. An odd little plant with clusters of peppery yellow flowers on a leafless ridged stem, was the broom spurge *(Amperea xiphoclada)*, pushing up among the yellow flowers of large-leaf bush pea *(Pultenaea daphnoides)*.

We saw no 'roos, but plenty of tracks on the sandy path and in the ash of the newly burned brackenny scrub — of wallabies, pademelons and snakes. Most numerous were those of the big blue-tongue skinks *(Tiliqua nigrolutea)*, a deeper tail trail scoring the softer furrow made by the plump body, with a tracery of little footmarks along either side.

There were splendid views from the flat granite slab of the summit — out to our own little island with its satellite Reef Island and the rugged outline of the Strzelecki Peaks away to the right. Spread before us was the whole gamut of islands dotted around Franklin Sound, with the solid lump of Cape Barren as a formidable backdrop.

Away to the east was the dark swirl of the notorious Potboil and the white horses frolicking over the nearby sand shoals, with the high peak of Babel Island further north, frowning down on Storehouse and Cat Islands at its foot. These lay off the pristine beaches of eastern Flinders, where long sand spits separated a line of placid lagoons from the spray-fringed sea. We could even make out the myriad forms of black swans and lesser waterfowl dotting the surface of Logan's Lagoon, which was later to be designated a RAMSAR wetland site of international wildlife significance.

This was a fine place to see the sunset, with some pretty odd black clouds scudding across the orange expanse, but their evil portent proved a false alarm: they had come and gone before we could "Run for the boat" as Derek suggested. The baker's parlour was a welcome place in which to partake of refreshments while admiring Lynette's shell collection and being presented with some superb paper nautilus shells *(Argonauta nodosa)*, picked up locally, six for each of us.

My only encounter with these exquisite Cephalopod or octopus egg-cases had been on volcanic White Island in New Zealand's Cook Strait, where I was mutton-birding with Motiti Island Maoris and in no position to collect such fragile treasures. By dint of careful packing, I got the paper-thin coils, some the size of a tea plate, safely back to the UK and they adorn my mantelpiece still, forty years later.

On Flinders Island these eggshell-thin trophies are brought in by the westerlies for a period of a few weeks only in early May, with a bumper crop coming ashore about every seventh year. The female octopus sails with her fragile boat until her eggs are laid and she may then abandon it to wind and tide, so that many drift ashore. They are very vulnerable to wave damage, but such exquisite objects inevitably command high prices in the tourist market, so they are avidly sought by the islanders during their brief landfall.

The *pièce de résistence* was Joe, the opportunist brush-tail possum *(Trichosurus vulpecula)*, who came cantering over the corrugated iron roofs of the bakery every night to receive his stale bread and jam buttie. He sat atop the roof ridge, like a big tabby cat, with splaying ears and a squirrel's tail, but was shy of strangers and stayed on the ridge tonight. Derek hung onto the gutter with one hand and banged the roof with the other, this the 'come hither' signal although likely to frighten the life out of more timorous beasties. Lynette climbed over the water tank onto the roof, but had to cross it to deliver supper, which he took daintily in his forepaws to nibble, squirrel-fashion.

Down through the trees to the dinghy, we found that the wind had dropped and we rowed across without incident, but that was not the last of the evening's excitements. Out checking the mutton birds into their burrows at 10.30 p.m., we were presented with the glories of the Aurora Australis. I had just missed seeing this several times during my year in New Zealand and had never witnessed the Northern Hemisphere's Auroroa Borealis, so this was a treat indeed.

At first it looked like a battery of pink searchlights diffused by mist, radiating from behind Cape Barren. Then it started wavering, as the once all too familiar wartime searchlights never wavered, and the beams were joined with frilly curtains of pink and red, varying in intensity as they danced across the night sky. We were too bemused even to think of going in for our cameras!

3 Manuka or Broom Tea-tree *Leptospermum scoparium*

4 Eastern Water Rat *Hydromys chrysogaster*

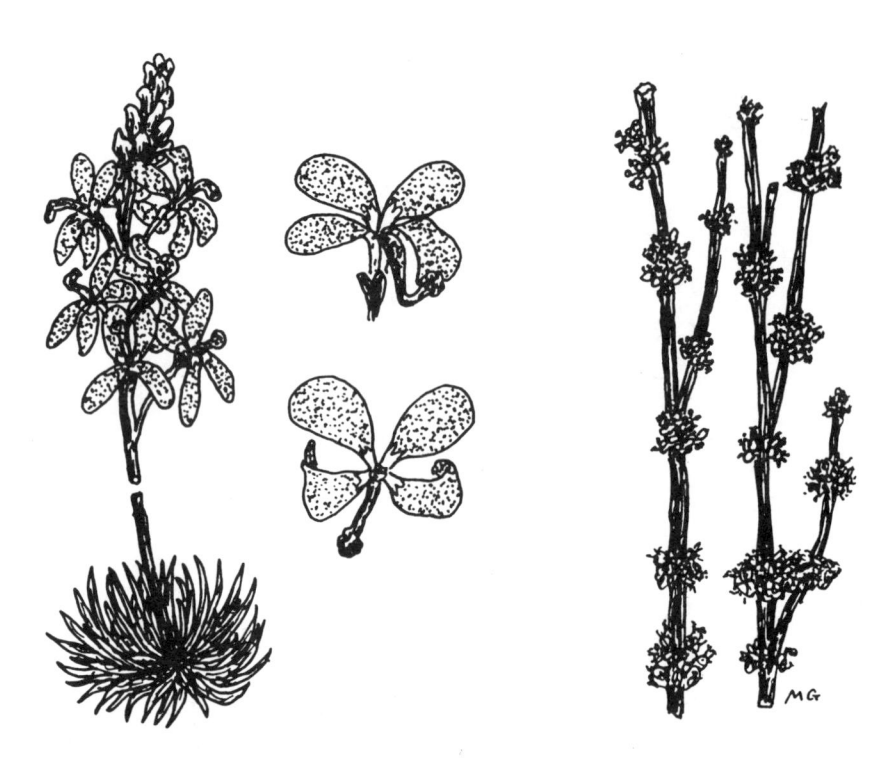

5 Grass-leaved Trigger Plant *Stylidium graminifolium* and Broom Spurge *Amperea xiphoclada*

2. BLACKBOYS, WOMBATS AND POSSUMS

Two days later, Derek managed to acquire a vehicle suitable for rough country and took us on the promised 'roo hunt. He shut up shop at five and we set off in an ancient truck, charging across open country to avoid the ruts of the track, and making short work of the low tea-tree scrub that stood in our way.

Very soon we were among a great stand of grass trees or blackboys *(Xanthorrhoea australis)*, each provoked by a recent fire into producing an eight foot tall spike of creamy yellow flowers, parallel-sided and not a bit like a kangaroo tail, which has been suggested as a more suitable name than blackboy for these modern times. Those which had failed to recover from the fire bore a distinct resemblance to a tousle-headed hunter, the black spike from a former flowering raised aloft as a spear.

Striated black and white New Holland honey-eaters worked methodically around the flowers, sipping their sweets, these often referred to as yellow-wings because of their bright wing flashes. Those spikes which were ripening their circlets of ginger-brown nutlets were providing supper for a lively flock of yellow-tailed black cockatoos. These clung vertically, extracting the seeds with their awkward-looking but efficient beaks and taking little notice of us. When the ginger nodules came away in bunches a foot was brought into play as a hand.

Brittle brown marbles of varying dimensions lay in clusters on the sand below — a cross between the molten dribbles from an iron smelter and a Malteser. (I don't think we knew about Maltesers forty years ago: my diary likens them to aniseed balls or gobstoppers.) These were consolidated globules of resin, not just drips, as may leak from certain wattles and pines, but sap that fizzed out and balled up when a fire went through.

Canon Brownrigg, writing in 1870, quotes an earlier visitor on the subject of blackboys in the following terms:

"Five to seven feet high and as many in circumference, leaves three to four feet long, flower spikes five to ten feet high, thickly clothed with hard scales and small star-like white flowers, except for about eighteen inches at the base which is bare. All trunks are charred from burning off of the scrub.

"An abundance of red resin used in the manufacture of sealing wax and French-polish is exuded. This substance fills up the spaces left by the decay of the flower stems and by injuries and is also lodged round the base of the trunk, which is thus defended from an excess of moisture.

"The blanched base of leaves obtained by beating off the head of a grass tree that has not yet thrown up a flower stem is pleasant eating and has a nutty flavour."

This is the only reference I have seen to the edibility of the plant's crown.

It savours somewhat of 'millionaire's salad', which is the tender growing tip of a felled palm tree.

Two evenings before Derek had taken us into the yard where yacca gum was harvested from the grass trees lopped on Cape Barren or cleared from future farmland on Flinders. As in tree ferns, most of the trunk consists of tightly packed leaf-bases. These were a shiny rufous below the charred surface and impregnated with resin from which shelac was extracted for use in varnish making. There were heaps of various sized pieces, from pineapple-like chunks down to a powder with the consistency of sand, the state in which the product was bagged up for sale. The bigger bits solved the mystery of the unidentified objects washing ashore on the outer isles.

The tallest heap of yacca fragments lay beneath the outlet of a Heath Robinson-style crusher, used in the extraction of the resin. The body of the machine was fashioned from four fourteen-gallon oil drums, joined end to end, with the final chute cut from the side of another. Wheels alongside both this and another wooden contraption behind suggested some sort of internal screw. No doubt Derek explained how it all worked but I have forgotten during the intervening decades. The apparatus was surrounded by heaps of waste 'slag', said to contain more gum than that extracted.

The resin industry, which was more important to Cape Barren Island than Flinders, had peaked in the early 1920s, but was still being carried on in the late fifties in more desultory manner. When I was in this yard again two years later, in 1960, it was all over. Some of the Cape Barren grass tree butts lay rotting in sacks, others were being used as fuel to soften saplings into a state of suppleness to weave into crayfish pots. Tar-like yacca gum oozed from cracks in the glowing brazier, which was another holed oil drum pierced obliquely by a metal pipe containing the 'withies'. I couldn't help feeling how useful some of that might be for caulking the seams of "Half Safe", which was still playing up, as in past years.

The making of wicker work cray pots in this yard outlived the extraction of yacca gum. Long metal cylinders were filled with water and the material to be woven and heated over a wood fire. As in Western Australia, cane was used for the neck of the pot, 'bushwood' for the body, slender saplings of manuka or coast tea-tree *(Leptospermum laevigatum)* in this case. The pots were fashioned on templates resembling long-stalked wooden mushrooms.

After photographing the cockatoos, we headed for the eastern lagoons and bumped along a narrow isthmus to the sea. This was poor sand country, under ten to twenty feet high tea-tree scrub with sedge and bracken — secondary growth after fire. Australia was not yet tree-conscious, and there was tremendous wastage of timber still, the burned standing stumps bulldozed into heaps and burned again, although there were moves afoot to fell the native eucalypts, saw them into firewood logs and load them into the holds of the Tasmanian cargo vessels, which often returned from the islands empty or in ballast.

Many hundreds of black swans, chestnut teal and other ducks disported themselves on one of the lagoons, while the other was virtually empty, except for a few large white egrets and darker white-faced herons pottering along the edge. The difference was a matter of depth. The waterfowl were dabblers and could only feed where they could reach down to the weedy bottom from the surface. All were shallower than usual in 1958, due to drought, the bordering mud baked hard, the marsh vegetation dry and stringy, with a shrunken river under a rickety bridge which we crossed with caution.

The circling water plants had retreated with the retreating water, among them the Tasmanian endemic, *Nablonium calyceroides*, a white button daisy growing almost flush with the ground and confined to the Bass Strait Islands and a few wet sites on the West Tasmanian coast. The fragrance of water mint, *Mentha diemenica or gracilis,* assailed our nostrils, from both the normal and the thyme-leaved variety *serpyllifolia*. There was blue lobelia anceps and sticky yellow bartsia *(Parentucellia viscosa)*, which is closer to home in the Mediterranean.

We had moved back through the splaying fronds of red-fruit saw-sedge *(Gahnia trifida)* into mixed scrub, featuring the handsome cypress pine *(Callitris rhomboides)* and prickly broom heath *(Monotoca scoparia)* when Derek spotted a wombat *(Vombatus ursinus)* 200 yards away. He was gone like a flash, his once white sandshoes twinkling over the sand as he bore down on his portly quarry. Too blocky and short of leg to muster a great turn of speed, the animated digging machine, that has earned itself the name of badger in the islands, nevertheless made it to a sheltering burrow at the same time as its pursuer. Derek tried to grab it by the tail as it shot underground, but the dimensions of a wombat's tail detract from its efficiency as a handle and the fugitive remained holed up and unmolested.

This one had found a burrow ready-made. On another occasion I watched a wombat digging in a sandbank while two men with spades failed to keep up with it before it found haven among a tangle of tree roots. That one, too, went free, but others were caught and kept as pets, befriended by the family dogs.

The whole landscape was liberally supplied with broad-mouthed burrows, resembling the ancient setts of British badgers, and wombat droppings were everywhere. These were blocky and square-ended, like the animals which produced them. Dung pellets from the more streamlined wallabies were more elegantly tapered. Chubbily rounded rabbits (a species happily absent from Flinders Island) produced spherical dung pellets. Was this just coincidence?

There were plenty of wallabies about, the larger Bennets and smaller rufous or pademelons. In little more than an hour's stroll we saw close on twenty, despite their preference for feeding under cover of darkness. They seemed to be everywhere, emerging from behind dune tussocks and popping out from close-knit scrub. Was it my imagination or did they thump the ground with their hind feet in warning, like the more familiar rabbits, before loping off?

Derek pointed out features of their tracks in the sand. 'Roos are well named as Macropods or big-feet, the distance between the heel and the foremost of the modified toes quite considerable. Their 'hands' only touched ground when they were pottering and were a more orthodox shape.

The wombat's footprints were as chunky as would be expected from its general lumbering shape: those of the echidna had long slender toes to match their spines, one of their hind claws a formidable tool for grooming the intractable coat. Thirty-seven years later, on this same ground, we saw six echidnas *(Tachyglossus setosus)* in as many minutes, and there was no indication that the marsupials were getting less.

The tracks threaded between the last of the summer's flowers — silver everlastings *(Helichrysum dealbatum)*, variable groundsel *(Senecio lautus* now *S. pinnatifolius)* and trailing blue-flowered love-creeper *(Comesperma volubile)*, which looks like a pea but is actually a milkwort. The coast wattle bushes *(Acacia longiflora var. sophorae)* Derek referred to as 'boobialla', a name which is better reserved for the real boobialla *(Myoporum insulare)*, with starry white flowers. The flattened leaf stalks or phyllodes of the wattle are the same shape as the shinier leaves of the other and have led to the shared term, despite the wattle's dusty tassels of yellow flowers in spring and pods in summer. Similarly a whole lot of evergreen shrubs get lumped together as 'tea-trees' in island parlance.

On our return we dropped off octogenarian Arthur Harland who had accompanied us with his twelve-bore gun.

"I always carry this, so I can shoot any snakes I see."

We managed some flashlight photographs of the brush-tail possum tonight, some of us joining him on the roofs that were his nocturnal stamping ground. Eric and Joe finished up in the swaying top of a tea-tree before we adjourned for titbits from the bakery and to pack our paper nautilus shells in sawdust and wood shavings for safe transit.

Peter, another helping out with the bird counts on Fisher Island, had put a hurricane lamp at the end of the slip to guide us back. It was very dark and very eerie, the dipping of the oars in the mirror-calm blackness the only sound to break the sort of silence that is but a memory to most of today's city dwellers.

* * * *

Next day we spent on Spences Reef, but went ashore again on the 22nd for a possum hunt with Derek, for ring-tail possums this time as Eric wanted to take one with him as a pet. There were innumerable errands to attend to first so, while waiting, I was taken to morning tea in Leila Barrett's dimly-lit cottage, "Rookery Nook", west of the jetty.

Leila had been harbour master and much more during the war and was a great character, described to me by Dr Dominic Serventy (who had not yet materialised) as a good friend to Fisher Island. A good friend she proved indeed, particularly when I was there on my own, always ready with a cuppa when we came ashore, wet and dishevelled, or rowing out in a borrowed dinghy to deliver messages or food items. We all thought of her as "Auntie". Sadly, she has passed on, but her white weather-boarded cottage, abandoned after her time as unfit for habitation, still stood among its high protective hedges in 1995.

Eric scooped me up and we set off in an elderly van with Derek and the fourteen-year-old bird-watcher son of the postmistress. Following the coast road towards Badger Corner, we peered over a fascinating stretch of beach and marsh where black swans browsed sleepily on the eelgrass *(Zostera)* and a huge flock of oystercatchers was gathered, both pied and sooty, all headed upwind, lest their pristine plumage get ruffled.

We dropped in at a holding where the farmer's wife and her five offspring introduced us to their pet pademelon *(Thylogale billarderii)*. He was a new acquisition and still shy of humans. A rich red-brown and about eighteen inches long, he got slightly longer when Derek grabbed him by the base of the tail and dangled him upside down, snarling, spitting and hissing like a hunter rather than the hunted. Thirty-seven years later I watched Derek pick up another in similar manner in his wildlife sanctuary, this an ailing animal which he was treating for weepy eyes. With a tail like that, it is scarcely surprising that it gets used as a handle.

"Oh yes. Plenty of ring-tail possums here."

The oldest son, Tony, fetched a sack and we set off in search of father, a handsome, well-spoken half-caste, or more correctly quarter-caste. We found him driving a tractor with a sled of logs behind. The logs were not in transit, they were a tool, like the great iron balls being dragged across the bed of the future Kariba Lake in Central Africa at that time to clear the bush. He drove through tall tea-tree bushes, crushing them to earth, so that they would dry out and he could set fire to them a few days hence, then work the ash into the soil with a heavy disc plough. There was a big acreage to be broken in here and sown to rye-grass and clover, like so many other millions of acres throughout the temperate world.

Glad of a break, he came across, shook hands all round and led us off into a particularly dense spinney. There were plenty of ring-tail possums' nests, collections of sticks ten to twenty feet up, these inhabited throughout the year, although most of the young would have been weaned by now. Bushes were shaken and saplings climbed, barefoot, but they yielded nothing more substantial than a photo of the backside of a fleeing possum, waving its white-tipped tail derisively.

We moved on into a scrap of doomed marshland, an eerie place of oozy brown creeks littered with fallen logs like sleeping crocodiles and shaded by tree ferns. The scented paperbarks *(Melaleuca squarrosa)* grew close together, their papery wrappings slightly charred by fire, so that we got covered with soot as we squeezed between them. The arboreal marsupials were quite at home in the labyrinth of branches and we fared better here, one of the pert-faced residents being popped into the bag for a gentle habituation to the domestic way of life.

I emerged from the thicket, peering over my shoulder to brush the charcoal from my new anorak when the farmer yelled a warning. Turning, I found myself gazing into a pair of unblinking beady eyes and saying "What a beauty" instead of widening the three foot gap that separated us. This was a four foot long copperhead snake *(Austrelaps superba)*, the alacrity with which Tony leapt out of its way reminding me that it was not to be trifled with. Back in the vehicle, we passed two black tiger snakes *(Notechis scutatus)* on the road, each about the same size and equally poisonous. The island's third species, also with unpleasant venom, was the white-lipped whip snake *(Drysdalia coronoides)*.

Derek had left his dough to rise and had to be back by one, but our young companion persuaded him to stop on the way back to catch a black and white jumping spider, which progressed in hops of about six inches and proved extraordinarily difficult to waylay. The lad bore it off in Dell's headscarf and transferred it to a tin — one of those queer 'pets' that budding male zoologists like to have about their bedrooms.

After collecting our stores, we took him out to Fisher Island with us for hot soup and a look around. We left him happily screwed up in the hide by the sooty oystercatcher's nest, his eyes riveted on the sleeping bird. Asked later how he had fared, he broke into a broad grin and gave vent to that most expressive of Aussie comments: "My word!"

Tuck came in soon after two o'clock to drop us off on the tiny crested tern reef near Little Dog Island, with its shags and Pacific gulls, so the lad had a good day.

6 Grass Tree or Blackboy *Xanthorrhoea australis*

7 Wombat *Vombatus ursinus*

8 Mammal Tracks, Wallaby, Wombat and Echidna

3. THE SEAMIER SIDE OF ISLAND LIFE

As the weeks went by I made some good friends on Flinders Island, but learned more of the nitty-gritty of life in these remote parts. To the newcomer seeking adventure it was an island Utopia, but there was another face to Lady Barron, not all was roses and 'roo hunts. My diary for 8th February 1958 expands on some of the less-favourable aspects.

The West Australian teachers had left on 23rd January and I had been on my own on Fisher Island since then, although getting picked up for visits to others by various passing boats. There was no two-way radio, it was just a matter of hitching lifts — or being offered one unexpectedly, the louder the hail the better. My new acquaintances, particularly Tom Langley, who had been appointed as my 'keeper' by the absent Dom Serventy, kept an eye open for my smoke signal requesting help, but I never had recourse to use it.

When I bucketed in on this particular Saturday the usual mooring rope had come adrift and I was very wet by the time I had located it, hiding among the Posidonia sea-grass. It was two inches diameter and thirty yards long, not the most manipulable of objects, but I managed to make it fast to a tree after attaching my painter and finding a hold for the anchor. I was being watched by Derek Smith's mother from Devonport, sitting half-hidden under a bush knitting.

"Aren't you lonely over there on your own all this time?"

They all asked that: the answer was "No, the days aren't long enough."

There were surveys and analyses to be done, notes to write up, card indexes to be updated, plants to sketch and press and usually a sunny corner out of the wind in which to carry out these jobs.

Derek appeared with Arthur Harland, who passed on to his neat black and white boat, seaworthy again after a long spell on the slip for repairs. The craft had gone firmly aground on Lady Barron beach at the start of a fishing trip. Derek told the story with relish. After bringing Arthur ashore in his dinghy, he and Trooper Bailey decided to have some fun at his expense and contacted the broadcasting service at Launceston on the police radio transmitter. Over the air on the next news bulletin, which they made sure Arthur was listening to, came the sad story of

"Mr Harland, retired British miner, who had run his boat onto a rock in Bass Strait and had to abandon her to her fate as the tide fell and left her stranded."

"And was he hoppin' mad!" exulted Derek.

The three least of the Smith tribe accompanied me on a botanical skirmish along the shore, as far as an interesting peaty cliff sporting two insectivorous sundews *(Drosera auriculata* and the dwarf *Drosera pygmaea)*, and trigger plants. I learned more than just botany from the small fry.

Back in 'town' the store was crammed with people in the most disreputable and often filthy workaday clothes. There were few occasions demanding respectable garments and living conditions were crude for most. Houses boasted few comforts, sometimes not even an armchair, and much of the furniture was knocked together from old packing cases and fish boxes.

Conveniences were minimal. Every man made his own arrangements to row out in an often-borrowed dinghy to dump his rubbish in the sound. They dug pits to receive the contents of their Sanilavs and fitted up guttering and rain tanks which delivered water to a knee-high tap by the wood-fired stove, served by no sink or outlet pipe and with washing-up gear hung in the trees outside. True we did the same on Fisher Island, but that was a temporary camp, not a permanent way of life.

Services such as mains water and electricity were non-existent. The fortunate ran diesel-fuelled generators, the rest used Tilly lamps and candles, as we did on Fisher Island. The only public amenity was the telephone.

"Yet the place is awash with money" they said.

Cray fishermen habitually earned a thousand pounds a week at this season (two thousand dollars) — a great deal in 1958. Graziers were said to be making money hand over fist with the sale of sheep and cattle reared on paddocks won cheaply from the bush before land values rose with the coming of the government's land settlement scheme. Most farmers and fishermen had other jobs in connection with the agricultural bank at Whitemark, as contractors, middlemen for goods brought in by air freight and resold at remunerative prices, house-building, storekeeping, driving the school bus (a necessity, not the luxury of modern townsfolk), delivering letters and much more.

Most ran brand-new cars or had a couple of trucks skulking in their yards, yet they lived as our ancestors of long ago, in primitive cottages sometimes no more sophisticated than the shacks inhabited during 'the season' on the mutton bird islands. The usual answer to "What do they do with their money?" was "Drink it." — The litter of beer bottles scattered around large and small islands alike being testament to this. The men worked hard, often showing commendable courage in an adverse environment, and were happy to 'live rough'. The unfortunate women had to go along with it.

How different it was when I came again at the end of 1995. Most then lived in neat new houses with colourful, well-tended gardens, water on tap, huge deepfreezers, television aerials and video recorders and a new issue of mobile phones.

"Guess where I'm ringing from? I'm walking round my kitchen" from one proud new owner. "I'm taking the call in the garden" from another.

The Aboriginals enjoyed a higher status in the nineties than the fifties. Earlier attempts to hide any 'touch of the tar-brush' had graduated to the flaunting of any native ancestry, the dignity of ancient lineage giving citizens a stake in history — which had run for relatively few generations since the first permanent white settlement.

The Aboriginal meeting hall and leisure centre, built on the site of the plain concrete store at Lady Barron, was regarded as the finest building on the island. Tatty seaside paperbarks had been tidied into a semblance of esplanade style parkland. Inhabitants were waking up to the possibilities of tourism, but, happily, had not so far suffered its damaging impact. It was judged that the number of visitors would remain small because of the limitation and cost of plane seats to bring them. Fewer people moved on the sea now than in the first half of the twentieth century, when cargo boats such as the *"Naracoopa"* serving the coastal ports carried a few passengers, and there were no moves to bring tourists in that way. The 'Roaring Forties' were a great dampener to sea travel for pleasure!

I had a sumptuous crayfish lunch that Saturday in Leila Barrett's atrociously dark, smelly, grossly overcrowded and highly inconvenient yet homely hovel, which nobody bothered to salvage after her death. This once much-loved hideaway now provides sanctuary for creatures of the wild, the garden leafier and even more overrun than before.

While the long-term inhabitants behaved acceptably, if not always too properly, there were other, tougher characters about. During the past five years more and more boats had been coming in to exploit the riches of the seas and Lady Barron was now the gathering ground for vessels of unknown calibre from all round the south-east corner of Australia.

They plundered the rookeries for mutton birds and penguins to bait their craypots — even the fast diminishing gannets of Cat Island which were finally exterminated as a breeding colony. Often the jetty was piled high with the fly-blown corpses of wallabies killed with similar intent — these contributed by some of the most respectable of the landlubbers, who sold them to the cray fishermen.

Dr Serventy arranged to have someone on Fisher Island all the time the birds were ashore, to prevent some of his precious ringed and laboriously documented research subjects going the way of so many others.

"Sure as eggs, if you spent a night ashore here someone would sneak in and pinch your firewood."

I wondered why it hadn't been filched while awaiting transit on Lady Barron beach, but was told that the offshore islands were more vulnerable.

"They never know who's about here, watching."

Five tough looking weirdos were eating bread and cheese by the 'factory' warehouse, where they were unloading superphosphate from the *"Naracoopa"*, a two-masted trading vessel plying out of Hobart. They stared at me long and hard, as if I was something out of the ark, too uncouth to acknowledge my "Goodday", and stared some more when I returned, one managing a lewd wolf whistle. Dr Eric Guiler of Hobart, had said that Fisher Island was not the place to be at the end of the birding season, when the birders raked in the big money and went off on a king-sized binge until it was all spent. He could be right, but Dom Serventy had appointed 'Honest Tom' Langley to keep an eye on me!

When I was back among the crowd in the store swigging a fizzy drink from a bottle, we were startled by a nearby explosion. Everyone surged out to look. The superstructure of a fishing boat at the jetty was on fire. There were two on board: one had been filling the petrol tank, the other making tea on the Primus, rather too close! They were taken off, burned about the face and with singed hair. Soon after the flames were quelled Harold Holloway and another were ripping off the cabin roof and repairing the wiring.

I was soon ready for off and Harland, proud to have his boat serviceable again, greeted me with "My boat will soon be afloat. I'll give you a tow over."

"My boat will soon be sunk: she was half full of water when last seen" was my reply. The trouble with "Half Safe" was that if you left her in the water she got wave-battered and if you took her out the planks shrank as they dried so that the sea seeped in through the seams when she was launched. There had been a goodly force of water on the way over, the tide rip turning me broadside on and causing me to row mainly on one side only, finally shipping the port oar altogether.

When I got to her the water was up to seat level and the oars floating perilously near the gunwhale. One of the Smith twins lent me a bucket and I got to work, while the faithful Leila went off to put wood on the fire and bring me hot tea. As the tide was making, I decided to step in, nearly scuppering the whole caboosh. Too late, I remembered about shifting cargoes. Standing not quite amidships, I found the waters inside and out joining hands over the port beam. Hastily I moved over and water flowed in to starboard. Gently I eased myself into the middle, until I had an inch of freeboard each side. I baled furiously and was finishing off with a meat tin when Leila arrived with the tea.

I thought I should be able to make it across before she filled up again so I put my boxes of stores, clean laundry and bedding aboard and set off. Harland's boat was still high and dry, but many willing hands pushed me out. I only wished they had been there when I reached the other side. Tide and wind were moving opposite ways and my course was not a little erratic as I tried to accommodate both. (I had risen to be captain of student rowing, as well as swimming and gym, in the postwar years, but racing rowing, even on the sea at Aberystwyth, had little in common with this.)

Struggling to meet the slip at the right angle, I felt my muscles could do no more, but somehow they did, there was no alternative. I heaved a sigh of relief that I hit the right spot at all, and got one leg out of the boat and balanced on a knee-deep pile, but slid off this into deep water as I tried to get the other over her side. (This was a three-man boat, not a single skull dinghy!)

Still clinging to the painter, I managed to ease her round and haul her up, bit by bit. The fact that my luggage was piled on the anchor rope as the only way to keep it out of the bilge water, didn't help. The greasy wire cable from the winch had a life of its own, forming animated coils like a writhing python. With a man at each end it could have been simple. As it was I alternated between pulley and winch, putting my whole weight on the strongly resisting handle. Inch by inch "Half Safe" responded, her burden of water not helping, as she was too heavy to tip single-handed.

It took me nearly an hour with block and tackle before the operation came to a halt with a confusion of ropes wedged firmly under the keel. The sooty oystercatchers shrieked their disapproval of the whole episode and the resident gulls chortled derisively. When I finally lay back to recuperate, I found I had a cut foot, a slit thumb and a grazed thigh backed by a spreading purple bruise. The folk who had been watching anxiously from the shore dispersed. I had made it! Those stores, however wet, would have to last me until my muscles were back in working order, or until Bill Mollison arrived to share the chores.

How much easier life is now. When I visited Fisher Island in November 1995 "Half Safe" had long ago met her end. We travelled in a tiny featherweight inflatable which would have been a delight to row, but which we didn't have to row because she was fitted with an outboard motor. It would have been child's play to haul her up but we didn't have to haul her up: she chugged back merrily to the shore to bring my friend across.

Life had moved on in Lady Barron in those thirty-seven years — to a world of videos and mobile phones, lightweight and mechanised craft. No wonder fewer families were 'birding' by then. That is an industry which cannot be mechanised and there are easier ways of earning a living in this feather-bedded age.

9 Ring-tail Possum *Pseudocheirus peregrinus*

10 Bennets Wallaby *Wallabia rufogrisea*

11 Creeping Monkey Flower *Mimulus repens* and a white button daisy *Nablonium (Ammobium) calyceratum*

Chapter Two

FLINDERS ISLAND: BIRDS, LAGOONS AND MOUNTAINS

1. SOME NEW ANGLES ON THE MUTTON BIRD

My first spell on the islands came to an end in early March; but for only three weeks: by the end of that month I was back, for the 'birding' season.

Tuck took me into Lady Barron for the plane, although feeling pretty groggy after a day off with dysentery. Once ashore, with *"Tassie"* safely at her moorings, he had plumped down under a paperbark tree to watch his son offloading concrete blocks at the jetty. Was there a touch of envy in his rheumy eye? Age will tell, even for the seemingly indestructible.

I despatched my herbarium specimens air freight and adjourned to 'Rookery Nook' to change into my city togs. Tom Langley was also bound for Melbourne and we headed for Whitemark together in one of his trucks. There was no hurry and he showed me something of his 250 acre farm tucked in a valley under the Strzelecki Peaks. He hoped to change over to dairying eventually, but it produced only beef at present, "Because it has to run itself." He had appointed Jerry Addaway from Berkshire as farm manager, but Jerry didn't like snakes and had opted instead to serve behind the counter in the store. The estate was at present in the charge of a hoary little individual reputed to be the oldest cattleman on the island.

"Well known to the police" he grinned.

"Well known to everyone" Tom corrected him.

Whitemark was the main cattle centre and made no mean contribution to Australia's beef stocks, the meat travelling on the hoof. Animals were swung aboard in belly slings, as I had seen them being swung ashore at Port Welshpool on the Victorian coast. Lady Barron exported cattle too, but her claim to fame was as the cray fishing and mutton-birding centre.

We flew out, eight of us in a ten-seater aircraft, with sunshine highlighting the sprawl of islands below. The final outliers in the Furneaux Group were the two Sisters Islands off the north-east of Flinders, their towering cliffs very different from the smooth low granite mounds in Franklin Sound. Soon we were over the Gippsland coast, with its bewildering jumble of sandy spits and rocky headlands.

My Melbourne destination was Alexandra Hall, the university's residential ladies' college, where I was soon to become a tutor. I was ushered into an elegant afternoon tea party for the Far Eastern contingent of young ladies from China, Malaysia and Vietnam, all meticulously exquisite in their national silks. (I had not yet orientated to the fact that in Australia what has always been the Far East becomes the Near North.)

At dinner I found myself sitting at high table in an academic gown, recollecting that there were such things as table napkins and butter knives. It seemed unreal after two months of eating from frayed newspapers, swatting blowflies, ants and errant crabs.

Life at the Ladies' Hall of Residence was very formal in 1958, emulating the ancient universities of home. During my most recent experience of university life the year before at Massey, in New Zealand, the young men came to dinner in shorts, hiding their lack of ties with high-necked pullovers. No doubt the wearing of gowns has been dropped long since in Melbourne, as in most emporia of learning.

On 29th March 1958 I flew back to Flinders Island, from Melbourne this time, first through a fudge of cotton-wool whiteness, then a tumult of dark grey. Yesterday had been Melbourne's coldest March day for ten years: it seemed that winter was setting in early. The best the plane could offer in the way of refreshment was Coca-Cola, an international institution which I abhor, but I got a belated breakfast of beef sandwiches and coffee at the Interstate Hotel in Whitemark.

Jerry Addaway had come to collect me with his attractive three-year-old son, Michael, and eight-year-old daughter, Christine. The hot rubbery smell of overheated brake linings wafted into the truck with increasing intensity.

"No good stopping for help here," said Jerry as we passed farm after farm.   "They're all away at the mutton-birding."

The 'season', it seemed, had started two days before, at the end of a debilitating heatwave, but those had been two days of deluging rain and howling gales, so not much had happened yet. Eventually he found an occupied house and phoned.

Another of the Island Store's trucks arrived in due course, with a mechanic of whom it was said, "If anyone can fix this thing, Frank can."

The ailing truck got back just fifteen minutes after the rescue vehicle! During the inevitable morning tea with Leila Barrett, I met another of her many brothers — Captain Barrett of a cattle boat, storm-bound at Whitemark.

No-one was birding so far on Little Green or Mount Chappell Islands, but there were ten sheds occupied on Great Dog Island and two on Little Dog, with the Babel figures unknown. Tom Langley, Dom Serventy and his assistant, Bill Mollison, were on Babel awaiting transport back — this delayed by Trooper Bailey's various non-functional two-way radios; three 'crook' machines having been despatched on that day's plane for repair.

Also on Babel Island was an inspector from the Tasmanian Fauna Board, the licencing authority, who would stay with that bustling community for the whole season instead of making surprise visits, as to the others. In addition there were two film crews, one from Tasmanian Television and the other from CSIRO (The Commonwealth Scientific and Industrial Research Organisation) which financed most of the Serventy-led mutton-bird research.

The teams had already been on Fisher Island filming Dom banding a shearwater chick, a young penguin losing the last of its baby down and some illegally taken cray bait washed up on the shore. The last consisted of sixty adult mutton birds and three penguins, some still in an old bran bag, while a further fifty-three were found floating on the sea on the way across from

Lady Barron, jettisoned when the inspector's boat hove in sight. The miscreants were not, of course, locals, Jo Greeno having seen Victorian fishermen stealing birds from Babel Island.

The Babel workers came and went in a barge, but there was no daily collection of processed birds from this most inaccessible of the commercial outposts (which lay on the wrong side of the Potboil), all the proceeds being salted down in barrels. These eventually found their way to the Lady Barron 'factory' where they were checked, re-salted and re-packed for export.

A good proportion of the birds from the islands in Franklin Sound were brought in fresh daily in metal-bound wooden boxes measuring about 18 x 12 x 8 inches. These, ready plucked, were inspected in the 'factory', re-packed in cardboard cartons and air-freighted to be sold fresh in the poulterers and fishmongers of Tasmania, Victoria and New Zealand.

I picked up a sack of stores and got a lift out to Fisher Island with Tuck, who was taking a party of birders and their household effects to Little Dog Island, racing up to see if the key was in the door of the hut before letting him go.

For the next four hours I was spitting and polishing, the hut being in the sort of state one would expect after several weeks of all male occupation. (Those were the bad old days when men gloried in their inability to cope with the finesses of the domestic front, although the 'field types' with whom I associated were past masters at getting by on the culinary front.) Firewood had been stacked but not chopped, so I got busy with the axe, my muscles complaining after their weeks of inactivity.

But where were the several dozen boxes of matches that lived on the shelf? I remembered seeing half a box in the stationery drawer: thankfully they were still there. I soon had a fire going and water heating, lighting my evening's candles from splinters of she-oke held to the flames with pliers. No way could I let it out now.

Numerous bowls of hot water went to the scrubbing of shelves, boxes, tables, floors and windows, until the place was fit to live in and look out of. I spread my sleeping bag under Bill's, both double bunks having got back into the living room in readiness for the cooler nights of autumn. Supper of tinned meat and fresh veg was under way when a boat seemed to be heading in from the east, but it veered away: my fellow islanders were not on it.

Tuck had arranged to drop me off at Woody Island on his mail run the next day and I was up betimes and shivering on the rocks, wearing all the clothes I could muster, at the appointed time, but *"Tassie"* sped past and there was no response to my yelling and waving. Maybe he thought it too rough to loiter off that outpost for the paltry sum of fifteen shillings.

I spent the day with histograms and drawings and, at 5.30 p.m., sighted a strange, blunt-nosed craft wallowing her flat-bottomed way through a westerly running sea from the direction of the Potboil. This must surely be "the barge". It was. She nosed into the north-east boat harbour, but couldn't quite make it and backed out again to manoeuvre into a more favourable position. Serventy and Mollison were crouched under a tarpaulin in the bilge water, sheltering from the seas which slid in and out through the landing door in the bow. As the craft edged into a taller granite slab, a seaman threw me a rope and Bill, barefoot, followed close behind. Together we shoved her off the shelf where she had lodged and the doctor and the gear came ashore. Both men said they would remember that voyage!

I threw fresh logs on the fire and regaled them with hot coffee, 'D.L.S.' repeating his delight at being 'home again' in "Yolla" as he gradually thawed. ("Yolla", proudly emblazoned over the door of our quarters, was Aboriginal for mutton bird.) Soon he had an array of tins of meat, vegetables and soup bubbling merrily over the glowing logs. They had been sleeping on the concrete floor of the 'factory' on Babel Island and were glad to turn into their bunks after an evening of gossip.

* * * * *

We went ashore next morning, me to botanise, the two men to busy themselves with hammer and nails in the back yard of the store, knocking up boxes to house live mutton birds. These were bound for Dom's home territory of Nedlands, Perth, in Western Australia for observations on the gonad cycle and onset of fertility.

Scientists had always been intrigued by the close synchronisation of the breeding cycle. Like an explosion of gametes from massed coral polyps on the Great Barrier Reef, everything happens at once, despite the astronomically large number of birds involved. (The short-tailed or slender-billed shearwater *(Puffinus tenuirostris)* vies with the related but smaller Wilson's storm petrel as candidate for the most abundant bird in Australia.)

All the hens lay their single egg during the short space of ten to twenty days — from 20th/22nd November to the end of the month or, at the latest, 2nd December. This routine is invariable, from year to year and from rookery to rookery, in spite of vagaries of weather pattern — and even day length, because nesting latitudes range between Southern Tasmania and Ceduna in South Australia. Nor does it vary over the decades, early observers from 140 years ago recording similar dates.

In a paper published in 1956 in the Proceedings of the Zoological Society of London, Volume 127.4, Marshall and Serventy had suggested that ripening of eggs and sperm must be triggered by day length, and this, not in the breeding area, but earlier, on the trans-equatorial migration down the Pacific Ocean from their off-duty fishing grounds in the Arctic. This migration in itself is anomalous, the species exceptional in breeding in the WARMER of the two regions between which it commutes.

In Britain we are very geared to thinking of our wintering geese and waders going to the chilly Arctic to breed; our summering swallows and warblers to the warmth of Africa to winter, so this in itself is intriguing.

Gametogenesis, the formation of eggs and sperms, begins while the mutton birds are still in the Northern Hemisphere so that the breeding organs are well developed before they reach the southern breeding grounds in September. If gonad development is triggered by day length, this implies that it happens with DECREASING light as the birds move from the long summer days of the Northern Hemisphere to the twelve-hour cycle of the Equator. Other birds are more often triggered by the lengthening days of spring.

Mating occurs on arrival, when the previous year's burrows are being cleaned out for re-use, to the accompaniment of a cacophony of nocturnal display calls. The domestic quarters in order, the birds adjourn to sea, while the fertilised egg enlarges ready for the 'big week'. The hen lays only one, but this weighs eighty-five grams or a sixteenth of her body weight.

There is no possibility of another if the first fails: insemination and fertilisation are too exact to allow of any replay. Even on arrival at the breeding rookery, the male testes have started to shrivel and become impregnated with fatty waste products. In one of a number of papers on the subject, Dom points out that no other bird is known to show such rapid testes collapse.

To test the theory of dependence on changing light regimes in the Northern Hemisphere, he had taken twenty Bass Strait adults back to Nedlands the previous year, 1957. Their gonads came into breeding activity after a year of pampering in captivity — just as they would have done if they had looped around the Pacific Ocean to Alaska and back, so that rather put paid to that theory.

Shearwaters are not unduly disturbed by handling, as we had found during concentrated studies of Manx shearwaters on Skokholm Island in South Wales, and Dom's Nedlands birds took readily to being hand fed on small fish or strips of larger fish. I could picture the feeding sessions, having had the good fortune to join one of Steve Cress's teams feeding puffin chicks on Eastern Egg Rock off the coast of Maine in New England. We fed the American birds on capelin, cut obliquely lengthwise and stuffed with minerals and vitamins that they might otherwise have lacked. Those chicks had been moved south from Canada and installed in artificial drainpipe burrows on an island deserted by puffins years before, in the hope that they would return there to breed when their time came. They did, lured by hand-painted decoy birds, and brought others with them!

Dom was taking thirty birds this year and some of these would be subjected to artificial light regimes, to see whether these really did affect their internal clocks. There were endless possibilities for further experiments. Would they construct burrows and lay eggs so far from their traditional ancestral sites, would they lay without burrowing. Where would any chicks hatching return when they were ready to breed, and would this differ according to whether they were released over the Indian Ocean off Perth, the Pacific Ocean off their normal haunts or the Southern Ocean which connected the two? Dom's mutton bird studies did not go into abeyance when he left our delectable summer isles.

12 Lady Barron Store in 1958

13 Prickly Moses, *Acacia verticillata*

14 Insectivorous Sundew *Drosera peltata* and parasitic Dodder-laurel *Cassytha glabella*

2. SOUTH-EASTERN LAGOONS

While Serventy and Mollison were busy with their bird boxes, Frank Henwood, harbour master at Lady Barron from 1960 on, took me to nearby Scotts Lagoon. This was one of the few freshwater lakes on the islands and a permanent one. Most of the Flinder's lagoons were ranked along the eastern side and separated from the sea by vegetated sandbanks which could be breached in time of storm. Even if salt water did not flow in, they were subject to blown spray and showed a tendency to brackishness.

Scotts Lagoon lay well back from the coast opposite Hays Point, the outlet stream percolating through scrubby land to Factory Beach or Henwood's Beach, making the community one of trout rather than flounders. On this morning it was alive with birds. There were stately flotillas of black swans, black duck, black coot, black shags and black clouds to match, but showers were brief and fitful sun peered through the enveloping shroud at intervals.

Although not prone to drying out in summer, the lake level rose in winter to inundate the encircling grassy flats which had been closely grazed during the thirstier months. Frank left me in the adjacent brackenny scrub, with a warning to beware of wild pigs and snakes. I saw neither until I got back to his garden, where he had broken the back of a four-foot snake on his return.

The close turf of the flats was sprinkled with the crimped circular leaves of moss pennywort *(Hydrocotyle muscosa)*, each of five wedge-shaped segments, and the tight yellow flower discs of water buttons *(Cotula coronopifolia)*.

'Snapdragon' blooms from the spreading stems of creeping monkey flower *(Mimulus repens)* and the rosettes of swamp mazus *(Mazus pumilio)* mingled, although the first is more characteristic of saltmarshes, the second of freshwater. Both have mauve flowers, but the double central boss is yellow in mimulus and white in mazus.

The tiny plants of mudwort *(Limosella aquatica)* were almost as invisible as the ones which turn up occasionally in British wetlands. There were pink flowers of willow-herb *(Epilobium billardieranum)*, dusty heads of cudweed *(Gnaphalium)* and hoary sprouts of glaucous goosefoot *(Chenopodium glaucum)*, the plants probably boosted by blown spray.

So much of Australia's native vegetation is twiggy and unwelcoming, that it was good to see so many 'softies' reminiscent of home. This theme was carried back into the 'dogwood' *(Cassinia aculeata)* scrub by small coast daisies *(Brachycome parvula)* and scarlet-flecked running postman *(Kennedya prostrata)*. Blue flowers of black-anther flax lilies *(Dianella revoluta)* were progressively replaced by shiny blue berries. I was by no means familiar with all that I saw on that visit, but specimens went off to the Museum in

Melbourne for confirmation or identification.

Henwood regaled us at lunch with stories of wrecks he had known and lent us a book entitled *"Wrecks of Tasmania"*, pointing out that he knew of at least twenty not mentioned by the author. We took turns later reading about the more local ones by the light of our sizzling Tilly lamp.

After lunch he took me to a beach where he collected cuttle bones for his hens, as others collect them for their canaries. These porous internal skeletons, with which the cuttlefish can regulate their buoyancy, were cast up in profusion on Flinders Island.

He showed me a bed of fossil shells and other ancient specimens illustrating fluctuating sea levels during ages past. From far inland he had collected seashells, showing that that ground had been inundated by the sea. From Petrifaction Bay, close to Lady Barron, he had fossil wood, suggesting that a former woodland there had been overrun by the sea.

I spent the afternoon in Henwood Bay and on a little tidal island offshore. Cloying stems of climbing lignum *(Muehlenbeckia adpressa)* looped over the boughs of coast tea-tree *(Leptospermum laevigatum)*, while brilliant wine-red flowers of Senecio elegans spread down to the fleshy stems of Black's glasswort *(Salicornia blackiana)* on the shoreline. Purple and white ivy-leaved violets *(Viola hederacea)* mingled with small poranthera *(Poranthera microphylla)* of the spurge family. Cryptic silvery cushions of hairy centrolepis *(Centrolepis strigosa)* were pathetically tiny members of the lily family clustered in freshwater seepages.

When Bill was rowing us back in the evening, I put my hand in the bag on the stern seat beside me and something wriggled. Henwood's snake, appropriated for scientific investigation, was not dead. Bill administered two more wallops when we got back. These animals are difficult to extinguish, the muscle reflexes continuing for a long time in the back half. It was weighed and measured and opened up for stomach contents, which were, as so often in reptiles, nil, meals being few and far between, although often large.

Next day I was off with camping gear to join the birders on Big Dog Island and visit some of the smaller reefs where Wilson's storm petrels nested. I returned in due course with a party of hunters who had been shooting Cape Barren geese on Big Woody Island. They came aboard with their swag from the north-west bay and I shared the deck with the once handsome birds, grieving over their soft grey plumage, stubby primrose-yellow and black beaks and pink legs.

Half an hour after Dom had greeted me back, Lew Bailey brought the British research couple, John and Pat Warham, to join us from Cat Island, along with a great deal of bulky kit which they were hoping to ship out to Launceston on the *"Naracoopa"* or the *"Prion"*. While we juggled with camp beds and mattresses, the strains of music wafted across the moonlit stretch of water separating us from the Flinder's shore. It was Easter Saturday and the folk not away on the birding were having a beach barbecue.

Everyone was in high spirits as we launched our boat to join them. Dom and John took an oar each, Dom back-paddling at intervals and blaming John when we started going round in circles. 'Honest Tom' Langley, as he was generally known, was playing host, his blue eyes twinkling more brightly as he got progressively merrier and more amorous.

All was in light vein except for the hammer and tongs discussion between Dom and Johnnie, a Latvian or Lithuanian fisherman, on the vagaries and inconsistencies of the State and Commonwealth Fisheries licencing restrictions. Johnnie waded in again every time Tom tried to break it up. One could not help feeling that the fisherman was trying to enlist Dom's support after being caught with mutton bird corpses on board during a police search, following the washing-up of more filched bait on Big Dog Island.

Knobbie, another Baltic fisherman, who captained "The Barge", not too expertly, some said, had been roped in as principal chef and fire devil. He had protested vehemently, making off with: "No! I no go to barbecue. I fed up with you all," when he was finally persuaded and became the sulkily silent king pin of the whole affair.

He sweated over a blaze of driftwood and discarded notice boards, spreading his chops and steaks on the wire frame of a discarded bedstead placed over the top. They tasted good, even the ones that had adventured temporarily into the ashes. Soup was heated in billies and served in mugs, potatoes were fried and served with savouries and the drink flowed freely. We sat in a semi-circle around the fire on old blankets, the sea lapping close to the glowing embers. We danced on the flat granite slabs to the accompaniment of a radio-gram and a piano-accordion played by the policeman's goose-hunting son.

There was much hilarity and it was past one o'clock when the little island — no more than a pimple on the glistening calm — called us back. We hauled the dinghy in from where she rode her anchor chain and paddled across. No homecoming mutton birds were checked into their burrows that night!

We had planned a return dinner party for Easter Monday, with eleven guests invited to share our roast lamb and bring their own vegetables, but there was a gale blowing by then, so we dined alone.

* * * * *

It was Frank Henwood again who enabled me to see more of the lagoons two years hence on 22nd February 1960. We had always known the extensive and irregularly spreading south-eastern one as Potboil Lagoon, but the official terminology when it joined the international list as a RAMSAR site was Logans Lagoon. My hopes of getting there again on my 1995 visit were dashed because the bridge on the only negotiable road leading into it had been destroyed in a fire. This was no doubt good for the wildlife, as visits from the sea were unlikely with the Potboil so menacingly close and it was a long hike after leaving a vehicle.

My 1960 visit was in lieu of one to Cameron Inlet and others to the north, no-one knowing at that juncture that Logans was to be selected as the special one. (Perhaps my list of plants contributed to the choice, as there seemed to be little plant recording going on at that time.) Our approach to the others was barred by a pall of smoke from a rampaging bushfire.

It was disappointing to find that Logans was fragmented into separate parts, most of them almost dry — as, indeed, it was again in 1995 according to hearsay. Some of the bed was white with caked salt, some scattered with muddy hollows in the sand, where the last dregs had lingered and dropped their load of silt. Fish had expired as water evaporated from the dwindling puddles where they had taken refuge.

Stranded water insects had proved a bonanza for insect-eating birds and the entire lake bed was honeycombed with their footprints, but most had gone now that the feast was over. As the invertebrates converged on the last scraps of water, predators had no longer to range far for prey, until all lacked for oxygen and they lost interest.

Bugs and beetles could fly away, dragonflies, damselflies, mayflies and the like too, if they happened to be at the right phase of their life cycle. The puzzle was, where to go, with the whole island in a like state of desiccation. The winners were the ones that could expire, secure in the knowledge that the eggs of the next generation were safely buried in the mud, awaiting the life-giving rains. Molluscs had fared badly and great drifts of tiny cone-shaped shells had built up like banks of orange shingle, while the sand was littered with other shells of many descriptions.

We saw four live Bennets wallabies and two dead ones, come, perhaps, for a last comforting drink in their final sickness. With no natural predators, sudden death came to the fit only from men seeking cray bait. Inspecting the animals at close quarters, it was interesting to see how much coarser their coats were on these dry sands with their spiky vegetation than were those of the moister Strzelecki foothills, which were quite silky by comparison.

There was one dead Cape Barren goose, but parties of live ones were around all afternoon, the largest a flock of twenty-two. Some were grazing the succulent but probably quite saline saltwort *(Salicornia quinqueflora)* and the fleshy leaves of trailing jointweed *(Hemichroa pentandra)*, another member of the saltbush family with meagre flowers scattered along the stems.

Wild pig footprints mingled with those of wallaby and wombat — these the issue of those escaping from or released by early seafarers. Small and large cat-like tracks remained unidentified. Water birds lingered on: few other places would have suited their needs better in this drought. Five Pacific gulls pottered on the outskirts of the seventy strong flock of silver gulls. There was a Caspian tern, two pelicans (not often seen around the islands), black swans and various kinds of duck. The little patch of bushes that had survived the fires gave sanctuary to three green rosellas, ten goldfinches and a scattering of silver-eyes.

Thick scrub barred our way to the sea, but we managed to push through to a smaller lagoon to the south which was not quite so dry, wishing that the wallabies which had made the tracks we followed were taller. Tantalising glimpses of Vansittart or Guncarriage Island came and went, but we failed to break through to the sea.

Turning, we emerged, streaked with charcoal from former fires, to find that more than a hundred yards of lagoon bank were now burning, the flames engulfing the only remaining green patch of eucalyptus and acacia. This had been lighted after our arrival by a gun-happy truckload of youths who were out after geese, but had so far bagged only a young pig.

The fire was advancing with alarming speed and sundry reports and crackles rose at intervals to a roar as more fuel came to feed the flames. Grass and heath beyond the spinney was tinder dry, but too sparse to burn as fiercely. More dense smoke billowed up to merge into the yellow pall hanging over land and water alike. At no time in the past four or five weeks had the islands been entirely free of fire.

Fortunately Frank had stayed with the truck and he moved it progressively away from the conflagration, the last move having to wait until after the grass had burned out so that he could close in behind the blaze to pick us up.

Three days later he succeeded in getting us to the more northerly lagoons. Five black cockatoos were circling over the freezer shed behind the jetty when we joined him. Rica Erikson, author of botany and local history books from Western Australia (and a fine hostess and flower guide, as I later discovered) occupied the front seat. Her farmer-husband, Syd, John Thompson — then of the Zoology Department at Melbourne University, later a professor in Sydney University — and I perched on the back of the truck, ducking as branches swept across the cab roof to flick playfully around our necks. We wished we had brought pillows to ease the humps and bumps.

A wrong turn and we found ourselves backing out of a swamp. Some of the rippled grey sand of the lagoon beds looked deceptively like water, and supported all the birds seen three days earlier, plus some pied oystercatchers. Of more interest were the wild pigs, hairy and almost black, with long pointed snouts.

"Escaped from some of the early wrecks" quoth Frank, "but with a dash of blood from early settlers' pigs gone bush."

We drew up alongside two on the north shore of Logans Lagoon. They regarded us with interest, then trotted off, little concerned. From our experience on a flashlight trip after possums, they were no more wary at night, standing their ground under a fusilade of shouting and whistling. They can be dangerous if cornered, but were no match for a man with a gun, as shown by a dead animal a little further on, shot just for 'sport' with no attempt to butcher it for use.

There were several halts for botanising, the heath plants in better fettle than the amphibious ones. I already had a list of seventy-seven plant species from Logans Lagoon back from Jim Willis and staff at the Victorian Museum in Melbourne, so there was not a lot new to be found in this hostile spell of weather.

We passed on to fossick along the east beach towards Babel Island, collecting shells, sea urchin tests, cowfish skeletons, Posidonia balls, sponges and other treasures of the sea. A half mile stretch of bush separated the parched lagoons from the creaming sea and on this we spotted three wallabies, a juvenile echidna and a wombat disappearing into its burrow. Other finds were semi-fossilised bones and calcareous root concretions of past dune flora, exposed by blowing sand after a long period of burial and petrifaction, as natural lime replaced the organic tissues.

The afternoon was still young so, after inspecting a dead tiger snake on *Paspalum dilatatum* grassland, we visited a roost of black-faced cormorants alongside the Samphire River, between the lowest bridge and Petrifaction Bay into which it empties. It was dusk and the old blue gum and a number of swamp paperbarks already bore a load of birds. These rose at our approach, circling uncertainly overhead with a characteristic swishing of wings.

Sweet bursaria *(Bursaria spinosa)* was co-dominant with the paperbarks but obviously of the wrong conformation to accommodate the ungainly feet of the cormorants, all four toes of which are connected by the web, not just three as in gulls — which are not partial to tree-perching in spite of this. Perhaps it was because the bursaria branches were so generously draped with a parasitic tangle of dodder laurel *(Cassytha)* stems, but the native hop bushes *(Dodonaea viscosa)* were also avoided by the birds.

Another tree roost of black-faced cormorants which we had visited earlier was beside Scotts Lagoon, the trout of whose fresh waters would supply some tasty breakfasts when the birds awoke. We were more accustomed to seeing these black and white birds roosting at ground level on the pigface *(Disphyma australe)* of Reef Island. Obviously they are as adaptable as the cosmopolitan large black cormorants which are equally at home, for nesting as well as roosting, in tall trees or on the ground.

The Samphire River roost had been in occupation for a long time to judge by the tatty, guano-fouled state of their perches, many of which were dead. Although several hundred yards from the sea, the rain of fishy excreta had killed the indigenous understorey plants and stimulated in their stead a seaside-type community dominated by bower spinach *(Tetragonia implexicoma)* with seaberry saltbush *(Rhagodia canolleana or baccata)* and South African boxthorn *(Lycium ferocissimum)*. The most abundant herb was the cosmopolitan, fast-growing chickweed *(Stellaria media)*, which is characteristic of bird colonies throughout the temperate world.

Following the river to where it emptied into Franklin Sound, we explored Petrifaction Bay, criss-crossing the black tertiary basalt of the intertidal flats collecting fragments of fossil wood. These were a shiny brick red or buff colour, very different from the calcified woods of the other shores, less brittle and much older. Swarms of little crabs sheltered beneath them, while Cape Barren geese mingled with the swans on the mud lying in pockets of the flattened rock surface — an indication of the unusually good degree of shelter enjoyed by this embayment of the shore.

15 Swamp Isotome I. *fluviatilis* and yellow water buttons *Cotula coronopifolia*

16 Short Purple Iris *Pattersonia fragilis*

17 Small Poranthera *P. microphylla* and Hairy Centrolepis *C. strigosa*

3. EXPLORING THE STRZELECKI MOUNTAINS

The day that we ventured into the wet sclerophyll forest of Flinder's southwestern heights was, like so many others, earmarked originally for something quite different. Dom Serventy and I were anxious to work together on the two western islands of East Kangaroo and Big Green, where the Tasmanian Fauna Board was particularly interested in the interaction between grazing and birding, but it was not to be.

The expected boat did not arrive, although the weather was perfect. It had been anchored at the top of the tide and was now firmly aground and likely to be so for many hours yet. Leila Barrett rowed out to us with the bad news and suggested that we all go for a mountain picnic instead. Pat and John Warham, after weeks of roughing it on the wind-denuded outer islands, were all for a change of scene, so we packed food and went ashore.

Bill Mollison drove one of the Island Store's trucks out on the Trousers Point road to 'Honest Tom's' farm, where we took off across a paddock, gleaning a big haul of mushrooms as we went and stashing them in a corner to pick up on the way back. Supper assured, we plunged into the tea-tree thicket which obscured the vast mass of Devonian granite ahead. This was forested below and shrub-covered above. The upper shrubs thinned to twiggy heathland, through which thrust great shoulders of naked grey rock. These sparkled intermittently as their quartz, felspar and mica crystals captured the sun's rays and winked them back. Their wind-scoured surfaces yielded few rootholds for plants, however tenuous.

It was odd that the range should offer both the lushest and the most barren of the island's landscapes. Several factors contributed but the two main ones, the depth of accumulated soil and the exposure to the elements, were dependent on gradient and altitude.

The mountains rose to only 2,407 feet (756 metres), but they did so abruptly, from the much younger quaternary sands and clays of the low-lying coastal plain and terminated above in a scenic line of jagged peaks worthy of much greater ranges.

No doubt the peppermint gums and other eucalypts had formerly spread across Honest Tom's fields, which were not sharply demarcated. Along the boundary between reclaimed land (or, more correctly 'claimed' land, as it was not Tom's to start with, despite our blithe use of the term) and the unclaimed was a belt of scrub.

Inroads by the beef cattle kept the trees at bay, but the animals were defeated by the ability of the white kunzea, the bushy needlewood and dagger hakea *(Hakea teretifolia)*, which seemed able to produce a plethora of branches where the tips had been nibbled. The spines of the hakeas were a particularly effective deterrent to browsing. Observing this, early settlers had introduced that spiniest of all hedge plants, the South African boxthorn, and had lived to regret it. In summer this produces a luscious crop of baby tomato fruits, beloved by all the fruit-eating birds on the island. They dined richly, flew off and defecated the pips across pastures new. These were as viable after ingestion as are the tomato pips which escape from British sewage works to produce stands of tomato plants on the river shingles downstream from effluents and leaks. Boxthorn thickets sprang up everywhere and proved recalcitrant monsters when it came to clearing them.

At first our path led through dry sclerophyll forest of she-okes and lowland peppermint gums. Higher up these graded into manna gums and Tasmanian blue gums *(Eucalyptus viminalis* and *Eucalyptus globulus)*. Tiny streams cascaded from above and, as the canopy thickened, humidity rose and we saw our first tree ferns.

These were mostly soft tree fern or man fern *(Dicksonia antarctica)*, but there were some fine specimens of austral king ferns *(Todea barbara)*. It was strange after being on the sun-blistered outer isles with their salty succulents, to see such lush fern gullies in the middle of Bass Strait.

The only ferns most of the islands could muster were harsh stands of bracken *(Pteridium esculentum)*, their hard, overwintering fronds much tougher than those of British bracken which live for only six months, dying away completely in winter. Strzelecki was more like the familiar woodlands of Wales, the illusion strengthened by the splaying fountains of mother shield ferns *(Polystichum proliferum)*, so like our hard and soft shield ferns. Another here, the leathery shield fern, had recently been separated off from the others as *Rumohra adiantiformis*.

The less flamboyant pendant fronds of *Pellaea falcata* were like an oversized version of our maidenhair spleenwort, except that the ginger lines of spores were ranged around the leaf margins instead of in oblique lines on their backs. Strzelecki's screw ferns *(Lindsaea linearis)* seemed a screwed up version of our mountain form of hard fern, smallest of the Blechnums.

One for which we have no counterpart was the scrambling coral fern *(Gleichenia microphylla)*. As vigorous as the more cosmopolitan bracken, the repeatedly forked fronds seemed indestructible, every tip having the power to divide into another pair of leaf segments to create a tangle of leathery bead necklaces.

We even came across some of those fragile treasures, the filmy ferns during the course of the day. Clinging to old mossy tree trunks or fallen logs, they were more like mosses themselves than ferns. The rather lop-sided fronds of the veined bristle fern *(Polyphlebium venosum)* came to our notice first, huddled in deep shade by a tinkling waterfall. Later we came across one of the three species of *Hymenophyllum*, a genus which occurs in Britain's wettest forests, but only rarely. This was the austral filmy fern *(Hymenophyllum australe)*.

As we ascended, the path began to dwindle, as walkers who faltered at the gradients turned back. Our attention was diverted from the plants as we picked our way over fallen trees and scrambled up rock outcrops. Never were we unaware of the bird life, however.

First there were yellow-throated honey-eaters and golden whistlers, the resonant, needle-thin call of the latter putting me in mind of New Zealand bellbirds. There were brilliant red flashes of flame robins and blue ones of superb fairy wrens, where there always seem to be more of the dashing cocks than the dowdy hens. Not all the cocks are drones, or mere songsters, however, the young males helping to feed chicks (that they have not fathered) in the communal family nest.

Other denizens of the forest were grey fantails and white-eyes or silver-eyes. Later there were scarlet robins, less brilliant than the flame robins and more like the robin redbreast of the Christmas cards. Dom, one of the old school of taxonomists, wanted a specimen of honey-eater and whistler for his collection. He extricated his long-handled pistol from its holster and handed it to Mollison.

"Go get that bird, skinner boy!"

(He had recently returned from an African safari where he had had black skinned skinner boys to do his bidding.) Bill proved as efficient at shooting small birds in dense undergrowth as he was at most things, his competence leading later to a distinguished career in organic-orientated conservation in New South Wales. Two small corpses were lovingly transported back to Fisher Island, skinned and stuffed by the master scientist.

The Strzelecki Peaks are now a national park, where such behaviour would be unthinkable and where it is a sin even to pluck a flower. Times and attitudes have changed over the years — and very much for the better.

We encountered no mammals, we were too many and too noisy, but there were plenty of tracks and a few corpses floating down the streams. Lunch was eaten in a pleasant streamside clearing by some prickly currant bushes *(Coprosma quadrifida)*: cold lamb sandwiches, tinned beetroot and raw onion, biscuits and cheese and blackcurrant cordial. And so onwards and ever upwards, with pauses on open bosses of granite to view the ever nearing peak ahead and the ever widening vista behind. Flower clusters of white swamp heath *(Epacris paludosa)* gleamed from dark corners, with less spectacular bushes of *Monotoca glauca* of the same family, its tiny cream flowers hiding among the leaves.

Cheesewood or banyalla *(Pittosporum bicolor)*, with pale stalked flowers, was as often rooted in the bases of tree ferns as in the leaf mould. This and the lemon bottlebrush *(Callistemon pallidus)* of wet seepages are two of Strzelecki's specialities, another is the rare *Hakea epiglottis*.

Where the blue and manna gums dwindled at about 1,600 feet (500 metres) the mountain pepper *(Tasmannia lanceolata)* began to appear, bearing circlets of black berries like ivy, but beware those berries! Take the tiniest nibble, then spit the fragment out and the residual taste will go on getting hotter and hotter in the mouth until one is reaching for the water bottle.

Tall sassafras *(Atherospermum moschatum)* trees with flowers scattered along the twigs as in Monotoca but with larger leaves, occupied gullies, casting the cool shade needed by the underlying ferns. Sassafras belongs to the mulberry family.

Stinkwood *(Ziera arborescens)*, with its three-fingered leaves, like laburnum, grows on the seafront at Whitemark, but is more characteristic of these heights. Another with a wide altitudinal range is the so-called dogwood, which is a daisy bush, unrelated to the true dogwoods of Canada and Europe.

The orchids which we were told to look out for, we failed to find, but I caught up with them thirty-seven years later with Doreen Lovegrove, one of the volunteer curators of the Emita Historic Museum. In my mid-seventies by then, and at the end of a long day of exploration, I was no longer headed for the heights, merely ambling along the first part of the Strzelecki trail.

Over a stile and across a paddock pimpled with mounds of kikuyu grass, whose stringy stems had climbed the wire fence to convert it into a solid leafy barrier, we plunged into a long tunnel of magnificently blooming kunzea bushes. Ascending a gentle incline along the left fork, the hard water ferns and others began to increase and derelict tree boughs 'bloomed' belatedly with growths of branched grey lichens.

At the first creek crossing we came upon the prize in full bloom, streaked rock orchids *(Dendrobium striolatum)*, their lemon-yellow petals streaked with pencil-thin lines of red, the boss on the lip crisply white. Flowers were held six inches above the boulders, backed by thick mats of grass-like leaves draped down the rock faces.

They grew near the plunge pool of a small waterfall which was cascading down the narrow gully of a natural chute. The beer-coloured fluid, stained by organic matter, and possibly also limonite, frothed into soapsuds before gathering to cross the track and sluice down through a little grove of soft tree ferns, some of which looked the worse for wear and one completely dead.

Two black pipes led from the pool, to supply two settler families on the farmland below. Red-fruited saw-sedge splayed under the streamside paperbarks, but we saw few other plants and no birds, although the strident calls of black currawongs and black ravens penetrated the stillness imparted by the all enveloping leaf canopy.

It was wonderfully mild in the shelter of the trees, in sharp contrast to the rumbustious gale howling outside. This was November and spring should have sprung, but it was quite wintry still. Looking back after re-emerging from the kunzea tunnel, we saw a gaunt yellow scar on the grey granite above. A large chunk of hillside had recently got dislodged and come tumbling down. Doreen, an enthusiastic hill walker, was going up to investigate on the morrow if the weather allowed. I flew out before she left, hoping that she wasn't being blown away when she emerged from the comforting embrace of the gum trees.

On our first sortie into the forest with Leila and the Warhams, the going was much rougher. The branch with which Dom supported himself on one of the steep drops, broke and he slithered down the wet earth bank to finish in a heap on the stream bed. Although he was not a casualty, we started talking about reincarnation.

Dom elected to come back as a mutton bird and, later, probably in a subsequent reincarnation, to write his memoirs under the title of "*I was a surface egg.*" At least he knew all the answers already and how to roll down a burrow out of the way of illegal egg collectors. I thought I would return as an albatross, one of the royals on the New Zealand mainland, away from the worst of the southerly weather.

We made several stops on the way back, one to admire a great concourse of oystercatchers on a sand spit, another to investigate a wealth of heathland flowers carpeting the ground beneath a fine stand of grass trees. Here were hakeas and epacrids, hazel pomaderris *(Pomaderris apetala)* and blue olive-berry *(Elaeocarpus reticulatus)*, with white bell flowers developing into blue berries among leaves up to six inches long.

The guitar plant *(Lomatia tinctorium)*, named for the shape of its dry fruits, grew as bushes, like the hakeas when covered with their terminal tassels of flowers, but the leaves were leathery and divided instead of being formidable spines. Straggles of Australian clematis *(Clematis aristata)* softened the outlines of many of the shrubs.

Screw ferns sprouted from wet peat, the first-formed fronds flat to the ground, the sparse sporing spikes erect. With them was a neatly regular club moss, *Selaginella uliginosa*, and insect-eating sundews, with the disembowelled remains of their victims lodged among the leaf tentacles that had imbibed their liquefied entrails. Here was another pennywort, the hairy *Hydrocotyle hirta*, growing with austral brooklime *(Gratiola peruviana var. pumilla)* of the speedwell family. The pale pink tubular flowers snuggled into the leaf axils making this the sort of plant one should look for in English woodlands. It seemed strangely at odds here with the harshly angular horny cone bushes *(Isopogon ceratophyllus)*.

18 Veined Bristle Fern *Polyphlebium venosum* and
Austral Filmy Fern *Hymenophyllum australe*

19 Yellow-throated Honey-eater *Lichenostomus flavicollis* and
Sassafras *Atherospermum moschatum*

20 Mountain Pepper *Tasmannia lanceolata* and
Striated Rock Orchid *Dendrobium striolatum*

Chapter Three

FLINDERS ISLAND: SEAFARERS, FARMERS AND NATURALISTS

1. OF SHIPS AND STRAITSMEN

By mid-December 1958 the sheep on the outlying islands had been shorn and the wool was baled, stacked and awaiting collection. Tuck Robinson was roped in, as ever, his launch *"Tassie"* admirable for the job but his dinghy much too small to accommodate the big bouncy bales. Just one of these would effectively exclude even the wizened and wiry Tuck from squeezing in alongside to man the oars.

That was where our cumbersome *"Half Safe"* came into its own. When he borrowed our boat for ferrying wool bales he had us too, 'us' on this occasion being me and the six foot four inch, thirteen stone nine pound Bob Tilt of CSIRO. We boarded *"Tassie"* at 6.0 a.m., our bread and Marmite breakfast in hand (probably Vegemite in this country), the forecast break-up of the fine spell having brought Tuck well head of schedule. *"Half Safe"* was made fast astern. Some of the smaller reefs carried only a few sheep, but, even if there was only one bale, it had to be picked up.

On one of these trips we came upon the remnants of William's boat, the *"Elma"*, wrecked off Vansittart or Gun Carriage Island, some said on purpose. She was reputed to be near breaking up point, even with the most expert of handling, and her owner was rumoured to believe that the insurance money might be worth more than the boat.

Beyond the island, firmly stuck on the Vansittart Shoals, were the remains of the steel ship, *"Farsund"*, which had carried no more than a ballast of sand when she foundered here in 1912.

During 1958 the *"Merilyn"* had run aground on Goose Island, after being pensioned off as the Manly Ferry, where she plied under the name of *"Narrabeen"*. Her plight was due to fog, not rough seas, and her crew rowed safely ashore to be picked up later by the police boat. She was carrying boxes of gelignite, which the marine authorities envisaged taking on a life of their own as the ship broke up and drifting around as floating mines, an unpredictable hazard to shipping. *"Merilyn"* had therefore to be blown up.

When the official party went to salvage the £1,500 engine and other valuables before scuttling her, they found that the local fishermen had forestalled them, and had even bodily removed the wheelhouse. Unfortunately for them, someone let the cat out of the bag while on the beer and Trooper Bailey was led to the swag, hidden in the bush half a mile or so from Lady Barron, where it had been landed under cover of darkness. Needless to say, no-one came forward to claim it. At least the officials rescued the propeller and part of its shaft, these being put on display later at the Emita Historic Museum.

Heading south for Apple Orchard Point, we passed the sturdy cargo vessel *"Prion"*, stuck fast on the rocks of Tin Kettle Island. She had been there for some days, out, like us, to load wool, but she had gone in too close. Although not a total loss, like the others, it looked as though she would be there until the next fortnight's high tide lifted her off. She was rescued intact and lived a long and happy life thereafter.

Thirty-two years later, in January 1991, as a tourist on the little paddle steamer *"Lady Stellfox"* at Launceston, I heard our skipper drawing attention to three old cargo boats which had plied to and from the Bass Strait Islands. They were drawn up alongside a wharf where the River Tamar broadened out below the basalt walls of Cataract Gorge, but I looked in vain for the familiar lines of *"Prion"*. The skipper remembered her well.

"Pensioned off," he said, "after her long and distinguished battle with the Roaring Forties."

From which I took it she was still afloat somewhere, like an old horse, put out to grass.

Not all were that lucky. On 18th December, 1958, the very day that we saw *"Prion"* aground, the fisher folk and others in Lady Barron were glued to their short wave radios, listening for news of any survivors of the ninety-three tonnes *"Willwatch"*, sunk without trace in the western Bass Strait the previous day.

On board had been Captain McCarthy, Mac to the folk here, and five others. Captain and engineer had six children between them and three of the others were mere boys, of sixteen to eighteen. *"Willwatch"* had been in trouble with colossal seas, her forecastle full of water and the deck cargo shifting in the early morning among the Hunter-Trefoil Island group off King Island. The crew were plugging holes ripped in her side with blankets; the forward bilge pump was blocked.

The boat was sixty-four years old and this had happened before, but Mac had brought her limping into port to be dried out. This time was once too often. The little wooden ships of the day were gallantly pliant, riding what seemed impossible seas, but the sea always held the master card.

Weather was from the south-west on this day, where all the sheltering land might have been, but *"Willwatch"*, now low in the water, had not the stamina to turn round and head into the maelstrom, so had to run before it, out into the open strait. Calls had come at about twenty minute intervals.

"Decks awash. Don't know how long we'll last."

"Position deteriorates."

"I've ordered the crew over the side in life jackets."

First the dinghy that might have acted as a lifeboat was stuck, then they got it free but couldn't get it launched. No way could the terrified horses in horse boxes on the deck among fifty sliding petrol drums have survived. The fifty drums went over first.

There were ships speeding to the rescue, but none close enough to see her rocket flares in the wild conditions prevailing, till all had been used. Captain Mac knew that even the last one had not been seen, but he remained calm.

"I'm still here, but I can't hold her now. The sea has her."

A little later, through a lot of static, as the ship rolled and bucked her last: "It looks as though this is it. See you later. Cheerio."

No more messages came!

The gallant men who sailed those lissom wooden ships through the tempestuous waters of the Roaring Forties, the straitsmen and others, were a race apart, achieving astonishing feats of bravery in the ordinary course of a day's work, to keep the cargoes coming and going. Often they looked death in the face, and were prepared when it came for real.

Next day the search was officially called off and there was a lot of head wagging among the fraternity who had waited in vain by their radios for news of a respite. There were just three and a half hours between the first SOS and the final farewell. This was too little for any of the other vessels braving the storm, and under duress themselves, to arrive, but why had the RAAF plane not reached the spot until nearly an hour after the last distress call?

The talk was angry, and subdued, as we headed for Apple Orchard Point, passing the green, two-masted cargo boat, "*Sheerwater*", en route. She, too, was to come to a sudden end along that treacherous North Tasmanian coast, lost after hitting a reef off the mouth of the Tamar River.

Was this the reef, by Georgetown, where the oil tanker "*Iron Baron*" had foundered towards the end of 1995, after the pilot had come aboard but before he reached the wheelhouse to take over. When I got to Flinders Island just after the wreck, I learned that James Luddington and others had been engaged on a rescue mission to save penguins fouled by the oil that streamed out of the stricken hull. Because of the set of winds and currents, these were coming ashore on some of the outer Furneaux Islands, principally those south of Cape Barren, but some drifted through into Franklin Sound and a few round the north of Flinders. Five per cent of the penguin population and the odd albatross were affected. The boat was eventually towed out into Bass Strait and sunk in deep water.

Even the so much stouter "*Naracoopa*" died with its boots on eventually, blowing up and disappearing beneath the waves off Port Lincoln in South Australia. Both she and the "*Sheerwater*" were gone before 1975.

Talking with one of the knowledgable ones in 1995, I was told that sixty-eight wrecks have been pin-pointed around the islands, but the locals claim there to be well over a hundred. Names of some of the smaller islands such as Tuck's Reef and Jack Mansell's Reef are said to have been given in memory of local seafarers who had wrecked their boats on them.

* * * * *

The naming of Apple Orchard Reef where Tuck dropped me off that morning was a mystery. Nothing seemed less likely to grow here than apples. I learned from Tuck that a large part of the island had once been covered by bushy kangaroo apples *(Solanum aviculare)*.

"Hard to get through, but the fruit's good to eat, like cape gooseberries or little tomatoes."

Both are of the same family, the first ensconced in orange Chinese lanterns. Tuck hastened to add that the similar fruits of the spiny Sodom's apple *(Solanum sodomaeum)* were poisonous, as were the stems and leaves of kangaroo apple.

Bob stayed on *"Tassie"* to help Tuck with the wool bales, which he was collecting from one of the Cape Barren Island woolsheds in a bay just beyond Apple Orchard Point. I had an hour and a half to explore 'my' delightful little island.

The eastern part was riddled with storm petrel burrows, penetrating the all enveloping bower spinach *(Tetragonia implexicoma)* at an average density of four per square metre. Numbers tailed off towards the sea and towards the sizable nesting and roosting ground of the big black-backed Pacific gulls alongside, where life would have been untenable for such vulnerable little birds. They were no bigger than swallows, and trying to locate their nest holes among the sleeping predators at dead of night would be a frightening experience.

Little blue or fairy penguins burrowed among the tussocks of coast spear grass *(Stipa teretifolia)*, where I flushed some Cape Barren geese, but there were no mutton birds, just sooty oystercatchers and caspian terns around the periphery.

We wanted to land on the smaller reef between here and the point, but Tuck was unfamiliar with the surrounding shoals and clouds were building up with a freshening of the wind. It was important not to get the wool wet, with sea spray or rain, so he promised to find a way in with someone more knowledgable and bring me another time. The wind was getting chillier. I slithered into the hold between the hessian-wrapped bales and the deck and wriggled around to where Bob was dispensing elevenses. The best of the day had gone, but we'd made it this time.

Trying the previous day, we had got only just beyond Little Dog Island when Tuck decided to turn back rather than risk a douching. He dropped Bob and me off in "Half Safe" near the scatter of islets lumped together under the term Samphire Islands. The mighty Bob did his St Christopher act getting me across the shallow tide rip dry shod.

Samphire Islands were well named, being little more than humps on tidal flats of white sand and flat black basalt rocks, outliers in Petrifaction Bay off the mouth of the Samphire River and very much within the sea samphire realms as far as vegetation zones went. They were too vulnerable to inundation to provide nesting habitat for birds other than a single pair of sooty oystercatchers, but these had succeeded in bringing off a couple of chicks.

We put up huge flocks of curlew, dotterel and other waders that were feeding on the mud flats in such numbers that they were difficult to count. Here also were two pelicans. After wading and rowing around the islands, tabulating the meagre salt-tolerant flora, we moved in towards the Flinders Island shore, following the curve of Petrifaction Bay to finish up at the little shop and replenish our stores.

There were just as many cargo and fishing boats around when I was here again, thirteen months later, some registered here, some from other ports. Many fished with nets, some set cray pots around the island rocks — selling their catch, not as crays but as lobsters, regardless of the lack of the big succulent claws which make the best eating. Others took shellfish from the seabed.

Nine fishing boats were drawn up at Lady Barron jetty, which was piled high with fresh wallaby carcases for cray bait. The *"Naracoopa"* put in at 11.30, necessitating a certain amount of give and take to afford her enough wharf space, the fishermen having to double up. Her efficiency at discharging cargo was commendable. No sooner had she made fast than one of the three trucks for the Agricultural Bank was swung onto the wharf, a small tractor lowered into it and the two driven off immediately for Whitemark.

Agent Frank Henwood started lumping crates of fruit and vegetables off, assisted by four or five cray fishermen, while the *"Naracoopa"* crew dealt with the main cargo of bags of fertiliser, this continuing until well after dark.

Finally, when the young sickle moon was suspended high over the Strzelecki Peaks, the hard-working crew crept into their bunks, but the ship's lights flashed on again soon after 3.0 a.m., beaming through "Yolla's" half open door. The winches clanked into action, but only for a spell, then the inanimate noise changed to an animated one. Bleating of mutton-on-the-hoof mingled with the caterwauling of the mutton birds overnighting on the tussocks outside. And not all the noise drifting over the water was from the sheep, as the big flock was driven, cajoled and cursed ashore. (In those days masculine language was usually modified in the presence of females, but these early morning workers had too much on their minds to think of possible listeners of the fairer sex lurking on offshore islands!)

By 5.0 a.m. the mutton birds had left and the *"Naracoopa"* was edging her way unobtrusively out into the still grey light of dawn. Like the nightly passing of the shags, she came in from the west and left to the east. She would be moving back to Hobart along Tasmania's eastern sea board, calling perhaps at Coles Bay, Maria Island, Tasman Island or wherever her services in the picking up and putting down of cargoes were needed.

* * * * *

Entrails from the dismembered wallabies on Lady Barron jetty floated into Fisher Island's North-east Boat Harbour, attracting the attention of silver and Pacific gulls. Later in the day, when the ebb left the bulging intestines high and dry in crevices, large crabs got busy tweaking bits out with sharp pincers and transferring the revolting, half digested contents to their mouths with apparent relish. There is no accounting for tastes, but thank goodness for Nature's sanitary squads.

A whole swag of 'roo bones, picked clean of meat, was lodged in a gully. This was a later stage in the clearing up process, probably finished off by the maggots which metamorphosed into the plague of blowflies which had invaded "Yolla" the previous day, then disappeared as rapidly as it had come. Today and for most of the following week, the island was alive with more attractive insects, large dragonflies and black and orange butterflies which found no problem with the sea crossing.

Two boats circled the island while I was watching some spur-winged plovers scrawtching overhead. One was about its usual business of laying cray pots, the other was towing a water skier — a first for these waters as far as I was concerned.

Next morning I experienced a visitation from the Launceston Aero Club. An ominous roaring close above caused me to drop my paper on Vegetation Cycles and race outside "Yolla" in time for the next salute. The little Auster plane circled the island four times, a round face wreathed in grins peering out of the cockpit every time it swooped over. On the last, most daring sweep, our chimney nearly went the way of all flesh and the grin was replaced by a look of concern as the machine tilted skyward in what seemed the nick of time and, with a friendly flick of the tail, was off in the direction of Whitemark. Such a visitation from the skies was typical of spontaneous Aussie warmth. I assumed it was from my new-found friends in the Agricultural Department who used the planes in the normal course of their duties. Dave Paton, an agricultural officer from Launceston had flown in with me the week before to join Geoff Dimmock of the CSIRO Soils Division who was doing a comprehensive survey of island soil quality.

It was two days later, on 6th February, that I heard a distant human voice requesting Bill to wake its owner at six next morning. It sounded to be on my threshold, but came from the black and white *"Argonaut"* which had just pulled in to the shadowy Lady Barron pier. We enjoyed few of these still moonlight nights when sounds spanned distances as though they did not exist.

Even the mutton birds were not whooping in tonight as they did on darker nights when there was nothing to fear from wakeful gulls. The only sound was the querulous murmur of their offspring from underground, a persistent squealing, like the sound of invisible waders on distant mud flats.

This was the calm before the storm. At dawn there was not a ripple to be seen. *"Tassie"* chugged past under a brooding sky at 7.45 a.m. and in less than ten minutes was swallowed up, along with Little Dog Island, as part of the heavens made an unexpected visit to Planet Earth. Forked lightning played magnificently among the Strzelecki Peaks, visible only in the narrow strip of sky which lay below the heavy black pall hanging over the summits. The storm was centred in the west but ventriloquial thunder claps rolled in from all around. Daylight was effectively extinguished. Even nearby Reef Island and massive Big Dog Island disappeared in the menacing gloom.

And then the wind came. The randomly perched cormorants and sooty oystercatchers on Reef Island swung around to head into the westerly blast. The pied oystercatchers on Potts Point crouched close to the ground and the seven musk duck gave up their gentle offshore cruise, circled overhead and were gone with the wind.

Spreading eddies and ripples formed ominous patches on the oily black of the sea and suddenly the surface was whipped into white-capped rollers, despite the small area of fetch. Nothing seemed petrified in Petrifaction Bay during that whirlwind twenty minutes, but then the rains came in earnest, flattening out the sea as rapidly as it had risen. For the first time since my arrival, the welcome sound of water pouring into the rain tank was heard. I tried not to think of all the gull guano that was going in with it. This was my drinking water. Work stopped on the *"Argonaut"* as the crew dived for cover.

The rain ceased but the wind had come to stay. The noble Tuck turned tail and a bedraggled *"Tassie"* came bouncing back to bob agitatedly at her moorings for the rest of the day, the sea rising again as soon as the deluge ceased. The ease with which the seas can make here is quite extraordinary. The *"Argonaut"* lay inert all next day, with the waves slapping up her side and over the deck. She did not indulge in the rapid turnover achieved by the hardworking crew of the *"Naracoopa"*. Eventually, with all her bags of lime off-loaded, she was away with the tide early on the 8th February.

21 Pacific Gull *Larus pacificus* and old Sailing Ship

22 Wilsons Storm Petrels *Oceanites oceanicus* commonly seen at sea

23 White-backed Magpie *Gymnorhina tibicen*

2. WRESTING A LIVING FROM THE LAND

When I returned to the islands on 26th January 1960 the folk at Lady Barron were anxious to hear about my Antarctic experiences. I had sailed on the Danish polar vessel, *"Thala Dan"*, as one of the first four women ever to join the men of ANARE (The Australia and New Zealand Antarctic Research Expeditions) in the field. Four of us fitted nicely into a four-berth cabin. Since the 1959-60 trip women have been present on most of the annual visits to the southern bases, but it was an innovation then, and so newsworthy.

It had been hot and dry here. During most of my first week a fire was burning on the south-west corner of Flinders and another on Cape Barren. The first was the worst for some time, starting at Trousers Point and spreading up into the Strzeleckis. The Cape Barren fire burned longer and was joined by another near the jetty. Acute fire danger warnings were being broadcast for Victoria, although Sydney's heatwave, with its twenty-five deaths and over 100 heat collapses, was over.

"Half Safe's" planks had contracted under the onslaught of the merciless sun. She filled with water within five minutes of being launched and I left her anchored off the west side of Fisher Island, bravely, but only just, keeping her head above water, while the gaps narrowed.

Thirtieth of January was quiet and sunny, just right for the Saturday shopping. Despite four days of submergence and yesterday's bailing, "Half Safe" was still a quarter full, but sped around the north-east point on the incoming tide when emptied, as though propelled by an outboard motor. I was ashore at 8.0 a.m., an hour before the village came to life and four hours before either bread or fruit, for which I had come, would be available.

I passed the time of day chatting with Derek Smith's tame galah, who had only time for an occasional brief comment between gobbling down the green fruits of the New Zealand mirror plant or taupata *(Coprosma repens)* in which he roosted. There would be small chance of any of these travelling to Fisher Island in a gull's crop, as so many had before, their issue setting up a thriving colony along the back of the hut. (On my 1995 visit, this outlier had spread horrendously, although repeatedly cut back over the years.)

The galah's companions were a white budgerigar and a three-year-old boy with a toy bulldozer. When asked to keep the "brrrr brrrr brrrrs" quieter he replied, logically enough: "But I can't or the bulldozer won't work!"

News from the grown-ups revealed that Honest Tom Langley had given up the store and moved to Launceston, although there were rumours that he would be back for the mutton-birding. Jerry Addaway had taken over the store and the store planned by Trooper Bailey for his son, Don, was no nearer completion than it had been thirteen months before.

By the following year Tom and Jerry had swapped roles, as their namesake cartoon characters so often do. Tom was back in charge of Lady Barron store and Jerry had left to set up his own enterprise on the mainland. Don Bailey had at last opened up his rival store near the jetty.

In 1960 we had opportunity to get to know something of the island's farming. My companions by that time were Michael Ridpath of CSIRO in Hobart and his petite French wife, Paula, and Minette Ross, a colleague in the Botany Department at Melbourne University during my year's exchange lectureship there. Our guide and informant was Atholl Dart, who farmed, as Tom Langley had, in the lee of the Strzelecki Peaks — a grazier and a contractor doing major land clearance tasks for others.

On the day of Minette's arrival, 23rd February, he took us all up Vinegar Hill, a must for newcomers. The summit lookout was only 323 feet (107 metres) above the jetty, but the views were superb and it would have been a sin to miss them. As our cameras clicked, he told of his colour slide collection and invited us to go and view it the next day. It was touch and go getting ashore, but we made it and Atholl drove us to his holding, which was quite near to Whitemark.

A bored mob of steers and heifers stared curiously as we went into the welcoming warmth of a log fire.

"Gum roots. They burn longer, slower and hotter than branches."

Like the iron-hard mallee roots along the margins of South Australia's dry country. Atholl was a bachelor and we were welcomed by his spryly energetic eighty-year-old "Poppa". Beside him was a bookcase of fascinating reading matter and a Norwegian phonograph, which language our host was learning preparatory to receiving emigrants from that country. The evening of pictures thrown onto a wide screen left no doubts about Atholl's skill as a photographer, both on Flinders and among the mountains of Norway, where he had holidayed recently and hoped to do so again.

By eleven p.m. the wind had risen alarmingly.

"It would be madness for you to go back tonight. You must stay!"

We had hauled the boat well above high water mark, so there were no worries on that count. After two hours' more slides and more tea, we distributed ourselves around spare beds, sofas and carpets and settled for the night, with a doubled sheet apiece. A possum had crept in under the eaves to sleep in a warm corner by the chimney and was very much part of the house party, seeming very close as he shuffled around during the night.

"Poppa", who looked after the beef cattle and sheep and milked the Jersey house cow, was astir at 5 a.m. I woke the others at six, as we had an appointment with Tuck for several days on another island at eight. We ate home grown fried eggs while admiring the spacious views, one right across the island to the peaks of Babel.

A week later, back from our camping trip on Little Green Island, we met Atholl again for a conducted tour around the island's farmlands on the most appalling roads. None of the Flinder's roads were sealed at that time as the population was too small to be adequately represented in parliament.

(approximately 1,200, 350 of whom were school children). Members from other parts couldn't care less.

The sixty trucks belonging to the Agricultural Bank were the chief churners-up of the road surfaces and they were registered in Hobart, so Hobart got the benefit of their road tax. The Flinders Island cars, one to every four of the population, were reputed to be more per head than anywhere else, yet most of the roads were excruciating. This was a price one paid for being a pioneer.

Pausing by Chew Tobacco Creek, Atholl pointed out how to assess different qualities of land. Bigger trees and denser scrub grew only on the better soils, where the shrubs to look out for as being those denoting fertility were hazel pomaderris, 'dogwood' and tree everlasting *(Helichrysum dendroideum)*, also an understorey of Bass Strait fireweed *(Senecio capillifolius)*. These only turned up on the poorer land after superphosphate had been applied.

Perennial ryegrass and clover leys varied greatly in quality and our guide stressed how much better it was to leave the land fallow for a year, or even two, after clearing, to allow time to get rid of the inevitable regrowth before sowing the valuable seed, then stocking only lightly at first. He abhorred the practice followed by the Bank Scheme of sowing and stocking straight away and creaming off the virgin goodness of the land in a crop of fat cattle before passing it over to the settlers for them to deal with the weed problem.

White turnips might be grown as a nurse crop and grazed off as the grass pushed through. Oats as a nurse took too much from the soil.

"Two to three hundredweights of super with the necessary micro-nutrients and this land will produce as much as Table Cape in North Tasmania, which is selling for £200 an acre." And a great deal more in the nineties.

Atholl thought the Bank had not only overgrazed but bought over-extravagantly. They started with pure shorthorns, crossing these with Aberdeen Angus from New Zealand. Later, as in so many other parts of the world, Herefords became the favourites. The fat stock were exported to Tasmania, usually before the settlers moved in, often to blocks with no houses on them. They worked for the Bank until they had earned enough to buy.

Unlike the settler scheme on King Island, no qualifications were needed to be a settler. No capital was necessary and the earlier proviso of having to work for two years on a farm elsewhere had been waived. Eventually each was provided with a house, a water supply, two windmills and a loan to buy stock.

"There's one I could name, owes £7,000, and just lazes away his time doing nothing about it!"

Water availability had been ascertained before Dimmock's soil survey was completed and all farms could rely on good water about three metres below ground or less. Only a few areas suffered the all too prevalent Australian curse of salinity.

We visited Stewart Harley, newly settled on sandy land near Nelsons Lagoon. Five hundred acres was a usual size of holding, but Harley farmed 720 acres of these porous soils, running a flock of 350 sheep on land that would more comfortably have accommodated only 250. These were

Pollworths, that are still the most popular breed thirty-five years later. Pollworths were three-quarters Merino; half bred Merinos were known as Corriedales.

His somewhat scatty sheepdog was not in the business of obeying orders when there was something more interesting to do. At present he was chasing three sheep in and out of a concrete culvert under the road, in an entertaining version of canine hide and seek. Stewart was still employed full time at the bank, working on his holding at weekends.

He was currently suffering a plague of grasshoppers, the population being estimated at two to three per square foot or twenty to twenty-five per square metre. The insects were not as destructive as their big brothers, the locusts, but they did not confine their attention to pasture plants.

Figuring on their menu were bracken and the leaves of boxthorn hedges, to which they were quite welcome. More reprehensible was their liking for the bark of lemon trees, wallpaper, upholstery, curtains and loaves of bread left on posts by the baker for collection. Farmers' problems can be more than meets the eye of the casual passer-by.

The hills backing Stewart's farm held alluvial tin, while silver was suspected to lie hidden in Silver Hill. Perhaps, if farm pests got the better of them, the settlers could take up mining. Tin mines had operated on Flinders Island at one time, but yields were small and the prices dropped, so the mines went out of business — as did the Cape Barren islanders who sluiced tin out of the Rock River. A little silver has been found, and a few specimens of gold — at thirty to thirty-two ounces to the ton of rock — but no-one can find the elusive reef from which these might have come. The best find so far has been some tiny fragments on the beach west of Badger Corner. Soft brown coal deposits are said to occur fifty feet (16 m) down.

Moving off the sands, we came to a better watered area where strawberry clover *(Trifolium fragiferum)* was so lush that the associated ryegrass seemed to be pushing through with difficulty. There had been three feet of water lying here in winter, before the broad open drains were dug. No tile or mole drains fed into these but the water table had been effectively lowered. A few reeds, the cosmopolitan *Phragmites australis*, lingered in places and the land was too wet still for sheep, which contracted bad infestations of "worm".

Before being broken in, this land had carried a mixture of tussock grass, sedges and reeds and was a favourite with the Cape Barren geese. These moved onto the larger island when their small nesting islands dried up with the advance of summer. As grazers, they sought out fresh green forage — just at the time when the farmers needed it for their livestock — this not enhancing their popularity.

Times were hard anyway by 1960, the livestock markets in severe decline. The freight charge on cattle travelling to Melbourne was £12 a head, to Launceston £8. This was acceptable a few years before, when fat cattle were selling at £75-80, but the price was said to be as low as £30 now. The value of sheep meat and wool had also halved in the past three years or so and freight charges were still rising.

The farmers felt that the crews who manned the cattle boats, earning £80 a month and their keep, should have been on to a good thing, but there was a very rapid turnover of these sailors. Some just didn't put in an appearance when their ship left the home port. Three of the six on the current boat had recently left because they were unable to go to the pictures on Saturday nights. There were two sides to life at sea, as to everything else.

The main spectacle of our day out with Atholl Dart was the witnessing of the aerial spreading of top dressings of fertiliser. It was Sunday, but that signified not at all, the important thing was that there was scarcely a breath of wind. Allowance still had to be made for such little breeze as there was, the fields being covered in thirty feet (14 metre) strips, slightly displaced to allow for drift, although the little planes flew so low that this was minimal.

Ground staff loading the super phosphate into the planes earned £40 a week, the pilots, for obvious reasons, more. Three men aboard each truck were emptying the bags of fertiliser into the hopper, one manned the hoist which emptied the hopper into the aircraft as it taxied alongside. Even since leaving the mainland, the artificials had been handled many times, on and off trucks from the store, on and off the boat, into and out of the island warehouse, on and off the trucks and on and off the plane.

The ration for each plane was seven hundredweights on a hot day such as today, nine hundredweights when cooler, more the previous year when safety standards were laxer. Although the target field was currently three miles away, the turnaround time was only three and a half minutes in the air and one and a half on the ground. Atholl said it was sometimes even less. There were a couple of craft, so the pilots could give each other a breather without slowing the operation down.

I learned that the recent aerial salute to which I had been treated was from the farmers' representative on the Tasmanian Fauna Board, a member of the Launceston Aero Club who had come over to watch the stripping of some grass seed that he was buying for his farm at Port Hedland.

From the loading site we drove to the reception area where farmer and ex-pilot Johnnie was acting as marker, with a big white kitbag held above his head every time a plane approached. Thirteen manly paces to one side and he sat down to await the next.

"'Tis tiring. You get up and you sit down and you get up again. Mad as a two bob watch. I'm so busy I don't know whether I'm Arthur or Martha. Gets me flat out, like a lizard drinking."

There was much more in this vein; a wealth of Australianisms as picturesque as the traditional Cockney rhyming slang. And we had an hour and a half in which to be entertained, as this was the lunch break and the two pilots had flown back home for theirs. When time was up Minette took a turn as 'marker boy', with the idea of confusing the pilot with her very short shorts.

By now, in 1960, the Agricultural Bank was nearing the end of its opening up campaign. Twenty thousand acres had been cleared this year but only five thousand were scheduled for next. After a certain amount of re-ploughing, the Bank would hand over to the State. When the job finished Johnnie had ideas of taking to his plane again to help the duck shooters, by keeping the birds low within range of their guns. I couldn't help feeling that, with an Auster roaring through the skies at them they would be more likely to make a prompt exit. Perhaps he would round them up and bring them back, sheepdog style.

Our next port of call was Summer Camp, the headquarters for the Bank's eighty-three crawler tractors, and the source of a welcome pineapple juice after imbibing so much flying fertiliser. Rows of compact bachelor quarters among the big machines made this look like a mining or lumbermen's camp.

Belatedly we ate lunch at yet another of the Bank's sites — a sand pit this time, where shell sand was scooped up for dressing paddocks newly cleared from the more acid peaty heaths. This was a fine white sand with eighty per cent of calcium carbonate, mostly as pulverised shell fragments, but some from calcareous concretions accumulated around organic detritus. Much of the shelly material was from marine deposits laid down when the site was under the waters of Bass Strait during geological history. The usual dressing was one to two tons per acre, then a further two to three hundredweights per acre of purer calcium carbonate, probably of slaked lime possibly of quicklime, when the seed was sown.

South and west from here, we emerged onto the coast at Marshall's Bay near Emita, about halfway up the west coast — a magnificent stretch scenically — and travelled south through Whitemark to Atholl's farm. A man of big machines, contracting out his services for those needing major jobs done, he took us to the western mountain foothills, where he was excavating a huge dam in the dark sandy soil. He wasn't 'at work' this Sunday evening but he gave us a demonstration. The bulldozer roared into frenetic activity, great in noise but slow in speed (like the earlier three-year-old simulator). Michael climbed aboard and the two men trundled the mechanical monster back and forth across the great hole, pushing giant gobs of black soil ahead of it and toppling this neatly over the brink onto the newly cleared heath beyond. This looked exceedingly sandy. Would the dam hold water, or would they have to line it with puddle clay, like our old canals at home?

On the way there we had passed a certain Joe shooting a black tiger snake on the road. We rounded off the day by visiting the island's most famous beauty spot of Trousers Point, where we caught up with Joe, a lawyer, and his companion, a new Australian, baiting a fish trap with the dead snake. On the way back to Atholl's farm, where "Poppa" was entertaining a Methodist minister, just flown in from Melbourne, we stopped to watch a huge disc plough at work.

Afternoon tea and then a tour of the farm, to admire some prized polled Hereford milkers with sturdy calves at foot. The grazing was good, but I couldn't help being saddened by the standing skeletons of once noble blue gum trees among which the Herefords gained their healthy gloss. People must eat and the land must provide. Farmers and conservationists must always compromise in an effort to strike an equitable balance before it is too late, as in so much of the earlier settled world.

A highlight of the final miles back to our dinghy and a very different facet of the Flinders landscape was the sight of thousands of clamouring starlings jostling for a foothold on the gaunt limbs of their roost trees — isolated forest monarchs spearing up from recently cleared land: natives spared to open their arms to these querulous invaders from the Old World.

A covey of twelve brown or swamp quails scattered ahead of the vehicle. This is the commonest of three kinds occurring on the island. Less common are the stubble quail and the painted button quail. A nankeen kestrel was hunting in the vicinity of Lady Barron as we launched our craft.

24 Swamp Honey Myrtle *Melaleuca squamea*

25 Love Creeper *Comesperma volubile*

26 South African Boxthorn *Lycium ferocissimum*

3. NATURALISTS AT LARGE

Dr John Thomson of Melbourne University Zoology Department joined me on Fisher Island on 8th March, 1960. He was studying mammals at the time, changing subsequently to genetics at Canberra and later to a world-wide study of bracken, based at Sydney. The recent discovery in Victoria of leadbeaters possums, thought to be extinct, had brought possum studies into fashion and he wanted to acquaint himself with the Flinders Island animals. Derek Smith was ready to oblige, as always.

The two of us came ashore at the appointed hour in a borrowed dinghy, our own being under repair. It was small, disappearing between the long slow swell waves passing smoothly beneath from the port beam, so that a worried Derek watching from the land kept losing sight of us. He made for the jetty, seeking a rescue vessel, but came at a jog trot when he saw that all was well. Frail the little "*Nyla*" might appear, but she rode the waters as buoyantly as a gull and was much easier to handle than her cumbersome counterpart, which had been built for duck shooting on table-flat marshes. It was good, too, not to be up to our ankles in bilge water.

The weather was not what we would have chosen for possuming and there was a sharp rain squall as we beached the dinghy, but there was little more that evening. Daughter Lynette and Captain Ross Campbell of "*Victoria II*" joined us for many windy miles in pursuit of our uncooperative quarry.

Derek drove with his eyes following the spotlight that played on the bushes alongside. Ross, in the front seat, kept an eye on the road and a restraining hand on the steering wheel when Derek appeared to be following the lure of the light into trouble.

The possums were supposed to be feeding on the bulldozed mounds of blackboy stumps on newly cleared land, but had chosen the easy option tonight of keeping out of the wind and out of sight. We were proceeding afoot when we spotted our first — up a gum tree. Ross shinned up, as on his more familiar nautical rigging, to shake him down, making alluring offers of a free ride to Melbourne. John took up a strategic position below, with stout "butterfly net" at the ready. Derek, with professional abandon, leaned against a neighbouring tree trunk with folded arms to watch the amateurs, remarking: "This is going to be fun."

It must certainly have appeared so to watching possums. The candidate for admission to the university hit the ground with a thud. John's net hit the ground alongside with another and then there were bodies flying everywhere. Quite a while later the quarry was 'playing possum' in dense cover, as possums should, and his pursuers were extricating themselves from situations which they would have regarded as unattainable in the normal course of events.

Our next target was sitting on a mound, posing nicely for cameras which we might have brought had it not now been nearly dark — in a way that possums never did when cameras were to hand. This time we went at it more scientifically, encircling the mound so that the animal had no chance of breaking free.

While the marsupial gazed in goggle-eyed fascination at the zoologist who had just materialised in front of him, Ross crept unsportingly up behind and dropped the net over his head. A squirm, a scuffle and there were once more bodies racing everywhere. Some finished up in the same thicket, others were scattered round the open flat trying to lighten their darkness with inadequate torches. Possum II probably went into a huddle with possum I and had a little chuckle about the learned folk who were studying possumkind.

Shoes abandoned in the chase were retrieved and there was a considerable interval while all the eyes which gleamed from the darkness had the reddish glow which denoted wallabies. Some were far apart and obviously bovine, one pair belonged to a black and white puss, foraging some ten miles from the nearest habitation and lucky, indeed, that we carried no firearms. Foraging feral cats were among the least popular of mammals.

We flushed a few quails and larks from the long grass and conjured up images of wombats and wild pigs, which turned into blackboy butts as we got nearer. Only the one which snorted and made a half-hearted rush at the supposed antagonist, then scooted away at high speed was genuine.

When almost back to Lady Barron, voices were suddenly raised in unison, triggering a squealing of brakes and grinding of wheels on gravel. A cascade of bodies flowed over seats in the effort to envelope an inoffensive beastie gazing dreamily into the headlights, mesmerized by the sudden intrusion into its ordered nocturnal world. Still dazzled, the possum turned and bolted, but was run to earth in a patch of scrub and grabbed by the scruff of the neck. He squeaked in protest, but was popped ignominiously into a sack as the party reassembled in triumph. Derek, lounging unobtrusively in the background, leaving the fun to his guests, asked if any of the speedsters remembered getting through that fence.... Nets and torches retrieved, we continued on our way.

There was a final skirmish in the scrub near Petrifaction Bay, where all that glinted in the darkness proved to be that most characteristic part of the Australian scene, the abandoned beer bottle. And so to Derek's for a welcome cuppa.

Percy the possum proved to be the silver-grey phase, not the Tasmanian black (which is usually a dark chocolate-brown). He quietly pondered his fate on the living room floor, learning quickly that there was no easy way out of his current predicament and no point in threshing around. This placidity was equally well shown by wild koalas newly winkled from their tree perches on Phillip Island a few months later. Marsupials, even devils, are not noted for their ferocity, which is maybe why they got squeezed out by the more pushy placentals from other parts of the world.

Possum was later consigned to the wash house with the talking galah. We can only surmise what they found to talk about during the long blustery night

— a night which we spent in Derek's parlour, having brought our sleeping bags in anticipation of not being able to return. We had to wait for slack water at the turn of the tide next morning, so walked up Vinegar Hill first, enjoying our belated breakfast of steak and kidney pudding and beans the more for the exercise.

The weather remained unsettled and John needed more possum material before Friday morning's plane, so he took off straight away with food and camping gear to tide him over the next twenty-four hours. He spent the afternoon picking up skulls around the lagoons with Ross and Arthur Harland and was spared the necessity of more skulduggery by shooting to obtain skins when he learned that he could obtain the data he sought from Silas Mansell's pelt collection.

This he did the following Monday, discovering that there are none of the typical Tasmanian black possums on Flinders Island, only variations of the Victorian silver-grey. The blacks on Wilsons Promontory had been introduced so did not form a geographical link between the two as had been postulated.

The evening hunt became a 'bring 'em back alive' exploit and Percy found himself with three playmates at the end of it. Derek drove the four possums to the airport and exchanged them for CSIRO's Ukrainian Dr Myckytowycz (Mycky to everyone here) and Ted Hesterman, so there were four of us to lunch on Fisher Island. Ted tried out his fishing rod in the afternoon, 'to get the feel of the sea', but it was tinned steak for supper. Chess became a new institution in the nightlife of the island.

* * * * *

Our next night ashore on 14th March was spent with Atholl Dart. The four of us went armed with sleeping bags this time and were conducted first around some new land which Atholl had acquired to the south. After refreshments we set off on foot to investigate a limestone cave at the foot of the range bordering his paddocks.

This opened out within the low entrance into a spacious chamber with broad stumpy stalactites hanging from the roof. Earth had accumulated on the floor and no earlier formed stalagmites pushed up through the deposits. Seepage along cracks imparted a pinkish ferric tinge to the rocks and microsculpting on the walls formed intricate patterns, like frost on a window pane. Tunnels led off in various directions, inviting further exploration.

We had hoped to find bats, but there were none, and no tell-tale guano. Two of the smaller insectivorous species have been recorded on Flinders Island. The lesser long-eared bat *(Nyctophilus geoffroyi)*, a widespread species, the Tasmanian ones slightly larger than those of Western Australia, and the forest eptesicus bat *(Eptesicus vulturnus)*. This last genus includes the serotine bats of Europe, but is not mentioned in the Australian zoologists' 'bible', Troughton's *"Furred Animals of Australia."*

This author records no fruit bats further south than the New South Wales'

Victorian border, although stating that one, the little reddish fruit bat *(Pteropus scapulatus)*, which feeds mainly on eucalyptus flowers "is a great wanderer and may fly as far as the Victorian border at times".

It was of particular interest, therefore, when John Nield recorded a fruit bat on Big Dog Island a few years before. This had appeared during the birding season to feed on a pile of rotting apples tipped out on the beach.

"I thought it was a vampire, come down after the dead mutton birds."
Nield had caught it, fed it on apples for a couple of days and then let it go, but it came back. He re-caught it, kept it awhile and later sent it off, live, to a zoo near Hobart, where it was reported to be still doing well.

My first day in Australia in 1995 included a visit to the Melbourne Botanic Garden by the River Yarra, where I was astonished to see hundreds of fruit bats dangling in the branches of palms, gums and poplars. It was early October, a day of watery eyes and runny noses with both me and my companion wishing for gloves. From reading Troughton and from observations elsewhere, I had assumed fruit bats to be tropical. It seemed not.

"They have always been here" I was told.

Most were wrapped in their leathery black wings — suspended rectangles, but there were a few flutterings and the occasional take-off. When they left to feed on the plentiful flowers of wattles, gums and bottle-brushes with the coming of night, it would be even chillier.

Back in Atholl Dart's cave we found fresh dung of small mammals, likely to be either pouched mice *(Antechinus minimus)* or New Holland mice *(Pseudomys novaehollandiae)*, both of which are recorded from Flinders Island. The faecal pellets supported starry growths of white candelabra-shaped fungi like evanescent versions of the familiar candle-snuff fungus of rotting wood.

John, our professional entomologist, was in his element, collecting the creepy-crawlies from the cave walls and floors. We all joined in. For more than an hour the cave echoed with the hunters' cries of "What's this?" "Here's another." "Come quick, before it gets away."

Most characteristic were the bright brown cave wetas, members of the cricket fraternity with long wispy antennae and slender rangy legs, very like ones I had seen in the Princess Margaret Rose Caves of coastal South Australia. Small springtails (Collembola) hopped blithely across the rock faces among scuttling silver-fish (bristle-tails or thysanurians), such as we see scooting across our carpets indoors.

Grey-black slaters (an outdoor version of the familiar domestic wood lice) trotted past shiny black millipedes and smaller black ticks. Preying on the more vulnerable were several kinds of spiders. Most sluggish were the brown flatworms (platyhelminths), which had special memories for me from my student days, when these animals appeared in all our lecture notes as bloody helminths. Such are the snares of taking down dictation, but it made a useful swearword in the days when the prefix was not in such general use as when I reached the great southern continent.

Some of us were to return later with live traps to capture and identify the small mammals producing the dung. On that visit John collected the black phase of a white-lipped whip snake, also earthworms and different kinds of ticks. Cave plants were restricted to a few mosses.

Shallow excavation brought to light the canine tooth of a wombat, several of which creatures had made their homes in the cave floor. Their burrows were large and the entrances trampled hard by constant use. They led deep into parts of the underground tunnels inaccessible to humans. The barks of Atholl's dog faded to virtual inaudibility when he went in after them, suggesting an extensive labyrinth, probably ready-made, not that wombats needed help on that front.

Laurie Walkier of "*Victoria II*" had told me of a pet wombat that scratched its way through a hefty front door, burrowed under the house and came up through the floorboards to raid the pantry for sugar and other delicacies. On our first visit we emerged from underground into a steady drizzle and clambered back up the slope, noting the landmarks which Atholl pointed out so that we could locate the spot again.

A brush-tail possum was sighted on the roof of the grain shed as we approached the farm and the zoologists prepared for battle. This one got away, but there were three more inside, tucking brazenly into an open sack of wheat — a habit which did not endear them to the farming community. Two of these, an adult and a large joey, were caught and popped into a bag, protesting loudly.

On subsequent visits John bagged two more alive and a further four with Atholl's rifle. The four live ones were given a lethal dose of chloroform the following morning as he already had four for breeding experiments and insufficient facilities for housing more. The deceased would supply skins for further colour comparisons and skulls for a study of developmental stages as they included different sized youngsters. Killing such charmingly furry creatures is never pleasant but was justified now on the three counts of their over-population, their role as farm pests and the contribution which they might make to science. With no natural predators to keep numbers within bounds, populations could easily get out of hand.

This part of the island was suffering from another population explosion — of grasshoppers. Atholl showed us the damage to his pastures and a boxthorn hedge stripped entirely of its leaves during the passing of the locust-like hordes. He corroborated what I had heard earlier of these creatures — one of the plagues of Egypt.

"Why, the hoppers'll eat the paper off the walls when they've finished everything else!"

But help was at hand, in the guise of enormous flocks of silver gulls which had descended on the invaders like the gulls that have saved more famous enterprises than this in the course of history. Gulls are not among the best loved of birds, but there is no denying their usefulness at times. I was put in mind of the flocks which descend on our home pastures when the winged ants are swarming on muggy summer days.

Back at the farm we enjoyed hot baths — the first for nearly eight weeks in my case — and climbed into our sleeping bags for the night. Not all the possums had been routed. At least two were scuffling and sneezing on the roof when I gained semi-consciousness in the small hours.

Next morning we breakfasted on home-grown roast lamb and potatoes and settled the vexed question of the 'spear-grass' of ancient literature and modern hearsay. We allocated it, not to stipa or the silver tussock poa, but to great brome *(Bromus diandrus)*.

Organising ourselves into a reception committee, we drove into Whitemark to meet the three VIPs off the plane: Dominic Serventy, king of the mutton birds, Eric Worrell, Australia's snake man and TV presenter, and Russell (Tas) Drysdale, famous artist and much more, all of them Furneaux Group addicts. Our intention of smartly presenting arms was foiled when Dom chose not to be associated with the disreputable crew leaning over the rails and stalked past, trying to look like a city gentleman. As Derek had brought only one transit vehicle and Atholl had left, he couldn't get away with that for long, however. We dropped John off at Atholl's gate. He was to spend the morning skinning possums and catch the next plane to Melbourne.

Back on Fisher Island, I set about preparing a buffet lunch for eleven, but the population was not to stay at that level. Mycky and Ted were off for a two-week camping session on Big Dog Island and the Westralians left that day for Perth.

27 Brush-tail Possum *Trichosurus vulpecula*

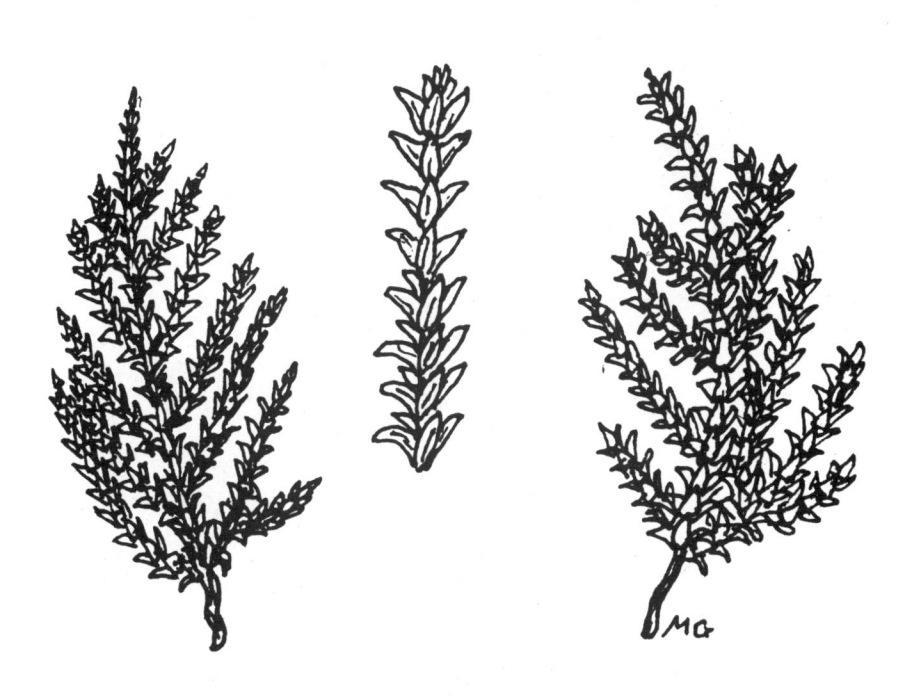

28 Swamp Club Moss *Selaginella uliginosa*

29 Common Flat Pea *Platylobium obtusangulum*

Chapter Four

FLINDERS ISLAND UPDATED

1. OLD ACQUAINTANCE: NEW SANCTUARY

After those early years in Australia I sailed for home in 1960, allowing myself six months on the way to see something of Africa, a fascinating continent which I was to visit many times subsequently. At first I worked on some of the commercial guano islands around the Cape of Good Hope, then hitch-hiked across to Nigeria, sight-seeing on the way. Back in Britain and immersed in my new job in the University of Wales, it was many years before I managed to return to the Antipodes, although the longing was always there.

On the occasions in the eighties and nineties when I succeeded, I travelled widely in mainland Australia, to some of my old haunts in the Centre, the West and the Great Barrier Reef, but mostly on well-worn tourist trails. I even managed a couple of tours of Tasmania, but Flinders Island seemed beyond reach and certainly beyond the ken of British travel agents. I knew I could fly in if I could muster the cash but, with no expeditionary backing and the unlikelihood of any of my old mates being still around after so long, I might be stuck in Whitemark with no road or boat transport.

Good friends in Victoria investigated and came up with a contact address — James and Lindsay Luddington, English settlers who had fallen for the island's charms and stayed to show others round by land and sea. After that all went smoothly. Things had changed on the Furneaux Group, as well they might in thirty-seven years. Tourism was becoming a potential source of income, although muted by the separating air miles. It was now possible to hire cars or four-wheel drives, even boats, and the range of accommodation had widened.

No longer would I be dependent on the inhabitants allowing me to unroll my sleeping bag on their floors. A friend in Victoria, alerted to the previously unknown possibilities, elected to join me there. She flew in from Melbourne, I from Launceston, at the end of a fabulous car tour of Tasmania with good friends from our 1959-60 Antarctic visit.

It was early spring in this hemisphere and I had been in the southern continent for nearly six weeks, acclimatising myself to the cold winds spawned in the Southern Ocean, which dogged us even on magnificent Kangaroo Island off South Australia, as well as in traditionally cooler sites such as the Otways. Not all Australia conforms with the traditional pommie idea of hot red dust and scorching sun. My flight to Flinders Island was slotted between storms but, thankfully, there was some blissful weather to come.

"Air Tas" had moved base for the week but, after a few false starts in the ANSETT and Flying Doctor air terminals, I was away in the little eight-seater plane by 6.45 a.m. on 6th November 1995.

"They had an inch of rain on Flinders in nine hours last night."

This while helping myself to tea from the waiting room urn. Five of us squeezed into our seats, bending low and easing along the central aisle.

"It's going to be a bit bumpy today. I'll try and avoid the bigger holes."

This from the pilot as the little craft leapt away so much more blithely than the usual lumbering tourist planes. I dreamed myself back on the sprightly little Tiger Moth that had taken me around the Hunter-Trefoil group of islands at the other end of Bass Strait so long ago.

Once we had lifted through the cloying cloud masking the radiating ribbon development of Launceston, we settled into a belt of clear air between this and a sullen grey stratum above. The apricot hue of post-dawn sunlight filtered through the rift between and a watery sun pushed through briefly but soon thought better of it.

Holes in the cloud floor revealed vistas of ultramarine flecked with patches of sheeny white, like the dark bogs of Connemara with their silvered pools and tarns, but they went on for too long. These were not the boggy heaths of Flinders Island but the menacingly dark waters of Bass Strait inhabited by veritable herds of foaming white horses. Wybalenna Island off Settlement Point appeared with a long line of surf trailing into the uninviting depths, then came a circular yellow bay patched with dark sea-grass and we were heading into the south-easterly winds to the Whitemark airstrip, through sheeting rain.

A cloud of spur-wing plovers took off as we roared down, then some silver gulls, but the half dozen spur-wings near the new, partially built reception area, took no notice as we taxied gently to a halt, no more of an intrusion than a mini-bus. The pilot came round to the passenger door to release the four island residents. To me he said: "You hang on here, Lindsay'll come out in the car".

She did, so my initial re-baptism with Flinder's rain was brief.

"We haven't had weather like this for months." The usual story! I told her about the inch of rain. "Oh great! We so badly needed it. We haven't had any decent rain for two years. The grass is scarcely green, even now, at the end of winter." Seeing that I was not sharing her enthusiasm for the deluge, after waiting for so long to visit, she added. "It started suddenly: maybe it will stop suddenly. It does."

My friend, Joan Preston, and I were to be the first visitors in a brand-new guest house being completed by Irene Slaven and her partner Chris Arthur, who was one of the island's national park wardens. We could not have wished for better. It was self-cooking accommodation, within easy reach of the Whitemark shops and with iron rations in the fridge, including a box of eggs with blue shells laid by some newly acquired hens from South America.

There were vases of kunzea, stinkwood (which doesn't smell) and purple groundsel, also a splaying feature of blackboy leaves, like green knitting needles. Many blackboys, it seemed, were affected by the rampant *Phytophthora fungus* which used to conjure up visions of the Irish potato famine, but had recently become a major pest of trees, though blackboys were scarcely trees. Paper nautilus and balone shells adorned the mantelpiece, a whale vertebra the hearth and decorative twists of driftwood dreamed of their sojourn at sea in an alcove. Sofas, armchairs, books, all mod cons: everything a traveller could need.

Irene piled more logs on the wood-burning stove (a feature of every house or cabin visited so far, in Victoria or Tasmania) and I settled in front of the blaze to draw specimens collected in Tasmania while waiting for the Melbourne plane. A kerfuffle in the garden brought me to the window for splendid views of three green rosellas, seeming more yellow than green against the dark *Coprosma* leaves. Some familiar 'London' sparrows were battling with the elements and starlings were being blown from their rooftop perches.

News travels fast on islands and Derek Smith, large as life and as bushy-tailed still as his beloved possums, had sent a message asking me to contact him. He had moved from the bakehouse in Lady Barron to a single-storey building near the Whitemark jetty. We were given instructions: "Turn along the seafront and continue towards the pier until you reach the most dilapidated house in the row. It looks deserted and is guarded by two Dachshunds."

Not the same ones, but no doubt of the same much cherished line.

Fortified with home-made soup, brought to us through the rain, Joan and I set off to find Derek. Umbrellas were out of the question. We bent our heads to the squall, detoured to survey the strand and turned in through a little wooden gate by another burgeoning New Zealand mirror tree, its leaves even shinier than usual as rain streamed over them.

Derek opened the door and we sized each other up silently to see what nearly forty years had done to once youthful faces and figures. I found him not so different from my slide of him clasping a wombat to his chest in 1958, just a little less willowy. He didn't let on how he found me.

His sense of humour was undiminished. After a few preliminaries he took me to the door to enquire the species of the tree outside. It was covered with spent tea bags dangling from every twig like a colony of mini-fruit bats. I suggested *Coprosma teabageri* as seeming to fit the bill.

"The product of years. Grandchildren compete to see who can fling them the furthest."

In the years between he had stopped shooting wallabies to sell as crayfish bait and capturing animals for export to zoos and become an active conservationist. Like so many dedicated naturalists, he had started as a hunter, learning to respect his quarry and changing from poacher to gamekeeper.

Hating cruelty in any form, he was the power behind the Patriarch Trust Conservation Area and it was he who had located a suitable site when 8,000 dollars were donated to set up the trust. He chose an abandoned farm of around 250 acres (100 hectares) east of the North, South and Middle Patriarch peaks beyond the Darling Range. This was on the east coast flyway of palearctic waders commuting between their arctic breeding grounds north of Japan and their Tasmanian 'wintering' grounds. It was also a haunt of Cape Barren geese, whose low population was in need of a helping hand and which shared the string of coastal lagoons with waders, swans and ducks.

Only part of the farm had been cleared, the rest was under native scrub. Paradoxically, the geese preferred farm pastures to natural vegetation, so more grass seed was sown and an electric fence erected to deter the ever present and ever hungry wallabies. Grass needed fertiliser, much of which the ever resourceful Derek conjured up from roadsides. As a good countryside sleuth he had pin-pointed over the years the places where this commodity was most likely to fall off the backs of trucks. Best were corners which could be taken at speed because of good visibility, so that the law of inertia took over.

Volunteers joined paid farmers in the excavation of water holes and erection of mounds for sentinel geese and the sanctuary was officially opened in November 1980 as a conservation area under the umbrella of the Tasmanian National Parks and Wildlife Act. It was claimed as the first privately owned bird refuge created in Australia by local people with no government assistance. There are residential facilities for humans as well as birds and the site is an official bird banding station.

Derek was never one to mind bad weather and we had too few days at our disposal to waste time waiting for better, so we set off in borrowed waterproofs in his ancient blue car, of which a great deal more was expected than of most. (An interesting feature of Flinders Island vehicles was that the two petrol pumps, one at Whitemark and one at Lady Barron, sold only old time leaded spirit. New cars needing unleaded were not catered for. It looked as though everyone would have to buy new cars simultaneously when the supply was modernised.)

We headed 30 km north and west around the north of the Darling Range. Cock pheasants roamed nonchalantly through the rain, as contented as in an English winter, and spur-wing plovers stood in for the lapwings which might have co-habited with them there, one pair with some bedraggled chicks. The bronze-wing pigeons seemed ordinary enough, but the feral breeding populations of peacocks and turkeys added a bizarre touch.

"Christmas coming up. The locals pull them out of the trees where they roost. A bit tough though."

An outsize human effigy dangling in roadside bushes — part of the Derek image — welcomed us at the end of the gravel track where birds and mammals gathered for the hand-out of vegetable peelings and stale bread that their benefactor was expected to bring.

St Francis, patron saint of animals, himself blessed by the local priest, dispensed blessings from his island shrine on the nearby pool. On closer inspection he proved to be a man of clay, fashioned by the skilled hands of one of his most faithful disciples, whose life was now dedicated to animal welfare — like those of his veterinary forbears.

The spring-fed pool gave sanctuary to shelduck and other waterfowl and contained rare Tasmanian mudfish *(Galaxias cleaveri)*, which were first recorded on Flinders in 1983. These are related to the better known mountain trout *(Galaxias coxii)* and the common jollytail *(Galaxias maculatus)* which are also present.

Among those gathered about the entrance of the A-framed visitor centre tucking into the offerings of apple, lettuce and carrot, were Cape Barren geese and a solicitous mother pademelon with a joey in her pouch. Derek grabbed one of the bigger wallabies by its hind legs to treat its ailing eyes. Two rain-sodden superb blue wrens were grounded by a muddy puddle.

"Poor little buggers. Fancy having to feed a family in this."

When we went inside he closed the door firmly behind us.

"Came here once, opened the door and blimey — talk about a council meeting! There were wallabies sitting all round the table and one on top. The door had blown open — weather such as this. They'd gone in out of the rain and it had slammed shut. Just as well I came or they'd have eaten the posters and photos."

He pointed up under the eaves.

"Welcome swallows nested there, on a tiny shelf two inches wide." He held up two fingers. "I put a wider shelf up next time and when they'd finished a pair of wood swallows moved in and built on top with a different colour mud. I've never known that before."

Among the wildlife and literary exhibits was a little book which he had written depicting the life of children in the old days of sealers and Aboriginals and at the present time, the proceeds of sales helping to run the sanctuary, which operated on a shoestring. Upstairs were the sleeping quarters where visiting naturalists spread their sleeping bags and a great spread of blanket-covered mattresses which could sleep endless children head to tail, and provide facilities for much horseplay in the doing. Derek enjoyed the many parties of school children who visited, particularly those from the towns, who knew so little of this way of life that was second nature to him.

At sixty-nine he scarcely qualified as a patriarch himself but was very evidently the father figure of the Patriarchs Sanctuary. In at the beginning and the innovator and craftsman producing the necessaries over the years, he found time to devote to the day-to-day running and spreading the conservation gospel to the younger generation. It should have come as no surprise to find that he had been awarded the much coveted Australia Medal for his services to conservation — the presentation ceremony held at the sanctuary. May he long remain at the helm. When he reaches his eighties he should qualify as the fourth patriarch!

He enthused about the young and reminisced about the old.

"We're almost the only two left now. Dom Serventy, Eric Worrell, Tas Drysdale; all gone. Leila Barrett, Tuck Robinson, Arthur Harland......" his voice tailed off. Others, John Thomson, Bill Mollison and John Warham among them, were currently pursuing distinguished careers elsewhere. Atholl Dart had sold up and moved to pastures new.

Noreen Riddle, a young water colourist and member of a mutton-birding family in the fifties and sixties, was now married and working part-time in the local hospital. We knew her best for her series of paintings depicting stages in the bird harvest, which were now of historic interest. She had given the originals to Dom Serventy and the museum folk on Flinders were trying to trace them.

I wrote to Dom's brother, Vince, well-known author and broadcaster, when I got home, having failed to raise him on the phone when in Sydney, and learned that they were safely lodged either with the RAOU (Royal Australian Ornithologists' Union) or in the state archives in Perth (Dom's home town). Many of us had Kodachrome copies and mine, at least, remain unfaded.

Noreen continued to go birding at the family hut on Big Dog Island. She enjoyed it still, although suffering a damaged wrist the previous year. I ran her to earth later on and she gave voice to nostalgic memories of the old days. "It was wonderful, the birding. Nobody worked very hard. We took time off when we liked, did a bit of beachcombing, had a party or just lazed on the sands. Some of the work was distasteful, but there were compensations. Just like a holiday."

There was a parallel here with the former annual exodus of hop-pickers from Hobart up the Derwent Valley and from London to the Kentish oast houses, although some of the birders worked for themselves and not for wages.

Noreen's wrist had healed and she was painting again: evanescent seascapes and wind-tortured landscapes that captured the wild yet magic spirit of the islands perfectly. Her studio and living quarters, surrounded by a brilliant flower garden, lay just back from the Lady Barron shore east of the new concrete wharf built in 1969.

It had commanded a beautiful view until BP built its oil reception depot at a little distance in front. She had planted a she-oke which blocked the eyesore at first but this was getting leggy and needed help. Since 1984, when mains electricity came to Lady Barron, less oil had been needed for the individual home generators, which were costly to run, but on which most people depended. Mains water supply had also come that year.

Passing by on the sea in the *"Strait Lady"* later in the week, James Luddington had pointed out the blocky modern vessel that brought oil in for island use. It was not a tanker, the fuel came in barrels (as the mutton birds had departed) to be pumped into storage tanks. Close by was a more traditional wooden craft, painted black.

"She's a hundred years old, built of huon pine. It went scarce after that but there was more about when they felled the trees before flooding Lake Peddar for the hydroelectric scheme."

Drilling for oil had been going on in Bass Strait, in the Bass, Otway and Gippsland Basins, for three decades, in a mix of volcanic and sedimentary rocks, the first well being opened in 1965.

On our return from the Patriarchs, still in blinding rain, Derek shot off up a side track to his favourite forest on Walkers Hill Lookout, a peak in the Darling Range where a two-way radio link with Melbourne and Launceston had been established in 1948, using diesel-operated equipment. He drew up in a fine stand of Tasmanian blue gums towering skywards, the loose spiral patterning of the bark enhanced by the rain streaming down them.

"Reckon this is how the whole island looked before burning and clearing."

Then, pointing to some big trees with badly burned butts.

"I can't think how they keep standing. Our other big gums are manna gums *(Eucalyptus viminalis)*, with rough bark at the base of the trunk. Some call them white gums. That's where the rare forty-spotted pardelotes are."

Striated pardelotes are common on the island, the spotted pardelote less so, but more than the elusive forty-spotted. Irene had been out with a party of bird-watchers, spotted pardelote spotting, and they had found none in the manna gums where they were previously recorded but had come upon them accidentally in others. They concluded that the birds commute between suitable stands of trees.

Pardelotes pick insects from the leaves and also eat lerp and manna, which is a white substance produced by the trees in response to insect attack. The birds are of special interest in being confined to a few islands off the east of Tasmania, principally Bruny, Maria and Flinders, having evolved from the spotted after the severance of the land bridge connecting Tasmania to Victoria.

30 Wind-trimmed Coast Beard Heath *Leucopogon parviflorus*

31 Cape Barren Geese *Cereops novae-hollandiae*

32 Forty Spotted Pardelote *Pardalotus quadragintus* and Manna Gum *Eucalyptus viminalis*

2. SETTLEMENT POINT AND WYBALENNA HISTORIC SITE

The deluge that continued unabated through the next night, was not confined to Bass Strait. The morning's newspapers reported "Floods in South-east Australia": "Four hundred evacuated from flooded homes in Gippsland." The islanders were ecstatic.

"It's truly marvellous. How we needed it. It hasn't rained like this since 1989."

We met Lindsay Luddington in the supermarket.

"James had to leave his boat in Whitemark. He'll be taking it back to Lady Barron tomorrow and you can join him and see some of the islands."

In the event he returned that same day, in response to an emergency — a heart attack on Cape Barren Island — bringing the patient to Lady Barron for road transport to Whitemark and the plane out.

The rain eased a little and after an early lunch, Irene Slaven drove us to the site of the earliest settlement, at Wybalenna and Emita, picking up Doreen Lovegrove, one of the volunteer museum curators, en route. Doreen's water supply, an open well, hidden among trees in a corner of her plot, had been brimful until two years ago. Then the water table started going down. Now it was dry. We were shown the evidence; island pride dictating that we be assured of the good weather as well as the bad.

I was intrigued to learn that her property had previously been owned by 'the bottle man', whose obsession with glassware had led him to construct walls, gateways and minarets of beer and wine bottles set in cement. He had moved on to King Island, where he had done the same again and where I had photographed some of his efforts on a repeat visit there in 1991. A small world indeed. None of his Flinders Island efforts had been allowed to survive, although it had been a mammoth task removing them.

We drove north up the Palana Road to Settlement Point, to look at the beach where sealers, convicts, settlers and Aboriginals had come and gone during the eighteen hundreds. This was the place where materials for building the settlement that was supposed to save the remnants of the Tasmanian natives had been landed.

Padding out along the line of the crumbling wooden jetty on Lillies Beach, it was apparent that a considerable depth of sand had been swept away in the recent storm. The base of each wooden pile, formerly protected below sand level, was in almost pristine condition, but the next section above was badly eroded, the tissues torn by waves armed with the coarse granite shingle of which the beach was composed.

The parent granite that was slowly being pounded to sand, stood up as mighty boulders, patterned with the black, orange and grey lichens that adorn rocks in that order (from the base up) on so many of the world's shores. The orange *Gasparinnia murorum* covering the rocks from high water mark up through the splash zone, was redder than usual today after absorbing so much rain. Only the previous week, I had travelled along the coast of the Bay of Fire in Northeast Tasmania, a bay deriving its name from the crustose, flame-coloured plants.

Glistening quartz veins scored the granite and Doreen drew our attention to the dark inclusions or xenoliths in the pale crystalline rocks. These were finer-grained than the matrix and reached the size of rugby footballs, the junctions between dark grey and pale buff clearly defined. 'Xeno' implies a foreigner or stranger, as in xenophobia, and these were foreign rocks — still granite but differing in texture from the rest. Doreen explained.

"The intrusions are small masses of granite that cooled slowly, so that they were caught up in a subsequent magma flow and carried on to cool within the coarser-grained material extruded later. They are best developed in Sawyers Bay, just south of here, but occur all the way down to Blue Rocks."

Some of the granite that had been hidden under the beach sand before the storm bore a thin coating of more recent yellowish limestone. This had drifted over the igneous rocks as sand in past aeons and later become lithified as a softer limey sandstone. Now it was being eroded away again as the sea gained access. Most had gone from the upstanding boulders.

While gritty sand had been drawn out to sea in the backwash of the waves, lightweight flotsam had been brought in and stranded. I was specially impressed by the enormous number and large size of the cuttlefish 'bones', which are common enough components of driftlines, but seldom in such profusion. Some get hung in bird cages because of their high lime content and peckability, but there was lime and to spare here for all who needed it. The relics were from the giant Bass Strait cuttlefish, *Amplisepia apama*, whose remains are found along both sides of Bass Strait.

Irene told us of a major cuttlefish mortality around the islands a few months earlier, when hundreds of the porous cuttlebones that enable their owners to regulate their buoyancy, were floating erect, with the lighter, pointed end uppermost. Disintegrating flesh trailed away from the old internal skeleton to which it had clung in life. Albatrosses, which normally feed on the live animals, had been swooping down to feast on the unwholesome remains without damaging the bones. The two kinds most commonly seen were the black-browed and the shy albatrosses, but five species have been recorded in island waters.

My brushes with Mediterranean cuttlefish as food had left much to be desired, the experience resembling the chewing of rubber bands. In my early days on Flinders, cuttlefish were regarded as fit only for bait, but they have been coming into favour in recent years as human food. Taiwanese fishermen attract them to their boats with lights after dark, seeking out the long-bodied Gould's or arrow squids *(Notodarus gouldii)* and the more sought-after southern calamaris *(Sepiotenthis australis)*, where the lateral flanges which undulate when they swim are attached right along the body instead of only at the tail end. The group as a whole is famous for the clouds of black 'ink' which animals produce when threatened, so cuttle fishermen and cuttle fishing boats get pretty grotty.

The limpets *(Cellana solida)* were also bigger than normal. As the tops of vacated shells started to erode away, they began to resemble outsize keyhole limpets. Ear shells lay around, their nacreous linings less brilliant than the blue-green paua or *Haliotus iris* of New Zealand. They are called abalones here, as in America. Two kinds, the black-lipped *Haliotus ruber* and the green-lipped *Haliotus laevigata*, are now the basis of a commercial fishery, started in 1964 after my previous stays. The shellfish are prised from the rocks by divers and processed in the fish factory at Lady Barron.

Again my ventures into eating the black, leathery flesh in New Zealand, were not a success, despite the animals' other name of mutton-fish. The 'meat' looked and tasted like the rubber of which tyres are made, even after removal of the tough border and a good pounding. Only the batter in which they were fried was edible.

There is a market for anything fishy with the overpopulated Japanese nowadays and the lustrous shell linings are used for making novelties, their colour a muted pink or that of milky opals. Sea urchin tests on the beach were not from the edible kind. Some were oval, the sort that we call sea potatoes or heart urchins *(Echinocardium)*; others were like little round sand urchins *(Psammechinus)*.

We walked south along the lower driftline and back along the upper where the lighter flotsam had been thrown out of circulation. Here was a wealth of fingered and fluted sponges in many shapes and sizes, crimped and spiralised sea mats and many kinds of shell caught up among feathery red seaweeds or the brown sargasso weed that was so amply supplied with air floats.

The principal vegetation below the tide mark on this sandy shore was the big sea-grass or strapweed, *Posidonia australis*, named after the sea god, Posidon, rather than the true seaweeds, which prefer rocks. Ripped from their hold by the waves, many fronds had washed ashore and piled together in soggy brown banks.

The softer tissues had rotted away from material torn asunder before the recent storms, leaving a mass of harsh leaf fibres which became balled up by the waves into featherweight spheres and egg shapes, which were bowled around by the wind like oversized Ping-Pong balls. These are the Posidonia balls so familiar around the Mediterranean and other warm seas, where they often get mistaken for fruits. Some have a shoot base as a nucleus within, but most here show no obvious starting point when broken open.

A live cockle was lumbering over the sand, with siphon extended. We helped it into a wet hollow, then crossed over Settlement Point to Port Davies, where the coast dipped into Cave Beach on the north side. Doreen remembered when the old timber jetty was standing proudly above the tide. Now the walkway and crossed beams had gone, leaving only the denuded uprights protruding from the waves like a broken-down fence.

"If they'd built a breakwater out from the point here, this would have made a better haven than Whitemark."

Two black currawongs watched us warily as we drove away inland, to where tiny Tasmanian thornbills foraged among scented paperbarks.

* * * * *

Nearby Wybalenna, just inland of Peajacket Hill, was where well-meaning but misguided missionaries had tried to succour the last of the Aboriginals rounded up around Tasmania and give them a decent life, but their charges, divorced from their land and their culture, persisted in dying off. From the start of the project in 1833 only forty-five remained by 1847. These were removed to Oyster Cove near Hobart, where the last one died in 1876.

It was a sad sad story, aggravated by European diseases, invading sealers, stolen stores and pig-ravaged vegetable gardens. Most of the farming was done by convicts, the Aboriginals remaining as hunter-gatherers until all the wallabies within reach had been hunted out and food was crucially short. They also collected mutton birds and eggs from the colony among scrub and tussock near Port Davies jetty. This is the only mutton bird rookery on the Flinders mainland and the fact that it survived here, so close to the major predators — man — says much for the resilience of these long-lived birds to inroads on their progeny.

The natives' houses had disintegrated long since, been excavated by archeologists and covered up again, being discernible now as mounds of grass-grown rubble. Only the brick-built, shingle-roofed chapel remained — restored by the National Trust in 1974 after years of use as a woolshed. We went into the bare interior, where services, even weddings, were sometimes conducted under the original rafters, the building having never been deconsecrated, even when it housed only the earthly shepherd and his sheep. Welcome swallows nested under the roof at both ends, the urgent squeals of the hungry chicks, the only sound in the big empty building.

Moving uphill to the old farmhouse, we waded through a thicket of iris leaves dotted with a few late flowers, mostly blue, a few white. It must have looked quite splendid a few weeks before, in October. An old mulberry tree grew beside the well tucked in against the shabby building.

"It's so lush it must send some of its roots into the well. We all come here for the fruits in season."

There were bougainvillea and other remnants of the former garden — also what was reputed to be the oldest brick-built outside dunny in Tasmania, well away from the house. A huge wombat burrow disappeared among the spreading roots of an ancient tree beyond the disintegrating pallet fence.

The farm had been built of bricks filched from the Wybalenna settlement. There is little suitable clay for making bricks on Flinders Island, but the Aboriginals had fashioned theirs from the muddy bed of a nearby lagoon and lime from the seashore. Other, harder, bricks had been imported. Most modern buildings are of concrete.

Further up the hill was an old shearing shed with different levels of slatted wooden floor and ragged walls where campers ripped off loose planks for their fires. Doreen's curatorial urges were roused by the hundreds of fragments of blue and white china washed free of soil in the recent rains and scattered throughout the site. We helped her gather scraps of the jigsaw for piecing together later. It was illegal, even for museum curators, to dig for archeological specimens, but there was no law against collecting from the surface.

Downhill again to the old cemetery, over alien grassland speckled with star clover and dove's-foot cranesbill, we wandered among the tombstones. One commemorated the first white child to be born in the Furneaux Group and who had lived for only eleven years. Another was erected to a young woman who had died with two infants in her arms when her crinoline caught in the rigging of the ship that had brought her to spend Christmas with her soldier husband, who awaited her onshore. (How good humans are at bungling things. It should have been apparent to the most stupid that crinolines and sailing ships are scarcely compatible!)

Derek had been called in recently to an undermined headstone to remove the wombat which had burrowed into the loosened earth to share quarters with the mouldering bones. Only the white inhabitants had marked graves. There were two more members of the old families still alive, who wished to be buried here, then the cemetery would be closed.

The short tenure of European colonisation was brought home when Doreen mentioned that the recent birth of a baby in one of the families represented had brought the number of generations on Flinders Island up to eight — about the maximum achievable in this young country. No wonder my forester friends from the Otways, who had recently cycled round Europe, thought the Roman aqueduct at Pont du Guarde to be inconceivably ancient!

The unmarked graves of the Aboriginals had been lost track of, their burial ground a grazed field until recently. They were located after the grass had been mown and the evening sun picked out the humps. Most are said to be empty, the skeletons sold to medical and scientific institutions in Europe or reburied by their own kind, but a memorial to them had been erected by local Young Farmers' Club members.

* * * * *

A few kilometres up the coast, beyond Marshall Bay, we came to the Emita Historic Museum housed in an old school room and the associated outbuildings. This was a treasure house of the past, tended by volunteers from the Furneaux Historical Research Association, with more to interest the visitor than most had time to absorb.

Among the natural history exhibits the shell collections and some artistically fabricated 'shell samplers' were of particular merit. In the human history sections sealing, mutton-birding and shipwrecks were made much of, the story of the *"Sydney Cove"* and the incredible journey of crew members which followed her wrecking being particularly poignant.

It is fitting that the historical records should be housed here, as Emita and Wybalenna were the first parts of the island to be settled, losing their claim to become the capital, some say, because the pub was built at Whitemark and a pub is a great draw! Both districts boast fertile limestone soils, easily cleared and farmed, and there are records of some fine beef animals being shipped out from Emita wharf. Limestone hills reach to 650 feet (200 metres) above the museum.

An involvement in more modern history is Emita's proximity to Wireless Hill, where the first ship to shore radio link using Morse code was inaugurated. The tall mast was fashioned from planks of Oregon pine shipped from Victoria, rafted ashore and hauled to the site by bullock team in 1913. This Morse code exchange remained the only contact with the outside world, apart from sea passage, until the first battery-operated radio telephone link was installed in 1942.

The old system of smoke signals continued on the lesser islands, where I received instructions quite early in 1958. One fire = help needed: two fires = doctor needed: three fires = a death. Today's local attractions are not only historic but scenic, Emita Beach and Allports Beach, with Watermark Rock offshore, being popular holiday spots and a coastal reserve.

We emerged from the yellowed records within the museum to a now sunlit garden where a brown skink had crept from shelter and was basking gratefully on the verandah. The widow of the deceased founder owner of the museum, Mr Fowler, living in the house up the hill from the exhibits, had recently died. Doreen had been in the habit of sipping tea with her after spells of duty and took us up now to enjoy the riot of colour in the garden which she had so loved, but which was fast becoming overgrown.

There were pelargoniums in every possible hue, red, blue and Jerusalem sages, Spanish broom, orange hibiscus, yellow lilies and many more, following the show of spring bulbs. Her hens still wandered on free range, in no fear of predators, with foxes, dingoes and devils absent. A local man came daily to feed them and water the pot plants.

It was an idyllic spot. The repeated calls of a white-throated butcher bird in a pine tree mingled with the chortling of introduced carolling magpies. Long drawn out whistles came from firetail finches and a grey shrike thrush was spotted. A noisy posse of endemic green rosellas came careering through, as they had at Wybalenna Farm. An eastern spinebill, one of the more distinctively marked honey-eaters, hovered around some yellow dogwood *(Pomaderris elliptica)*.

The paddock between museum and garden was of coarse buffalo grass, probably *(Stenotaphrum secundatum)*, mounded into reddish tumps between the criss-crossing trails of a busy community of wallabies.

"Wallabies won't eat this. A pony might help to keep it down."

It seemed another world, fitting into the fifties more than the nineties, but I had never managed to get this far north in those early years.

33 Bladder Pea *Gompholobium hugelii*

34 Tasmanian Thornbill *Acanthiza ewingii* and
Scented Paperbark *Melaleuca squarrosa*

35 Eastern Spinebill *Acanthorhynchos tenuirostris* and
Yellow Dogwood *Pomaderris elliptica*

3. TROUSERS POINT AND THE SOUTH

Just as Ayers Rock epitomises the 'Red Centre', so Trousers Point is the chosen ambassador for Flinders Island. Not only is it a beautiful seascape in its own right, but it is glamorised by the dramatic backdrop of the Strzelecki Peaks alongside. I had managed to get to it only briefly during my previous stays on the Furneaux Group, when none of my exploits ventured into the northern three-quarters of the island beyond Whitemark.

The day of my visit to Trousers Point in 1995 was phenomenally windy, with the broad highways of Whitemark as exposed as any. When Joan and I set off for town, our heads tilted sideways to make breathing possible, a plump young lady came bowling along the road towards us at a rate of knots. The cry came on the whistling air as she was swept past.

"Have you seen a sheet of paper coming this way?"

We hadn't, not in the last several hundred metres. She had a long chase ahead. Doreen was alighting from her open yellow truck a little further on.

"I lost my notes this morning. No way could I catch up with them on foot. I had to follow in the truck."

Another despairing islander, who had just been blown off her feet, recognised us as strangers and proffered the information: "These can go on for three weeks. Everyone gets more and more irritable."

Like the Provencal Mistral in the South of France. But, like the little girl with the little curl, when it was good it was very very good — and the change could happen within the hour.

At one o'clock, after retrieving my errant laundry from the woodpile, I set off with Irene and Doreen in the yellow truck for Trousers Point. If the passenger seat was to windward when she stopped, the driver came racing round to help steady the cab door.

"These can get buckled or ripped off if you don't hang on!"

Like the one I had failed to save on a land rover in the Hebrides.

In summer the little sandy coves around the mushroom-shaped headland are favourite bathing places with the locals. Today we had them to ourselves. The water looked as translucently turquoise and inviting as any in the Caribbean, but we were not tempted, turning our coat collars up instead. I had come in early spring to see the flowers at their best, but early spring carries a tail-over of late winter gales.

The old sailing ships relied on their persistence to speed them round the globe, but none could beat their way back against them. Another silver lining to these rumbustious natural phenomena was the settlers' ability to harness them to power the wind pumps which brought vital water from underground — an important asset when electricity was home-generated at considerable expense.

Trousers Point is wooded and geared to holiday-making, with sheltered camp site, barbecues, water supply and dressing sheds. The reception areas of the 'Organic Toilets' are provided with capacious air vents to facilitate aerobic decomposition, a method of disposal which fails in wetter areas, where dampness can exclude the necessary oxygen.

The area is a coastal reserve of a hundred hectares — part of the Strzelecki National Park, coming under the control of the National Parks and Wildlife Service — successor of the old Tasmanian Fauna Board.

Our first view of the pristine coves, ringed about with the lurid orange of the lichen-rimed rocks, was backed by the sparkling waters of Franklin Sound, with Mount Chappell Island to the right and the immensity of Cape Barren beyond. To get the classic view with the mountain backdrop, we needed to go out onto the headland and look back.

Foam-edged waves were creaming in over the untrodden sands and splattering into the tangled branches tumbling from wooded clifflets in the little inlets. On the bluffs the water swooshed in silver cascades over limpets and barnacles, to moisten the half-grown mussels which crowded into each available cranny where their guylines or rubbery byssus threads could gain a hold.

The principal shade trees were she-okes or she-oaks, known as Casuarinas until recently, when allocated a new name of Allocasuarina. On the acid granite soils the black she-oke *(Allocasuarina littoralis)* was predominant, its ridged green twigs stoutly erect and the shape of the tree tending to conical.

One had been sawn off close to the ground, exposing an interesting cross section in which the radiating lines of the medullary rays were sharply etched by weathering and reached right to the centre, with none of the usual demarcation into dead heartwood and living sapwood. It was highly decorative: slices would have made wonderful stool tops. I was intrigued to learn later, therefore, that this durable timber is prized for cabinet making, ornamental joinery and veneers — which would cut across the rays.

The other common she-oke able to withstand the strong winds and salt spray, was the drooping *Allocasuarina stricta*. This has pendant twiglets and more of a mophead crown. It prefers limey sands, such as occur immediately north of Trousers Point in Fotheringate Bay, where limestones overlie the granite. These are weathering like those of Settlement Point, but more ornamentally into the fairy-tale sculptings that are so well seen along the coast of Victoria across the Strait.

Undershrubs included sea box *(Alyxia buxifolia)*, a soft-leaved Olearia, a brown-flowered Pomaderris, a green-flowered Correa and a yellow-flowered Pimelea. Some of the coast tea-tree buds were swollen and hairy. Opened up, they revealed the squirming maggot hatched from the egg of a gall-forming insect, exploiting a handy ecological niche which harmed the host plant scarcely at all.

Prolific greeny-grey lichens on tree branches pointed to purity of air and high humidity. Some boughs were draped with broad-leaved scrambling lignum, others with finer tangles of blue-flowered love-creeper. Silver everlastings romped across the forest floor, sharing the seaward margin with seaberry saltbush, whose leaves lack the mealy greyness of most of its relatives.

Butterflies flitted through the sheltered camp ground, lingering at the furry flowers of coast beard heath *(Leucopogon parviflorus)*. They included a few whites, but most looked just like the painted ladies that come winging up to Britain from the Mediterranean each spring. They were, indeed, painted ladies, a species which is widespread in temperate localities and present in all continents except South America.

These southern ones commonly travel the thousand miles between Australia and New Zealand — an incredible distance for such fragile creatures with a wing span of only six to seven centimetres — although no doubt wind-assisted. They are among the greatest of insect travellers. Less stalwort butterflies might well have been grounded on such a day.

A prettily patterned brown moth sat on a boobialla bush, waving his splendid, comb-like antennae in an attempt to pick up the scent of a potential mate. He seemed to be having little success. All scent might be gone with the wind today.

Birds, apart from the bevy of oystercatchers out on the point, were skulking in shelter. Least elusive were the superb blue and jenny wrens and the silver eyes. A little back from the picnic area was a pool noisy with the croaking of eastern banjo frogs *(Limnodynastes dumerilii)*. It needed a little imagination to equate the calls of these big warty grey creatures with the twanging of a banjo.

The lower section of a wooden stairway leading to one of the beaches had been ripped away by the waves, leaving a sheer drop to the sands. Just another job for the wardens, repairing the ravages of winter for the bathing parties of summer. During our week on the island, they were busy in hard hats with some tree clearance.

We moved on down the coast to Big River Ford. En route we crossed the most magnificent display of flowering kunzea bushes that one could hope to see, in or out of a garden — an even-aged stand, the bushes forming neat domes two metres across, with ample space to move between.

"Seven years ago this was a bare ten-acre field. Not burned since."

Nor grazed, by the look of it. This was a striking example of how quickly — and how beautifully — untended land can revert to bush. The parallel at home is the advance of hawthorns — which can be equally lovely — over chalk downland after the withdrawal of grazing sheep.

Outcropping granite here showed some fine big crystals. The milky white ones were quartz. Feldspars included both white plagioclase and pink orthoclase. There was darker biotite and clear muscovite, which glinted in the sun. An exposure where the track dipped down into Big River Ford showed grey expanses of granodiorite, with a more granular texture, contrasting sharply with the rest, and due, presumably, to separation during the cooling process.

The tea-coloured water burbling across the ford was shaded by swamp paperbarks ornamented with drapes of parasitic dodder-laurel. A handsome gum had been planted nearby, the broad opposite leaves not confined to the juvenile foliage. Erosion by the swollen waters made the ford impassable, but this route was classified now only as a fire trail, although following the old track to Lady Barron. There had been talk of damming the flow above the crossing, but nothing had come of this.

The gravel road which we followed out was lined with black peppermint gums, yellower-green thickets of cherry ballart *(Exocarpos cupressiforme)* and the bright flowers of gorse bitter-pea *(Daviesia ulicifolia)*. Veering off sharply through an open field gateway, the game little truck trundled up an uneven grass slope that was being invaded by bracken — an abandoned farm plot with the remains of a homestead.

The locals called this Belladonna Point, and it was easy to see why, although the earlier massed pink of the Belladonna lilies was now represented by fat green seed capsules pushing through a deep sward of daffodil-style leaves, as invasive as the Wybalenna irises. This was no doubt a garden escape: perhaps the peacocks were too, but they stalked among bristling thistle heads now instead of the formal garden trappings with which we associate them.

Matting the turf in places was yellow wood sorrel *(Oxalis corniculata)*, with elegant trefoil leaves. This is the most popular candidate for the Irish shamrock and I thought it might have been brought by some homesick Irishman, but it was, in fact, regarded as a dinkum native.

Our wanderings took us to a circular pool surrounded by dense scrub. Windows in the narrow belt of trees along its further shore provided tantalising glimpses of blue sea beyond. A king-sized wombat scuttled into the cover of the lagoonside paperbarks and this was by no means the only one.

As we sidled round the narrow strip of turf between the swollen waters and the encroaching branches, it became apparent that scores of animals must have been using this little oasis as a watering hole during the long drought. The ground was as thick with droppings as that around a sheep trough — oblong 'barrels' from the wombats, oval 'grapes' from the big wallabies, 'cherries' from the little ones, 'currants' from suspected potoroos and 'sausages' from some unknown donors; all among a maze of footprints.

That the water was likely to be fairly permanent was shown by its content of one of the more delicate of the water milfoils, probably *Myriophyllum salsugineum*, although three others have been recorded on the island. Tiny herbs were incorporated in the newly submerged sward, but were giving away none of their secrets until the water withdrew again, allowing them to flower. Immersion was a necessary forerunner and it was rumoured that six inches (15 cm) of rain had fallen in the peaks above during the past week. (That was the extent of my stay, this being my last day.)

From here to the start of the Strzelecki Track, along which we explored a little, Irene and Doreen were discussing which residents had moved in and out of the hundred acre plots that we passed. They seemed to know them all — a prerequisite of island life, where everyone knew what so-and-so might be doing at a certain time of day, as well as most other things about them!

It seemed to me that most of the plots were now semi-derelict, with quantities of brush as well as the planted shelter belts of dark marcrocarpas and brilliantly flowering Spanish broom. This was where both 'Honest Tom' Langley and Atholl Dart had farmed, but it was more overgrown than I remembered.

Dogs are not allowed in national parks so, while Doreen and I visited the striated rock orchids, Irene walked Rasta, her little cross Australian terrier bitch, along the road, as she had done when we were in the Trousers Point reserve. The previous day, when we had all visited Fisher and Great Dog Islands in superb sunshine, Rasta had been left behind and allowed a special 'walkies' afterwards. This was to the 'Orchid Patch', a small area of state forest famed for its ground orchids.

We were not lucky with these that day, although plenty had been flowering on the Tasmanian mainland the previous week. Most of the suspected wispy flower stems proved on inspection to be the sporing spikes of screw fern. There were nice clumps of many-leaved sundew, bursting into flower above the stickily predatious leaves, pink bells *(Tetratheca)*, golden guinea flower *(Hibbertia)* and pink heath *(Epacris impressa)*, Victoria's state flower. The bright firetail finches of the forest were also busy in the gardens when we got back to Whitemark.

When out with Derek Smith a few days before, we had passed a giant grass tree, which he though might be three thousand years old.

"Never flowered, never burned, never alters."

A veteran indeed, but that's a long time to know. Another fine roadside specimen was in danger of being felled during hedge-trimming operations, but Derek persuaded the farmer to put a label on it instead.

"Now everyone stops to look, learn and photograph."

Beyond a bank of saw sedge and scrambling coral-fern was a stretch of road lined with splaying tufts of pampas grass *(Cortaderia argentea)*, now categorised as an official pest on the Tasmanian mainland.

"The boffins want us to grub it all up. Afraid of it getting away into the bush, but it can't do any harm here. They used to encourage us to plant it, for shelter belts and for cattle forage in time of drought. The animals'll pull away at it when there's nothing else. Was said to be only one sex. Now there's a new strain from New Zealand and we're getting vigorous hybrids."

I thought it looked rather decorative, and an effective wind barrier.

"Shrubs have never flowered as well as this year. Must be the two dry seasons: not enough rain to get down to the roots and produce real growth."

That was hard to take in the current deluge, but the tea-trees, paperbarks and particularly the *Kunzea ambigua*, were certainly in fine form.

"All that used to be bush. Now its ryegrass, cocksfoot and Yorkshire fog. The fog should never have been brought."

It probably wasn't, intentionally. This noxious weed-grass has a way of getting around on its own — disliked by all grazers and eaten, even by rabbits, only when they are starved of most else.

"Ring-tail possums aren't doing well. They need trees and so many have been cleared. Brush-tail possums are becoming ground feeders. We see them right out in the open as never before. In a few thousand years they'll be wallabies!"

As if there weren't already enough of those. Derek was evidently a believer in adaptive evolution. Tree kangaroos had gone the other way.

The big overpopulation of Bennets wallabies, and to a lesser extent of pademelons and brush-tails, was demonstrated by the road casualties, which were everywhere. The number of corpses seemed at first to bode ill for the species but, in fact, showed the opposite. There was very little road traffic, not enough for the introduction of modern gimmicks such as traffic lights, so the large number that got hit must be but a tiny fraction of the number that didn't.

Sadly, since the arrival of the dreaded cinnamon fungus *(Phytophthora cinnamomi)*, from West Sumatran cinnamon trees via mainland Australia, all did not look so rosy for the plants. It is a relative of the even more catastrophic potato blight *(Phytophthora infestans)*, that caused the Irish potato famine of 1845 and the resulting wave of emigration, and another of these malevolent microscopic fungi has just moved in on Britain's alder trees.

On Flinders Island the pathogen is affecting the various heaths, Banksia and pea flowers that add so much colour to the summer landscape and, most specially, the unique Australian grass trees or blackboys. Grasses and sedges are unaffected and are likely to take over and create a gloomier ground flora where marked tracks lead muddy-booted walkers from infected to unaffected areas.

"Not many of the original land settlement scheme people are still here. Most sold up and went to the mainland. The few who stayed bought up the other properties for sheep and beef and now have spare farmhouses that they want to hire out as holiday homes. No good unless by the sea: holiday-makers who come to islands want beaches."

Back in Whitemark, Derek took us on a brief tour of the booming little town, pointing out the old and new hospitals, library, post office and golf club house.

"Only 700 people here now." (The official figure a decade before had been 1000). "Too many of everything: everything duplicated."

Better than too few, surely. Availability of amenity facilities could give a useful boost to future tourism.

36 A Wild Pea *Dillwynia glaberrima*

37 Starry-leaved Daisy Bush *Olearia stellulata* and blunt-leaved Heath *Epacris obtusifolia*

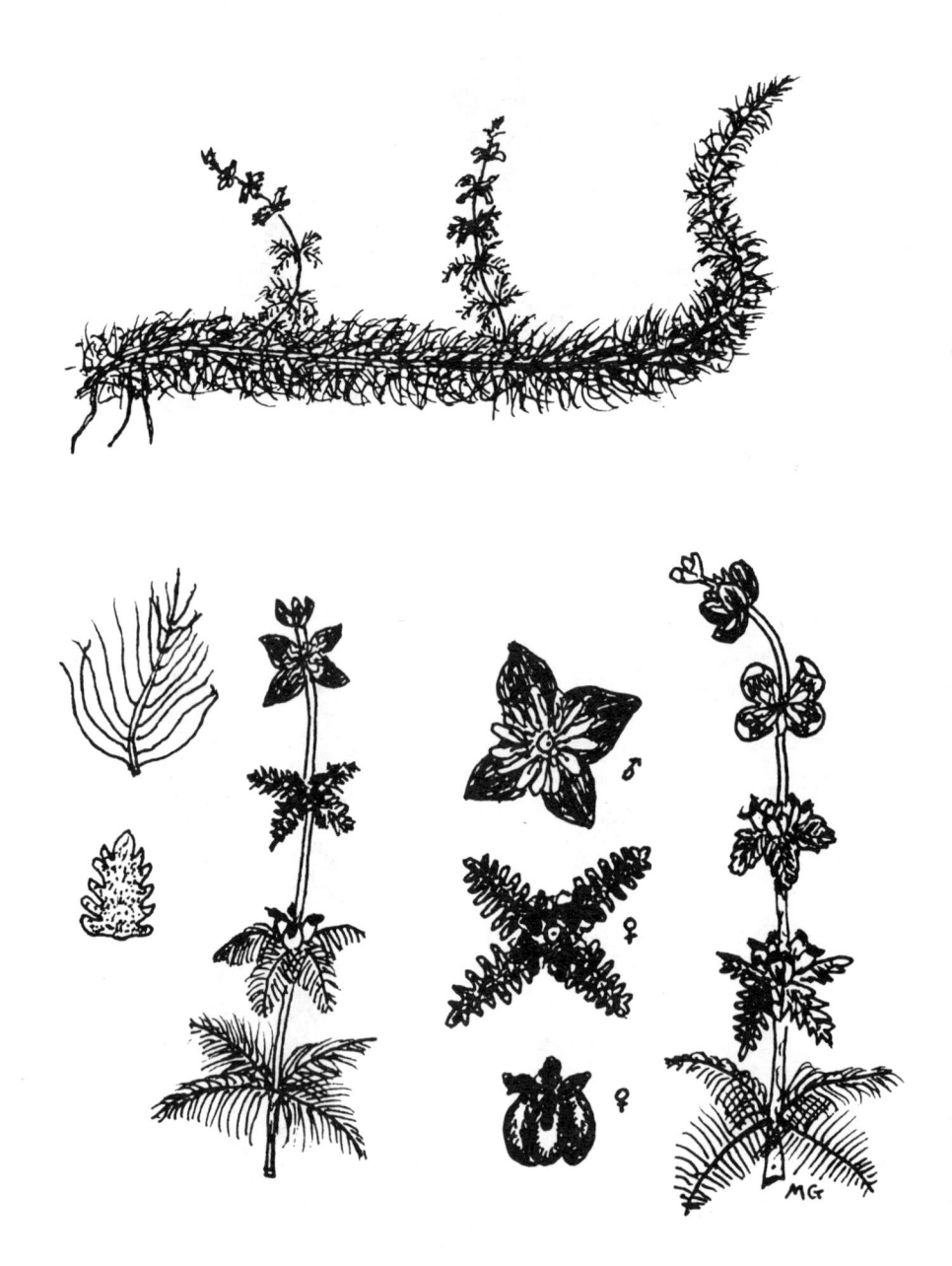

38 Water Milfoil *Myriophyllum salsugineum*

Chapter Five

FLINDERS ISLAND: FILLING IN MORE GAPS

1. WEST COAST TOUR

Our third day on Flinders Island in 1995 started grey and drizzly, but the tentative glimmers of sunshine gained in confidence and eventually transformed the silver seascapes into miracles of blue and gold. We were taken north by Lindsay Luddington, with ample opportunity to dip into odd corners where wildlife treasures might be hiding.

From the Palana Road we turned back south down the peninsula to Long Point. To our left was a broad area of white clayey saltings with the appearance of a lagoon, but this was an inlet of the sea, providing free access to the restless waves. The tidal range varied between nine and twelve feet (three and four metres), but the flatness of the bay floor ensured that a vast spread was exposed twice daily. This seemed bland and empty, but probably harboured untold invertebrate riches, invisible to us but a vital source of nourishment to resident and migrant waders and waterfowl.

Slipping through an old stock fence, we investigated the bordering saltmarsh vegetation. At first we were in a low scrub of shrubby glasswort *(Arthrocnemum arbusculum)*, its stems as fleshy as those of the shorter herbaceous *Salicornia* but with woodier cores and a more rangy growth. With the glassworts or samphires in the forefront were Austral seablite *(Suaeda australis)*, glistening saltbush *(Atriplex billardieri)* and halberd-leaved orache *(Atriplex hastata)*, their succulence exhibited in leaves rather than stems.

All are members of the saltbush family and belong to genera which turn up worldwide in salty places, their exclusiveness a pointer to the rigours of the habitat, with high salinities and fluctuating water levels that few can tolerate. It is reassuring to meet old friends or their near relatives so far from home and realise how much little Britain has in common with her larger counterpart 'down under'. A link with the ocean was provided by the Neptune's necklace seaweed drifted in on the making tide from rocks at the bay mouth.

Observing us with interest from the roadside wires was a kookaburra, the first of five encountered during the day. A cohort of shrieking green rosellas sped past, these the only parrots here apart from the yellow-tailed black cockatoos, which create such a hullabaloo just before rain. Pheasants pottered so unconcernedly along the verges that I was not surprised when Lindsay said, "They are seldom shot, but suffer from feral cats, which are."

The rocks at the tip of Long Point were of hardened quaternary sands and clays instead of the granite that we encountered on most of the headlands, their relative softness no doubt responsible for the sea's incursion to form the inlet.

Drifts of empty bivalve shells, including a few scallops, had collected in pockets, with a sprinkling of tops, winkles and whelks. Little purple clusterwinks *(Littorina unifasciata)* huddled in rock niches at the top of the tide, above spreading beds of horse mussels *(Modiolus pulex)*.

We rejoined the Palana Road, dipping down to the beach again at the coastal reserve of Blue Rocks. Everyone called this Sawyers Bay, sometimes corrupted to Lawyers' Bay in deference to the two resident lawyers, but it is Arthur Bay on the definitive map.

It was one of Derek Smith's favourites and he brought me here to see the sunset on my last night, after a showing of the video film made of the mutton bird industry in 1957; the year before my appearance on the scene, but starring many of those I remembered. Having no video player at home, he took me to his daughter's house near Wybalenna, armed with a generous supply of 'takeaway pizzas' from the Whitemark bakery — an innovation unheard of in his own days as baker.

His engineer son joined his fisherman-farmer son-in-law as we ate, then the two went off to check on a couple of dolphins which had come ashore the night before. They were two males, apparently bonded, one beached and the other swimming around distractedly just offshore. The ranger and helpers had managed to tow the stranded one out to sea and the two wanted to ascertain that they had got away. Too often when these creatures' inbuilt sonar fails them on gently shelving shores providing no satisfactory 'bounce-back', it is likely to do so again, so that rescues are in vain.

But, back to our day trip with Lindsay. A group of spur-wing plovers rose from a bank of shells and sea-grass balls as we approached the sea, where we walked but briefly among saltbush and boxthorn before sprinting for cover from a sudden rain squall. Then the sun broke through again, the blue dome above streaked with bubbling cirrus and flowing mares' tails that told of high altitude winds. We had to slow down to avoid the sleek Hereford cattle straying from the broad grass verges and the conversation turned to farming.

James and Lindsay Luddington ran cattle on a small hill farm, where they had problems with bracken poisoning. With so much of the noxious fern about, one feels that cattle should have learned that it is to be avoided, but we have the same problem on our Welsh hills. Lindsay told us, however, that the alkaline juice from bracken fronds assuaged the pain of ant bites, so it seemed it might be good for something.

Until recently they had owned a 3,000 acre lowland farm in Happy Valley, keeping sheep as well as cattle. They bought old Pollworth ewes due to have one more lamb, weaned the lambs and took a wool crop from the mothers. Then the bottom dropped out of the wool market and they sold up and concentrated more on the boating side of their tourist venture.

They knew what they were about, having lived and farmed sheep for five years on Big Green Island, before deciding that it was time to rejoin their fellow man. James had formerly farmed in Norfolk: Lindsay had grown up in Porlock, Devon, where her ex-army father ran an equestrian training school. They had emigrated independently, meeting up here.

Feral turkeys ambled contentedly around the fields where wild pigs sometimes put in an appearance.

"There are still plenty of wild pigs in the Strzeleckis, AND on our farm. My husband and son shoot them, as they dig up the paddocks. You can't eat the old ones, but the youngsters, penned and fed for three weeks, are delicious!"

The roadside sward where we made a convenience stop was patched with white, blue and even pink *Pratia irrigua*, one of the lesser fan flowers. Other tinies were slender speedwell *(Veronica gracilis)*, golden guinea flowers growing flush with the ground and mats of very English-looking scarlet pimpernel. Not much larger were the stunted trumpets of pink bindweed *(Convolvulus erubescens)*.

Towering over the rest were white spikes of 'candles' *(Stackhousia monogyna)* and white flag or butterfly iris *(Diplarrena moraea)*. This was the only time I saw the iris on Flinders, although it had seemed such a common roadside plant throughout Tasmania and on the larger islands such as Bruny. It was a delightful spot, with the craggy hills of Killiecrankie rising to the left and the two peaks of Mount Boyse ahead.

One of the finest coastal features which we visited was the much photographed Castle Rock in Marshall Bay, which is named after the "George Marshall", run aground in the Kent Group in 1862 and brought here to be beached. Crew, passengers and cargo were saved but the ship remains — buried in the sand.

Castle Rock is a parallel-sided granite tor, split horizontally across the middle and dwarfing the admiring folk gazing up from the beach below. Were it not for the brilliant covering of orange Gasparinnia lichen, it would be reminiscent of the Dartmoor tors. The smaller, but still man-high boulder to seaward is below the lichen zone and shone a silvery blue in the lurid light of a passing squall.

A feature of the beach-back here was the profusion of mauve sea-rocket *(Cakile edentula)*. The calcareous shell sand so well fitted to its requirements extended far inland as lightly vegetated dunes. Any major scrub destruction might initiate disastrous sand-blows. Fortunately the scars left by fires were small and were being healed by succulent-leaved swards of variable groundsel and coast twin-leaf *(Zygophyllum billardieri)*.

Other yellow blooms were supplied by the leek lilies. The larger *Bulbine bulbosa* produced handsome spikes among sheltering scrub, in contrast to the smaller *Bulbine semibarbata* of the coastal sands and outer isles. Candles and the cosmopolitan sea spurge *(Euphorbia paralias)* speared up among low button-bush *(Calocephalus brownii)*, with purple-flowered Swainson's pea *(Swainsonia lessertifolia)* trailing between. Taller scrub included boobialla, daisy bushes, coast wattle and the usual tea-trees and beard heaths.

A little way down a track leading inland was a notice which read WINGAROO NATURE RESERVE. This occupied one of those sun-kissed stretches of open heath which are so much richer in their variety of wild flowers than any of the shaded woods and denser scrubs. Beneath the organic surface was an impermeable layer able to hold the recent rain on top and the thirsty bog flowers were making the most of the lavish water supply.

Among those resembling small twiggy tea-trees were six-petalled wiry bauera or 'dog rose' *(Bauera rubioides)*, five-petalled pink swamp heath *(Sprengelia incarnata)* and four-petalled lilac bells *(Tetratheca pilosa)*, which shares the name of black-eyed Susan with other quite different flowers. Both pink and white common heath grew alongside blunt-leaved heath *(Epacris obtusifolia)* and candles. There was common flat-pea *(Platylobium obtusangulum)*, with sharp-pointed arrowhead leaves, small parrot-pea *(Dillwynia glaberrima)* and a bush-pea *(Pultenaea daphnoides)* with the unlikely name of native daphne.

Botanically it was poles apart from the limey dunes we had so lately left. Occasional erosion faces revealed a greater depth of organic detritus — the undecayed remains of vegetation spanning aeons of time. Beneath this soggy surface lay the dark silent world of an ancient archive, which only those with the know-how and ability to recognise preserved pollen grains could unravel. It was as though we stood on the colourful flyleaf of a coded history book, waiting to be deciphered.

Our wanderings were accompanied by a chorus of burbling frogs and one of the tracks we followed disappeared under water, as three streams came careering in at right angles from higher ground alongside. Some of the paperbarks clustered round this depression had mauve flowers — the swamp honey-myrtle *(Melaleuca squamea)*. Moist ground was blanketed in parts by spongy white lichens, whose intricate branchings I associated with more permanently wet moorlands in western Tasmania, but there was none of West Tasmania's characteristic button-grass — or pin-rush, as Lindsay called it.

Very striking above the peat-stained waters, were young shoots of coast banksia *(Banksia marginata)*, covered in bright ginger velvet and almost as decorative as the yellow bottle brushes which would follow. This has for long been regarded as the only banksia on the island, but Derek told us that a patch of *Banksia serrata* with saw-edged leaves had been found recently.

Out in the open were some of the only tall blue fan flowers to be found in Tasmania, *Dampiera stricta*. One of two which could be termed 'architectural plants' was the spikily angular horny cone bush *(Isopogon ceratophyllus)*, some with a central cone, some with a lemon-yellow flower cluster. The other was the even smaller, flatly symmetrical bog club moss, *Selaginella uliginosa*. The starry daisy bush *(Olearia stellulata)* stood out, but the prize for beauty and abundance must go to the pink *Sprengelia* swamp heath.

North of Marshall Bay the coast bulges westwards to Frankland, beyond the Paps. Killiecrankie Bay — quite a tourist honeypot, but one which we did not have time to visit — is tucked in north of the headland. This is where the famous Flinders Island topaz is found, associated with the granite and pegmatite and referred to as Killiecrankie diamonds or crystal. Joan and I were already acquainted with these attractive stones, having chatted with an elderly lady in Whitemark who had been diving for them until recently, sucking them from the sand of Killiecrankie Bay with a compressor-driven pump.

The stones are a fluoro-silicate of aluminium, usually colourless, but sometimes tinted blue or pink by potassium or manganese impurities. Some are faceted, with liquid-filled bubbles or slivers. They are semi precious, harder than glass or quartz, softer than sapphire or diamond, but harder than most other topaz. A rich source has been the alluvial deposits and tailings of the old Mount Tanner tin mines, but they can also be found in waterworn pebbles on and off the granite foreshore and in the mouths of peaty river creeks. Cut stones can be bought in the gem shops, uncut ones sought with sieve and shovel on organised trips to appropriate spots, such as Mines Creek or Diamond Gully.

On our outward journey we pressed on to the north coast, but on our way back we enjoyed a walk at a glorious stretch of shoreline known, inexplicably and inappropriately as the Dock. Anything less like the traditional idea of a dock would be hard to imagine. As well as the splendid jumble of promontaries and reefs sprawled across the intertidal sands, the rugged yellow pile of Mount Killiecrankie rose to the south. A window of blue sky glimmered through a hole in a lofty rock pile, while away to the north, beside the few houses that comprised Palana, was Blyth Point.

The sun was blazing by now and my camera clicked greedily, recording orange-painted granite monoliths, close-packed paperbark trunks, evergreen mountainside, Craggy Island offshore and much detail on. Spreads of Neptune's necklace seemed to grow from shingly sand of disintegrating rock, but this was just a thin layer on a level granite platform. Long fronds of *Phyllospora* had been helped ashore by the firm oval floats to lie among the cuttlebones. The beach had been piled with shells the previous week, according to Lindsay, but most of these had been swept out to sea by the storms, only the heavier cone shells remaining in any quantity.

After preliminary beach exploration, we dipped back into the fringing paperbarks, the contorted trunks of which writhed skywards in such proximity that almost no plants found sufficient light to grow below. The only life seemed to be the perennial bracket fungi and dark-loving invertebrates. It was quite eerie, I almost expected to come across a band of trolls cogitating in the gloom.

Picking our way through the litter of fallen trunks and branches, we emerged where a pair of black currawongs watched our every move critically from an outlier of the scrub and rosellas shouted, unseen, in the undergrowth. The seascapes which opened up outside were almost as intricate — etched in black and silver as we looked into the sun, blazing in blue and gold when we turned around.

39 White Butterfly Iris *Diplarrena moraea* and
Large Leek Lily *Bulbine bulbosa*

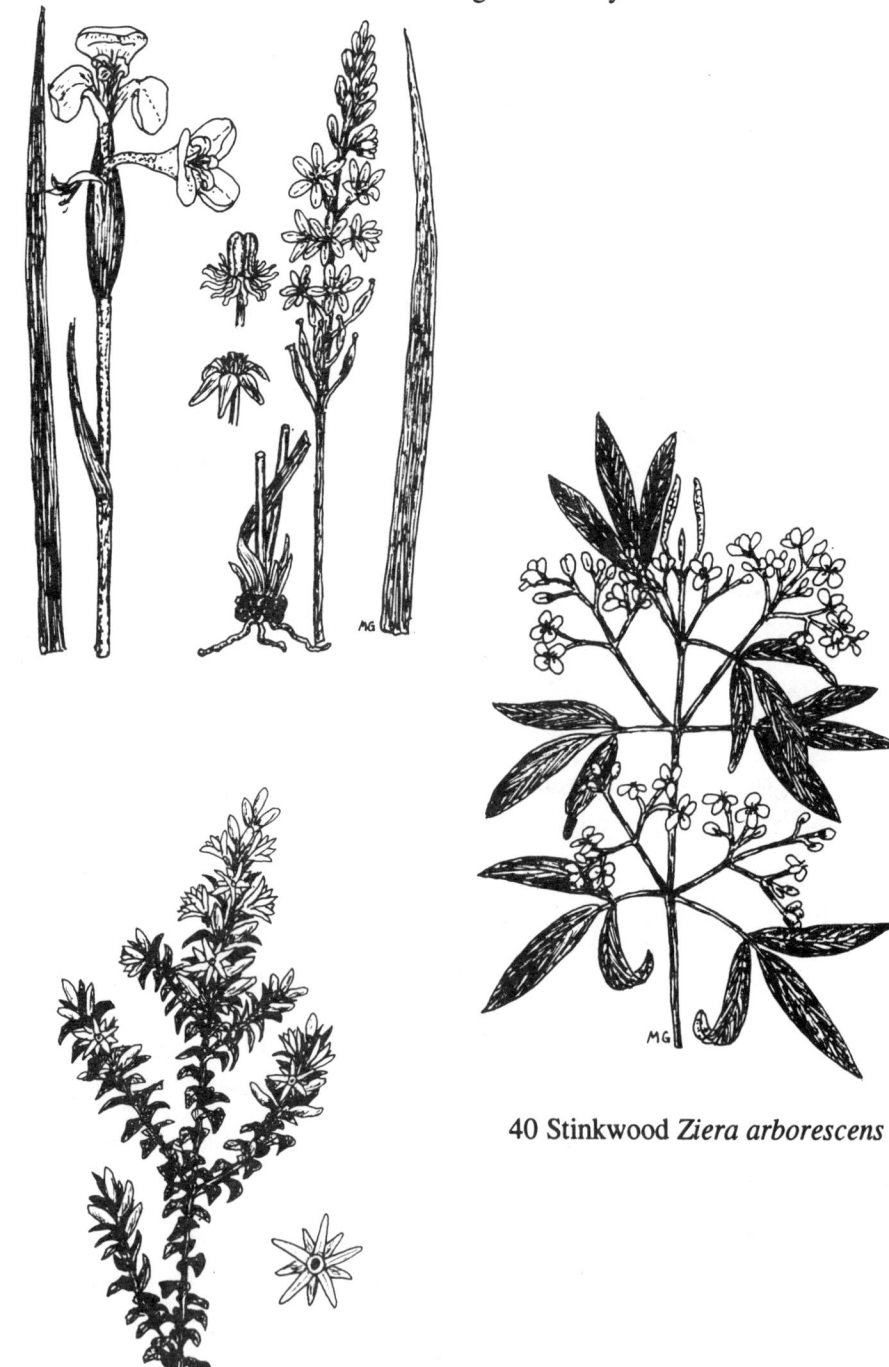

40 Stinkwood *Ziera arborescens*

41 Swamp Heath *Sprengelia incarnata*

2. SPEWINGS OF THE TIDE IN THE NORTH AND EAST

The afternoon was well advanced when we stopped for lunch on the north coast of Flinders Island, watching a posse of screeching terns hovering over an offshore islet. We shared our granite platform with some triangular crayfish caufes. These were high and dry. When in use the slatted wooden crates float almost completely submerged, as holding pens for crayfish between catching and sale.

They were much abused in the late fifties, being filled with crayfish caught illegally before 'the season' opened. Unfortunately the long imprisonment with no food meant that the flesh shrank inside the unshrinkable shells by the time they could be marketed, so weight did not match up to size. (Modern cray fishermen would not, of course, descend to such ploys.)

Moving on, we passed a series of holiday homes, half-hidden among the paperbarks lining the estuary of North East River. This was a favourite place with the islanders for Christmas holidays. The road petered out among bushy *Helichrysum* and *Olearia*, within sight of the little low lighthouse on Stanley Point, the island's northern extremity. The terrain was low, slabby granite, accommodating a helipad.

Purple noon-flower *(Carpobrotus rossii)* pulled itself up through coastal beard heath, and bidgee-widgee *(Acaena anserinifolia)* surged unstoppably along the path. There were none of the noxious bur-fruits so heartily disliked by graziers at this season, but the budding balls of flowers gave promise of trouble to come. We padded out through short everlastings to view the two Sisters Islands offshore.

Closest and largest was the two-humped Inner Sister, occupying 630 hectares. A sheep-grazing lease was taken up here in 1884, the grazier's family getting stores half yearly from Launceston. To supplement these, and the bread baked in cast-iron camp ovens, they harvested 20,000 mutton birds annually, these and their eggs eaten stewed or boiled, with more birds put away for winter, smoked or salted. The bulk were salted and sold in Launceston for ten shillings a hundred to offset the cost of other essentials.

Hares were introduced in 1890 to provide sport for visitors, and they persist still, alongside the native wallabies and possums. These are the only hares in the archipelago and rabbits, mercifully, are confined to a few of the outer islets. In view of this, it was surprising that one of the more vociferous participants at the Whitemark Council meeting on our last evening should have recommended introducing the new rabbit Calcivirus that had 'got away' from its experimental island in South Australia with two reporters and was the talk of the media.

There were, of course, no foxes, nor in Tasmania anywhere, despite several tentative introductions. It has been suggested that they failed because Tasmanian devils are attracted to their lairs by the discarded carrion and go inside to dispose of the cubs.

Lying away to the north-east was the Outer Sister (405 hectares). This was first inhabited in the 1830s. When the settler's Aboriginal wife died in childbirth her baby was said to have thrived on lightly coddled cormorant eggs! Cormorants were still to be seen, winging their way low over the waters of Sisters Passage with the Pacific gulls. There were also a few pelicans. As on the Inner Sister, the paddocks are burned to improve the grazing, but both scrub and mutton birds survive. Both are now mutton bird reserves.

We moved over to the mouth of North East River, where two young men in wet suits were coming in with their surfboards. The sun was out now and I flushed no fewer than three skinks enjoying the warmth which had been in such short supply of late. Pied oystercatchers pottered on the beach, probing for molluscs, but the silver gulls were standing around on the sand, apparently quite replete, like gorged cattle killing time after a substantial feed.

As we moved up-river the beach became more and more littered with marine detritus. While sand and shells had been drawn away from the western beaches by the storms, the eastern ones seemed to have been on the receiving end. We became beachcombers in earnest, picking over the flotsam and jetsam, much of it still alive, and trying to identify the unidentifiable.

Dr Isabel Bennett, one of our female foursome with the Antarctic Division thirty-seven years before, had surveyed the marine life at the mouth of North East River and pinpointed the site as a meeting place of organisms from further south and further north. The big bull kelp *(Durvillea potatorium)*, arching above the water at low tide, was an outlier of populations growing in the frigid Southern Ocean. The brown wrack *(Phyllospora comosa)*, borne inshore by its firm oval air bladders, was a Pacific species characteristic of the coast of New South Wales. Other seaweeds, olive brown with resilient velvety branches half a metre long, were new to me and fascinating in the knobbly intricacy of their design.

Animals torn from their hold and rolled up the beach fell into two main categories — the 'heavyweights', consisting of solid jelly lumps, and the 'lightweights', spongy or hollow.

Best known and most numerous of the jelly lumps were the ascidian sea squirts known as cunjevois *(Pyura stolonifera)*. Usually these are exposed only by the lowest tides and they really do squirt. Lean over too far when feeling their vital statistics with the fingers, and one may get a well-directed jet of water in the eye.

Companies of cunjevois sit erect on downshore rocks like chunky, two-nozzled vases, the nozzles being inlet and outlet. Some give shelter in their hollow, meshlike interior to little red sand fleas. These cause them no harm, living in a commensal partnership. Rock fishermen commonly collect cunjevoi for bait.

Only the larval phase, which is a bit like a tadpole, with the precursor of a backbone, is capable of swimming, so the displaced individuals would not be able to re-establish themselves. They and the rest were destined to form a feast for scavenging gulls if these could penetrate the firm enwrapping 'tunic' which has given the group as a whole the name of Tunicates. But the gulls, it seemed, were already too satiated to bother.

Other jelly blobs strewn on the sand were elongated Sipunculids, clean-washed by the waves, yet mildly repulsive in their obesity. Sinuously bulging, milky-white worms, they were transversely ribbed and longitudinally wrinkled, bulbous at one end and tapered at the other. One identified later by Hope Black from a photograph was *Phascolosoma noduliferum*. This bloated marine worm was fifteen to eighteen cm long with a protrusible proboscis and mouth at the narrower end. The waste outlet was not at the further end of the body tube, but amidships. Detritus feeders, the animals live buried in sand or mud, their uprooting suggesting that a considerable amount of sea bed must have been on the move. The British *Phascolosoma vulgaris* is thinner, yellower and more transparent.

Most ornamental of the jellied specimens were the shining white clusters of cuttlefish eggs, *Sepiotheuthis australis*, their firm texture not unlike that of their mother, but pure white, yellowing with age. They were attached end to end in rows of six to eight, the groups connected by their tapering necks into bunches of forty to fifty. Each string of eggs was ten to twelve cm long, the splayed cluster fitting neatly on a dinner plate.

The variety of sponges in the featherweight flotsam thrown to the highest levels was an eye-opener to someone used to the humbler encrusting or rounded sponges of North Temperate waters. They varied from closely aggregated scrolls the size of tennis balls to slender branched forms half a metre long.

Sycon, a limey sponge, is a genus found also in Britain. The Flinders specimens were small balls of tightly packed, slightly branched clubs, the British are chubbier, scarcely branched and more solitary. Those were a furry buff grey, with a crown of spines at each tip, the Furneaux ones were pink and shiny.

Clione, a boring sponge, is also common to both regions, fashioning a maze of narrow chambers and tunnels in oyster shells and limey rocks. They grow as an enveloping mesh over the substrate chosen by the free-swimming spat and sport an unassuming brown or yellow livery.

Tethya, a third genus common to both sides of the world, is also small and rounded, but generally brighter. Another North East River genus of modest proportions was *Thorecta*, but nothing we can do in the North approaches the long, sparsely-branched beauties of the Flinders sands.

Neatly rounded sea urchins cast up with the melée were identified as *Amblyneustes ovum*, the test remaining bristly around the top, even when the main spines had gone. A more exciting find was a slate pencil urchin, with smoothly flattened, pencil-like appendages instead of the usual sharply pointed spines. Always before, I had associated these with the Tropics.

Sadly, time is finite, and we had to drag ourselves away.

* * * * *

Next day, after a long morning at sea in Franklin Sound, Irene and Doreen brought us again to the east-facing coast to view more of the spewings of the tide. They had hoped to show us Logans Lagoon — a wetland reserve with no water — and Cameron Inlet — a bird sanctuary with no birds — where we saw but a single swan, but we ended up on the coast a little further north.

Turning off the Memana Road at Lackrana, we followed the Cameron Inlet Road as far as it went, curving up the coast towards Sellars Lagoon, arguably the biggest on the island. We were beyond the narrow, sometimes blocked, entrance of Cameron Inlet here, heading on foot along the open coast of the Tasman Sea south of Babel Island.

The driftline was quite different here and more spectacular. At North East River it had been mostly animals, scattered over the sand: here the same amount of fauna was dwarfed by great banks of seaweed, ripped loose and thrown ashore in tangled confusion. In some places the seaward side of the continuous bank of weed was vertical and the height of a man — the sort of accumulation more often seen beside the great sea-grass meadows.

Here the substance was not of the Posidonia strapweed but mostly the much more substantial oarweed or bull kelp, some of this brought, perhaps, from beyond Cape Barren. Every other conceivable type of weed, red, green or brown, was intertwined, with another, rather special kind lying on top. These were spongy dark green balls resembling the *Codium bursa* of the Mediterranean. They could be up to twenty cm across, although usually smaller, and seem to swim around under their own steam, possibly to avoid sea urchins, which relish their flavour.

Shapes of those on the Flinder's shore varied slightly. *Codium lucasi* formed neat spheres the size of tennis balls: *Codium mamillosum* balls were a little more elongated with a slightly depressed 'waist' and an orifice at one end. I have come across no popular name for these distinctive growths, the obvious one of 'sea balls' having been appropriated by the Posidonia balls. Other *Codium* species here were the commoner, fingered shape of *Codium fragile*.

Many animals were enmeshed in the tangle, some living on and struggling to free themselves. One such was the scarlet hermit crab, *Eupagurus sinuatus*, with bright blue eyes on long stalks. This had been winkled out of its protective shell but sought in vain for another. The only shells visible were unaccommodating halves of bivalves; this chap wanted something a lot more substantial to hold two to three inches of curving body.

Oddest of the fish was the sea dragon, *Phyllopteryx taeniolatus*, an ornate version of the better known sea horse, itself a more complex digression from the pipe fish. These were a handspan long, the tubular snout beyond the bulging eyes and the slender neck between the 'ears' and the 'shoulders' both almost as long as the tail.

Blue-tinged bladders of Portuguese-men-of-war *(Physalia physalis)*, which is almost cosmopolitan in warmer seas, had been cast up with the rest — with or without some of the tangled stinging trailers. The bladders are sometimes called 'bluebottles' (polythene ones for preference) — a more fitting candidate for the name than the familiar blowfly style bluebottle.

Among the displaced cunjevois were some related colonial sea squirts, remarkable for their starry surface patterning rather than the double-spouted vase shape. One such compound ascidian was the yellow *Sarcobotrylloides*. Like squashed rubbery balls now, these had been encrusting in life. They put me in mind of our star ascidian *(Botryllus schlosseri)*, where the tiny golden individuals are grouped around a central exhalant hole from which waste water is expelled, each embedded colony resembling a miniature sunflower. Our British *Botrylloides*, though more similar in name, is differently patterned, with long ellipses instead of stars.

Other white but more barrel-shaped Sipunculid worms here were *Themista cymodocae*. A Holothurian, *Paracaudina australis*, was white instead of the black of the better known sea cucumbers or trepang of the Tropics, like an even more bloated Sipunculid.

One of the sea urchins here was indistinguishable from our British *Echinocardium cordatum*, the sea potato, which is known to occur here. Most of its time is spent buried well down in the sandy sea bed.

From the many colour slides which I sent back to Australia for identification, Hope Black managed to name some of the riot of sponges, but others eluded her. Hands of finger sponges, *Chalinopsila*, reached to three times the size of human hands. Fittingly more elegant were the mermaid's gloves *(Haliclona)*, a familiar kind on our South Wales shores. *Phyllospongia calciformis* came in the form of a slightly fluted cup; other species of this genus took the form of fans. Two kinds of *Thorecta* appeared in the randomly taken slides and a probable *Mycale*, plus others defying identification.

Apart from a few mud oyster shells *(Ostrea angasi)*, solid objects were scarce. Probably most had dropped out of the gelatinous mass as it writhed its way ashore. Of particular interest was a stony white colonial corallite, *Pleisiastrea versipora*, the limestone skeleton a series of circular openings surrounded by fine radial plates ranged side by side. Their substance was that of reef corals, although the true reef builders seldom get beyond latitude 28°S, where sea temperature is unlikely to fall below 68° F. A few Gorgonid sea fans, themselves pliant, horny corals, were also present.

More fascinating to my mind were the encrusting sea mats, with white limey skeletons. Those forming spiralised collars up to three inches long around slender twiglets were *Densipora corrugata*. Each colony consisted of closely aggregated individuals in little limestone boxes — hence Polyzoa, for 'many animals'. A soft mat of tentacles was extruded as they fed — hence Bryozoa for 'moss animals'. Each specimen was basically a tight spiral of ridges and furrows, increasing from two to eight cm long and from half to one and a half cm wide, the older ones with fan-shaped flanges. These grow in shallow water and I had been finding them on the west coast, but had not come upon such interesting shapes anywhere else.

More treasures were to be found by flipping aside the massed weed. Although this was a calamitous mortality for so many, it gave me a feeling of elation that there was so much more left in these waters than in the over-fished and over-polluted seas around the Northern Hemisphere's more ancient centres of civilisation. These casualties, like the car-killed marsupials on the island's roads, were but the tip of an iceberg, telling of greater riches unseen.

Among the most lightweight of the casualties was a creature not entirely of the sea — a fairy prion, with black beak, legs and tail contrasting with the soft blue-grey plumage. Among the heaviest was the find that excited our museum curator most. This was a great irregular lump of coal, which she and Irene managed to carry back to the van between them.

Only a little further up this coast, the *"City of Foo Chow"*, a coal-carrying vessel of 1034 tons, had come ashore after striking Beagle Rock in 1876. Doreen was convinced this must be some of her cargo, given up by the sea after 120 years. She would have none of our suggestion that it might have gone overboard from a coal-burning steamship subsequently.

Loaded with this and other treasures, we stumbled back through the threadbare line of dunelets, which were loosely held by sea spurge, saltbush and marram grass, to the extensive sand flat behind. This was covered with circular clumps of succulent, round-leaved plants having spikes of white flowers resembling squat 'candles'. We had none of us seen these before, but they proved to be, indeed, coastal 'candles', *Stackhousia spathulata*.

This was not on the island list of plants but, if it was a new arrival, drifted in on a spring tide, it would have had no trouble in spreading across the low-lying flat once the meagre row of sand tumps was breached. It was certainly strikingly dominant by the end of 1995. This open community graded into a closely grazed turf sprinkled with tiny flowers of coast brookweed and dwarf yellow buttons.

We kept our eyes open throughout for the triangular fossilised shark teeth for which the area is famous. These survivors from Pliocene times are stained black by minerals, but we searched in vain today.

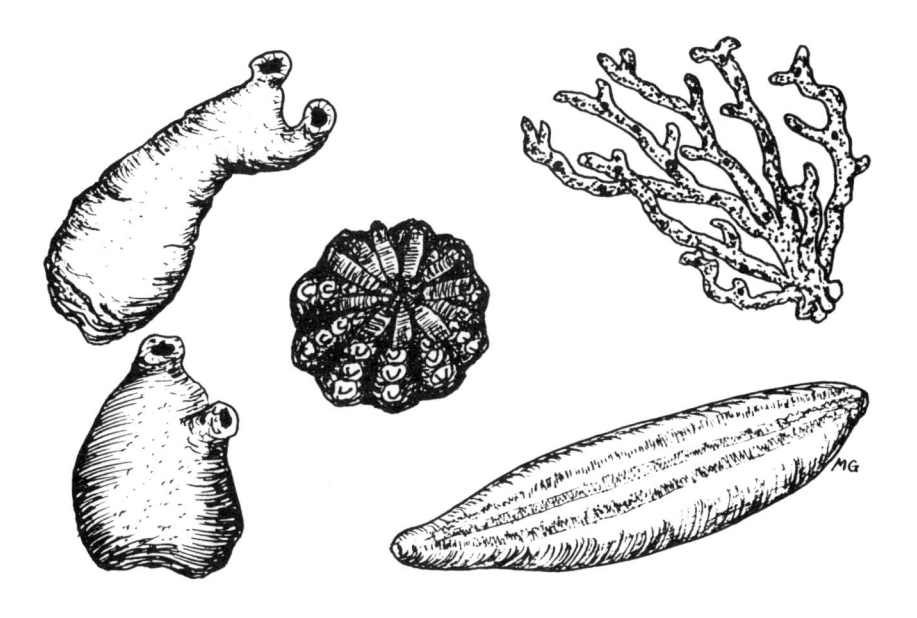

42 Cunjevoi Sea Squirts *Pyura stolonifera*, Pencil Urchin *?Phyllocanthus irregularis*, Mermaid's Glove Sponge *Haliclona* and a Holothurian *Paracaudinia*

43 Cuttlefish Eggs *Sepiatheuthis australis*

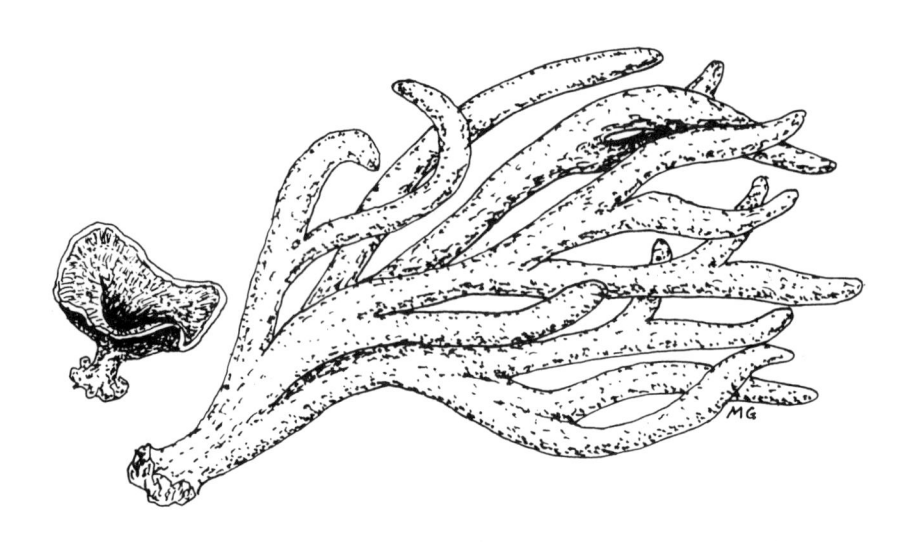

44 Cup Sponge *Phyllospongia* and Finger Sponge *Chalinopsilla*

3. FRANKLIN SOUND AND SOME ISLANDS REVISITED

Leaving the aftermath of the ocean's fury behind, we moved south along the inner shore of Cameron Inlet. The long sandspit across the water kept Father Neptune and his boisterous retinue at bay, allowing the severely wind-trimmed thicket to take heart and burgeon into woodland.

This was the Locarno Wildlife Reserve, where duck shooting was illegal, but we came upon a duck shooters' camp as we pushed through the trees, trying to see if the lagoon was really as birdless as it seemed.

The hovels, for they were little more, resembled open-sided birders' huts with the most primitive sleeping and cooking equipment. This, we were told, was a traditional site for browned-off male citizens to come and work off their frustrations with guns: an activity impossible to police.

Almost every part of this supposedly remote landscape was put to use. As we crossed Chew Tobacco Creek, Doreen had commented: "Lovely white sand here: we used to collect it for making cement."

We didn't make it to the water but obtained fine views of swamp harriers, kookburras and swallows. Most impressive, however, were the echidnas, eight in all, mostly quite dark but one a light sandy hue. One stop was to photograph a magnificent tiger snake, sunning itself on the highway. From behind it was as black as the six-footers on Chappell Island, but from the side it showed a row of light yellow triangles poking up from the paler belly, rudiments of the tiger stripes of the mainland one that I had photographed a few weeks earlier in an Otway Mountain sandpit. There was neither black nor yellow on that one, a modest four-footer — the banding being in brown and fawn.

The official name of the tiger snake is *Notechis ater*. In the fifties and sixties they were referred to as *Notechis scutatus*, but Eric Worrell later separated the robust Chappell Island race as *Notechis ater serventii* in Dom Serventy's honour.

By this time we were on our way to Petrifaction Bay, east-facing like the last two but much more sheltered, being tucked into the flank of Adelaide Bay behind a scatter of islands. This Tertiary Vesicular Basalt had received a lot less drift than the others. Most of the displaced organisms were small, like the egg capsules of dog whelks, or lightweight, like the ornamented mermaids' purses (egg cases of skates or rays.) There was also the sad remains of a diving petrel, the dark waterlogged plumage given individuality by the broad bill and bright blue legs and feet.

The dotterels were very much alive, racing over the tidal flats with legs twinkling like those of sanderlings. Petrified wood was scarcer than I remembered, the fragments no bigger than walnuts but showing beautiful graining. This was a muddier shore than most, so soft in places that we were jumping from one rock slab to the next.

Shellfish were as numerous as ever, but were predominantly of one kind, the neatly symmetrical pyramids of gold-mouthed conniwinks *(Bembicium auratum)*. Attractively patterned with circular rows of humps, most were a khaki colour. They darkened with age, possibly from sulphides in the anaerobic mud, although each was firmly clamped to the black rock. This species is typical of sheltered shores.

The softer substrate again produced mainly one type of shell, these almost circular and an inch across. White outside, with only a delicate tracery of criss-crossing furrows, they were a rich purple-black within. Striated dog cockles *(Tucetilla striatularis)* seemed to fit the bill, but there are many similar kinds, all with white interiors, which might have got stained black, but scarcely that regal purple.

* * * * *

The morning's weather had been dreamlike in its perfection, sunny and windless with scarcely a ripple on Franklin Sound, but a sea mist clamped down in the afternoon. Dark clouds rolled in from the south-east and there were a few spits of rain. The morning we spent at sea with James Luddington and the blissful weather lasted through our belated lunch on Vinegar Hill's viewpoint, from where we watched the haze swallowing up Cape Barren Island and creeping across the water to Flinders. By nightfall that tranquil expanse would be whipped up into a frenzy of white horses.

We had presented ourselves at Lady Barron jetty at 8.30 a.m., Doreen, Irene, Joan and I. Boxes of gummy shark and larger than usual stripy garfish were being manhandled onto a runabout truck from a fishing boat. James, helping with the carrying, was building up a big game fishing enterprise. Two others hired out boats at weekends, one a teacher, the other a full-time builder.

We were taken to Fisher Island two at a time in a bouncy little inflatable with outboard motor, and stepped ashore like ladies on sunkissed granite, moistened by scarcely a ripple. I had lived on this scrap of land for so many months that I must have known every bluff and every plant. It seemed to me that little had changed as I moved across the rock platform, trying not to crush too much of the crimson-leaved, magenta-flowered jelly-bean style pigface, which clashed so stridently with the sheets of orange lichen in an outrageous riot of colour.

There were few residents now, with only one researcher, Iryneji Skira, (from Hobart University) making widely spaced observations of the ringed birds — keeping up the continuity of records for over forty years. This was not too long, with individual ringed birds living for thirty-five years or so.

Stepping over bright tufts of leek lily, silver everlasting and tall coast daisy, I made my nostalgic way to "Yolla". The building stood four square to the winds, as it always had, now newly painted in camouflage green. The back room with its two double bunks and the minuscule toilet block were as before, but there were now two galvanised water tanks and a tap releasing their contents into a sink. The meat safe had been replaced by a kerosene fridge and the wood stove was no longer the mainstay for cooking, being superseded by a gas stove.

The card index, detailing the birds and plants over the decades, occupied the same corner of the table under the window, although I have a feeling that much of its substance was now on computer. Were those the same marine knick-knacks on the mantelpiece that I remembered?

Bushes of fringed beard heath as well as the coprosma behind the hut had increased enormously. Some had been grubbed out and dragged to bare rock for disposal. Permission from the National Parks Officer was necessary before it could be burned.

Where the pair of red-capped dotterel had brought up their spherical, long-legged chicks each year, was a party of between forty and fifty birds. It would be nice to think they were of the same family line as those whose fortunes I had followed so long ago. They took off and circled, tilting like shearwaters, to show first the white belly and then the mottled back, before landing like a cloud of white butterflies on the most seaward outlier of Reef Island.

This was the only rock not already occupied by the age-old colony of black-faced cormorants. The pigface-quilted island centre was sprinkled with idling Pacific gulls. There were still very few Dominican gulls about according to James.

On the other side of Fisher Island where the sooty oystercatchers had nested in front of the cramped little hide, three were standing in a shallow bay with a white-faced heron and trio of silver gulls. A pair of musk ducks sailed into the picture, with another pair and a single further out, the drakes' misshapen heads unmistakable. Foraging singly until recently, the springtime hormones were flowing, bringing partners together.

Then came the mountain duck, flying directly towards the Darling Ranges, necks outstretched and distinctive white markings plainly visible. More followed, then a few small contingents of Cape Barren geese.

The brooding calm of that idyllic morning was heavy with memories, the scene almost overpowering in its timelessness and permanence. It seduced the senses with its vibrant colours, red, yellow, green and blue, and the muted bird calls. Fisher Island was an insignificant scrap of land in an all-embracing arm of the sea, yet it was of major significance to the many who had helped with the mutton bird project when the research was in its infancy.

Fate could not have set the scene more enticingly in that week of gales and rain. Or was it James Luddington I had to thank, for picking the only quiet period for our visit? This was "Goodbye" to something that had become an integral part of me. At my age there was little chance that I should ever return.

* * * * *

Back at Lady Barron's smart new jetty, we transferred to the big game fishing launch, *"Strait Lady"*, bound for Great Dog Island. Climbing the ladder to seats behind the upper wheel on the cabin roof, we settled to enjoy the tranquil scene. The big new warehouse and processing plant by the pier grew steadily smaller as we headed out between deserted tree-lined bays to port and the tussock-clad island of Little Dog to starboard. This showed the black scars of a limited burn.

"The tussock hasn't regenerated because of the long drought, but it'll soon be greening up now."

Little Dog was privately owned and still produced harvests of mutton birds.

With the general change in attitude towards wild harvests, there was a dwindling market for birds in the 1990s, as well as fewer people willing to collect them. Most of those taken at present were "skunned". Instead of the plucking of feathers and scalding to remove residual down, the feathers, down and subcutaneous fat were pulled off altogether, along with the skin. Carcases were opened out, kipper style, and exported fresh-frozen instead of salted or smoked. The harvest was still many weeks away and the huts drowsed in the soporific sunlight.

A large dark shape overtook the *"Strait Lady"* — an eagle or harrier — then another, showing more white, this a young sea eagle, which made more appearances as we closed in on two sets of Great Dog birding huts. This island was the main source of harvested birds at present.

The launch's mooring buoy had been uprooted in the storm and lost without trace, but it was high water, so we were able to move inshore and make fast to the one used by the birding family's dinghy. We dropped off two by two into the inflatable and headed for the bluff beyond the more easterly settlement. To save getting wet feet in a beach landing, we did some bottom-shuffling across a granite face and sidled round the bushes between gently lapping wavelets.

The Cape Barren geese pottering on the low sward in front of the buildings took off in panic and the watchful pair of black currawongs croaked their disapproval but held their ground. The pair of little ravens in the tall she-okes made themselves scarce, while a family of young starlings complained hungrily from their nest in the ceiling of the processing hut.

I went into the gloomy interior to change a film, but found nowhere clean enough to put the camera down. The place was filthy, a soft coating of bird down clinging to every well-greased surface and dusty cobwebs stretched across the thick layer of fat around the scalding vats. Were all those surfaces still used in the "skunning", or was that residual squalor?

The room with the cooling racks was a little more savoury. Outside were bulging sacks of pickling salt and stacks of metal barrels in all the familiar chaos of the fifties and sixties.

We escaped into the sunlight, to be replaced immediately by the fussing starlings, their beaks crammed with squirming fodder. A broad path led obliquely up through the rookery between overgrown tussocks matted together with fog grass and bower spinach. The only other plants sufficiently robust to fight their corner were the papery white everlastings, some tinged crimson. These formed big clumps quite as beautiful as the yellow cultivar planted in the shelter of the huts and nourished by a combination of human waste and bird processing effluent. At a few places mats of wild clematis were romping across the grass tops, effectively barring access.

Nervousness on the part of the National Park wardens had prevented them from granting permission to burn and the ungrazed rookery vegetation had got out of hand. Alongside the path bird burrows penetrated the ground at the rate of about one per square yard, but fewer were visible beyond. The hairy, cloying fog grass had choked many burrow mouths, sometimes preventing the entry of birds caught in its meshes and greatly hindering the people trying to take the progeny of pairs which had made it.

With so much dead trash and sun-dried growth, no-one dared give the go-ahead to burn now. Flames that might have passed swiftly through an open community would now create a hot fire and burn everything, leaving few stools or seeds to regenerate. While the thousands of birds needing holes might continue to inhabit those penetrating bare blackened sand, there would be a big risk of erosion and an influx of all the undesirable, easily dispersed weeds like thistles, cat's-ear, hawkbits, and ephemeral grasses. Had lack of the traditional management spelled the end of the bird harvest — even of the birds themselves if the mattress got too dense to penetrate? It was a sobering thought: only time would tell.

We came down from the hill and took the other main path through the scrub. On a broader stretch, under kunzea bushes loaded with blossoms, the scattered goose dung around the huts increased to a squishy carpet. This patch of open ground must be where the geese congregated to roost. There was no food to tempt them, the only ground level growth being a few fawn toadstools. They, too, would be excluded from the blanketing tussocks and denied fresh green sprouts in the overgrown lanes between.

A few silver-eyes flipped among the white flowers of the coast paperbarks or poked along branches shaggy with old man's beard lichen. She-okes dominated much of the scrub, reaching right to sea level on the bluff where bower spinach climbed up all available supports.

Some of the sticky hop bushes *(Dodonaea viscosa)* bore circular red fruits, winged like those of elms, but the real beauties were the long spikes of kunzea flowers. These spread from ground to treetop, bristling with the feathery white stamens which distinguished them from the real tea-trees with which they are often lumped. I had not been particularly conscious of these before, but most of my visits had been between December and April when the show was over. Springtime on the islands was a new experience and one which drew to a close all too soon as we re-boarded the *"Strait Lady"* for the return passage.

Although suffering frequent fires in the past, much of, Great Dog Island, as of the other principal mutton bird islands of Little Dog, Little Green and Babel, had been spared the depredations of grazing livestock, because of the poverty of the soil derived from the underlying granite. Islands used more specifically for grazing, like Big Woody and Tin Kettle Islands and Big Green and Kangaroo Islands to the west, had more fertile soil, derived from their capping of post Tertiary sandy limestone which forms a crust over the granite, as on some of the lower lying parts of Flinders Island. The Siluro-Devonian quartzites and slates are much more restricted on the archipelago as a whole.

For six short days only I had been on the Furneaux Group in 1995 (from 6th-11th November) with the weather far from helpful for most of this time, but I had awakened happy memories of that earlier chapter in my life. Thanks to friends old and new, I had also had the chance to learn something of the 'mother' island of Flinders which I had seen so little of while on the seas and outer isles in my more youthful years.

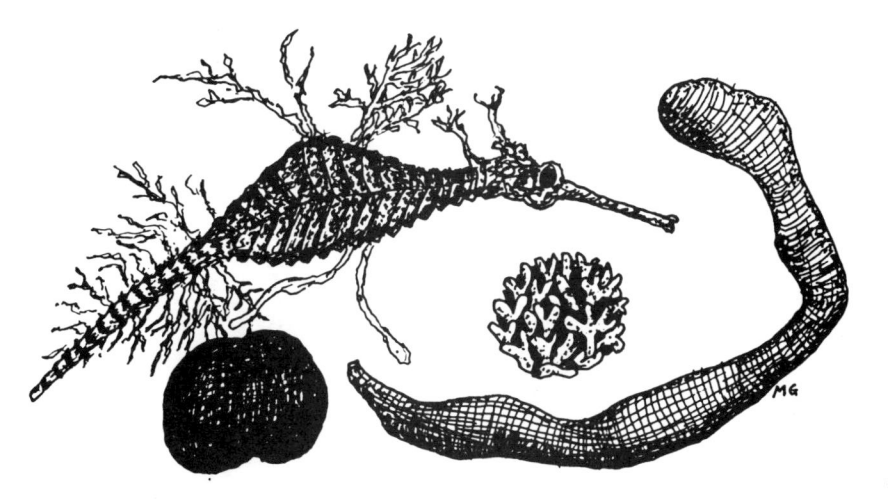

45 Sea Dragon *Phyllopteryx taeniolatus*, Green Algal Ball
Codium mamillosum, Sponge *Sycon* and Sipunculid *Phascolosoma noduliferum*

46 Portugese Man-of-War *Physalia physalis*

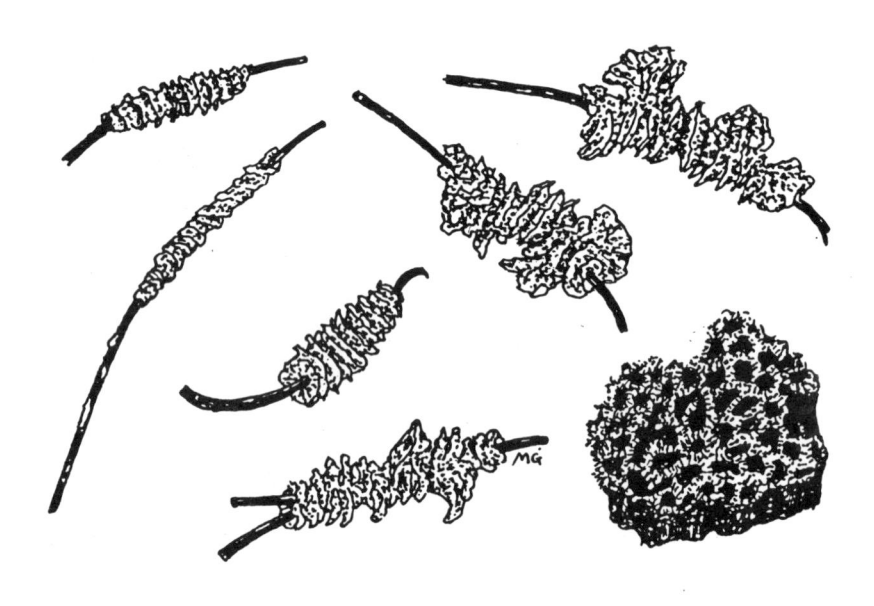

47 Encrusting Moss-animals *Densipora corrugata* and Corallite *Pleisiastrea versipora*

Chapter 6

STOCK RAISING ISLANDS ACROSS FRANKLIN SOUND

1. CAPE BARREN ISLAND

My first visit to Cape Barren Island was on *"Tassie"*, with Eric and Dell Lindgren. Skipper Tuck Robinson knew all there was to know about these waters — except, perhaps, where all the shifting shoals were currently lodged, but his knowledge was essentially local. The fact that New Zealand occupied more than one major island was news to him!

Cape Barren lay three hours' chug away, so we had a chance to get our bearings en route. While no-one at home has heard of Flinders Island, Cape Barren is familiar to every bird-watcher, because of the famous Cape Barren geese at the ornithological Mecca of the Slimbridge Wildfowl Centre in Gloucestershire.

There was something romantic about the name anyway, that stuck in the mind. It had a bleak, antarctic feel, bolstered by half-heard stories about its population being the last survivors of a lost race. In fact, we saw no geese on the island, those from the populated corner where we landed having no doubt gone towards the survival of the gun-happy survivors, but there were plenty flipping around islands passed on the way.

From the long wooden jetty, the other passengers headed inland for the little settlement. We three followed the shoreline west. With only a fortnight's Australian experience behind me — and most of this in dry farming country — I found myself in a vegetation bearing little resemblance to that of New Zealand's coastal scrub, that I had recently got to know. My companions were from Western Australia — a land apart — so were little help. Cape Barren and Flinders were the only areas here with much wooded country. The smaller, grassier islands, I found easier to come to terms with.

Even Cape Barren had been repeatedly and ferociously burned over the decades — initially to facilitate hunting the wallabies and pademelons. All the good timber trees had gone, the once fine silver peppermint gums adopting a stunted mallee form if they managed to regenerate from persistent basal ligno-tubers.

Captain Flinders in 1772-1774, described the island as 'high, rocky and barren', but an 1880 visitor wrote of it as 'Thickly timbered with gumtrees and she-okes, while scrub, tall grass trees and tea-trees extend from the water's edge to the interior.'

The bushes climbing the 2,235 ft (687m) high Mount Munroe now, were patchy and my photographs show great smooth faces of bare silver granite. Cape Barren seemed a very appropriate name. Alluvial tin has been found on Mount Munroe, but mining activity in the late nineteenth century was short-lived. Killiecrankie style topaz has been picked up in Kent Bay in the south — the site of the first sealers' settlement.

There are no rabbits on the island, although plenty occur on Clarke Island to its immediate south, the third largest of the group. Nor are there wild pigs or goats and sheep are said not to thrive (although we later took a considerable number of wool bales from Apple Orchard Point). Cattle rearing was possible only by supplementing their copper and cobalt intake, while fruit and vegetables were cultivated on a small scale.

The mainly half-caste (actually quarter-caste or less) Aboriginals were hunter-gatherers still rather than farmers, relying heavily on mutton birds, none of which nested on their own island. They had left few geese, but might have gleaned other waterfowl from the extensive lagoons along the eastern seaboard and supplemented their diet with sea foods, not least of which were the inshore crayfish.

It was very hot and we wandered idly back and forth, turning stones in a lizard hunt and keeping a weather eye open for snakes. Most revealed only hairy crab spiders and their offspring. Our commonest backboned finds were mottled rock lizards *(Egurnia whitii)*, plump little fellows six to seven inches long. We kept two in captivity for a few days on Fisher Island, feeding them on blowfly maggots fattening on some sausages removed from the meat safe. They loved these, but refused adult blowflies and were overcome with panic when offered a large bouncy frog. I never fathomed whether this frog lived in our sealed rain tank (the only fresh water on the island), had swum across the sea or, like the Stephens Island frogs in New Zealand, got by without any free water for spawn and tadpoles.

The seashore provided richer pickings, including some fragile, undamaged 'sea eggs' or urchin tests. We sat in the shade of a great boulder, sucking oranges and drinking cordial, watching the big Pacific gulls. These were using their intelligence, flying up to drop shellfish on a granite surface, to break the shells so that they could reach the contents. Many tries were needed, but they persevered and were rewarded in the end.

Ambling back, we sat among the silver gulls on a beautiful little beach, with dogwood and daisy bushes behind and translucent water separating us from Long Island just offshore, to await Tuck's return.

On another visit in late February, we were able to explore some of the Cape Barren sand dunes. I was with Bill Mollison this time and Tuck was to drop us off at Woody Island, but it proved too rough; he was afraid he wouldn't be able to get in to pick us up, so we continued with him.

Wafting across the sea from the north-west was a cloud of thistledown, spawned on Big Green Island and posing a headache to come for some island grazier. From south to north came a scattered flock of white-rumped tree martins, moving in little parties of eight to ten and diverting slightly to rest on Little Dog Island.

About a week earlier there had been a movement of welcome swallows and these were still coming through in dribs and drabs, two perching on the eastern rocks when we set off from Fisher Island. As we passed the various islets, we counted the grazing geese and learned something of their history from the skipper. Then sea water came slopping inboard at increasing intervals and we went below, along with three other passengers, MacDonald a dentist, Geoff Barrett and the local parson.

"Just as well you wear a waterproof collar!"

The young Church of England minister, stationed in Whitemark, travelled to Cape Barren every fifth weekend to conduct a service and in-between to visit the sick. He was very used to boats, helping to haul the sails as required.

It seemed he had been out from London for only five years and had not chosen to be posted to Flinders Island, surely one of the most unusual parishes in Australia. He found it rather dull after a while and had just applied for and been appointed to a new parish — only to be offered a post as ship's chaplain, which he really coveted, not least because it would enable him to get home occasionally, passage paid, to see his parents. He was now wondering how he could ditch the new parish. Even holy men have their problems.

While still some way short of our destination, we ran aground. Resorting to trial and error, paramecium style, we succeeded in backing off, to the accompaniment of helpful shouting from all and sundry. Soon after, we stuck fast on another sandbank and the crew settled down to await the rising tide. Bill and I cast hungry glances at the nearby coast, and Tuck detailed Barrett off to row us ashore, arranging to pick us up four hours later at the jetty.

We moved up the beach, through silvery spinifex grass and sea rocket, to explore dunes faced by sea fescue *(Festuca littoralis)* and topped by coast daisy bush *(Olearia axillaris)* and dune thistle *(Sonchus megalocarpus)*. An imposing promontory clad in tea-tree and bordered by sea box lured us back. Crested terns nested among pigface and coast spear-grass on Ned's Reef off Ned's Point to the east, beyond Doughboy Island.

The sand we traversed was alive with reptiles — a white-lipped whip snake, lissom and slender, and three kinds of skink. Largest was the three-lined skink *(Leiolopisma trilineata)*, the kind that lived also on Fisher Island. Then there was the metallic skink *(Leiolopisma metallica)*, exhibiting a dull bronze glow, and the oscillating or spotted skink *(Leiolopisma ocellata)*.

Mollison concerned himself with the animals, I with the plants, the specimens I brought back bringing our list for the two visits up to 123. We paused only for a lunch of crayfish and lambs tongues, but time passed all too quickly. Returning west up a low sand cliff we were in pastures burned brown by the sun, the only green the broad-leaved buffalo-grass *(Stenotaphrum)* and Ross's noon flower. There were cattle, horses and sheep here, but none would eat the acrid noon flower, which stained the clothes if sat upon in error.

Pushing through boxthorn and coast beard heath we heard anxious shouting and lingered for but a few words with the group of half-castes gathered outside the school to see 'the scientist with the great ginger beard and the lady doctor from England'. Later we learned that our co-passenger, MacDonald, was inside, extracting a tooth from a recalcitrant nine-year-old who had broken into the school the day before and enjoyed himself breaking gramophone records and other valuables. He had decided to skip the dental inspection, but a sound box on the ears from Mac had changed his mind.

A gentler, summertime scene greeted us at the jetty head. On a small pony cart by the wood pile was a curly headed Aboriginal youth with a load of cooking fuel for transport to Babel Island for the birding season. Brown-skinned youngsters in bathing togs were splashing in the crystal-clear waters, with a European albino, whiter than white in contrast to his swarthy companions.

The cargo ship *"Prion"* was in and groups of men chatted on the wharfside, enjoying back-slapping yarns and ribald jokes. It was an uncomplicated world, drowsing under the caress of the sun.

* * * * *

It was to be two years before I got to Cape Barren Island again and then only briefly. Because there were no mutton bird colonies here, this was not on our work schedule so, although the second largest island of the group, we saw little of it. Alec Ross picked four of us up in Tuck's boat on a scenically blue but distinctly chilly day at the end of February 1960.

Minette Ross and I had just time to walk smartly to the settlement and on to the cemetery. After all the unfavourable tales we had heard, we were quite pleasantly impressed by the standard of housing, at least from the outside, the clothes and smiles of the inhabitants. Only when we asked for photographs were there signs of truculence. John Thomson, visiting a week later, was depressed at what he termed 'the dereliction of this human backwater'. It was not backwater enough for world news to pass it by and we were amused by the comment of a black woman at the jetty.

"Have you heard about the engagement? Princess Margaret to a joker named Jones — photographer or something. We'll really have to be keeping up with the Joneses now, with Mrs Jones one of the six best dressed women in the land."

Things were better in 1960, now that imports of alcohol were limited to 'the few that could be trusted'. Tuck had had problems when the people were allowed free passage on the mail boat and unlimited booze.

"Except for three or four families, the 150 souls on the island live for drink, doing as little as possible. Silas Mansell has a boat, a few farm, the rest live on the dole or pensions. Youths marry young, around eighteen, but their wives soon leave them."

I heard the story of a riot in *"Tassie*'s" hold, when Alec Ross, crewman, vowed he "Wouldn't have gone down there for £50. They'd kill you." Tuck had to.

"They were abusing the women something terrible. I got down just in time to see one knocked out." He managed to quell them by threatening to return them to Cape Barren and send the police out.

"They promptly went to sleep: it's a terrible thing, the drink."

The trouble was the lack of resources and the squandering of such as there were — mostly earnings from the bird harvest. Every so often their plight hit the public press under headings such as "Cape Barren Islanders on the verge of starvation". One such occasion arose from the plea of the bush-nursing sister to the Red Cross for powdered milk for the starving babies in late June 1959, this still needed, even after "*Sheerwater*" arrived with four tons of supplies, including food, to break the famine.

Milk was flown in by George Munroe of the Tasmanian Aero Club. He arrived half an hour behind schedule, because of bad weather.

"I was hit by squalls of up to 70 mph," he reported. The school teacher, possessor of the island's only vehicle at the time, was not at the airstrip to receive it, so the consignment was left, and he made for home with all speed.

Such reports were usually followed by other articles with headings like: "Only one solution to Island's problem". This was the mooted deportation of the population and its assimilation into those of Tasmania or King Island.

As one reporter put it — not very elegantly: "If they could be removed from the island where there is nothing to do but do nothing, they would have a chance of being somebody!"

"Too many of the islanders treat Cape Barren as a haven" said another. "They have boats but they don't fish and most of the money they earn is frittered away."

The problem of under-nourishment had been partially addressed by the government between 1948 and 1955 by the provision of school meals.

"I would close the school and the hospital" said the minister concerned. "To force from the island those willing to work."

But isolation, colour prejudice and lack of education had so far mitigated against their integration into other communities.

In the event, the school was re-equipped and granted a second teacher and, by the mid-eighties, the island had a solar-powered telephone service and a twice weekly mail plane, to replace the indomitable but now deceased Tuck Robinson. With only a short week in the Furneaux Group in 1995, I was unable to catch up with the current situation, but these problems tend not to go away entirely

48 Echidna *Tachyglossus setosus*

49 White *Kunzea ambigua*

50 Grey-backed Silver-eyes *Zosterops lateralis* and Drooping She-oke *Allocasuarina verticillata*

2. VANSITTART AND PUNCHEON ISLANDS

My solitary breakfast of egg, tomato and fried bread was rudely interrupted on 10th February 1958 by a throaty yell. A mast was visible above the daisy bushes and I hurried out to see Bill Barrett paddling the dinghy in from "*Tassie*".

"Vansittart and Puncheon Islands. Thought you might like to come."

They gave me a quarter of an hour to pack lunch and make ready.

The weather was overcast, the clouds soon lifting, so that the sun blazed down on us all day. Bill was dropped off on Little Dog Island, where he had some guttering to fix and carpentering to finish in readiness for the birding. Tuck, Alec Ross and I swept east along the south coast of Big Dog Island, then cut across to Ross's property of Vansittart, a big island covering 1,500 acres (600 hectares). It is the largest island in Franklin Sound and near the eastern entrance. The northernmost part of Cape Barren Island, Puncheon Point, reaches out close to its southern shore: to the north is the notorious Potboil.

The "Vansittart" for which it is named, was a small government cutter which helped with Strzelecki's original exploration, but it is known to some as Guncarriage Island, after its high point of Guncarriage Hill. Alec Ross grazed his flocks here, but had had to battle with coarse vegetation to get the island back in shape after earlier grazing lapsed.

Because of its fertility and good fresh water, it was colonised quite early in the history of the group, sealers, with their Aboriginal wives, supplementing their living here with vegetable gardens. From 1831 the island supported eight adults, seven children and 600 goats and exported mutton birds and vegetables, including potatoes, to Launceston.

Our companion's ancestor, Alexander Ross, had emigrated from Scotland to salvage the cargo of the 1691 ton "*Cambridgeshire*", wrecked on Preservation Island in 1875. The crew escaped with their lives and much of the valuable cargo was rescued, but not by Ross, most falling into the hands of the Cape Barren islanders. (The sea passage from Britain left plenty of time for this). It is on record that the locals indulged in wild parties by the light of bonfires of sperm wax candles, ill-treating valuable Broadwood and Lipps pianos with sticks, under the influence of the overproof spirit drawn from the ship's kegs. Who wore the ball gown intended for the wife of the then governor of New South Wales is not recorded — nor what happened to the gold that constituted a goodly part of the ship's value.

With or without any spoils from the wreck, Alexander Ross married and settled on Vansittart, running sheep and cattle and working the farm with bullocks. He opened a store and post office for the seafaring community, providing hospitality for any marooned by bad weather. His more lasting legacies to the island are the long lines of stone walling.

His family later tried their luck with the wreck of the sailing ship, *"Farsund"*, grounded on the Vansittart Shoals in 1912 and never refloated. They bought and stripped her of anything of value, but they, too, lost money on the deal, the vessel having been vandalised. Even sails, cordage and tow ropes had been wilfully slashed and the 'cargo' was no more than a ballast of sand. She was insured for considerably more than she had cost new and the crew swore they would never again sail with the captain, so she may well have been put ashore on purpose for the insurance money.

To get rid of the coarse herbage which had taken over the farmlands by the time our current member of the Ross family took over, Bennet's wallabies were run on it. These thrived, breeding so fast that they had to be shot out before Alec could follow up with his cattle, sheep and horses. He had been burning off the tussock and sowing foreign pasture plants.

"Almost every kind of grass I could lay hands on, and Dutch and clustered clover and sheep trefoil." (This last is the yellow-flowered *Trifolium dubium*.)

"Wonderful good grazing in the spring, but no good now in the summer. 'Western wolf' was all over the island once." (I failed to run this remarkable name to earth, although all the graziers used it, and produced widely varying descriptions. Frank Henwood thought it most likely referred to Italian ryegrass, a lush hay species.)

These were habituees of softer climes, not taking kindly to the drying summer suns of the Sound. Concentration of soil salt may have had a lot to do with their seasonal demise, coupled with over-grazing, because most of the erstwhile grassland was now converted to a ground-level carpet of the rosette-leaved buck's horn plantain *(Plantago coronopus)*.

In Britain this species is essentially coastal and extremely resistant to heavy grazing, leaves which rise to twenty-five cm in optimum conditions abandoned in favour of ones cleaving to the ground, where they suffer trampling with impunity and cannot be levered up by grazers, beaked or toothed.

Dead stalks of Vulpia, Danthonia and brome grasses told of a greener spring. Wisps of Cynodon and buffalo grass that were still green had attracted hundreds of Cape Barren geese, which fed across the plantain carpet, leaving it soiled and flattened but intact.

The geese were able to satisfy their two principal urges here — the privacy of the small outlying islands and the lushness of the sown grass swards which they normally had to risk going to Flinders Island to find. No wonder Vansittart was popular with them. Buck's horn plantain suffers similar goose grazing pressure on some of its native Scottish and Irish islands where arctic geese over-winter, and is as tolerant of generous helpings of goose dung as it is of blown sea salt.

Another sign of grazing pressure on Vansittart was the almost complete absence of succulents, which, unless acrid, like the large noon-flower, are likely to be more palatable than their fibrous neighbours. Chief associate of the maritime plantain was the spiky blue or white sea holly or prickfoot *(Eryngium vesiculosum)*. Others surviving by their modest growth: were alien storksbill and sheep's sorrel and native kidneyweed.

The geese seemed to prefer these plantain swards to the greener grass of the slightly brackish water meadow between valley and lagoon, where the salt-tolerant *Distichlis distichophylla* dominated. There was less plantain here and others were tiny — twin-flower knawel *(Scleranthus biflorus)*, yellow wood-sorrel and dwarf sea-celery — or coarse, like the *Brachycome diversifolia* daisies.

The thousands of mutton birds formerly present were here no more. Alec thought they had been over-harvested, but they were finally exterminated by wild pigs rooting out their burrows and eating the eggs and chicks. An attempt was made to reinstate them, artificial burrows being dug and stocked with twenty brooding adults and their eggs. These were soon deserted, the adults presumably homing back to their old site after their first fishing expedition, to wonder where their egg had gone! Imprinting with a new home territory is not so easily achieved.

In 1870, before Alexander Ross arrived, Brownrigg reported that the waters of the large lagoon at the base of Guncarriage Hill had entirely drained away. This was probably seasonal, as it was still recognisable as a lagoon ninety years later, a somewhat salty one.

Essentially grassy, it was surrounded by tall sea rush or a low turf of moisture-loving sedges and spike rush *(Eleocharis)*, with the two mauve 'monkey flowers' *(Mimulus repens* and *Mazus pumilio)*, also *Wilsonia rotundifolia* with close-set leaves.

There were more water-lovers in the ditch draining the lagoon into North Bay. Among the knob sedge *(Carex inversa)* was crantzia *(Lilaeopsis australica)*, a small mud-dwelling member of the carrot family, and three kinds of water buttons, the yellow-flowered, white-flowered and creeping. Also of interest on this north side were lobelia, a spurrey *(Spergularia media)* and an Austral bluebell *(Wahlenbergia gracilis)*.

Of the eighty-one species recorded on this hurried visit, thirty-eight per cent were alien introductions. The luscious globe fruits of one of these, the South African boxthorn, had attracted a chirruping flock of white-fronted chats. A skylark leapt from almost underfoot as I hastened back to the dinghy.

* * * * *

My next landing was on Puncheon or Puncheonhead Island a little to the south-west. Alec warned me repeatedly about snakes. "Tigers! Not just ordinary tigers but nasty spiteful tigers. They swim over from Cape Barren there."

Nothing if not a Job's comforter, but I took note — and care — and flushed only lizards and brown quail from among the tussocks.

The shallows extended far from the shore and *"Tassie"* lay well out. I was put onto a reef, from where I had to paddle in over excruciatingly knobbly black rocks and sandy gullies bristling with sharp-edged shells.

This island, too, was grazed — with forty sheep — this number regarded as its maximum carrying capacity. The animals scarcely touched the dominant silver tussock once they had nibbled off the first young green of spring.

"And that doesn't fatten them. They'd starve rather than eat it when it's old."

They ate it, nevertheless, on some of the islands I visited, notably Mount Chappell. Cattle and goats are less fussy.

Once again, there were scarcely any palatable succulents left and thirty-seven per cent of the forty-nine species seen were foreign weeds. The usual mounds of bower spinach were replaced by low rounded humps of sticky boronia *(Boronia anemonifolia)*: on Vansittart their place had been taken by button bush. Instead of the usual samphire and seablite around the periphery, the shallow mud deposits over the pebbles bore mats of creeping brookweed. Norfolk Island pine, Macrocarpa and New Zealand mirror bushes had been planted near the house for shelter.

A sailing boat hove to alongside *"Tassie"* as I browsed among the plants. It was manned by the Aboriginals who had the grazing on the island and, very naturally, wanted to know what I was at. I came upon them later examining the sheep, to supplement whatever explanation they had been given. They had intended staying the night, but the weather was cracking up and they left soon after us.

Going was easy in the mutton bird rookery on the western side, as it was threaded by stock tracks. The tussocks had not been burned for many years to stimulate new growth, so were getting a bit threadbare. Nor had birds been harvested in recent years, but 6,000 to 7,000 were taken annually not so long before. Bidgee-widgee was rife — a menace to both birds and sheep.

Tuck was punting the dinghy in for me all too soon and I splashed out to him through thousands of bright yellow, blunt-nosed toad fish lying in the shallows. They were oddly lethargic, trusting, perhaps, in their pattern of spots for camouflage, and shooting off only when brushed against.

"No good for anything," said Tuck. "Not even bait."

Maybe those toad fish knew nobody was after them. I never tired of these sand and rock shores, with their wealth of different starfish, sea urchins and crabs, including the fascinatingly swift-footed rock crabs *(Leptograpsus variegatus)*.

* * * * *

My skipper, like the dark-skinned shepherds, was getting worried about the weather and he allowed me only a quarter of an hour in the shaggery of Puncheonhead Reef a few 100 metres off, and that grudgingly.

Small and low-lying, the plants were subjected to plenty of salt spray as well as guano from both cormorants and gulls, but not to grazing. They were quite different from those of the neighbouring sheep-dominated island. Succulents were in the ascendency and aliens were down to eight per cent.

There was a neat zonation of plants up each side of the central gully which almost divided the reef in half. Nearest to the infiltrating sea water was herbaceous glasswort, then shrubby glasswort, passing into seablite, then pigface and finally stipa tussock. Pigface and spinach ran right through the silver tussock above and sea celery was much chunkier than the feathery-leaved relicts surviving in crevices on Puncheon Island.

A depauperate, red-leaved type of the mesembryanthemum dominated the area occupied by the black-faced cormorants. To deal with the concentration of minerals in the soil, the leaves of this were swollen with so much internal moisture that they were almost as broad as long. In 1995 I came across the name of jelly-bean plant for this form. It could scarcely have been more apt.

The nest of a pair of Pacific gulls was surrounded by several hundred crab claws — the only part of the horny shell too hard to be crushed and recycled as a crop pellet. As with other gulls, each pair seemed to have its favourite food, so that meal leftovers were surprisingly uniform for such omnivorous birds. 'Jelly beans', spinach and sow thistle grew in actual contact with the nest.

Tuck had intended to wait for me in the dinghy, but decided he had better go back and help Alec with *"Tassie"*.

"It's coming up westerly. He's going to get blown ashore."

They cruised back and forth as I scuttled round, writing, photographing and memorising in the usual race against time. In twenty minutes he was back, shouting as lustily as his elderly lungs allowed. I came at the double, pushed off and hopped in as he bawled at Alec to move in a bit. Alec wasn't budging. He disliked rocks.

"For God's sake don't go the other way." We tumbled in over the stern.

"Quick now: there's dirty weather. We shan't get home."

"Tassie" was well under way by the time he had made the dinghy fast. There are plenty of occasions in these waters when the adrenalin flow is boosted, even for the most seasoned of habituées. Seldom a dull moment!

I sat on deck for a while, swathed in oilskins, but went below when Tuck scrambled to the bow to jam the hatch tight where water was pouring intermittently into the hold. He passed me a kerosene tin for a seat and settled himself on a dry patch of floor to starboard.

Long before reaching Little Dog Island, we spotted a narrow plume of smoke, several hundred yards long, blowing on the wind from a tiny fire at beach level, signifying where Bill Barrett awaited pick up. It was a full quarter of an hour before we saw the man himself. I realised why I was so often told about signal fires. Such smoke plumes were always investigated by passing boats as Tuck was renowned for forgetting his calls on return voyages. I resolved to carry matches in future.

Several hours later, back on Fisher Island, I was washing in the altogether, silhouetted between the candles and the window, when I saw a pair of trousers, highlighted by a torch, advancing from an unaccustomed direction. I did a quick cover-up, my visitor the more embarrassed, responding to my greeting with "Good night", as though about to leave.

It was young Holloway, come to say they'd be sailing for Cat Island at 8 or 9 next morning (with the usual Lady Barron sense of time), and could take me. I had been ready and waiting with camping gear time after time for a promised boat which never came. Holloway's didn't.

I rose at 6. a.m., dealt with rubbish, Sanilav contents, washed, scrubbed, packed, sorted, brought the oars up out of the rain and was still waiting at 10 o'clock. Wind had freshened and gone to the east, the worst possible direction for Cat Island, on the wrong side of the Potboil. I was not surprised when two boats, one of them Holloway's, veered off into the western passage. There was no way he could let me know, however willing. How much simpler life is now with radio telephones and the like!

Gathering an armful of logs from the wet woodpile, I lit a roaring fire, greatly helped by the kerosene can, and settled down to label seven boxes of coloured slides, to remind me of sunnier days on islands off New Zealand.

51 Pink Bindweed *Convolvulus erubescens*

52 Four Grasses, *Deyeuxia quadriseta*, *Paspalum dilatatum*, *Echinopogon ovatus* and *Lolium multiflorum*

53 White-fronted Chat *Ephthianura albifrons* and
'Couch' Grass *Cynodon dactylon*

3. TIN KETTLE AND WOODY ISLANDS

I was landed on Tin Kettle Island in the perfect calm of a sunny morning, with the usual warnings from the doleful, direful Alec Ross, JP. It started with the usual "You be careful now" and ended with "Oh my word!" The middle part today was not about spiteful snakes or slippery rocks but: "You mind those cattle. Wild as hell. Would charge you as soon as look at you."

In fact they wandered round quite placidly, eyeing me with the mildest of curiosity.

Most of the island shores were sandy and the west side was one big sand dune system, but with no bird burrows. Tuck Robinson had been the grazier on Tin Kettle Island for sixteen years and he confirmed that there had never been any shearwaters or petrels here, just a few penguin burrows in the North-west.

On the commercial bird islands, where the Poa was all-embracing, it formed tall, separated tumps, earning itself the name of silver tussock grass. Here the combination of burning and chomping by cattle resulted in a more muted form, as on parts of Cape Barren Island, suggesting that the digging of burrows between the plants had a lot to do with the tuftiness.

Where tussocks persisted, twenty-three Cape Barren geese were grazing the short green turf between, nipping the sweet young shoots from around the thistles and *Lepidosperma gladiatum*, the commonest of the coarse sedges. Brown quail were about but snakes were said to be scarce and I saw none.

John Nield, the current grazier, claimed there to be Silurian slates here, as well as the headlands of granite. He maintained that the sanding was due to blowing from the sand flats between Tin Kettle and Woody Islands. Subsequent erosion, initiated by the cattle, was causing this to blow away again to expose good ground underneath.

In his earlier days, he had planted marram grass to stabilise the loose sand backing the north beach, but it was too low and washed out. He planted again higher up, Kikuyu grass *(Pennisetum clandestinum)* this time. Now he had done a U-turn, realising that it was better to let the sand go, as the soil underneath was of so much higher quality. I was reminded of the grazier on Cape Schanck in Victoria, who actually 'cultivated' and harrowed his dunes to facilitate the loss of sand, so that he could farm the land that it had buried.

Some of Tin Kettle's blow-outs on the west were thirty metres across, terminating inland in sand cliffs up to four metres high. The dune fescue, although lacking the extensive underground stems of some of the other sand-binders, had fibrous roots extending for four to five metres, these exposed as a fine mesh when the sand was ripped from under them. The displaced sand might be waylaid by other clumps of the same, building up into mounds from which only the tips of the flower spikes protruded. A fine collection of limey concretions of past dune vegetation had been revealed on bare patches. If sand went to leave mainly granite, the most likely plant was button-bush.

Nield ran both cattle and sheep on the island, the former doing a good job on the new sprouts of tussock grass after the biennial burn. Rye-grass and three kinds of clover had been sown in parts and regenerated after fire along with the unwanted but all too prevalent Yorkshire fog grass. Buffalo grass had been sown round the huts because it remained green all summer and minimised the fire risk.

"It's hard and stock don't like it that much, but they'll eat it when hard pressed."

Grazing had effectively eliminated all succulent plants except Ross's noon flower, apart from a few stragglers tucked away in crevices — enough to repopulate if grazing pressure alleviated. Thirty-eight per cent of the ninety-three species listed were aliens, some planted but most a spontaneous influx of weeds.

More worthy elements of the flora included common onion orchid (*Microtis unifolia*), small-leaved clematis and the fine-leaved *Apium filiforme* as well as the commoner sea celery. Shrubs such as bottle-brush, 'dogwood' and coast and twiggy daisy bushes, survived rather better than on most of the bird islands.

Two cudweeds, *Gnaphalium candidissimum* and *Gnaphalium luteo-album*, grew in a damp dune slack grazed by sheep. A dune seepage in the south was richer, because cattle coming to drink had added a goodly quota of dung to the sand. Growths included *Pratia platycalyx, Lilaeopsis, Lobelia* and water buttons.

By the time my boat was due, quite a big sea was running from the west and I had to follow the dinghy round to the other side before it could be beached. At the oars was a smiling young 'Abo' from Cape Barren. It was common practice for one of the younger passengers to do the pick-ups to save the muscles of the aging captain and crewman. Everyone handles boats with expertise in communities such as this.

Tuck changed tack completely on the subject of the bird harvest as we sped back to Fisher Island with the swell behind. Yesterday he had been boasting how thoroughly he collected his birds, putting pegs in to divide the ground into squares and feeling in every burrow. Today, having twigged that I disapproved of wholesale slaughter, it was: "Of course, we don't take them all. We stop at 12,000."

He suggested that the only way to prevent over-harvesting would be to limit the catch to a proportion of previous ones, offenders to be 'found' £100. Bully for them: or could he have meant 'fined'?

The season was well advanced when next I went to Tin Kettle Island on 6th April. Tuck was ferrying a party of locals out to his birding hut on Great Dog Island for a picnic. They were dropped off first, a pretty twelve-year-old half-caste girl running back to the boat with a swag of birds for Tuck and his friends, plucked, scalded and de-legged, but with wings and head intact.

Four more passengers were put off on Little Dog Island where Tuck's son had his birding hut. John Nield and I went on to Tin Kettle, he armed with a spade to clear the blocked seepage and allow more water into the livestock's water hole.

He took his black cattle dog with him, mindful of the time when he had been marooned on the island for three days and forced to kill and eat one of his own sheep. Without the dog he would have been hard put to it to catch this.

"Good with both cattle and sheep," patting the animal's head. "And a good retriever. He'll even dive to collect Cape Barren geese if I shoot them over the sea."

His master pitched him overboard as we neared the land, remarking that he hadn't had a bath lately, and the dog paddled ashore with anxious glances over his shoulder to see that his master was following.

We had dead geese on board on our return voyage and the dog sniffed them with interest, then snuggled up beside them — for warmth or companionship. These were not Nield's birds. We had three 'hunters' on board. They shot not only for the pot, but blazed away at cormorants and gulls as well as edible targets, egged on by the women during the early part of the trip and leaving several bloody corpses on the hitherto unsullied bosom of the deep.

Black-faced shags fell most frequently to the gun-happy islanders. It is said they are attracted by gun fire. One circled the boat nine times, through a barrage from three shotguns. There must have been some near misses, but he just shook his feet, flipped his tail and pressed on. Inevitably he fell at last, after costing his killers a goodly sum in cartridges.

* * * * *

They were spending the day on Big Woody Island, as I was, but I let them get well clear before I bent to my botanising. Woody (or Anderson Island) lay due west of Tin Kettle, and was about the same size. As its better-used name implied, it had once been covered with trees.

All through the day, startled geese were flying out to sea, but none had the sense to stay away for long. I realised why as I came upon more and more nests, some solitary, some in groups, most surrounded by thistles and nettles, including the scrub and small nettles *(Urtica incisa* and *U. Urens)*. They had home ties to bring them back.

The largest number together was twenty-one, but there were obviously many more. When I spotted birds skulking among the rushes, I refrained from putting them up. Most escaped the guns. The total 'bag' for the day was only four, little more than one apiece.

Mutton birds had formerly nested here, despite the prevalence of scrub, but had been rooted out by feral pigs, as on Big Green and Hummock Islands. A hundred pigs had been run on Big Woody Island for a few years, according to local report. All three of these islands were now grazed by cattle and sheep.

Spur-wing plovers complained throatily from the shoreline, their cries mingling with the equally raucous ones of crested terns and the so-called 'black jays' or currawongs. More pleasing were the trillings of several skylarks and the 'peeping' of north-bound wood swallows. Despite the considerable amount of residual scrub, I saw few of the bush birds that were still relatively common on Great Dog Island.

Canon Brownrigg, writing "*The Cruise of the 'Freak'*" in 1870, stated that Woody Island, formerly covered by dense scrub, had been completely denuded by fire. Now, ninety years later, an even-aged stand of swamp paperbarks had regenerated on the eastern slopes and was nibbled back only around the edges. Most of the rest was now open, apart from a few sweet bursaria bushes and white correa. The sheep and cattle introduced after the pigs, were blamed for the destruction of the 'barilla' and 'box', these the local names for coast saltbush (*Atriplex cinerea*) and seaberry saltbush (*Rhagodia baccata*).

Brownrigg comments that, although mutton birds occurred on the wooded islands, they were seldom found in any but the cleared spots. Local graziers spoke very highly of the present quality of the herbage — in spite of the Cape Barren geese, which others maintained fouled the pastures. In fact goose dung and sheep dung were concentrated together on the shorter, denser swards so sheep, at least, were not put off.

"We must burn, or the tussock gets out of hand. Cattle fatten well on the young growth: even sheep." (Not everybody's opinion.)

There had been no sowing of ryegrass, but native grasses and clovers came in after fire and I saw veritable swards of clover seedlings on my April visit. The coastal belt of succulents had been grazed out, climbing lignum replacing the bower spinach that so often scrambles up into the shrubs where it is not eaten back. Only where goose fouling was sufficient to deter grazing, did I find any spinach.

Bracken grew around the two buildings on the south beach and thirty-seven per cent of the eighty-four species seen were foreigners, although the most noxious, as often, was the native prickly bidgee-widgee. Dunes were not nearly so prevalent as on Tin Kettle Island and most were stabilised with knobby club-rush (*Scirpus nodosus*) or dune fescue.

A board-lined pool, only two metres across, had been constructed in a natural seepage for the cattle to drink. Lesser duckweed floated on its surface and the grassy sward round about carried the usual willowherb, lobelia, water buttons and celery, these surrounded by pale rush (*Juncus pallidus*).

Over seventy per cent of the plants able to tolerate the worst of the goose-fouling were aliens. Five of the most abundant are characteristic of heavily grazed sites in Britain, so sheep may have played a part in stimulating them here. A stranger among the pommie invaders was South African Capeweed (*Arctotheca calendula*). Lying between latitude forty and forty-one degrees

South, Franklin Sound showed a preponderance of North European weeds over those from Mediterranean climes that was not entirely due to the predominantly Anglo-Saxon settlement. The frigidity of British latitudes is mitigated by the warm waters of the Gulf Stream — an amelioration not felt here in the South — although rumour had it in 1996 that the North Atlantic current was cooling!

* * * * *

North of Big Woody Island lay Little Woody Island, covering forty acres, and between the two was Mid Woody Island, of a mere two acres. I visited these eight months later, in mid-December. Little Woody was a commercially useful island, but Mid Woody retained more natural features.

This smallest islet sloped gently up to the granite of the south-east — a mixture of grass and succulents, as on other ungrazed sites, but with the addition of white Correa and Austral storksbill *(Pelargonium australe)*. The first formed a low scrub, the second huddled among big boulders. Leek lilies, both large and small, sprawled across rock outcrops and a large area had been invaded by bower spinach. Eighty-three per cent of the thirty plants listed were natives.

Numerous white-faced storm petrel burrows penetrated among the grass tussocks. These small birds add little guano to the soil and do not stimulate the spinach as mutton birds do. On Apple Orchard Reef, where they burrowed among that for preference, the grassy areas had been taken over by Pacific gulls.

There were no mutton birds on Mid Woody Island, but blue penguin burrows were frequent, either in dense Correa thickets or insinuated under boulders. At this stage of the year breeding was well advanced. Seven burrows with well-worn tracks leading to them were found to contain well-grown chicks.

No goose nests were spotted, but it looked as though the island was used as a roost by moulting birds, most of the open areas being fouled and trampled and strewn with discarded feathers.

Invertebrate life breeding in the resulting bird slum, had attracted a little flock of fifteen starlings, which may have been nesting in the rock crevices which they frequented with easy familiarity. Fifteen sooty oystercatchers shared the coast with three pieds and some Caspian terns.

Little Woody was ostensibly a stock island, but had been ungrazed for many years until two weeks before my visit, when Tuck had put thirty sheep on. It was unburned apart from traces of a small recent fire. Sixty-six plants were listed, thirty-six per cent of these 'followers of man'.

Cape Barren geese used the island almost as much as they did the reef, enjoying not only the many introduced grasses and five different clovers of the paddocks, but ripping sea celery from its tenuous hold among the rocks, while studiously avoiding the acrid noon-flower alongside. It seemed they were after the nutty fruitlets, as most of the foliage was discarded and wilting.

Other favourites were the three-sided fruitlets of the dock *(Rumex brownii)* and, fortuitously, the seeding heads of Yorkshire fog grass, whose hirsute leaves were spurned. Leek lilies were particularly tolerant of goose pressure, as they were of gannet pressure on Cat Island. More unexpected was the Austral hollyhock *(Lavatera plebeja)*.

The several goose nests found were made of knobbed sedge covered with a generous layer of white down. Some of the glossy eggshells remained on the feather mattress where the chicks had hatched — up to half a dozen per nest. They were relatively unsullied, considering that the nesting season is usually June to September, much earlier in spring. Perhaps these nests belonged to late breeders. The goslings, being nidifugous, would have left home very soon after hatching.

Penguin burrows were thickest among the spinach nurtured by the run-off from the goose-fouled slope above, but the island hosted neither shearwaters nor petrels. Several skylarks suspended in the blue vault, were carolling away irrepressibly. The inevitable white-fronted chats foraged at ground level, seemingly on the yellow seed heads of the suffocated clover *(Trifolium suffocatum)*, which were more conspicuous at this end of summer than the plants themselves. The starling flock here was slightly larger and two pairs of sooty oystercatchers were still nesting. Small skinks scuttled everywhere — more numerous in December than in February.

Soil was black and peaty and strewn with granite chippings, with fewer of the more prevalent sands. While probably more retentive of moisture, the few shallow pans had dried out, to be colonised by a red-leaved form of glaucous goosefoot among water buttons and kidney-weed.

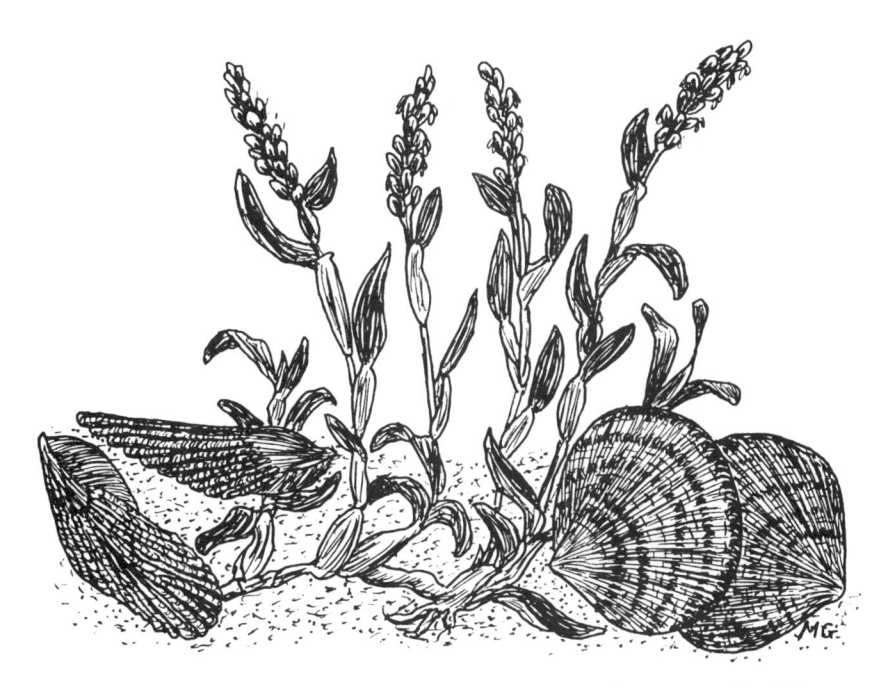

54 Rough-beaked Mussels *Hormomya erosa*, Flame Dog Cockles *Glycymerus flammeus* and Buffalo Grass *Stenotaphrum secundatum*

55 Yorkshire Fog *Holcus lanatus*, Great Brome *Bromus diandrus* and Marram Grass *Ammophila arenaria*

56 Yellow Wood-sorrel *Oxalis corniculata* and Australian Salt Grass *Distichlis distichophylla*

Chapter Seven

FISHER ISLAND: HOME FROM HOME

1. SHEARWATERS, OYSTERCATCHERS AND HERON

Fisher Island, latitude 40° 10' South and longitude 148° 16' East, occupies just over two acres at high water and nearly three at low water. Like most of the smaller islands in Franklin Sound, it is modestly rounded, nowhere more than six metres high and with neither tall cliffs nor spreading sands.

Smooth granite rises gently from the tideline and dips as gently beneath it, reaching to no great depth towards Lady Barron. Indeed, so many reefs and shoals became exposed on low spring tides, that we felt we might almost have waded across for the Saturday shopping. The island seemed little more than an excrescence on the sub-littoral peneplain stretching across Adelaide Bay.

It was this very shallowness that caused us to be cut off on occasion. The depth was insufficient to accommodate the swells that came rolling in from the west, unannounced, subjecting our marine environment to rapid changes of mood. Wave-break started far from the shore as the waters over-rode themselves and hidden snags reached up to tweak at boats sliding into the troughs.

The island had been named in 1941 by the Lands Department in honour of Police Sergeant George Fisher who, from 1926 to 1934, had been the first to mark its mutton birds and monitor their comings and goings. Lying conveniently between the commercially harvested islands and the port where the spoils were landed — and supplies could be obtained — and with its own manageable population of birds, Fisher Island was the obvious place to base the subsequent long-term study of their biology.

This was launched in 1947, jointly by the Commonwealth Scientific and Industrial Research Organisation (CSIRO) and the Tasmanian Fauna Board. Fisher Island had already been declared a fauna sanctuary in 1928. Before this it was rather too handy for raids on the eggs and fledgelings and the population suffered accordingly. There was a time, too, when goats were pastured there. "Yolla", the researchers' living quarters, was built in 1948 and a back room added in 1956.

In such a small area it was possible to know the position of every mutton bird burrow and keep tabs on their occupants. To this end Dr Dominic Serventy, research chief, invited naturalists to man the island for as much of the five month breeding season, from November to April, as practicable. They usually came in pairs, often from Western Australia, which was Dom's home base and far enough away to make this an enticing holiday destination. There was usually no shortage of willing recruits.

On clear dark nights, when the clamour of myriad shearwaters came wafting across from Little Green Island, the bird monitors were catching thirty to forty birds per session. Eric Lindgren erected a coffin hide over a burrow from which a replaceable 'lid' of turf could be removed from above the nest chamber. On alternate nights, when he was not 'on patrol', he would lie in this with camera and flash gun trained on the sitting bird. With no ingress of light, the bird seemed more comfortable than Eric with this arrangement. He lay head downward, the surrounding tussocks preventing him from choosing a more comfortable angle for his coffin.

Inevitably some periods were not manned. If I was in residence I attempted some sort of coverage but I was not normally involved in this side of the study. With so static a population of birds, the data from before and after the lull could be linked with small margin of error in the continuity of activity.

A pair of observers would be out for two hours after dusk when the birds were making landfall and for two hours before dawn when they took off to sea again. Birds plumping to earth or emerging from holes were picked up and their ring numbers noted. This gave data on the frequency of visits and whether by cock or hen, and pinpointed changes in the sequence as incubation progressed through the chick-feeding stage to the starvation period before the youngster fledged.

On the bright moonlight nights experienced during my first week on the island, few shearwaters came in, probably for fear of the predatory Pacific gulls, which slept lightly, if at all, when visibility remained good. Rafts of birds assembled some distance offshore well before dusk, sometimes in spectacular numbers, but most of these were bound for Little Green Island.

It was not dark until 8.30 p.m. but birds started moving in quietly from 8.0 p.m. onwards, flying low over the sea to circle the island two or three times before plopping down and scurrying into their burrows in haste, as if they knew ornithologists were lying in wait. Some were better at orienteering than others, slipping home with little more than a rustling of the tinder-dry grass or the occasional exchange of crooning calls with their partner within.

Parent birds knew the location of their nest without having to see it and would scratch around on top of a sleeping bag trying to get through if we lay across a burrow entrance when sleeping out on other islands. Fortunately they were persistent enough to wake the sleeper so that they could be allowed in. The clamour coming across the water from Little Green Island was all-embracing on still nights, like the banshee wailing of a wandering army of disembodied spirits. Not only were there vastly more birds there but the lack of monitoring removed any need for secrecy.

Before 4.0 and 4.30 a.m., just before dawn, from the third week of January onwards, the noise increased on Fisher Island and changed in tone. A squeaky creaking, like a rusty wire clothesline aggravated by the wind, mixed with the more usual crooning: the chicks' farewell, perhaps, to the departing parents.

White-faced storm petrels sped low across the island in the dark, en route for Spences Reef and other islets where they nested in thousands.

Daytime coverage of the shearwaters consisted mainly of reaching into burrows, all of which were numbered, to record when the single white egg metamorphosed into a downy chick. In 1958 the first recorded hatching was on January 10th. Because of the close synchronisation of laying time, this activity was crammed into a relatively short period. Teams present before egg laying could check when the pairs came ashore to spring-clean the old nests and when they finally returned to lay after a prolonged spell of building up their resources at sea.

The Fisher Island birds became so habituated to frequent handling that they took little notice, although there was a tendency for their burrows to be longer, up to two metres instead of the more usual one that made reaching in by the harvesters such a practical proposition on the bigger islands.

Three flying suits were provided for warmth during night patrols and one of these I appropriated to augment my two thin blankets, my sleeping bag (of warm mutton bird down) being still in transit from New Zealand. The two double-decker bunks were in occupation on my arrival and I had borrowed a folding, iron-framed stretcher bed from Trooper Bailey, this NOT the last word in comfort.

The small toilet block alongside "Yolla" was furnished with a shower consisting of an elevated kerosene tin which one filled with water before entry. On pulling a WC type 'chain' water was released through a nozzle at the base — all at once. If not well soaped before, it was too late after, unless one could persuade a mate to bring some rinsing water. As this came from the precious roof supply, such extravagances were not encouraged. With the sea so close, we had plenty of opportunity to rinse off, if not to soap down.

One sleeping bag and two bedspreads were out of circulation, being draped over a camera tripod as a hide for watching the resident sooty oystercatchers. During my early days on the island these birds would shriek blue murder, as only oystercatchers can, every time someone approached the nest, but they soon got used to us. On an island that small it was needs must. Soon they would feed nonchalantly almost to our feet if we remained still.

I particularly liked the way they cocked one leg over their back between the wings to scratch the neck and head, and I forthwith christened them Scratchy and Sooty. It was easy to tell them apart as the bill of one was orange and the other pink.

Favourite foods were the dark banded periwinkles or australwinks *(Melarapha unifasciata)*, thousands of which crowded at the top of the tide. Just any winkle wouldn't do. Once a prey animal had been selected the bird would trot long distances, holding it in the tip of the long beak rather than drop it in favour of another. The effort involved was not in locating the food, but in dealing with it.

The mollusc was placed on a rock with the horny lid or operculum uppermost and as many as a dozen chisel-like blows delivered to shatter the shell. The contents were winkled out delicately in several pieces, only a fraction of the potential gape coming into play during the tweaking process. Beak length had been evolved for deep probing — for cockles and other buried treasure — rather than for dealing with big mouthfuls.

Sometimes the oystercatchers foraged on the island's only beach, hauling tiny unidentifiable morsels from the sand. The woodpile provided a ready-made hide for observing these activities. Tiring of this, one might move inshore to probe for invertebrates among the silver tussock grass, or fly off to Little Green Island for a change of scene. Very occasionally, when all was calm, I had the unusual experience of seeing them swim, despite the lack of webbing on feet fashioned for wading.

The two blotchy brown eggs, more finely tapered than gulls' eggs, were not attended constantly but were never allowed to cool. They had been there at least since the New Year and the first egg chipped on January 24th. My diary shorthand of "Egg chip Friday" set me wondering in later weeks as to why I should be on about egg and chips when Friday was fish day!

A small black bill appeared through the break on the morning of the 25th, accompanied by a flow of infantile cheeping, although the inmate was lying upside down in its prison. I turned it up the right way and, at 6.30 a.m. on Sunday a damp chick was lying beside its unhatched sibling. It was dry and fluffy by 10 o'clock, apart from a bare, unfeathered strip along the backbone.

The second egg had chipped by then and next morning number one had left the nest and number two was in the powder-puff stage. Eggshells had been removed from the nest — a seemingly unnecessary precaution as this was soon abandoned, the second chick spending even less time there than the first.

During the ensuing days the family stuck close together, the adults piping intruders away and the chicks 'freezing' on command, relying on their excellent camouflage. On Monday night they were brooded among the samphire but they might settle down anywhere. The parent, having none of their offspring's cryptic colouration, would rise, shouting, at any disturbance, the chicks tumbling out from underneath and scuttling for cover, while the second parent ran back and forth as a further distraction.

The chicks allowed themselves to be picked up without batting an eyelid, quite free from fear, the parents meanwhile standing quietly nearby, but running away when the chick was put down, either to lure the youngster from me or me from the youngster.

The resident red-capped dotterels never got as blasé about disturbance as the sooties. Twinkletoes and Tinkabel (or Dot and Little Dot), the two chicks, were a delight to watch when active, their feet twinkling over the granite, but were as quick to 'freeze' on command as the bigger youngsters. When thus immobilised, they made fine photographic subjects: when picked up they nestled snugly into the warmth of a cupped palm, gazing pertly at their admirers with no manifestation of alarm in the beady black eyes framed by white down. We did not ring them, having no rings small enough.

During mid-February I was on my own for a long spell when a letter from the absent Dom asked if I would try and get information on the three and four-year-old birds that returned to their natal plot at this time of year, although not yet old enough to breed.

These had no burrows, so hung around on the surface, but were not used to being handled and put up a commendable fight. I emerged from my first evening's sortie honourably scarred after my tussle with 12506 and 20407.

Waking at 4.0 a.m. to a pandemonium of shearwater calls, I tumbled into some clothes and emerged into the warm darkness. It seemed I was too late. Lines of birds were moving along the corridors between tussocks to bare granite surfaces, beating their wings long before their feet left the ground for the long swoop out, like swans taking off from a lake. They only just cleared the waves, having small powers of lift and no high point to use as a launch pad.

Before the last had gone the south-eastern sky was flushed a deep orange and I lingered to watch a splendid sunrise. Flaming colours engulfed the sky behind Little Green and Vansittart Islands, streaked with scars of dark purple, then fading to the palest opal.

I climbed back into my bunk, but sleep was out of the question now with the sun blazing in at me. The stillness of the ocean called and I made my way to North-east Boat Harbour to swim, as I had done twelve hours before. These jaunts had to be at high water. Low tide necessitated a wade through broad stretches of sea-grass meadow full of invisible stingers to reach water deep enough for swimming. By that time I would be in the main shipping channel and in danger of being washed away to another island.

Mooching along the edge, plucking up courage to take the plunge, I was aware of hundreds of little round sea urchin tests no bigger than golf balls. Leggy crabs, broader than long, scuttled sideways out of the pools, like giant prawns.

This was oystercatcher territory and Sooty and Scratchy pottered back and forth staring in bewilderment at this new species of grampus causing such a flurry in their private paddling pool. They constantly picked up tiny pebbles or strands of *Posidonia* sea-grass and dropped them again; a 'displacement reaction' that they often engaged in when disturbed from their routine and not quite sure how to react.

Human parallels can be drawn — the patting of an immaculate hair-do and unnecessary blowing of nose and clearing of throat before a public entrance. I had to chuckle when they joined in pursuit of a detached air bladder of a seaweed, which kept bowling along just out of their reach as they lunged at it — a strange reaction for birds feeding habitually on practically static shellfish!

It was glassy calm at this hour, except where the tide raced past the North-east point — a time of day when the reflections of rock and island might have been on a sheltered valley lake. Summer days often started this way, in a miracle of beauty, but the sea surface was inevitably ruffled a few hours later as the sun-warmed land sucked cool air off the sea.

Lazing on a rock slab to dry off, I had opportunity to watch a lone heron hunting lizards. The long neck appeared over a rock just behind me, followed by a grotesquely lean body and stilt legs, with the bill pointing straight ahead. An ecstatic wiggle of the neck, a lightning thrust of the bill among flowering

Pelargonium and a skink was struggling crosswise in a strangling vice.

The squirming victim had to be juggled into position for swallowing — a long job, achieved during a walkabout. Once gulped down the heron came back for more, but spotted me. Again that neck wiggle as it peered suspiciously before flapping slowly past, neck tucked in and legs extended. Ten minutes later it was back, prowling round the dinghy.

I had not seen the spur-wing plovers lately, but every morning a flock of fifty pied oystercatchers took off on the ebb and made towards Petrifaction Bay, where they foraged among the eel grass, *Zostera tasmanica* and *Zostera muelleri*, repairing to my safer roost when driven up by the incoming tide.

57 Short-tailed Shearwater *Puffinus tenuirostris* and egg

58 Sooty Oystercatchers *Haematopus fuliginosus* displaying

59 Silver Gulls *Larus novaehollandiae* displaying aggressively

2. VISITING BIRDS AND ABSENT BOATS

The bird-watching teams were interested in more than just shearwaters and other birds were ringed if they could be caught. Silver gulls, which came for kitchen scraps spread on "Yolla's" granite forecourt, were an obvious target. Now and again we set a clap net to catch the unwary and record their vital statistics for the island's card index.

The apparatus, a fisherman's leftovers, resembled a tennis net, with one long side weighed down by stones and the other elevated obliquely on stakes. Springing the trap was achieved by pulling an invisible length of nylon fishing line from the shelter of the doorway, to topple one of the stakes and bring the net down on the feasting birds. Most were too quick off the mark and the catch seldom exceeded two or three individuals.

It was not long before we could recognise the pair which had decided the patch belonged to them, to be defended against all comers. Sometimes the food lay for a while before anyone noticed. When the plot owners spotted the booty they alighted alongside and made such a defensive gullabaloo that others read the message as "Come quickly, grub up" rather than the intended "Keep off".

While the dominant pair was displaying to demonstrate ownership, wily underlings nipped in and took all that was worth taking, leaving the noisy ones with only their aura of self-importance. Meat leftovers were most prized and these lightly-built gulls would try to swallow a chop bone when the crop was already bulging with gristle and fat.

As the shoulders were hunched and the bill dipped to the ground in the first part of the display, the beak remained clamped onto the bone and the call came out flavoured with lamb. When the shoulders went down and the beak came up for the second part an opening just a fraction too wide would allow some cheeky antagonist to snatch the unswallowable morsel for itself. With so little in their favour, it is remarkable that such bones were regarded as edible at all, but gulls are gullible and never learned.

The Pacific gulls, or 'man-eaters' as Leila Barrett called them, although so fierce with smaller creatures, were cowards when it came to approaching people. They seldom alighted on the feeding patch, but would sail overhead and swoop on any smaller gulls flying up with booty. They were given a good run for their money, but the prize was usually dropped eventually, to be caught by the assailant in midair, chop bones and all.

The young of both species were on the wing by mid-February, but had no chance of titbits while their elders and betters were around. They just paced or hovered, squealing enviously.

Both species and all ages were present when we tipped edible rubbish out of the dinghy at sea. They preferred their meals made to measure. Presented with a whole loaf of mildewy bread, they had no idea what to do with it, allowing it to sink unmolested to the ever watchful fish and crabs. The guttural grunts of the Pacifics, so different from the caterwauling of other black-backed gulls, took a lot of getting used to.

The few blue penguins on the island were flipper-tagged and their progress monitored. The short stocky legs were seldom visible, even when the birds were not sitting back on their haunches, and numbered metal tabs clipped to a flipper were easier to read with binoculars.

Parent birds came faithfully every night to feed their pair of lusty chicks, which were near to fledging during my first days on Fisher Island in the second week of January. Full-sized, with the last wisps of baby-down being pushed off by feather growth beneath, the twins would emerge from their burrow to greet the homecoming parent enthusiastically. Both adults and young retaliated boisterously when handled, delivering lightning blows with the workmanlike beak.

For a considerable period black-faced shags would come winging across the island around seven each morning from their roost away to the east, just twelve hours after heading the opposite way the night before. There would be about 110 in the main flock, with some twenty late risers about a quarter of an hour later. Their daytime destination was in the direction of Samphire Island, none dropping off to join those roosting on Reef Island, which seemed to belong to a different population.

In fine weather they flew high on a straight course, closely packed. When battling into a headwind with rain squalls, they were scattered in a wide-ranging rabble close to the sea surface. It was every bird for itself then, with no regard for orderly formations, some individuals getting blown back, tail first. To avoid the full ferocity of the westerlies, they would swing away over Fisher Island into the shelter of Petrifaction Bay and follow the coast around to their feeding grounds.

A couple of young black-faced shags, with lighter, more mottled plumage than the breeders, had a regular sleeping place on the seaward rocks of Fisher Island during my initial stay. They were always there early and late, with heads tucked back among the shoulder feathers.

One was sick and so easy to approach that I could sit beside it stroking the feathers of its back without waking it. An unguarded movement on my part and the neck would uncoil, the eyes meeting mine with a rather bemused expression, but no attempt was made to escape.

On one occasion it dropped its body from the vertical to the horizontal and spurted a well aimed jet of chalky guano in my direction, then tucked its head in again and appeared to go back to sleep. It eventually died and, on investigation, was found to be full of worms.

Its corpse was used to bait our two crayfish pots and there was a small adventure getting these set, an oar lost in the process having to be dived for. Any oars other than those of the notorious "Half Safe" might have been expected to float!

The crayfish did not converge on the corpse with any show of enthusiasm: they preferred fish heads. Something, probably crabs or prawns, cleaned the shag carcase so meticulously that the skull, attached to ten inches of vertebral column, graced "Yolla's" wall for many weeks after.

The lee of Fisher Island was a favourite place for musk ducks to while away the time when there was a brisk tidal flow further out. They would sit the water for hours at a stretch, the leathery lobe dangling under the drake's bill creating a bizarre outline against the silvered background. The females lacked this ornamentation and were smaller than their mates, which are the largest of Australian ducks.

The birds seldom flew and when they did the wings seemed to be too small for the body. Instead they dived frequently, cormorant fashion, in search of the shellfish and other sea-bed organisms that sustained them. The tail feathers were straight and stiff, the body long and lean and they floated low in the water, often fluttering and splashing to resemble cormorants even more closely.

Although barred and freckled, they appeared black against the light, occupying the ecological niche of the marine scoters of my home seas, although more often to be found on fresh water. The call was a goose-like honk rather than a quack and they are often cited as the odd ones out among their kind.

Particularly splendid were the chestnut-breasted shelduck or mountain duck, a medley of chestnut, green, white and dark. These flew over at times but never alighted, favouring fresher water on the Flinders Island lagoons.

Black swans and Cape Barren geese passed occasionally, pelicans and great white herons much more rarely than the white-faced herons. From about the 20th January groups of twittering welcome swallows would fly over and the starlings nesting on Reef Island would commute to Fisher in search of food.

Every so often a fierce looking white-rumped marsh harrier would quarter the island to see what was about, although there was little in the way of small fry except the numerous fleet-footed skinks which, at three to four inches long, seemed a suitable size. Sea eagles were seldom so bold as to visit when we were in residence and our only other predators apart from the gulls were the big orange and white water rats. These swam across from the mainland and were blamed, rightly or wrongly, for the loss of shearwater eggs and chicks from the Home Rookery.

* * * * *

On 23rd January I refused a tow back to Fisher Island behind *"Tassie"*, which was delivering a load of firewood, and got myself across in fine style but had the usual problem on arrival. Making *"Half Safe"* temporarily fast, I crested the rise and sought help. Bill Barrett obliged, scratching his head in perplexity as he got to grips with the situation.

"How the hell are you supposed to do this on your own — or even get her? That's a three-man boat: two at the oars and a crew man for steering and landing."

It was nice to know I was not quite as inadequate as I felt! We worked very hard to get her up between us.

Towards evening the sea calmed and I sat on the rocks by the new woodpile luxuriating in an island to myself. Cattle were being moved along the road ashore and their agitated bellows and the cries of the drovers came wafting across, muted by distance. Later, as the sky blazed into one of those colourful sunsets that are so much a part of this evocative seascape, the breeze brought strains of music from a cargo boat moored at the quay.

Even spending a penny became a pleasure. By making use of the running water of gullies cleaned by every tide instead of the static Sanilav, I could watch the marine life going about its everyday business instead of reading stale news items in last week's papers.

I no longer had to read in bed until 9.0 a.m. to avoid disturbing the night workers, so I reorganised my day to use the magic hours after first light. Having moved my sleeping quarters, I was awakened anyway by the sun blazing in onto my pillow.

Tuck and Barrett came next day with another load of wood. They had missed high water and most of the logs were rolling back into the sea. I guided them to a deeper venue and fetched some planks that Eric had used in his coffin hide to lay across the gully into which the logs slid when they moved round. They still had to be thrown clear of high tide level, but at least we didn't have to fish them out of the water. Sweat streamed from old Tuck's forehead and next day he was complaining of stiffness, but he never gave up.

I produced refreshments and soon after their leave-taking Leila Barrett sculled across in a minute dinghy with the meat and vegetables that Tuck had forgotten to bring and to collect his jacket which he had forgotten to take.

As promised by Dom, the ex-harbour mistress was to become my fairy godmother. It mattered little that she came disguised as a witch in darned slacks, worn sand-shoes, shapeless blouse, unruly hair, ineffectually restrained by a bandana and lipstick awry. She had a heart of gold. We talked of this and that, outside and in. I had just time when she left to finish my 'exposure transect' from west to east before dusk closed down.

Next day I spent on Little Dog Island. The following morning Leila arrived as I pegged my laundry out, bringing mail, two old newspapers, a bottle of fresh cow's milk and a newly caught pike, streamlined like the familiar river fish of home. Commenting on the easterly change in the weather, she prophesied that my long-awaited trip to the Cat Island gannetry was likely to recede yet further into a nebulous future.

I was fast learning the uncertainties and frustrations of being remote from the hub of activity. Trooper Bailey had been delegated to organise my transport, but he was usually away on some unexplained business or seeing to matters on his farm, leaving neither messages nor instructions. Boat after boat had gone out in that direction recently, but none had come in to pick me up, however urgently I had been instructed to have my camping gear packed and ready. Information was always conflicting.

Another dinghy headed my way after Leila had gone. A small boy was rowing an almost unrecognisable Tuck, resplendent in his Sunday suit, collar and tie and a trilby hat!

"Jo Greeno's sailing for Cat Island in the *"Betty G"* tomorrow morning between nine and ten," he called. "Get your kit across to Lady Barron by nine."

I walked back to "Yolla" and came face to face with my pike: something of a problem as I was better at catching fish than at cooking them. Fried fish needed batter and I had no eggs. I would poach it. And why not some powdered milk in the water, and butter and salt? Things were looking up; but surely white sauce was thicker than this. I cast my eyes along the shelf. Sure enough, flour and cornflour. I selected the latter, heated up yesterday's sprouts and onions and produced a repast of which I could be proud, topped off with pears and cream. Only subsequently did I learn that the end product was improved if the ingredients were added in a different order.

At 6.30 next morning I was launched into the elusive Cat story once more. Disposing of rubbish and leaving everything shipshape, I loaded my gear into a delightfully dry boat, forgetting that she had been out of the water for long enough for the seams to have opened up. Despite all re-balancing of equipment on the way across, I was shin-deep in water on arrival and the two loaves of bread and towel in the bottom of my rucksack were sodden, with the precious camera balanced high and dry on top.

An elderly, bewhiskered Mr Hendrick, ex-harbour master, gave me a hand. "'*Betty G*' isn't in yet, still at her moorings in the bay named after her skipper." He looked in horror at the amount of water in the boat and hailed a small boy. "Here lad, bail 'er out. A tin in each hand." Shouting to a couple of seamen on the wharf to give us a help up, he continued muttering about the boat. "Allus told 'un it was too heavy. Ridiculous for one. S'pose beggars can't be choosers. Reckon the bereaved salmon poacher was better off with a cheaper substitute."

One of the fishermen cast scornful glances at the small boy with his two corned beef tins and set to himself with a four gallon kerosene tin. In genuine pursuit of information, I asked what best to do with "Half Safe".

"Put 'er on the bottom and catch crayfish in 'er."

I said no more.

Then panic, a bailed-out rowlock. We peered into the matted sea-grass embedded in black ooze. A shipping company had recently offered a £300 reward to anyone who could lift a sunken propeller beside the wharf and the diver who volunteered sank in mud up to his middle and gave up. But, by a miracle, we found the missing part.

A bellow from one of my helpers raised a bystander on the jetty. He was gazing contemplatively into a barrel and returned to this all-absorbing activity, like a fortune-teller gazing into a crystal ball, after lending a hand with the heaving. I took, oars, rowlocks and hut keys to Lew Bailey's wife for safe keeping — Lew being away in Tasmania — and Jerry Addaway gave me a lift to the jetty with my fresh stores.

"Sorry, no fresh fruit or veg. There never is for the Cat Island lot."

Leila joined me, a distrustful look in her eye as she watched Greeno coming and going in his big new van.

"Trouble with these fishermen is they've got too much money. He's come in three times in the last eight days with £3-400 worth of crayfish each time. They don't care whether they go to sea or not. He's not going; you mark my word."

At 11.30 even his newly arrived crew man didn't know whether they were sailing or not. Midday brought the man himself, with a big grin and no apology.

"I don't think I'll go after all. It would be nice to drive the wife to the Launceston plane for her shopping — and see the boy off to boarding school." Then as an afterthought: "I'll be back and ready to sail this evening, if you hang about."

Ready, yes, but unlikely at that time of day. I murmured something about my wasted preparations and he suggested I sleep on his boat to save re-launching, but Leila dissuaded me.

"You'll likely be sleeping on *"Betty G"* all week."

She rowed me back arranging for Tuck to collect me if the long-awaited trip ever materialised.

Greeno didn't want the responsibility of my gear, knowing that he didn't want me either, so we stowed it in the wheelhouse of the *"Lady Merle"*, which wasn't due to sail until Wednesday. Her skipper, a doctor's son, who got more money fishing than in the professions, always went east with his two Lithuanian crewmen and the local 'bad lad' of Neolithic appearance, so would take me.

The *"Betty G"* did not, of course, sail as promised and the weather then turned easterly. Too rough, I thought, for the *"Lady Merle"*. I was horrified, therefore, when I saw her leaving the wharf at midday, the scheduled hour for departure, and curving in my direction. Seldom have I achieved so much in so short a time and I was packed and ready to receive her as she came abreast of the island. But she was going west! I wondered if my camping gear had gone west too, but hoped it had been lodged at Bailey's.

Two days later *"Lady Merle's"* dinghy arrived with my baggage, the oarsman saying it had set in easterly and there would be no Cat Island for a long time yet. There wasn't.

This sequence of events was so typical of the uncertainties of island life that I had become inured to it long before my arrival in the Furneaux Group. It is no wonder that islanders become happy-go-lucky, accepting what comes with a minimum of forward planning.

60 Pied Oystercatchers *Haematopus longirostris*

61 Drake Musk Duck *Biziura lobata*

62 Chestnut-breasted Shelduck or Mountain Duck *Tadorna tadornoides*

3. SEA LIFE AND FISHERMEN

My male colleagues occasionally caught parrotfish from the Fisher Island rocks, as a welcome adjunct to our meals. Cantankerously the fish most anxious to take the hook were quite inedible and returned for another nibble, however often they were thrown back. Eventually the frustrated fisherman would transfer them to another pool, away from temptation.

When the state of the sea allowed, we took every chance of visiting other islands, so the opportunities for replenishing our supplies at the Flinders' store were limited. We dug deeply into our cache of tinned steak and kidney puddings and wished we had enough flour to make something that would stand in for bread but could be made without an oven.

Sometimes we were reduced to eating mutton birds — for long months pickled in brine and soaked well before cooking, but not well enough to remove the horrendous amount of salt. I had enjoyed the New Zealand mutton birds (sooty shearwaters) — even the fishy ones, which I regarded as the answer to a maiden's prayer for a kipper without bones, but not these. Most of us gave up less than halfway through.

Fortified with less exotic fare, we re-set the crayfish pots, baited with the greasy remains, and the crayfish needed no second bidding. They were immune to high salinity and enjoyed grease. The handsome orange captives were brought in a day later and popped in the firewood box while water was boiled in the four gallon kerosene tin which had failed very early on to act as the ablutions shower.

While the mutton birds were disappointing, smaller than the New Zealand ones and sold in Island Stores for 4/- each instead of 5/- the pair, the crayfish left nothing to be desired. I voted them every bit as good as the ones fed me by the Motiti Island Maoris and the West Australians maintained that each was as big as two of their native animals.

It seemed that West Australian fishermen might come this far to fish. We met one at the jetty with two triangular caufes floating alongside. He told us he had been nabbed by a Fisheries Inspector the day before for being in possession of undersized crayfish. Maybe they looked right by his standards.

At that time the crayfish or southern spiny rock lobsters *(Jasus lalandii)* were exported from Lady Barron whole, not canned on the spot as in North Tasmania. They were said to be at their best in January. While the closed season for males was only two months (September and October) that for females was five (June to October inclusive).

That was when the hen crays that had attained breeding stature, at three to five years old, were 'in berry', carrying a load of pinkish orange eggs. Ten weeks after laying, these hatched into free-swimming larvae, not destined to settle on the sea floor for a full year.

There were also fishing restrictions in November when the moult took place, the animals very vulnerable for a full week then until their new exoskeleton hardened up. To conserve minerals, the old skeleton was eaten, as deer on lime-deficient soils gnaw at their shed antlers.

In March and April the fishermen said the crays came inshore and hid under rocks where they were difficult to locate, and catches were poor. Many of them 'slipped' their boats then and took a holiday, or painted and pottered. When fishing, echo sounders were used to distinguish rocks from sand. Where there were rocks there were likely to be crays.

On our travels around the islands we often came on rows of pots attached to a line suspended from red and white floats and marked by a flag. An average boat might carry thirty pots. Spear guns and hooks were banned.

Not all the fishing boats drawn up by the high-fenced loading ramps for cattle along the wharf were after crayfish. Blue-eyed trevalla were brought in from deep water and surface swimming fish caught nearer the shore included gummy shark and school shark, snoek and school whiting, salmon and garfish and flathead and flounders from the sandy shallows.

For some strange reason, 'shark' is a dirty word on the culinary front and must always masquerade under another name. Gummy shark, by the time it gets to the Whitemark Hotel, has metamorphosed into 'flake'. I found this quite delicious in 1995, but 'a rose by any other name would have smelled as sweet'. Dogfish, our smaller UK sharks, are marketed under the misleading and flattering name of rock salmon!

The flatfish were said to be easier to catch at night, when they slept a little above the sea bed so that nets, including trawls, go under the majority instead of only those roused from the sand and trying to escape. Another advantage is that young, undersized fish are thought to sleep just below the surface, so are not netted at all.

Arthur Harland was a great one for 'floundering' on a small scale. We would see him wading through the shallows at night with a torch and sometimes respond to his shouted invitation to row across and join him. He splashed back and forth with a spear in one hand and a bulb mounted on a four foot pole in the other, this powered by a battery strapped to his back. The broad flat outline of a flounder spreadeagled on the sand made an easy target, and he would catch turbot and mullet as well. We enjoyed specimens of all as additions to our Fisher Island cuisine.

Arthur had not been born to a sea-going life, although he was the proud owner of a motley array of mummified sea dragons, sea horses and pipefish, as well as his fine shell collection. An octogenarian now, he was an ex-miner from Birmingham, about as far from the sea as he could get in the UK, but claimed to have been born at Balmoral Castle, sired by the chief forester.

The Scottish connection had been perpetuated by a brother ten years his junior, who, he said, had advanced from private to general in the British Army and was currently a governor in the Hebrides. Resident on the Isle of

Skye, he shared Arthur's enthusiasm for natural history and was the author of a book on wild flowers. Arthur himself was a world traveller and a great storyteller, the stories losing nothing in the telling!

He was undoubtedly a good field naturalist and wildlife photographer and a picker-up-of-unconsidered-trifles, like many of us on Fisher. His own shell collection was inspired on a visit to another, vine-growing, brother in Western Australia, when he had been commissioned to pick up shells for Mrs Greeno. He did swaps with dealers. For every paper nautilus shell which he despatched, he got back ten shillings' worth of shells from different parts of the world.

His naval son had added contributions from Port Moresby and Arnhemland. For saving an elderly Chinaman from drowning, he had been given a pair of intricately carved pearl shells about eight inches across, one of which he passed on to his father.

When Sir Peter Scott of Slimbridge Wildfowl Trust, the World Wildlife Fund and much more visited the Furneaux Group in 1957, Arthur was anxious to meet him and got an appointment at the Whitemark Hotel. I had an account of this episode, which proved to be a non-event, from Derek Smith, who was never at a loss for words.

"Poor old sod. He worshipped the ground that Scott walked on, but the great man couldn't be bothered. Arthur had so many baths first that he shone and reeked of Lifebuoy soap. Got all togged up in his best. Looked like Marilyn Monroe, his breast pockets stuffed with colour slides to show the major domo, but Scott sent a man down to say he had a slight cold and was not available! When people remonstrated later his comment was 'I came to see the geese, not the people'."

Pointing out what was named Scott's Reef in Peter's honour, Derek commented: "Used to be Billy Goat Reef. They're two of a kind!"

Even the great are fallible.

Pike in my book had always been the toothy top predators of freshwater fisheries: the marine pike off Fisher Island were a novelty. Both Derek and Arthur used to come out in their dinghies to troll for them. The only thing that stopped them, apart from rough seas, was a lot of floating weed, which wrapped around the lines and snagged on the hooks.

When Leila Barrett walked me along the shore to meet the elderly Hendrick, we found his dairy farmer son visiting for a day's pike fishing. His three curly-headed daughters, aged seven, nine and eleven, were enjoying a last day on the beach before returning to school after their seven-week summer holiday.

The son quaffed a flagon of whisky and three pints of stout and walked out, quite steadily. A while later we watched him whizzing back and forth across the bay in his mechanised dinghy, trailing a line.

"Much too fast for pike" said his father. "But he won't be told."

He kicked over a stout bottle on the floor. "I hate the stuff."

Hendrick, like so many of this maritime fraternity, had marine treasures draped around his walls. The prize specimen was a giant crab caught off King Island. The two ultimate joints of the bigger claw were both eight inches long, dwarfing the sea dragon alongside.

Our host described the mob of silver gulls that had descended on the plague of 'army worms' (or moth caterpillars) that threatened the island crops, polishing them all off. Black swans, he said, were now so numerous that they had been taken off the protected list and were likely to fall to anyone with a gun.

"And swans make good eating, too" — this last with a reminiscent smile. "The open season for Cape Barren geese is two months, but they're shot willy-nilly. Some of the poachers bring back eighty at a time, including youngsters not yet able to fly!"

Evidently the Fauna Board made laws which had no parliamentary backing and were impossible to enforce. The latest law that people were complaining about stipulated a minimum complexity for the mutton birders' houses, costing at least £1,000, and insisted on water tanks holding a thousand gallons instead of the previous 400. As one MP was heard to ask: "How long are you there: four weeks or four months?"

School summer holidays had recently been changed so that they no longer coincided with the birding season. This meant that mothers had to stay back with the children and many of the fathers would not go to the islands if there was no-one to cook for them, so the industry was already on the wane. The islands were state owned, so the Fauna Board was losing licence money.

From 22nd February 1958, I shared Fisher Island with Bill Mollison, whose enquiring mind embraced animal life in general and limpets in particular at that time. He was an enthusiast and a field man, not an academic, having left school at fifteen to get to grips with practical fishing and forestry. Adult matric was obtained at evening classes, followed by a first-year university course at Hobart before he launched out into shark fishing in Bass Strait. He became involved with wildfowl and duck shooting laws and was one of the very few to have seen a Tasmanian wolf or thylacine in the wild.

Currently he was employed by CSIRO as Dom's field assistant and I learned a great deal of nature craft from him, both in Bass Strait and in the Tasmanian backwoods. We lost touch when I returned to Britain, but, about thirty years later, he appeared, large as life, on British television as a leading conservationist and organic horticulturist in New South Wales.

We did a Box and Cox act when we were not visiting other islands, as most of his observations were carried out at night. I moved into the back room for uninterrupted nights and he retired there to sleep by day, while I occupied the all purpose living room. There was never a dull moment when we came together, with so many ecological problems to argue about. Could we, for instance, control barilla and bracken with rotary slashers and chisel plough, or what was the effect of feldspar hardpans on grazing wallabies? He was already hooked on organic matter and we burned tins of Fisher Island soil on top of the wood stove to assess the percentage by weight of inflammable humus.

Marine life was more active by night than by day and Bill did a lot of collecting after his mutton bird patrols, the spoils pickled in formalin and sent off to a certain 'Scotty' for identification. When he collected before the bird check, I would go too.

Only one species of squid had been recorded in these waters at that time and he had already caught several others off the islands, so there was great excitement when we spotted two small white ones cruising just offshore. They are better known now and are brought up in trawl nets from deeper water.

Bill tried to catch this pair in a hand net lined with fly wire, while I stood ready with a bucket of sea water. Trying not to get his feet wet, he missed them, cursed his luck and promptly fell in, cursing some more for not getting wet in the first place. We saw no more squid, but plenty of other animals.

First-comers were pale blue garfish with ridiculously long snouts, cruising fast in formation, then brownish fish with sharp pectoral fins, ogling clownishly like goldfish. Prawns and shrimps, transparent and almost invisible by day, were much easier to see by night as their eyes shone in the torch beam like orange fog lamps.

Crabs were out in a big way, three types, not including the brown scuttlers of the daylight hours. They seemed not to mind the light and we spent long minutes crouching over them watching the pincers busily scraping food from the limpet wigwams and transferring them to the sideways operating jaws. They fed only from the limpet shells, probably because the limpets had themselves scraped off all the algae and encrusting animals from the rock faces. The safest place for potential food items to grow was on the 'lion's' back, out of reach of the rasping tongue.

The crabs' tastes were catholic. One in the bucket, after four thwarted attempts to climb out, set about the six inch long garfish that had died when Bill trod on it accidentally. Pincers worked methodically, stripping off the skin and pulling at morsels of flesh, leaving the tattered remains only when completely satiated.

We had a duplicate of this species for pickling, so this individual was left overnight to enjoy more of the feast. When he tired of the orgy, he pattered out to the toilet block to sleep it off. The crabs led us a goodly dance over the rocks, clinging with incredible tenacity to the slightest crevice with their many pointed toes.

So enamoured was Bill with this sport that he started marking them, 'tattooing their telsons' or the abdomen that was held so closely under the thorax that it could not be bent outwards with a finger. A crab, in effect, is a lobster folded tightly in half, the male's undercarriage triangular, the female's rounded and equipped with feathery appendages on the enfolded surface to hold the egg clusters.

One admirably calm moonlight night, sitting watching the twinkling lights on distant Flinders and veritable legions of stars, we spotted what looked like a monster white jellyfish steaming in our direction. Anticipation mounted but, as it sailed by, we identified it as waste paper from *"Prion"*, anchored at the jetty opposite. Beauty is, indeed, in the eye of the beholder!

Intrigued by a persistent rasping noise, we got down on hands and knees to discover that this came from stationary limpets, left high and dry by the receding tide but still rasping away with the zigzag radula as when they were scraping their way across underwater rocks on their grazing forays. No wonder there were depressions in the granite where they habitually roosted during the ebb.

The incongruity of our attitude, ears close to the rock listening intently at dead of night, suddenly struck us as funny and we collapsed laughing — although well aware that scientists do dafter things than this. There was something about island life: inhibitions fell away as we harked back to a Utopian childhood, unfettered by the trappings of normal decorum. This was particularly evident in Dom Serventy himself, always eccentric, but behaving with the abandon of a naughty schoolboy when let loose among his beloved mutton birds.

Ever ready to experiment, Bill got some blue paint to mark both limpet shells and their position on the rock. Contrary to expectation, we found that some returned only to the same general area after each foray and not to the selfsame shell-sized depression. The mean resting position was higher after a high spring tide and the bigger limpets roosted higher upshore than the smaller ones — the opposite of most marine animals. We wondered what the micro-pasturage would be like above the level of normal tides. To our eyes it seemed non-existent.

On another night our prize catch was an octopus with tentacles eighteen inches long — more than a convenient handful as Bill's gloved hand tried to push it into a container. As fast as one tentacle was stuffed in another came snaking out. It would not have been caught if it had not grabbed the handle of the net in annoyance, and it continued in the part of the aggressor.

Bill told of his encounter with a really big octopus when he was shark fishing at the age of fifteen. He had thrust repeatedly at the animal's body with his spear, but freed himself from the enwrapping arms only with difficulty. His seniors told him later that he should have reached in for the stomach and pulled his adversary inside out. South Sea Islanders bite them between the eyes to quieten them! The worst course was to hack off the arms one by one, the captor always tiring before the octopus did.

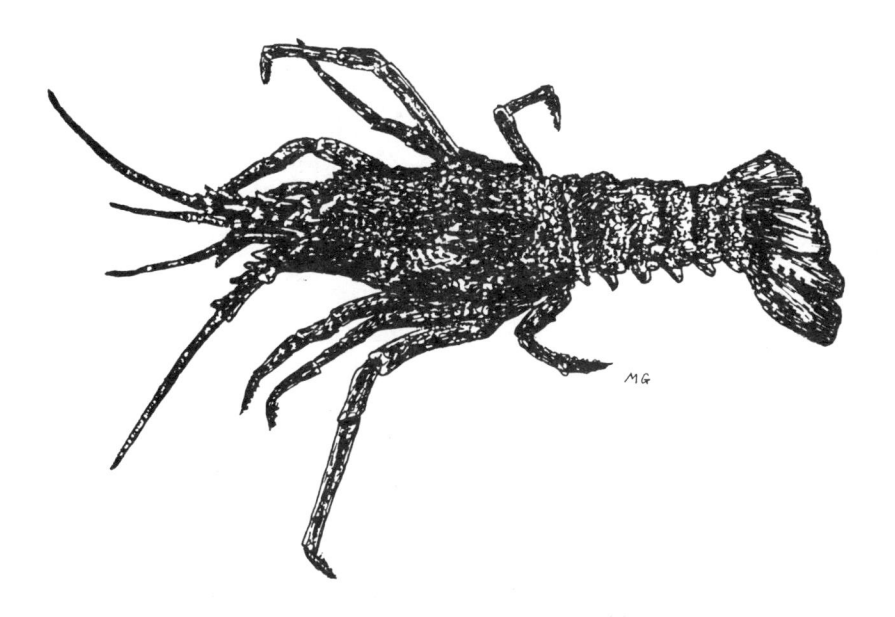

63 Crayfish or Spiny Rock Lobster *Jasus lalandii*

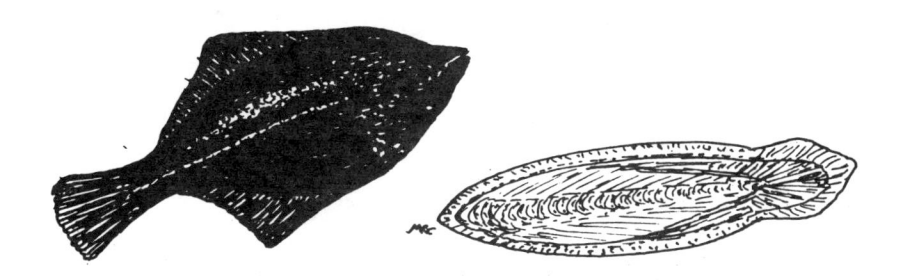

64 Flounder *Pleuronectes* and Cuttlefish *Sepia* 'bone'

65 Painted Lady *Phasianella*, Keyhole Limpet *Amblichilepas* and Orange-edged Limpet *Cellana*

Chapter Eight

FISHER ISLAND AND THE HAPPY HERMIT

1. LIFE ON THE HOME FRONT: HUMAN, AVIAN AND FLORAL

It was nine months before I came to Fisher Island next, at a different season, with a new generation of birds coming off the production line. The sooty oystercatchers, tame as ever, had laid two eggs a few metres from last season's nest and a lone red-capped dotterel's egg was perched on a pile of shell debris west of the hut.

A precocious starling 'flutterer' was out of the nest, hopping uncertainly among the boulders, but making no serious attempt to fly. The shearwater whose crumbling burrow entrance had been repaired with a length of earthenware drainpipe, had absconded and laid her egg in a nearby burrow, resenting the intrusion. Or was it the triangular hide, erected over her chosen, lidded, nest chamber that she resented?

My initial companion this time was the lofty, sandy-haired Bob Tilt of CSIRO — a great man to have at the oars of "Half Safe". He was as fascinated by the marine life as Bill Mollison had been and on his first evening we were out photographing a charmingly undulant pink sea slug. We then fell to gathering some of the prettily marked pink and red painted lady shells *(Phasianella australis)*, which were also a feature of Possum Boat Harbour on the main island.

On our first trip with Tuck we failed to make the desired landing as his newly overhauled dinghy had been lost two days earlier in a storm and he could find no water deep enough to bring *"Tassie"* inshore. We trolled for pike over the stern instead, but located the errant craft skulking in a bay before the day was out and took her in tow again.

The ensuing heat wave ended on 11th December, when 0.96 inches of rain fell on a troubled sea. This was the day that Dom Serventy elected to join us, but Bob managed to get him across. I plied the dripping pair with hot soup on their arrival, followed by braised mutton bird from the cask under the concrete base of the rain tank and not so salty this time after prolonged soaking.

17th December saw another display of the Aurora Australis; a paler version than I had witnessed before, but thrilling, nevertheless. The reds were more fleeting, among shimmering muslin curtains of white, veering between warm cream and electric blue in constant waving motion. It brought to mind the first couplet of Roy Campbell's poem on this phenomenon entitled "The Flaming Terrapin".

"Zigzags of scarlet; combs of silver flame
Shivering in the darkness, went and came."

His next two lines bore little resemblance to what we witnessed, savouring, like the title, of poet's licence or the liberty to fantasize.

"And fifty hues in fierce collision hurled
Blazed on the hushed amazement of the world."

Just four hues was nearer the mark tonight, delicate hues but sufficiently all-pervading to make the star-spangled void away to the north seem even blacker.

Two days later the new Cat Island gannet wardens joined us on Fisher Island. A retired couple, the Dunns, they had been selected from thirty-eight applicants answering the newspaper advertisement of ten days before. Like so many here, they were English immigrants, in Hobart now for eight years. With them was their younger son, Morton, a Hobart University student with a rowing blue, which would stand him in good stead in the weeks to come.

We had a magnificent sunset to show them, but no aurora. That night was particularly dark, with car lights flashing near Vinegar Hill and ships' navigation lamps rocking gently across the sound. Few shearwaters were calling on the evening bird patrol, but there was veritable bedlam at 2.30 a.m. The Dunns would become better acquainted with this banshee caterwauling from the well-named Babel Island as they settled in on Cat Island in its shadow.

* * * * *

I had travelled widely around the islands of Western Australia and the Great Barrier Reef and been South with the Antarctic Division before I came again to Fisher Island on 26th January 1960.

On the plane from Melbourne, Dave Paton, a Launceston agricultural officer resident on Flinders Island for seven months, recognised the name on my luggage and made himself known. With him was Geoff Dimmock of the CSIRO Soils Division and between them they clued me up on things I should know and presented me with some welcome beans and tomatoes — Island Stores showing the usual shortage of fruit and veg.

Trooper Bailey was nursing an injured toe, which he had bumped on some part of *"Aralla"* in a rash moment of activity. Among his complaints of Penicillin rash and having to do a job in Whitemark in the middle of several weeks' sick leave, I gathered that he would be unable to take me across. Young Holloway obliged, with Tuck as crew man. "Half Safe", which had filled with water within five minutes of being launched, was anchored off the slip, bravely but only just keeping her head above water while her thirsty planks imbibed liquid as avidly as when they had been part of the living tree.

A prolonged heat wave had left everything tinder dry. Even the leather-leaved shrubs and succulent herbs were sadly wrinkled, as in old age. Temperatures soared to 101 degrees Fahrenheit. The layer of congealed milk and other nasties on the main working surface cried out for attention, so my first job was to light the fire, heat wave or no heat wave, for hot water. It took half an hour of vigorous scrubbing before the pattern on the oilcloth covering the dining table-cum-writing desk emerged.

While the last inhabitants had not been over-zealous on the house-wifery front, they had left the shelves well stocked. It was thirty-nine days since the last occupant left and the sugar had taken on a life of its own since then, heaving restlessly on its shelf like a suppurating volcano. And so began a long war against ants, which seemed to dislike only cocoa. The packet of Mylex bags contributed by Dave Paton provided a useful first line of defence but it was only a matter of time before the marauding horde forced a passage.

The evening patrol revealed no mutton birds on the surface, but a feeble voice from the bowels of the earth assured me that the entire population had not perished of heat.

Next day saw an unusually high mid-morning tide covering the whole of the eastern platform and submerging the boat mooring under two to three feet of water. I missed the cheery piping of the oystercatchers, but other birds were up to expectations, onshore and off, where musk ducks still idled on the sea and cormorants cogitated on Reef Island. A young Pacific gull and a young starling had come to grief on the rocks.

On the 28th the oppressively hot hush of the early morning proved to be the calm before a storm, which blew me to a standstill when I ventured outside and sent clouds of stinging spray across Snake Gully.

About 130 cormorants hurtled across, flying high with the wind behind, and ten turned back, only to be blown on with the rest, tail first but almost as fast. Two stayed above the island for a while, tacking, with a view to landing, but gave up and allowed themselves to be hurled away to leeward towards Scotts Reef. "Half Safe" was grounded comfortably on a cushion of sea-grass at low tide, for a well-earned rest after the tempestuous tossings of the morning.

The family of young starlings in "Yolla's" roof added their hungry yelps to the noise of the wind as they demanded more and yet more from hardworking parents forced to forage at ground level or risk being blown away with small hope of an immediate return. Bigger birds fared better, twenty-one silver gulls converging for their breakfast snack and twenty-three pied oystercatchers whiling away the high tide on Potts Point. The plump, four inch long fish on which a black-faced cormorant breakfasted had been caught off the slip in the calm of the early morning.

The gale continued through the night, swinging a little to the south-west, so that I had to move "Half Safe" to a less choppy mooring. A marsh harrier was exulting in some hang-gliding on the updraughts and some swallows were hurled past by a following wind.

With March came a heat wave, temperatures rising to eighty-four degrees Fahrenheit on the 3rd. This was a sultry day of cloud with the promise of thunder, when my temporarily prostrated torso became a landing pad for flying ants. These moved in tandem, in a brief orgy of mating, the little ones riding the more substantial queens-to-be, which tolerated only one passenger when in flight but were besieged by as many as five on alighting. The resulting frenzy resembled the jostling of toads struggling to perennate their kind in the chilly spring months at home.

Ants swarm on days of high humidity and this day produced the odd phenomenon of a rainbow after the sun had dropped behind the cloud bank over the Strzeleckis. Only the two ends of the arc were visible, these very bright. One grew out of Vinegar Hill, seemingly out of the fire that had been blazing there all day, the other from the south end of Little Green Island.

Two swans came flying out of the spectacularly stormy sunset which followed and there were other birds about. An unusual visitor was a little raven and there had been fly-pasts of ducks and curlews, swifts and swallows, egrets and herons, with a nan keen kestrel over the jetty opposite. As the storm died a sodden loaf of bread washed ashore attracting four Corvids, nine young Pacific gulls and a mob of silver gulls.

The singing of a magpie mingled in the hush of the subsequent dawn with the raucous notes of spur winged plovers and currawongs on the adjacent shore, while a hundred pied and thirty sooty oystercatchers took off from South Point into a crimson-flushed dawn.

Three new plant species were added to the Fisher Island list at this time, bringing the total up to ninety-five — not bad for a mere two acres, although it is unlikely that these were all there simultaneously. Most aristocratic was the native box *(Alyxia buxifolia)*, its fleshy fruits, like mini, two-stoned plums, no doubt brought by gulls, which enjoyed the orange pulp and spat out the stones.

They were blamed for the influx of the New Zealand mirror plant *(Coprosma repens)*, which had similar orange fruits to which they were very partial. This was a popular hedge plant in Lady Barron and gulls feeding there brought a succession of seeds, either expectorated as crop pellets or defecated in a white blob of uric acid.

Already I had noticed the spread of the bushes, not only across the grass behind "Yolla" but through the moribund coast wattle thicket to the east. By my 1995 visit it had made huge inroads, despite the efforts to rip much of it out.

There was none at all in 1952 when the vegetation had been mapped by Glen Storr of Western Australia, a formidable and delightful fifteen stone ornithological colleague of Dom Serventy. A mere twelve years later it was the most important shrub on the island. This rapid advance was mirrored by that on the Three Sisters Islands off Devonport in Northern Tasmania, where it had become the main plant since a silver gull colony took up residence there. Photographs taken by the local bird man, Les Hill, showed negligible amounts before the influx of the nesting birds.

It is significant that two of the other four shrubs on Fisher Island also bore edible fleshy fruits, white on the coastal beard heath *(Leucopogon)* and dark red on seaberry saltbush *(Rhagodia)*. Both were much the worse for wear after the drought, but replacement saplings were pushing through. The starry-haired daisy bush *(Olearia stellulata)* had fluffy seeds likely to have been brought by the wind. How the pea seeds of the coast wattle had arrived was anybody's guess.

Coprosma seeds coughed up by gulls were seven mm long, flattened on one face and with a triangular flap which broke away to reveal the two purplish seed-halves or cotyledons within a straw-coloured shell.

On 8th February a silver gull had obligingly coughed up a crop pellet into the bucket below the winch. This consisted of forty *Coprosma* seeds and a few beetle remains in a mush of skins, the fleshy parts squeezed off and swallowed. I soaked the seeds overnight and planted them in peaty soil in a box, the better to observe their germination stages.

Nothing happened for several weeks — when a fellow resident who enjoyed rock fishing tipped them out to use the box for his bait! The seeds were rescued and on 12th March the cocoa-coloured cotyledons had separated to release the tender roots. So, too, had some from a newly produced gull pellet. This, evidently, was 'the season', with or without an incubation period.

While it is pretty certain that the gulls brought the plants to open areas of the island in the first place, it was equally evident that the starlings spread them around, and into bushed areas not frequented by the gulls. When the young starlings fledged from their nest in "Yolla", they divided their time between the clumps of mirror plant and coast wattle, where young seedlings were springing up like mushrooms. If further proof was needed, it could be found in the contents of the smaller, neater crop pellets which they coughed up to make room for the next intake.

The other two plants new to the island were lucerne or alfalfa *(Medicago sativa)*, one of the Flinders Island crop plants, and a grass, *Agrostis avenacea*, both near the woodpile and presumably arriving with the logs.

It was around this time that seedlings of a sea-grass began to appear in the intertidal zone, but which one, *Posidonia* or *Cymodocea*? Wild flower books tend to gloss over these marine plants all too briefly. The one-seeded fruits were borne on flattened, leaflike stems up to half a metre long, leafless except for clusters of bracts immediately beneath.

These were washing up on Flinders Island too. When Frank Henwood came to help us with the boat at Lady Barron during the week of my find, he brought a box of the fruitlets with him, these more obviously Posidonia.

"In all my years as harbour master, this is the first time I've seen them wash ashore in numbers like this!"

It seemed there was a bumper harvest in 1960: or a bumper storm to do the harvesting and cast the crop ashore.

Fruit production was closely followed by germination — from deep down on the sandy ocean floor, to little embayments of our island coast. *Posidonia oceanica*, this southern plant's Mediterranean counterpart, can grow in water as much as a hundred metres deep, but ten metres is the greatest depth that I have seen quoted for the Australian species. The Furneaux Group is almost as far south as this goes and it is confined to the north coast in Tasmania.

I needed to conduct no germination experiments, this miracle of new life was happening all about me. Some of the youngsters held fast to their chosen spot, others, ripped out by the tide, were cast onto the piles of severed fibrous leaves that have inspired another name of 'fibre plant', the fibres outlasting the rest to get rolled into the familiar 'sea balls'.

The single cotyledon was green and fleshy from the start, nourishing the infant plant with both stored parental and newly manufactured nutrients. Juvenile leaves developed no more than a sheathing base, the green leaf blade appearing only on later ones.

* * * * *

One morning, after throwing the daily three buckets of sea water into "Half Safe" and watching this flow out of the seams almost as fast, I was moved to take up my pen. It seemed unfair that the powers that be could finance a plane to take two soil surveyors from Flinders Island to Cape Barren when the strait between was full of fishing boats, but could not afford a few pounds to buy a small dinghy. Like Little Miss Muffet, I sat forthwith on a tuffet (the feminine of tussock?) and lapsed into doggerel, to work the cumbersome craft out of my system.

"HALF SAFE"

So you've come to do research from the Fisher Island base!
What you'll soon find out is that the boat is a disgrace.
It's there to let us row across to Flinders' Island Store
But is leaky as a sieve, so this is more than just a chore.

Some trials and tribulations are enough to make one weep:
The Fauna Board won't buy a boat — they got one on the cheap.
Filched it from a fellow who had shot illegal duck
And thought that they had got themselves a little bit of luck

But oh how very wrong they were, how very very wrong
To think they'd got a bargain 'cos they'd got it for a song.
They didn't have to use the thing, they didn't have to row.
I wish just one of them would try and then, perhaps, they'd know.

When she's put into the sea she fills straight up with water
And the one who's got to bale her out says things they didn't orter.
And so would you if, as you baled, the water came in faster
And you began to wonder whether boat or you were master!

It isn't only when she's been for weeks up on the slip
That you have to pay a man good cash to hire you a ship
'Cos her seams have opened wide as the planks between have shrunk
And once into the sea she's on the way to being sunk.

You leave her in the water for several days or weeks
And haul her in and bale her out, but still the B thing leaks.
You let her go and watch her fill, in hope the planks will swell
But still the water gushes in. You think "Oh go to Hell".

But, after days of no more veg and mildew on the bread
You know you've got to go ashore, for woman must be fed.
The chances are the wind doth howl, the tide is streaming past
But you know you've got to go and you've got to get there fast.

Because midstream is not the place to have to stop and bale;
You get swept half a mile off course while busy with the pail.
But if you just row doggedly on you find your seat's awash.
To say the boat's a bit of luck is just a bit of bosh!

The chap who named the boat "Half Safe" was being optimistic:
A "Quarter Safe", I would have said; he got the wrong statistic.
But see you're always in the half that safely stays on top
Each time you have to go to Lady Barron shop.

But this is not the worst of her, the worst thing is her size
(And the Fauna Board's so proud that they got such a massive prize!).
She'd happily accommodate quite six or eight or ten
And when you have to haul her up you need a team of men.

And when you're on the isle alone and are but woman weak
The outlook when you get back home is most exceeding bleak.
If fortune fair has favoured you to reach the slip alright
And you've leapt into the icy sea and made the mooring tight.

The next stage is the problem, how to get her high and dry —
A time when lonely woman weak for hefty man doth sigh.
The rope's undone, the pulley's on, she pulls with all her might
But, tug and strain, she does no more than pull the pulley tight.

The oars and rowlocks moved away, the anchor laid aside
And all the water baled right out to help the boat to slide —
Back to the pulley rope she goes and pulls with might and main
But might and main are not enough and all her work is vain.

If there was but a tin of grease to ease the friction points
She might make headway, but there's not; just rust in all the joints
And snags upon the slipway where the boat should glide so smooth
And all the strength that she can muster fails to make it move.

And so the hated rusty winch with tangled wire cable
Is sought to help, although she knows that she is quite unable
To free the rusted coils and use it as it should be used
And will have to use the pulley rope — a rope that's much abused.

The handle of the winch is high, she has to get above it
So climbs upon the cairn of stones, but still can scarcely move it.
But slowly, slowly, inch by inch, the wretched boat is moving
The fact that will can master muscle slowly, surely proving.

And so, when nigh an hour's passed, the boat is where it should be
But the tangled, matted pulley rope is far from where it could be:
It's jammed up tight and cog's release just doesn't help at all.
She strains upon the handle, wishing she was twice as tall.

But then, at last, she stretches out upon the friendly granite,
The boat made fast, but boatman now has very nearly had it.
She knows it will be many a day before she tries again:
Her aching muscles tell her that it's too much of a strain.

She sees Tuck's little dinghy bobbing lightly on the water
And thinks "With very tiny sum, the powers might have bought her."
Where are the men of planning in the CSIRO
That for the sake of so few pounds they let her suffer so?

She thinks of all the many pounds that she has had to pay
To get to Fisher Island when there was no other way.
Those pounds which she could ill afford, she had too few to spare
But which fishermen demanded as their just and proper fare.

But no doubt we will muddle on, as we've always done of yore
Ignoring common sense and using brute force as before.
Till "Half Safe" really bursts a seam and sinks beneath the wave
And we'll hold a joyous funeral beside her watery grave!

66 Fruits and Crop Pellets of Taupata or
New Zealand Mirror Plant *Coprosma repens*

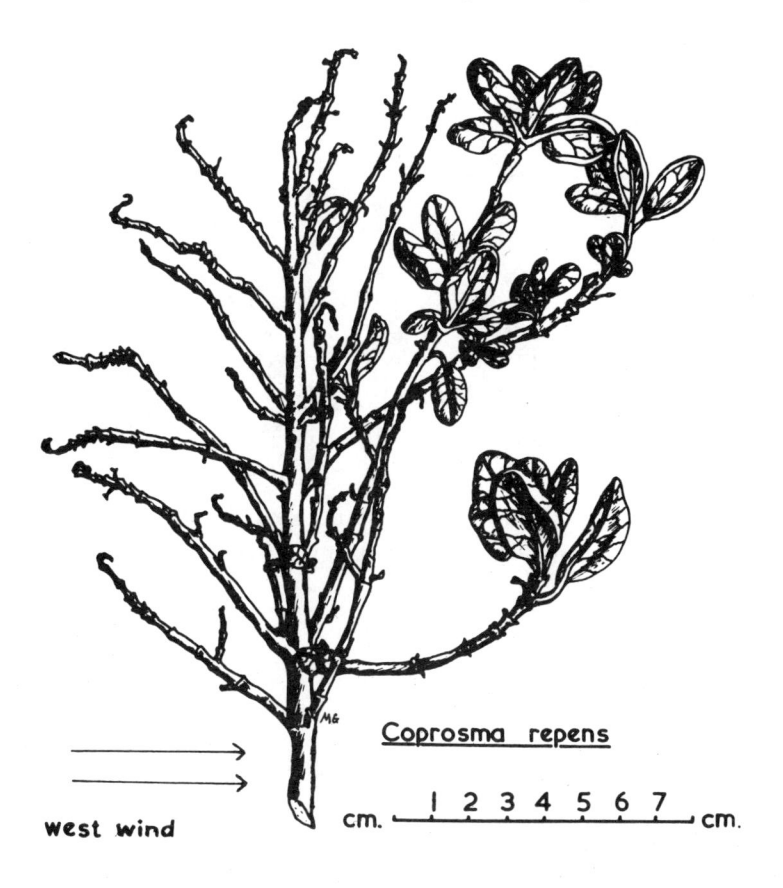

67 Wind-scorched Taupata *Coprosma repens*

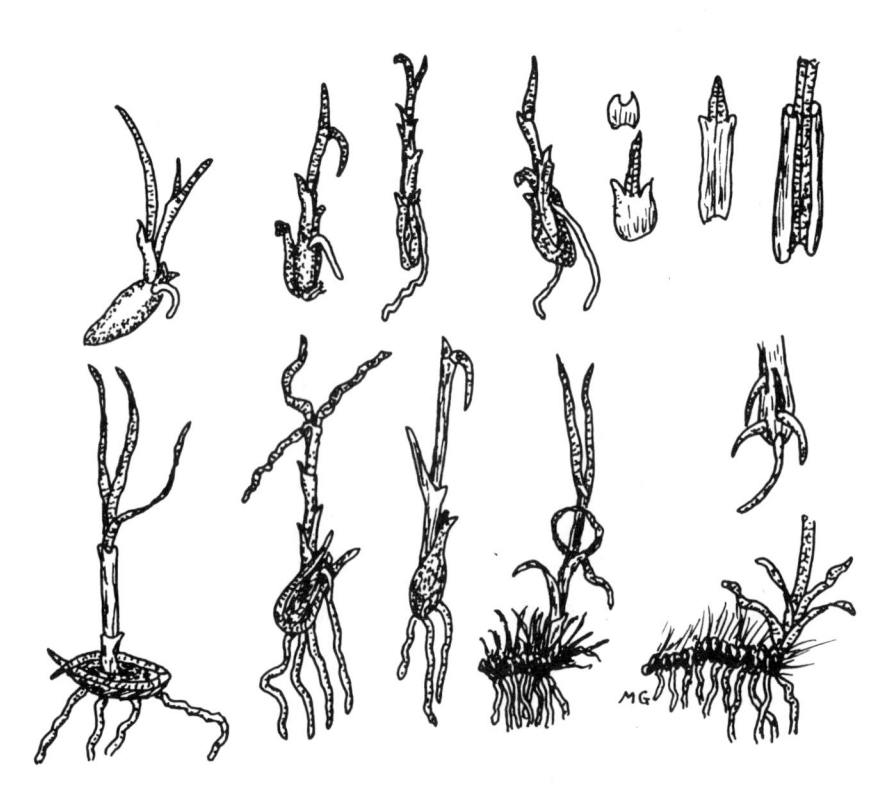

68 Germinating Strap-weed Seedlings *Posidonia australis*

2. OUR RESIDENT MUTTON BIRDS

For me, as a botanist, Fisher Island was just a convenient place to stay while I radiated out to other islands for surveys of sites grazed and ungrazed, burrowed and unburrowed, burned and unburned. For the folk engaged in the mutton bird studies, it was the hub of their activities.

In the decade from 1947 when the current study began, the entire mutton bird population of Fisher Island had been banded (or ringed). The total of 1,196 bands used signified fewer birds, because some of these were replacements for lost identification marks. For the first three years copper leg bands were used but these, like the aluminium ones commonly employed for land birds because of their lightness, were unable to withstand corrosion by sea water and scuffling in the burrows by wearers unable to stand erect because of the backward displacement of the legs to aid swimming. Shuffling along in a squatting position entailed considerable abrasion and few bands lasted for as much as three years.

A change was made to Monel metal bands in 1950. These were much more durable, as they had need to be with birds living for thirty or forty years. Both resident adults and fledgelings on the eve of their departure for the sea were ringed on Cat Island as well as Fisher.

On the commercially harvested islands only a random sample of fledgelings was marked each March, just before the harvest began, and it was hoped that the harvesters would hand in any rings from the birds which they caught to give information on the percentage take. The veracity of such data was suspect, not only because harvesters might seek to avoid censure for taking too high a toll, but because burrows most accessible to the ringers were also those most accessible to the harvesters. Perhaps the one factor would cancel out the other...

The ringing yielded data on various aspects of the birds' lives. Some would provide figures for longevity, as well as the age that breeding maturity was reached: also whether birds were faithful to their chosen mate, to their original burrow and to their natal island. This was a simple matter to check where burrows as well as birds were numbered.

Even more valuable, but harder to come by, was information about their trans-equatorial migration between breeding seasons, as these depended on recoveries elsewhere. In fact, most of the foreign recoveries were of first-year birds which became casualties, either from an insufficiency of food or an over-sufficiency of gales or a combination of both. The least experienced, immature birds are inevitably the most vulnerable and their corpses sometimes wash up on East Australian beaches in large numbers.

A migration route had already been postulated by observations of unmarked birds, both at sea and stranded on alien shores. A remarkable figure of eight pattern had been traced around the Pacific Ocean across to New Zealand, back to Japan and north to wintering grounds in the chillier seas of the Bering Strait and off Alaska, but this had to be modified in the light of subsequent recoveries.

First records of the species had come, uncharacteristically, from the non-breeding territory in the North. The first sighting was by a Russian in 1755, the first painting, among ice floes between America and Asia, was done in 1778 and the first surviving museum skin was taken off Alaska between 1787 and 1791. These early records reflect the greater number of mariners sailing high latitude seas in the North than in the South during that era.

The shearwaters' home run might be down the Californian coast and across the great ocean to New South Wales. Only on this westerly lap are the flocks usually denied the benefit of a following wind. This is a zone of constant South-east Trades and this was the ultimate test of their fitness. If the krill and anchovies on which they depended were in short supply during this crucial period, there could be heavy mortality among the younger birds.

Southern bluefin tuna depend on the same sort of food. When this dwindles the tuna are able to go elsewhere, as the birds headed for home on a tight date schedule are not. It soon became evident that New South Wales fishermen could not expect good tuna catches if many mutton bird casualties were washed up, this being a sure sign of famine. In 1939-40, when tuna were most abundant and bird casualties fewest, there was an unprecedented glut of anchovies providing luxurious feasting for both types of predator.

Subsequent ringing recoveries up to the end of the twentieth century have modified the route as postulated by Serventy in 1953. Data from Japanese fishing vessels have shown that the majority of birds move north up the western side of the Pacific to Alaska and back down the centre, converging on the Australian coast as before, but not necessarily via California.

Sadly, the data from Japanese fishermen too often came from casualties. As established by Everett, Pitman and Johnson in 1993, short-tailed shearwaters are among the most abundant sea birds on the salmon drift net fishing grounds. King and Ogi in 1984 calculated that between 132,000 and 281,000 mutton birds were drowned annually in the drift nets, this level of slaughter continuing until December 1992, when drift netting was banned on the high seas outside the 300 km EEZ (Exclusive Economic Zone) of individual countries. Thereafter the number drowned in the nets, in both the Northern and Southern Hemispheres, dropped to around 40,000 a year.

In one of these fisheries seventy to eighty per cent of the casualties were fledgelings and accounted for nought point two per cent of the mutton bird population. In the Southern Hemisphere an unknown number, mostly adults, were being caught in the Southern Bluefin Tuna Fisheries within Australia's 300 km EEZ according to Rosemary Gale of the Tasmanian Parks and Wildlife Service.

Losses of albatrosses, porpoises and dolphins by similar means are more widely publicised, but this catastrophic waste of the world's bounty can occur among any of the air-breathing, deep-diving animals which inhabit our seas.

By my mid-1990's visit, the mutton bird population of Fisher Island had dwindled for another reason. Lady Barron by this time was a thriving urban community, blazing with lights now that individual generators were no longer the only source of electricity, and many of the fledgelings leaving the island on their maiden flight flew into the lights and died. It seems possible that a population too squeamish or conservation-orientated to kill the birds directly, might still be dining on them.

Irynej Skira of the University of Tasmania, whom I had the pleasure of meeting in 1985, carried on the Fisher Island work where Dominic Serventy left off after his last visit in 1976, twelve years before his death. Irynej provided the continuity of record keeping and was still at it in 1995, with all the resident birds ringed and stricter laws in force in relation to landings, with their threat of the trampling of burrows.

During the years between silver gulls had been using Fisher Island for both roosting and nesting and had spread halfway across it, killing the vegetation and battening down the topsoil hindering the opening of new burrows. They perched on the hut roof and fouled the contents of the drinking water tank — a reprehensible practice, as they fed largely on offal from the fish processing factory at Lady Barron. Poisoning had pushed the tide of gulls back by my November 1995 visit and the plant cover was well on the way to recovery.

At the beginning of the 1960 season, it seemed to me that the Fisher Island mutton birds had been roaming the oceans on migration for long enough to have forgotten that the frequent handling in their nesting colony did them no lasting harm. The early-comers fought back, so a special contraption was devised to hold them while the ring number was being read.

The idea was fine: a metal cone with two slots to allow the legs to poke outside, but the actuality was a non-event. The apparatus became known as 'The Thing' or 'The Infernal Machine' and its ineffectiveness when I was doing the patrols alone, moved me once more to fabricate some frustrated doggerel verse. When Dom insisted that I press on with the task in hand the dialogue went something like this:

THE THING

"But this cruel task I've done before" quoth Mary with distaste.
"My hands and wrists get pecked quite raw and all my pains are waste
Because, when birds have ceased to maul as much as they can reach
They flap off with triumphant call and make towards the beach."

"But Fisher Island birds are tame," quoth Dom, the expert birder.
"They've been conditioned to their fame; they know we would not murder;
And so they treat us gently now, as they themselves are treated.
So, when they jab their beak at you, just take it you are greeted!"

And so 'The Thing' grew 'neath his hand: a tapered thing of metal.
"Just pop the bird in as you stand, like dormouse into kettle,
Then pull a leg out through a hole and read the number on it;
Just write it down and, 'pon my soul, you'll find you've gone and done it."

So, nothing daunted, Mary tried. The thing she held in one hand,
But knew quite well that Dom had lied when trying to find the leg band.
Her spare hand round the bird did clasp, her third was on her notebook.
Her fourth held pencil, fifth held lamp — but what a hopeless outlook!

The bird at last was in the cone, but way beyond the leg slits.
It moaned a most distressing moan as she hauled upon its tail bits.
A leg came out: there was no ring. Another blank. "Oh bother!
What use is this confounded thing; I don't know one from t'other."

At last two legs came out at once, but still they were not numbered.
Unlettered, yes, but not a dunce, now he was unencumbered.
The broad end of the thing was wide and freedom lay beyond.
He turned himself about inside: a whoop and he was gone.

There was more, but that sums up the situation fairly accurately. Fundamentally the apparatus was too big, with ample room for the bird to turn (as worms are prone to), but not enough to be pushed in unless the wings were pinioned first. The keyhole slits were the wrong way round and the loop for attaching to the belt useless, as night patrols were conducted in siren suits or oilskins without belts.

I was unlucky with the victim that inspired those verses. An unringed bird had to be a newcomer to that closely monitored scene. No wonder it wasn't conditioned to being handled like the old-timers. Even a licenced ringer, which I was not, might have had trouble single-handed.

I fared little better, however, with seventeen-year-old 12247, picked out by my torch beam as it peered expectantly round a tussock. A respected patriarch of the island hierarchy, mated faithfully to the same partner for the past ten years, he knew the routine and waited patiently to be picked up.

But this was not like the old days. He took as great an exception to the 'infernal machine' as I had. Shedding all traces of decorum, he disappeared into its interior with a shriek of consternation. In all his respected career, he had never been subjected to such an indignity! A spread wing came out through each leg slit and, using them as pivots, he described a couple of youthful somersaults.

I helped him out and, to his lasting credit, he seemed not to associate those gentle rescuing hands with the strange engine of terror. Whatever his thoughts, if any, he sat quietly while I smoothed his ruffled feathers and read his ring number. Maybe Dom was right, his birds WERE conditioned. He and his disciples had worked a little miracle in making silk purses out of those free-spirited sows' ears.

Another unringed bird picked up was as unruly as the first, falling out of the funnel twice. Too late, I realised that it was unringed and in the same place as before, outside burrow number 188, and in all probability the same bird. There was no question of feather stroking here. It slipped rapidly into a burrow — probably someone else's — leaving the pale moonlight to the distant calling of waders that seemed to be passing in huge numbers.

* * * * *

From 9th February 1960, after a fortnight on my own, I was to enjoy the stimulating company of Michael Ridpath and his French wife, Paula. Newly emigrated from Surrey in the UK via the ANZAAS scientific meeting in Perth, Michael was swapping his study of wood pigeons for the British Ministry of Agriculture for one on the Tasmanian native hen for CSIRO. They had bought a house in Hobart as a base for Tasmania-wide field work.

Michael had been asked to send a bacteriologist three live shearwater chicks by air, to enable a suspected infection to be investigated. These could obviously not be taken from the fully documented Fisher Island study group, so they planned to spend a night on Little Green Island and arranged for a boat to get them to Flinders in time to meet the 8 a.m. mail bus for Whitemark. Needless to say, it didn't work out that way. The folk who say, "Oh yes, you'll be on the Furneaux Group. Send us a few birds by such and such a time," can have little idea of the complexity of the logistics involved.

There was no chance of Tuck getting them to Little Green Island under the changed wind pattern and torrential rain: he was fully occupied making three attempts to board his boat to move her to a safer anchorage. Unable to reach it in his own little dinghy, he had to engage the services of a motorised cray boat, whose propeller was out of the water for much of the time, making for haphazard steering.

In view of the sheeting rain, it was just as well, as we had failed to get a key to the Green Island hut and had only one tarpaulin between us: fine for sleeping out in dry weather but not in this. I cried off when they finally went, because we could only muster half a dozen cordial bottles for drinking water and that was barely adequate for two. There was a rain tank, but this was hermetically sealed, and we had no wrench to prise the rusted tap open.

When they landed on the opposite shore, ten geese honked their way across to Fisher, returning after half and hour. Michael and Paula brought back no chicks, but, between them, they had picked up four ringed birds on Little Green that proved of more immediate interest.

One, ringed on Fisher Island in 1950, had been missing, believed lost, for the eight years since 1952, proving that breeding adults may change islands in mid-career.

The first case of such infidelity to the natal island was recorded by Dom

Serventy for number 12458, a cock bird breeding on Fisher Island in 1951 and 1952 with the same mate, but found, assumed breeding, on Little Green Island in 1954 two-thirds of a mile away. His original spouse remained faithful to Fisher Island, but changed partners at least every second year. Could she have been difficult to live with? Dom's early records showed that, by far and away the majority of birds returned, not only to the island of their birth in subsequent seasons, but to the same part of it and often the same burrow. By 1984, however, it had become clear that only forty per cent of the breeding population on Fisher Island had hatched there themselves. (Serventy and Currie, 1984).

Two other birds picked up by the Ridpaths were two-year-olds ringed as fledgelings, one on Great Dog Island and the other on Fisher Island — proving that youngsters prospect on islands other than their own and that they did so at an earlier age than had originally been thought. Maybe this exploration of new sites was why they had been missed earlier, when only three, four and five-year-old pre-breeders had been found ashore.

Recoveries of ringed one and two-year-olds off the New South Wales coast had shown that these youngsters accompanied the main population on their migration from the northern summer where they wintered to the southern summer where their elders bred, but it was suspected that they remained at sea while in the South.

Three and four-year-olds came ashore regularly, but later in the season in January, February and March. Non-breeding five, six and seven-year-olds, and a very occasional fourth year bird, came in with the adults at egg-laying time in November and December, but were off again in January when the chicks began to hatch. (If we chose to be anthropomorphic, we might wonder if they were escaping the possibility of being expected to help with the feeding.)

The Ridpath's fourth find was a four-year-old ringed on Babel Island, ten to fifteen miles away from Little Green. Were these youngsters seriously considering setting up home in foreign parts, or were they merely sowing their wild oats, we wondered?

As a botanist interested in the spread of wild plants from island to island, I had always pooh-poohed the idea of seed transport by these essentially ocean-going birds, believing them to come ashore on one island only. It seemed not. They were as likely to sow their wild weed seeds as other young things. While they fed only at sea, with no possibility of depositing seeds in crop pellets or dung, there was still the more remote chance of carrying weed fragments on plumage or legs.

As valuable providers of data for the scientific records, these four special individuals were not sacrificed to the bacteriologists, so another expedition was undertaken to Little Green Island. We paddled the birds obtained across to Lady Barron, to find that the 8 a.m. mail bus ran only on Monday, Wednesday and Friday. There was just time to intercept the 8.20 a.m. school bus at the crossroads, where Derek Smith's daughter, Lynette, was the prefect in charge of a bevy of lively five to fifteen-year-olds. The bus driver accepted the mutton birds, the unstamped mail and some loose cash with equanimity, as though he did this sort of thing every day.

Before shopping and loading the dinghy with stores, we went to inspect a supposed shoreline gull roost which proved less populous than it had seemed. The white give-away smudges assumed to be guano, turned out to be lichens. On the return journey we dropped off on Reef Island, where the caspian terns which had successfully brought up a brood, had created a large bare patch in the carpet of pigface.

By 1995 a pair of the rare white-fronted terns had moved in to breed on Reef Island, where it seemed the black-faced shags no longer did so, and two pairs of crested terns had nested on Fisher Island.

On 1st March, after seeing a fellow islander off on the school bus for the plane, I got into conversation with the Fauna Board's mutton bird health inspector, who was seriously worried about the quite uninhibited taking of birds for cray bait and the lack of policing. This was done so blatantly that skippers chatting to each other on the ships' radios would announce that they were just off to Babel to get more birds. The local watchdogs, including the Cat Island wardens, had been supplied with radios which worked on a different frequency band and so could not latch on to the illegal practices. The trooper had a tendency to be away in Launceston during the crucial periods or turning a blind eye. We, on Fisher, would have been happy to have a radio working on any band to save reliance on smoke signals, but that was no more likely than the acquisition of a manageable dinghy!

Penguin populations were becoming seriously depleted as well. Mauled penguins washed out of cray pots, found their way onto the beaches, while pots found to contain penguins remained unclaimed, although they could often be identified by their position.

"Caufes all over the sound: full of crays for weeks before the season opens and boats coming in with four to five full loads during the first few days of legal sales, in spite of losses to octopi and others" said Frank.

Perhaps the near extermination of crays would be a means of saving the bait species. Fortunately it didn't come to that: both birds and crayfish seemed to be doing fine during my 1990's visit.

69 Development of Short-tailed Shearwater Chick *Puffinus tenuirostris*

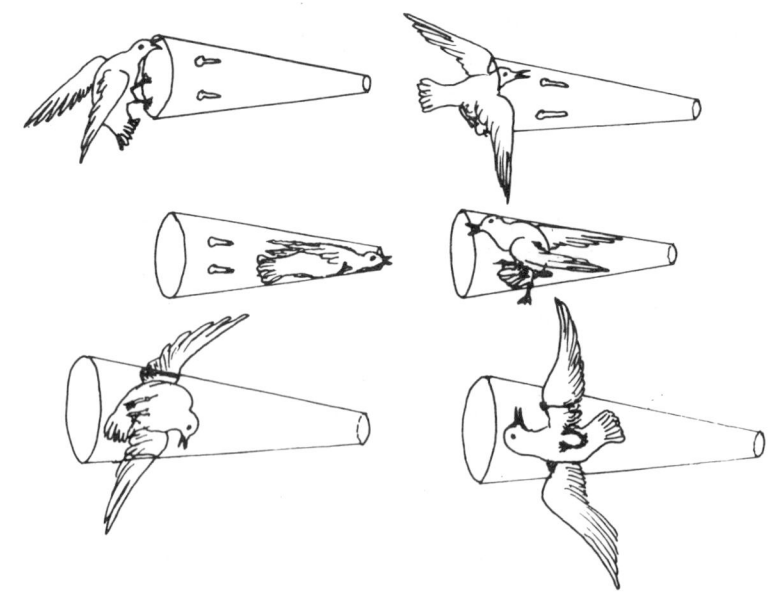

70 "The Thing"

71 Shearwaters *Puffinus tenuirostris* taking off at dawn

3. LIFE BETWEEN THE TIDES

One calm moonlit night, I introduced Michael and Paula to the awesome nocturnal raspings of the limpets. The big, orange-edged *Cellana solida* were much the commonest, forming an intermittent belt around the island, although preferring tumbles of boulders which provided differently angled feeding opportunities. Almost as large were the pyramidal *Patelloida alticostata*, moving, with the others, across the green films of *Rivularia australis* algae and sporelings of green *Enteromorpha* and red *Bostrychia mixta*.

Limpets avoided downshore rocks coated with limey tubes of marine worms, *Galeolaria caespitosa*, where the going became uncomfortably rough. Nor were they willing to graze across the rugose shells of the rough-beaked mussels *(Austromytilus* (or *Hormomya) erosus)* which clustered around South Point.

Fresh from my capers with 'The Thing', I wondered idly about the keyhole shaped slot in the shell apex of the keyhole limpets *(Amblychilepas javanicensis)*, which reminded me of the apical gap for poles in an Indian tepee. It seemed to defeat the object of manufacturing a limey tent against the outside world.

When the animals were submerged, a little 'chimney pot' protruded through the keyhole, this a siphon used for the expulsion of unwanted fluids. On the hoof under water the living mantle flowed up the outside of the shell, as in ambulant cowries, whose shells remained so unblemished and highly polished in consequence.

Siphon holes appear again, in duplicate, in the abalone or ear shells, biggest of all the limpets, whose shells show the rudiments of a spiral leading on to the helix of the typical snail form of single-shelled molluscs. Here the holes are in line, new ones forming as the shell grows and the old ones fuse shut. There are usually five holes open at any one time for penetration by the exhalant siphons.

Fisher Island supported a population of the brightly hued Emma's ear shell *(Neohaliotis* (or *Marinaurus) emmae)*, as well as the more widespread blacklip or knotted ear shell *(Notohaliotis ruber)*. This last grazes over the rocks as limpets graze, but also reaches out more adventurously to pull in sea-grasses and seaweeds floating past.

This is when they are most at risk from predatory fish nipping in to take a bite of some of the exposed flesh. Mostly they 'cling like limpets', only moreso, and can only be prised from their hold with a stout tool — not by fingers, which could easily become trapped, as by a giant clam.

Only when clamped to the rock among sheltering kelps are they virtually immune from enemies other than eagle rays, sting rays or even large parrotfish, which have teeth capable of crushing their shells. Little ones are vulnerable to many predators, from crayfish and octopus to starfish and even whelks.

Another species, the greenlip ear shell *(Haliotis* (or *Schismotis) laevigata)* relies almost entirely on capturing sea-grasses and the red seaweeds which grow attached to these, scarcely bothering to graze and generally avoiding green and brown seaweeds.

During my three seasons on Fisher Island, no-one was particularly interested in abalones, except as pretty shells for ashtrays or pin trays, but a commercial fishery started up four years later in 1964. Catch size and the number of catchers were severely limited and licences to catch were expensive. Such firmly clamped animals cannot be dredged from the sea bed but are sitting targets when it comes to prising them off with hand tools, so the haul needs to be regulated. Divers may locate them down to depths of twenty fathoms (forty metres).

Another local shell fishery concentrates on scallops, the largest of which is the king scallop *(Pecten meridionalis)*. These are dragged from the sea bottom in a pair of dredges, each catching some of the animals disturbed by the other and making a jet-propelled escape by opening and closing the paired shells in underwater flight. There were hand-processing plants for these at Lady Barron and just outside Whitemark, where producers had to meet their export quotas, so that there were few left for the locals. The scallop fishery was closed in 1987.

A quite charming creature which we came upon occasionally was a five to seven cm long salmon pink butterfly crayfish. The golden pinpoints of light reflected from the stalked eyes of the myriad shrimps, sparkled like a bevy of female glow-worms soliciting partners out of the sky.

These transparent but vaguely mud-coloured crustaceans clung to the rock with their hind claws while waving exploratory white pincers ahead, ever busy, transferring edible morsels to the mouth faster than our eyes could follow.

What were remarkably visible in the torchlight were the living components of the plankton soup in which they lived, many of the organisms pale and wigglesome. We felt that a strainer would have been a more effective method of gaining a meal than those animated pliers.

The shrimp population, almost unnoticed by day, was enormous. Each animal, three to four cm long, was spaced only twice this distance from its near neighbours in all directions — like delicacies spread on a table for the pleasure of larger diners.

Fragile red and yellow crabs clattered over surfaces peopled by larger, purple-clawed ones during the day. These tweaked their food from the rocks, leaving others to strain the goodies from the water, their pincers working like clockwork, as though encountering no shortage. Both pincers were used for feeding, but only one for locomotion. They gave the impression of short-sightedness, showing no reaction to a hand moved in front of the stalked eyes, but scurrying to safety at the slightest rock tremor.

I amused myself some nights by allowing a foraging crab to walk onto my foot, then lifting it into the air and watching the perplexed search for a safe passage hence. The imperturbability of nocturnal crabs was in sharp contrast to the wariness of their daytime counterparts.

Fingerling fish flipped from rock to rock while larger ones flicked the water into silver flurries further from the shore. Occasionally a fourteen-inch fish, transversely striped in brown and buff, would move past, these not the common toadies but more elegantly salmon shaped.

Small octopi ballooned past, the octet of arms pulsating like a rubberised parasol. The bright green encrusting coral was something of a surprise, the chlorophyll-packed polyps forming bright stars in the limey matrix, the colonies more or less circular and up to twenty-five cm across. Arthur Harland presented us with a fluted lace coral of exquisite beauty and much more delicate than the reef builders of further north.

Most obvious on our daytime forays, apart from the ever present acorn barnacles and molluscs, were the big, pink-spined sea urchins. We never tired of watching the synchrony of the prongs as these ambled across the sea bed. My mind returned inevitably to the 'sea eggs' served up by the Motiti Island Maoris as hors d'oevres to a memorable repast of mutton bird and suckling pig.

It was odd that we were seeing these as commonly as we were, because both *Amblypneustes ovum* and *Goniocidaris tubaria*, the two species present, usually live in five to ten fathoms of water and come to light most often in fishermen's trawl nets, although obviously at home intertidally here.

February 10th brought a low spring tide when we waded round to our hearts' content finding new treasures. The pipefish suspended vertically and almost invisibly among the sea-grass had been thought by our recent companion, the dentist, MacDonald, to be a new species.

Innocent looking tufts just exposed by the tide were liable to shoot out a jet of water. Investigation revealed jellified purple sea squirts or cunjevoi *(Pyura stolonifera)* below the camouflaging weed, sitting so peaceably on the sea floor that the plants had no more difficulty in growing on them than on the shells of the ponderously ambulant limpets.

The encrusting ridged sponge, *Hymeniacidon perlevis*, its grey colonies up to a foot across, cushioned more sea squirts and yellowish tufts of the frondose weed, *Gelidium australe*, whose UK counterparts are dark red.

It was the more shapely sponges drifted in from deeper levels that I found most fascinating. They came fluted, flanged or fanned, cup-shaped or branched, red, orange, pink, blue and every permutation of yellow and brown. Represented were *Thorecta, Peysonellia, Stelospongia* and many more.

The *Posidonia* seeds located three weeks before were now, in the third week of February, germinating in regimented rows along crevices and in platoons on shingly mud lower down. Fleshy green cotyledons showed little deflation, even when the first leaves were eight to ten cm long and creeping stems had begun to creep forth. With noontide temperatures consistently up in the eighties and unlimited water, food manufacture was keeping up with growth needs, with no necessity to draw on parental supplies.

The twenty-second of February 1960, scout and guide thinking day, brought news of the birth of the queen's second son, Prince Andrew, and the death of Viscountess Mountbatten. I spent part of it sending three stinky wallaby carcases on their way. They had been gently fermenting for days in an embayment of the south coast. Gutted, they had probably been jettisoned from a cray boat when they got too high to tolerate. Contentedly squirming blowfly maggots were providing a bonanza for the birds.

I guided them out with a stick, helping them on their way down channel with hurled stones when I lost touch. It was a revelation, watching them, to realise the complexity of back-tracking in the swirling coastal currents. Was it only my imagination that the stalked eyes of crabs deprived of many days' rations glared so balefully from among maggot-strewn tufts of sodden fur?

Next day we knocked up sightings of 118 sooty oystercatchers and fifty-seven pieds, two of the latter swimming just offshore. This they achieved with competence, riding quite buoyantly, but they had difficulty taking off, flapping valiantly along the water surface to no avail. Instead of turning back to wade ashore and join the rest, they went paddling and flapping downwind towards Little Green Island until lost to sight.

Tasmanian native hens, which resemble our moorhens, have neither foot webs nor flanges, but are expert swimmers, both on and under the surface. Not so the great white egret that called today, the first I had seen on Fisher Island, but with legs so long that there was no need.

* * * * *

At the end of the month, after a spell camping on Little Green Island, we entertained two locals and learned more of our marine neighbours. One, with a name sounding like Orrie Broome, worked as a crayfish packer and part time fisherman. The other, Norman Perrott, was the son of the Englishman who was always busy carpentering and painting around Island Stores.

Perrott was round quite often in his little boat catching fish of one to two pounds weight, probably the metallic blue garfish. With an average catch of twelve a day and a price of three shillings and tuppence a pound, he could make £3.6.0. a day or £20 a week: small beer compared with the takings of cray fishermen, for whom a single big six pound cray might be worth £1.10.0.

Our visitors said a Bennets wallaby costing 7/6 would bait six pots, a rufous wallaby three, but others doubled these figures. No doubt bigger bait attracted bigger takers. They feared, like others, that crayfish would soon be fished out now that they were located by echo sounders. Thirty-five years later, however, the industry seemed still to be in a healthy state.

Nobody bothered to collect crabs, with so rich a harvest of crays for the taking, but crabs took each other. It was not uncommon on our night prowls to see a big crab tweaking the legs off a little crab one by one and carrying the legless body off with a gloating expression in the fierce little eyes. Crabs can grow new limbs if allowed to live until the next moult, but only if a decent proportion of the original ten are available for locomotion in the interim.

The two fisher boys told us that salmon and tuna were plentiful around Cat Island at that time and were being located from spotter bi-planes, whose crews saw the shoals as moving shadows.

It was seldom that mutton birds regurgitated food except directly into their chick's gullet and we were surprised when three broke this rule on one of our night patrols, allowing us to inspect the food. Instead of the expected mass of shrimpy krill, we found several fish fillets, each about ten cm long, embedded in grey slime. Was this usual, we wondered, or was the large size of the prey the reason for the premature ejection by the parent or rejection by the chick?

On leap day, February 29th, when Michael and Paula had left, Perrott presented us with the great grandfather of all crayfish. It was too big to have been caught off our shores and was probably a Babel animal escaped from one of the caufes. While he finished getting his pots up, we drowned our prize in cold fresh water and boiled up sugar and sea water in the camp oven. The appendages were stowed into the pot with difficulty, but the instructions to take it out in half an hour were ignored, because it was all hands on deck then to avert a crisis. The ebb had left Norman's heavily built pine craft with outboard motor settled firmly on the sea bed and it needed a combined effort to get it back into the water, levering and heaving with poles.

Three of us dined on the cray's legs, then we moved outside to the gulls' eating place and, with their help, demolished some of the bittier foreparts. There was still enough left for me on the morrow, although Minette Ross, my companion at the time, took the whole tail back to Melbourne. All but the tail would have been wasted if this animal had been processed with the rest.

Norman, who was farming in Oxfordshire before emigrating with his parents eight years before, said he sometimes got pipefish in his pots and promised to bring us some, in case they were the suspected new species. After finishing lining in and re-colouring Glen Storr's 1952 vegetation map, which had faded almost into oblivion during its eight years hanging on "Yolla's" wall, Minette and I did the mutton bird round. One of our catches (12398) was a cock bird who had been breeding in the Home Rookery for the past eleven years. Another caught a week later (12302) was also an old faithful, recorded regularly for the past twelve years.

The night of 6th March 1960 saw the last wallowings of "Half Safe". After weeks of westerlies we were experiencing the tail end of a freak easterly storm which had hit Sydney, breaking up a surf boat there and stirring things up generally. Savage rain squalls smacked at "Yolla's" windows and sent silver cascades through the roof onto the table. I feared for the boat and was glad I had retrieved oars, rowlocks and baler before retiring.

It was high water when I woke, to find she had dragged her anchor but that the safety line had held. During a brief battle, during which the sea-filled hull did nothing to help, I satisfied myself that she was fast again. She had fought gallantly against this thing that had hit her, but it was a losing battle. A land-lubber boat, spending most of her time out of the water, she was no better fitted to weather this sea than I was to get her out of it.

Both the middle seats had broken away from their stays, water gushed through an open seam to starboard every time she rolled and daylight was visible through the portside seams. Despite all the unkind things I had said of her in the past, I was sad to see her thus. She was no more responsible for her inadequacies than I was and she HAD served me, if wetly, for three seasons. Every true Englishman has a soft spot for a boat and it was, perhaps, fitting that the one who had been alone with her for so long should witness her fall.

Three seams were wedged open with small stones and shells, one plank had split across and she had spread to such an extent that the cross seats were now much too short to be lodged back in position.

Breakfast went down in gulps. I was already in mourning, the thoughts of that 'joyous funeral' somehow inappropriate. I had a mind to tear up those earlier verses: Dom would suspect me of sabotage. "*Tassie*" was beached in Petrifaction Bay, only the top of her crazily angled mast visible, and Perrott was no longer tending his pots. It was a poor lookout for next week's visitors. During the evening I managed to waylay Murray Holloway, who thought it all a huge joke and suggested we might get the use of the police boat's dinghy for the next week.

""*Aralla*'s" just back from Launceston and the skipper'll need a week to recover."

It was high water, so Murray took "Half Safe" in tow. Her contents swilled aft and her bow reared out of the sea like a breaching whale. A flock of around 400 waders converged in a fly past, a fitting funeral cortege — or would some ill advised person attempt a repair?

John Thomson, zoologist, arrived on schedule. There was no question of using "*Aralla*'s" dinghy. Lew Bailey brought John across in a dinghy borrowed from a fisherman without permission, knowing that he could be lenient with himself if the matter was reported to the police. We both went back with him and spent several hours zigzagging among the boating fraternity, to emerge finally with an extended loan of "*Victoria II*'s dinghy, "*Nyla*".

By mid-March 1960 things began to get busy on Fisher Island. Myckytowycx, Hesterman and Thomson were whisked off to Great Dog during breakfast on the 12th and I was left with a Mad Hatter's tea party as I moved from one cup of coffee to the next. Two farming couples from Western Australia, Syd and Rica Erikson and Walter and Alison Meston, were expected later in the day, so it was just as well the others had gone if we were all to fit. I went across in "*Nyla*" — a splendidly easy row — and we made two journeys to get the gear over, with a walk up Vinegar Hill in between to see the panorama at its brightest and best.

The bush was full of blue wrens and we saw flame robins and English blackbirds. This was normal enough, but the three black cockatoos which later preceded a flight of geese over Fisher Island was a first for me, so far out to sea.

The Great Dog trio reappeared after a few days for stores and then left; the four Westralians returned home and the VIP trio arrived: Dom Serventy or "Der Ruthless Fuehrer" as he was known at the time, Tas Drysdale (artist) and Eric Worrell (Snake man).

The men sent me down to the shore to sing an alluring "Lorelei" when Norman Perrott made the first round of his pots. I returned with two fine crayfish, ten shillings each, and even the mutton birds had to take second place. There was insufficient rain water left in the little tank for death by drowning, so Dom killed the crays by inserting a scalpel in the central nerve ganglion in the mid-back. People scurried to get sea water and firewood and the bigger cray was stowed into the camp oven. We demolished the lot except for a few scraps earmarked by Tas for fish bait and Dom for rat bait. The second went the same way next day, then Frank Henwood presented me with another, laced with tomatoes and home-grown grapes, when I went ashore. Riches indeed!

The store could produce no batteries for Drysdale's electric shaver. A big torch battery was run to earth and Dom held onto the contact while Tas shaved. This was a penance for insisting on rowing us ashore in his usual muddle-headed way and running us aground. After retrieving his lost trilby from the sea, I waded thigh-deep to push the boat off, but refused to do so again in my best trousers when the same thing happened on the way in to a social evening. Eric volunteered and pushed us back and forth over the shoals until Dom could be dissuaded from seeking a new route.

It was a hilarious evening, thanks in no small part to our charming snake charmer's charm. He was always in need of more snakes, which he milked for their venom to produce a vital supply of anti-venene for snake bite sufferers. His stays in the Furneaux Group were partly holiday and partly for stocking up with new venom supplies. He paid Derek Smith £2 for every live snake over four feet long, £5 each for wombats and £2.10 for wallabies, plus expenses. Not long after, Derek produced two wombats — filmed on the fowl run fence looking like chubby koalas.

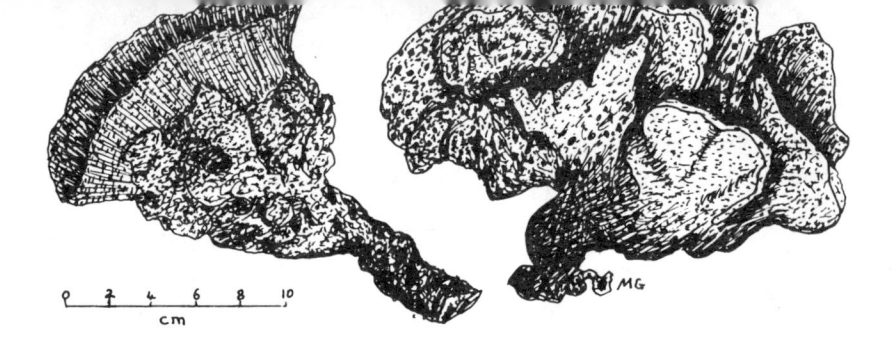

72 Funnel-shaped *Thorecta* and Fingered *Peyssonellia* Sponges

73 Black-faced Cormorants *Leucocarbo fuscescens*

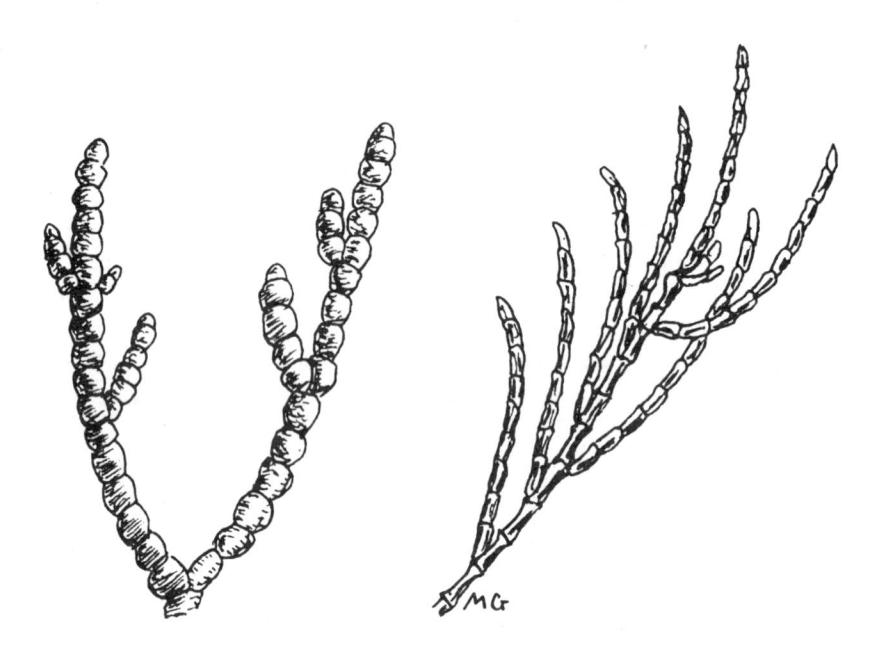

74 Black's Glasswort *Sarcocornia blackiana* and Beaded Glasswort *Sarcocornia quinqueflora*

Chapter Nine

GOING TO THE DOGS

1. ROOKERY FIRES ON LITTLE AND GREAT DOG ISLANDS

Eric, Dell and I were squatting on the deck of the police boat, "*Aralla*" on the first of three January visits to Little Dog Island in 1958. We were headed south-west, our craft nearly twice the size of Tuck's "*Tassie*" (forty-eight feet as opposed to twenty-eight feet) and the ride was that much smoother and drier on this account.

Silas Mansell, Trooper Bailey's usual half-caste crew man, was 'on the beer' and not available for work, so two small boys, Rex and George, were standing in. Silas, a boat owner himself, crewed for various skippers, but the cash acquired in the process burned a hole in his pocket if not immediately transformed into alcohol and taken internally. The big money earned during the mutton bird harvest was expended in one glorious autumnal binge with his contemporaries.

Rex and George assured me they had ten brothers and three sisters and that the whole tribe went birding for six weeks from mid-March — or had done until now when the long summertime Christmas hols were deferred until March to fit with the local culture. (I thought back to the potato-picking October holidays of home.) The withdrawal of this concession to conform with mainland schools, as from 1958, was posing many family problems.

No-one on Flinders could be expected to take on fifteen unruly youngsters while Mum and Dad went birding, and youngsters denied the fun of their accustomed spell of untrammelled freedom on their island were likely to wax more unruly than usual. It looked as though there would be a lot of absenteeism from the classrooms this year.

Most of Little Dog's 200 acres was one vast mutton bird rookery, but the number of birds taken annually was steadily decreasing. Around thirty-seven years before, in the early 1920s, the annual take at harvest time was 90,000 birds, 30,000 passing through each of three family birding huts. Twenty years later, in the early 1940s, 80,000 chicks were exported. Now, in the late 1950s, numbers varied between 15,000 and 30,000, depending on who you were talking to. These were the product of only two establishments, the third having burned down.

It was estimated that, to avoid the feared imposition of restrictions, only half the leg bands from slaughtered chicks were returned to the research project, so it was difficult to assess the present status of the population. With so long a period of immaturity, too many chicks could be taken for six or seven years before any diminution in the number of breeders would become apparent.

"Chicks are taken almost to the last bird. The stock is fast dying out." This from Lew Bailey.

"Six or seven burrows empty to every one full this year — but the burrows in the fog grass on the east of the island have been empty for ten years." This from Tuck Robinson, whose family harvested both here and on Great Dog Island.

"Thirty thousand birds from forty acres on Little Dog and the same number from forty acres on Great Dog. Plenty of burrows in box", (seaberry saltbush) "barilla" (coast saltbush) "and fennel" (fireweed *(Senecio capillifolius)*), "but can't get at them. These are the worst possible to go birding in, but the birds like them alright." This from Tuck again.

These patches of denser vegetation might have proved the birds' salvation if the annual cull had become too drastic, but the industry seemed to be dying a natural and painless death with the increasing affluence and changed attitudes of the nineties. Just as the wildfowling for gannet and puffin chicks on the Scottish islands had died long before!

"Grass burning is very severe. Sometimes the whole island is set on fire at once. Then none of the burrows are hidden, so none of the young birds are missed."

Except, hopefully, those in thick underbrush. It seems it had always been thus during the past century. Canon Brownrigg wrote in 1870: "Little Dog Island has no timber. It is occupied solely for the sake of its rookery, but it is a pity measures are not devised to prevent the wholesale destruction of mutton birds which is periodically occasioned by the reckless burning of the grass which covers the rookery."

No farm livestock had been grazed on Little Dog for over forty years, so these could not be blamed for the deterioration.

Such abuse of the environment by humans had left a very artificial plant cover. While the overall dominant was the native silver tussock grass, over a third of the eighty-nine species listed were introduced weeds. Two of the four cudweeds recorded were aliens and unusual intruders were the cape gooseberry or Chinese lantern *(Physalis peruviana)* and a catchfly, *Silene gallica*. The sparkling South African ice plant *(Cryophytum (Disphyma) crystallinum)* grew with the related pigface and noonflower and another pink-flowered succulent, the purslane, *Calandrinia calyptrata*.

The few patches of scrub spared by the fires consisted of coast beard heath, coast wattle, boobialla, white correa and box, as well as tea-tree, paperbark and kunzea, these sheltering smaller, more vulnerable plants. High moisture content of the coastal succulents rendered them less flammable and an effective firebreak where growing in sufficient quantity.

The most saline areas, disliked by the majority of weeds, had retained the most natural vegetation, with lobelia and sea celery on the salty south-west corner and a lush sward of creeping brookweed with the samphire in the north-west. Shore spleenwort *(Asplenium obtusatum)*, an unusually salt-tolerant fern, penetrated crevices to within thirty cm of high water mark.

Destruction of the vegetation by fire left the sandy soil open to erosion, bringing the granite close to the surface, so that shearwaters might be left with inadequate soil depth for burrowing. The extent of erosion since the last fire was only too apparent where the basal twenty cm or more of the grass stools were quite unsinged, having been buried when the fire passed.

The extent of previous erosion was shown by the coarse residual shingle perched high up on the blackened columns of fibrous roots from whose summits the hard yellow leaves splayed. The tufts often became mushroom shaped due to abrasion at the base by the granite shingle, denuded of the cushioning sand by the wind.

Noon flower or spinach straggling across the desecrated surfaces sometimes compensated for the loss of cover, allowing birds to tunnel under their matted stems. Here they were invisible to potential enemies, but their very invisibility made them more vulnerable to trampling.

I almost stepped on one, which scuttled off along its leafy tunnel with a startled squawk. The clean white egg was undamaged. Replacing the bird on top of it, I beat a hasty retreat before it could take fright again.

It was a real scorcher and our Fisher Island contingent waxed a deeper shade of pink as the day advanced, from the heightened blood flow within and the burning rays without. The coastal dune sands were too hot to touch, except where shaded by spinifex grass or barilla, and too dry and friable for burrows to persist for long without collapse.

Botanising my laborious way uphill to the crest of a rise, a magnificent panorama opened out ahead, a limpid blue bay eating deeply into the tawny expanse of sun-scorched grass. At the junction of the two was a pristine beach of untrodden sand, worthy of any Caribbean Isle. Severed sea-grass fronds were banked high in odd corners.

Mottled waders foraged among the debris, rising as one to wheel and circle in the vibrant heat haze. A hundred flecks of fugitive white would tilt simultaneously to an almost invisible motley of buff and brown, then change to white again. These soon returned to the feast but the Cape Barren geese headed away into the blue void. The goslings were fully fledged now and the discarded nest material dispersed and trampled.

* * * * *

A chill wind was blowing when I visited Little Dog a week later with Tuck, the Furneaux summers as fickle as those of Wales. My survey areas were all on the windward side and I suffered as much from cold as I had from heat on the last visit. I made for a sheltered beach for lunch and luxuriated in the sun's warmth before finding diversion in a sheltered bracken patch.

Several hours after the agreed pick up time I was still shuttling from point to point looking vainly for a boat. It came eventually, the skipper apologetic at having forgotten me. Soon after delivering me, *"Tassie"* had run into a crayfish pot, unsportingly placed in the fairway, and had fouled its propeller. Tuck cut it free, thereby sacrificing the pot, but the dog ends necessitated him running at half speed.

Then a radio call came through from his intended destination. "Don't come: there's a regular gale blowing out here."

Glad to be spared a long slow voyage, he headed back to Lady Barron, jettisoned mail and passengers and unravelled the offending propeller. He spent the rest of the day bringing in a mob of sixty sheep from Great Dog Island. Fifty were lowered into the hold and the others towed behind, ankle deep in bilge water, in the dinghy.

He disliked this job, in spite of many helping hands, as it was a major operation cleaning the boat afterwards. Sheep respond to the fleece-raising experience of being rounded up in the way that all frightened creatures will! The outer dung had been thinned by sea water, but there was a generous layer in the hold.

While swilling down for tomorrow's passengers, the skipper remembered that he had not yet finished with today's and took to sea again. I had difficulty attracting his attention above the screeching of terns on the offshore reef, but was soon safely perched on the gunwhale, hanging on to the yard arm as we rocked our way home.

Twenty minutes after being landed on Fisher Island, we could still see the top of his mast bobbing up and down beyond Limpet Rock and went to see what was keeping him. All aboard were swearing and heaving at a trapped anchor. It was obviously not their day. They were on the point of cutting the rope and coming back for it on tomorrow's low tide.

Eric offered to give it a heave from landward if they could get the anchor rope to him, but neither of the boatmen were practised with a lasso and it fell short every time, although he waded in waist deep. They finally made it by starting the engine and nosing in so close that the mate feared they'd be leaving the boat here overnight as well as the anchor. With three of us heaving from the shore, the offending member came free at last.

My visit to Little Dog Island on the 9th April 1958, was unplanned, like so much else. Dom and I were to be dropped on Woody Island from the Cape Barren mail run, but it was too rough to go all the way, so the drop off went by the board too. I divided my attention between pressing plants and watching Dom stuff two small birds, deftly manipulating the pathetically fragile corpses, using arsenic paste.

In the middle of operations Tuck arrived with the news that he had to collect Fenner, the Fauna Board Health Inspector, from Great Dog and transfer him to Little Dog, and could drop us off on Little Green — one of the Fauna Board's problem islands, where we had things to look at. Dom declined: I accepted. In the event I didn't get there either, finishing up on Little Dog with Fenner.

Tuck hovered offshore while I carried the week's bread up to his son's birding hut, finding everything there very neat and tidy and the table laid for a meal. Back at the boat father took me to a spot he thought I ought to look at, because there were no burrows there and he wondered why. This proved to be in the south-west — and I had planned to go east to keep out of the brisk wind.

The deep penetration of my iron rod showed that this was not one of the areas lacking burrows because of insufficient soil depth. As far back as last century, Little Dog had been regarded as the most over-burned of all the islands, but fire could not be blamed here. Around 1862, in Brownrigg's time, there was a group of lads who periodically set fire to the grass when the shearwaters were in residence and the sea around held a number of dead birds, injured in the fire and unable to make a good getaway. Perhaps the deep soil was unburrowed because there were too few birds left to burrow!

I crouched out of the wind for lunch, getting covered in charcoal from the blackened grass stubs in the doing. When I returned to the birding shed, as arranged, the boat had gone. The reason was yet another fire.

"Gran'dad and the inspector've gone rushing off to a big rookery fire on Great Dog. It's near his hut. There's little they can do but they want to know what's going on."

The wind-tousled, sun-browned child returned to her game in the sand as though this sort of thing happened every day.

Making my way along the north coast, I saw sheets of orange flame rising ahead of towering plumes of black smoke emanating from patches of scrub, while less menacing blankets of white surged erratically from the tussock grass.

It transpired that the fire was on Dave Nield's rookery. Dave was against fire as a management tool and his tussocks were skirted with brittle sheaths of old leaves, which went up like tinder. Mercifully, neighbouring areas of green, sprouted since an earlier burn, had acted as a firebreak.

Bracken, one of our greatest fire hazards in Britain, where it withers to a trash of dead fronds in winter, is much less inflammable in Australia, where it remains winter-green. The optimum time to use fire on the islands is in May, soon after the birds have left, this giving the maximum period for the vegetation to regenerate before they need the cover again.

The inferno had started on the upper part of Dave's rookery, destroying some twenty-five acres before burning itself out. The story emerged later. The rookery owner had lighted a cigarette, thrown the match away, got down to haul a bird from its burrow and turned to see several square feet of grass alight. He rolled on it but failed to quench the flames, merely singeing his chest. One unguarded minute and the damage was done.

He rushed for assistance, but nothing could be done. Later, Tuck told us, he was in tears, blaming no-one but himself and saying they could jug him if they wanted to — it being illegal to fire a rookery at this crucial time. Trooper Bailey, who had made all haste to the blaze, along with several other boats, deemed it an accident, with no action to be taken.

A team of men went over the burrowed ground as soon as it had cooled off sufficiently and found that no chicks seemed to have been injured in their underground fastnesses. The grass was so inflammable that the fire had passed swiftly, not igniting the peat, nor lingering to heat the air in the burrows for more than a brief spell of discomfort and no doubt alarm for the inmates.

Men and women, mostly half-castes, flocked from all over to lend a hand, although their rookeries were to windward and in no danger. Tuck commended them afterwards on their prompt action. They had strung out across the forefront of the fire, pulling tussocks and throwing them back, to make a linear fire break.

The house was burned down, but most of the contents were saved by a willing team, passing things from hand to hand. The two sleeping quarters and all the processing huts remained unscathed. A woman with two kiddies had panicked and sheltered, unwisely, between two boulders over which the fire had to pass, but a man spotted them just in time and got them down the beach to the others.

Dave said he would go on birding and the health inspector offered his family hospitality in the old homestead which he had shared with me the previous week. Neighbours were rallying round and it was likely that all would be well, although unlikely that the house could be rebuilt for this season, despite the short time in which such things were sometimes achieved, with all hands to the hammer and saw.

Evidently the chief danger of such a conflagration was to the homecoming adult birds. These were attracted through the darkness to the lingering flames, like moths to a candle, even if these were not on the nesting area, and might fly into them and get shrivelled up like so much chaff.

It was a sight such as this that had greeted Fauna Board inspectors on a visit to Great Dog after one of Barrett's wildfires and had resulted in them banning his sheep from the island. There was an area today that the islanders deemed in danger of igniting and causing one of these nocturnal holocausts, so they fired it then and there and made sure it was burned out before the onset of night.

All this I learned afterwards. While the blaze lasted I sat on a tiny dune above granite eroded into arches and tunnels on the north-east corner of the neighbouring Little Dog, with half my attention on the fire and half on the offshore reef, where a party of red-capped dotterels consorted with gulls and terns. These dotterels are almost indistinguishable from the little rufous-crowned plovers of Europe, which just impinge on the south-east shores of Britain, where we know them as Kentish plovers.

Squatting later in a patch of scrub, I was butted three times in the backside by something very small but very determined. Rolling over, I found my 'attacker' to be a mole cricket, a hardy little creature determined to have a go at removing anything which got in its way.

All of an inch long, with wings only half this, the intrepid labourer set about constructing a burrow, digging rapidly and elevating a pile of earth clods with a diameter equalling its own body length. When the clods were touched, it backed out to see what was afoot. When its tail was touched, it burrowed furiously on, to surface at a little distance before looking back. Did I discern an anxious expression on that horny face?

It was five o'clock before I detected *"Tassie"* bucketing back from the scene of the fire and got my chilled body back to life in the strenuous trek to meet her. One of Tuck's granddaughters, a prefect at the Flinder's school, embarked with us and we picked up a cheery snub-nosed boy of eleven from Willis's hut — a typical "William", with shirt tails hanging from his pants and underclothes from his kitbag. They were headed for a week of lessons, but would be back on the island ere long.

75 Erosion after Fire, leaving inadequate soil for burrowing

76 Stools of Silver Tussock *Poa poiformis* after fire and erosion

77 Pelicans *Pelecanus conspicillatus*

2. BIRDERS' HUTS, GEESE AND OTHER WILDLIFE

Two macho-looking rams were tethered to the mast on a subsequent visit to Little Dog Island, these charged with the duty of upgrading the genetic makeup of future stock on Cape Barren Island. I was put ashore on the north-west corner, with six hours to pick-up time.

After busy spells on saltmarsh and sand dune, I sank back on warm white sand for a behaviour study of Cape Barren geese. The birds were obviously suspicious of my intentions, but were also inquisitive. Four tapered heads appeared over a shelf of rock, the wary stares leaving me in no doubt that I had been spotted. But curiosity overcame their fears and they worked steadily towards me, only half their attention on the leaf munching and grass pulling as they came.

Eventually, the onset of cramp and a slight disorientation with my laterally distorted view of the shimmering world of sun, sand and surf, got the better of me and I squirmed into a more comfortable position. One terrified honk from four throats in unison and the birds were gone. Geese were coming and going along the west coast throughout the day. As many as 150 might pass together but most flocks were of thirty to forty birds.

While tending to move over to the Flinders farmlands as the smaller islands dried up, the geese were not dependent on fresh water — even for drinking. They can tolerate brackish or full sea water, having, like gannets and other sea birds, a salt excreting mechanism built into the skull. Salt is extracted from the drinking water and accumulated in glands above the eyes, from where it is excreted as a nasal drip. On days as hot as this one, the water turned to vapour before it could drip and salt crystallised out on the snub noses.

This facility enables the birds to deal with the salty sap of seaside succulents and I had watched them feeding on glasswort and *Hemichroa* by Logans Lagoon and nipping off leaf tips of pigface on the islets. They nevertheless showed some preference for soft freshwater growths, favouring strawberry clover from the wetter lands above other clovers, also irrigated lucerne crops, although varying their leafy diet with seeds, including those of grasses.

Dr Eric Guiler, who I was to get to know later in Hobart, had conducted an aerial census of geese on the outer islands the previous year, 1957, published in *The "Emu"*, Volume 57, part 3, 217-221. He had estimated the population to be around 2,000, occurring especially on grassy areas backing beaches. While breeding occurred also along the coast of Victoria and South Australia as far as the Recherche Archipelago in Western Australia, the Furneaux Group hosted the main population, with birds avoiding the more exposed islets along the Tasman Sea.

His counts were made during the bird harvest in late March, so many geese must have been scared away from the commercial islands, and he saw none on Little Dog. Highest counts, of 470 and 440, were made on Badger Island and Woody Island. Big Green and Vansittart were next, with 255 and 220; Goose Island and South-east Flinders yielded 100 each, with ninety on Chappell Island and smaller numbers on Isabella, Tin Kettle and Kangaroo Islands.

The chief breeding islands were Badger, Big Green, Goose, Chappell and East Kangaroo, with nesting concentrated between June and September. During this phase the pairs were strongly territorial, seeing off all comers. And they could be quite formidable, with their wing span of five feet (1½ metres), stout lunging necks and a bulk of eleven to twelve pounds (5 — 6 kilograms).

They are practically the only geese in the Furneaux Group but, seen with others in wildfowl collections, their shape is unmistakable, not least because of the short cone-shaped beak with basal yellow cere. They belong to a group apart, lying between geese and ducks, like the more lightly built shelducks.

The open season for geese lasted three months, during which the daily legal bag was limited to six birds. Unfortunately this was impossible to police and many birds were taken during the closed season. These might be goslings, as yet unable to fly, or, more seriously, old birds, loath to abandon the nest they were tending. The goslings exhibit little fear and it was easy to approach within gunshot, particularly in a boat.

Sergeant George Hanlon, Fauna Board Field Police Officer on mainland Tasmania, told me later that 300 nests were destroyed on Chappell Island that year by the owner, who alleged that the geese were fouling his grazing lands. Although illegal, this act of vandalism was repeated in 1959.

My Little Dog lunch spot, sheltered from a stiff breeze by a backing boulder, could scarcely have been more magic, with the romantic outline of peaks before and behind and the ethereal, reflective sea between. It was a good day for birds, too, with sightings of a banded goshawk as well as the more commonplace white-breasted sea eagles and marsh harrier. There were quail, dotterel and hirundines and a scatter of penguins which had escaped the bait collectors.

After examining two more plant communities, I worked my way back over the summit, where a patch of scrub surrounded by a firebreak of bare granite had survived. *"Tassie"* was racing in under full sail with a following wind and I had only just time to find a disembarkation rock with a sufficient depth of water alongside.

* * * * *

There were few snakes on Little Dog Island, probably, it was thought, because there were few lizards on which to feed. Had these suffered from the frequent fires? Things were said to be different on Great Dog, so for my first visit there with Lew Bailey, I donned a pair of sheepskin-lined, knee-length flying boots lodged in "Yolla" as snake boots.

Lew was headed to Cape Barren to value a farm and dropped me off on the west end of Great Dog promising to return at five. This gave me plenty of time for goose watching and to explore the birders' huts, which would not be occupied for another two months yet.

The first hut I entered had the usual two-tier chicken wire bunks like the one I was sleeping in on Fisher Island. The walls of off-white asbestos sheeting were spattered with crop oil, this probably just as well in view of the hazards of airborne asbestos fibres that came to light subsequently, and there was fly wire over the ventilators.

Sacks of salt, fused into solid cakes, were piled on the floor and spread on a corrugated working surface supported on two-metre timbers. An outhouse was stacked with empty barrels in which prepared birds would be packed in brine. Pushing past a leaning tier of folded sacks, I entered another room to sink knee-deep in feathers — evidently regarded as unsaleable. How the spiders and other creepy crawlies were enjoying that cosy insulation! Spades, forks and shovels leaned on soiled plank walls and rainwater tanks were brim full; roofed, but with the entrance pipe dipping into a perforated funnel in which the precious fluid could be seen.

A second establishment contained a living room with wood-burning, cast-iron stove and tin sink over a boarded cupboard, now a handy perch for starlings wishing to relieve themselves. One wooden bench had collapsed, but there was an old kitchen dresser, table, chair and form and the walls were papered with news sheets the right way up for some light reading and topped by a pictorial map of Australia.

All rooms were floored with tussock grass — like the rush floors onto which Henry VIII flung his discarded meat bones, while empty plonk bottles and other debris poked from a pile outside. A homely touch was the toy boat made from an old kerosene tin and a short wide bunk on which the children slept, four deep. Gaps between walls and roof were stuffed with old rags; gaps in a corner cupboard with dry grass. Nevertheless, the rampant bower spinach had found a way in through the chinks and advanced across the floor, attenuated, but still quite green.

Goose guano came right to the doorstep, even inside in places. I was told later that geese were incurably inquisitive and that wildfowlers sometimes attracted them by concealing themselves and elevating above their hiding place first a white flag and then a red, turn and turn about. Geese seemed always to be around the settlements when these were empty, probably attracted by the short grass. Even the downy fog grass was preferable to the scratchy tussock of the rest.

These buildings had been erected in a pretty bay sheltered by offshore reefs, where the sea ran up over golden sands to rocks almost at their doors. It was an idyllic spot in which to enjoy the simple life.

Skinks, mostly the three-lined variety that we had on Fisher Island, darted across the thresholds and wove through the neatly stacked firewood at the top of the beach. These were long and lean, their legs reduced to the size of matchsticks and almost invisible, but powering tremendous bursts of speed.

The mountain 'dragons' *(Amphibolurus diemensis)*, while not much longer, about four to five inches, were chunkier, with quite hefty limbs both back and front. A blunt snout and high forehead gave them an odd appearance and the name of dragon must have come from the line of triangular black spines running along the back. They were more arboreal than the rock skinks, scuttling along tea-tree branches and proving so tame that they would sit on an extended hand, enjoying the warmth.

The next establishment visited was fitted with cross-slatted wooden bunks and the same floor coverings of grass and feathers, like an outsize bird's nest. Spinach had invaded again but was doing best in the toilet a little way back uphill. The disengaged door swung loose on its hinges, allowing enough light in for pigface, as well as this more shade tolerant species, to take hold.

I returned to the pick up point a little before five for a quick dip, adjourning to the shade of a rock to total up my transect figures. It was nearly three hours before "*Aralla*" hove in sight.

Lew was apologetic. "My word. That farm we had to value. We walked and walked and walked. My word!"

My fellow islanders had almost given me up, but had a good hot meal waiting.

A few weeks later I was landed on the north coast of Great Dog Island and took the opportunity to explore the grounds of the deserted homestead. This was a grander affair altogether, a government house, and locked. It was for the use of Theo Barrett, who had the grazing rights on the island, although it was said he had never lived there.

"Like all the rest, he's too well heeled. The £1,000 a year he gets for his Great Dog wool is just a drop in the ocean."

A drop which might evaporate forthwith as he was threatened with eviction from the island on three counts. Firstly he was never there to see to the maintenance of the house; secondly he let his sheep stray into the rookeries, although this was an island boasting stock-proof fences; and thirdly, he let his management fires stray into the rookeries when the birds were in residence.

It was early February and he had paid rent until the end of April. The government had no intention of reimbursing him and he had no intention of moving without reimbursement so it was stalemate at present. In the event, he was allowed to stay, with a slightly diminished quota of livestock.

The house was surrounded with unkempt gardens and orchards, being overrun by a tangle of loganberries, vines, nasturtiums and geraniums. Birds had eaten all the cherries and cherry plums and most of the soft fruit, as Tuck had predicted,

The branches were alive with friendly grey fantails, more colourful than their name suggests, with rufous breast and throat set off by black and white patterning on head and gorget. Others were firetail finches, with crimson beak and rump, and perky yellowish silver-eyes.

My task today concerned fence line ecology, comparing the swards to either side of stock-proof barriers. I had gained the summit of Big Hill, keeping a wary eye out for snakes in the metre-high tussock, when I spotted "*Tassie*" leaving Lady Barron quay. She was going to be on time for once. I raced down the hill, slithered through the coastal scrub and scrunched across the rocks. It would never do to be late when the skipper always made so much play of being on time on the few occasions when he was. He had to make a wide circuit round Spences Reef as the tide was low, so I made it.

Next time we set out under a sunny blue sky, but "old lady Ross" was no happier than usual.

"It's alright now but it's going to get bad. I don't like that sky. My word! Look at those wisps and mares' tails."

He shook his head violently and just caught his false teeth in the nick of time, coughing an embarrassed cover-up while I studied the far horizon.

"It's going to blow. You'll not be going to Rabbit Island. We may have to get you off in a hurry and you'll be nowhere to be found. Anything could happen!"

It didn't, of course, the sky-borne mares tossing their tails all day in the upper air without eliciting a response from the foaming white manes of their brethren in the sea. I was duly landed on Big Dog, at the east end of 'the hard ground' in the north, this implying ground with no burrows. The heat was stifling and, after sweltering through a rookery beset with spiny-headed mat rush *(Lomandra longifolia)*, I dumped unwanted kit at a birders' hut and concentrated on scrub woodland to benefit from the shade.

The first wood I entered seemed to have drawn curtains around itself against intruders, the bower spinach climbing to three metres in the marginal branches, nourished by birds tunnelling in its base. Enjoying the cool interior were a grey shrike thrush and two English blackbirds. Brightening the gloom was a cock flame robin, resplendent in crimson and black, but his mate no more colourful than the brown thornbills feeding through the tea-trees. Those kept up a raucous cheeping as they foraged.

Outside again, over a fence and through bracken and tussock, I flushed several coveys of brown quails, each about a dozen strong, and more English starlings. The next wood was unburrowed and lacked the protective curtain of spinach.

Squatting down to write notes on the understorey, I was aware of something large moving in the undergrowth. Expecting a cow, I was surprised when the perpetrator of the noise proved to be an adult Bennets wallaby. He must have seen me but seemed not to care, grazing his way across the brittle grass to within a few metres.

At intervals he plucked a sprig of provender and sat up, squirrel fashion, holding it in his forepaws to eat. Then he spent a full ten minutes at his toilet, as fastidiously as any cat, first his hands, then his face, working forwards from the back of the ears.

It was at this juncture that he took exception to my intrusion, thumped the ground several times to warn his non-existent fellows, and loped off. This was not a mere thumping of the tail, as a beaver might, but of the hefty hind feet, rabbit fashion. Nevertheless, he shadowed me for the rest of the afternoon, moving back and forth on a parallel track. I congratulated myself on having such an affinity with the wild but learned later that this animal scarcely qualified as wild.

Many years before, when the house was occupied, he was one of a pair introduced in the hope that they would breed. Neither had been seen for several years and they were thought to have died. Perhaps this one was lonesome for a companion near his own size. I, too, progressed on two legs, with nose going frequently to ground to probe some new puzzle.

I still had things to do when I was aware of a chugging engine and penetrating whistle twenty minutes before time. Crashing through the woods and along the beach to collect my kit, I found I was further west than I thought and had quite a bit of rookery to negotiate. My progress through chest-high tussock and fireweed, stumbling into burrows and tipping forwards on hands and knees, was rowdy enough to send all the snakes in the vicinity gliding to safety. The only thing left behind in the hurry was my bag of plant specimens.

The season was well advanced by my next Great Dog visit and, while I was ashore, the boatmen sailed on to raid Theo Barrett's orchard. They returned with a fish box full of damsons and crabapples. Their wives would be busy tonight making jelly.

I, meanwhile, had been investigating some old whalers' try pots at one of the birding establishments, cast-iron cauldrons in which mutton birds had formerly been boiled down for their oil, as penguins were on the sub-antarctic islands when the seals ran out.

In the bottom of one was a dejected shearwater sitting in three inches of slimy green water. I rescued it, getting pecked for my pains. Bedraggled and disgruntled, but still spunky, the bird flapped along the ground to a patch of undergrowth to preen. It might have got clean quicker by going to sea, but it was low tide and the beach stretched away for an intimidating distance, uninvitingly bright and hot for a creature accustomed to be ashore only under cover of darkness or underground.

Use of try pots for mutton birds was a natural sequence to the collection of blubber by sealers and whalers. They usually wanted only the fat from under the skin and round the kidneys. After plucking, the birds' legs and wings were removed, the body split along the back and the skin pulled off with the subcutaneous fat attached.

With the modern 'skunning' of the 1990s the flesh is kept and the skin is the waste product. A century before it was the other way round. The carcase might be flung into the try pot with the skins or discarded. If kept, they were separated and jointed into breast and legs, after the crop oil had been squeezed into the pot to boost the fat.

A hundred birds yielded about a gallon of liquefied fat and an average to good year in the latter half of the nineteenth century provided around 3,000 gallons. This was burned in lamps, as whale oil had been, and used for lubricating machinery. An important sales outlet was to sawmills, where the fat was used to grease the skids over which the big timber slid.

78 Birders' Hut with brick chimney on Little Dog Island

79 A Skink *Leiolopisma* and Stunted Pigface *Disphyma crassifolium*

80 A Mountain Dragon Lizard *Amphibolurus diemensis*

3. I JOIN GREAT DOG ISLAND BIRD HARVESTERS

It was on April Fools' Day, when the fruit harvest was over, that I came again to Great Dog with camping gear, to experience the bird harvest at first hand. As we approached the shore the two health inspectors appeared in response to Tuck's throaty bellow and helped us in.

I was to join them in the lower of the island's two old homesteads, which we reached along a track winding through dusty bracken. This was a finer edifice than the birders' huts, with elevated verandah atop a flight of wooden steps, but was long-abandoned and almost empty of furnishings.

The men were sleeping on sackcloth which sagged, hammock fashion, across timber bed frames. Two of the three seats were old boxes, the third had hessian stretched between two oblique planks for the back and more to pad the seat. This was the easy chair, the easy applying to the manufacture rather than the comfort. A bamboo table with boxwood top had the legs shod and capped with metal bottle tops

Food boxes were piled on a tin sheet out of the way of mice. It was these, not ants and blowflies, which were the main problem here, but numbers were diminishing, as they emerged at night to help themselves to bait poisoned with 'Ratsak'. It was not uncommon to trip over a comatose mouse in the half light of the early morning which filtered through an exceedingly dirty shaded window. Scarcely the expected abode, this, for health inspectors.

Fenner spent a fortnight here, then swapped with his colleague for a fortnight on Babel Island. Great Dog had formerly been overseen from Flinders on a daily basis, but this was unsatisfactory as the birders could see the boat approaching and behave accordingly. Under the new system they could be taken by surprise on an overland approach.

My quarters were more frugal, but I had the choice of two double beds, one with boards nailed across the frame, the other with a reinforced sheet of wire netting slung across a rusty iron bedstead and furnished with a brown mattress stuffed with bracken and pine needles.

I plumped for this and fluffed up the pine needles, finding it a great improvement on my Fisher Island couch of sagging chicken wire. The stuffing came from a nearby shelter belt of pines to the west and another exotic tree, a macrocarpa, overhung the chimney, causing the cooking fire to smoke. The days of this were numbered, its removal part of the renovations planned by the government body which owned the dwelling and had earmarked £100 for a tidy up.

I had been invited to stay with the Riddle family, one of whom, the young Noreen, had produced the collection of watercolours depicting the mutton bird harvest, replicas of which Dom Serventy had shown me long before on one of his rare visits to London. They had a full house, however, so it was decided I should join them by day to see how the harvest was tackled.

The track to their shed was quite tortuous, through straggling woodland and clearings, so that it was as well that I was led thither by the inspectors, who visited each of the twelve families working on the island at least every other day. There had been opposition from the birders when this practice started, but the quality of the product had been going downhill, and with it the asking price and total sales, so it was to their advantage in the long term.

Previously no attempt had been made to keep the blowflies off, so the carcases were badly fly-blown. They were cooled on the floor instead of racks and had patches of down clinging to them. Now the sheds were fly-proofed, with double doors in crucial places. The odd fly which got in, despite the now routine swishing of a bunch of bracken fronds when the door was opened, was quickly dealt with.

The work team at Riddle's hut was five strong, under the leadership of the swarthy, curly-headed Bill Riddle and his wife. There was daughter Noreen and two helpers. Christine was a young English girl who had come out in her teens with her family to a farm on Flinders and had been birding for the past four years.

Bruce Bessemann, with whom I tagged along around the rookery, owned a wood pulp business in Launceston, but deemed the mutton birds worthy of an annual visit to the Furneaux Group. He was a New Zealander, his ancestor having emigrated to Nelson and been roped in immediately on arrival by a police boat to help fight in the Maori War. Bruce moved to Flinders in 1946 and from there to Launceston, so was introduced to mutton birds before wood pulp and had retained his fascination for them.

The men worked out in the rookery, collecting; the women in and around the huts, processing. I sipped coffee in a room floored with tussock grass newly cut from the tracks and papered with coloured magazine pictures. Every available corner was stacked with tinned food. Cooking was done on a kitchen range, with chunks of blackboy as fuel, and some crisply aromatic loaves of bread had just been taken from the oven, while home-made rock cakes accompanied the coffee. I lunched with them later, on leftovers of yesterday's excellent mutton bird 'poy' (it took me a while to translate that into 'pie').

My days were divided between rookery and huts. Old Mr Riddle worked more slowly and thoroughly than Bruce, but both were pretty slick at the start, where birds were numerous — a dozen chicks being taken in as many minutes.

Bruce showed me how to tell which holes were occupied — often the least obvious ones, with grass partially veiling the entrance. Big holes were often empty, either too public or the result of a roof collapse. Wherever the young man flung himself down and reached in there seemed to be a chick to be hauled out.

Other birders might extend their reach with a stick tipped with a twist of wire but the Riddles deemed this unnecessary. Birds were usually within an arm's reach of the opening and, if not grasped firmly on first contact, would scuttle on down the burrow and were left. Wire could tear the skin and damaged birds were no longer acceptable commercially. Dom used a stick with a padded end to poke down the Fisher Island burrows, maintaining that the chicks nibbled at the pad so that he could tell that the burrow was occupied with minimal disturbance.

The captive was held by the neck just behind the skull with the first two fingers of the right hand. A sharp downward flick would break its neck, death being instantaneous except for a few cases when a second flick was needed. Adult birds were never taken. If pulled out they were flung into the air and headed off to sea.

Later, during the starvation period, the adults would have deserted the chicks to live on their puppy fat, but now, at the beginning of April, there were still plenty ashore. If the chick came out first, the adult stayed in the burrow, unlikely to emerge until nightfall. If they were handled much in an underground mix-up they might regurgitate any food not yet fed to the chick.

There was great excitement when a pure white bird was pulled out. These were rare and this one was replaced. Perhaps it would produce another in due course: more likely its outstanding appearance would lead it into trouble.

Occupied holes were easier to locate later in the season when abandoned chicks came out to exercise their wings and scuffed up the sand around the entrance. After a few nights of this, they would leave, making their way downhill to the sea if this was fairly close, or uphill to the convenient eminences of Bald Hill or She-oke Hill to gain the necessary height to get airborne.

They took the easy route where practicable, along the man-made tracks, and sought refuge by day in trackside holes, making collection that much easier. A succession of chicks could be taken from the same accessible holes on consecutive days and towards the end of the season the harvesters concentrated their efforts on the low and high points where their quarries were converging. Although the rookery was 'gone over' two or three times, a lot of birds must have been missed in the homogeneous mass of tussocks with usually no system of marking.

With such huge takes one must inevitably wonder if enough are left to keep the population up. As ringing brought in more data on the longevity of breeding adults, however, it was apparent that a very small percentage of survivors would be necessary to make good the losses. By the 1980s, forty years after the ringing started, a few Fisher Island individuals had been recorded breeding for thirty to thirty-two of those forty years. Hen birds producing thirty or so chicks over the course of a lifetime allowed for a very healthy surplus over the replacement of themselves and partner.

In the late 1950s we believed that cock birds first bred at the age of seven and hens at five, but the accumulating data has shown that they are usually older. First breeding might be at any age from four to fifteen years, with an average onset of maturity at seven point three years for males and seven for females.

The vast numbers of untended surface eggs which appear in glut years are laid by unmated pre-breeders, so are infertile. It seems that the physiological ability to lay develops before the social ability to find a consort!

Breeding six-year-olds have little success and a third of the birds failing to rear chicks will divorce and try another partner the next year. Wooller et al in 1988 showed that the median survival time after first breeding is nine point three years, giving an average life expectancy of only sixteen to seventeen years, this figure pulled down by losses at sea, principally of one-year-olds. By any standards, the thirty-eight-year-old on Fisher Island was a great survivor.

In 1995 Irynej Skira of Hobart University published a figure of twenty three million mutton birds currently breeding in 250 colonies, 209 of these in Tasmania. The largest was Babel Island, with two point eight six million nesting burrows. Great Dog had 952,000 burrows and Trefoil Island off northwest Tasmania 700,000.

During the second half of the nineteenth century, after the extermination of most of the seals, mutton birds were the economic mainstay of 200 Aboriginals and 200 whites on the Furneaux Group. By the first part of the twentieth century harvests were tailing off and there was a general expansion of the birds' breeding range in Tasmania. By 1985, 106 colonies had been designated as reserves: with commercial harvesting of birds permitted under strict supervision on seven of these and non-commercial harvesting for home use on seventeen.

Natural mortality, mostly from starvation, is reckoned to be around ten per cent per annum and chicks hatch from sixty per cent of the eggs laid. Commercial harvesting takes only seven per cent of this annual increment of chicks, with a further 100,000 chicks taken non-commercially. Thus the annual take is well within the "Sustainable Yield" — a phrase much bandied about these days in relation to fish stocks and timber reserves.

But, back to the Great Dog Island of forty years ago. Each birder carried a five feet long wooden stake, sharpened at both ends. When about a dozen birds had been transferred from the right-handed neck flicks to the left-handed neck hold, these were impaled on the stake through the lower jaw and the stake balanced across the shoulders.

Forty five to fifty-five birds were regarded as a full load. With each weighing up to two pounds in a good year, this meant a burden of around a hundred pounds — quite enough when the walk back to the hut might be as much as half a mile. Bruce was glad to rest his load between the paired forked poles driven into the ground at strategic intervals along the tracks. Irynej gives the mean weight of fat chicks as 800 gms. (1.76 pounds), almost twice that of the parents, despite sometimes as much a sixteen days between feeds.

The weight of chicks varied according to the season and date, rising in a series of minor peaks during the growth period after each feed, with a slight fall as some of the energy intake was dissipated in respiration and defecation. The all time high, when chicks weighed more than adults, fell off as they absorbed their baby fat prior to departure, and it was these leaner birds that the birders used to stock their own larders for the year ahead.

Nineteen-fifty-eight was a good season and all the birds were plump. It had started badly, with stormy weather during the last few days of March, when only a few bedraggled birds had been hauled from the dripping tussocks at great personal discomfort.

Back at the hut, Bruce lodged his stake across horizontal bars on a holding rack. Pulling birds off one by one, he squeezed out the stomach contents with finger and thumb into a kerosene tin. The grey, half-digested food was known as gurrie or gurry and was dyed orange by oil from the proventriculus — as orange as the egg masses squeezed in similar manner from the other end of hen salmon in fish nurseries.

After the mess had settled, the oil was decanted and strained through thick sacking into a metal drum. The residue was carried down the beach and tipped out for disposal by gulls, crabs and tides.

At this stage the oil looked like tomato ketchup, but Bruce assured me that it would resemble port wine more closely after further settling time. It is a secretion, not a late stage in digestion — the equivalent of the fishy orange fluid which had been squirted at me more than once when I had approached unwisely close to Northern Hemisphere fulmar petrels!

One of its chief commercial uses in 1950s Australia was as suntan oil, marketed as 'suntan oil from the royal bird of Tahiti'. If some of the Sydney bathing belles who smarmed it over their browning torsos could have seen it at this stage, they might have had second thoughts. By the nineties, with the increase of skin cancer and decrease of protective ozone, the need was for screening rather than browning.

It was also used in medicine, particularly for colds and chest complaints, but it had no special vitamins or enzymes and was probably as ineffective as rhino horn is when employed as an aphrodisiac. Like the fat, it was useful against rust and was said to have been employed by sailors to calm troubled waters. Some dairy farmers had been known to skim the cream off their milk and replace it with mutton bird oil before feeding the skimmed milk to the calves.

Young birds found on the surface by day were likely to be sick. One which I came across smelt foul, had yellow fluid oozing from the beak and cloaca and a hard lump near the vent. Birders believed that chicks picked up small hard objects as gizzard stones or ballast before leaving the burrows and that the body rejected anything toxic by building up a hard concretion around the offending object, like an oyster walling off an irritant in a pearl.

Sufferers were known as limy birds and the birders expected about one in a hundred of those taken to be affected — often more in the bracken patches. These were discarded.

"One limy carcase in a cask of salted chicks will spoil the whole lot!"

The problem was currently being worked on by Dr Myckytowicx, a vet employed by CSIRO, who sometimes joined us in "Yolla". He disagreed with the birders' theory, although unable to come up with a firm cause. The hard lumps were formed by excessive uric acid and they might multiply to completely block the lower part of the alimentary canal — when the bird would be unable to excrete waste food and would inevitably die.

In a paper of 1963 (CSIRO Bull VII 1) Mycky writes: "The reason for the formation of the uric acid concretions is still obscure and it is not known whether they are due to impaired motility or to the abnormal nature of the contents."

He suggests that it might be related to gout — a frequent disease of fowls, turkeys, pheasants, geese and other water birds, caused by deposition of uric acid. The question remained open, however, as he continued to test for bacteria, viruses and other pathogens and to examine blood, intestinal contents and discoloured body fat. At least the condition seemed not to be transmitted from one bird to another.

After removal of the oil and gurrie, Bruce threw each bird through a hatch in the wall of the processing building. This hatch resembled an oversized cat flap and was curtained with hessian. Noreen took over inside. She was an expert plucker, practised since early childhood. In hot weather she sat on the doorstep at this task, with a sack across her lap. A few deft pulls and all the contour feathers were stripped away, leaving only wing and body quills and the adherent body down. Another shed I visited had three pluckers at work, perched on old fish boxes and ankle-deep in feathers and fluff.

Noreen's plucked birds went through another sack-covered hatch to Christine, who cut off the legs — a job often done by quite small children supplied with lethally sharp knives.

Next in the team were the scalders: Mrs Riddle, often with Bill, whose greying mop of hair made him eligible for a spell now and then from the hard work in the rookery. They sat one each side of a small copper in which hot water bubbled over a blackboy fire; this imported fuel giving a quicker and fiercer heat than the home-grown she-oke available on Great Dog. Each straddled a box with a hessian-covered plank protruding between their knees as a table.

Birds, held by their wings, were dipped, tail first, into the boiling cauldron and held there for a minute. Water was flicked away and the now loosened down smoothed from the long breast with a single wipe of folded hessian, the rest cleaned off with the palm of the hand. I found this fascinating to watch, as the bedraggled grey corpses were transformed in a twinkling to very edible-looking dressed poultry.

This was when negligence might invite fly strike, but the cleaned bodies were despatched through another hatch into the fly-proofed cooling room, newly built this season and leaving nothing to be desired. Noreen and Christine had, by this time, moved in there to lay the bodies out along a vertical series of wire netting racks, with the heads and necks dangling over the front. Birds cooling from earlier were dealt with in the 'opening process'.

Like the scalders, the two girls sat on boxes with a plank protruding forwards as a work bench — stabilised by their weight on the back end. Beside each was a pile of untreated birds and a box or sawn-in-half barrel in which to put treated ones. Between them was an old style zinc bath to receive the offal.

First the tail with adjacent fat was chopped off, then the head removed and the belly split open. A few deft strokes with a frequently sharpened knife removed the entrails, sometimes leaving the heart and kidneys, but never the liver. On occasion the hearts were put aside to be made into a pie for a special treat.

Lastly the wings were removed with a double cut each side and the bird cracked open along the spine like a filleted kipper. These were stacked face to face in pairs alongside the regiments of fresh birds on the cooling racks. When the zinc bath could hold no more debris, the girls took a handle apiece and carried it down the beach to empty at the edge of the tide.

As the morning progressed the heaps got steadily further away, following the ebb. The bonanza was shared by the two gull species onshore and a school of mullet offshore. Currawongs, the so-called black jays, joined in the feast, although pre-eminently fruit-eaters rather than the carrion-eaters suggested by their crow-like demeanour. Silas Mansell blamed these birds for spreading the noxious African boxthorn seeds that had taken over much of his rookery on Babel Island.

Needless to say, birds, fish and crabs between them, however willing, could not deal adequately with the sudden glut and the remains provided the perfect breeding ground for the blowflies that the inspectors waged constant war against. These had been tolerated in the past, in the hope that all the maggots would float to the top when the birds were put in brine and could be skimmed off when the barrels were opened.

The half-castes, even in 1958, cheerfully tolerated maggots in the birds taken from Babel for home consumption — as they did the maggots of fungus gnats that dropped from the gills of over-ripe mushrooms. We shudder, but why not, in a land where witchetty grubs are regarded by so many as a delicacy?

81 Bench Mark on Big Hill, Great Dog: View to NW of Little Dog

82 Try Pots in which Mutton Birds were formerly melted for their fat

83 Mutton-birder carries Chicks through Rookery

Chapter Ten

MORE OF THE ROOKERY ISLANDS IN FRANKLIN SOUND

1. THE ECONOMICS OF THE BIRD HARVEST

Late in the morning, Noreen emerged from the cooling room and spotted an unfamiliar boat dropping anchor offshore. "They've come for the fresh birds" she called.

These were collected daily once the harvest was under way, but this was the first time since the start on 27th March that the weather had been suitable. It was bad policy to get birds ready until a means of transport was assured so it was all hands to the pump now.

She and Christine busied themselves packing dressed birds in five stout wooden boxes. Each held forty, stacked in four piles against the white-painted interior. They were made fast with metal hoops hinged at the back and folding over the lid, to which the handle was attached.

Even in today's idyllic calm, matters were not too propitious for a boatman new to the area. The tide was well down and the extent of the shallows difficult to judge. Deeming caution the better part of valour, the skipper had anchored further out than he need, leaving his mate to cover the intervening distance under oars. It was not only a long row, but a long wade across an eelgrass meadow when the craft grounded 100 yards out.

The oarsman was well prepared, in short shorts — on other days he might be togged out in long thigh boots. He jibbed at carrying the full boxes back, with nowhere to rest their weight for a blow, and forthwith joined the three of us for a cuppa, while the tide made its leisurely way in across the sands. In due course he paddled out and brought the boat to a convenient rock platform, where many hands made light work of the loading.

The skipper, tired of waiting, had moved on to lie off the next hut, so what the mate gained on the roundabouts he lost on the swing of the oars during the long row back. Without a lookout in the bow, the vagaries of the channel caused him to get out and push more than once.

The team was definitely not making a fortune at this venture and it seemed likely that supplying the markets with fresh birds would prove uneconomic unless air transport to the commercial islands could be organised. Islanders could not rely on regular visits, sometimes having to unpack several hundred birds at the end of the day when transport failed.

The shuttle service charged ten shillings for every hundred birds transported and an average load was likely to be a thousand birds, leaving £5 for boat expenses and two men's wages. Often they spent so long waiting for the tide that their remuneration was less.

There was a greater demand for the product than the 400,000 — 600,000 birds currently produced. The pilot who flew mutton birds and crayfish daily to Melbourne said he could have disposed of twice as many to the poulterers and fishmongers. A good proportion of the total take remained on the archipelago for local consumption.

The inspectors stated that this was ranked as only a £60,000 industry and had far more than its fair share of government money spent on checking the produce. There was an ulterior motive, however, to help keep the Cape Barren islanders employed for at least part of the year.

Some were moving away to find jobs in Tasmania, often going into government housing; on the promise of which some of the former emigres were moving back to qualify for permanent homes themselves. Most of them did their birding on Babel Island, but three sheds were not working there in 1958, owing to labour costs and the new standards that had to be met.

Some of the Babel sheds were the responsibility of whites, who paid their coloured workers' wages — a considerable proportion in advance, to enable them to stock up with tucker for the duration. It had become increasingly common for labour to fall out with management and change sheds, so that the new boss had to pay for services already paid for by another.

If one can believe all one hears, they were just as likely to fall out with the new firm, and sheds might have to close down for several days for lack of sufficient hands to work them. I failed to discover what happened when master as well as workers were half-castes and unlikely to be able to subsidise advance payments.

Families took up residence on Babel about ten days before the season opened, to clear tracks through the rookery, cut firewood and prepare the huts. The tendency was to work well for the first few days of harvest, but for enthusiasm to wane as the days' hauls became smaller and boredom set in.

Matters were worse on snake-ridden Chappell Island, where 200,000 birds had been a regular take early in the twentieth century. Even if a mammoth project to remove the snakes was launched, it seemed unlikely that birders would be found to take it on. Most of the old hands had died or were too old for such taxing work, while the younger generation could earn bigger money more safely with the Agricultural Bank scheme on Flinders Island.

The old buildings no longer came up to scratch and no-one was likely to want to fork out around £800 for new ones conforming with government regulations and then search around for a team of workers. The Chappell Island grazing lease was about to come up for auction, this seeming a more practical form of land utilisation. There were 788 acres (319 hectares) of good sheep land there, with the starting price for a year's rent of £150, but an expected price nearer £650.

On Great Dog Island all twelve birding sheds were still in business, but the inspectors assured us that at least £600 per annum more could be raised in grazing licences than in birding licences. All rookeries were yielding fewer birds than formerly, but the Great Dog families were not wholly dependent on birding for their income. Most had farms or other businesses on Flinders Island and the birding was regarded by many as an annual spree or working holiday. This view was still held by Noreen Riddle nearly forty years later and she was continuing to enjoy birding as a vacation activity in 1995, when her paintings of island scenes, wind-tossed or sun-scorched, were as popular as ever.

The 1958 premonitions had proved correct, with Great Dog being the island to carry on the ancient tradition. Already, in 1958, none of the eight sheds on Little Green Island were working and only two of the three on Little Dog.

The Riddle family took about 12,000 birds from their twenty to thirty acres, which stretched from Bald and She-oke Hills down the east side of the scrub to the north coast. They received up to £6.12 per 100 for fresh birds and £7.00 per 100 for salted ones — a better price by 12/- (12 shillings) than the previous year — which was as it should be, with the birds plumper than usual. Fresh birds were selling for as much as 5/6 each in Hobart.

According to Tom Langley, a considerable number of birds was exported to New Zealand, to supplement the 30,000 sooty shearwaters collected there by the Maoris, mostly from islets off Stewart Island. They went salted, in barrels containing around 400 birds or drums holding around 100. Most were headed for Auckland Province in the north, these being furthest from the local supplies. Practically all were bought by Maoris, who were currently paying 4/9 per head.

The orange oil was fetching 3/3 per gallon and feathers were worth less than 4/- a pound to the birders although £1 a pound after cleaning and processing to eliminate the all-pervading odour. These were valuable long before the days of down sleeping bags and there was a time when the birds were harvested primarily for their feathers in a gruesomely primitive manner, according to Brownrigg's *"Cruise of the Freak"* (1870).

It was customary then to drive the victims into a pit six to seven feet square and lined with bark, to prevent them digging escape burrows. They were guided in by brush fences extending a few 100 yards from the seaward corners, with a man posted at the end of each. Parties of beaters flushed the birds out and "birds would hurriedly crawl and scramble down before the pursuers, but only to be taken by thousands in the snare". When full the pit had been covered with bark to smother the birds, any still alive when this was removed being despatched with sticks. It took about twenty-five birds to produce a pound of feathers.

Mutton birds had been harvested in Tasmania from early colonial times, as a natural follow on from sealing. The sealers were white, their wives black and the inheritors of the industry were their half-caste offspring, who became known as the Straitsmen. By the 1950s it was coming progressively more under white domination — something which had not happened in New Zealand, where only Maoris and their descendents, who held traditional rights, were allowed on the bird islands.

Short-tailed shearwaters had always held a special place with Australians, as the only bird species harvested commercially for food and probably the most numerous of any. The immensity of their numbers was first noted by Captain Flinders in December 1798. He encountered them off Three

Hummock Island at the other end of Bass Strait, but it was appropriate that the principal island of the group where the main harvests were taken when settlement began, should be the one to be named after him.

Flinders computed the size of the flocks to be upward of a hundred million birds. Writing in the *"Victorian Naturalist"*, volume XXVIII, 11, in 1912, Joseph Gabriel checked his calculations and reckoned this to be too low, adding an extra thirty-two million birds. Gabriel records that, in the Furneaux Group alone, 800,000 birds were taken each year in the early part of the twentieth century; "This harvest being practically their principal means of livelihood." More were taken from the Hunter Group in the west and Phillip Island in the north.

He firmly believed that the population was well able to withstand this enormous cull, despite the taking of adults as well as chicks on Chappell Island and large numbers of eggs on the Kent Group and Cape Woolamai on Phillip Island. He could have been wrong, there being a steady annual decline during the 1950s. Numbers quoted at that time were 583,000 in 1954, 443,00 in 1955 and 312,000 in 1957, with the downward trend continuing.

Following an afternoon with Bruce in the Riddle's rookery, I returned to the processing sheds to observe the final stages of salting down and clearing up. A metal-lined tray at table height in the cooling room was used for salting. Coarse, off-white crystals were tipped onto this from sacks and prepared birds thoroughly rubbed in the mass. They were then packed spirally into wooden barrels whose capacity varied from 150 to 350 birds, each plump breast fitting into the hollow of its neighbour's back. The centre was filled with folded birds and the mass covered with hessian and left to settle, the blood and salt draining down to form a crimson brine.

Later the bung amidships was removed and the brine drained out to this level, the stream cleverly deflected into a kerosene tin along the blade of a sheath knife. This was done to prevent leakage when the upper hoops were removed to loosen the uprights and allow insertion of the barrel head or lid.

The birds were counted as they went in and the number chalked on the outside. In one instance I watched five removed and the '330' replaced by '325'. The lid was then hammered in place, the loosened hoops knocked back into position and two smaller ones added above. The height of barrels varied, the ends being sawn off when they got damaged, or the girth diminished by removing a split plank, the hoops replaced by smaller ones.

Filled barrels were rolled out to the top of the beach, laid on their sides and the bung removed, so that they could be topped up with brine — half a cupful at a time towards the end, as this seeped down to find its own level. Any birds failing to get submerged turned 'rusty'.

Extra brine was made by adding salt to sea water until this was concentrated enough to float an egg or a potato — not a bad egg as this floated anyway in fresh water. This gem of information I gained from Dom Serventy, who insisted on taking a potato with him when he went birding on Little Green Island. The brine was strained through hessian into a storage barrel, from where it was dipped as required. Each addition created a beer-like froth on the dusky fluid within.

Some of the 'early birds' consigned to brine were to be shipped out the following week to Launceston, most sent on their way by Island Stores in Lady Barron, but Bruce would see his own barrels out to retailers when he got home. Often, he lamented, the retailers spoiled the birds by opening the barrels in the wrong way and he would be sending a man to show them how it should be done this year. The proper way was to drain the brine out to the level of the bung to allow loosening of planks for lid removal — after which the hoops must be replaced to make a watertight seal for topping up with brine again. Birds kept their quality only if submerged and the uppermost had to be weighed down with a brick to prevent them floating to the top.

The autumnal April day ended with Christine swilling the salting bench down with buckets of sea water. Robinsons had dug themselves a freshwater soak behind the beach ostensibly for this, but the health inspectors suspected it was used for other purposes and regarded sea water as quite adequate and more hygienic. Bruce busied himself raking up soiled tussock grass and feathers and strewing new grass on the cooling racks and floors. The girls discarded their shoes and took boxes down to the sea to scrub clean.

Bill Riddle was straining the last two kerosene tins of oil into drums, tipping the gurrie and residual oil out on the beach; sacrificing the extra few cupfuls of oil that would have surfaced by morning in his desire to get all shipshape by the end of the day.

They gathered round their evening repast and I moved off into the dusk, laden with de-fatted mutton birds which supplied all but two of my remaining meals on Great Dog. As I picked my way homeward through scrub and tussock, the languid moonlit world seemed strangely quiet after the bustling industry and blood and guts of the day.

Vistas of star-bright sea came and went through the tracery of branches, but the peace was short-lived. Soon the adult shearwaters started whooping in from the black rafts that had been gathering on those shimmering expanses. I crossed an open brackenny area where the inspectors had been prospecting earlier for a possible airstrip, to avoid the tedious waits for boats that they suffered at present — and also to aid the regular delivery of fresh birds.

They had dined when I got in, thinking I would be eating with the Riddles, so I fried and consumed my bird in isolation. Before retiring I wandered round the moon-drenched paddock, dodging the swoosh of passing wings and listening to the cries of welcome from burrow occupants as their supper loomed closer. And so to a blissful night in a sleeping bag of mutton bird down from which all traces of odour had been removed, allowing me to savour the sweet smell of the pine needles in my mattress.

84 Squeezing Oil and Gurrie from Mutton Bird Chicks outside hatch

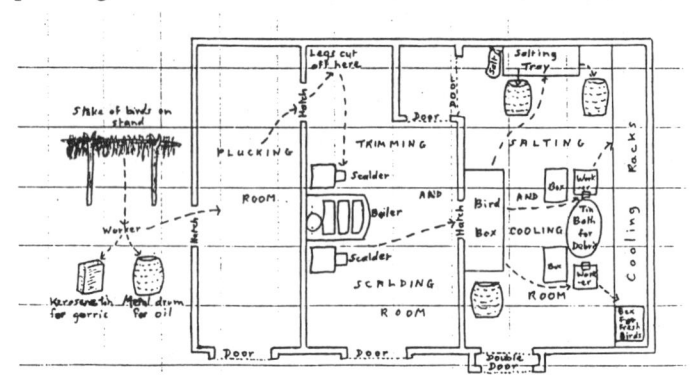

85 Diagram of typical Processing Shed

86 Boiler for scalding Mutton Birds

2. ON AND AROUND THE DOG ISLANDS

My companions in the homestead left at 7.30 one morning, their plans radically altered at the eleventh hour, as so often. Tuck was to drop them at Lady Barron, from where the senior member would pilot the little government plane to inspect birders on Trefoil Island and the junior would stock up with stores and move onto Little Dog Island. I went down to see them off and ask if Dom would be joining me on the morrow, as arranged.

We were met with the news that the plane had come to grief the previous day in a bad landing on Babel Island. The propeller had been knocked off and the undercarriage damaged by a malevolent shelf of granite hiding in the grass. The pilot, unhurt, had got back to Flinders Island on "*The Barge*" and boarded the scheduled flight to Launceston to get new parts.

The Trefoil Island visit receded into an unscheduled future and Fenner decided to stand in for his colleague on Babel Island instead. The old ecological adage of "Adapt or Perish" applied to all of us here! Adaptability and a willingness to change course at the drop of a hat were vital to survival in this sort of life. I returned to re-heat my panful of mutton bird and tomatoes and busied myself with field notes and the composing of a seventeen-verse poem on "Hard Ground" for the Fisher Island log book, at Dom's request.

John Nield had come ashore to visit sheds which he leased at opposite ends of the island, manned by half-castes. He stopped to chat. Taking a lively interest in natural phenomena, he had much to tell about Tin Kettle Island, where he held the grazing lease.

I botanised during the afternoon in a partially derelict rookery, where some of the burrows in the fast-eroding soil had roofs no more than an inch thick, held together precariously by a fibrous mat of grass roots. A hoary-looking type by the name of Davies came by, his shirt greasy from carrying stake-loads of birds. He expressed astonishment at the sight of a spreadeagled stranger reaching into burrows, and presumably up to no good. But this rookery was not his, he was just passing by to see if the boat he'd left below the homestead was still at its moorings. Health inspector number two was back from his day on Little Dog when I returned, so we combined forces in the preparation of our mutton bird stew.

It was more mutton bird for breakfast, after which we set off together, calling first at Willis's establishment. Set well above sea level among shade trees, this seemed an ideal holiday cottage, with a line of laundered baby nappies fluttering in the breeze. There were no employees here, this was a family affair, with five-year-old Gillian cutting off the birds' legs and two boys, even younger, spreading cleaned birds on the cooling racks.

The uppermost shelf held the fruits of the previous night's fishing trip in the dinghy — flounders, flathead, mullet and pike. The scalding fire was again of blackboys, bought from the Cape Barren islanders.

From here we visited Robinson's shed on the south side — a less highfalutin setup than the family concerns and worked by paid labour. One of the dark-skinned ladies was openly hostile, but Robinson, Tuck's brother, was affable enough, walking with us almost to the summit of Big Hill to show us a special white chick. It was not an albino, having dark eyes, pink legs and an orange beak, its handsome white down liberally sprinkled with orange oil from within by the time he had finished handling it.

There had been a white chick in this burrow for five consecutive years now and the lives of all had been spared. The men had not been up there at night to ascertain whether either, or even both the parents were white, as seemed likely, with no normal dark chicks being produced for at least five years, possibly longer.

When I eventually got back to Fisher Island, I found Dom Serventy and Bill Mollison quartering the rookeries on hands and knees, pegging out the burrows and ringing the year's crop of chicks. There were alarmingly many addled eggs and a number of eggless burrows which Dom blamed firmly on the marauding, sea-going water rats. I learned later that the two of them had gone round the larger island of Babel twice on their hands and knees, snakes or no snakes, on an earlier occasion.

Bill Riddle had had other stories to tell of the eminent scientist as a young fisheries officer on a research vessel plying round these islands. "Pointy Spanish beard, pith helmet, eyeglass, the lot!"

Perhaps that was when he first fell in love with the mutton birds, which he had insisted on studying ever since, although detailed by his employers to conduct research on rabbits. Whatever our eccentric friend did, he did with might and main, to the exclusion of almost all else!

We rounded off that day with a party ashore, during which fisherman, Keith Williamson, asked me for the photo of his boat which he had seen me taking awhile before. Since then there had been a minor explosion and a fire on board and the boat had later piled onto an offshore reef and broken up. Something was needed to remember her by! He complimented me on my prowess with "Half Safe" on rough seas. Soft soap, or sincerely meant? I hoped the latter. Such praise from a professional seaman, if not latterly a very successful one, was praise indeed.

We adjourned from the beer mugs at Derek Smith's place to Jerry Addaway's, where Mrs Nichols was helping to peel a huge mound of freshly gathered mushrooms, and joined her postmaster husband, a retired lieutenant-colonel from the British Army, sipping sherry.

'Honest Tom' Langley sauntered in to discuss my prospects of getting to Kangaroo Island. Hiring of boats, as well as taxis, was one of his sidelines, despite the twinkling comment of: "The thought of charging you anything when I look into your eyes never occurs to me."

Whereupon Dom leaps to his feet with: "Them's fighting words, Tom." It was that sort of an evening.

Bill Mollison, togged up in some more than usually respectable clothes from Tom's wardrobe, outstayed us by several hours. Dom and I took an oar apiece in "Half Safe". Bill borrowed a dinghy and was well launched before discovering that he had only one oar and had forgotten how to skull over the stern. It took him a long time to make it across, paddling Indian fashion, first one side and then the other. He was adamant that the amount of alcohol consumed had nothing to do with his erratic progress. Early next morning we towed the offending boat back before it was missed.

When next I was on Great Dog Island, nine months later, in December, it seemed strangely deserted without all the bustle of the harvest. We landed at Robinson's shed, where Dom wanted to show me the effects on the plant life of a new land rover track opened up from north to south.

On the way in, Tuck landed us on all three of the Spences Reefs. Silver gulls and blue penguins were confirmed as nesting on the eastern reef, white-faced storm petrels on the others, but no mutton birds. On the way out he dropped us on Penguin Island, where we recorded more petrels, some caspian tern chicks and a few gulls' nests.

Cape Barren geese met us on the Great Dog beach and two white-breasted sea eagles were sailing, vigilant, over their nest in the eastern tea-tree scrub. Dom and Bob Tilt busied themselves ringing mutton bird chicks while I collected samples of sand and peat for later analysis. I was intrigued how most of the burrows in Yorkshire fog grass sloped up towards the surface within the entrance. Birds seemed to regard the mat of roots and dead leaves as adequate roofing. Certainly it excluded the light, but might lead to disaster if anything, even as light as a sheep, walked across the top.

It was mid-March in 1960 when I came to Great Dog again, helping to land a load of casks for mutton birds processed in the Willis sheds. John Nield punted us out to *"Tassie"* and Tuck took us into the Lady Barron quay, where our two visiting West Australian farmers were in their element rolling and heaving the barrels aboard.

The onshore wind was in our favour when we arrived on Great Dog and the empty vessels were heaved overboard to make their own way ashore. Many hands dragged them out onto the banked sea-grass and rolled them up the beach. Mrs Willis and her son showed us round the premises, which they had decided to lease out to another team — from Cape Barren — during the coming harvest.

Other huts were changing hands and Tuck took Nield to move his equipment from one which he was abandoning to another which he was taking over. This was next to his other holding, making for greater convenience in working.

The farmers, used to closely grazed paddocks, seemed not to enjoy floundering through the tussocks to find birds to photograph and emerged onto the beach with undisguised relief. We followed the shore to Riddle's hut, where we turned inland, losing the badly overgrown track in the scrub, but finding our way eventually to the Homestead paddock, where a patch of belladonna lilies bloomed in pink profusion.

Members of the Willis family had lived there in 1908 and it was far from new then. Its age was very apparent now, the back entrance blocked by a tangle of brambles. Three of the research team, Mycky, Ted and John, were due to be taken off, and they were on the beach with their gear by the time we got back.

* * * * *

Little Dog Reef lay off the south-west corner of Little Dog Island, but it was its opposite number on the north-east that I found most rewarding. This was extremely noisy and was loosely tethered to the main island by an interrupted reef, menacing as a dragon's jaw. Tuck always gave this a wide berth when landing us.

On my first visit, his grandchildren, helping their mum and dad get the hut opposite shipshape for the harvest, ran down the beach waving and shouting, fearing that he was giving them the cold shoulder, but they got their visit from Gran'dad while we were investigating the bird life.

The translucent water over the white sand was as clear and colourful as a chlorinated swimming pool. Tuck scarcely ruffled its surface as he ferried us in, two by two, sculling over the stern with a single oar, an art which he had perfected by much practice over the years.

Black-faced and little pied shags took off in a magpie cloud as we rounded the point and a skein of the cosmopolitan large black cormorants, which frequent most UK shores, sped past across the shimmering surface. A mob of crested terns rose as a body, but remained suspended, screaming invective. They hovered, seemingly motionless, although leaning on the wind, flying into the air stream at the same speed that it was pushing them back, so that their ground speed was nil.

Slightly bigger than the white-fronted terns of New Zealand, these had greyer backs, and the black head feathers ruffled into a crest behind the yellow bills. It is this same species, *Sterna bergii*, that goes by the name of swift tern in South Africa.

Now the third week in January, the mottled brown chicks, about thirty of them, were three-quarters grown and able to trot nimbly over the ground, or bob, light as corks, on the calm water. As we landed on the leeward side, the chicks that took to the water did so to windward and were soon drifted back and deposited on dry land like so many feathered shuttlecocks. Here they remained and we took care not to panic them again.

Adult birds soon came to ignore us and continued to fly in with fish, picking their own offspring from the huddle or crèche where the youngsters congregated after leaving the nest. Feeding rituals proceeded undisturbed, under a battery of cameras poorly concealed behind a large boulder.

Four kinds of fish were being brought in, these averaging three inches long. They were held singly, crosswise in the bill. There were yellowish flounders, flattened horizontally and reddish fish flattened vertically. Others resembled well-grown sardines and there were transparent tiddlers like whitebait, great shoals of which habitually milled around under the Lady Barron jetty. The spectacle was delightful, but the noise horrendous: terns have such scratchy voices. The streamlined forms were the epitome of grace, but the raucous cacophony of cries created bedlam.

Since the créches of young birds had formed the nesting sites had been little used, but were still heavily fouled, the former covering of pigface, spinach and samphire wilting under the strain.

The granite feeding tables of the Pacific gulls were spread with hundreds of broken shells, almost exclusively finely tapered whelk-like, white spindle or murex shells *(Fusus)*, averaging three inches long. These were very solidly built and must have been dropped from a great height to be smashed as they were. Shellfish this size usually live in fairly deep water and gulls are surface feeders, so their abundance posed a problem as to how the gulls might have obtained the live specimens.

They would have had no trouble in reaching the few abalones, whose empty shells lay among the murex. These lived at extreme low water, but would need a powerful jab to loosen their hold, even if they were out grazing. Once dislodged, the saucer-shaped shells would not have to be opened.

The shags did not nest here, using the island only as a roost. They favoured the north (seaward) end and returned to some offshore boulders there to await our departure. Terns tended to move seasonally between Neds Reef off the north-west of Cape Barren Island, Cat Island and the nearby Storehouse Island. We had reports that the Cat Island colony contained few birds this year. Perhaps some of their former members had moved here.

87 Boxes of fresh Mutton Birds going off by sea

88 Rare White Mutton Bird Chick, fifth in succession in the same burrow

89 Large Black Cormorants *Phalacrocorax carbo*

3. LITTLE GREEN ISLAND: A ROOKERY REPRIEVED

Although the 212-acre island of Little Green was our nearest neighbour, it seemed inordinately difficult to get there. Boatmen, like carpenters and decorators, preferred jobs big enough to pay reasonable dividends.

Arthur Harland had arranged to take Bill Mollison and me across one February Sunday, but his boat was firmly aground until floated off on the midday tide. As we waited disconsolately on Fisher Island, munching the packed lunch made from week-old bread the consistency of cardboard, Bill was at pains to point out that Arthur was a Pommie, so I couldn't blame the lackadaisical Aussies this time.

We envied the complacency of the nearby sooty oystercatcher, whose head was tucked into the shoulders in simulated sleep, but whose one bright eye had us under constant surveillance. Harland's boat bobbed derisively on deep water just across the strait, but her master was away beyond the jetty, helping to free a fishing boat that had run ashore in the previous day's gale. He was crewing on one of the three vessels that had rallied round to tow it off on the peak of the tide. We gave up and busied ourselves moving the woodpile out of reach of that same tide.

There was no sign of him next morning, so we rowed ashore, to find that he was away driving the school bus — everyone seemed to have so many irons in the fire here, whether ostensibly retired or not! Derek Smith was pushing his boat out, but we had no luck there either. He was off trolling for pike, but was too much of an inshore fisherman to risk having to go as far as Little Green twice. Tuck was not available: he had potatoes to dig.

"They're going green for want of getting out of the ground."

We prevailed upon him, however, to come and fetch us in the evening if we rowed ourselves across. Derek towed us out to Fisher, where we packed newly acquired bread, crayfish tail, tinned tomatoes, fruit cake and the essential pop bottles of water, and set off before the increasing choppiness got too much.

It was hard splashy going, with Bill at the oars and me bailing, but we made it, sliding upwind of the pole marking the submerged reef and pausing for breath in the island's eastern lee, while watching the stately progress of four black swans — as at ease on the sea as on the lagoons. Edging up a samphire-filled creek, we left the boat on a long anchor rope, to allow for the tide, and paddled in across sand cushioned with eelgrass.

Little Green Island was noted for its healthy population of copperhead snakes, so we saw to it that our passage through the thick, bush-studded tussock was a noisy one. We flushed four copperheads, of burnished bronze flecked with orange sun glints, and a drabber whip snake, but no tigers. It is likely that none of these occur on this island.

Leila Barrett blamed the abundance of the copperheads for the recent decrease in the shearwaters, maintaining that there had been fewer snakes when there were cats on the island. She thought the cats should be reintroduced, as they preferred snakes to birds, but, fortunately, she was alone in this belief. Feral cats are seldom welcome under any circumstances.

A patch of low-growing grass, hollyhock and purslane in the south-west was being used as a feeding ground by a small flock of geese, which seemed to be concentrating on the seeds of the big quaking grass *(Briza maxima)*. We found crop pellets containing the grains, but these could have been coughed up by either gulls or geese.

Coursing back and forth across the island, we crested an eminence to be greeted by a fine panorama, embracing the Spences Reefs, Big Dog and the imposing profile of the Strzeleckis. The tide was well down when Tuck's boat was sighted and we had a long wade trundling the dinghy over smooth granite slabs and Posidonia beds, sometimes sinking shin-deep in oozy mud.

It was April when I joined three others to go mutton-birding on Little Green Island — ostensibly for live prey. Thirty more adults were required for the CSIRO labs at Nedlands, Perth. These came back in boxes, but spent the night loose in the Fisher Island toilet, being re-boxed for air transport the next day. 'Honest Tom' supplied us with a barrel for edible chicks, half of these destined for the Fisher Island store and half for Miss Barrett, who was as experienced in birding, as in much else. We took our own supply of blackboy stems, collected on the Flinders' heath during a recent plant hunt.

Eight months later we were there again, rowing across on the spur of the moment to make the most of an idyllic calm. It was mid-December, with Dom Serventy and Bob Tilt ringing adult birds and me collecting soil samples. So much of the vegetation had recently been consumed by fire, that we were all filthy — particularly Bob, who had been spreadeagled most of the morning reaching birds out for Dom to ring. Our tasks completed, a sea bathe took priority over food.

Another fourteen months and I was able to spend longer on Little Green Island, in company this time with Michael and Paula Ridpath and Minette Ross. We hedged our bets, towing "Half Safe" behind Tuck's *"Tassie"*, 'lest he forget', and leave us stranded. It was still early in the day as we unloaded the camping gear on an east-facing point.

Banded goshawk and sea eagle looked down censoriously and a blackbird fled, giving voice to its hysterical alarm call. There were curlew, dotterel and quail, swamp harrier and all the usual coast birds. Near the landing was a cast snake skin and a dead snake, both coppers, alongside a dead shearwater. We failed to work out how both snake and bird had died together and whether the sloughed skin belonged to the deceased.

After a busy morning, we grilled steaks over a driftwood fire and washed them down with coffee. The afternoon proved wet and gusty, gamin breezes tweaking paper from our grasp and sending it spiralling out over the sea. Having been up since before six and with a long night's work ahead, Minette and I retired to the tent for a snooze. The wind did not rob us of sleep, but we woke to find that the oar used as the back tent pole had collapsed and the canvas had sagged down on top of us, limply held by the boat hook used as the other pole.

Righting matters, we were in time to produce grilled bacon and eggs for the two who had braved the elements. The storm passed and we clambered to the nearby viewpoint to admire a superb flame-coloured sunset, like a monstrous bushfire behind the Strzeleckis. A host of mutton birds were swirling over the blood-coloured sea, rising and splashing down, as though impatient for the light to fade and allow them safely ashore.

Penguins among rocks by the camp were getting tuned up for their nightly performance of trumpeting and growling, a sound that was audible on Flinders across the water on still nights. We were loath to leave the motley colour display, but a nippy wind eventually drove us back to the warmth of the campfire, which Michael kept permanently stoked with driftwood,

At 8.30 p.m. we girded our loins for the first round of the rookery. Although this was a recognised 'study area', the birds were by no means conditioned and were exceedingly agile. We wore miners' head torches, to keep our hands free, and clicked our records onto an automatic counter.

After an hour and a half, we had collected 130 birds between us, two of these already ringed. One of them was the last to be picked up as we returned to the fire, but was also the first at the start of the next sortie, a hundred yards further on. Sustained by mugs of hot chocolate, we rested our weary limbs for an hour and then set off again, knocking up a similar total of birds on our second round.

At midnight I crawled into my sleeping bag for a couple of hours, fully clad except for boots. Mike donned his flying suit and did likewise, but the other two spent their waiting time by the fire crunching toast and marmalade and swigging more beverages.

I woke at half past three, to perceive the others returning from a third sortie for more toast and drinks, and was just sufficiently awake to hear Mike saying they would be off again at four. I determined to stay alert until then, lest they leave me to sleep again, but my next view of the world was of a fiery dawn blazing through the open tent door, its brilliance mirrored in the glassy sea.

Three dark forms were silhouetted against the glow: the workers were back. Minette stumbled into the tent and was asleep almost before touching down, but the Ridpaths strolled hand in hand along the dawn-fresh beach — young lovers with a romantic Utopia for themselves alone. They returned an hour later, Paula's French vivacity undiminished by her gruelling night. In fact, after spending half her time leaping crazily over tussocks, grabbing at grounded shearwaters, she had settled down to watch the private life of a particularly noisy pair of penguins. She flagged out soon after and lay, dead to the world, stretched on a lilo in her full kit — flying suit, boots and gloves.

Michael remained on his feet, seeing to the fire — which disappeared a while later under a foot of water, as an unusually high tide seeped up the crevices on either side of our dining slab. We rescued the last glowing embers and brewed some coffee, leaving the two girls to sleep on.

The night's catch totalled 363 birds, seven of which were already ringed. Three of the seven had been ringed on Little Green Island, the other four on Fisher Island. Three of those were ringed there as fledgelings and had been recorded back on Fisher Island as three and four-year-olds, prospecting for nest sites, but had chosen to move to the neighbouring island when it came to the real thing. This was, I think, the first evidence of a definite site change, and not because all the burrows on their natal island were in use.

The fourth Fisher Island bird had been ringed as an adult and had bred on Fisher Island until 1952, but had been missing from there during the subsequent eight years, so infidelity to site, and probably mate, might occur later. Perhaps the bird had disliked the constant monitoring.

* * * * *

Birds suffered less disturbance on Little Green Island, where there had been no commercial birding during 1958, 1959 and 1960, although there was still some egg collecting and birds were taken for crayfish bait. All the rookeries were on the coastal slopes, making it easier for poachers. Some forty acres of the island centre were unburrowed and surrounded by a dilapidated wire fence.

Cattle had been grazed there for an unknown period until removed fifteen years before, and Tuck blamed these for treading in many of the nest holes in this enclosed central paddock where they were originally confined. Twenty to thirty cattle were run here and a photograph taken in 1938 showed grazing sheep. Subsequently cattle had roamed at will over the whole area.

Coast wattle was encroaching onto the old grazing plot through the broken fence and other shrubs taking hold were dogwood, coast beard heath and coast tea-tree. An attractive sward of the velvety pink hare's-foot clover *(Trifolium arvense)* was noticed.

The number of habitable burrows far outstripped the number actually inhabited, according to those who had taken harvests there, yet many eggs were still laid on the ground surface. Were these the product of young birds, I wondered, not yet geared to what was required of them in the full breeding routine? Subsequent studies proved that they were.

Tuck told us that teams from seven sheds had been working in 1926, averaging 17,000 birds each — a total of 119,000 — then, later, six huts, taking 20,000 each or slightly more in total. J. E. C. Lord, in his *"Report of the Furneaux Islands"*, written in 1908, quoted a similar annual take for 1907, when thirty-three people were involved in the harvest.

The two huts left in business in 1956 were said to have collected 31,000 between them; the sole remaining team in 1957, gathering birds over the whole island and taking 16,000.

An article in "*The Hobart Gazette*" of 15th December 1891, stated that Little Green Island was reserved for mutton-birding except for two freehold blocks, consisting of forty-one acres belonging to T. W. Barrett and sixteen acres to H. Taylor. The reserve had not been released for grazing since 1897 and was generally regarded as having been greatly damaged by the livestock, even as far back as the end of the nineteenth century.

Cattle were necessarily more of a menace to an underground population than lighter-footed sheep. If the soil was sandy, the chief threat was from collapse: if clayey, it was consolidation to the point where burrowing became impossible.

Sand, much of it probably blown from the beaches, accumulated on coast-facing slopes. In the central paddock the soil was a dark peaty loam of much finer texture. Burrows there were considerably wetter than elsewhere, possibly because the higher clay fraction held onto more water. In spring they were as wet as those of Snake Gully on Fisher Island, which sometimes contained standing water.

Frequent burning destroyed the colloidal organic fraction of the soil and the subsequent wind scour of the bared surface removed the finer particles first. Aggravated by excessive fires, there might be only coarse sand and granite shingle left near the top, making it too unstable for burrowing. It may be that no burning at all allowed the soil to develop too far the other way, and so lose the friability that made the average rookery so burrowable. There is a fine line here; an ecological razor edge between the moisture retention that makes for good livestock grazing and the 'workability' that makes for easy bird burrowing.

The running of cattle was made possible by a water hole that occurred at the east end of the paddock and a marshy area in the low-lying west, where birds had been flooded from their burrows by the rains of December 1958, when a considerable area was under water, although chicks were reared here successfully in dry years. Pale rush and Yorkshire fog did well here and yellow buttons formed an intermittent ground cover, grading upwards into clustered clover.

Fog grass in the central paddock was second only to silver tussock, with alien cat's ear and sheep's sorrel the main subordinates, followed by quaking grass and knob sedge. Fifty per cent of the twenty-two species there were foreigners, as opposed to only thirty-eight per cent of the ninety-four species recorded on the island as a whole. Around the north-east shed, the dozen most abundant plant types and sixty-six per cent of the total of twenty-nine were of alien origin.

* * * * *

Little Green Island remained reprieved. By the 1995-96 birding season the only harvests being taken were from Great Dog Island, one of several to have been furnished with an airstrip by then for the more immediate export of processed birds.

Babel Island, which had once supported twenty-eight of the fifty-eight sheds working in the Furneaux Group (Skira, 1990, 1994) had only three sheds remaining in the 1960s, one in 1984 and none by 1991, following a diminished take of 3,200 birds in 1990. The island's remoteness has caused it to be priced out of the market. Transport costs were by now prohibitive because of the dwindling boat traffic and the lack of anywhere flat enough to build an airstrip.

All birds taken have to be salted and there is a limited market for these nowadays. Not only are landsmen jibbing at toiling in the rookery: modern seamen are not prepared to face the hazards of loading and offloading on unfriendly shores as their predecessors were.

Ten of the sixteen remaining birders in 1990 were Aboriginals and eleven of the twelve in 1994, only one of these with any other job. Nevertheless the continuance of the harvest — as part of Aboriginal culture — is regarded as vital from the social and psychological point of view and has been part of the political tangle to ensure sovereign rights to the natives regarding their traditional ways and food sources. This was finally resolved in parliament in 1995 and the coloureds have been given jurisdiction over Babel, Great Dog and Chappell Islands as part of their more widespread takeover of crown lands.

The new owners want to make birding on Great Dog Island into a commercial undertaking, although few are keen on reaching into burrows for the fledgelings. Rather would they take them off the surface at night — a practice long since illegal because of the difficulty of telling youngsters from adults now that they have lost their down and are of similar or greater size. There is no problem on the grounds of numbers, the population being described as "enormous", because of the dwindling takes.

Current findings are that fifty to sixty per cent of the burrows contain chicks, only seven per cent of which are taken — this being well within the safe calculated limit of a thirty-seven per cent take. The maximum permitted harvest is unlikely ever to recur, so it seems that the bird population is safe from human exploitation for the foreseeable future.

Unlike the world's fur seals, which were nearly exterminated, and America's passenger pigeons, which were, the mutton bird hosts have weathered the years of human onslaught almost unscathed. It will be interesting to see what happens to the surplus, as the already prodigious estimated twenty-three million breed on, almost unmolested.

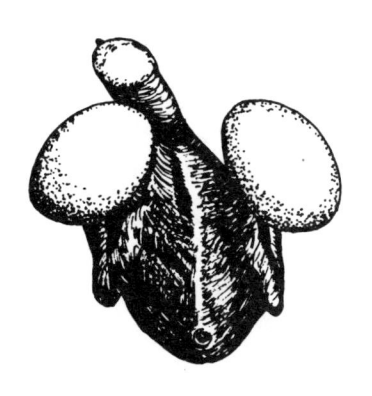

90 Cormorant Chicks, early stages of development

91 Bower Spinach *Tetragonia implexicoma*

92 Old Man's Beard *Clematis aristata*

Chapter Eleven

THE BABEL GROUP AND CAT ISLAND GANNETRY

1. SUCCESS AT LAST

Babel Island and its smaller satellites, Cat Island and Storehouse Island, were as important to the mutton bird industry in those early days as the sites in Franklin Sound, although more difficult of access. They lie almost halfway up the east coast of Flinders Island in the less protected waters facing onto the Tasman Sea.

Sellars Point, north of Sellars Lagoon, reaches out towards them and must have joined up when sea level was lower. The Babel Passage now is a treacherous jumble of shifting sandbanks which restrict and anger fast-running seas. Nevertheless, men have occasionally crossed on horseback at slack water of low tides.

Babel Island is the largest and nearest to the land, occupying 1,100 acres (445 hectares). Sellars Point is low and sandy, but the peaks of the three Patriarchs reach skyward just behind and the double summit of Mount Capuchin rising to 662 feet on Babel Island seems to be an outlier of the same group.

Cat Island is lower, at 105 feet, and smaller: seventy-four acres or thirty hectares. It lies a little further out and was home to a dwindling population of gannets as well as many other sea birds. It is dumbbell shaped, the two rugged halves connected by a sandy isthmus, where the wardens had their primitive living quarters.

Storehouse Island to its south is even smaller and was originally Strawhouse Island, from a thatched hut erected there.

The name of Babel was given to the whole group in 1799 by Captain Matthew Flinders. He wrote: "The island is inhabited by geese, shags, penguins, gulls and sooty petrels, each enjoying its separate district and using its own language. It was the confusion of noises that induced me to give the name Babel Islets to this small cluster." The 'geese' might have included solan geese, the old name for gannets, as well as Cape Barren geese,

His expedition was the first to make inroads into the fauna of Cat Island: "Where Mr Bass went onshore and brought off a boatload of seals and gannets." By 1958 the fur seals there were in even poorer shape than the gannets, the once thriving colony reduced to a single lonely individual known as Josephine.

My first visit was on 12th January, 1958 on the *"Aralla"*, which took three and a half — four hours each way, leaving us only a short time ashore. The voyage included a passage through or round the notorious Potboil — another treacherous jumble of sandbanks off the south-east corner of Flinders Island, where Logans or Potboil Lagoon nestled in the shifting sands of the shore.

As we approached it, a great yellow bank breasted the water like a stranded whale, with waves churning along its flanks. Silas Mansell stood in the bow, sussing out the best passage and waving the helmsman to port or starboard.

We made it through rather wetly and turned north alongside golden beaches dotted with pelicans. With us on *"Aralla"* was Arthur Harland, who had spent two seasons of three months each on Cat Island wardening the pathetic remains of the once splendid gannet colony. The present wardens were the English couple, John and Pat Warham.

The gannets, formerly present in thousands, had been reduced to eighteen pairs at this time by unprincipled cray fishermen taking them for bait. Nesting on the ground surface, they were 'sitting ducks', easier to come by than burrow-dwelling shearwaters or penguins or the more excitable gulls and terns.

This group had been the only accessible colony in Australia and could have been the archipelago's most spectacular tourist attraction — the more numerous burrowers being invisible by day and creating no visitor draw. As so often, the greed of the few had ruined it for the many.

This was my first experience of gannets in Australia, my several attempts to visit those on Lawrence Rocks off South-west Victoria having met with as little success as those of local ornithologists. I had, however, been one of the multitude of tourists visiting the birds at Cape Kidnappers and elsewhere around the coast of New Zealand.

The Australasian gannet, shared by Australia and New Zealand, is one of three species. The other in the Southern Hemisphere is the Cape gannet of South Africa, where I was to have the privilege of working in the vast colonies exploited commercially for their guano.

The North Atlantic gannet is shared between North-west Europe and North-east America and my student days in South Wales had involved a number of landings on Grassholm Island off the south-west of the principality. The fortunes of the gannets there were headed in the opposite direction. In the early 1950s the little twenty-two acre island held 3,000 nesting pairs. By the early nineties the colony had increased to 30,000 pairs — a phenomenal growth, leaving little room for further expansion.

"Aralla's" skipper had told us to bring mugs, knives, forks and spoons. The mugs were useful for morning tea en route, the cutlery was a joke. Lunch, when we finally got to it in late afternoon on the return voyage, was bread-based and needed no tools.

We were landed on one of Cat Island's sandy beaches, with instructions to be back in an hour and a half, this leaving no time for food. Warden John replaced Eric's sandals with gum boots, as a precaution against snakes. There was only one species here, the black tiger, but they were here in numbers. Warden Pat, who acted as my guide, avoided the denser tussocks and beat those ahead of her booted footsteps with a stout stake tipped with strong wire ending in a broad fork. This was useful for pinning a too bumptious snake to the ground while an escape strategy was worked out.

The gannet colony, when we finally circled round to it, was pathetic, an anticlimax after my experiences in crowded Welsh, Scottish and Irish gannetries. We managed a circuit of only half of the island today, but I would soon be back for a longer period. The other party had already returned to the landing beach and we were bundled unceremoniously aboard the dinghy while the skipper muttered dire predictions about the state of the tide at the Potboil.

My first thought when back on board was for food and I dived below for my cheese and vegemite, washed down with cordial. It was cold and wet up aloft, so I curled up on one of the bunks. When I woke in the early evening, it was to learn that it had been impossible to get through between the Potboil and Flinders and that we had sneaked round the outside, taking care not to get embroiled in the Vansittart Shoals beyond.

* * * * *

My return to Cat Island with much needed stores for the Warhams was long delayed. Their boxes of provender languished on Fisher as snag followed snag, and I threw out progressively more of the mildewed oranges and tomatoes, whose vitamin C was among the would-be recipients' primary need, I separated eight cracked eggs from sixteen good ones and stewed the steak which was fast approaching its 'sell-by date'. Stale loaves, which I could have done with the previous week, were broken up for the gulls.

When at last a dinghy arrived with the news that the *"Lady Merle"* would sail between 12.30 and 1.30, I Sellotaped the newly-opened milk tin, cushioned the cracked eggs, scoured the billies, dowsed the fire and carried all the crates down to the slip.

At 1.30, when I found time to raise my eyes from the tasks in hand, I realised that the blue sky was no longer with us and that some very dirty weather was on its way. There was just time to get some of the more vulnerable stuff back to "Yolla" when the storm broke. And what a storm. All the pent-up energy of a sea held back by a contrary wind came roaring across the sound as that wind let up. In less than a minute visibility was down to a few yards, rain was pouring in through cracks in the roof and foaming seas replaced the calm of the morning. Father Neptune had once more timed his show of power to prevent me from getting to Cat Island.

A persevering gull tried time and again to perch on the tipsy notice board which had been saying nothing for several years, but it was blown off every time. Then the wind subsided, but not the waves. Once more I must sully my meticulously cleaned premises.

When I ventured out to find what the storm had brought in, it was to find instead what it had taken out. All the bigger, less manageable logs from the woodpile, that the men had left as far downshore as seemed safe, had taken off. Some had drifted against North-east Point and I waded in to spend the next hour or so making a new stack there, throwing the lumps up the rocks in stages.

After lugging the rest of the gear back to the hut to dry out, I was ready for supper, but the well-douched fire refused to relight. The Primus stove needed pricking, but there were no prickers. Broom bristles and pins proved too thick and nylon fishing line too flimsy, but the unravelling of some old wire gauze did the trick at last. Unfortunately the resulting flame was too fierce for either cracked scrambled eggs or the toast to go with them.

Next morning dawned calm and blue. Nothing could stop the *"Lady Merle"* now. Nothing did. At 5.0 a.m., before her skipper thought I would be awake, I spotted her slipping out of port in the opposite direction. There was only one other boat left at the jetty, a visiting two-masted schooner — and so perished another hope.

The afternoon brought the low spring tide that goes with a full moon; inimical to boats in inshore waters, but with plenty to interest the marine biologist that I became after working out my latest valence squares.

As a host of constellations began to twinkle across the night sky, the tide moved in over the flats and hundreds of shearwaters spilled in behind along the silvered path of moonlight. They fluttered, moth-like, back and forth and up and down, ghosted by their reflections on the sea below. When they plucked up courage to move in, they came silently, not to alert lightly sleeping gulls. It was the oystercatchers which piped through those long light nights, as though they felt the day had forgotten to fade.

It was more than a month after my first visit that I finally made it to Cat Island to stay. A boy in a dinghy announced that Trooper Bailey had a load of cement for Babel Island and would call for me at 5.0 a.m. next day — 15th February. It was panic stations to get organised in a later than usual dawn, but I was well ahead by the time the puny light from my candle was obliterated by an ensemble of red and purple streaks. We were away by 6.0 a.m., the deck cargo of building material dwarfing my mound of bedding and stores. Some of the paper sacks had already split and we took care not to trample any of the fast-setting grey powder into the cabin below.

It all seemed too easy this time. Bailey's promises of transport had an uncanny way of falling through. Soon after I boarded, Sergeant George Hanlon, field man for the Tasmanian mainland police, emerged from below, and I realised why. The Tasmanian Fauna Board intended building a superior homestead on Babel Island for use during the birding season and the contractors had sent workmen up from Hobart months before. When no building materials appeared they had been withdrawn.

George Hanlon, who I was to come to know well during subsequent travels around Tasmania, had been sent across to get things moving. A former resident of Whitemark and an experienced boatman, he knew his way around and had soon mobilised Bailey and three fishing boats. By 6.0 a.m. the morning after his arrival, all were loaded up and on their way. He had been blessed with good weather, but George was not one to let the grass grow under his feet, come wind or high water.

He was a fine bushman, one of the few to have had an authentic sighting of the Tasmanian tiger or thylacine — and achieved wonders in bringing some semblance of law into the outback, despite an impossibly large area of ground to be covered. I owed much to him during those first years in the South. A great guy to be with, he was kindly, competent and cunning in outwitting both wild animals and wild men.

Very conscious of his lack of schooling, he would tell of times when he was unable to go at all in winter, because he had neither boots nor overcoat. He lamented not being able to get higher in the police force, because the exams were beyond him. In reality, he would have been a great loss to the force if he had been promoted beyond the present post of field ranger that he filled so ably, with his cleverly thought-out traps for miscreants. I never enquired if he was responsible for confiscating "Half Safe" and landing it on the Fisher Island lot!

With us today was half-caste Silas Mansell, who had birded regularly on Babel Island until five years before. He had pulled out when labour got too pricey.

"Can't get even a boy now for £150 the season" (which lasted five weeks).

He trailed a line over the stern, fitted with a lethal looking but unbaited hook, hoping for barracuda. The line was bitten through and the hook lost but nothing was brought aboard.

A black-browed albatross caught up with us and followed hopefully in our wake. Even in the absence of waste from the catch, we might have stirred something up, but evidently not. A few stretches of sea were crowded with mutton birds, which can only be nocturnal when on land. Most spectacular, however, was the school of about fifty dolphins, leaping out of the water and diving beneath the boat. The graceful animals stayed with us for about twenty minutes — for the sheer fun of it.

"Always love to see dolphins" exulted Silas. "We took them for bait — with a harpoon." Was there anything they didn't take?

Fortunately the rest of the school was expected to make off when one got into difficulties, so only singles were taken. Today's long fence nets for tuna trap and drown far more, taking an untargeted, completely wasteful toll!

Bait seekers were a lawless lot. Gannets, mutton birds and penguins were slaughtered wholesale — even on Storehouse Island, in full view of the Cat Island wardens, who were helpless to stop them without a boat. Fishermen had exterminated the cormorant colony on a stack between Cat and Storehouse Islands, maintaining that the birds were taking too many fish.

A bullet, hopefully intended for a gannet, had hurtled through the wall of the warden's hut on Cat Island, narrowly missing Arthur Harland, seated within. Another had gone through his water tank and he had had to boil drinking water from brackish cliff pools for five days until a boat arrived with more. This was brought in old molasses tins that had not been properly washed out, so that it soon fermented in the hot sun and became undrinkable. Arthur was back to boiling the green-scummed brew from guano-fouled pools!

Those gun-happy years, when truckloads of booze-stimulated toughs hurtled through the bush at night, potting at kangaroos, rabbits or anything else that appeared in their gun sights, human or otherwise, are hopefully a thing of the past in these more enlightened nineties.

By 9.0 a.m. we had safely negotiated the Potboil and were chugging through the narrows between Cat and Babel Islands, turning into the north-west corner of Babel towards Monument Point where the new house was to be built.

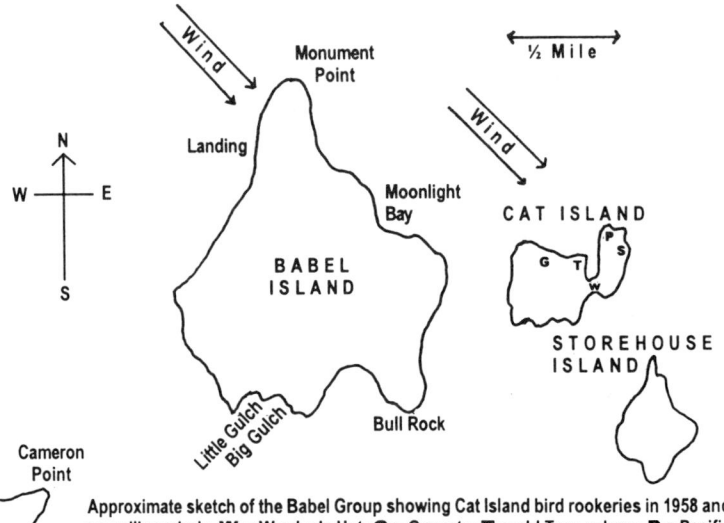

93 Map of the Babel Group

94 Aboriginal rowing water tank into Babel Island

95 Cormorants in flight

1. Land cleared for polled Hereford cattle.
Whitemark, Flinders Island, 1960

2. and 3. Unloading roan and brindle cattle
from the deck of *"Prion"* 1959

Plate I

4. Loading superphosphate for aerial top dressing. Flinders Island

5. *Kunzea ambigua* on Big Dog Island

6. Grass Tree fruiting spikes damaged by Yellow-tailed Black Cockatoos

Plate II

7. Yacca Gum crusher, Lady Barron. The Grass Tree material from Cape Barren Island

8. Grass Tree leaf bases from which resin is extracted

9. Yacca Gum exuded from Grass Tree in bushfire

Plate III

10. Derek Smith with newly-caught Wombat, 1958

11. Brush-tail Possum: a Tasmanian 'black' from Mount Wellington

12. Echidna or Spiny Ant-eater

13. Pademelon or Rufous Wallaby Joey whose dam has been shot

Plate IV

14. Trousers Point. South-west Flinders Island, 1958

15. Granite Peak above Dock, North-west Flinders Island, 1995

16. Castle Rock, Marshalls Bay, dwarfs beach walkers alongside, 1995

Plate V

17. Mutton Bird or Short-tailed Shearwater and egg in nesting burrow

18. Adult Mutton Bird in the hand. Note tubular nostrils

Plate VI

19. Eric Worrell (squatting), Dom Serventy and Tas Drysdale ring a Mutton Bird chick on Fisher Island

20. Silver Gulls wait for breakfast outside the Fisher Island research hut

Plate VII

21. The author with "Half Safe" on the Fisher Island slip. Reef Island and Strzelecki Peaks beyond

22. Blue Penguin chick and Austral Storksbill on Scotts Reef

23. The author after rowing to Big Dog Island, 1959

Plate VIII

24. A Cape Barren Islander prepares for
the bird harvest on Chappell Island

25. Bill Riddle carries Mutton Bird chicks
in on Big Dog Island

Plate IX

26. Paper Nautilus shells

27. Collection of sponges from Fisher Island

28. Marine treasures, Fisher Island

Plate X

29. Crested Terns rise from Tuck's Reef

30. Tuck's little boat off a Crested Tern colony in Franklin Sound

Plate XI

31. Crested Terns with fish

32. Cape Barren Goose

33. Remnant of the Gannetry on Cat Island, 1958

Plate XII

34. Eric Worrell bags a black Tiger Snake among Chappell Island Barilla

35. Painting Goose Island lighthouse

36. Ross's Noon Flower

Plate XIII

37. Doleritic Columnar Basalt, Tasman Island, South-east Tasmania

38. Coast Cheeseberry or Pink berry on Tasman Island summit

39. Exhausted cow after swimming to Bruny Island from SS *"Cape York"*

Plate XIV

40. Maatsuyker Island lighthouse and Brownie,
off South-west Tasmania

41. Maatsuyker Island, South-west Tasmania
Temperate rainforest vegetation

Plate XV

42. Corner of Steep Head Island, North-west Tasmania, viewed from 'Tiger Moth'

43. Calcareous concretions exposed by erosion on King Island dunes, North-west Tasmania

Plate XVI

2. ALL GO ON BABEL ISLAND

Babel Island, while closer to the shore than many in Franklin Sound, was more oceanic. Mobile components of the sea bed had been scoured away to bedrock and the great claw holdfasts of the bull kelp were the only grappling organs devised by plants able to maintain a grip. Here were no sandy flats of sea-grass and eelgrass.

Shining brown 'oars' of the *Durvillea antarctica* oarweed swirled back and forth with the ebb and flow of each wave, rhythmically mesmerising in their endless pendulum swing. I was minded of the writhing masses that surged to and fro off subantarctic shores, squeezing the homecoming penguins from the restless, rubbery carpet, tiddlywink fashion, like corks from a bottomless bottle.

Not all the holdfasts held fast all the time and it was just such seaweeds as these that had been ripped from their anchorage to pile man-high along the opposing shore of Cameron Inlet, where we had our glorious beachcombing binge on my 1995 visit.

The boy who rowed me ashore made heavy weather of the journey as the octopus-like coils tugged at the oars. Outboard motors fared little better as the strands wrapped around the propeller blades. The tide was falling, so things got worse rather than better as more and more of the snakelocks surfaced.

Looking back from the rugged mounded shore on that blue and gold morning, I beheld a dimpled expanse of sea, with every dimple throwing back moving shafts of light, like a spill of diamonds. Four powered launches idled on the dancing carpet, wavelets lapping along their sides and sending heliographs to heaven.

Four dinghies plied to and fro, one bright with new blue paint, another of pristine fibre glass. The more manageable inflatables had scarcely been invented then. A brand-new craft in maroon and pale blue, with outboard, had been towed across behind the police boat for use by the builders and was now pulled up beyond reach of the waves, on smooth granite.

I went off for two hours' exploration of the hinterland, returning to such a scene of bustle that I hitched a lift back to "*Aralla*" in the lightly bobbing fibre glass dinghy to get my camera and record some of it for posterity. Just moving around the island had left me hot and exhausted. The men were sweating and cursing, as they toiled through the uncooperative ebb tide to get the stuff ashore. Most were fishermen or policemen: the builders were supposed to be doing this, the rendezvous between the two parties being at 9.0 a.m.

The legitimate workmen were being flown in to make a beach landing on the opposite shore and walk across. The plane had come on time, but there was too little sand exposed to accommodate it. As the pilot circled back to

Flinders, the land-bound workers scowled up at the grinning faces of those aloft, who waved approval and encouragement as they saw their allotted task diminishing by the minute. By the time enough beach had been uncovered for the landing, most of the labouring had been done.

Heavy planks were being carried up over treacherous seaweedy rocks, balanced on men's shoulders: sheets of corrugated iron needed a team effort. An Aboriginal stood at the oars, ferrying in a thousand-gallon water drum, which left precious little room in the boat for him and his mate. Wheelbarrows full of a motley of gadgets and fixings were being trundled up through the impedimenta of boulders, but everything was dumped as close to high water mark as practicable. Silas worked like a slave and deserved the long beer which disappeared in a single, ecstatic gulp.

"A good man that. Can steer a compass course, which is more than most of them can."

He met me as I returned from a second sortie inland.

"See many snakes?"

I hadn't, actually, but I'd been aware of a lot of rustling grass ahead of me as they made off. He told me that the old horse passage from Babel to Flinders could be negotiated by truck at low springs.

"The processed mutton birds sometimes go off that way, but the families and heavy gear have to go by sea — in spite of transport costs of hundreds of pounds going to the boat owners! Trouble is, there's no track for the last few miles," and, of course, no roads on Babel Island. Having travelled that country with Derek Smith on 'roo hunts, almost as far as the low water crossing, I was inclined to think that there were more than a few miles on the Flinder's side without tracks.

A Victorian skipper, who had offered his services free, manoeuvred another monster water tank onto a Tasmanian boat which had been hired at the going rate. This was to be taken to the other side of the island. I was back on board *"Aralla"* by then and we chugged round behind, for Hanlon to brief the builders, who had by this time materialised on that distant shore — and stayed there. The tank safely landed, the fishing boat went off to check its cray pots and Hanlon rowed in to tell the builders what was expected of them. He came back fuming.

"They think they'll install the water tank first as they're here, and camp the night. Asked the police boat to go back and get their tucker! I told them where they could go!"

On the ensuing lap to Cat Island the hungry crew went below to dismember crayfish and hunks of bread. I stayed aloft, meaning to eat after landing on Cat Island, but accepted a succession of succulent cray legs passed up through the hatch. It was a long time since that 5.0 a.m. breakfast.

* * * *

The landscape of Babel Island was subtly different from that of islands in the Sound and not only because of the greater exposure. Less burning was practised here, but shearwater density was unabated. Silas said the birds were everywhere, this not quite true, as there were soil-less granite knolls covered with scrub, but they seemed more crowded than on islands visited so far. He didn't hold with burning as a management tool.

"Rookery always the same when you come back to it if you don't burn. Don't have to make roads through the tussock like on Great Dog."

Certainly there were few of the burned black stools with a foot or more depth of soil blown away from the bases to make them twice as tall. Here most leaves sprouted at ground level instead of way above. Going was difficult. In parts I trod through at almost every sixth step, often deeply enough to pitch forward onto vegetation which I dearly hoped, harboured no snakes.

There were two birding sheds where the materials had been put ashore and another ten scattered around the island. Seventeen processing sheds had been worked here at one time, each taking some 15,000 birds — "But there were plenty left" according to those in the know. Two shops had functioned on the island at that time to service the needs of the harvesters. Many of the birds were taken back to Cape Barren Island to tide the workers over the months ahead, but others were exported to New Zealand.

At one time seventy per cent went to supply the Maori market, but sales were to fall off and the distributors found themselves with a frozen stockpile. By 1986 outlets were drying up and the annual bustle of activity that had added the human babble to that of the birds, was officially at an end, although birds were still taken for home consumption.

The coastal fringe of succulents was broader than I was in the habit of seeing, the plants eking out a living from smaller depths of saltier soil than could be tolerated by most. Pigface was the hardiest, its form varying greatly from site to site. Where most exposed, it tended towards the 'jelly bean' form, the beans almost spherical in their plumpness. At the other extremity were long-leaved plants sheltered from both wind and sunlight in crevices.

Far-creeping stems of this and its near relatives would advance over plants on their inland flank, transforming spiky tussocks into smooth domes. Noon flower and spinach rose gradually to tapered seaberry saltbush and barilla, forming a partial windbreak for severely wind-trimmed coast wattle and boobialla.

Daisy bushes and tea-trees favoured more inland sites, with wild hop, kunzea, paperbarks and clematis. Soil was seldom deep enough for burrowing in the scrub patches investigated, but several mutton bird corpses were found strung up in the branches. Most birds learned to alight just outside and scuttle in among the spinach drapes along well-worn tracks.

Silas corroborated this, except where the scrub was of South African boxthorn "Brought by they damned black jays!" This could completely smother rookeries, excluding first the birders and then the birds. The thorny tangle was cut back at intervals but was still advancing.

"If I could've got hold of some waste sump oil from the Agricultural Bank, I'd've burned that lot off long ago!"

Silas still had a use for fire as a management tool.

Such small dune systems as I encountered were huddled in the lee of rising ground, the sand partly stabilised by grey humps of cushion bush. Other composites included three daisy bushes, three everlastings, five cudweeds, *Cassinia* 'dogwood' and *Brachycome*, as well as cat's-ear, fleabane and various dandelion-type weeds.

In 1958 the Babel plant list stood at 111 species, twenty-eight per cent of these foreigners. Cat Island had seventy-two, including seventeen per cent alien and Storehouse Island forty-three of which fourteen per cent were alien. Less common Babel shrubs were pink berry *(Cyathodes juniperina)*, tree broom heath *(Monotoca elliptica)*, *Correa reflexa* as well as white correa, sweet bursaria, sea box, coast banksia, cherry ballart and large-leaf bush pea.

In the valley behind Monument Point I came upon a cluster of wooden crosses, poignant memorials to wrecked sailors who had lost their lives on those treacherous shores. Some may have been from the *"Williamstown"*, wrecked in 1858, or from the *"Planter"*, lost in 1877 — the same year that the coal-carrying *"City of Foochow"* went ashore just to the north of Cameron Point. In 1880 the *"Jane Helen"* became a casualty off Babel.

Next day, across the water on Cat Island, I came across the last few timbers of *"The Tasman"*, wrecked in January 1951 on the southern rocks west of the wardens' hut, the remains fit now only for firewood.

Beyond Babel's lonely graveyard was an area that had once been cleared, an old stockyard, perhaps, rife with weeds. Most rampant was the yellow sow thistle, overtopping spear thistles on the rolling mat of downy grey fog grass. Both were shedding silky clouds of thistledown, wafting seeds to pastures new. Nearly three-quarters of the species here were aliens, and the locals — kangaroo apple, native nettle, grass and saltbush, were scarcely the choicest. A former scrub was indicated by blackened tree boles.

The lush growths, stimulated by nutrients from man or his livestock, had attracted numbers of Cape Barren geese, whose sausage-shaped droppings added to the general fertility. Mutton birds burrowed under the short-lived sow thistles but few had broken through the fog grass.

The other interruption in the predominant cover of tussock grass was the silver gull colony. Current occupation ensured that this was liberally guano-fouled with most of the former plants dead. The rain-stimulated aftermath was yet to come. Incomers at present were native leafy peppercress *(Lepidium foliosum)* and the cosmopolitan black nightshade *(Solanum nigrum)*.

"Aralla" followed the coast of Babel for a while and then struck east to Cat Island's southern beach. Hanlon rowed me in and John and Pat Warham waded out to help with the kit and stores. We manhandled the stuff up the line of planks over the low dunes and settled down to poached eggs on toast and an exchange of news and views.

They had been here since mid-November: three months, with no human contacts other than a passing seaman or a flying visit from Lew Bailey. The 8.30 a.m. radio exchange with Mrs Bailey kept them in touch with what was going on in the outer world of Flinders. It was a lonely life, particularly for anyone as talkative and outgoing as Pat, who was without her husband's fanatical dedication to his ornithological investigations.

Their sojourn on Cat Island was part of an eight-year long tour of Australia from Britain, divided between the pursuit of science and the pursuit of sufficient cash to make that a possible option. They travelled from place to place by camper truck, living rough, and this was the first scientific post for which they had received any remuneration, and this slight enough.

The past five years they had spent in Western Australia, mostly on offshore sea bird islands and in what they referred to as 'the tropical wap waps', studying marsupials. John, lean, sinewy and bearded, was formerly an industrial chemist, with a fascination for wildlife photography and a fine collection of slides and prints. These he sold, to help the budget, along with magazine articles. Two books arising from his British work were "*The Ominous Owl*" and "*The Techniques of Bird Photography*".

Both were prolific writers and a jointly-produced taste of their Australian adventures, "*Wild Islands of the West*", had recently gone to press. Later I was to read accounts of Australian mammals and "*They Fish Australian Seas*" in the *Royal Geographic Magazine*.

Few had John's patience to spend long hours in bird hides, waiting for the best shots, and fewer had his stickability to labour in the docks as a stevedore when money was short in the early days. Pat, as dark and Spanish-looking as John was fair, was a trained nurse — an ideal partner for a somewhat hazardous life in the outback — and a profession always in demand and able to keep them in funds when times were hard. She indulged in photography on her own account and wrote articles on their adventures for magazines, as well as checking the Cat Island shearwater burrows, organising the domestic front and typing notes and scripts for John.

Both kept diaries, his on the bird behaviour and scientific front, hers on the often more intriguing facets of human behaviour. Their lively sense of humour and courage to tackle all that their chosen lifestyle could throw at them — from snakes and rough seas to sandy deserts and heat exhaustion — brought them a wholesome sense of satisfaction and achievement.

They never returned to Britain to settle, but, after that first eight-year tour, they went back for long enough for John to gain a degree in Zoology at Durham University. This was the one place where ornithology loomed large on the academic syllabus and where sea birds, particularly, were ably dealt with by Dr Bill Bourne, who had roamed the world in pursuit of these evocative creatures himself.

When fully qualified in his chosen field, John was offered a lectureship in Christchurch University, New Zealand. He is still there, retired now, in his early eighties, but retaining a footing in Academia and still producing scientific works, particularly on that least known and most elusive group, the petrels, shearwaters, prions and albatrosses.

Now and again we see them in their homeland, as in the summer of 1996, but they are firmly rooted now in the Antipodes. Their long university vacations have enabled them to indulge their wanderlust, which was always centred around the ferreting out of new ornithological facts.

Their lives, like those of so many of my contemporaries in the fifties and sixties, were fraught with excitement and uncertainty. In retrospect they could scarcely have been bettered, but those who get a lot out of life usually put a lot in. There were the hard moments too, and the dangerous ones: times of discomfort and deprivation, when they must have craved a juicy steak or a long cold drink.

If they ever become chairbound — and there is little sign of it yet — they will have a wealth of memories to draw on and savour again a range of sights, sounds and activities that most folk only dream of or experience on their television screens.

During my first evening on Cat Island, I explored alone along the dunes to the austere granite of the south-east reaching out towards Storehouse Island. Even after such a halcyon calm as had lasted throughout the day, big waves from the Tasman Sea were hurling themselves onto the eastern rocks. The overspill from the last high tide lay in puddles, imprisoning blue fragments of sky on the face of the earth. Sheets of spray nurtured a specialised salt flora, but the bay behind the point was as calm as ever. Even islands as small as this can be sites of great contrast.

We were not under canvas here, but in a two-roomed hut, like "Yolla". I spread my stretcher-bed in front of the kitchen fire, moving it into the back room on top of Pat's before breakfast. We dropped easily into a routine during the eight days of my stay, each setting off after breakfast about our own business, to compare notes over tucker on our return.

96 Leafy Pepper-cress *Lepidium foliosum*,
Coast Candles *Stackhousia spathulata* and Sea Celery *Apium prostratum*

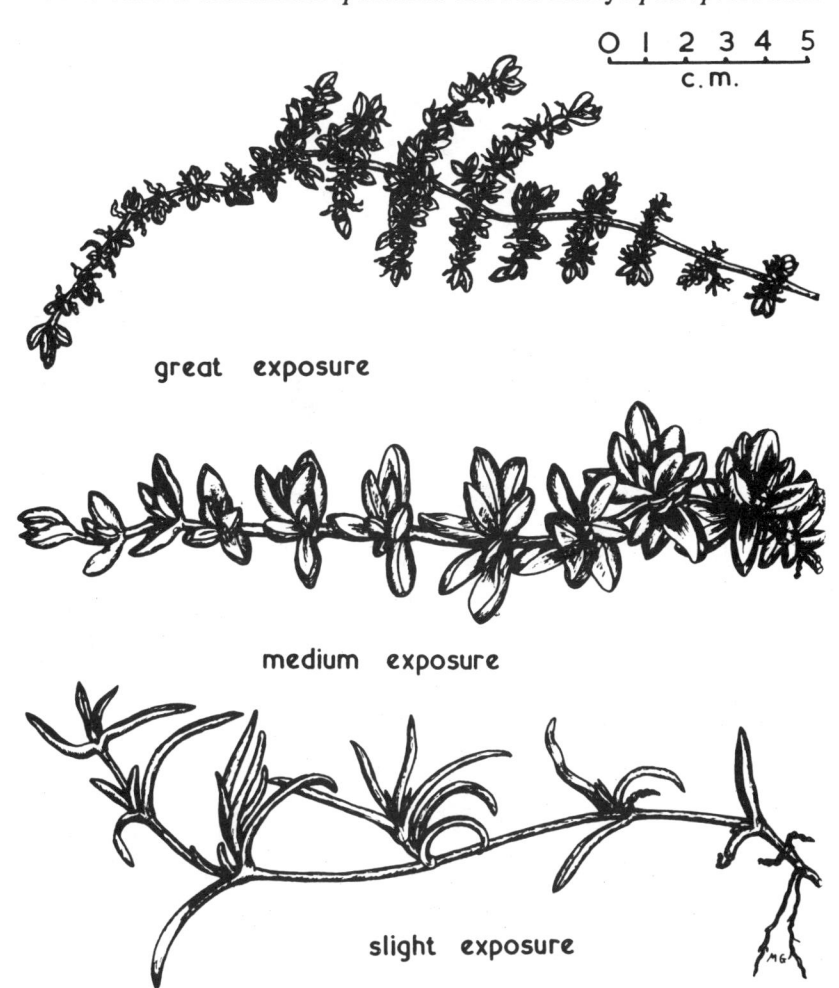

great exposure

medium exposure

slight exposure

97 Pigface *Disphyma crassifolim ssp clavellatum*:
three forms in relation to exposure

98 Gannets *Morus (Sula) serrator*: mutual preening

3. CAT ISLAND GANNETS

On my first morning on Cat Island, after partaking of boiled eggs lodged in photographers' eggcups — cardboard film cartons, cut crosswise — I got no further than the local sands. I found in them the sort of full-blown dune system that I encountered elsewhere only on Tin Kettle Island. Between the anaemic green of the sun-bleached Poa tufts the sand was paved with the russet-gold of scorched herbs and strawey grasses, punctuated by bushy grey tumps.

White-fronted chats were rattling away merrily in the low scrub, their staccato song having given rise to the local name of tin tack bird. Their nests were small and grassy, in the tops of tussocks, one which I came upon being empty and dishevelled. When I showed it to Pat later, she said that a trio of chicks had hatched in it but, three days later, the nest was empty and a contentedly sleepy tiger snake was curled up below. This was not such a substantial meal as the preferred mutton bird chicks, which were everywhere for the taking, but the naked morsels would have provided a less fishy flavour as a change.

In the afternoon I found my way by a devious and difficult route to the gannet colony, 150 yards from the sea and eighty-five feet above it: a mere twenty feet below the island summit. It was blatantly bare. Birds had gone from most of the area and vegetation had replaced them only marginally. The rest was evidently too impregnated with guano for plants to grow and too firmly trampled for shearwaters to burrow.

While all around was sandy, the ground in the gannetry was a sticky black peat topped by a shallow layer of clay, whitened by uric acid from the droppings. The denuded area was bordered by an intermittent belt of flowering leek lilies, their vegetative parts a deep bronze colour. Uncommon elsewhere, these small pioneers were notoriously ornithocoprophilous, which jawbreaker, being interpreted, comes out as 'ornitho' = bird, 'copro' = dung, as in its fossilised version of coprolites, and 'philous' being loving.

Neighbouring vegetation consisted of fleshy mounds of spinach and seaberry saltbush and mats of spurrey and *Calandrinia*, grading back through fireweed, austral hollyhock, austral storksbill and a giant brome grass *(Bromus unioloides)* to the silver tussocks of the sand.

The plantless area accommodated sixteen gannet chicks, the issue of eighteen nesting pairs. Round about was a gaggle of juveniles and unpaired birds, totalling about eighty in all. When the wardens arrived the previous year, they had found seventeen adults shot — presumably just for fun or target practice, unless the despoilers had been disturbed before they could collect the spoil!

The chicks I watched on 16th February in 1958 were well grown, but some still wore their white down. Others had shed this, the darkly mottled feathers below pushing it off as they grew. They would be wearing a semblance of full adult plumage after only two years — the change occurring in half the time taken by North Atlantic gannets, which mature in four years, but retain a few black patches into their fifth or sixth year.

When the colony was larger, most of the youngsters would have been away to sea by now, small groups such as this apparently lacking the necessary stimulus to get going briskly at the start of the breeding season.

The Cat Island gannets had made the acquaintance of man less than 200 years ago and this was the start of their undoing. Their discoverer, Bass, in 1799, helped himself, bringing birds back to his ship, presumably to feed the crew. During the ensuing century little is known of the interaction between the two species. With sailors always hungry for fresh meat, one can only guess that any encounters were not to the birds' advantage.

The next recorder to put pen to paper was Thomas Scott in 1828. He was a Tasmanian surveyor who left a handwritten MS and a printed broadsheet entitled "Furneaux Islands: a short Geographical memoir thereof, taken from the Information of James Campbell, Boatman, Hobart Town, August 1828".

Campbell seems to have confused the islands somewhat. He refers to "Gannett Island: No trees, rocky. South end sandy. Water in ponds. One mile round, a round island". Another reference is to "Cat Island. A rocky seal island, long and narrow. A quarter of a mile round, no trees".

It is possible that this may refer to the elongated smaller eastern section of the dumbbell shaped whole, the mariner having missed the narrow sandy neck across the strait. Of Babel he writes: "Babel Island: five miles round, trees and scrub. Rock all round; high land, plenty of water in ponds". The mention of water is significant. In the absence of streams, ponds must serve to replenish supplies for drinking.

The next visit that we know of was by Victorian naturalists in March 1893 — when 2,500 pairs of gannets were counted, the nests some thirty inches apart in a rookery fifty yards across and 150 yards in circumference.

Campbell (1901, p.984) published a photograph of the gannetry, with birds extending well north of their present position.

In 1907 the seaweed nests were stated to cover roughly an acre on an original site estimated at two to three acres. The island's 1901 lessee made occasional visits to collect guano and bird numbers then were reckoned to be undiminished from two decades earlier, constituting the largest gannetry in Australia.

From the 1830s into the 1930s guano was being removed right up to the occupied nests and the visitors reported seeing a heavy toll of eggs and young being taken by Pacific gulls when they put the adults up. In 1919 an RAOU (Royal Australian Ornithologists' Union) camp out on Flinders Island recorded the start of the decline, but the main rot set in just prior to the Second World War, when both the white fish and the crayfish industries received a boost.

Prior to that the slump — said to be worse here than in the UK — had ensured that few men had the money to invest in boats and fishing enterprises.

With the rising demand for fish in Australia and cray tails in America, things changed. There were big prizes to be had and the unscrupulous started casting covetous eyes on the tamely trusting birds, that were so much easier to come by than more traditional bait from the sea.

By the 1935-6 season the area occupied by birds had shrunk to about a fifth of an acre, this holding 800 to 1,000 adults and some 500 chicks. Then the Tasmanian Fauna Board maintained a guard on neighbouring Babel Island during the breeding season to protect birds from fishermen and in 1937-8 800-900 young were counted. To help the cause 146 Pacific gulls and forty-three tiger snakes were destroyed.

Despite all precautions, there was considerable chick mortality that year in a bad storm, and again in 1938-9, when 1,000 chicks had been estimated in mid-February and 1,028 nests counted on aerial photographs. Sadly, the wardens were withdrawn at the onset of the war, not to be reinstated until many years later, when the population had fallen dangerously low.

When Dom Serventy visited in 1948 there was evidence that 400 pairs had nested, but he found no young gannets at all — "Only a wooden waddy with a shaped handle and broken iron hook with which cray fishermen had evidently been gaffing the young, and probably the adults too. The whole rookery was deserted, but early next morning about 120 adults were roosting on it." He found the same situation in 1949, assuming these two years to have been without issue of any matured offspring at all.

Serventy appealed to the fishing community in an article "Spare those Gannets, they point to Pilchards," in the *"Fisheries News Letter*, Vol. 8, No. 5" of August 1949, but it fell on blind eyes and the slaughter continued.

In 1951, 140 pairs tried to breed; in 1952 about 130. Serventy appealed again to the marauders in "Saving the remnant of a Gannet Colony" (*"Fisheries News Letter*, Vol. 12, No. 11" in 1953), but to no avail. He quoted the incident of a reputed gannet stealer being wrecked on Cat Island in a south-easterly, with loss of life — a coincidence which the locals related to the old nautical superstition that bad luck will inevitably come to anyone who harms the sea birds with which he shares the hazards of the deep.

In those days most of us studied Coleridge's *"Ancient Mariner"* in school poetry classes, whether we lived in seafaring communities or not. The moral was that retribution must be suffered for evil acts against our fellow creatures. How true that rings today, as we battle with the many repercussions of the misuse of our environment, on sea, land and air!

The very next year, 1953-4, all the chicks produced by the remaining fifty pairs were killed. "The island was deserted. Just a few dead birds lay around among the footprints of the raiders!"

From 1955 wardening was resumed and Cat Island was declared a sanctuary. The notice board acquainting visitors of this fact bore the proviso: "Heavy penalties are provided for infringements, including confiscation of offender's boats and gear." But first catch your man.

Forty-three chicks fledged in 1954-5, forty-six in 1955-6 and only fourteen in 1956-7, so sixteen in 1957-8 from only eighteen pairs was as much as could be hoped for. As Serventy was at pains to point out in his articles, "The great majority of fishermen deplored this shocking vandalism and the raids were undoubtedly caused by a few rogue individuals who were better out of the industry." He also pointed out the value of gannets as markers for shoals of tuna and pilchards, but subsequent developments first the coming of echo sounders and then radar — pulled the mat from under his feet there. That age-old partnership between birds and man, had become redundant, like so much else, to be followed by the depletion of our fish and fisheries on a world scale.

During the late fifties, the warden and the police boat used low-cycle radios that prevented their messages being intercepted by the fishing boats, so that *"Aralla's"* whereabouts could remain secret up to a point, but with little effect. In subsequent years things seemed not to have improved and locals were lamenting the loss of what might have been the biggest tourist pull the archipelago had to offer.

It was the accessibility which would have served paying visitors that was the undoing of the Cat Island colony. At Lawrence Rocks, where gannets nested on the larger of two almost impregnable basaltic islets off Point Danger near Portland, numbers were increasing during the 1950s. W. B. Hitchcock in 1952 counted 406 pairs: John McKean in 1960 counted 605 pairs and in 1961 639 pairs. Bad weather prevented him from landing in 1962 and 1963, but observations with high-powered binoculars from mainland cliffs showed that the area occupied by nesters had enlarged. (McKean, 1966. *"Emu"* Vol. 65, No. 3, p.159.)

* * * * *

There was plenty to see and, with so few birds, I could concentrate on individuals. I settled to watch the half-grown youngsters soliciting food from their parents. Adults seemed to dislike regurgitating and John said chicks would sometimes coax for several hours before they got anything. If a bird was startled, a fish the size of a herring might be coughed up onto the ground, usually headless, because the head went down first and was digested first. This may be what the seemingly unwilling adults were waiting for, the bony headgear being the least palatable for introducing into juvenile gullets.

Such jettisoned food was not retrieved. The chicks would pull it about a bit but lacked the wit to recognise it as a meal. Nothing, of course, was wasted, but the gulls were the gainers. They also comprised a useful sanitary squad, because it was the discarded fish which attracted flies, not the guano, which soon dried and hardened.

The slighter, nippier silver gulls minded their ps and qs, however, when they were among the bigger birds, knowing where they must draw the line. John had seen one of them have its leg broken by the jabbing bill of a gannet.

An adult taxi-ing in over the bare ground spotted me as it alighted and brought up two large pike, which lay neatly side by side, both headless, so this bird may have been loitering with intent. How long, I wondered, did it take for the head to disintegrate and detach. John had seen local sea salmon being brought in sometimes and a chick might get more than one fish in a single feed if the homecoming parent had fared well.

When a chick was startled into regurgitation, it was likely to be fish soup which came up, but this happened only twice, even when we were ringing them a day or two later.

The Warhams shared a dawn-to-dusk watch the next day, to see how often each individual chick was fed. The hide, resembling a latrine tent, was installed twelve feet from the nearest nest. Most got two feeds a day, usually in the early morning and the evening when the adults changed places. Fish were delivered not only fresh from the sea, but also sometimes from the adult which had managed to resist the chicks' demands during their long vigil at the nest.

When the chicks were young feeds had been more frequent and the fish necessarily smaller. The watchers reported sluicing noises as the adults strove to bring the fish back up from warm watery depths. Regurgitation seemed troublesome. John noted that half the attempts to deliver were unsuccessful and twenty per cent culminated in the food being slurped onto the ground.

He recorded forty-five fish delivered in thirty-three feeds, the chicks averaging two point eight fish each during the fourteen hours' watch. I was fascinated observing the young heads disappearing into the open maws to intercept the goodies before they were lost to the exterior. Afterwards most submitted to a bout of preening from the solicitous adult.

Kazimier, Wodzicki and Moreland examined vomits from Cape Kidnapper's gannets in New Zealand (*"Nottornis"* Vol. VIII, June 1966). The regurgitated food included squid, horse mackerel, anchovy, sardine, garfish and needlefish. Gannets in the New Zealand White Island colony which I had visited the previous year took barracuda, horse mackerel and anchovy.

The usual greeting ceremony was always indulged in at the homecoming but the insistent "urrah urrah" type clamour that is part and parcel of larger colonies was half-hearted. There were excitable squawks and grunts when a squabble broke out but somehow the expected zest for life normally shown by these macho fishers seemed muted in accordance with their depleted status. I tried to discover what the nests were made of but the material was unrecognisable, each chick apparently seated atop a concrete tower of guano.

On the occasion of the annual chick ringing I was sent ahead to find out what I needed to know about the vegetation, which encroached very close to the nests, these having been made in one corner of the great bare patch. The boss man wanted us all to leave at the same time after the ringing, to give the birds a chance to sort themselves out. I was shown an easier way than the one I had stumbled along originally, the inland turning marked by a surprisingly visible pebble perched on a boulder.

Some of the youngsters were big enough to go flapping off prematurely so John marshalled his helpers into strategic positions as we advanced slowly, putting the adults up quietly at a time when few of them were in, before the arrival of the unoccupied bystanders with the evening changeover.

Pat and I had been schooled in how to catch and hold, getting a firm but non-throttling grip on the upper neck as soon as convenient. Innocently juvenile our quarry might be, but those four-inch beaks could do a lot of damage in a short time. We wore leather gloves but the chicks had an uncanny ability to aim at the wrists above.

One of us would pinion a bird to the ground while our licensed ringer fitted the stout edge-to-edge leg ring with special pliers. The other would move circumspectly round, gently shepherding back to base those that had floundered off into the tussock grass. At the crucial moment the nearest would be grabbed and the wings tucked in neatly in readiness for the next ring.

Some birds responded to handling with a snake-like hiss of expended air, a sort of gasp. Looking into an open beak I perceived an unrestricted tube leading down to uncharted depths. Was this something to do with the involuntary inflation of the lungs to cushion the impact of diving from a height, I wondered, or just a convenient receptacle for whole fish. John told us that respiratory squeaks and whistles often issued from grounded birds as they flapped their wings in front of the hide.

All sixteen youngsters were dealt with satisfactorily and left wearing rings nos. 130 13102 to 130 13116 inclusive. Where possible, they were replaced on their personal pedestals.

Retreating to a discrete distance, we watched the first of the wanderers heading back home, and adults returning to reassure them that all was well. We then hurried back to roast beef and Yorkshire pudding, my first for many a long day. What it was to have an oven! By next morning all the chicks had returned to the correctly numbered nests, but it was John who read the numbers to be sure, the birds knew by other means.

This type of disturbance is only justified if there are recoveries of ringed birds and there had already been a few. Four banded as nestlings on Cat Island in 1954 were recovered at Eden in New South Wales three and a half years later by Robert Carrick. This supported the belief that there was a tendency to move to warmer waters and as a group of contemporaries. Another bird was recovered in Tasmanian waters by Hitchcock in 1963, three years after it had been banded on Cat Island.

While not strictly migratory, gannets from New Zealand fly across the Tasman Sea to winter with others of their kind in South and East Australia. These return to their natal colonies at three years old, but may not breed until four or more.

Gannets are strong fliers. With an air speed of 35 mph, even nesters could travel 470 miles in their off duty spells during incubation, this reducing to about 225 miles when there was a chick to be fed. In stormy weather they fished near the island and it was a joy to watch their arrow-like descent from the heights onto prey. Sometimes they exploited surface fish shoals, joining gulls, terns and pelicans when there were easy pickings near the top.

Even at this stage of the nesting cycle, birds would sometimes come in with a beakful of seaweed or locally gathered leek lily to add to the nest. Preening took up a lot of their time ashore — of themselves, their partners and their offspring. The head was used as an oily mop, after passing it over exudations squeezed from the nipple of the preen gland with the bill. To scratch the head, the foot might be brought up under the wing and it was amusing to see them doing this in flight, as well as when firmly settled on the ground.

In this year of 1958 the first of the sixteen banded chicks left on March 8th, its parent remaining until the 21st. There is no withholding of feeds in a final starvation period in gannets as in shearwaters. The chicks wandered around during their last earthbound days, less harassed by neighbouring adults than in a normal-sized colony, but they returned to the nest to be fed.

Their final departure was not easy. In precipitous colonies, like that at Lawrence Rocks, the take-off was, literally, as easy as falling off a cliff. Cat Island birds had to walk from their almost level nursery, weaving through the tussocks down to a suitable launch pad. Even adults had problems taking off on calm days, making a flapping run across the empty ground but not infrequently coming a cropper among the grass, to waddle back to the open patch for another try. There was no running through those formidable tussocks for creatures properly skilled only in movement through air and water.

When birds passed out from the nests as I worked on the cliffs, I noticed that they flew straight into and through several waves and indulged in wing fluttering like starlings in a puddle. This was their method of bathing to get rid of grime picked up ashore, grime that very soon obscured the numbers on the leg rings of chicks which had no opportunity to wash,

Their homecoming was not much more graceful than take-off. As they stalled to lose air speed, their bodies were arched upwards, with heads and tails sagging and big webbed feet pushed out in front to absorb the impact. They ran the gauntlet of neighbours' beaks if they misjudged their landing spot. It said little for the powers of imagination imprisoned in the tight fetters of instinct, that they continued to nest so close together, when there was all that Lebensraum for the taking.

It was also extremely unfortunate that the plot of ground that the surviving remnant of the colony occupied was close against the marginal tussock grass. Had they opted for the centre of the great bared arena, they would have been spared the horrors of a fire which swept through the island in May 1983.

A letter received from John Whinray tells of this disaster. Thirteen adults with eggs or chicks had been counted in the colony a few weeks earlier and six adults stayed through the conflagration to protect their chicks, they and their offspring being burned, along with the eggs. This left no more than four or five breeding pairs — a pathetic remnant of the five thousand present at the beginning of the century.

The tragedy is that the blaze was completely avoidable. An engineer had decided to burn the old batteries — wet cell, twelve volts — from the automatic lighthouse which had been erected since my visit in 1958 on the rise not far south of the gannetry, instead of taking them out with him on the helicopter.

The blaze got out of control, killing tens of thousands of mutton birds and penguins in their burrows, as well as the gannets and who knows how many reptiles and other lesser life.

The National Parks and Wildlife Service knew only too well of the fire hazard in tussock grass, but had insufficient resources to man all the island sanctuaries adequately. The grubbing out of a few tussocks by the nesting area might have saved the gannets, if not the great host of underground dwellers.

In an article in *"The Examiner"* of March 17th 1984, Whinray reported less than three hundred pairs of gannets to be still breeding on rocks off Tasmania. By 1996 the picture was brighter, with about fifteen hundred birds on the Counsellor Reefs south-east of Clarke Island and around four thousand on Judgement Rocks in the Kent Group, halfway to Victoria.

On my visit in November 1995, I heard that forty concrete replicas of gannets looking skywards and earthwards were being hand-painted and set out on Cat Island as decoys to lure others in. There were likely to be few survivors bred on the island available to take up residence again, but perhaps some of those wanderers from New Zealand might be tempted to join the dummies. Over the past few years some young birds had been settling, as though to prospect for sites, but there were no nests as yet, only hopes.

The decoy method has worked for Dr Steve Kress in New England, enabling him to reinstate Atlantic puffins, common terns and guillemots (murres to the Americans) on islands where the original populations had been exterminated by seamen. On Eastern Egg Rock in Maine, his painted puffin decoys were backed up by pufflings flown south from Newfoundland and transplanted into around two hundred artificial nesting burrows.

Near the start of this project in the first half of the 1970s, I had been fortunate enough to briefly join the team of volunteers acting as surrogate mums by feeding the puffin chicks with capelin. The new colony which built up was partly of these chicks, hand-reared on the island, and partly of birds reared elsewhere and attracted in by the decoys.

An unexpected spin-off from this project was the use of the man-made burrows by leach's fork-tailed storm petrels. Eighty-four of the two hundred or so burrows were used by nesting 'stormies' in the 1996 season, this representing seventy-five per cent of the known population of a hundred and thirteen pairs.

Importing and handfeeding young gannets on Cat Island would prove a very different kettle of fish, but the decoys seemed to have a good chance of succeeding. Only time will tell.

The second season of the project, 1996-97, bore no fruit, despite the constant playing of taped gannet talk recorded on the Pedra Bianca gannetry, in an effort to entice newcomers to touch down. Occasional landings and tentative nesting behaviour were the only results and no chicks had been hatched in the thirteen years since the unfortunate Department of Transport fire. The decimation of the Cat Island gannetry by unscrupulous fishermen has been repeated the world over. The best known example must be that of Bird Rock in the Gulf of St Lawrence. When Audubon visited there in 1833, he reckoned there to be a hundred thousand pairs of North Atlantic gannets nesting on the flat top of the rock and another fifty thousand on the sides.

In 1869 the Canadian government built a lighthouse on the rock, making the summit accessible to seamen who, in the thirty years to the turn of the century, had practically wiped out the hundred thousand pairs on the top by clubbing them to death. Government protection finally stopped the slaughter and birds are spreading upwards again.

All power to the efforts at reinstatement on Cat Island.

99 Gannets: Scissoring display and sleeping

100 Gannets: Development of Chick

101 Gannets coming in to land

Chapter Twelve

CAT ISLAND'S OTHER WILDLIFE

1. SNAKES, SKINKS, GULLS AND TERNS

Although the Cat Island wardens of twenty years before had killed forty-three black tiger snakes, regarding them as a potential threat to the gannets, it is doubtful if they were. Snakes are quite slender and, while equipped with expanding jaws, have no means of breaking up their prey, so all but the smallest chicks are too large to swallow. John Warham had never seen a snake on the open ground of the gannetry in all his hours of watching from the hide. "I reckon the gannets would make short work of any that ventured too close."

He was stationed on the island from 14th November 1957 to 5th April 1958, so would have been there when the chicks were quite small. It seems that only a large snake is likely to break the shell of a shearwater's egg, which would be an easier proposition than a gannet's egg. Nor can they tackle a fully-grown shearwater fledgeling. Adult shearwaters may be killed defending their young — dying from an injection of the potent venom within a minute — but they are not swallowed. A snake may have a problem just dragging a dead adult out of the burrow in order to reach the chick for which it had sacrificed its all.

Opinion is divided, but the islanders regard the black tiger snake, the only species present on Cat Island, as the third deadliest in Australia. They ranked the Queensland taipan first and the death adder second. The makers of a wildlife film on Chappell Island, shown on BBC British Television in 1996, reported the Chappell 'tigers' as eighty times more venomous than rattlesnakes — with no explanation as to how they reached this figure.

John assured me that they were quite docile unless antagonised, but admitted to having met one that very day that had raised its head menacingly and tried to emulate a cobra in a puny attempt to spread the 'hood' behind the lidless eyes.

No shearwater burrow is proof against their entry but, if the intruder found the occupant too large for a meal, it might snuggle up against it for warmth. Cold blooded by nature, the creatures are dependent on external heat sources to warm them into activity. One can only hope that the shearwater chick is unaware of its bedmate's lethal potential. Most animals have a very acute reaction to snakes.

Experienced birders have been heard to say that they can tell if a snake is in the burrow down which they are reaching because of the extra chill. Nevertheless, where snakes are prevalent, they move their hand in close beneath the roof of the burrow. The snake must be above its quarry when it strikes, the venom dribbling down the paired fangs in the upper jaw. A canny birder can grab it from above, haul it out and fling it away over his shoulder!

Perhaps to reassure me, John pooh-poohed the tales of large numbers of the reptiles on Cat Island.

"A man would have a job to catch five in a day."

Notwithstanding this, I saw five in my first afternoon, all catchable — had I had a mind to catch them.

I was sitting writing at the top of the beach when the first rustled into view. This was the biggest I had yet seen, a sinuous black beauty, highly polished, with lemon-yellow markings curving up from the ventral side. At least they did not add invisibility to their menace. As top predators they had nothing to fear, but they might have stalked their prey more effectively if they had merged more closely with the background.

This snake was only about three metres off, but it spotted me first and had turned away when I became aware of it. More than one metre of body followed the mean little triangular head into a labyrinthine button-bush.

An almost simultaneous whispering of the grass behind me was made by a comparative whipper-snapper. I rose and sidled after this one with camera at the ready as it slithered away, seeming to have difficulty gaining a purchase on the loose sand grains. Although only about thirty cm shorter, this was much thinner. The other was still visible, but not close enough to get a shot of two for the price of one.

It is said that what the eye doesn't see the heart doesn't grieve over, but I was more worried about the snakes I didn't see than the ones I did. I felt quite unsafe scrabbling up the burrow-pocked, tussock-tousled slope to the gannetry, prey to fears of the unknown as I floundered onto all fours with monotonous regularity.

During the ascent I saw two more snakes and at least a dozen skinks, along with sibilant motions of the Poa that might have been caused by either. All seemed hell bent on getting away, but I was not sorry to emerge onto the open terrain of the gannetry.

On my return I was blasé about encounters with the cold-blooded menace. Night was falling: it was much too cool for them to be around now. Not a bit of it. Number five glided off ahead of me. Over supper John informed me that he often encountered snakes on his night rounds. My preconceived idea of good snake weather as those breathlessly muggy days when the perspiration fails to dry was obviously fallacious. Other observers had recorded snakes as disappearing underground when the mercury shot up and emerging to feed in the cool of morning and evening or after rain.

One of these was Cashon, a taxidermist from Hobart University who had done a spell on Cat Island as warden. He had found birds, skinks and beetles in snakes which he had killed for museum specimens. Poultry was only on the menu seasonally. For other parts of the year when they were not hibernating, the staple diet here was the small *Leiolopisma* skinks and lesser members of their own kind.

Just after my final snake of that afternoon, I spotted its possible quarry — two fluffy brown balls among the short-lived pink purslane which bore a generous crop of edible seeds. These materialised into brown quail chicks. They scuttled off and I came upon two adults, rooting among kidney-weed

(Dichondra repens). Even these were only ten cm long. These game birds were abundant on the island, nesting among the tussock bases.

Since Arthur Harland's day the wardens had fed the quail in front of the hut with rice grains scattered across the sand. Other sand scratchers were native water rats, frequent visitors to judge by the proliferation of footprints, which showed them to be much bigger than our mental image of the brown sewer rat.

Less frightening than the tigers and eminently more friendly were the blue-tongue skinks *(Tiliqua nigrolutea)*. That specific epithet of black-yellow linked the two species colourwise, but they had little else in common apart from their reptilian affinities. In fact the blue-tongues sported a background colour of medium brown, more like the mainland tiger snakes.

Our usual idea of a skink is of something long, lean and quick off the mark, despite much reduced legs. Blue-tongues have none of these characters, being plump in relation to their thirty-five to forty-five cm length, heavily built with chubby legs and slow of gait. I prefer to think of them as blue-tongue lizards or southern blotched lizards. Their dry country counterparts are the better known stumpy-tails, which present a similar image whether coming or going. Blue-tongues are well distributed on Cat, as on many of the islands. They are easy to pick up for close viewing and as happy as pussy cats to enjoy the warmth of a human lap. Fully grown blue-tongues can make short work of shearwater and penguin eggs.

* * * * *

Pacific and silver gulls nested on the north-east promontory and eastern rocks. This was a spectacular coast, the white browed rollers swashing in over time-smoothed granite and roaring back into gullies. Plants stayed well clear of the froth and bubble, leaving bald slabs that were part land, part sea bed.

Some of the crystalline expanses served as gull dining areas, the uncleared leftovers an assortment of crab appendages, shells and disintegrating bundles of vegetable matter containing viable seeds of an incoming generation.

Most prevalent of the shells here were the slightly curved plates separated from the big chiton or coat of mail shells, which resemble overgrown woodlice plastered to the rocks in life. Each animal has eight sections to the dorsal armoury, connected by a rough encircling leathery girdle. These measured two by one inches and were dark outside with sky-blue linings, surprisingly thick, like warped dominoes, the spots abraded by the waves. They must have been quite a tough proposition to dismember and this was achieved by the larger black-backed gulls.

The crop pellets of plant matter had been coughed up by the smaller silver gulls, which were currently feeding on the soft red fruits of bower spinach. The hard yellow seeds were discarded as indigestible, some with a wisp of red flesh attached. Tolerant of both salt and guano, they would readily germinate when washed into crevices.

Other fleshy fruits available to the birds were the orange ones of boxthorn, the jettisoned pips flattened, like those of tomatoes, and the dark red ones of seaberry saltbush which yielded a scattering of small black seeds.

Nests of about twenty pairs of silver gulls were tucked into hollows a little further south, these containing eggs or small chicks, but I saw no youngsters of the size that had been visiting us on Fisher Island of late. It looked as though breeding time with gulls was not closely synchronised as it is with shearwaters.

It transpired later that this was a second attempt. The main colony lay further north and this contingent had peeled off in early January to make a fresh start. The wardens had come up with no explanation for the move. Plants, like nests, were largely confined to depressions and included the usual succulents, plus Austral stonecrop *(Tillaea sieberiana)*, green and robust in the fertilised soil. Lobelia and the alien cottony white cudweed *(Gnaphalium candidissimum)* also favoured the proximity of nests.

Many adult silver gulls had died, their corpses unpredated, and there were also dead penguins and mutton birds, as though some avian disease had struck. Was this, perhaps, the reason for the new start? One bird with an egg and a small chick had no partner as the others had. He or she was particularly belligerent with intruders. Would it be able to rear the twins alone?

The Pacific gulls had nested much earlier and the mottled young were as big as their pied parents. There were fewer than Nature intended, as the wardens had been around during the incubation period in November pricking eggs, to prevent all from hatching. As with the big black-backed gulls of the Northern Hemisphere, which prey on auks and other sea birds, it was good management practice to keep their numbers within bounds.

Isolated pairs of both gull species were scattered along the coast. Unlike gannets, these did not need the stimulus of a crowd for the sex hormones to work. Both gathered in a communal roost above the gannetry, keeping watch for expectorated fish.

When Arthur Harland was wardening here, he noticed that gannets were more readily alerted when the gulls rose en masse than when potential predators of their chicks passed over. He put this down to the fact that a rising cloud of gulls was usually triggered by the approach of people and it was these that the gannets feared, the satellite birds providing an early-warning system. The gulls, which are by no means stupid, had learned to associate human intrusion with a bonus of fish brought up in panic, so hung around, waiting for the main chance.

Gannets took little notice of a passing sea eagle or harrier, watching the passage of the former but largely ignoring the other. Harland saw a dark, unidentified bird of prey carry off a young gannet and later found two harriers feeding on one. Cashon observed a sea eagle eating a recently killed gannet, but had no proof of the cause of death.

Moving through the gullery, I flushed two newly-hatched oystercatchers, rescuing one from a brackish pool into which it fell in its hurry to get away.

The other got temporarily lodged in a crevice, but struggled through a gap and scuttled off, as full of bounce as before its four metre drop. Such downy morsels are almost weightless and fall softly, like tree ducklings making the initial exit from their arboreal nests. Thirteen pairs of sooty oystercatchers were breeding on Cat Island and an unknown number of pieds.

Several hundred pairs of crested terns had bred on the north-west corner of North Bay when Arthur Harland was wardening the island in 1954-5. The old site was in two halves and was still very obvious, marked by the dense growth of brome grass *(Bromus unioloides)*, with spinach on the bared soil and noon flower on the rocks.

The following year there were none on Cat Island, the birds having moved to Storehouse Island. In 1957-8 terns were flying round prospecting early in the season and settling momentarily, but they did not nest. A new colony was discovered on a reef off Little Dog Island that year but was not big enough to account for all the several hundred pairs.

They were still not back on Cat Island in 1958-9, the year when large tern colonies appeared on Tucks Reef and Inner Possum Boat Harbour Reef in the Scotts Reef Group. Most tern species are notoriously fickle in their choice of site — possibly a canny way to evade over-wintering parasites. It seems that these were no exception.

102 Leek Lily *Bulbine semibarbata*

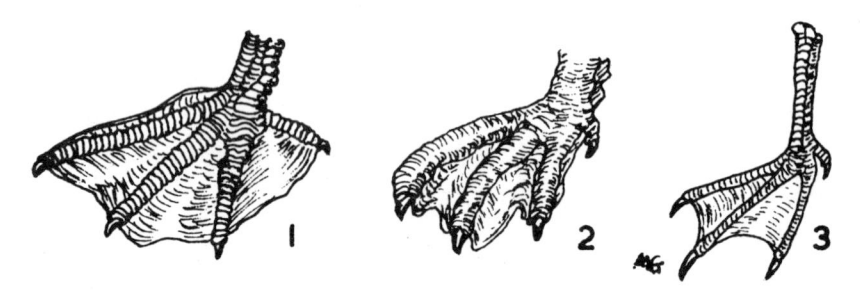

103 Feet modified for swimming: Cormorant, Penguin, Tern

104 Feeding chicks of Gull and Shearwater

2. FUR SEALS AND SHEARWATERS

Governor Hunter, writing of an exploratory voyage in 1797, refers to the wealth of seals on the Furneaux Islands. "I sent in the schooner *"Francis"* Lieutenant Flinders of the *"Reliance"* (a young man well qualified) in order to give him the opportunity of making what observations he could among the islands. This he did, discovering at the same time great herds of seals."

Captain Matthew Flinders in the *"Norfolk"*, with a crew of eight in 1798, was the first to establish that Bass Strait was a throughway, as the naval surgeon, George Bass, had suspected, and not just 'a deep bay of shoals', as thought by Tobias Furneaux. Bass, who was with him, landed on what is thought to be Cat Island. After enumerating the birds, including "the pied offensive shags", he states: "The rest of the island was appropriated to the seals".

More tales of "Islands teeming with seals", a potential rich harvest of skins and oil, had been brought from the wrecked *"Sydney Cove"* in 1797. Yet by the end of the 1950s the seal population was down to one! Cat Island's lonely Josephine was the only seal which I saw on any of the Furneaux Islands during my three summers there.

Charles Bishop, captain of the eighty-ton brig, *"Nautilus"*, lost no time in moving in and setting up a sealing base at Kent Bay on the south shore of Cape Barren Island — this said to be the second British settlement in Australia.

He sailed away, leaving fourteen men building huts, hunting fur seals — to the extent of 9,000 skins in their early sorties — and making vegetable gardens. Little ships came back to transport the skins and oil to the markets, while men were left to continue the killing, skinning and rendering down the blubber, sometimes for prolonged periods fraught with hardship and privations when relief ships were delayed or wrecked.

The fur seals, unfamiliar with predation on land, allowed a close approach and were 'sitting ducks', like the gannets. Other enterprises moved in, the employees of one concern collecting 28,282 skins and 410 tons of oil in sixteen months! There was no conception of maintaining a breeding nucleus for long term harvests. Like the gold rushes of equivalent times, it was a matter of 'grab all and get out and the Devil take the hindmost'. One observer reported 300 seal pups left to starve when their mothers were butchered!

Governor King of Sydney brought a semblance of order into the wanton exploitation by Australian and British crews, but this went out of the window when lawless American ships arrived for a share of the plunder. The slaughter continued unabated.

Elephant seals *(Mirounga leonina)*, the first to be exterminated, have not returned — nor to King Island in the west of Bass Strait. Fur seals and the shorter-coated white-maned hair seals or Australian sea lions *(Neophoca cinerea)* were hunted to the last few animals and the ships went away, seeking ill-gotten gains elsewhere, mostly around New Zealand.

Nine white sealers remained behind on the islands, taking unto themselves ten coloured women, six Tasmanian Aboriginals, three Australians and one Maori. Their line of descent became known as 'the Straitsmen', their issue now inhabiting and radiating out from Cape Barren Island. They lived from land and sea, hunting wallabies, gathering mutton birds, beachcombing, fishing, building boats and growing vegetables. The tough environment bred tough men, lawless and undisciplined, but with the courage and endurance to survive in an environment hostile enough to defeat most.

The only seal in the archipelago's mammal list for the 1980s is the Australian fur seal *(Arctocephalus pusillus)*, formerly known as *Gypsophoca tasmanica*. Was Josephine the last survivor of the old, doomed population or the vanguard of a new influx from waters beyond?

Numbers did build up, fortunately not quickly enough to levels to tempt the sealers back. The idea of conservation of stocks and sustainable harvests was generally accepted in the second half of the twentieth century, so the animals were left in relative peace. By the mid-eighties about 6,000 were hauling out to sun themselves on the granite slabs, the bulls forming the nucleus of growing harems. Moriarty Rocks, east of Cape Barren Island, came to hold their main colony.

By the mid-nineties fur seals had also built up to around 6,000 on Kangaroo Island off South Australia, where they have been increasing steadily at the rate of about six per cent a year. The dark pups are dropped in mid-November in the Furneaux group, a month or so earlier than on Kangaroo Island. They are nourished on milk that is more than half cream, staying around the islands with their dams for a whole year, while the bulls go off to sea to build up their aggressive urges in time for the next breeding season, when the seeing off of rivals will take priority over feeding.

While competing with man for fish and crayfish to some extent, seals partly justify their existence with the fishermen by eating large octopi which prey on crayfish.

Josephine hung around her favoured corner of Cat Island and could be relied upon to be there when I visited. She preferred to be out of the water, obviously enjoying the sun. Although wary compared with fur seals encountered elsewhere, she was too young to remember the slaughter of the bad old days. Probably it was her isolation which made her nervous, her kind being essentially gregarious when opportunity allows. The absence of a pup suggested that she had not had contact with others in a functional harem.

A few months later I was able to walk freely among the breeding white-capped hair seals of Fisherman Island off South-west Australia, the cows brushing past me quite unperturbed on the narrow tracks through the bushes where they had dropped their pups, affording me scarcely a second glance. Only the bulls challenged me. This was a 'new' population, previously unknown to fishermen or scientists as far as we could ascertain. It is likely that the animals had not encountered humans before: they certainly had no fear of them.

In 1995 I met the same species again, now forming a tourist attraction on Kangaroo Island. Wardens did not allow the public very near, but the animals seemed as unconcerned by the gaping crowds, which did them no harm, as were those others of thirty-five years earlier, who had no knowledge of man's potential for destruction.

I had to stalk Josephine very slowly and got no closer than five metres on my first visit before she spotted me and elected to make herself scarce. Probably I should have made my presence known before getting so close.

Not badly frightened, she was soon back. The waves were rising and falling about three metres and she waited for an extra big one to sweep her well in, scrabbling up the rock as it receded. She was not very mobile for a sea lion. These are normally much nippier on land than the true seals, which are unable to turn their hind flippers forwards to lift the body above the ground to walk. Successive waves swished around her hind quarters, but she made it back to her former snoozing spot, regarding me suspiciously but evidently not anticipating anything untoward.

Each time I spoke she turned towards me and uttered a deep-throated sea-lion bark before relaxing again, sometimes rolling over to scratch languidly at her tum with the knuckles of a hind flipper.

After a short sleep, she decided to go back to sea, hanging head-downwards over a splashy brink waiting for a suitable large wave into which she could plunge without risking too high a dive. Soon she was water-sporting, corkscrewing as seals do, raising her fore flippers out of the water and bouncing up high enough every so often to get a good look at me. She had a sore mouth, pinkly mis-shapen, as though she had fallen foul of a fisherman's hook, but it did not seem to bother her.

I had a similar experience with Cape fur seals *(Arctocephalus capensis)* off South Africa, getting to know surviving singles in 1960 but joining boat-borne tourists in 1994 to see many hundreds gambolling on and around offshore islands, these showing an even more spectacular recovery after the cessation of seal hunting than their Australian counterparts of Kangaroo Island.

Closer to the Furneaux Group, I was able to see large numbers of seals through the tourist telescope on Victoria's Phillip Island when on a visit in 1989, the animals clustered on the seven acres of Seal Rocks offshore. This colony had not dropped so low, however, being estimated at 5,000 in the mid-1950s by the Victorian Fisheries and Game Department (McNally and Lynch, January 1954).

One thousand to fifteen hundred bred on the Glennies and Ansers off Wilsons Promontory at that time and there were some 130 on Lady Julia Percy Island and Lawrence Rocks off West Victoria and a maximum of 800 on the Skerries of East Gippsland. These figures applied after the culling of up to 2,000 in the late 1940s.

Culling then was not for furs but to pacify disgruntled fishermen, who regarded the seals as rivals, food items including crayfish and barracuda as well as squid *(Loliga ethridgei)*. Lesser prey were crabs, octopus, sea cucumber relatives, echinoderms, parrotfish and other unidentified species. This data came from the examination of 246 seal stomachs, only 138 of which had any contents.

Sadly I had no seal encounters in the Furneaux Group on my 1995 visit, but I was glad to learn that they, too, are increasing from that bleak period of near extinction in the late 1950s.

* * * * *

Mutton birds were as numerous over much of Cat Island as they were on Babel Island, but there was no harvesting here and no burning, so the vegetation was denser and the fire-prone spinach more prolific, so that it could be used as an indicator plant to show where the birds were most prevalent. Average burrow density throughout the colonies was about one per square metre.

It did not need many nights here to appreciate why the islands had been called the Babel Group. The clamour was completely distracting. On my second evening I secreted myself in the quail hide at 5 p.m. to watch the quails' evening activities. Dusk came early, beating the quails by half an hour, but by then the nocturnal pandemonium had set in — 'each bird calling in its own language'.

The shearwaters came streaming in from the offshore rafts where they had been gathering in thousands, black forms swooping against the pinks and yellows of a watery sunset, with long glides and intermittent wing beats, shearing the tussocks as they sheared the water. These big mobs seemed to arrive earlier and leave later than smaller ones, so that they were easier to observe while there was still light to see. Many would plop to earth before the birds below ground started calling, so could not be guided in by voice recognition. Strong numbers engendered strong confidence: any catastrophe was likely to befall the other chap.

We would sit fascinated at supper time as the mob swirled outside, their plumage momentarily catching the feeble glow from the Aladdin type lamp. The sky was dark with birds over Radio Hill, where the aerial had been erected, and over the main west block of the island where burrows were thickest, but there were inconceivably large crowds also over more sparsely populated tracts.

Sundry individuals crashed into the aerial or the fly wire over the window with a resounding thud, but seemed little the worse for it as no casualties were found next morning.

The Warham's had several research projects in hand. Pat had twenty-four burrows under observation to record comings and goings of birds from the sea. Every day she erected a fairy fence of small twigs across the entrances, doing the rounds each morning to see which had been deranged by passing birds.

Her burrows were chosen at random before egg-laying began, but all came to be occupied and all were visited regularly, sometimes nightly by the owners — even the one from which the egg disappeared. Some of the entrances were almost closed by the occupants, which sat inside pulling any plant life within reach towards them. Burrow mouths might become encircled by grass blades, some had twigs, earth and other debris scraped in until they resembled smaller, storm petrel burrows.

The nestlings had a greater urge to gather nest material than the adults and we saw quite tiny tots at the burrow entrances, more intent on pulling plant fragments in to their small known world than in prospecting the big unknown world that they would soon be launched into beyond.

John had a hide over an excavated burrow where he lay above the orifice, watching activity by the light of a red torch beam, which the bird took no notice of. He recorded that his particular chick had not been fed for six nights in succession. In some related species the gap between meals may be as much as a fortnight, suggesting that the food, when it comes, must be very nutritious.

His particular starveling was in no way inhibited in its journeys to the hole entrance to drag in more bedding. Maybe it instinctively sensed that external body warmth would compensate for the sparsity of inner fuel. It seemed that the parents were cooperating by piling fresh plant material just outside, but this type of behaviour was by no means normal.

To prove participation by the chick, we put lengths of red and green wool outside. The green was taken in during the first night, the red not until the third, but all was accepted. This chick did more building than most adults; a racial harking back, perhaps, to nest-building ancestors more akin to our fulmar petrels of the North.

Some shearwaters, like the grey-faced petrels that I had found nesting among arum lilies on Moko Hinau Island in New Zealand, nested as often on the surface as in burrows and some of the Furneaux shearwaters made do with dense vegetation, proving as versatile in this as rabbits. Others would sometimes sleep all night on the ground surface with no attempt to seek cover.

Many birds deposited their eggs on the ground surface, but these were not incubated and were soon picked up by gulls, ravens, currawongs or magpies. The birds disliked daylight when ashore, even birds in short burrows tending to desert if too much sunlight diffused in.

Leila Barrett had stories of eggs laid on beaches and grass on Big Dog Island. Silas Mansell was heard to say that 'the ground was white with eggs' on Babel Island but John thought that surface eggs, though large in number, were small as a percentage of the whole. (Even in the mid-1990s the estimated population was twenty-three million.)

The main spectacle of numbers was in the early mornings when the birds left for the sea. On windy nights they could rise into the airstream almost anywhere, but on still nights they needed help. We watched at one four metres high rock where countless birds came scrabbling up each night to gain the necessary elevation to get airborne. John had waited here with camera and flashlight and achieved some splendid photos of birds piled on top of each other as they queued to take their turn in the dawn launching.

With numbers as big as this, the state of the moon seemed immaterial to their comings and goings: there were as many crowding in on moonlight nights as on dark ones. The warden's observations were beginning to show that homecomings were more closely related to good fishing opportunities. If there was something to bring home they would bring it.

This was borne out by more frequent visits to the nests in rough weather, when the shearwaters fished close inshore with the gannets. If the flotsam and jetsam embroidered with the blue floats of Portuguese-men-of-war was any indication of the amount of krill and other goodies in the inshore waters, there would certainly be good feeding opportunities close by. One might even envisage the comfort of a burrow to be more alluring than those restless rollers, even to such pelagic creatures as mutton birds!

105 Australian Fur Seal *Arctocephalus pusillus*

106 Australian Fur Seal harem

107 Short-tailed Shearwaters *Puffinus tenuirostris* in flight

3. PENGUINS AND MATTERS MARINE

Penguins resemble fur seals as they skim past the wake of a boat and they are not a lot more mobile than seals when on land. Although bipeds, like other birds, the backward displacement of their short legs to facilitate swimming has necessitated the erect stance on land that is the prerogative of humans.

The stance is not quite erect in the little blue or fairy penguin *(Eudyptula minor)*, which leans forward when walking, as though anxious to arrive. When they are really anxious, they resort to a mammalian gait on all fours, their flippers as useful in rowing them along the ground as are those of a sea lion. These are the motile power when at sea, the big flat feet being used as rudders. Few birds walk or scuttle as penguins do, but most have their legs attached amidships on a horizontally held body and not alongside the tail.

I never tired of watching the chunky little birds coming ashore in the hour before dark — almost as readily up the sloping rocks as the two main sand beaches. They were less confident on land than in their natural element, although their chief predators, seals, struck only at sea. Enemies on land, apart from unpredictable man, were more of a threat to eggs and chicks.

Most would hesitate as their feet bottomed out, allowing each wave to swirl around their stumpy backsides as they looked nervously around for danger. Birds taking fright on the lower beach would flee back to the haven of the sea. If they were more than halfway home, they would scuttle precipitately to the safety of the burrow.

During my sojourn on Cat Island in mid-February, breeding was over, the chicks most closely observed having left for the sea at the end of January. At a little over three weeks old they had started emerging from the burrows to squat outside or pluck up courage to toddle around in the vicinity. Between eight and nine weeks old they had finally taken off to sea, some still wearing a neck ruff of grey baby down over the sleek blue of the new feathers.

Adult birds stayed away at sea when released from their parental duties, enjoying only a few weeks of freedom to feed none but themselves before having to come back for the moult. Unlike flighted birds, their feathers do not come out singly or in matching pairs, but in furry mats. During the process they lose their waterproofing so would get chilled and waterlogged at sea. This entailed a starvation period ashore lasting seventeen to eighteen days, while the greyish tousled mat sloughed away to reveal the smooth metallic blue beneath.

It was mainly these birds that I was seeing in February. Non breeders, juveniles from other years or unmated singles came in first, followed a week or so later by the breeders, which had more leeway to make up after their domestic chores. Sometimes a pair would arrive side by side, suggesting that they had spent the intervening weeks at sea together. These might return to their nesting burrow or, like the non-breeders, find a suitable hideaway nearer the sea.

They did not remain in these often inadequate shelters and the sight of a bedraggled, half-dressed bird sitting disconsolately on a growing pile of discarded feathers was not uncommon. Maybe they only looked miserable, but their enforced fast of nearly three weeks was not conducive to complete wellbeing. No doubt they had stocked up with fish quite adequately before coming in, but there was a very visible shrinkage of those white tums as the days advanced.

Although spasmodic matings continued long after the chicks had hatched, such pastimes were over now — but not the vocalisations that went with them. I would stroll out after supper with a camp stool and settle to pry on their private night life. The three display phases known as 'half trumpet', 'full trumpet' and 'ecstatic' were as likely to be indulged in as a welcome ceremony in mid-February as a lead up to coition in December or January.

The half trumpet display was directed forwards, the body often held at a low angle with the flippers spread sideways and (presumably amorous) growls issuing from the open beak. In the full trumpet, which usually followed, the head was thrown back and the flippers might meet behind where the waist would be if they had one, while even more boisterous calls issued from the upflung beak.

Mutual ceremonies of this sort might culminate in a circular dance, not quite cheek to cheek, but facing each other, heads bowed decorously and the stumpy little bodies raised on tiptoe, as they tripped around each other in a pas de deux, with flippers held wide.

Calls given as birds advanced up the beach consisted of a sound between a bark and a cough: of the sort that came drifting in from the groups at sea. These were probably contact calls, keeping members of the group in touch. Other causes for the various sneezes, donkey brays, pulsating growls and surprised shrieks were contacts with partners or rivals or a response to external alarms. The muscles of their fat little bodies would ripple and throb in sympathy.

Penguins were numerous on Cat Island, although living in loose community, their burrows more widely spaced than those of shearwaters. As with rabbles of frogs, when one started calling, others joined in. Each defended its little plot within the colony, feeling the need to trumpet its authority over the home domain. Even mutton birds did this, although their patch of Mother Earth might be less than a metre across.

One of a pair I was watching wandered off, leaving the other squatting contemplatively. This one perked up when a neighbour started emulating a jackass, but answered only softly in a muted, feminine voice. (I had decided she was female by now.) Advertising territory seemed to be none of her business. She settled onto her fat little tum and awaited the return of himself, with befitting decorum.

On windy nights the trumpeting was less urgent and came from within the burrows. Either the birds wished to escape the blast or realised that its noise would drown any attempted communication. With all sheltering inside there were no trespassers to be warned off anyway. Their withdrawal was not due to the human watchers, who dimmed their torches with red paper.

I came in one night to report a great clattering of corrugated iron reminiscent of the racket made by penguins I had lived with on Kapiti Island in New Zealand. The perpetrators slid repeatedly down the artificial surface to clatter back up. John's response was: "Oh that must be Tubby and Bessie. They haven't been in for some nights now."

He could imitate the penguin calls to a nicety and on one occasion persuaded an unattached male to try to mate. It was not his whole person that attracted the amorous bird, just the enticing shine of his dew-drenched gumboots. The little fellow, his hormones thoroughly roused, made love in the only way he knew how. Squeezing between the two potential mates, he took his pick, sidled closer and beat an exited tattoo on either flank with his hard little flippers. He slapped away, giving no indication that the slightly rubbery response was less feminine than he could have hoped. I couldn't help thinking of the attentions paid by swashbuckling male bumblebees to the bee-like boss of a bee orchid flower. Sex-crazed males are so easily duped!

The inmates of two penguin burrows were taken into temporary custody while John made removable lids for their nest chambers and erected a lightproof hide over each. The burrow entrances remained untouched and the lids were not removed until he was safely inside the lightproof hide, so that the reinstated occupants would sense nothing amiss as he observed their shadowy activities in a red glow.

He marked one of each pair with a dab of blue paint on the white bib and the other with yellow. Even the expert could not tell the sexes apart until he saw them mating. One pair reared two chicks under his eagle eye, the other pair only one, as the second egg proved infertile. This couple became very confiding, if this is the right term to use for creatures with such a low level of intellect, even on bird-brained standards.

Chicks were certainly not very bright, spending most of the day when not snoozing uttering chirruping whimpers that advertised their presence to friend and foe alike. They greeted the returning adults with boisterous calls in their rush to plunge the beak deep into the fish-holding maw. An adult wishing to evade too much attention might lengthen the burrow a little by scratching the earth away with one foot at a time, shearwater fashion.

Long periods were spent preening, immaculate plumage an essential for sea-going creatures needing to maintain their body temperature in chilly depths. The nipple of the preen gland near the tail was squeezed to obtain oil for rubbing over the coarse, bristly feathers that were so different from those of other birds; with nothing approaching wing primaries or tail feathers.

Male and female preened each other and both preened the chick, helping to loosen the down to expose the waterproof coat beneath, but failing to dislodge many of the ticks. Self preening helped the moult and hastened their return to the sea to feed. Stupid they may be, but penguins are very endearing, with their irresistibly human stance, mammalian style coat and startled, jackass-like braying.

* * * * *

There was no legal stipulation regarding the size of water tanks on Cat Island and our two were much too small. Pat and I spent a lot of time trekking to the beach to fetch sea water for cooking vegetables, washing up and cleaning. While soap refused to produce a lather in salt water, there was no such problem with detergents. It would have taken more than a little salt to quell the frothing of the Teepol which we used.

The carrying of water from Harland's brackish pools for ablutions and laundry had been abandoned when storm waves swept into them, making their contents as salty as the sea — moreso after a few days of evaporation. Thus it was that we welcomed the two occasions when the heavens opened and the tanks were topped up, along with all available buckets and kerosene tins placed to catch the overflow.

I was due to be collected after the second cloudburst, but a southerly buster was propelling outsize breakers into South Bay. It looked as though Cat Island was going to be as hard to get off as to get on. Lew Bailey's voice crackled cheerily through the static on the morning radio 'sched.', pointing out that he had known such conditions to last for six weeks at this time of year and that he had the doctor and the dentist waiting to get to Cape Barren Island as soon as it let up. I was happy to stay where I was, but had yet to visit Chappell Island and time was running short.

We wondered how the lost yacht was faring, the one that had set out from Hobart to Adelaide and was several days overdue. A couple of days back a four-engined RAAF bomber had flown low over the island in thick mist, and into the cloud surrounding the pinnacle on Babel Island at about 300 feet. It looked dangerous and we thought it was in trouble and trying to make a forced landing. We learned later by radio that the pilot was searching for the missing boat and had come down to investigate a couple of fishing boats holed-up in the lee of the island.

Hopefully the yacht would not share the fate of the *"Tasman"*, wrecked to the west of the hut seven years earlier in January 1951. When the gale suddenly blasted into action on that occasion, a crew man broke his arm in the rush to get the anchor up to move away from the rocks. In the time it took the others to splint it, the tumult took on a new lease of life and the boat ran ashore. The injured man lost his life. The other three reached land, one badly scraped on the barnacles. They took up residence in the wardens' hut and attracted help four days later with smoke signals: three for a death. Fortunately they had a watertight box of matches — not only for the smoke signals, but to light brushwood fires to cook mutton birds, their only source of nourishment.

Beachcombing after our 1958 storms, we had good hunting with marine animals, but no driftwood like the handsome plank we had lugged up from the North Beach a few days before. Gnarled offering from the dune scrub kept our cooking fire alive all day, providing warmth for frozen fingers and drawing the moisture from sodden clothes.

We were beguiled by the behaviour of some whelk-like molluscs feeding on small fluted limpets. They sidled onto their prey, the horny lid of their shell moved aside to allow the foot to embrace the limpet with one half while holding tight to the rock with the other. With a long, strong sideways pull, they slowly levered the limpet from its hold, the pair tumbling back onto the pool floor as one. There the shell was twisted, so that the predator's horn-like process curved over to penetrate the soft flesh and apply suction. It appeared to be a hollow tube, as small gobbets of black limpet about one mm across could be seen gliding upwards through its transparent walls, the system resembling an overhead line of miniature, slowly moving coal buckets on a mine site.

The evening sky, suffused with sulphur-coloured clouds, boded well for the morrow, which dawned blue and gold, but brought no boats. Lew's airborne voice announced that the Potboil was bad and that he was also stalling with the doctor and dentist. It was a great day for farming! We employed ourselves taking compass bearings and pacing distances in an attempt to map the island, there being no aerial photos available to provide a semblance of greater accuracy.

I kept a weather eye open for driftwood and was rewarded by a far-travelled plank, covered in blue-shelled goose barnacles with long black 'hose pipe' attachments. If planks could talk, what tales this might have told of its origins and wanderings.

A night of wind and rain heralded a morning that was no better. The sky had darkened like a bruise after a brief let up at dawn, so we were surprised when Lew's radio-borne voice announced his imminent arrival, with Bill Mollison and MacDonald, who was taking a few days off from examining school children's teeth. These two had come for the ride (seven to eight hours) rather than to see Cat Island, being allowed only half an hour to talk with the Warhams over cups of tea. Dearly though they would have loved to see the gannet colony, it was not to be. Nor were we three Cat Islanders allowed the promised landing on Storehouse Island.

All too soon, we were wading out with the gear. Silas would take only one passenger, with the dinghy so heavily laden that water swilled in over the stern. Bill and I adjourned to a slightly quieter corner of the beach for a drier pick-up. Up anchor and we were away, waves soon clawing over the gunwhale with white-padded paws, while parallel furrows streamed behind, as from a plough.

We retired below, to be brought up again by an ear-shattering yell from Lew. No worry. He had nosed into the south-east bay of Babel and was bellowing messages to the workmen domiciled there to build the new house. There was much cursing and gesticulating ashore when *"Aralla"* had to circle out to avoid being pushed in too close. The men thought we had gone, their own messages undelivered.

We were thankful to retire again, to eat, talk, read and write notes — almost a wasted voyage for the two trippers. Had we had a function on deck, we should no doubt have savoured the experience of the Potboil passage to the full, but the excitement of repeated douchings with cold sea water soon loses its appeal. *"Aralla"* edged round inside the maelstrom, hugging the Flinders' shore as close as her skipper dared, and we were edging in to Fisher Island just before dark.

It was good to be home again, despite the muddle of the foregoing bachelor reign, with food, ants, pliers, lamps, cameras and notebooks littered in homely confusion, but plenty of dry matches for warming things up.

108 Pied Oystercatchers *Haematopus longirostris*

109 Little Blue Penguins *Eudyptula minor*:
Half Trumpet and Full Trumpet display

110 Awkward Gait due to backward displacement of legs:
Penguin and Shearwater

Chapter Thirteen

LESSER SEA BIRD ISLANDS IN THE SOUND

1. WHITE-FACED STORM PETREL COLONIES: THREE SPENCES REEFS, RABBIT AND PENGUIN ISLANDS AND ISABELLA REEF

On a world basis, the smaller the island the less interest it is to humans and the more likely it is to be colonised by sea birds. The great spreads of mutton birds on so many of the sizable islands of the Furneaux Group are an obvious exception, but other birds prefer the lesser reefs, be they nesters in the open, like gulls, terns, shags and geese, or in burrows, like storm petrels and fairy penguins.

Whenever opportunity offered, we arranged to be dropped off at these more spectacular sea bird gatherings in Franklin Sound. Currently neither graziers nor mutton birders used these islets for economic gain and they were seldom visited. Even the purloiners of cray bait and the poachers of shearwaters or their eggs did better on the bigger islands.

During my three summers on the archipelago I was able to land at eight colonies of white-faced storm petrels or frigate petrels *(Pelagodroma marina)* here and compare these with those of the Mud Islands and South Channel Fort in Port Phillip Bay, Victoria, and seven on islands visited in South Western Australia. These were West, East and South Spences Reefs off Little Green Island, Rabbit Island and Penguin Island off Great Dog Island, Apple Orchard Reef off Cape Barren Island, Mid Woody Island between Big Woody and Little Woody Islands and Isabella Reef away to the west,

None of these are more than a few acres in extent and their vegetation resembled that of other small islands enjoying similar shelter from the worst ocean squalls, with one notable exception. This was the growth habit of the dominant needle-leaved grass, *Poa poiformis*. The vernacular name of silver tussock describes its growth form almost everywhere else, but on the petrel islands it formed level swards of soft, blue-green shoots rather than tussocks.

The temptation to think of this as a different species was firmly quashed by the late Jim Willis of the National Herbarium in Melbourne and other botanical experts who processed my specimens. I never got around to growing the two forms side by side under experimental conditions, to determine whether they were genetically distinct or merely responding to different environments. Nor could we solve the conundrum: Did the petrels move in because they preferred the bluish mat to the yellowish tussocks, or did the grass respond to their presence by adopting the different growth form? The other principal plant of the petrel colonies, the bower spinach, remained true to form.

Where soil depth allowed, the petrel burrows occurred commonly at the rate of two to four per square metre, and as many as nine entrances were observed opening onto a plot of this size. Many were no longer than thirty cm and most were only five cm across at the entrance, opening into a larger nesting chamber within, this lined with grassy bedding. Larger entrances with smaller tunnels leading away inside were almost certainly abandoned penguin burrows which had been taken over by a group of neighbours.

For some undiscovered reason, shearwaters were not present on any of the petrel islands, so the smaller birds could not utilise the leftovers of their larger relatives. This was particularly striking as so many of the other islands apart from the two inhabited ones of Flinders and Cape Barren were occupied by the larger birds. White-faced storm petrels visited on Western Australian islands cohabited with the little shearwater *(Puffinus assimilis)* and the wedge-tailed shearwater *(Puffinus pacificus)*, while dove petrels and diving petrels shared islands in the Glennies and Ansers Group off Victoria's Wilsons Promontory with short-tailed shearwaters.

The Furneaux stormies started excavating, either in soil or matted vegetation, in October. Subsequent scratching to keep the burrows free from spring and summer plant growth showered fine soil across the mats and these soon grew over to obscure the entrances when the petrel chicks left in March.

On Apple Orchard Reef these platforms were contributed to by penguins as well as petrels, forming firmly elastic roofs to burrows beneath. While the delicate hooves of sheep might step through these, the big flat feet of the principal associates, Cape Barren geese, were unlikely to do so while the stiff Poa or Stipa leaves retained their springiness.

The geese seemed to home in on the petrel colonies to graze, preferring their sort of turf, and the ground became fouled with their droppings. Goose nests were seen on some of the islands and fifteen goslings on Rabbit Island. Silver gulls and crested terns sometimes cohabited with the petrels, along with the occasional caspian tern or oystercatcher, and there seemed to be a special relationship — not to the petrels' advantage — with the fearsome Pacific gulls.

I located these large black-backs in any number on only two of the thirty-three islands I visited in the Furneaux Group and both were petrel islands. In each case the gulls had established their gathering grounds on sites vacated by the petrels. They, too, appreciated level swards for loitering, lounging and looking, although their nests were tucked among neighbouring tussocks which gave better cover for eggs and chicks.

Intensive use created a crust of dried guano, coloured by a film of green and blue-green algae, as a false floor on top of flattened grass. Sprouting through this — as around the Cat Island gannetry — were robust stands of bronze-leaved leek lilies, flowering most profusely where hard-pressed. Two similar roosts on the northern slopes of Rabbit Island supported a few other succulents and Austral hollyhock .

Petrels withdrew when the gulls moved in or were forcibly ejected, either by the treading in of burrows or by predation. There is no doubt that the big gulls preyed on stormies, and not only on their two nesting islands of Apple Orchard Reef and Rabbit Island. Many gulls have individual feeding preferences and the occupant of an isolated nest on South Spences Reef had developed a particular liking for stormies.

Petrel burrows near this nest had been scratched out and the nest material, down and feathers scattered. Among the more usual food leftovers of crab claws, mollusc shells, caterpillar skins and the like were ten storm petrel carcases and the legs of many more. There were also broken shells of about twenty petrel eggs pulled out of desecrated burrows. More petrel remains were found at three other gull feeding sites in the vicinity.

* * * * *

Our most meticulously planned visits were likely to be cancelled at short notice while unplanned ones would be staged on the spur of the moment. Thus it was with the Spences Reefs. After I had waited in the rain from 8 a.m. to 10 a.m. for my first visit there, Tuck chugged to within shouting distance to point out that, although he might be able to land me, he wouldn't be able to pick me up.

"We probably won't make it to Cape Barren even."

He had a bevy of seamen aboard instead of the usual mixed passengers and they did make it, but had to put ashore four miles from the jetty and radio for a truck to pick up men and mail.

"Theo Barrett's going to Great Dog. He'll put you off and collect you at half four."

And so he did. Eric and Dell Lindgren decided to come and we were landed on Western Spences Reef. It was bitterly cold and we were wearing all we could lay hands on, including pyjama trousers under thin summer slacks. The East and West islands were connected by a low spit covered by every tide, but the South islet was permanently separated and inaccessible to us today.

The East and West Reefs proved to be honeycombed with the tiny burrows of white-faced stormies. Rather messy penguin holes were scattered throughout, more thickly than usual, and the more salubrious burrows thought to be those of shearwaters proved also to belong to penguins.

During lunch on the lee shore we watched sooty and pied oystercatchers and a black swan sailing the inshore waters. Seven goose nests were found on the West Reef and nine on the East Reef. A caspian tern's nest on the East Reef contained two young chicks and we counted forty-two occupied nests of silver gulls. All three of the common cormorant species were here, large black, black-faced and small pied. Some crested terns were diving for fish where little waves riffled over a submerged sandbank and a lone curlew was plunging its slender beak into the soft substrate of the isthmus.

The lower saltmarsh on this sand bar was home to Austral sea-blite, with creeping brookweed, common samphire and a few clumps of woody samphire. The upper marsh was carpeted with distichlis grass and sea celery, grading up through pigface and coast spear grass to the Poa and spinach of the main ground cover. Coast beard heath and coast wattle were wind-tattered, their branches shaggy with lichens. They enjoyed the partial protection of salt-scorched bracken below and climbing lignum above, as well as the inevitable rambling spinach.

These sightings were made on 15th December. It was 5th February before we managed to land on South Spences Reef, coming in at low water over intertidal swards of strapweed and eelgrass. We found the little petrel burrows to be as thickly scattered as on the other islets. A number of juvenile penguins had died from an unknown cause when almost fully feathered. The one goose nest contained broken rather than vacated eggshells and this was the island showing the worst predation of stormies by Pacific gulls.

* * * * *

On my first visit to Rabbit Island I was with dentist MacDonald. Tuck was off duty with dysentery and *"Tassie"* was skippered by Alec Ross and crewed by Geoff Barrett. Hardly a cloud cast its shadow on the gently heaving waters, but I had warned Mac of Ross's habitually dire forebodings and he behaved true to form. He gazed apprehensively at the sedate sky and shook his head dolefully. "I don't like the look of it at all. My Word! If it should blow up while you were ashore...." He left the rest unsaid, then added, "We won't get to Rabbit but I'll land you on Big Dog."

But Mac and I both wanted Rabbit Island and he finally agreed to look.

"Tuck said I wasn't to do anything dangerous with the boat. If I can get you ashore it'll only be for a few minutes."

The sea got choppier in the cross currents over the shallows, but he hove to under the north side and gave us an hour. As Geoff rowed us ashore the familiar message came drifting over the water. "Mind those weedy rocks: they're slippery as Hell."

We 'mound' them and a while later saw him minding them himself as he trod gingerly up the north-west point towards a group of idling shags. Ross had a special interest in Rabbit Island as he was the grazier. For forty years there had been sheep on the island, but thirty years before twenty-five of them had been stolen.

"'Shook', they were. Just disappeared in the night and never saw no more of them. Never put any more on."

Now it was a lovely little island, with a good quota of succulents, its acres given over to storm petrels, Cape Barren geese and penguins. Stormies burrowed almost all over, many in the same sort of blue mat Poa as on the Spences Reefs, this threaded with trails of kidney weed. Mac set about estimating burrow density and reached into five burrows at random to find that all contained well-grown chicks. This was the last day of February.

An outlying colony in the south-west consisted of hundreds of tiny tunnels penetrating coast spear grass shrouded in pigface. On the eastern part the petrels burrowed in an amalgam of mat grass and bower spinach, a community which they shared with fairy penguins. Of the thirty-five plant species recorded eight were aliens, either leftovers from the grazing regime or brought from other islands by gulls or fishermen.

The northern slopes were most favoured by the other birds. Two areas mucky with excreta were shared by Pacific gulls and geese, white sploshes from the carnivores mingling with fibrous cylinders from the herbivores. These had left, there being nothing to hold them now that the green had faded with the advancing season. Some had moved onto a lusher patch of Italian rye-grass; others were nibbling at pigface leaves. Alec told us that fifteen goslings were raised here most years.

Black-faced cormorants roosted on the north side on guano-plastered rocks backed by leek lily and pink purslane, with *Brachycome* and groundsel type daisies, saltbush and hollyhock.

* * * * *

Penguin Island, visited in both February and December, is just under a sixth of a mile long, the northern and southern parts separated by a low neck which was partially taken up by a brackish pool. Sand banks had built up at either end, so it is likely that only the highest tides would break through. It was formerly known as Cooks Reef, after Cook, who owned the nearest birding hut on Great Dog Island, not much more than a stone's throw away.

Landing at high water proved no problem, but it was a long squelch through the eelgrass beds as reefs and sandbanks began to break surface before our departure. Tuck had come ashore but noticed *"Tassie"* sliding landwards along her anchor chain and scuttled back in the dinghy in haste, to take her out, stern first. The proud owner of a new thousand-pound diesel engine "Better than all those petrol jobs!", he had been dubious about leaving his crew man in charge. He refused to face the muddy shallows again and I had to find a suitable reef where he was prepared to pick me up.

Lignum and spinach sprouted from the blue mat of the southern portion, with pigface on the offshore cormorant stack. Barilla or grey saltbush was the upstanding component of the northern part, merging with *Lepidosperma* sword sedge in the north-east. Saltmarsh species of the low-lying centre were as before, some buried under drifted sea-grass leaves. Eighty-five per cent of the thirty-two species were native.

Petrel burrows were estimated to average one per square metre in the north and one per two square metres in the south. Both halves were frequented by geese, which had been nipping off the tips of pigface leaves, and there were a few old nests. Caspian terns and sooty oystercatchers were seen only on the beach in February, but the following December we found a nest of the big tern and those of a small colony of silver gulls. A litter of broken sea shells marked the Pacific gulls' dining area.

Storm petrels were MacDonald's favourite bird ever since he had worked on the commoner of the two British species on Skomer Island in South Wales.

He enquired of the powers beforehand if it would be alright to defend himself if one of the wee chicks attacked him. He did just that and was as delighted as a small boy with his prize.

He spent the evening on Fisher Island skinning and stuffing the mite for posterity, still with some of its baby down attached. The skin came off neatly, the specimen sprinkled liberally with borax, to avoid mess and deter beetles. The eyes, which occupied most of the fragile skull, were removed from within. Considerable dexterity was required and Mac's dental tools came into their own. I watched the wielding of the various probes and prongs with none of the usual forebodings. Wisps of cotton wool were pulled through the eye sockets from within, this being a skin for scientific study, not to be fitted with glass eyes and mounted in a case. While Mac completed the stuffing, Bill Mollison found the sex organs and proclaimed the chick to be a male.

* * * * *

Apple Orchard Reef and Mid Woody Island, two further storm petrel colonies, are referred to in chapters three and six. It was not until almost mid-April that I got to Isabella Reef. The gentle swell was ruffled by a plodding little breeze meeting us broadside on. Neither Tuck nor Alec were familiar with these waters, having had no cause to land before, but Alec had fished off the island and knew of one particularly nasty rock lurking on the sea bed. We were beyond the shelter of Franklin Sound and there were no sea-grass flats here. They eased the boat gingerly across the bouldery bottom, and narrowly missed grazing her paint on a whopper which loomed unexpectedly off the starboard bow.

"That's the one I told you about," yelled Alec.

A miss is as good as a mile, but Tuck's face was a study in worried concentration. He came ashore with me, to amble round one of the few coastal bits of the archipelago that he had not trodden before. Waiting patiently in the boat were an Abo boy and his deaf mute mother, bound for Cape Barren.

No sandy beaches were seen, although a little sand had drifted over the sea bed on the side towards the sound, transforming the overlying water from indigo to sapphire. The same bluish Poa mat predominated, any trace of past sheep grazing long since obscured. John Nield, grazier on the not too distant Tin Kettle Island, had told me that a dozen sheep used to be run here, but not during the past two decades.

We saw fewer petrel burrows than usual, but tell-tale depressions showed where the grass had closed in over the entrances. It was several weeks since the young birds had left for their pelagic life of 'walking the waters'. (The word petrel derives from St Peter, who tried just that, rather less successfully.)

When Dom Serventy visited Isabella Reef on October 23rd some years before, it was a different story. He found many hundreds of petrel nest holes in the "low, dense, soft-leaved, green Poa", some with freshly-dug earth outside. Some were less than a foot long, but completed burrows investigated ended in nesting chambers up to a foot across at the end of tunnels twice this length, their floors strewn with short lengths of grass as nesting material.

Twittering notes emanated from burrows which held a single bird and a yapping conversation from one containing two birds. He found remains of petrels outside five burrows — and a Pacific gull's shell-cracking midden in the North-west, these thought to be responsible.

They did not get off scot-free. He records two caspian terns swooping onto a pair of them on the water and continuing to harass the bigger birds when these took off. His field notes read: "The contrast in speed of flight was amazing, the terns being very much the faster."

His October visit yielded sightings of live and dead Cape Barren geese, two or three pairs of oystercatchers, a starling and a number of blue penguin burrows. In one of these a bird was seen and heard, in another an adult was sitting on two stained eggs and in another two birds were engaged in growling conversation.

In April the giant form of sea celery, which characterised the more oceanic islands, was among the thirty species recorded. Others of interest were the rare *Wilsonia backhousii* and dusty daisy bush. Droppings and shell middens bore witness to the continued presence of geese and Pacific gulls, although few were about at the time of our visit.

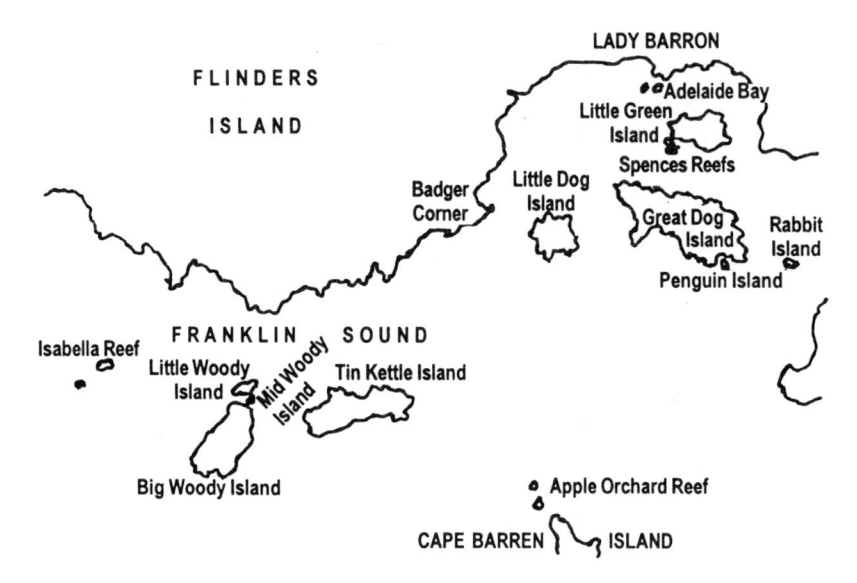

111 Map of White-faced Storm Petrel Colonies in Franklin Sound

112 White-faced Storm Petrels *Pelagodroma marina*

113 Silver Gulls *Larus novaehollandiae*

2. SHAG AND TERN COLONIES. REEF ISLAND AND TUCKS REEF

Surface nesting birds were distributed across a wider range of islands than the storm petrels. They could get by with minimal soil depth and plant cover and might occupy two sites concurrently — one for nesting and the other for off-duty birds to roost, away from the clamour. Terns are unable to roost at sea, as penguins, petrels and shearwaters do, becoming waterlogged if they settle, and the others showed a preference for dry land when idling and preening.

Our almost constant presence during the breeding season precluded Fisher Island as a gathering ground, but many took advantage of Reef Island close by. We could sit in comfort on our home patch and watch them with binoculars, sculling across occasionally for a closer look.

Terns, gulls and cormorants, as well as gannets, seemed to be running on a schedule two months behind their counterparts in New Zealand, so, when I arrived on the Furneaux Group in January 1958, I was able to witness a repeat performance, photographing unhatched eggs after fledgling chicks.

Most abundant on Reef Island were the several hundred black-faced cormorants with a more modest contingent of small pieds occupying the low island crest. A few silver gulls nested and, on my first visit of 8th January, we found a newly vacated starlings' nest. The owners were preparing for a second brood, commuting to Fisher Island for new nesting material.

Cormorants were present throughout each day, birds peeling off individually to feed as the last intake was satisfactorily digested, triggering the urge for more. They balanced on small rock excrescences, some with wings spread, and with beak and tail overlapping the fleshy carpet of jelly bean pigface that capped the island.

Because they headed always into the wind, plants to immediate windward of the perches shone a brighter red than those to leeward, which were often wilted, sometimes killed, by the powerful jets of guano headed their way. When the wind changed, plants that had escaped the worst of the effluent got just enough to give them a boost instead of laying them low. A bit like beer really.

During the first three months of 1960, the birds used Reef Island only by day, rising in the evening to join the mob passing from the Samphire Island shallows to the night roost in paperbarks by Scotts Lagoon. There were no shag nests on Reef Island at that time.

About 200 oystercatchers were currently using the area as a night roost, the majority moving off when the shags returned in the morning. Had they been waiting for the bigger birds to make way for them in this classic Box and Cox act? Pied oystercatchers outnumbered sooties and the two tended to keep to their own kind when sub flocks took off.

Such constant bird traffic was hard on the plant life, pigface winning hands down. Next came bower spinach and seablite with wisps of celery, Austral hollyhock and the related but alien tree mallow, which is characteristic of sea-bird vegetation in the North Temperate zone, as far south as the Mediterranean.

Honey bees made light of the sea crossing from Flinders during summer, to siphon nectar from the pigface blooms and load the pollen baskets on their hind legs with a protein supplement to augment the sugary fluid fed to the brood back home.

Situated such a conveniently short flap from the fishing quay at Lady Barron, Reef Island was an inevitable gathering ground for silver gulls on the lookout for the main chances. Only a fraction of those hanging around for a consignment of offal bred on the island.

In 1957 there were fifteen gulls' nests, but commonly around a hundred and sixty adults. Four pairs tried to nest on Fisher Island that year but only one brought off a family. A few years earlier there had been up to forty-nine nests on Reef Island, or down to as few as twenty-five. It was likely that the dwindling numbers were due to closure of the local fish cannery.

Caspian terns nested in a hollow on the summit in the 1959-60 season. The commoner crested terns used it only in transit — as did the sometimes huge mobs of red-capped dotterels and other waders. There was insufficient soil for any of the burrowing birds.

Reef Island was already a declared wildlife sanctuary back in the fifties but was not held sacrosanct by all on that account. Victorian vessels such as the *"Betty Elizabeth"* might anchor close by, her crew sidling up to the rocks in a fibreglass dinghy with shotgun at the ready. Spotting one of us watching from Fisher, they would wave feebly and pretend to tinker with the silent motor. When they thought they were unobserved, shots would ring out and cormorants would tumble, the corpses not retrieved if we made our presence known.

Their cray pots, no doubt primed with 'crooked bait', were let down haphazardly with untoward haste on one occasion when we drew up alongside their craft at sea, the 'we' including Bill Mollison, whose father-in-law was a Tasmanian inspector of fisheries. The local guardians of the law held few terrors for poachers, tipping them the wink if independent inspections were impending and not being above buying the odd crayfish out of season.

Sometimes, after a bout of bird photography from the sea, we would ease our dinghy into one of the low spurs of land running seaward from the little bird metropolis. Here, on sparkling sunny days, we might fall under a spell of enchantment watching handsome short-spined sea urchins, *Amblypneustes ovum*, their myriad sucker feet undulating in metronomic sequence. These enabled them to move over the eelgrass beds at a surprising pace and to right themselves if they toppled backwards to land the wrong way up. Most were purplish red, a few pale pink.

A smaller kind, *Goniocidaris tubaria*, had fewer longer spines, which tripled the animals' diameter. These, too, were red, but the spines pale yellow and distinctly thorny when viewed through a hand lens.

There were tiny red-brown starfish, *Patirella exigua*, ragworms, their many legs moving in synchronised rhythm, and many molluscs, including bizarre coat of mail shells, *Sypharochiton maugeanus*. Sands bordering their home rocks were softened by sea-grasses, including turtle grass, *Amphibolis (Cymodocea) antarctica* and the delicately stalked oval fronds of *Halophila australis (ovalis)*.

* * * * *

On 5th February 1958, I woke to a crimson dawn to find my watch had stopped. Looking critically at the haloed light effects, I righted it by guesswork and was delighted to discover that it was spot on. My sojourn in the wilderness was evidently bringing out my aboriginal sixth sense that I had presumed lost and gone forever in our headlong evolutionary scramble towards sophistication.

I had been waiting for more than two hours when Tuck arrived, full of apologies.

"It's them ole cows. They wasn't milked yesterday and we couldn't find them again this morning. My boy George, 'e took arf a day orf from work to look an' we still ha'n found 'em."

His cattle, like many others, were prone to wander at will. Groups of feral beasts were at large on Flinders Island and when these mooched past the farms the more domesticated milkers were tempted to join them and savour the delights of free range — unmindful of the fact that they would have to carry their master's milk with them. Time is of little moment here, to either man or beast. There was always another day tomorrow.

Our goal was Tucks Reef, lying between Little Green and Little Dog Islands, and named for the time when Tuck had run aground on its shores. It harboured the usual burrowing shearwaters and penguins, Cape Barren geese and a small colony of silver gulls. Visited ten months later, in December, the size of the gull colony had increased enormously and a vibrant mob of crested terns had taken up residence.

The twenty-five plant species, a quarter of them aliens, were unremarkable, with boxthorn, seaberry saltbush and tree mallow the only ones approaching underbrush size. The daisy flowers of *Brachycome* and fireweed brightened matted grasses and succulents. Penguins and gulls favoured the north side, gulls' nests insinuated into crevices. The four goose nests and the black-faced shags were in the south-west, the latter on outlying rocks.

Crested terns, unrecorded on our February visit, were present to the extent of some four hundred pairs on the west end the following season. Nests were rudimentary, little more than depressions in the vegetation, containing one or two eggs with no hatchlings as yet. The colony was in five parts, ascending from red-leaved pigface to mixed tussocks and succulents, but excluding

Ross's noonflower, which was common round about. With such a new influx of nesters, the vegetation was not the product of bird occupation but the type that they had chosen to move into.

About fifty pairs of silver gulls were breeding among coast spear grass. These, too, were at the cacaphonous start of their breeding cycle, not all the nests having their full clutch of three mottled brown eggs, although there were small chicks present in the Scotts Reef colony this very day. Gulls chose to nest among tussocks, terns in the open, and gulls were more widely dispersed within their colony. Two nests per square metre was the norm, whereas the terns averaged six per square metre, or up to a crowded dozen, perhaps as protection against Pacific gulls, whose main feeding ground was on the opposite side of the island.

Spinach was the commonest plant by the gulls' nests and the ground throughout was strewn with crop pellets of spinach seeds — a score or more coughed up around almost every nest. It was convenient that the birds could find provender without having to go out shopping, but these good times could not last.

The previous season's gull colony in the north was scarcely discernible, the spinach having got its own back by over-running the nests, the old growths boosted by germination of the ingested and disgorged seeds. Upstanding boulders in this area were still used as lookout posts, so the gulls continued to contribute a modicum of fertiliser. As often, the geese consorted with the bigger gull species on a north coast eminence.

These crowded bird islands were sheer heaven scenically. Our December visit was made on a day of blazing sun but ferociously cool wind. It was a matter of covering up, against cold and heat simultaneously, of anchoring the sun hat firmly under the chin and being generous with the sun-screen ointment.

When we hove to we gazed entranced at the massed white terns, settled among the brilliance of mesembrianthemum flowers. All heads pointed upwind, lest those pristine feathers get ruffled: the sky was a flawless blue, the cuprous waters as translucent as on any coral isle. *"Tassie"* was hard to hold in the stiff breeze, with anchors fore and aft, and the water was so clear that we seemed to be sitting on the sea bed far below.

As we stepped off the dinghy some eight hundred terns and a hundred gulls rose in a scintillating cloud — a frenzy of white wings, black-tipped, still headed into the wind as they hung, suspended a few metres above their precious eggs. We trod warily and they soon settled. They were inevitably excited by the novelty of human visitors, but had no reason to regard us as a potential threat. They were too agile to be sought by bait seekers and smaller than optimum anyway, when larger creatures could be hauled from burrows.

114 Silver Gulls flying over Nesting Colony

115 Crested Terns *Sterna bergii*

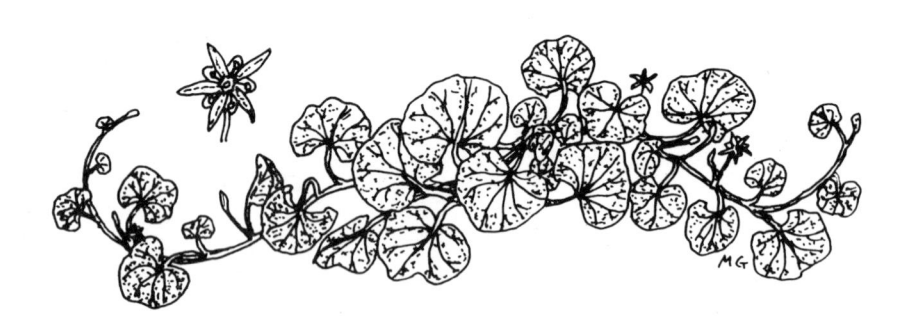

116 Kidney Weed *Dichondra repens*

3. BILLY GOAT OR SCOTTS REEFS

This group of islets, renamed on the occasion of Sir Peter Scott's visit in 1957, consists of four parts, aligned from north to south. The two central ones are the largest: Inner Possum Boat Harbour Reef lying to the north of the slightly smaller Outer Possum Boat Harbour Reef. To the north of both lies Jack Mansells Reef.

The southernmost, un-named, reef is little more than a rock, bearing scant soil and only a dozen species of plants, ten of these indigenous. While these grew fairly densely on the sheltered north-east face, we found no birds risking the onslaught of possible storms to nest there.

Jack Mansells Reef showed greater diversity, although barely a dozen paces across and little more than three metres above high water mark. The twenty-one kinds of plant had to tolerate periodic douching by salt spray and all were indigenous apart from two sow thistles and two grasses. We saw a silver gulls' nest and at least one occupied penguin burrow, also the feeding grounds of Pacific gulls and Cape Barren geese. Birds with looser ties to the islet were black-faced shag, white-faced heron and the two oystercatchers.

Inner Possum Reef is altogether larger, with half a dozen woody species — principally the coast wattle of the summit — and a stand of bracken on the sheltered side. Visits in February and December brought the plant list up to forty-six. Large numbers of gulls and terns nested here, along with the more widely distributed species, but most unusual was the pair of chestnut teal. Bob Tilt spotted their down-lined nest on our December visit. It was a metre down in a crevice near the island centre and contained eight white eggs, the size of a bantam's.

The slightly smaller Outer Possum Reef yielded only nineteen plant species, four of them shrubs. Many of the gulls which previously nested there had moved to Rabbit Island in the 1957-58 season and there were no terns. Burrows were numerous, a hundred of these said to belong to mutton birds, the rest to penguins, while goose droppings were everywhere.

Knowing our destinations to be little more than rocks, I had worn canvas sand shoes. It was a little disconcerting, therefore, to come across the sloughed skin of a large tiger snake soon after landing. I commented on this to Tuck when he sculled in to get me.

"You would! Alec Ross said to tell you to go carefully on these reefs. There's snakes aplenty swims over from Flinders. Why, only last week, one was coming alongside the boat with head stuck right up out of the water."

Ross had slipped up in his counselling this time, but was pleased to corroborate his skipper's words.

"A six-footer was killed on Inner Possum a few weeks back."

Then, in answer to my query: "Why Jack Mansells Reef? Tight he was: one night in the days of sail. Ran into it in his drunken stupor."

As we moved on towards the next reef, the portly JP jerked a thumb over his shoulder. "My first two wives came from over there: used to do my courting on these reefs. Sunday afternoons. My word!" The fat smile broadened as memories came flooding back.

I enquired how many wives he'd had.

"Only three. I've just divorced my third. She only stayed with me a fortnight." Then, lest I should get the wrong impression. "The first two died. Lovely women. My word! Lost one when she was thirty-four and the other when she was forty-four. Married the ole bitch when SHE was forty-four. Four's my unlucky number."

I gathered later from another source that wife number three had squeezed £1,200 out of her wealthy grazier spouse before departure. Another little bird let on that a fourth prospective candidate was in the offing, with one eye on Alec and another on the cash.

Before diving into the scrub and bracken of our next port of call, I gratefully donned Tuck's battered gumboots. While I was ashore the two men sailed back and forth trailing lines over the stern for pike, but caught none. On my return they commented on the beauteous flounders eighteen inches long, gliding over the sands only three feet below the keel — the absolute minimum for "*Tassie*" — on the falling tide.

"Tried those too, but got nowt."

I asked how one caught flounders.

"Lie flat on the deck and spear them."

I pictured the rotund Alec, rocking gently on his ample centre-forward. Perhaps the centre of equilibrium had not been stable enough.

Tuck waited for me on Outer Possum Reef, as it was a long pull back to the boat. I drew his attention to some useful looking baulks of timber and what seemed to be a door but proved to be the floor of a dinghy which had recently sunk. The boat had been retrieved, but was unusable without the decking. We stowed the treasures aboard, the longest spar protruding for'ward like a bowsprit. We lacked only the Viking maiden with swelling bosom to bring us good fortune. A couple of stalwort galley slaves might also have been useful on the long, strong pull to "*Tassie*". There was a fierce tide running and we got nowhere at first. I offered to lighten the load and let the timber go ahead, but Tuck didn't relish the double journey and made it in the end, wishing for his lost youth as muscles nearing their eightieth year took the strain.

On my initial visit to the islands in early February most of the nesting activity was over. It was a very different matter when I came again with Bob Tilt during the second week of December. Breeding was at its height then. Inner Possum Reef, particularly, proved to be another of those dream islands — alive with flashing white wings — absolutely made for bird photography. We had a full five hours to assess the lie of the land.

Terns were very much in the ascendancy, but we estimated there to be some two hundred occupied silver gulls' nests as well, although gulls were said not to have bred there the previous season. Nests were scattered almost throughout, although thinly distributed on the southern knoll and in the summit wattle scrub.

Most of the gulls' nests and all the terns' nests still contained eggs, but about ten per cent of the gull chicks had hatched. Bob quartered the island and ringed between forty and fifty of them, causing the downy mites to seek cover under the Austral storksbill, which plants were almost as closely associated with the nests as pigface, spinach and Poa. Once again the adults had been feasting on the scarlet spinach fruits and coughing up the seeds to add to the advancing mats.

This gullery was running to a later timetable than that on the Killarney Reefs of Victoria's Port Fairy dunes, which I had visited over two months previously, on 28th September, with local ornithologists, who were ringing chicks at the same stage of development.

We estimated the crested terns' nests to number about six hundred, mostly spilling down from the northern crest to a rather sick-looking border of overfed pigface along the lower edge where the powerful run-off accumulated. They were more crowded than the gulls' nests, among a jumble of small rocks and ephemeral plants.

Nest density varied, averaging from four to seven per square metre in the cliff sector and up to nine or ten per square metre in a few instances. Terns had not nested here the previous year, so had wrought no changes in the plants other than damaging those already established.

There was the usual heavy fouling by Cape Barren geese on a rocky knoll serving as lookout rather than nesting site, with the chestnut teal's nest not far away. Some of the resident penguins climbed to the summit, their walking tracks leading under tangled scrub into bowers formed by bower spinach and seaberry saltbush. Some birds were squatting in the tangle, not bothering with burrows. Others were sleeping under rock shelves or tussocks or in burrow entrances. Chicks had reached adult dimensions but were not yet feathered, their dove-grey down soft as a lady's powder puff.

Most of the shearwaters burrowed in the south-west, but neither species had attempted to dig in the hard ground under the bracken, where the cause of death of a number of shearwater corpses remained a mystery.

We were grateful for the shade of the southern rocks at lunch time, where we sat watching the geese foraging on Barrett's Spit and admiring the splendid flight displays of the two species of gull and two of tern.

There was a very low spring tide and we could have paddled across the eelgrass flats between the two Possum reefs had we had a mind to do so. A boat was anchored in the mud, its owner splashing back and forth on foot gathering legitimate bait. Another boat moved in to put down cray pots, each line of pots marked by a buoy and each buoy by a red flag.

Back on Fisher Island, Bob cooked yesterday's pike for tea while I sorted soil samples. All was quiet on the battle front with the ants since Island Stores had produced some effective poison. A while back they had invaded in thousands, even penetrating my final stronghold — a saucepan with a lid which actually fitted and in which I kept opened tins of fruit, jam and condensed milk. They seemed to enjoy our games of hide-and-seek through the multiple holes in the cheese biscuits which went by the name of Cheds.

When the remedy materialised, I took an unholy glee in watching my antagonists converge in their hordes to suck the sweetened hemlock. In a couple of days there were only a few strays left, wandering aimlessly, dejected and alone, among the last of their dead comrades.

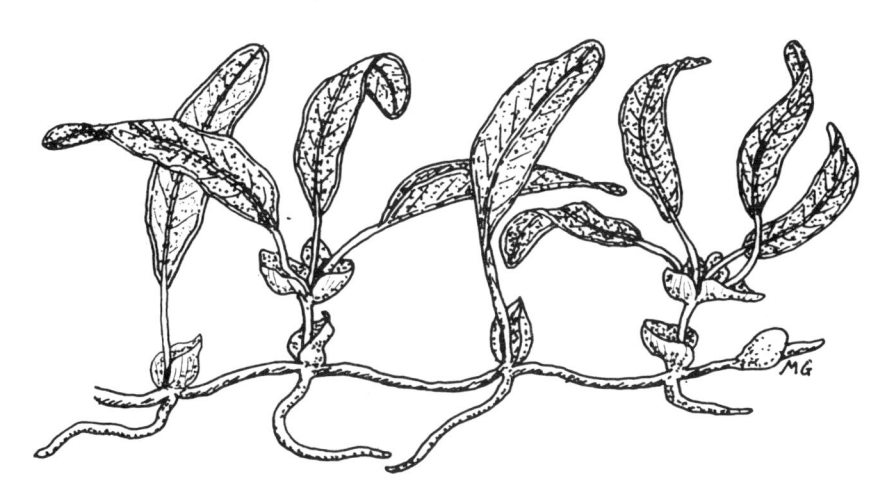

117 Sea Wrack *Halophila australis*

118 Abalone Shell, Brown Seaweed *Phyllospora comosa* and Sea Urchin test

119 Turtle Grass *Amphibolis antarctica*

Chapter Fourteen

BIG BLACK TIGER SNAKES

1. FEBRUARY VISIT TO BIG GREEN AND MOUNT CHAPPELL ISLANDS

Strands of liquid sunlight rippled across the tide as "*Aralla*" headed into a brisk westerly under an azure wind-wisped sky. It was 7.30 a.m. on 26th February 1958 and we were bound for a few hours on Big Green Island, followed by a visit to Mount Chappell. The launch edged north around the Strzelecki National Park, following the Flinders' coast almost to Whitemark before sweeping seaward again.

The 250 acres or just over 100 hectares of Big Green Island loomed low and grassy. It was used primarily by grazing sheep and was in a sorry state at this end of summer. The threadbare, sun-bleached sward was overrun by a bristling army of thistles, from which a gamin breeze lifted the wherewithal for yet more thistles and bore these away to spoil grazing lands elsewhere.

We anchored close inshore on the west side, in a haven sheltered from the westerlies by the similar sized Kangaroo Island. James Campbell, a seaman from Hobart visiting in 1828, deemed Kangaroo: "The best land of the islands. Abounds in woods — of she-oke — and has water in a lagoon. A low island; appears like two, having a low neck in the centre."

Big Green Island also boasts good land, the impoverished acidic sand derived from the granite mellowed by the Tertiary limestone overlay and generous helpings of mutton bird excreta. Bigger boats than ours used the western harbour to load bales of wool and live sheep for export. Fish of many shapes and sizes flitted beneath our keel, keeping the crew busy while Bill Mollison and I explored what we could of the island in the time allowed.

Campbell's 1828 impression of Big Green Island — as reported by Thomas Scott, surveyor — reads: "A long island without trees, inhabited only by birds. Is about three miles around. Water is found in holes. Sandy soil and a great many Botany Bay greens." Scott added a footnote: "The Botany Bay greens — a valuable plant for making barilla."

What, I wondered, was barilla? The only connotation I had heard for the word was as an alternative name for the glaucous-leaved grey saltbush, *Atriplex cinerea*.

Not until 1997 did I come across a chapter by John Whinray on barilla making in "*Plants and Man in Australia*", edited by two old colleagues of mine from my stay in Melbourne University — Dennis and Maisie Carr.

Barilla was the ash obtained by burning various saltmarsh plants to be mixed with beef suet and perfumes to make soap. The Flinder barilla or grey saltbush was the chief plant used in the Furneaux Group, along with seaberry saltbush. The woody glasswort or samphire was the mainstay of the trade in Tasmania where this covered wide stretches of saltmarsh and the other two were rarer. All these, *Atriplex, Rhagodia* and *Arthrocnemum*, belong to the saltbush family and are rich in potassium and sodium absorbed from the salty ground water. Herbaceous glasswort *(Salicornia or Sarcocornia)* has more than any but was a smaller plant so was less used. In the two glassworts the minerals are stored in the succulent stems — to the extent of 3,100 parts per million of sodium and 475 ppm of potassium in *Sarcocornia* and 2,750 ppm Na and 390 ppm K in *Arthrocnemum*. The other two hold rather less than half this amount, in leaves rather than stems.

The industry thrived from about 1817 to 1850 and was parallelled by the burning of kelp for soap and gunpowder on the Atlantic shores of Britain. Ash was sent to Hobart for manufacture and by about 1826 had supplanted imports from Britain.

Apart from soap making, the plants were boiled and eaten between 1804 and 1810 as 'Botany Bay Greens', along with some species of seaweeds by early settlers hard pressed for food.

By 1850 the barilla stocks, which took several years to recover from cutting, were insufficient to sustain the industry, which turned to chemically produced soda or alkali.

Canon Brownrigg in 1870 described Big Green as having "No timber and no grass except for four or five weeks in spring, when a fine but not very nutritious grass flourishes. The entire surface is literally covered with sow thistles and stinging nettles, with here and there barilla bushes and yellow everlastings. Sheep and cattle bred on the island thrive wonderfully, but those brought from Goose Island did not. The island is noted for prodigious numbers of venomous snakes. Record kept and, in eight years, upward of 800, some of considerable size, have been killed."

At this time, from 1849 and into the 1860s, the island functioned as a lucrative rabbit warren but, by 1872, the rodents had been wiped out. 1,200 were trapped in one year, 8,000 in eight years. By 1866 a further Department of Lands Survey stated that "There was not such a thing as a bush on the island". Nevertheless, ex-grazier Bill Barrett claimed that the island was covered with barilla and non-prickly box again in the late 1800s, suggesting the alleviation of grazing.

The original sheep grazers were Tasmanian Aboriginals settled for a short period at the Lagoons and catching mutton birds as an additional means of livelihood. Nowadays the sward is mainly of alien farm grasses, the presence of nettles and thistles suggesting adequate nutrient levels, but sheep wandered out to the northern reef islets for a change of diet when the tide was sufficiently low. They are a profitable undertaking still, breeding well and growing good fleeces. Then wild pigs were introduced, destroying many of the mutton birds, these eventually eliminated and replaced by sheep.

J. E. C. Lord, writing in 1908, gives more detail. He tells of "A splendid rookery in 1868. In 1883 between 15,000 and 20,000 mutton birds were harvested, but workers in 1907 reported having difficulty in finding 450 birds."

Bill Barrett thought the rookeries, which had never been large, to have been unaffected by sheep and had recently expanded to accommodate some 10,000 pairs of birds.

Indigenous vegetation had degenerated markedly by 1958, only a third of the recorded plant species being native. Not all the incomers were weeds, some were English grasses which had enhanced the value of the pastures for sheep. As far as we could judge on our all too short visit, the shearwaters seemed to be concentrated in the deeper soil of the depressions.

Some years later Big Green Island was declared a breeding sanctuary for Cape Barren geese and continued to be grazed by sheep, these cropping the sward to give the fresh new growth that the geese preferred. Among the graziers in the eighties were James and Lindsay Luddington, who have now moved to Flinders to farm in a more modest way and run a thriving tourist service by land and sea. Stocking rates quoted varied between two and six sheep to the acre, in contrast to Kangaroo Island where 600 sheep were run on 400 acres.

Kangaroo Island, too, was reported to carry 10,000 pairs of mutton birds in the fifties and sixties, in spite of similar, almost complete devastation of these by free-range pigs in the past. While Green Island's pigs reduced the mutton birds (some said to 4,000 pairs) it was the sheep which had so drastically changed the vegetation and we saw none of the usually so prevalent silver tussocks among the fourteen grasses recorded.

Soil depth was reputed to average forty-five to sixty cm. It had not suffered consolidation by livestock to the point where birds could not burrow any longer. Nest holes penetrated deeply and were even able to pass beneath well worn stock tracks with no hindrance. Indeed, the compaction might have helped deter burrow collapse when most of the protective vegetation had been eaten off or dried out in summer.

Island graziers found that sheep homed in on the rookeries to graze during the rainier period of winter and spring when the bird excreta was diluted and boosted lusher plant growth. The animals seemed to enjoy the prevalent soft brome grass and yellow wood sorrel but avoided the leek lilies. By our visit of late February most of the grasses were dead and they were having to be less choosy. Many had chosen to feed in sandier areas, where numerous penguins nested and even the spiky South African boxthorn had got nibbled back here to thirty cm or less.

* * * * *

Mount Chappell, the Island of Snakes, is the middle-sized member of the Chappell Group. Badger Island is considerably larger, Goose Island slightly smaller. This last sported a lofty lighthouse, which I was to visit later on the lighthouse relief ship. Badger Island was blessed with abundant fresh water and had been important for livestock rearing, with 300 Hereford cattle and 3,000 Polworth sheep, the latter continuing to graze there after it was designated as a conservation area in the 1980s.

A hasty lunch on *"Aralla'*s" deck and we were disembarking on the 788 acre (319 hectare) island of Mount Chappell. We stepped ashore on the eastern sandy beach, which provided one of the few breaks in the rugged granite coastline. Central feature of an island one and a half miles long and almost a mile wide in part was the cone-shaped mount, rising to 647 feet (198 m). I had expected extensive thickets of barilla and was surprised to find how open much of the terrain was.

We came upon a prodigious number of Cape Barren goose nests. Five to six hundred pairs were nesting here annually during this period, this and Goose Island being their main strongholds. We gave up counting after the first few hundred. It seemed that snakes were no more of a deterrent to these formidable sized birds than they were to the gannets of Cat Island. On the contrary the prevalence of snakes greatly reduced the popularity of the island for men with guns and the little ones were said to be snapped up by geese, which were not wholly vegetarian.

We investigated five inland nesting areas and two coastal feeding areas, noticing a drastic diminution of native plants and influx of undesirable aliens. The invading cohorts were led by the fluff-producing slender or seaside thistle *(Carduus tenuiflorus)*. The ratio of native to alien plants on the goose grounds was 1:2; on the island as a whole, 2:1. Very characteristic were two brome grasses and two goosefoots, the nettle-leaved *Chenopodium murale* and upright *Chenopodium urbicum*. Among indigenous species were scrub nettle, kangaroo apple and Austral hollyhock.

Many geese had converged on an east coast seepage and caused an overruning of much of the yellow water buttons by nettles, goosefoot, scarlet pimpernel and annual meadow grass. Among the granite chips of one of their feeding grounds in a clearing of the barilla, the chief, close-cropped food plant was curved sea hard-grass *(Parapholis incurva)*. More birds converged on the lush ryegrass around the birding sheds when the birders were not in residence.

Grazing by the adults and young from 500-600 nests takes a heavy toll of the most palatable grasses and was inevitably unpopular with the graziers, who killed large numbers of birds and destroyed eggs in the nests.

Chappell Island has always been something of a conundrum — "a puzzling problem admitting to no satisfactory solution". Graziers wished to graze it, despite questionable fertility, aggravated by a hard pan beneath the soil surface, brought about by alternate leaching and evaporation, and the lack of surface water for livestock. Conservationists were desirous of protecting the geese and birders wanted to harvest mutton bird chicks, despite the hazard of snakes. How was a balance to be struck between all concerned?

In 1868 Malcolm Smith of George Town wrote to the government asking "On behalf of the half-castes, that Mount Chappell Island be reserved for their use, it being centrally situated and a vast rookery of mutton birds." The government replied that islands in the Straits would be withheld from further sale, but that four blocks, of 40¾, 49¾, 40 and 40 acres had been applied for on Chappell and the survey fee and deposit paid on two of these, from which the applicants could not be displaced. These two blocks are still freehold.

In the same year Surveyor Hall, in recommending the sale of most of the rookery islands, described Chappell as the best rookery in the Straits, remarking that about forty persons were then engaged on it mutton-birding. This was the time when some of the other rookeries were being destroyed by turning pigs out on them.

Chappell's superior status was corroborated by Canon Brownrigg in 1870. He referred to it as the principal seat of mutton-birding operations with work beginning in earnest at the end of February. His description implies a greater bushiness than we found. "The middle is closely covered with barilla, "box" and everlastings, beneath which snakes to almost any extent may be found. Forty have been killed in one day. There is long coarse grass and an entire absence of trees. Where barilla forms sufficient shelter, birds do not form holes."

Smith's request for prioritising birding was granted. The *Hobart Gazette* of 15th December, 1891 stating: "All Crown Land in Chappell Island is reserved by Government as a hunting ground for mutton birds." In 1908 155 persons birded on the island, 110 of these half-castes: the approximate number of birds taken being 400,000.

Nevertheless, grazing was permitted concurrently. T. W. Barrett and J. L. Virieux worked the two freehold blocks, while the Fitzgerald Brothers held the whole of the "Reserve" under grazing licence for five months from 1st June 1908, and had at least 500 sheep on the central hump.

1908 is the year of J. E. C. Lord's Parliamentary Paper No. 57, he being then Commissioner of Police. Already there were disputes as to land use, the birders asserting that the running of stock was ruining the island and maintaining that there were not nearly as many birds as formerly.

"Running stock not only breaks in the holes and makes the ground so that the birds will not or cannot burrow, but that it destroys natural cover, thus exposing nests to crows and gulls which destroy thousands of eggs. Others argue that this is not so, but that stocking checks the spread of spear or oaten grass which has been on the island for fifteen or twenty years." (I suspect his spear grass may be one of the oat-like brome grasses.)

Information gleaned from various locals in 1958-60 pointed to there having been 1,200 sheep on Chappell Island for three six month periods during four years some thirty years before, circa 1927-31. These were regarded as doing no harm to the rookery and 8,000 to 10,000 birds were being processed annually in the eight sheds then working.

Cantankerously, when the sheep were removed the birders complained that "The rookeries have gone right back, the plants have grown up and the snakes increased."

Some 200 sheep were grazed at the time of my visits in 1958 and 1960, ostensibly on the two southern paddocks, but the dilapidated fence did nothing to restrain them and they were, in fact, distributed over most of the 394 acres, with little sign of their presence in the paddocks proper. No doubt there is a balance to be struck somewhere, and, by December 1996 a bill had been passed through parliament giving Aboriginals jurisdiction over Chappell, Great Dog and Babel Islands, for better or for worse.

Cast snake skins were everywhere, but I saw only three snakes on the uphill walk. February was one of their main feeding months before going into hibernation for the winter, but it was very hot and dry and they seemed to be waiting for dusk. The largest was spotted just in time, as I squatted to relieve myself after sidling off into the bushes.

This was a six-footer, a common size here, where some of the little ones are snapped up by larger members of their own kind, as well as by geese, and tend to be more secretive. Its head came up, weaving from side to side as its tongue flicked in and out, assessing the possibilities, but I fulfilled no aspirations for food and it glided away.

After this close encounter, Bill insisted on blazing the trail, beating a path ahead with a long iron rod, brought partly for this purpose and partly as a soil depth probe. Other such implements for deterring snakes, their use continuing into the nineties, were a long-handled rod like a shepherd's crook, the curved part fashioned to hook over a snake's neck rather than round a sheep's leg, pinning it to the ground, and the semblance of a lightly built, long-handled mallet with slender head, to imprison the reptile similarly.

Making our way through dense barilla with due caution and across open sheep paddock with gay abandon, Bill and I circled back to the beach and emerged at Walker's birding-hut opposite Badger Island, ostensibly to rifle the water tank.

We were thoroughly parched, but Bill halted abruptly, commenting admiringly on the guardian of the tank, no doubt there for the drips. It was the biggest poisonous snake of his lifetime, which had been a lot less snake-free than most. The magnificent specimen, as thick as his arm, wasted no time in slithering under the tank, but I took the precaution of kicking the metal before trying the ground level tap. To our disgust the vessel was empty, so we continued on our way dry, envying the geese, which seemed to find sufficient moisture in the moss of a peaty flush. This shortage of surface water mitigated against cattle grazing, although sheep thrived.

We discussed various management options during our three-hour reconnaissance, but converged on the shore again to cool our feet before boarding. Bill whipped the cover off the crayfish storage hold so that we could continue to do so on board. The hold was open to the restless swish of the sea and we sat on the edge dangling our legs in the cool water.

"Dangle over the side and you could get a toe nipped off by a barracuda."

We diluted our dregs of cordial drastically at the pump in the galley, getting well soaked inside and out before reaching Cape Barren to pick up MacDonald. As we sailed along the north shore of this largely wilderness island we considered its prospects as a habitat for red deer, to attract welcome dollars from wealthy American hunters. There was a move afoot at the time to introduce red deer into Tasmania, but the government wisely said NO, in view of the devastation they had caused in New Zealand. Cape Barren seemed a more likely candidate, good for little else, neatly demarcated, scarcely farmed and its rocky slopes not unlike those of the Scottish Highlands climatically. The land was already overrun with wild cattle, which could be hunted out before the deer were introduced. Presumably nothing ever came of this rather wild notion.

Ashore on Flinders next morning the talk naturally turned to snakes. We heard (again) possibly embroidered accounts of the corpses that had been carried off Chappell Island. There was the chap who had died of heart failure when he thought he had been bitten — mistakenly, as it turned out; of one who died because he imbibed a too generous helping of alcohol on his return to Flinders and another who got a double dose of poison by sucking the wound with a split lip.

Some of our informants had experience of seven-footers but the eight-footer (240 cm) seemed to be the record. One measuring 7'4" and another 6'10" had been lodged in museums, the killing of the latter, by an expert, not going according to plan. The killer picked it up by its tail in the approved manner and swung it round to crack its head on the barrel of the gun held in the other hand. Instead the snake coiled its entire length round the weapon so that he had to drop both and retire in haste. He employed the same technique another day, more successfully.

Skin widths of "whoppers" might reach fourteen inches or more according to the oscillating hands and assurances such as: "Without a word of a lie I reckon 'twas THIS much across."

Tuck sought to top them all with his story, but it was a little too tall. "Be'ind a boulder 'e was, on the beach. I crep' up and 'eaved a rock at 'im. Seemed to annoy 'im. Came for me, 'e did. I started off down the road at a sharp trot, stopping at the next telegraph pole to look round."

An eloquent pause — to build up suspense or think up the next move.

"When I looked round an 'undred yards on 'e were still coming for me, an' I didn't look round agin."

Every so often a shooting party was arranged to kill snakes on Chappell Island and Lew Bailey was fond of quoting their biggest kill ever, of 142 in one day. Mollison had plans for snake traps at strategic points around the island: a snake-proof fence diverting snakes into a sunken trap at the end. So far so good, but some brave soul would have to move in to despatch the captives in due course.

As since the days of Adam and Eve, the snakes were inevitably the villains of the piece, to be got rid of if possible, whether to benefit birds and birders or sheep and graziers. In the more enlightened days of the 1990s, this master race of reptiles is regarded as a conservation asset to be conserved at all costs as a valuable rarity, regardless of others' needs.

We adjourned to Leila Barrett's for morning tea and, just to keep the party going, a medium-sized tiger snake tried to join us. We might not have known had the Abo boy arriving with a message not let out a yell and departed pronto. Leila put her anti-snake board in place across the doorway, murmuring how fond these warmth-loving creatures were of snuggling up between the blankets. The snake disappeared under the house and Bill crept around with torch and stick but failed to catch up. These had their place on the island, but this one was uncomfortably close, although no new experience for our hostess.

120 Blue-tongue Lizard *Tiliqua nigrolutea* with flowering Pigface *Disphyma crassifolium*

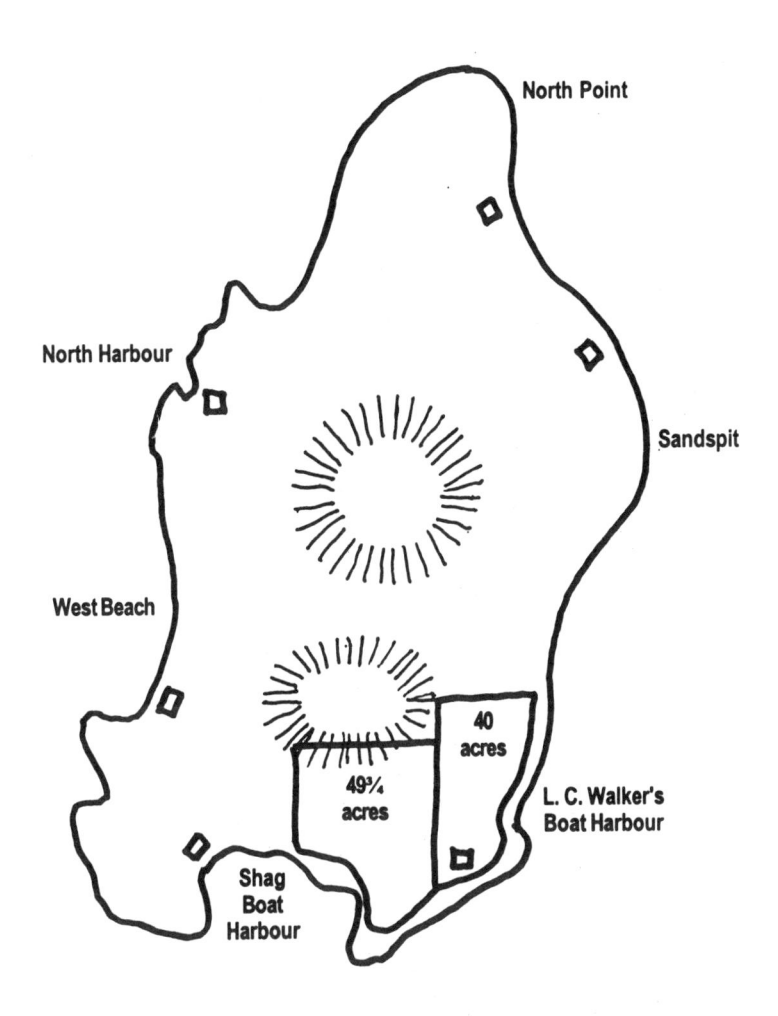

121 Freehand sketch of Mount Chappell Island

122 Austral Storksbill *Pelargonium australe*

2. WITH ERIC WORRELL IN PURSUIT OF REPTILES

It was not until Australia's snake expert, Eric Worrell, joined us on Fisher Island in March 1960, that the various reptiles fell into their rightful ecological niches in our understanding of the rookeries.

We were on Great Dog Island and he was finding fewer snakes than hoped. "Plenty of grasshoppers for skink food, but skinks scarce."

Skinks were eaten by snakes of all sizes and were almost the only living food available to young ones, which would be unable to tackle even newly-hatched mutton bird chicks until they were two years old.

Eric brought two snakes back to examine on Fisher Island. These were not tigers but juvenile copperheads, only eight inches (twenty cm) long and reckoned to be about eight weeks old. Let loose on the kitchen table for the cameras, they proved to be handsome miniatures, prettily marked in shining bronze, slick of movement and with constantly flicking tongues savouring the strange cooking smells of this new environment.

"Venomous from birth," quoth Eric, "but it's doubtful if their baby fangs could penetrate the human skin to inject the venom at this stage."

They are born in litters of twelve to twenty-four and are strongly cannibalistic. Youngsters of this vulnerable size led secretive lives, out of sight of their hungry relatives, and Eric had conducted a remarkable bit of sleuthing to spot these two, let alone catch them. Their principal foods are frogs and skinks and they need liquid water, as the island variety of tiger snakes does not.

There is little fresh water available on Chappell Island during dry spells and the tiger snakes have to manage by sucking dew from the plants. They also cash in on the phenomenon of internal dew formation, taking advantage of water condensing out at night on the protected surfaces of piled rocks. In adapting to their dry environment, they have come to need significantly less free water than do mainland tigers.

Among Eric's specimens from Great Dog Island were three pale-coloured brown tree frogs *(Hyla ewingii*, since renamed *Litorea ewingii)*, too large to serve as potential food for his copper coloured captive *Denisonia superba*, (since renamed *Austrelaps superba)*.

Chappell Island tiger snakes muster the energy to breed only every other year, their litters, too, being seldom larger than thirty or thereabouts. The infants are six inches (thirty cm) long at birth and their initial reaction is to wriggle off and make themselves scarce among the tussocks. Cannibalism was an ever present danger: they were just the right dimensions for sliding down the long and unrelenting gullets of their elders! Others might get snapped up by gulls, harriers, eagles, herons, currawongs or kookaburras, the last present only on the larger islands.

Eric found a couple of shearwater eggs sucked dry of their contents through small round holes.

"Not skink or snake damage. A rat — any sort of rat — would make a hole like that. Or just possibly the parent shearwater, by mistake."

His mission was to capture snakes to take back to his reptile park at Gosford in New South Wales for extraction of venom for antivenene. In the process they might disgorge their last meal, so he was in a better position than most to know what they were eating.

"Some disgorge rats, some odd pieces of fish or other marine animals."

British grass snakes catch live fish and frogs while swimming and black tigers swim competently in the sea, but Eric thought most of the marine animals were taken from tidal pools, the driftlines winding across the beaches or detritus pushed into crevices by waves.

"One of the remarkable things about tiger snakes is their willingness to eat carrion. Many snake species take only living food, and the few which take dead animals do so only if they are fresh."

It is likely that this trait was an evolutionary 'must' if so many snakes were to survive on scraps of land holding a vast amount of food for a few brief weeks and very little for the rest of the year. Another adaptation to this is the extended hibernation between the seasonal appearance of mutton bird chicks of the right size to swallow, this covering a far longer period than would be dictated by climate.

An evolutionary trend favouring mutton bird survival in this ecosystem is the close synchronisation of breeding, with all birds laying within a few days of each other. This has always been regarded as remarkable in ornithological circles. A wider spread of hatching would mean a longer period when chicks were a suitable size to be eaten, and so a larger number could be taken. Even a six foot snake can only swallow a certain amount in a limited time.

Chicks soon outgrow the threat of snake predation, after which snake and nestling can snuggle up together for warmth, with no harm coming to either. In modern times birding has fallen off on Chappell Island because of the snake hazard, so the reptiles have changed from enemy to benefactor by cohabiting. This was not always the case, however, many thousands of chicks having been collected there by thirty or more families since this most bizarre of the western world's surviving wild harvests was inaugurated in the 1870s — and before that, when chicks were important to the survival of the Aboriginals.

In an article for the "*People*" Magazine of 4th September 1957, Eric Worrell writes: "Because of the large numbers of snakes on Chappell Island, food for them is scarce, so, in the long months between mutton bird seasons, they live on mice, rats, fish from rock pools and carrion. They can fast for periods of several months."

The British Broadcasting Corporation's film "Deadly Liaisons" in the "Wildlife on One" series shown on British Television on 18th June 1996, told a slight variant of the Chappell Island story. The makers discounted the seashore as a food source and stated that, with no abundant rodent food, as was available on the mainland, the snakes must starve for the eleven months after growing chicks reached inedible size, this time spent mostly in hibernation.

The evolution of greater size in the snakes had the advantage of allowing bigger chicks to be eaten, so the biggest snakes with the widest gapes got fatter and were better able to perennate their kind. The survival of the fittest in this instance meant the largest — unlike that of the really big reptiles, the dinosaurs. The more a snake could eat in that busy month, the better were its chances, but about eight chicks was the normal maximum intake.

The film makers' claim that the Chappell Island snakes have doubled their size from the norm is somewhat overstated according to data available in Worrell's day, when they averaged one and a half times the size of mainland tigers. Their claim that "The shockingly potent venom is eighty times stronger than a rattlesnake's" also savours of an exaggeration, in view of the fact that it is considerably less potent than that of mainland tigers, although produced in greater quantity, but I know nothing of the potential of rattlesnakes.

On the plus side the film — a fascinating one, despite these small criticisms — depicts the special island tigers in the role of hero instead of the traditional role of villain that has dogged their passage from the Garden of Eden.

In making a case for the snakes' welfare, the write-up in the contemporary "*Radio Times*" points out that mutton birds remain Australia's most abundant bird species, although still harvested, and are under no threat, whereas the island snakes are in grave danger. Many hands are raised against them, whether in the cause of personal preservation or financial gain.

Demand for snake products is increasing. The skins are used for handbags, purses, shoes and the like, while the blood is valued in the Far East for its supposed medicinal properties. Export is illegal, but there are plenty of Asian buyers in Australia's cities and official protection is needed to ensure that this localised population is not wiped out.

In 1996 when the Australian courts handed Chappell Island over to descendants of earlier birding families it was hoped that permission would not be given for the suggested preparatory blitz on the snakes, before harvesting the chicks. There are other islands more suitable for birding, where the snakes live in less significant and dangerous numbers.

Tramping through tussocks on the various islands, Eric acquainted us with the finer points of sloughed snake skins, which might stretch to one and a half times their original length after being shed. The membranes which had covered the eyes appeared as shiny, curved discs and seemed to retain the same coldly watchful, soul-less expression. They were concave, the skins being turned neatly inside out, with the only opening at the mouth where the owner had crawled out. The old jaw coverings were folded back above and below and finished up at the rear as the refurbishing snake unthreaded itself, letting go of the tail tip last.

In the process of assessing whether these island tigers should be designated as a separate race, Eric busied himself counting scales — the little ones around the sides and across the back, discounting the laterally elongated plates of the underside. The number in a complete circuit was seventeen to nineteen, the same as in Australian mainland snakes, whereas Tasmanian tigers had usually fifteen to seventeen. The number running from head to tail, however, was more than in mainland specimens, about 185. Few of the mainland tigers were black, their tiger stripes in two shades of brown being very evident.

The more data the better before the new island subspecies of *Notechis ater serventii* was finally established. The name envisaged in 1960 was *Notechis scutatus yolla*, but the specific name was changed as well as that of the subspecies, which now no longer referred to the mutton birds but to the authority who had studied them over the years.

The endemic subspecies was described as "A giant robust race commonly exceeding six feet in length and bulkier in girth and bone structure than mainland tigers. Adults are mostly five to six feet in length as opposed to mainland tigers, which average four feet (120 cm)."

Potency of the venom had been analysed and called quits, mainland tigers producing only a third as much venom as island ones but of three times the potency. The differences have evolved during their long isolation and relative freedom from interference. Chappell Island has more snakes to the acre than any other known site, so it is understandable that food should be in short supply and periods of starvation long.

Matthew Flinders, explorer, named the island after his sweetheart, later his wife, Ann Chappell. I wonder if she was flattered when she learned of its main claim to fame?

Another of our visitors to "Yolla" was commemorated in a reptilian name. Russell or "Tas" Drysdale, famous artist and much more, was as addicted to life on Fisher Island as the rest of us and is remembered in the name of the white-lipped whip snake, then *Denisonia coronoides*, now *Drysdalia coronoides*. It seemed that this was sufficiently unique to have the whole genus named for the little Fisher Island fraternity, not just a subspecies.

Sometimes a deputation from Fisher Island invaded Lady Barron, whose characters usually turned out in force when "The Terrible Trio" of famous men, Worrell, Drysdale and Serventy, set foot ashore. On 21st March, while Eric was persuading sundry islanders to catch snakes for him, I wandered into the Walkers' domain.

A pademelon joey was produced from under the sofa and settled cosily into my lap, licking my arm for the salt — a mixture of sea splash and sweat. Its mother had been shot for cray bait and the little one had been adopted by the hunter's wife, who forthwith wore a garment with a large pinny pocket in front to serve as a pouch. Junior was little more than eight inches long and was being reared on milk, apples and fresh green grass.

I was rounded up by the trio and the four of us set off on a snake hunt around Scotts Lagoon, with Derek Smith and Ross Campbell. A herd of pigs had been at work, rooting up the ground and leaving ample irregularities for our quarry to hide among.

There were no tigers this morning, the eventual bag being two copperheads, two blue-tongue lizards and an assortment of smaller skinks and 'dragons'. Eric posed for the cameras, holding one of the copperheads by the tail. Dom asked how big it was and the reply came without hesitation. "Four feet seven."

Eric had held so many snakes at arm's-length before popping them in the collecting bag, that he could judge unerringly, by the way the wildly waving head skimmed the ground surface.

The other copperhead was already in the bag and he had trouble undoing the drawstring at the neck with one hand while controlling the new captive with the other, finally having to loosen the hitch with his teeth. He got Dom, not too willingly, to hold the neck of the bag open while he rummaged inside for another bag to be used for smaller creatures.

The opening was then lowered to ground level and, with one eye on the snake within and the other on the snake without, Eric bided his time until the threshing head turned towards the darkly welcoming retreat, then deftly brought the two together, allowing the newcomer to slide inside to commiserate with the other. The neck of the bag was jerked up and the drawstring tightened in a single movement. Such a simple operation, if you knew what you were doing, but there were few who wanted to know!

Soon after this, his hand and forearm, poised at shoulder height, took on the menace of a striking snake before they darted forward to tweak an *Amphibolurus dragon* from a twig. My modest contribution was another dragon, a juvenile not much more than three inches long, decorated with a striking diamond pattern along the back and the row of spines that made it a dragon. This was my first dragon hunt since I emerged from the realms of childhood fantasy: less magic than before, but just as much fun. One of Eric's recent films, shown on ABC Television, was called "We Have Dragons", the cameras blowing the wee beasties up to more traditional size.

A telegram had arrived that morning for Dom announcing that his middle son, Conrad, was arriving at Whitemark after travelling from Perth to Hobart on a British destroyer, as guest of the ornithologist captain. We piled into Ross's 'combie' and Eric drove us to the airport to collect him. Athol Dart, encountered en route, invited us back to lunch.

While the sausages spluttered in the pan, he informed us that he had seen a copperhead snake in the bottom of his well. Did we want it? Eric could never resist any such offer or challenge. He slithered down the pipe to twenty-eight feet (eight to nine m) and lodged himself across the shaft just above water level, but there were too many cracks in the wall where the snake could be hidden.

The dark water was plopping with frogs — this snake had dropped into a living larder — and a linen bag was sent down on a long wire. It waltzed up, lurching erratically as the six frogs within tried to jump in different directions simultaneously. They represented three different species, which, together with others captured a day or two before, made a complete collection of Tasmanian frogs less only four kinds.

The tally for the Furneaux Group was five, plus a toadlet, *Pseudophryne semimarmorata*. Another of the Hyla tree frogs, the green and golden, was *Litorea aurea*, the brown froglet *Ranidella signifera*. The two larger kinds were related: the spotted marsh frog, *Limnodynastes tasmaniensis*, and the burrowing marsh frog or eastern banjo frog, *Limnodynastes dumerilii*.

On the way back to Lady Barron the vehicle screeched to a halt and Eric's curly mop of hair disappeared from the driving seat as he leapt out to grab a copperhead on the road. It was already dead, although seemingly undamaged and fresh enough to give some of the passengers a nasty shock when it was dropped, squirming, onto the floor of the van beside the bagged ones.

By the time we had investigated the cormorant roost beside Samphire River, the tide was well in and our borrowed dinghy, "*Nyla*" was well out. We borrowed another to retrieve her and went across in two loads, not without the mishaps that are inevitable when grown men escape their wives and families to return to their prankish schoolboy days.

We were stormbound the next day, when we should have been on Chappell Island. Unless I had witnessed it, I would not have believed what a shambles four men with insufficient to occupy their restless hands could create in a small hut in a single day!

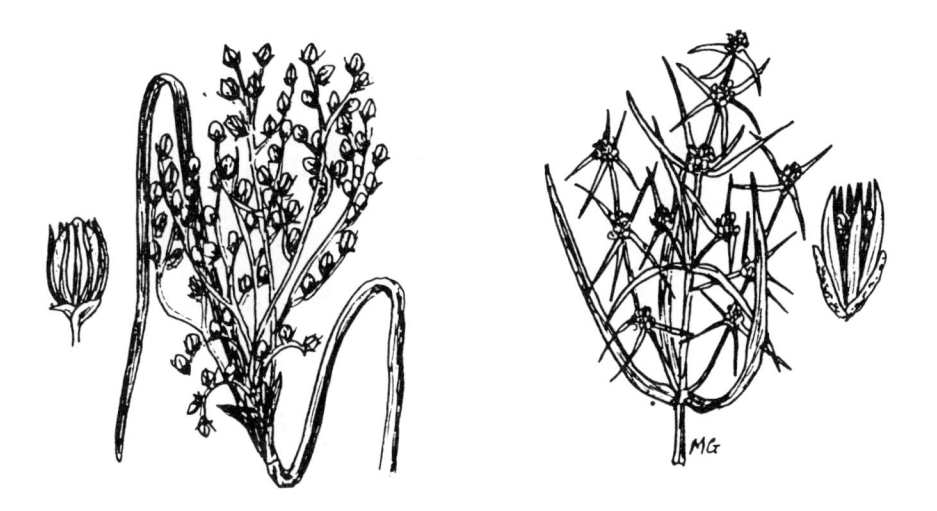

123 Pale Rush *Juncus pallidus* and Spiny Mat Rush *Lomandra longifolia*

124 Barilla, Grey or Coast Saltbush *Atriplex cinerea*

125 Seaberry Saltbush *Rhagodia candolleana*

3. CATCHING SNAKES ON MOUNT CHAPPELL ISLAND

Next day we were away. Everyone was up at 5.0 a.m. packing swags for an overnight trip, although Tas Drysdale was the only one with a genuine Aussie type swag. An experienced wilderness traveller in the empty lands of the North and West, his kit was stowed in a tarpaulin and rolled into a bulky weatherproof sausage.

Warm hearted and unconventional, he could rub along with anyone, however odd. He had a specially soft spot for outback weirdos, of whom he was wont to produce apt cartoons. Splendid character studies of some appear in the book *"Journey Among Men"*, by Jock Marshall and Russell Drysdale, published in 1962, this the tale of a journey through Australia's Red Centre.

He was born in England in 1912, returning to the family pastoral property in the Riverina at the age of eleven. In 1935 he opted to take up art as a career rather than farming and studied in Melbourne, London and Paris. By the fifties he was renowned for his paintings of the Australian Outback and had works hanging in London at the National and Tate Galleries, in New York in the Metropolitan Museum and in the National Galleries of New South Wales, Victoria and South Australia.

His colleague, Jock Marshall, was an equally redoubtable character, zoologist and explorer, born in Sydney in 1911, with part of his education in Oxford. He explored the New Hebrides, New Guinea and Spitzbergen and led the Oxford University Expedition to Jan Mayen in 1947. He had taught in the Universities of Oxford, Yale and California and at St Bartholomew's Hospital Medical College, University of London, where he was head of the Department of Zoology and Comparative Anatomy. Currently, in the fifties, he was professor at Monash University in Melbourne.

Anecdotal stories came trickling from Tas Drysdale as he went about his island tasks and we learned his opinions of the two famous Central Australian artists whom I had recently met in Alice Springs. These were the white Rex Battersby and the Aboriginal Namatjera — who had had the painting style of another world imposed on his colourful studies of the outback, although traditional, simple Aboriginal symbolism was finding its way back into the work of his pupils.

We sculled out to *"Aralla"* at 6.0 a.m. in two dinghy loads and Eric Worrell dispensed seasick pills as we began to feel queasy quaffing Arthur Harland's tea beyond the western end of Franklin Sound. Soon after 9.0 a.m. we were stepping ashore on the north-east corner of the Island of Snakes.

There was a slight swell where we landed and Eric hopped out onto a rock eighteen inches across, extending a hand for me to follow. There we stuck, clasped in each other's arms, trying to pivot round for me to make the next leap. When he enquired sweetly; "May I have the next waltz?" our helpless laughter almost precipitated a mini-disaster.

Lew Bailey was scheduled to collect the Cat Island wardens the following day and, having lost yesterday, our Chappell Island visit was cut down to a single day, but it was quite a day. As it turned out, Eric captured so many snakes in our seven hours ashore, that he needed no second day. He had said he would be happy to come away with twenty large specimens and he got almost twice this number, more than he could conveniently get back to New South Wales. It was hot and his collecting bags were stuffed so full of reptiles that seven died from suffocation.

Once ashore, taking stock, the men were appalled at the state of the vegetation. "The island's not just overgrazed, it's been mined. 1,500 sheep, scarcely any barilla — burrows broken in — snakes disappeared!"

One part had been ploughed and the trash burned off instead of remaining to give body to the sandy soil. Nothing had been sown so erosion had set in and thistles were running riot. But things improved as we moved away from this devastation. There was still plenty of barilla and 'box' elsewhere and the snakes seemed to have retreated from the despoiled areas into these.

There was no shortage of snakes, hidden in burrows, coiled among tussocks, even climbing into the bushes to warm up in the early sun.

"Barking 'Brilla the locals call it" said Eric. "Those snakes don't just hiss, they sneeze and bark!"

He tried to persuade us that the bigger ones were quite docile. It was good that he believed so, handling them as much as he did. I would have thought sluggish was a more apt description, the agility of the youngsters involuntarily sacrificed by the heavyweights.

It was well known that a snake in a burrow was more anxious to avoid a questing hand than to attack it and would crawl behind the chick if it had the chance. Attack, after all, did them no good unless it led to a meal.

Eric was in fine form but was completely worn out at the end of the day, as well he might be, if only from carrying an ever increasing load of snakes weighing three to four pounds each. The tension, often prolonged, during the actual catching, must have taken its toll of even the strongest nerves, but his were more resistant than most.

No snake taken was smaller than four feet long and most were a deal larger. There was no problem locating them, as they commonly lay, coiled up, on the ground surface, sometimes two or three together. We saw no small ones. It was only those over a certain size that could expose themselves, secure in the knowledge that they had no natural enemies on land and no need for an escape reaction. Man was a relative newcomer in their world, but they were well equipped to deal with him too. They could not have known, as Eric did, that the least of them possessed enough venom to kill ten men, the largest enough for twice that number.

Eric's technique was to grab them by the tail, six to ten inches from the tip, and pull, leaving the front end in the bushes trying to get away, or to dangle them at arm's-length, which, fortunately, left the rest of the captor just beyond reach of the lashing business end.

Thus held, the other hand could undo the stiff khaki canvas kitbag, which was furnished with a ring of small round holes for ventilation about twelve inches from the bottom. A drawstring of thin rope threaded through brass rings was carefully tied in a reef knot after each operation, since an assistant catcher had pointed out that a snake was crawling round the carrier's neck!

With the steadily increasing weight of the bag resting on the ground, the open neck was held invitingly towards the writhing, hand-held captive, but had to be dropped if the head shot across the top or dipped in and then out again, spurning the dark interior as a refuge. Perhaps the snakes already bagged — and there might be as many as twenty of these — were sending out warning messages.

Complete vigilance and instantaneous response on Eric's part kept him out of trouble and seldom did a former captive escape while another was being enticed in.

At mid-morning he transferred a dozen snakes from the kitbag to a flimsy looking white flour bag, almost as casually as if they were potatoes, and carried them into the shade to be picked up later. They were apt to strike through this material when they perceived a passing shadow: that was how Eric West had got bitten recently. It was the darkness rather than the impregnability of the canvas that prevented retaliation and the white bags were transferred to sturdier rucksacks for the journey home.

A lighter moment was when a five and a half foot snake evaded capture and slid into a burrow. After much excited squealing and hissing, it emerged with an angry mutton bird chick gripping it amidships. It was strange that the erstwhile prey should be so unafraid. Glistening drops of liquid venom on the lip of the bag showed what the bird might have suffered.

Another snake made it to a burrow which proved to be double ended and Dom was put to work at the back entrance to drive it forth. The two men changed ends several times, but the snake succeeded in giving them the slip and disappearing into another burrow, where Eric left it, as having earned its freedom.

Meanwhile Dom was ringing chicks, reaching into burrows bearing traces of grey fluff and not the smooth broad tracks of interlopers. He marked forty in all. Eric announced that nothing would induce him to put HIS hand in a burrow, in spite of, or because of, his unusual know how. He liked to see his adversaries. Conrad and Tas helped catch; I merely indicated new finds from a safe distance. Everyone survived.

The nearest we got to pandemonium was when six were sighted at once. My two were coiled together in sleepy repose and could wait: the other four were dealt with first. At one time Eric held three tails in one hand, but he passed two of these to others with instructions to leave their heads on the ground.

Tas Drysdale's was not to be thus lulled and lashed out at him. He lost his nerve and his grip, jumped clear and did a backward somersault over a boulder, a move which probably saved him as six feet of black lightning launched past his left ear. Dom let out a startled "Great God!" and even the imperturbable Eric looked momentarily worried.

Tas was on his feet again in an instant: it is surprising how fast one can move when there are man killers around. Eric handed him a more docile tail, which, all credit to him, he accepted, and went off after the miscreant. The snake tried it on again and proved quite a handful, but was pitting its small brain and four pounds of sinewy muscle against the expert and finished up in the bag. Tas's response to Eric's thanks for his help was "Well, I won't say it was a pleasure old man."

When the expert came to my pair, he had to disturb them to get them to unravel so that he could see which was head and which was tail. Grabbing a tail in each hand, he passed one to Conrad and both were swiftly dealt with.

I was able to get close views of snakes coiled in the barilla branches and noticed that almost all had a few ticks attached, like those which clamp onto cattle in the Northern Territory. These were buff-coloured and bigger than a flattened, shelled peanut. The tick's head was fastened firmly under one of the snake's scales, and behind it were tucked the obliquely placed and not very functional looking legs.

A dead snake, killed by man, had its tail eaten by birds, probably raven or currawong. After a scale count (seventeen) Eric popped its head into a burrow and a combination of scale arrangement and gravity caused it to slither slowly downwards as though alive. Remarking on the number of dead sheep, that had attracted a mob of currawongs, he said the snakes would have been responsible for at least some of the deaths.

We stopped for lunch at the wool shed which grazier/lessee/pub owner Moreton had offered us to camp in. While I cut bread and butter, which became liberally sprinkled with dark dust from the denuded sheep run round about, Tas, looking the perfect station hand in his broad-brimmed digger hat, organised the drink. He conjured up an empty beer bottle (never difficult where men gather in these parts), fixed wire round its neck and climbed up the fence to dip water from the tank alongside, while trying to kid us that this was full of decomposing flying foxes. The corned beef tins came in handy as cups.

Approaching the Mansell's birding shed after lunch, we spotted Fred and George Mansell and a muscular young half-caste, who were intent on reviving the birding this season. Only one of them would be reaching into burrows and he had had a dose of horse serum two months before and would be killed if antivenene was injected.

It was astonishing the risks these straitsmen were willing to take. They were a remarkable pair of old men, partly white but with merry brown eyes and hair, thick with grease, straight for the first four inches and then as crisply curled as any negro's. The young half-caste had already killed thirty snakes from around the house with a stick that morning, but it was never too late and they asked Eric into the hut to acquaint them with the use of the snake first-aid kit.

He rolled up one of the men's sleeves to show how to apply a tourniquet to bring up a vein in which to inject the serum — this not necessarily the arm which might have been bitten. Their syringe held only two cc instead of the required ten and the needles (unsterile) seemed a dicey fit, so they would have to have five goes, under difficulties. Demonstrating how not to inject air into the vein (certain death), he squeezed a droplet out before plunging the needle in. As he mimicked filing the glass neck of the ampoule, he stressed that it would be death to inject serum into the only man who would be bird catching, as surely as it would be death not to! This cheery soul seemed unworried.

"Why, I've birded on Babel for years and done this and that at sea, but I still keep going." Then, turning to Dom, as one birder to another: "You've gotta know where the birds are, that's what it is."

We looked around the two grass-floored rooms and saw where Eric West had been laid out on the floor with a beer carton for pillow, after he had been bitten. Eric Worrell showed us the spot where it had happened and the rock where Roy Gosse, too, had fallen victim, unfolding the stories of the two incidents as we walked.

A few years earlier the Mansell's shed had been worked by Roy Gosse, who played host to Worrell on his early visits to Chappell Island. As well as his farm on Flinders Island, Gosse held the grazing lease on Chappell, keeping stock there, year round, although the island was out of bounds to others except during the birding season.

On Eric's second visit, Gosse left him to it and went off birding. When the snake struck, he had the satisfaction of knowing that Eric was likely to be back at the hut and had demonstrated the most appropriate first aid the day before. Gosse was carrying a lance and a ligature for the first time. He hastened back to the hut, blood dripping from his wrist and a crude rope tourniquet twisted above the elbow.

Eric was on hand with antivenene and a more appropriate tourniquet. He sterilised the syringe, broke the top from two ampoules and injected the contents directly into a bulging vein. Going straight into the bloodstream thus, it was hoped that the system would be flooded with antidote faster than with poison. Pulse and respiration were kept under observation after removal of the tourniquet and Gosse made a good recovery.

It transpired that his antagonist was not in the burrow he was reaching down. Spread-eagled on the grass and struggling to get a grip on the chick, Gosse had thrown his free arm sideways onto a snake, which was startled into retaliating.

Eric's next move was to warn other birders to take extra care, these including his patient, who was back birding next day! His serum was running short, as he had had to use some on himself on the way from New South Wales, when bitten by a mainland tiger by the River Murray, and had had no time to replenish stocks.

Eric West, who was helping him to catch snakes, was the next casualty.

Usually, once in the kitbag, snakes stayed quiet, but this particular one was in a white flour bag and had bitten the man through the material, penetrating with only one fang. A single ampoule of 1,500 units of serum remained and this was back at camp. Worrell applied a tourniquet, slashed the wound with a razor blade and sucked and spat blood all the way back to base.

The tide was down, the boat beached, and there was nothing for it but to make the patient as comfortable as possible after administering the inadequate amount of antidote. His hand swelled, throbbed and blackened, his stomach pained and he was unable to eat, but was still alive by morning. The tide was low again and the boat had to be hauled on foot through the shallows for half a mile before he could be got into Whitemark for medical care. Apart from a dose of penicillin to ward off infection, nothing could be done. It was up to his own resistance. He won through but was laid up for several months.

Leaving the scene of these mishaps, we climbed to the saddle and circled inland. Raising our eyes occasionally from the grounded snakes, we gained superb views of sweeps of yellow sand, turquoise shallows and granite outcrops: a scene of serenity and calm contrasting sharply with the tension of past and possibly impending snake bites. Small parties of geese were everywhere. These were timid, rising well ahead of us, the only photos being of a youngster unable to fly.

It was not only Eric who was exhausted by the day's activities: we all slept soundly on the deck of "*Aralla*" on the homeward voyage. Back on Fisher Island, Dom and Tas mustered the energy to row ashore for mail, stores and tea with Gerry Addaway. Eric, Conrad and I lighted a fire, cooked a meal and retired early, oblivious to the gentle rustling of the newly acquired livestock stowed under the bunks.

126 Mutton Bird Chick and Black Tiger Snake *Notechis scutatus*

127 Black Tiger Snake *Notechis scutatus serventii*

128 Tiger Snake basking: Sea Celery *Apium prostratum*

Chapter Fifteen

FINAL FLING ON THE FURNEAUX GROUP AND BEYOND

1. LIVING WITH POISONOUS SNAKES

It was all go next morning getting yesterday's haul organised and preparing for the men's late evening departure on another island jaunt. Fully rested, after well-earned slumber, Eric Worrell extricated the seven dead snakes from the thirty or so live ones and consigned them to the spacious formalin tank after slashing them at intervals along the underside to allow the preservative to penetrate. These would be used later for analysis of stomach contents and scale counts.

We were all hauling scaly skins from our pockets and passing them over. The pile of 'sloughs' mounted to several dozen, increased by some taken from the bags of live snakes where moultings had occurred during the night. In the absence of twigs and tussocks, these had used their fellows to help scrape themselves free, but one had made a poor job of it and wore the crinkly covering like a crumpled polythene bag.

Several had a lobed red excrescence the size of a walnut bulging through the scales — an extrusion of the epithelial lining, probably of the rectum. This was evidently common in captive snakes. The writhing mass was divided between inadequate looking sugar bags and pillowcases and placed under the end of my bed, as being the best available unused space in our crowded quarters. I was warned not to tread on them, but was assured that Eric had never had any escapes.

I fervently hoped that he wouldn't have his first now, as I was to be alone in "Yolla" for the next few days. The stories told at intervals during the somewhat frenetic activities were not exactly reassuring. There seemed no end to the men who had lost out in their encounters with Chappell Island tiger snakes.

George Boyse, owner of a guesthouse near Whitemark, had shared a birding-hut on Chappell Island with his brothers during the early 1950s, going across to kill snakes before the birding season opened. On one occasion bird-catcher Moreton Maynard was late getting back. The search party found him stretched beside a burrow, pretty weak after being bitten. They dragged and carried him to the boat and got him back to Whitemark as quickly as possible, but he died soon after.

Sickened, the Boyse brothers sold their birding-shed to Arthur King, who worked it for a few seasons before he, too, came to grief. The nip on his finger as he reached into the burrow, he attributed to the chick's hooked beak, realising the truth only as he began to feel dizzy. He reached for his pocket knife to slash the wound, but dropped it in the grass. His sight fast blurring, he failed to find it, so he bit out the piece where the snake had struck. His mates found him and got him back to Flinders Island, but there was no hospital there then. He was made as comfortable as might be in a hotel bed, where he died five days later. George Boyse helped put him in his coffin.

Little Jimmy Murray was another who dared to challenge the tigers once too often.

"Used to catch snakes for sideshows in Tasmania. So short, he was, that when he grabbed their tails he had to jump onto a boulder to keep their heads off the ground and get them into the bag.

"Some crank in Stanley bet Murray that he wasn't game to let one of the snakes bite him. Murray took the bet and died in hospital. That was before the Commonwealth Serum Laboratories had developed their tiger snake venom!"

Worrell's work with the snakes was aimed at preventing as many such tragedies as possible by producing antivenene. He found his tigers quite docile after a few days in captivity. They took food readily from his hand, no doubt congratulating themselves on their good fortune. He fed them live rats, dangled by their tails over the snake's raised head.

At intervals he would take a snake by the scruff of its neck and induce it to strike a membrane stretched across the top of a beaker. The venom ejected dripped into the vessel to be used in production of the antidote. His life saving endeavours bore fruit from the start, two of the earlier victims of snake bite on Chappell Island to benefit being bird-catchers Billy Samuels and Jack Maynard.

Nevertheless, enthusiasm for birding on Chappell Island had waned several years before our visit, making the envisaged new start by the Mansell brothers the more remarkable. Even now only one shed remained in use where more than twenty had once been worked simultaneously.

In those days it was expected, and deemed desirable, that as many snakes as possible should be killed. When birding was at its height a policeman was stationed at each end of the island to pay a bounty of sixpence for every snake tail. Wily birders were not above collecting bounty from both officers before obeying instructions to cast the tails into the sea — from where they might well wash in again for another lucky bounty hunter. With 260 tails, including a few lizard tails for good measure, being presented twice in one day, however, this 'error' was likely to be caught up with.

* * * *

The four men left Fisher Island for Babel and Cat Islands at 8 p.m., sailing away into a seascape warmed by the reflected afterglow of the setting sun. In wakeful moments during the night I was very conscious that I was not alone. Squeaks and scuffles issued from under my bed as my semi-nocturnal roommates registered displeasure at their confinement. I hoped that they would remain confined and that they were unable to climb bedposts.

Plops and gurgles on the shelf emanated from wakeful frogs, while skinks and dragons produced soft swishings from the mantelpiece. Breakfast was accompanied by muted sneezes from under the table and a flour bag containing blue-tongue lizards walked into the middle of the room. It was all a little unreal to be the only free individual among so many patient captives; alone and yet not alone.

As I embarked on a writing session, Leila and Bruce, the army lieutenant who was part of the Riddle family's birding team, rowed across to measure the island's mutton bird barrel for new hoops. Had Eric asked him to check that all was well in this strange company? Bruce had rowed all the way from Great Dog Island, picking Leila up en route and she inveigled me into joining her on a similar marathon.

I collected her on Flinders an hour later and together we rowed round the west of Spences Reefs and through the choppy westerly tide rip to the Homestead landing on Great Dog. Bruce and others waved to us from the verandah and two of our research group, Dr Myckytowicx and Ted Hesterman, ran to the beach to help us in. Mycky, the Ukrainian, with his typical continental charm, presented each of us with a nosegay — a scarlet pelargonium filched from the garden, ringed by five yellow cat's-ear heads.

The men were camping, much as the health inspectors did, with hessian on boxes for seats, boards on boxes for dining and dissecting tables and boxes in which the scientific apparatus had been brought serving as food stores. Camp stretchers had been erected in the front room, the four poster with pine needle mattress that I had enjoyed spurned. To show the error of their choice, Bruce had just filled a big chaff sack with pine needles for his own bed in Riddles' birding-shed.

We left them for an hour's exploration, returning to find Mycky dissecting one of eight limey birds. They had expected more, these few having been taken from the ground surface after dark. Each bird had solid yellow masses of uric acid extruded from the urethra. After killing the birds, the vet took smears from the stomach contents in search of an autotoxin caused by the enforced constipation. Stones like gritty, chalky peas accumulated in the cloaca were part of the disease, but the spherical brown lumps in the greenish crop contents were a mystery with birds which are supposed to feed only on animal matter and plant plankton. Mycky decided they must be eating seaweed for medicinal reasons.

After a large communal lunch, we set off together for a tour afoot, calling at some of the birding-sheds. The noonday heat hung heavy over the parched land. All Nature seemed to doze in the oppressive atmosphere as we scrunched through the brittle grass. Even the shore birds were silent and we felt like noisy intruders, chatting of this and that between bouts of mopping perspiration. But not all was quiescent.

It was Ted who drew our attention to a pronounced tussle between two lean wasps, striped in black and white. They rolled over and over in frenzied combat, churning a small hole in the sand as they skirmished. The female object of their interest sauntered nonchalantly to and fro, quite unmoved by the extraordinary lengths that males will go to for the sake of sex.

It is fashionable to say nowadays that all living things have an urge to perennate their genes — items that I am sure these wasps had never heard of. Each time the combatants broke apart, they re-engaged immediately with a fearsome buzzing. By the time they let up the female had wandered off, proving how futile this sex urge can be.

At one shed we acquired a present of a blue-tongue lizard named George. A little the worse for wear after surviving a grass fire, some of his scales were singed and his toenails burned off. His ears contained small ticks and a few larger ones like swollen sultanas clung to his body, smaller and darker than those on the snakes. He ate the succulent leaves of the two mesembrianthemums, as well as insects and smaller lizards, but was unable to make use of birds' eggs unless their shells were already broken.

George nestled comfortably into my lap, clutching my thumb and forefinger in the crook of his short arm, and I nursed him on the way back — in a bigger boat, with our dinghy tied astern. He would become part of Eric's live collection. I tucked him against the mast while I went ashore for gear and returned to hear Tuck's small niece announcing excitedly that there was a goanna under the anchor chain.

George had explored further and was peering over the bow, as neatly aligned as a mini figurehead, wondering whether to make a dive for freedom. He decided against it and settled for a well-fed, fire-free life at Gosford Snake Park. I gave him a pillowcase to himself on my return and placed him beside others of his kind for company during the hours of darkness.

Two quiet days followed, with only the reptiles for company. The tigers wriggled their bags from under the bed during the nights and were swept firmly back in the mornings, while the young copperheads danced roundelays in their cardboard box under the table.

I opened up the jars of frogs and lizards at intervals to give them a breath of fresh air and a sprinkling of water. A lone skink which I missed died of desiccation and Eric used this animal on his return to demonstrate his theory that they, too, were dependent on absorbing moisture from internal dew formation among their sheltering rocks. Another skink had sloughed its skin but failed to break free.

"Even scruffier than Dom, 'fresh' from a birding expedition."

George was brought out occasionally for an airing and a snack. He still smelled unpleasantly singed but was much livelier than on our first acquaintance and something of a handful.

Life took on a different, more thought-provoking quality when Ted and Mycky returned three days later, and I got to know our Ukrainian friend better. He had none of the familiar British reserve, wearing his emotions very near the surface, and was as prone to delve deeply into the philosophies of life as to indulge in the usual Aussie pleasantries and horseplay.

He confessed to having expected a female who remained loyal to one as eccentric as Dom over the years to be equally odd. Instead, he found me quite normal, warm, teasable and pleasantly sympathetic, with all the desirable qualities of a good wife and mother! All very un-British, but nice, particularly as he spoke of his own wife with similar continental warmth. When we finally left Fisher Island on Murray Holloway's boat, Eric spotted me encircled by a Ukrainian arm and reassured the others: "It's only a shipboard romance. It won't last."

He, Dom and Conrad had homed in on a black fishing boat a few days after the others. While having no qualms about leaving me alone with the snakes, they expressed surprise that I seemed so little worried by them.

"Thought that must be a smoke signal summoning help as we came up the sound."

It was actually Ted, having trouble with the Tilly lamp, fortunately outside by the time the conflagration started.

The trio from Babel Island had brought a big tuna, about eight inches in diameter, and some barracuda, donated by fisherman 'Johnnie Lipstick'. Mycky and I had a blitz on vegetables while the others extricated the camp oven, rusty with sea water from the last crayfish cooking, and got to work scaling, gutting and de-boning. We dined royally, if somewhat messily.

Derek Smith laid on a party ashore for our last night on the islands. All the world and his wife were there, quite mellowed by the time Athol Dart set up his projector to show his slides of the local scene and Bavaria — a country familiar to Mycky — and mine of Sub-Antarctica and Noreen Riddle's watercolours of the birding.

Laurie Walker, captain of "*Victoria II*", slept soundly throughout and Ross Campbell brought in a little black pig for me to nurse. It was one of a litter he had picked up in the bush the previous day, with no sow in sight, although the piglets were barely twelve inches long. The pointy snout showed the relationship to Polynesian animals escaped from wrecks. The porker slept as soundly as Laurie until Derek introduced the dachshund, but the dog could not have cared less. There was obviously going to be no sport in this crowded indoor setting. Mycky and Ted went off to Atholl's to sleep, to relieve the crush, returning to join the melée of packing in the morning.

This was not a particularly orderly affair. Mycky, Conrad, Eric and I were going to Melbourne. Dom and Tas Drysdale were off to Little Green Island and Ted back to Great Dog with a new arrival. There were blankets to go ashore to be laundered, bush tucker to be sorted out and snakes to be stowed away. Eric was canny about this.

"People often offer to carry my suitcase, but never the kitbags. What they don't know is that I always put the snakes in the case: safer there!"

When interviewed by reporters at the take-off point, the formula was: "The snakes are coming along after."

When interviewed on arrival, it was: "The snakes have gone on ahead," allowing the porters to trundle his suitcases around with untroubled minds. He had many entertaining stories of unwelcome finds in his luggage in hotel bedrooms and other inappropriate places.

Everything had to be swapped to a different bag and the rest of us watched fascinated as individuals escaped from the thinly disguised piles of writhing muscle and headed across the bald granite in search of obscurity beyond. Russell and I had a bonanza with our cameras, the snakes so bemused by their recent experience that they posed admirably for photographs in their moments of indecision.

Among the blue-tongue lizards was a youngster, a 'drummer boy', with portly tum and disproportionately large head, this about a week old. Eric had been bitten by a whip snake on Babel Island, but assured us that a whip snake's venom was no more potent than a scorpion's.

The seven dead tigers were opened up to examine stomach contents. There were none, this being the end of March and falling in their main period of fasting. The only gut contents were shiny brown round worms two to three inches long, which Eric asserted and Mycky denied were the same as those found in sheep. All the snakes were infected but all were fat and well, or had been before suffocation, round worms causing less harm than tapeworms.

Two of the fattest proved to be pregnant. Tigers are viviparous, the young born alive and not hatching from eggs incubated outside the body as in some snakes. Eric extracted sixteen snakelets, ten inches long from one and six almost twelve inches long from the other. The latter, he said, were on the point of being born, the others would have been due in ten or eleven days. One of the large brood had two heads and deformed hind parts, this, apparently, not uncommon. Occasionally a two-headed snake was able to live, at least for a while, the two brains receiving the same messages and delivering the same orders.

We learned about litter size, mating time, gestation period and much more. Also that the average size of the snakes being exported was reckoned to be four feet eight inches (140 cm), although a number were over six feet.

Lunch was excellent, if somewhat chaotic: cold tuna and hard boiled eggs with tomato, beetroot and onion salad and two kinds of salad dressing, these Russell's speciality. The feast was disrupted by the arrival of Holloway's boat to take the first consignment of personnel. He was invited in and the men stalled for time with beer and coffee. Dom and Russell were the first to go. I packed their food, mindful of the fact that they had only firewater (whisky) with which to make their coffee unless they had a wrench to loosen the rusted tap on the water tank.

Things were a bit more orderly in "Yolla" when Holloway returned for the rest of us, and we infiltrated Lady Barron, paying our last respects to our good friends there, not forgetting wombats, piglets and talking galahs. Some would be returning next year but, sadly, not me. Soon I would be away to the guano islands of South Africa and my hitchhike north to Britain.

There was no time to take Conrad up Vinegar Hill, as planned. Derek drove us to the airport and Mycky took charge of my excess baggage, ascribing the overweight cost to 'the firm'. I looked my last — for thirty-five years — on my beloved islands, strung like yellow beads across the silvered strait.

They had become a part of me in those three years of coming and going and it was a wrench to leave.

Eric had his 'combie' at Essendon Airport, to ease the hassle of transporting the snakes, and he gave me a lift to my Melbourne destination. I was to see neither him nor Mycky again and now they are gone — perhaps to regions with neither poisonous serpents nor noxious diseases. As Derek remarked on my belated return in the mid 1990s: "We're almost the only two left."

I hope there will be wombats and dachshunds where he is headed when his time comes.

129 Superb Blue Wren *Malurus cyaneus* and
Native 'Fuchsia' *Correa reflexa*

130 Prickly Broom Heath *Monotoca scoparia* and
Blunt-leaved Heath *Epacris obtusifolia*

131 Boobialla *Myoporum insulare* flowers

2. GOOSE ISLAND LIGHTHOUSE RENOVATION

It was a year earlier, in March 1959, that I was able to explore Goose Island, the smallest of the Chappell Group at 241 acres (97 hectares). I was spending a month on board the 1500-ton Commonwealth Lighthouse Relief Ship, SS "*Cape York*", which had no business to transact on the main Furneaux Group, so I merely dipped in to the western fringe, seeing none of my old mates. We had sailed overnight from the tip of Wilsons Promontory, which reaches out into Bass Strait towards the archipelago and was part of the same in days long gone.

I emerged on deck into a Utopian dawn of gleaming sunshine and crisp blue sky. "*Cape York*" lay placidly at anchor on glassy calm water off the eastern shore of Goose Island, straining neither this way nor that at her moorings. Badger Island and the mighty peaks of Flinders lay to one side, the low southern part of Goose Island under its crimson blanket of turgid pigface to the other. Rising statuesque, if somewhat dingy, from the red carpet was the ninety foot (28 metre) high lighthouse, built in 1846. I had seen its light winking companionably for the citizens of nearby Whitemark and forming part of the chain from Swan Island across the dangerous waters of the Strait to Deal Island and Wilsons Promontory in the north. Soon I was to be allowed inside.

I slipped into the chart room to get my bearings, with the help of the first and third mates. Mount Chappell rose beyond the further point of Badger Island, concealing Trousers Point under the Strzelecki Peaks, with Kangaroo and Big Green Islands to the north, towards the Flinder's capital.

Captain Herriot came in while I was facetiously enquiring if there was likely to be a 'baggage boy' in the crew to carry my bags onshore. He offered his services, notwithstanding that 'the captain never leaves his ship when out of port'. When enumerating the items of equipment making a carrier desirable, I had been rash enough to mention my indispensable lemonade bottle.

"Whacko! It's going to be a St Trinian's picnic."

As the captain and I went over the side, a mocking voice followed: "Careful of the doctor's rucksack: there's a bottle of lolly water inside!"

Later, in the captain's absence, the deliverer of that warning commented, with an angelic smile: "So we've found a use for him at last."

The speaker had a master's ticket himself, and was sometimes in command, but there were insufficient ships in the service to keep all the skippers occupied and he was the odd man out at present. He would be leaving us in Hobart to fly back to a new appointment as marine surveyor.

Before we set off botanising, Captain Herriot showed me round the lighthouse, the business parts of which had already been partially dismantled by the refurbishing team. I was most intrigued by the sun valves which were responsible for kindling and douching the lamp. Each consisted of eight shiny brass and silver rods ranged round a central vertical black cylinder. They reflected the light rays onto this and the consequent expansion of the cylinder partially closed the valve which controlled the gas seeping through to fuel the light.

At a crucial degree of expansion only tiny pilot flames were left burning and the light went out. The mechanism of this gradual fading had puzzled us when camping on Wilsons Promontory and noticing the nautical beacon waxing steadily brighter during an afternoon thunderstorm to fade as the clouds moved on. So this was how it worked.

The whole of the Goose Island lighthouse, not just the sun valves, was automated. In a strategic position for Melbourne to Hobart shipping, it was said to be the most intricate of the automatic lights at the time and the only one of its kind. It was the pressure of gas from the cylinders that enabled the beam to revolve, causing the winking. In smaller lights the gas was fed through in jets, to produce flashings, on and off.

There were two full-sized lenses and two half ones. The tall gas cylinders, eighteen of them, stood at the base of the tower and were all connected by a single feed pipe of less than a centimetre diameter. This fuel supply lasted for six months, so the continuity of the beam depended on the twice-yearly servicing. The current visit was for a special overhaul, to include the five-yearly painting of the tower with two coats of white cement wash.

Hundreds of yards of thick rope — a commodity always in plentiful supply on working ships — were let down from the top of the tower. Three wooden cradles were hoisted up to the balcony and three pairs of agile seamen vaulted over the rail to occupy them. Buckets of cement wash were hauled up from below on thinner lines and the day's work began.

The cradles descended gradually as the men worked. At ground level half the circumference had been covered and they started again at the top on the other side. By 6 p.m. the first coat was completed.

The job was well under way when Captain Herriot and I set off along the ancient railway line connecting the light with a distant bay. This was well sheltered and was used only when it was too rough to make a landing nearer the light, as we had today, or when the gantry was needed to hoist heavy equipment ashore. Dragging the loaded trolley by man power, uphill all the way, was hard work and the track was known as the Convicts' Railway.

Goose Island light had not always been automatic and the ruins of the old lighthouse keepers' homesteads and outbuildings near the tower could be distinguished under the enveloping pigface. Only the foundations remained and, from the top of the lighthouse, they looked like the abandoned excavation of a Roman villa.

Behind the dwelling houses was the cemetery, with eight or nine graves — of keepers and mariners. The crew of the "*Cape York*" had put this is order on their last visit, freeing the memorials from cloying vegetation and burning off the Stipa tussocks. Variable groundsel had produced a sward of yellow flowers on the cleared ground in the ensuing six months.

A major tragedy had struck in March 1922 — at a time when the keepers had to row out to visiting ships to exchange outgoing and incoming mail and collect supplies. Families were accommodated on the island at that time and the third keeper's wife had ordered a feeding bottle for her new baby daughter. This need influenced her husband and the second keeper in their decision to venture out to the supply ship, the SS *"Kiltibanks"*, despite darkness and rough seas. They collected mail and stores, but the boat overturned as they struggled back through the breakers and both were drowned.

The *"Kiltibanks"* crew knew nothing of the disaster in the enveloping darkness and sailed on their way. It was a full week before the remaining islanders managed to signal a passing ship to report the deaths. There was none of the comfort of ship-to-shore radio in those days!

During that terrible week the head keeper managed to keep the light burning at night, lest there be more casualties, while the young widow did the work of the others by day, as well as looking after the baby, the only link to her lost spouse. The little girl grew up to become Mrs Patricia Daly, who returned to Goose Island in 1985 to visit the grave of the father she had never known.

Throughout the morning we were flushing gaggles of Cape Barren geese — unused to human intrusion in this far flung island fastness, which was not called Goose Island for nothing. The largest contingent was of 130 birds, but it was impossible to tell how many hundreds there might be in total — so readily did the flocks flip from place to place.

As far as we could estimate from the naval chart, the island was almost two miles long, top-shaped with rather less than a hundred acres of grassland on the higher northern block and around a hundred and fifty acres of pigface on the low-lying southern arm. There was plenty of room for the grey geese to merge into invisibility.

It was clear that they grazed the pigface leaves extensively, but, with so many people milling round on this part of the island, most took refuge in the grassy north during our two-day stay, or escaped to a little islet offshore. These were days of blissful, almost breathless, calm. When we returned a fortnight hence, winds were approaching gale force and the geese were sitting tight, not venturing up to do battle with the wind.

Their dung was impregnated with short hard fragments of the fruiting spikes of ryegrass, with a few of barley grass and plantain, these likely to leave more tangible remains after passing through the system than the fleshy pigface leaves. There was little fresh green in the grass swards at this end of summer and the birds were concentrating on the seeds.

This implied a water deficit, so it was no surprise to find congregations of birds in the damp flushes. Marshy areas stood out because of the pale mauve carpets of creeping mimulus or monkey flowers, co-habiting with *Lilaeopsis*. Some were fed by upwelling fresh water, where yellow buttons and blue lobelia were permeated by mudwort and bristle sedge; others were salty, with pink spurrey and glasswort.

An ibis, the first I had seen in Bass Strait, where both straw-necked and the white or sacred ibis are uncommon, was in evidence throughout the day. Sometimes its path crossed that of a lazily cruising white-bellied sea eagle. The two gull species were shattering the stillness with their wailing calls. With them were crested terns and black-faced shags.

Land birds were represented by pottering brown quails and grass-flipping white-fronted chats, some of these incredibly tame. Skylarks rose high into the still air, making the most of the freedom from wind as they trilled their messages one to the other.

At the West Gut, marking the junction of Northern Tump and Southern Peninsula, the captain took time off on a little sandy beach to gather shells, sea urchins and sponges for his children. Surprisingly, for a sea-going man, such opportunities seldom offered. Ships the size of "*Cape York*" usually made landfall in much more urban sites or lay off lighthouses on barren rocks which offered few such holiday havens.

As we moved into the northern block, the sward became littered with bits of the "*Merylin*" which had been blown up just before Christmas, after running into the island in fog.

"Radar is never infallible. There will be lighthouses for many years yet."

The captain spoke from the heart when he added: "Every mariner wants to see a tangible beacon rather than a smudge on the screen in front of him, and to know that there are men in the lighthouse, trained to lend a helping hand when needed. The "*Merylin*" was not that lucky."

Nevertheless, lights continued to be de-manned and automated, to save wages, causing the lighthouse ships to drop the victualling side from their maintenance calls — before being finally replaced by helicopters.

"*Merylin*" had been blown up to prevent the cases of high explosive which she was carrying floating away as a shipping hazard. It must have been quite an explosion. Mangled pieces of metal a quarter of an inch thick had been flung many hundreds of yards inland. Herriot mooched back and forth, identifying and pronouncing upon parts of ship and cargo, muttering darkly: "Of course they couldn't see the light. Obscured by fog."

Maybe radar was the answer after all.

Goose Island sometimes held sheep. Today we saw only two, very wild ones, skulking among boulders. No doubt their shyness had enabled them to elude the muster when the others were being taken ashore. Later in the day retired lighthouse keeper Williams told of the 'religious sheep' which formerly fed on the pigface around the lighthouse.

"Come evening, they all lay down for the night, head to wind, facing the westering sun. At intervals the whole flock bowed their heads in unison to pull at a strand of pigface — as though making obeisance to the sun. The boat's crew watched fascinated when this was pointed out to them. It seemed all the animals were on the same cud-chewing cycle."

By lunch time a heat haze had begun to gather, but the powerful ultraviolet rays penetrated this with unabated, eye-screwing, vigour. Herriot returned to the ship for a more substantial repast, leaving me and my lolly water in the shade of a rock, where I could watch the oystercatchers as I lunched.

The whole island was of granite, with none of the overlying sea floor deposits of softer limestone, as seen on Big Green Island. The northern part rose to about fifty feet, with piles of huge boulders, sloping down to the central gut delimiting the southern portion, which was transversely ribbed with shallow valleys.

In 1870 Brownrigg wrote: "Mutton birds abound on the island which, for its size, possesses about the largest rookery in the Straits Islands. Is less than 300 acres, fifty feet high. Tussocks and pigface. No trees." Of neighbouring Badger he wrote: "Well wooded. Has no mutton birds. It appears that mutton birds avoid wooded areas and, although occurring on islands with woods, nests are seldom found in any but the cleared spots."

The southern mutton bird rookery must have been a splendid sight when the pigface was in flower in spring, the swards as pink and extensive as the best of the thrift *(Armeria maritima)* communities in shearwater colonies along Britain's Atlantic fringes. Even now, with the flowers withered, the 160 acres of virtually this one species, was a remarkable sight, because of the reddening of so many of the leaves.

This had not occurred throughout. Instead the crimson formed an attractive mosaic, threaded with sinuous lines of bright green. The whole was arrayed, like a rich Persian carpet, when viewed from the top of the lighthouse. All the green corridors were riddled with mutton bird burrows, scarcely any of which occurred among the red plants, which grew with minimal soil, often creeping across bald granite and seldom on soil of burrowable depth.

The excess of red anthocyanin pigment was probably a function of water stress: the greening of the plants on the deeper soils due to a combination of the more abundant soil water and nitrogen from the guano. Both types bore fleshy fruits which were formerly relished by Aboriginals, as were the related ones of Hottentot fig *(Carpobrotus edule)* by native South Africans.

Where much soil was bared by the burrowers, variable groundsel and leek lilies gave contrasting flecks of yellow until the breach healed and they were squeezed out. Rookeries on the tussock grass of the northern slopes were unburned and those among coast spear grass included a number of penguins. Vacated nests of silver gulls were found just north of the lighthouse.

An interesting stranger in the north-western rookery was coast twin-flower *(Zygophyllum billardieri)*, growing with herbaceous kin of the saltbushes and Austral hollyhock. Dom Serventy, visiting some years earlier, had reported sheep to have eaten all the leaves of the storksbill within reach to expose the eggs of mutton birds nesting on the ground surface beneath.

The sun's orb flattened as it met the horizon on its passage west. I escaped from the card games in the officers' mess to go aloft and savour the night. The sky was of black plush, freckled with stars, the sea a sleeping giant, emitting not even a rhythmic snore.

The weather held and next morning the workmen were ashore early, giving the lighthouse its second coat of whitening — a less satisfying job than yesterday's, when the improvement was so immediately apparent. The lenses and reflectors had been overhauled and re-assembled when I climbed to the balcony with Charles Conway, regional lighthouse engineer, for colour photos of the crimson and emerald landscape.

At ten o'clock my companion shouted down to tubby little 'Bobbin' Ryder, lighthouse keeper from Cliffy Island, who was 'in transit' and acting as camp cook for the shore party, producing breakfast, smoko and lunch. The response was smoko for two being sent up in a dangling milk churn. It was halted at one of the cradles for the tin of milk to be turned the right way up, but only the billy of black tea reached us intact. In the biscuit tin was a glutinous mix of condensed milk, disintegrating biscuits and sugar-sprinkled mugs — which served us right for not going down for it.

The ship's officers had been using the pinnace for a fishing trip all morning. So engrossed were they, that it needed a blast on the ship's siren to alert them to the fact that a team of hungry workers had been sitting on the rocks waiting for the lunch boat for some time. Bobbin, the rotund, red-faced son of Lancashire, was catering only for the engineers and mechanics. The rest of us were duly collected and fed on board, then delivered back ashore — me to enjoy the rest of an idyllic summer day in a wilderness with a difference — carrying my own lolly water bottle.

132 Boobialla *Myoporum insulare* fruits

133 Goose Island Lighthouse

134 Climbing Lignum *Muehlenbeckia adpressa*

3. TO DEAL ISLAND IN THE KENT GROUP

From Goose Island *"Cape York"* headed south to the lights on Swan Island, Eddystone Point, Cape Forestier, Tasman Island, Bruny Island and along the south coast of Tasmania to Maatsuyker Island in the far south-west. It was 31st March before we steamed back to Goose Island.

A working party was put ashore at 6 a.m., the pinnace feeling its way through clammy mist and drizzle. The calm persisted but the magic and colour of our earlier visit had dissolved in the grey rain. By 8 a.m. a wind had sprung up from nowhere and waves were churning on the shore, so that it was touch and go bringing the seamen off for breakfast.

The second mate was in charge of the landing craft, but failed to prevent the engine spluttering to a standstill and becoming flooded with sea water. The davits for this boat were on the offshore side of the ship, but the boat was unable to work its way round to be hauled up. The pump was defunct and it was fast filling with water. Openings which should have let the water out were stuffed with hay, chaff and coal dust from former cargoes and Hughie, the new first mate taken on at Hobart, was too new to know that one of his essential jobs was to see that these were cleaned out.

Experts leaning over the ship's rail, watching the fun, took bets on whether the boat would go down. Others, more helpful, released her twin occupying the davits on this side and parked this on deck, so that they could haul the second boat up alongside until such time as she could be made seaworthy.

The block and tackle could not be lowered without a weight on it so our two good all-rounders among the able seamen, Geordie and Chick, sat themselves in a rope loop apiece, one on each side, and eased the tackle down to the swamped boat. She came up, with advice from all and sundry, but was swung aloft where it was impossible for the engineers to get to work on her.

Everyone stood well clear when the bung hole was freed and the contained sea water rushed out onto the boat deck, but the unexpected jet spurting from the engine exhaust took some unawares. The captain decided to up anchor and go round to the north of the island where it was quiet enough to deal with the situation.

Mechanics Kenny Baker and George Gough, had been left behind on Goose Island for later pick-up, their allotted task not quite completed. When they saw their hope of breakfast disappearing round the headland, they got busy preparing their own.

They caught and skinned five mutton bird chicks, fortunately in prime condition at this season, and collected driftwood for a fire. The drizzle had left the tussocks too wet to burn, so they helped themselves to shellite from the lighthouse to produce some useful flames. A grill was fashioned from an old bonlac tin and they settled to their repast.

Work finished, bellies full and fire douched, one of them shinned up the lighthouse to see where *"Cape York"* had finished up, and they shouldered their packs and made for the north coast. A lookout was being kept on board and a boat went in for them, getting them back in good time for lunch.

It was only six hours' steaming time to our next port of call at Deal Island in the Kent Group (sixty miles at ten mph), but we would arrive too late to do anything useful today, so we lay off Goose Island until after nightfall.

This was our second visit to Deal Island, and a quickie, to pick up principal keeper Colin Garreau with his wife and daughter and Alan, the second mechanic. There were no stores to land, as these came from the Victorian end of the voyage. Those which we had taken aboard in Hobart were for more southern lights.

The islanders came aboard and we were soon away, the swell flattening out as we ran into a thick bank of fog. It was eerie standing on deck blanketed in this silent world. We seemed very much alone in a vast empty expanse, but the ship's siren blared at intervals, in case there were others out there likely to stray too close.

We emerged from the enveloping pall as we passed the southern tip of Wilsons Promontory. The cloud was still present but had lifted, the underside of the white fleece undulating to match the contours below. The sight from sea level was as magic as its upper surface would have been from a plane.

Rodondo Island appeared as a scintillating cone rising from a level snow field, like a half-licked ice cream. The sea mist bulged upwards over the Ansers, repelled by an invisible force — heat emanating from the rock, perhaps — but was disrupted when it reached the mainland. Residual shreds of white had settled in the darkly wooded valleys as streaks and puddles, or as girdles around the granite peaks. The Glennies lay beyond its edge, sparkling in unobstructed sunshine pouring from a blue void.

* * * * *

Some weeks before we had homed in on the Kent Group from the opposite direction. Anchored off Cliffy Island for the night, our hopes of making a landfall there at dawn were dashed. Instead of the early call at six, I heard the clank of the anchor chain being winched aboard. A wind had risen in the night and Cliffy's steep rocky landing had become impossible.

"Cape York" swung about and headed back to finish a job at the tip of Wilsons Promontory, but the landing proved too difficult there too. By eight o'clock breakfast we were steaming on past Rodondo Island making for the Kent Group.

Rodondo's 198 acres (80 hectares) had broken from its former cloud cap and rose like a fluted pyramid from the turmoil of grey breakers, to a height of 1,138 feet (350 metres). Pinkish granite, smoothed by the waves and clad in deeper pink pigface, was steep and slippery, broken by no beaches offering easy access.

Only the intrepid few had landed there to explore the mutton bird colony and the homes of penguins, Pacific and silver gulls, Cape Barren geese and oystercatchers. Notable among these was a party of boys from Geelong College with John Berchervaise. They had found lizards and skinks, big old honey myrtles and tea-trees, beard heath, boobialla, she-okes, correa and much more, untroubled by man's exploitation or management.

Largely as a result of their findings, Rodondo was declared a nature reserve in 1976 by the Tasmanian Government. It comes closer to Victoria than any other part of Tasmania, lying only eleven kilometres from Wilsons Promontory.

We reached the spectacular Kent Group by midday and eased into the Murray Pass, with Erith Island and Dover Island to starboard and Deal Island to port. Despite the frisky wind, it was a blue sunny day and the prospect of the extensive haven into which fisherman Harry Brochie and another couple of crayfish boats had preceded us, was vastly pleasing.

I joined the first shore party at one o'clock, enjoying the luxury of a jetty landing and making the acquaintance of principal keeper Colin Garreau, who managed to spare time from the chores of victualling to acquaint me with some of his cherished wildlife.

Matthew Flinders had been the first white man to sight this magnificently craggy archipelago — in 1798. He named it the Kent Group after "The brave and accomplished sailor, William Kent". Later the name became associated with England's south-east corner and spawned others, like Dover and Deal.

Deal was much the largest island, at 5,000 acres (2,025 hectares), its mixed grassland, scrub and woodland sheltering animals as big as wallabies and possums.

Erith Island was well endowed with fresh water, enabling beef cattle to be fattened there by the holder of its 500 hectare grazing lease. The low causeway linking it to the indigenous scrub of Dover Island was known as the Swashway, presumably from the swash of the waves along its flanks.

Sea birds congregated on the lesser islands, particularly North-east Island, and a diminished colony of fur seals would soon be building up on Judgement Rocks.

Deal was the first island to be designated as a conservation area under the Tasmanian National Parks and Wildlife Service, followed by a recommendation for the whole group to be declared a state reserve. More recently archeologists are discovering that the indigenous humans also have a fascinating history, reaching back perhaps 8,000 years, to 6,000 BC. The rich marine life clustered round its unsullied shores must have helped to sustain them.

Colin kept an informed lookout for interesting happenings in this little unspoiled world and wrote Nature Articles for *"The Age"*. He collected rocks and shells, plants and bones and sent them off to the experts for identification. I was able to help with the fifty-seven alien plants, most of which were British, and our combined list for his well-endowed island amounted to 163 species plus fifteen mosses and liverworts.

It was not until after my visit to Flinders Island in November 1995 that I realised how few others had had the opportunity to look at the vegetation with a critical eye. A week or so after my return to Britain I received a letter from John Whinray, a botanist living on Flinders Island and making a special study of the Kent Group. Unfortunately I had not come across him while there and he only knew of my visit when it was all over and reported in *"Island News"*.

His first letter told how he had been writing around trying to find my address to ask about these early records. I would dearly have loved the company of a botanist during my stay, to remind me of all the plant names which I had forgotten during an absence of thirty-five years, but it was not to be.

He was collating all plant records for all the islands and told me that my brief sojourn on Deal Island had resulted in fifty-three new species (all checked in Melbourne herbarium) and a sighting of coast daisy bush which was the first since Robert Brown's visit in 1803. Among my other notable finds which he mentioned were *Wilsonia* on Vansittart Island, a 'first' for Tasmania, and coast twin-flower and spicy everlasting *(Helichrysum argophyllum)* on Babel Island, species thought to occur no further south and these some of the earliest collections for Tasmania. It was nice to learn that I had contributed, even if somewhat belatedly.

Whinray seems well fitted to pull all the information together. In one of his letters he writes: "To date I've been to 100 of the islands, from Hogan's Group down to the Swan Islands. In fact I went to Little Swan and Cygnet from Whitemark in a fourteen foot boat by myself: a memorable trip."

He divulged that there had been ten fires on Deal since my visit, one of them, in the wake of the 1972 drought, fierce enough to reduce the whole island to ashes.

While lighthouse stores and fuel were being offloaded, I had busied myself listing long-term residents and newcomers about the jetty. Then a short land rover jaunt took us to Colin's house and wife, who was a former employee of the CSIRO Forest Products Section. She was looking after a brood of infants at present, four of them belonging to an assistant keeper who had been taken off to hospital with an injured eye.

For forty-eight hours this poor man had languished on the island while Colin followed radio instructions from a mainland doctor, doping him with this and that to dull the pain of the split eyeball (fortunately only the white). Eventually, in dirty weather, Harry Brochie had come to the rescue and taken him off to medical care. Fishermen are more than just fishermen in this fraternity of the sea — just as lighthouse keepers do (or did) a lot more than keep the lights burning.

The Garreaus were scheduled for leave and had been poised to join us on *"Cape York"* as far as Hobart. Now they would have to stay to man the light single-handed until relieved on our return in a few weeks' time.

This was a station where the keepers lived on the fat of the land, killing their own sheep and cattle for lamb, veal and baby beef, milking their own cows and churning cream and butter. A bi-product was hides and a batch of these was spread to dry, each nailed at full stretch to the timber floor of a condemned house alongside the current homestead.

As so often in the homes of islanders, there was a splendid collection of natural history specimens — an inspiration to the son — now away at boarding school — and the four-year-old daughter. They were surrounded by books and completely fulfilled in their island life.

The lighthouse is a mile away from the house by land rover. It is claimed to be the tallest in Australia — as is Cape Wickham lighthouse by the King Islanders at the other end of Bass Strait. The Deal Island one stands nearly 1,000 feet above the sea at the south-west corner of the island, which measures two and a half by three and a half miles. We reached it along a steep, water-eroded track, with cracked bitumen easing the gradient on the last, most hazardous, stretch.

The lighthouse was built in 1848 and had served the seafaring community for 134 years when the Australian Department of Transport started formulating plans to abandon it in 1982. The light itself, at 304 m above sea level, has an impressive range, whereas the proposed replacement lights on two nearby islands would be only 100 m up and visible for shorter distances. As pointed out by John Whinray, who was opposing the plan, boats close to the group would be able to see neither, one being too far away and the nearer one hidden by the island itself.

As the only all-weather anchorage in North-eastern Bass Strait, the Kent Group is likely to draw shipping from all around when the weather is at its worst and the Professional Fishermen's Association of Tasmania, backed by the Victorian Fishermen's Association, were also opposing the plans. These men at the sharp end had plenty of tales to tell of how lightkeepers had been instrumental in saving lives.

Automated lights cannot keep a lookout for overdue boats nor check the safety of mariners in the neighbourhood nor phone for help when ships' radios fail. A more sensible move would seem to have been to equip the keepers with two-way radios tuned to channels used by seamen.

Whinray, in an article in "*The Mercury*" of 26th April 1982, stressed the importance of resident manpower in wardening the wildlife of the islands, which are regarded as some of the most important in Bass Strait, yet subject to wildfires lighted by vandals or worse. They harbour Australia's southernmost population of white-naped honey-eaters and several endemic plants.

Deal Island has a considerable area of peppermint gums and other woody vegetation, while Dover Island's rich flora inhabits one of the only two sizable scrub-covered islands little changed by man in Bass Strait. Fairy prion and diving petrel rookeries, as well as those of shearwaters, occur on North-east Island and Judgement Rocks in the south-west harbour a thriving colony of fur seals.

Even the voices of architects were raised in protest, pointing out that the lighthouse buildings still in use at the time were "The finest remaining group of early light station buildings" in Australia, classified by the National Trust of Australia and regarded as national heritage. How to continue the necessary day-to-day maintenance on an unmanned island? The main beneficiaries of de-manning would be the foreign shipping companies which cough up much of the cost, not the locals, human or otherwise. Money could be saved by returning to servicing the lighthouse by ketch instead of helicopter. Government plans for de-manning were deferred and those concerned fought on.

On my visit I went up the tower, ostensibly to admire the incredible views, but also to escape the bitter wind outside. Botanising my way back down the hill, I descended from the sort of salt-tolerant community usually found at the sea's edge, into heathy scrubland on the western slope. The noon flower and tussock of the wind-lashed summit received almost as much spray as they would have done within reach of the waves, and shrubs had not withstood the onslaught to regenerate after the likely disturbance when the lighthouse was built.

Geographically the Kent Group is Victorian rather than Tasmanian, so the presence of northerners like coast twin-flower was of little moment. Among the shrubs were drooping she-oke, silver banksia, narrow-leaved wattle, prickly Moses, large-leaf bush-pea, sweet bursaria, stinkwood, hazel pomaderris and a range of eucalypts, tea-trees, paperbarks, heaths and daisy bushes, in addition to the usual more salt-tolerant kinds.

White-lipped whip snakes were the only serpents here, although black tigers occur elsewhere in the Kent Group. Blue-tongue lizards and smaller skinks lazed or darted among the undergrowth. I saw nothing of the gannets nesting on Judgement Rocks and quartering the adjacent seas for fish. Whinray, who has been ashore there, reckons their numbers to be around four thousand.

Although the lighthouse shearwater colony and others on Deal Island were extinct — thought by Garreau to have been exterminated by sealers — the birds still nested on Erith and Dover Islands: mostly under bushes. I explored one of the defunct colonies, identified as such only by the excavation of bird bones sent off to Melbourne for identification.

Considering the density of shearwaters in their main stronghold of North-east Island, and the readiness with which the birds move from one island to another in Franklin Sound, it is remarkable that some had not returned to their old haunts on Deal Island.

It had been thus for a long time. Joseph Gabriel, writing in *"The Victorian Naturalist"* XXVIII in March 1912, commented on the crowded conditions on North-east Island which he and his club visited on 23rd November 1890.

"We found all the available nesting sites occupied by these birds. They were so thickly placed that, when in one instance I lifted up a bush, I found three shearwaters on eggs within the space of less than one square yard.

"On 25th November, two days after, Mr Carstairs and his two sons landed on that little island and gathered no less than ninety-three dozen (1,116) eggs. These eggs, Mr Carstairs assured me, were found on the surface of the ground and were, of course, deserted. They had no need to molest the birds in the burrows or under the bushes in any way and in all probability many more eggs might have been found for several days after."

Joseph Gabriel had the same thought that I had. He continues: "Now it stands to reason that the natural instincts of these excess laying birds would lead them to hunt for fresh grounds. North-east Island is very small and has but a limited space available for these birds. At the most, one thousand birds would more than crowd the available ground, yet we find that over eleven hundred have had to part with their eggs on being unable to find nesting places."

He refers also to Chappell Islands, where "The residents of the Furneaux Group gather annually no less than 200,000 birds. They gather very few eggs there but take some of the old birds during the egging time instead; yet, in spite of this seemingly suicidal policy, every year the birds appear as numerous as ever."

Shearwater eggs at that time were selling in Victoria for nine pence per dozen and "A man has to be an expert egger and work very hard to return him ten shillings per day for the four or five days available for the harvest."

Deal Island's vacated colony looked ideal for rehabilitation. Perhaps birds had tried in past years and been deterred by over-harvesting of their progeny.

All too soon it was time to leave. Even in East Cove across the Murray Passage, the sea was heaving mightily as we returned to the ship and careful timing was necessary to grab the Jacob's ladder as it swept past the reaching hands in the pinnace, or, more correctly, as we swept past the dangling ladder.

My first views of the Kent Group had been from the air in my transit to and from the Furneaux Group. On 6th December 1958, I was the only passenger on the plane from Melbourne, a thirty-five-seater DC3. Two-thirds of the seats from the front were loaded with freight and curtained off. We flew over a high ceiling of cloud, with frustratingly few breaks for observing the seascape below.

Seeing my interest, the stewardess brought the co-pilot back to me. He offered me space in the captain's cabin and said they would take the plane down so that I could see. We descended through the cloud layer to 3,000 feet: more would have risked a contretemps with the helicopter whose path was to cross ours over Deal Island.

From then on I had splendid panoramic views of Wilsons Promontory, Corner Inlet and the Glennies and Ansers. Tidal River wound across the sands to the sea, just as I had left it and I was able to pick out individual cattle among tussock and bracken on the largest of the Hogan Group, with the steep cliffs of Curtis Island sliding straight into the ocean away to our right.

The Kent Group was spread like a map, mysterious pale blobs on a darker background, with the lighthouse standing out like a shining knitting needle. We passed over the Sisters and Craggy Island, shaped like a broad-brimmed digger hat, with the steep faces well in from the coast, and dropped down over Settlement Point to Whitemark.

Only four passengers boarded the plane there for Launceston. Murray Holloway had brought a truckload of crayfish in to put on the first of the new freight planes to Sydney, so I did not lack for a lift south. On my return flight I was one of only two passengers in the thirty-five-seater, and it was a cloudless day, with no need to fly low to see the layout of the islands.

135 Starry and Coast Daisy Bushes *Olearia stellulata and O. axillaris*

136 Coast Twin-leaf *Zygophyllum billardieri*

137 Deal Island Lighthouse

Chapter Sixteen

MORE ISLANDS IN EASTERN BASS STRAIT

1. ABOARD SS *"CAPE YORK"* TO THE GLENNIE GROUP

My voyage aboard the fifteen hundred ton Commonwealth Lightship *"Cape York"* had begun on 12th March 1959. The vessel left Melbourne's City Wharf in the morning and put in at Number Four Oil Wharf in Newport Docks to stock up with fuel. I boarded her there, lowering my luggage down a horrendously steep gangway to where she lay, well below wharf level, on the ebb tide.

My fellow passengers were two engineers, engaged for lighthouse maintenance work, and a light-keeper returning to Cliffy Island after shore leave. We were away by two o'clock and I joined Charles Conway, regional lighthouse engineer, on deck, to watch the trappings of civilisation slip irrevocably away as we moved out along the Melbourne Roads.

Every available bit of the superstructure was occupied by silver gulls — each a double wing's length from the next, so that it could rise unhindered in the event of danger. Ornithologists call this "Individual distance" and it is meticulously adhered to when things get crowded, to get as many birds in as possible. Statuesque cormorants, like cardboard cutouts, lined booms and wharves and perched atop sodden piles.

It is easier to conceive the huge size of Port Phillip Bay from its spacious middle, when all shores fade into a nebulous distance. Here the black swans riding at anchor inshore gave way to mollymawks, this the sailors' collective term for the smaller albatrosses which abound in these southern waters and are not easily distinguished one from another. Their flight paths crossed those of feeding flocks of short-tailed shearwaters, probably domiciled in rookeries on Phillip Island.

A few of the smaller 'tube-noses' crossed our path, speeding low over the water. They are as diverse as those tubenoses of albatross size, although individuals are as rare as mutton birds are numerous. Only the diving petrels were unmistakable: the various sooty-backed petrels with white breast, neck and chin, evading identification by non-experts.

I whiled away an hour or so on deck with Mr MacKay, chief engineer from Lewis in the Outer Hebrides — as was the chief steward. MacKay liked to play the part of an old grouse-bag, always on about his ulcers, but he had a kind heart and a soft spot for females of any description.

His melodious Hebridean lilt took me back to happy sojourns on Scotland's Western Isles, as he pattered on about his fishing exploits. His big grouse today was sewage, and its effects on his potential takes. The Aussies, he insisted, were fifty years behind in these matters, notwithstanding those magnificent spreads of emerald green grass at the Werribee Sewage Works south of Melbourne, fed by sewage and fed upon by glossy-coated cattle;

these the envy of Sydney, which had insufficient flat land to do likewise.

Afternoon tea in his cabin included a glass of cow's milk — which precious commodity lasted out for six days, after which we suffered the noxious powdered variety so familiar on boats and cowless islands. But not for long on this voyage. At Swan Island we picked up Mollie, an amiable milch cow, for delivery to a South Tasmanian lighthouse keeper. She became my special charge, as I was the only one on board with experience of hand milking, after serving a five-year apprenticeship in Britain's wartime Women's Land Army. I adjourned from tea loaded with copies of "*The Stornaway Gazette*" to while away the hours afloat.

Until Mollie's arrival I had been the only female aboard with the forty males, but that seemed to bother nobody. All members of this sea-going fraternity, many of them wandering Scots, took me for granted, including Captain Herriot, who had greeted me with: "This is a working ship: you'll have to be one of the boys."

His crew included three mates, four engineers, a radio operator and a collection of ABs (able seamen) who ranked higher and more able than the OSs (ordinary seamen), not yet qualified to join in the night watches of four hours on and eight hours off. The night team consisted of two officers and four men. On deck were a mate to plot course, a man at the wheel and a man at the teapot — strictly the lookout, who passed this duty on to the mate when engaged on more important matters. Below decks was an engineer with greaser and assistant.

My cabin was in the lighthouse keepers' quarters, they, like me, being passengers as they went to and from their posts on terra firma. It contained a two-tier bunk, a 'sofa', a chest of drawers and a wardrobe. The communal bathroom next door had three washbasins, two laundry sinks, an iron on application to the steward, and two showers. These shot jets of water across the compartment at eye level to run down the further wall, until I got Kenny, the mechanic, to arrange things more usefully.

Once out through The Narrows between Queenscliff and Portsea, it became what the second steward understated as "a little choppy". Waves swirled across the floor of the toilet, doing a good job of cleansing. It was my own fault when they started swooshing across my cabin to douche the far wall and I hastened to close the porthole. I spent an interesting night sliding back and forth on my shiny-surfaced bunk.

Next day was calm, blue and sunny and I woke to find that we were lying south of Great Glennie Island, with Mount Oberon and the bulk of Wilsons Promontory away to the east.

We were just beyond latitude thirty-nine degrees south, on the verge of the 'Roaring Forties', but they were not roaring today. The double hump of the Great Glennie with its narrow central isthmus loomed two miles long and four and a half miles from the mainland, its 331 acres or 138 hectares now included in the Wilsons Promontory National Park.

The southern block rose to 455 feet (140 m) and supported a scrub dominated by she-oke with coast tea-tree, dusty daisy bush *(Olearia phlogopappa)*, boobialla and white correa. The more distant section was a sea of Poa tussock, relieved by Austral hollyhock, both heavily burrowed by mutton birds.

There was a cove with a landing beach on the sheltered east side and a hut above it, but the lighthouse ship had no business there, so I was able to get ashore only on the three smaller islands. Bird-watchers visiting the big island between 1968 and 1979, banded fifty-eight fairy penguins, thirty-four short-tailed shearwaters and sixty-one Cape Barren geese.

Ornithologist Ian Norman counted seventy-three geese here in December 1978, but states that many were being taken illegally by poachers and shearwater burrows were getting trampled by people landing from boats. Only two-thirds of the burrows investigated contained an egg. He reckoned the shearwater population to be around 400,000 pairs, the burrows thickest (at 0.83 per square metre) among the leafy peppercress of depressions, with few in the scrub. The penguin population was around 500 pairs, burrowing mostly among Ross's noon flower. Other sea birds which he recorded were ten pairs of sooty oystercatchers, 100 pairs of silver gulls and ten pairs of Pacific gulls, while twenty pairs of crested terns had been found nesting in the spring of 1967.

* * * * *

A *"Cape York"* shore party, which had been on Citadel Island since six o'clock, overhauling the automatic lighthouse, came back for breakfast at 8.0 and I joined them on their return. This was my first experience of the Jacobs ladder, which swayed erratically along the ship's side, with a pinnace dancing at its nether end. I gripped the ropes a little tighter than was strictly necessary and was rewarded at the bottom with: "You do that better than some of our ABs."

There was no way I could let the side down.

The men disembarked on Citadel Island and I was ferried across to Dannevig Island a little to the north. Jumping when the swell lifted the pinnace at an appropriate place, I landed on knees, elbows and chin, but was no more damaged than my dented wristwatch, which sped on, faster than required, as always on islands, where time, tide and sea captains wait for neither man nor maid.

I had three hours to explore this delectable little island of forty-eight acres (20 hectares), lying less than a quarter of a mile south of the Great Glennie and just over six miles from Tidal River on the mainland. Two-thirds of a mile long, it rose steeply to a central ridge 250 feet (76 m) high, the coarse-grained granite sloping almost unbroken to the sea on the more exposed faces. Soil was sparse and mostly at the southern end, but an incredible number of burrowing birds managed to find a living here, insinuating themselves under Poa tussocks or into rock crevices when there was too little soil to dig in.

The precipitous nature of the terrain limited penguins to the lower slopes among pigface and glasswort. Much more exciting were the fairy prions *(Pachyptyla turtur)*, birds that I had got to know during the year spent around the lesser islands of New Zealand. Unfortunately the ones I found were dead, the dove-grey feathers smirched and in disarray, but S. G. Lane found some breeding on the island in 1979 and it is probable that they were doing so twenty years earlier.

As intriguing as the fairy prions, were the diving petrels *(Pelecanoides urinatrix)*, another which I had not come across since leaving New Zealand. Both lived in smaller burrows than the penguins and shearwaters and there were several hundred of such, but no way of telling which species was inside. Lane recorded diving petrels nesting here on his visit.

Shearwater holes were everywhere. Wishing not to get carried away, I conservatively estimated around 4,000 pairs, but Ian Norman, being more businesslike about it in 1979, calculated there to be 44,600 breeding couples. I saw no shags, but Lane recorded thirty black-faced shags nesting on the sheltered east side in 1979.

Fifteen gun-metal grey Cape Barren geese grazed unconcernedly throughout my stay, but kept their distance. This was a habitual rendezvous, their fibrous dung pellets lying everywhere and several big grassy nests were tucked among the tussocks.

Navigators in the early years of the 1800s found them to be plentiful and so tame that they could be grabbed by hand or knocked down with a stick. To their cost, the birds make very good eating. By 1865 Gould wrote that in all its much sung habitats the species was by then "almost extirpated". By 1909 the few survivors had become extremely wary, taking off well ahead of any interloper and not settling within gunshot of cover.

Their shyness remained, hence their liking for the wind-shorn sweeps of bare granite on the seldom visited Glennies. Cape Barren geese seem to be better learners than fairy penguins or shearwaters — or is it just that they are more mobile and better able to put hard won knowledge to effect?

The southern island group, the Ansers, had been named for these noble members of the Anseriformes, as had Goose Island in the Furneaux Group. I had fine views of the first as I rested on the heights of Dannevig, with the calls of sooty oystercatchers and silver gulls wafting up from the shoreline, where twenty pairs of Pacific gulls were found nesting in 1980.

All these islands were of silver granite, great smooth sweeps of it, polished by the wind. Huge boulders were rounded by onion scale weathering, like the redder, more imposing Devil's Marbles near Tennant Creek in the Northern Territory. Crevice plants were few.

While some tea-trees managed to reach several feet high in the lee of bluffs, most remained prostrate, hugging the rock. Many attained great age, some died while quite small. Succulents, creepers and tussocks withstood frequent douchings with sea water and broad mats of glasswort, the traditional king of the saltmarsh, coated the summit!

I recorded twenty different plants and Norman added another five. Shrubs were sparse, but included sea box, white correa and kangaroo apple. Herbs were leek lily, angled lobelia, Austral and rufous stonecrops *(Crassula sieberiana* and *macrantha)* and tall daisies *(Brachycome diversifolia).*

Conditions were idyllic and atypical today, but I was soon to experience March gales as fierce as any of the traditional ones at home. Even now the quink-blue sea met the land in a necklace of creamy foam.

There were twelve sailors in the boat which edged in towards the rocks to collect me for lunch. The mate on watch was in charge, with a crew of two, the rest had been working on the Citadel light, spitting and polishing, painting and greasing. I got my timing right and landed in the space cleared for me, then slipped on some seaweed and skated under the bow seat into the bilge water. The ensuing good-natured quips were something I had to get used to, fast.

* * * * *

Back with the men after lunch, I was put onto the smaller island of McHugh. I made a neater job of the landing but found it slightly perilous scaling the granite ramparts above. The rewards were great.

This is the southernmost of the Glennies and part of the National Park, with restricted access. Covering over twenty-two acres (9 hectares), it rises to 211 feet (65 metres) and is a quarter of a mile long. Much was bare, most of the rest, tussocky with Austral hollyhock and storksbill, seaberry saltbush, correa, golden everlasting and straight wattle *(Acacia stricta)*. The eighteen species found were all natives.

A posse of geese took off in the direction of Great Glennie as I climbed. McHugh, like Dannevig, was honeycombed with bird burrows, those of penguins congregated where there was easy access to the sea.

Several scientists, Harris, Deerson and Lane, came ashore here a decade later and reckoned there to be a thousand occupied penguin burrows in November, with eggs, small chicks and fully-grown chicks present simultaneously. Their estimate of shearwater burrows was 6,200. Such counts are tedious and time-consuming and I usually took refuge in being a botanist when conscience told me that I should be making the attempt.

I did count several hundred smaller burrows among tussocks on the lower slopes, attributing these to diving petrels, as carcases of this species lay among them. The holes were shorter, as well as neater, not much more than eighteen inches long.

A dumpy bird hauled from a burrow was uncannily like the little auk of the Northern Hemisphere, except for the tubular nostrils on top of the chunky beak. Ecologically it is the southern counterpart of that arctic species, although penguins stand in for the larger auks. The diving petrels' legs are set well back, for use as a rudder, the motive power for swimming being supplied by the wings. They are even clumsier on land than are shearwaters, their flight fluttery and a long run needed for take-off.

I sent a dry carcase and a broken egg off to Dom Serventy on the Furneaux Group next day from the lighthouse on Wilsons Promontory, forgetful that, although a mainland station, access was by sea only. My parcel went off in Harry Brochie's boat that same afternoon, but we caught up with it two days later at Deal Island. It was then on its tortuous way to Port Albert in Victoria, although now more than halfway to its ultimate destination. I congratulated myself that it was for the record only and not a museum shelf. Islanders in those days had to practise patience.

Some of the small McHugh burrows could have belonged to fairy prions, several of which were found incubating eggs there in November 1978 (and ringed), more in November 1979. A few Pacific gulls nested, while sooty oystercatchers and black-faced shags were around, with the inevitable silver gulls.

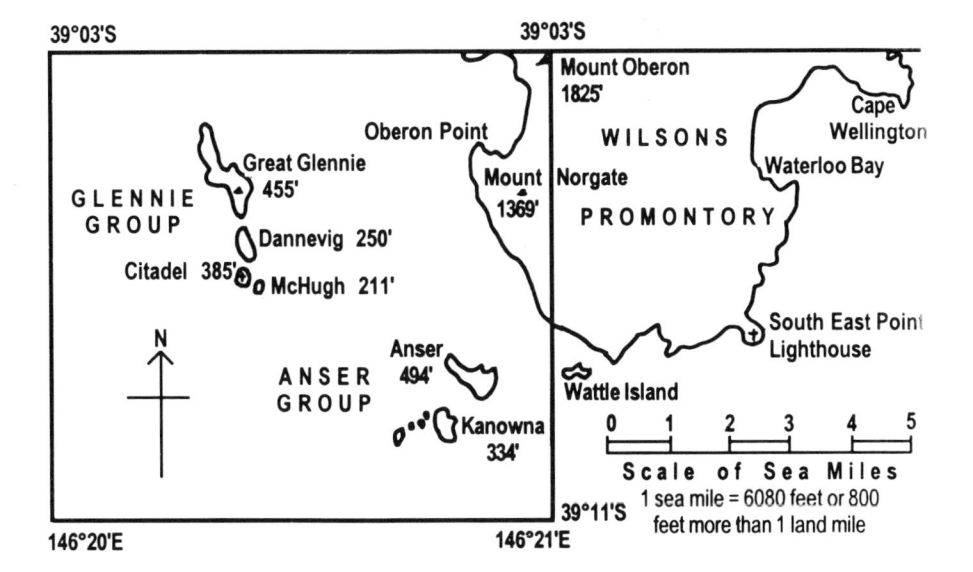

138 Sketch Map of the Glennies and Ansers off Wilsons Promontory

139 Cape Barren Geese *Cereopsis novaehollandiae* on Dannevig Island with SS "*Cape York*" and Citadel Island

140 Fairy Prions *Pachyptila turtur*

2. CITADEL ISLAND, WILSONS PROMONTORY AND THE ANSERS

At 'cuppa' time the pinnace collected me to join the men on Citadel Island. Sustained by a pint of black billy tea from a chipped enamel mug, I climbed the 356 feet (110 metres) to the summit. Citadel is the most barren of the four islands, occupying forty-three acres (18 ha) and rising directly from the sea to the crowning elegance of the square white lighthouse — unmanned then, as all but one of the Australian lighthouses were to be before the end of the 1980s.

There was much opposition during the 1960s and 1970s to the automation of the lights. Government maintained that 50,000 dollars a year were saved by taking the families off the lighthouse stations and the Australian Lighthouses Association had been formed to fight this policy. Each light automated caused job losses for the three resident keepers and their stand-ins when they took shore leave.

It also deprived the area of its nature wardens, weather observers and coastguard-style watchers, effective in raising alarms and saving lives at sea. The Association's first success was in 1981, when it was agreed to keep Maatsuyker Island lighthouse manned — this off the far south-west of Tasmania and one of our ports of call on this voyage. By the end of the 1980s such voyages as ours with the forty-strong band of men on "*Cape York*" had ceased, the servicing of lights being achieved by helicopters manned by just a few. Even little Citadel Island had found room on its summit for a helipad.

SS "*Cape York*" had succeeded SS "*Lady Loch*" but was not replaced: just withdrawn from service as the age of technology pursued its relentless course through the seventies and eighties.

Before this, in 1967, the automatic "white hut lights" were installed on Holloway Point on the north-east tip of Flinders Island adjacent to Stanley Point, and on Cape Barren Island and Cat Island. We visited the first in 1995. Squat and dowdy among low tumps of everlasting and *Olearia* daisy bushes and beard heath, it was unimpressive by Goose Island standards, although no doubt serving passing mariners adequately.

Small, solar-powered navigation lights had been set up around Franklin Sound by then: another link in the advance from that first of the radio beacons installed at the Cape Otway light in Victoria in 1937.

On Citadel Island stark granite surfaces were continuous from the helipad to the sea in parts, with no plants able to grow closer to sea level than about thirty feet on the west. So much spray was hurled at this side when the westerlies were doing their worst, that runnels had been scoured in the coarse-grained rock by the backwash, these channelling drainage waters into little rivulets. Annual rainfall measured at the Wilsons Promontory lighthouse was forty-one and a half inches (1,040 mm), with 50% of the recorded winds coming from the west.

Erosion along vertical joints had left upstanding rectangular blocks several yards high, these toppling eventually to add to the jumble of boulders on the beach. Granite shingle, like railway ballast, had collected in open depressions and such soil as there was contained a lot of big quartz crystals.

Only on the less steep eastern side, where shelter was afforded by the other islands, did vegetation approach near sea level. Surprisingly, there was sufficient to support rabbits. These had been introduced in 1913 to provide food for a temporary keeper when the lighthouse was first installed. An old photograph shows the vegetation to have been much thicker then. In 1959, I estimated the plant cover to be less than five per cent on all but the eastern patch of scrub. In conditions of such exposure, and the knowledge that the tea-tree scrub had been cut into, it is unfair to blame the rabbits for all the denudation, but they must have contributed to it.

When Norman and Brown visited Citadel Island in 1978 and 1979, they saw neither rabbits nor rabbit dung, nor any sign of their grazing, so it is likely that the rather precariously poised population had died out by then. They also recorded a marked recovery in the vegetation, except where irreparable soil loss had occurred in the north — as proved by the size of dead tea-tree stumps too large to have grown from the bare rock that remained. Elsewhere they found that the scrub had spread, recording twenty-three flowering plants and two ferns where I (albeit visiting in a drought) had found only seven flowering plants and one fern twenty years earlier.

The persistent fern was the blunt spleenwort *(Asplenium obtusatum)*, the newcomer, lamentably, was bracken — only two plants so far. Somewhat unexpected on my 1959 visit were two mosses, *Sematophyllum komomallum* and *Campylopus introflexus*, and a liverwort, *Marchantia cephaloscypha*. These would be boosted by the atmospheric humidity and not interfered with by rabbits.

Species surviving both rabbits and drought were pigface, variable groundsel, tall lobelia and a grass *(Danthonia caespitosa)*, along with the Poa, tea-tree and correa; all natives. Four of the newcomers were alien British weeds, but three were woody — coast wattle, sticky daisy bush *(Olearia glutinosa)* and a wattle relative, *Albizzia lophantha*. Perhaps their seeds or roots had been lying doggo until conditions improved. Perhaps they had come with the wind from Tidal River across the water, or other islands, perhaps with visiting humans.

I saw signs of burrowing penguins, but nothing else apart from the usual skinks. It seemed that these had a role to play in the food chain, as there were no less than three pale-bellied peregrines sailing overhead, on the lookout for supper. Norman and Brown suspected two peregrine eyries on the island, suggesting territories going off in opposite directions, to prevent belligerent encounters. By one nest was the remains of a fairy prion and not far off that of a diving petrel.

They found a lively colony of fifty nesting pairs of fairy prions, but breeding of diving petrels remained unproven. Nevertheless, it is good to know that these two uncommon species have such a substantial footing on the Glennies. Neither I nor Lane, who visited in 1979, verified shearwater presence, but

Norman and Brown found 111 shearwater burrows in the eastern tussock and a few elsewhere.

Penguins, I thought to be quite numerous and Lane found thirty burrows with breeding pairs and another fifteen with moulting adults, this an underestimate, because of the inaccessibility of many potential sites.

Black-faced cormorants came winging in from the sea, feet stretched well forward to act as landing brakes. A few Cape Barren geese, sooty oystercatchers and Pacific gulls were among the ever-present smaller gulls. The ubiquitous British blackbird was here too, some bold spirit having ventured across from the mainland, while Norman and Brown saw silver-eyes and olive whistlers. On my visit there were swallows, exploiting the unusual calm to hawk the flies metamorphosing from brackish rock pools.

My exploration of the island over, I found some swift footwork necessary to jump clear when the folk above jettisoned a trolley-load of rock ballast left over from 'flying fox' repairs — this the steep tramway leading from landing to lighthouse. I was also narrowly missed by a slithering length of metal cable when I was lowering myself backward down the rope to the departure boat in the evening. Those notices one sees around announcing "Danger, men at work" are not just cosmetic.

* * * * *

Supper on board was invariably tea and toasted sandwiches. Sleep, equally invariably, was achieved in the face of the clonkings, clashings and plumbing noises that are part and parcel of every working ship. The cooling water jet shot out to sea just above my right ear and everything that could be contrived to be noisy was. The heat below decks was suffocating, with one blanket one too many, but it was calm enough to have the porthole open and I slept the sleep of the exhausted.

While I did so, "*Cape York*" steamed past the Ansers Group and round the tip of Wilsons Promontory to anchor in Waterloo Bay to the east. This was the scene of a well remembered rescue of the McCoy Society, stranded there in camp the previous year. The rescue had been made by Harry Brochie, the same who took my petrel carcase for its tour of Bass Strait. The memory had not faded and the extent of his disgust was reiterated in both officers' mess and captain's smoke room.

"There's me, risking me life for them and overturning me fibreglass dinghy twice and what did they put on board first? Guess what." He paused for effect. "The bloody portable toilet. Hundreds of pound's worth of valuable equipment standing out in the rain and they had to salvage THAT! I was buggered if I was taking anything else on board after that — except bods." I quelled a chuckle. I had been part of the McCoy Society's subsequent stay on the prom in January 1959, in company with the offending toilet, but we had got away in good order that time, with no more than a wetting.

When I emerged on deck we were lying off the lighthouse on South-east Point.

This was built in 1859, the beam having a range of twenty-five nautical miles in clear weather. The advance party had already been ashore for two hours. The main task was to demolish the old wartime quarters of the Royal Australian Air Force and dump the rubble over the cliff — this taking a full two days.

I made the rock landing successfully, nipping smartly up the granite slab to avoid being caught by the next wave. The Scottish AB who had appointed himself as my assistant was well and truly caught. He came racing up the slab with a gleefully chuckling wave curling round his shorts and up under his armpits, coming to a breathless halt with: "There'd a' bin a flow o' language then if ye hadna bin there."

It was a constant source of amusement on board, the way men admonished each other to watch their language in the presence of a lady. I'm sure it did them a power of good!

Browsing gently along the eastern shore, I ascended the hill dominated by a spectacular granite boulder, fifty feet high and split in two by lightning in some fearsome storm. The western side of the point proved as barren as the western sides of the islands. Not so the landscape generally. On the low extremity where the lighthouse stands, connected to the main promontory only in the north-west and rising to 381 feet (117 metres), I listed 180 different species during my short walk. True, eighty of these were alien 'weed' species around the lighthouse, leaving only 100 dinkum natives, but this was a great many more than on the islands, where isolation, wind and spray and bird burrowing combined to suppress plant life.

Much of the bare granite was the outcome of fires which had swept through the area in 1930 and 1951. Previous to this, the officers told me, the whole area had been scrub covered, with no bare rock visible from the sea. Now the west side was scarred by deep erosion channels and most of the finer particles had washed away, leaving a matrix of granite chippings with dusty organic soils confined to crevices.

The leafless broom spurge dominating the low western heath was the prostrate form found in Western Tasmania. Drooping she-oke formed little spinneys in the south, these grading into coast tea-tree on the east.

Wallaby grazing was severe in parts and there was plenty of rabbit dung about. The grass-leaved trigger plant seemed to be the most constantly grazed species, but even the acrid noon flower was nibbled. In the absence of nesting birds, the woody species approached quite close to the sea — regardless of spray — coast spear grass and silver tussock being compressed into a narrow belt above the coastal fringe of succulents.

The Ansers lay about a couple of miles offshore to the west — seventy-four hectares of Anser Island and thirty-one hectares of Kanowna Island. The first, which is a mile long, is almost 500 feet (152 m) high, the second, at half a mile long, gets to 312 feet (95 m). About one and a half miles from Anser Island is the sheer granite monolith known as Skull Rock — higher than Kanowna at 371 feet (113 m).

Fairy prions bred on both the larger Anser Islands, along with the usual shearwaters and fairy penguins. Diving petrels nested on Kanowna, where a dead white-faced storm petrel has also been found — Cape Barren geese and an unusually large colony of twenty pairs of Pacific gulls bred on Anser Island.

Kanowna hosted a thousand or more Australian fur seals, which pulled ashore in the north, where they had flattened a considerable area of silver tussock — limiting the seaward spread of the shearwater colony. Anser differs vegetatively from the others in being more than half covered by a herbfield of Austral hollyhock and seaberry saltbush.

A skein of geese flew past my viewpoint on the mainland, some forty strong, headed for the quiet of the islands. Black-faced shags were engaged in desultory fishing offshore and sooty oystercatchers were feeding on mussels. They caught these unawares with the shells open, just before the falling tide left them high and dry, attacking first the muscle controlling shell closure, so that they were unable to clam up on them.

I happened in upon the principal keeper and wife at the lighthouse just in time for that old Australian custom, afternoon tea. A beautiful collection of seashells was on show and plants of various sorts adorned the enclosed verandah of this cosy, well kept haven in the wilderness.

Not all, it seemed, were so content. I was accompanied to the tip of the peninsula later by two small boys, part of the family of eight of one of the assistant keepers. Mama was away in hospital producing the ninth! The ten-year-old explained that he and his mum didn't like it here — too cold in winter — and that they were going to Queensland as soon as the current baby was big enough to travel. He seemed not to have twigged that the succession of babies too small to travel was still in the pipeline.

Papa, a cheery, burly soul, normally attended to the schooling (by correspondence course) of the six oldest. He had joined the lighthouse service quite recently in order to get a house large enough to accommodate the ten of them, plus come what may. Previously they had been living in two houses. Few young keepers could afford a house when first married and the lighthouse service solved the problem if they were the right type — just as the Antarctic Division did for men saving up to buy property.

Down at the point the wreckers were indulging their destructive urges to their heart's content, with much clattering and shouting. I climbed into the jeep with them at knocking off time, for the perilous passage down the steep ramp to the landing.

Sunday for me was a day of rest, writing up notes, pressing plant specimens, chatting with Chief Mate Lines, in the chart room and McKay at the back end of his inevitable fishing line. The demolition had still a long way to go by nightfall, but it was decided to move on to Cliffy Island, as the weather promised to crack up and there were light-keepers waiting to be swapped. We forthwith chugged off eastward and anchored off Cliffy at ten o'clock.

141 Cape Barren Geese *(Cereopsis)* in flight:
SS "*Cape York*" and the Ansers

142 Sooty Oystercatcher *Haematopus fuliginosus* and
Sea Rocket *Cakile edentula*

143 Tattered Coastal Paperbarks *Melaleuca ericifola*

3. GABO AND CLIFFY ISLANDS

Ships' captains must, above all things, be versatile and able to change plans at the drop of a hat — or the slap of a wave. With forty on the payroll, time spent on the voyage costs more money than fuel for steaming extra sea miles, and we had recourse to zigzag across the strait in an illogical manner to find places peaceful enough to hole up in and get on with the job. Thus it was that we came next, not to Cliffy Island but to Gabo.

Gabo Island lies only four to five miles from the New South Wales border, off the sandy lagoon and dune country of Mallacoota. It is bigger than the islands visited previously — one and a half miles from north to south and two-thirds of a mile across, occupying roughly 420 acres (170 ha) and rising to 171 feet. Telegraph Point, the nearest part of the mainland, is only a few hundred yards away and many years ago the island was accessible from here across a connecting sandspit at low tide.

The island loomed large outside the porthole at daybreak and we went ashore early, to find ourselves among thousands of penguin burrows, where birds swarming in at dusk spread over the dunescape of the northern sandy neck. It was warm and there was much to be done. By midday I was well away on the eastern shore — too far from the jetty to return for lunch — so I sustained myself with home-grown blackberries and watercress.

Feral cats were obviously having a ball at the birds' expense. The light-keepers had told me that the last of the mutton birds had died out two years before, but I came upon a small colony in the east and another in the west. Examination of the eastern rookery showed most burrows to be abandoned and overgrown. In an area containing forty occupied nests I found the dead remains of thirty birds, apparently, freshly killed. Fourteen of these (just the wings and skeleton) had been taken to an unburrowed peaty hollow six yards across by the marauder. If the progeny of former lighthouse keeper's cats continued to prowl, the island it seemed that the two remnant shearwater colonies were doomed to extinction.

Penguins were a tougher proposition as pussy prey, but during subsequent years the Gabo penguins fared little better at the hands of marauding cray fishermen. At all too frequent intervals outraged reports appeared in the press, telling of hordes of penguins taken from this unusually accessible colony to bait the cray pots.

Most burrowed among noon flower, little else except buffalo grass being able to withstand the high degree of disturbance and guano. These graded out through tussock grass and sedge to bracken and so to the heathy scrub and peaty hollows of the island centre. Every isolated pocket of nesting burrows inland showed the same concentric zonation, which illustrates the incompatibility of native heath plants and burrowing birds.

A few sheep and cattle were grazed on the island, but these lived mainly on the buffalo grass around the lighthouse, leaving the heathland to its own devices. Tea-tree was dominant of most, with banksia and wattle. The rather unimpressive leafless broom spurge was again the first of the heath plants to come in as the noon flower faded out, its tiny clusters of brown and cream flowers no match for the brilliant magenta of the other.

Sweet wattle *(Acacia suaveolens)* and coast wattle were interspersed with red-flowered dusky pea *(Kennedya rubicunda)* and running postman *(Kennedya prostrata)*. There was Victorian heath, tree broom heath, prickly geebung *(Persoonia juniperina)*, cranberry heath *(Astroloma humifusum)* and poverty raspwort *(Haloragis tetragyna)*, with twiggy daisy bush *(Olearia ramulosa)* and satin everlasting *(Helichrysum leucopsideum)*. I found 136 species of flowering plants in all, forty-one of these aliens.

The heathland was fairly unadulterated, in contrast to the disturbed rookery areas, where some of the less usual interlopers were black nightshade, creeping wood sorrel, small-flowered mallow and Capeweed. Some, like spiked mint, cape gooseberry and a fig tree were garden escapes.

Sheep's sorrel was characteristic, this a sure indicator of acid soil in its native Britain, as indeed are most of the Gabo heath plants in Victoria. The parent rock was siliceous, an attractive rose-pink granite dominating the north coast and the barren east point, where the forty-eight metre high red granite lighthouse sent out its warning of reefs and shoals to coastal shipping to a distance of twenty-six nautical miles.

Where scrub had been cleared under the telephone lines from landing to lighthouse, climbing plants such as love creeper and twining glycine *(Glycine clandestina)* grew with rough fireweed *(Senecio hispidulus)*.

By the time I reached the lighthouse the sun had been overtaken by a great bank of cloud and a chilsome wind had sprung up. I took refuge, and afternoon tea, with the principal keeper and his wife in their big rambling house. The blackberries tasted much better made into jam and spread on buttered scones under a generous dollop of home churned cream from one of the house cows.

Neither the principal keeper nor his wife were much more than five feet two inches tall, a cheery elderly couple who loved island life but were due to retire the next year. They proposed to live as close as possible to their island retreat on the adjacent mainland.

A minimum deposit of £2,000 was required on a house at that time, a sum that they had managed to save while enjoying the free housing that was an obvious incentive to joining up. Regional lighthouse officer Conway was adamant that new recruits were warned of all the snags before joining and most settled well, meticulously observing rule number one — that the light must be kept going at all costs, even when this meant turning it by hand all night in the event of a breakdown. The keepers in their turn sang Conway's praises, well pleased with the way he did his best to supply their every reasonable need.

Peering through the telescope at a passing cargo ship from Britain, I could not but contrast this way of life with that of the mainlander. During my island career I had been involved with keepers from West Wales to New Zealand, on 'family stations' and 'bachelor rocks', and had heard few grumbles.

Gabo Island, on the corner of the continent, is the turning point west or north for coastal shipping and a lighthouse was started here in 1845, fourteen years before that on the continent's most southerly point at the tip of Wilsons Promontory. Unfortunately the money ran out after two years and the work stopped. It took the wrecking of the barque-rigged steamship, *"Monumental City"*, with the loss of fifty-five lives, to get the project going again.

For nine years the light shone from a hastily rigged wooden tower before today's handsome red granite edifice took over. Red arcs above the main light warned mariners not to turn too soon, while these were still visible.

The Gabo light continued to be manned when so many of the lighthouse men were being laid off at automation. If a lighthouse site is too small for a helicopter to land, as is the Bishop Rock light off the Scilly Isles in Britain, a helipad is built on top of the tower, so that maintenance engineers can drop in directly from the sky to see to the smooth running of the works.

On Gabo there was still the personal touch, the friendly quips on the ships' radios, warnings of the unexpected and administration of first aid where needed. This personal involvement was manifested on 18th December 1982, when a contestant in the solo round-the-world yacht race was wrecked on the island. The yachtsman, Desmond Hampton, managed to get ashore and it was fortunate for him that the light was still manned, so that he found immediate aid.

It was a mile's walk across the island to the landing and I was about halfway when the brewing storm broke. As I arrived, drenched, at the departure point, a boat was speeding off to the ship. One of the two assistant keepers leapt off the tractor and ran onto the jetty, gesticulating for it to come back. It did, saving me an hour's wet wait for the next, which came in for the two engineers. There was another wetting in sea water on the return passage, but one cannot be wetter than wet and hot drinks and toasted sandwiches would be coming up soon.

There was a mainland light to service on the morrow and we spent the day anchored off Cape Everard, while the men worked on the Point Hicks lighthouse. We lay 110 km east of the eastern end of the Ninety Mile Beach, but the coastline was still a bland, unbroken stretch of surf-washed sand and half-vegetated dunes.

Conway had been instrumental in stabilising the blowing sand around the lighthouse by planting coast spinifex and kikuyu grasses, this rendering the tractor track from landing to light more stable. Just around the corner rose the Captain Cook memorial.

No bird colonies were known here, so I did not go ashore. The most fascinating hours were spent peering over the ship's rail with 'Chiefy' at the wide assortment of marine creatures, many of them phosphorescent, even in daylight, when rumpled by passing water currents.

* * * * *

A banging on my cabin door soon after five next morning was followed by "Up, if ye want to go ashore on Cliffy".

Awhile later, as we undulated over the aftermath of the storm in the hard worked pinnace, the sun rose as a fireball above the horizon, flooding the world with crimson. I thought smugly of how much beauty the lay-abeds miss.

A not too easy landing had been made easier by the blasting of footholds from the granite in critical places, and I was soon away up the rock dome which occupied nineteen acres (8 ha) and rose to 140 feet (43 m). We were further from the mainland here — fourteen miles (22 km) — but were on the more sheltered, eastern side of Wilsons Promontory. About 400 x 300 yards (370 x 260 m) of island was bounded by cliffs towering a sheer 100 feet (30 m) on the south and east, with more gently rising gradients elsewhere.

Shearwaters were concentrated in the Poa tussock south of the summit lighthouse, the only place where soil was deep enough for burrowing. Elsewhere chunky pigface, glasswort and groundsels — crept over the rocks and buck's-horn plantain, plumbed crevices with its long taproots.

Blunt spleenwort was here again — equivalent of Britain's only maritime fern, the sea spleenwort. It has characteristically fleshy yellow-green fronds based in crannies, always coastal and often douched with sea spray. When cultivated in more hospitable garden soils, it burgeons into a prolific green tuft resembling the shining spleenwort *(Asplenium lucidum)* so closely as to cast doubt on its existence as a separate species rather than a coastal variety of the other.

I reckoned there to be only about 100 shearwater burrows and the colony was still small when Hope and Dunk visited in 1967, but Mike Harris and Dearson, who visited in 1978, estimated 6,300 burrows. This sharp increase might be attributable to the automation of the lighthouse in 1971, with consequent evacuation of people and animals. The light had been manned for a century, with all the wear and tear concentrated in the small area of deep soil, plus the depredations of cats and dogs. (A delightful roly-poly black puppy was part of the 1959 establishment, with a lot of nefarious deeds to be perpetrated as he grew from puppyhood.)

In 1886 lighthouse keeper Dunk sent diving petrel bodies and eggs away for identification and the Melbourne Bird Observers' Club had recorded fairy prions here in the distant past.

The diving petrels came ashore in June and July to prepare their nest sites and laid eggs towards the end of July. Both species would be easy prey for cats and dogs and have not been recorded since. Now that the birds have the place to themselves, apart from occasional helicopter visits to service the light, it is possible that these smaller petrels may recolonise.

Mattingley recorded silver gulls on the island in 1938 and about 100 pairs were nesting in 1959. On the 1978 visit only one lone pair was present. Perhaps the colony had moved to the mainland, where the pickings around the burgeoning tourist camps or urban rubbish tips provided a more lucrative living.

The small population of penguins, formerly present, seems to have left the island. Some were about in 1938 and 1959 but none in 1978. Small flocks of Cape Barren geese came and went and there were the usual sooty oystercatchers, stalking across the shore, prising open mussels and other small shellfish rather than the oysters that their name suggests should be their favourites.

Guano from the gull colony fouled but enriched the waters of the little brackish rock pools in their breeding areas and initiated a mini food chain culminating in thousands of wriggling mosquito larvae. Some of these had metamorphosed, invading the *"Cape York"* in clouds, to complete their life story with a boost of seamen's blood.

At 8.0 a.m. I joined the engineers, mechanics and relieving lighthouse keeper in the principal keeper's house, for a hugely satisfying breakfast. The head keeper sported the enormous ginger beard so commonly produced by men 'in the field', regardless of hair colour. Off afterwards for more botanising, until time for departure.

As we sped towards the ship there was a yell from the shore asking if 'one of the girls' could come aboard. Chief Officer Lines at the tiller muttered some uncomplimentary quips about females in general, glanced covertly at me and added: "Ones who wear skirts". Nevertheless, he turned back and she came aboard, skirt and all.

Lighthouse keepers' wives and daughters often refused to climb the Jacob's ladder and were swung aboard from the pinnace in a big oblong basket, but this lass made no bones about it, so Lines need not have worried. I conducted her on a tour of the ship, the blind leading the blind, as we pulled out towards the tip of Wilsons Promontory, where the rest of the day would be devoted to completing the demolition of the old air force base.

Seals were basking on northern rocks under the Cliffy Island gullery, but this was not a breeding colony. The other islands of the group lay to the west and north of the lighthouse site. They had no history of habitation by man, goats, dogs and cats, so their wildlife was in better shape.

Mutton birds nested in profusion among the tussocks of Rag Island and Seal or Direction Island. The other two, Notch Island and White Rock, were little more than granitic extrusions, with scant soil or plant life to accommodate animals.

The anchor came up at sundown and we settled into the next leg of the journey across Bass Strait to the Tasmanian lights, me making up a canasta four in the captain's cabin, with his Nibs, Conway and engineer Brian.

Our route took us approximately along the more easterly of the two underwater ridges, now sunken, but in times past connecting Tasmania to mainland Australia. The westerly ridge passes north from the opposite corner of the island state, through King Island to the Mornington Peninsula in Victoria, leaving the Otway Basin to its west.

The easterly ridge surfacing as the Furneaux Group, turns towards the west there to surface as the Kent and Hogans Groups and join up with Wilsons Promontory, leaving the Gippsland Basin to its east. Between the two is the Bass Basin, sometimes cut off from the sea for prolonged periods in geological time, when land deposits of sandstone, shale and coal piled up on its floor. Fluctuations in sea level as the continental plate slid north, carrying the region away from Antarctica, have amounted to as much as 585 feet (180 m) as icecaps built up, trapping water, or melted, releasing it into the sea.

The last retreat of the icecaps, bringing sea level up to isolate the island groups as we know them today, occurred around 10,000 years ago. A complex story of change has been unravelled by marine geologists.

Gazing into the darkened waters dividing around "*Cape York*'s" bow, the depths yielded none of their secrets. To mariners they could be as benign or treacherous over the ridges as over the basins, and the archipelagos could be havens or hazards.

144 Automatic Lighthouse on Citadel Island, view north

145 Dusky Coral Pea *Kennedya rubicunda*

146 White-fronted Tern *Sterna striata*

Chapter Seventeen

SOUTH WITH "*CAPE YORK*" THROUGH THE TASMAN SEA

1. SWAN ISLAND, EDDYSTONE POINT AND CAPE FORESTIER

The often stormy waters of Banks Strait separate Clarke Island, the most southerly of the Furneaux Group, from the north-east corner of Tasmania, twenty-five miles away. Lying off the larger land mass and twelve miles east of Cape Portland, is Swan Island, with Little Swan and Cygnet Islands to its west.

Big Swan comprises the most seaward hazard to ships following the east coast of Tasmania to pass west of the Furneaux, and was the obvious place for a lighthouse. The need for this, and others on Goose and Deal Islands, was first pointed out in 1841 by the Governor in Hobart, Sir John Franklin, who, as an ex-naval officer, was well aware of the dangers, but nothing materialised for four years. It took two shipwrecks claiming four hundred and twenty-three lives, the "*Mary*" and the "*Cateraqui*", before the go-ahead was given.

Swan Island was the central of three lights in a straight line through Banks Strait, with Goose Island to the north and Eddystone Point to the south. It beamed its first warning messages in 1845 from a tower eighty-five feet (28 metres) high.

While Goose Island harbours geese, Swan Island has no swans, but a few pelicans nest among the more run of the mill mutton birds, oystercatchers and gulls. The island is now a designated Heritage Area.

"*Cape York*" hove to off the Swan Island jetty on the morning of Sunday 22nd March 1959. Viewed from the deck, the island appeared like a monstrous sand heap, with dunes piled over smooth dark rock, two-thirds of them mobile, with bare sand patches vulnerable to every wind that blew.

The previous motive power for haulage work had been bullocks — two Friesians, one black and one Devon Longhorn which: "Jumps fences like a racehorse, but won't go when saddled and mounted by a would-be jockey."

Today it was a miniature caterpillar tractor standing about three feet high which came to meet the boat. Mobile dunes extended from coast to coast, only partially stabilised by bracken, grass and sedge. No way could wheeled traffic cover the considerable stretch of loose sand between lighthouse and jetty and any attempted road might well be undermined by the first gale. There was, however, an airstrip at the other end of the island, where the fortnightly supplies came in.

Elongated from west to east, Swan Island is approximately two miles long and half a mile wide, covering around six hundred acres and rising to a hundred and nine feet. Fortuitously more rock was exposed where the lighthouse was needed on the eastern point. Elsewhere it surfaced only where the sand was washed or blown away. We were off the granite now. This was dolerite, fine-textured and with a slaty cleavage.

The dunes, as always with so much space waiting to be colonised, were rich in plant species. I listed a hundred and four in the morning, from the eelgrass of the tidal sands to the swamp paperbarks of the centre. One of the commonest was marram grass, presumably introduced as the world's most efficient sand-binder, although going out of favour in the Australia of the nineties, in favour of indigenous species.

Tasmanian coast everlasting *(Helichrysum gunnii)*, knobby club-rush and sword grass (both actually sedges) were helping the bracken to hold the western dunes, with a little coast tea-tree and South African boxthorn. Sheep and cattle, which seemed to have the run of the island, came to drink at moist hollows containing yellow buttons, mauve monkey-flower and streaked arrow-grass and areas of tussock had been burned.

I worked my way across to the lighthouse, below which was a colony of about five hundred pairs of silver gulls. Nesting was over, with only a small legacy of fully fledged young still hanging around the rocks below. From the profusion of angular yellow seeds in the fabric of the nests and spilling from the disintegrating crop pellets, it looked as though these had been brought up on bower spinach berries.

Three pairs of pelicans had nested regularly on the north coast during past years, arriving about 15th March and staying only until the gawky young fledged. They used rocks so windswept that I could scarcely stand up straight — and I had not thought it all that windy today. Certainly Swan Island seemed to collect more than its share of what was about.

Crested terns idled below the gullery and coordinated squadrons of small waders, resembling black-capped dotterels and referred to locally as sandpipers, fed across the tidal sands.

Climbing the lighthouse tower, I spotted light-keeper George Gough conferring with Conway on the airstrip. Heading their way to find out where the mutton bird rookery was, I was directed to the far corner of the island and hurried thither with time at a premium, as always. Skylarks trilled aloft and a nan keen kestrel hung motionless — a mobile unmoved by the draught — watching the grass for movement. Was it after a skink, I wondered, these being much the most visible of the small ground life.

I spotted the dark shapes of two tiger snakes on the Yorkshire fog grass of the rookery — these no doubt availing themselves of the shelter of the bird burrows and partaking of the odd poultry breakfast in season.

I was to be picked up at the jetty by the boat bringing the keeper back from lunch on board, but the smoke room conviviality was protracted and this arrived an hour behind schedule. I was very cold by then and could have wished myself back in the comparative shelter of the rookery had I not been entertained by a cow fur seal which came nosing around the jetty to keep me company. She was obviously used to people in this location and had no fears.

When the boat materialised George Gough and mechanic Kenny Baker emerged from under a dripping tarpaulin. I took their place, spray slopping noisily onto my cover all the way back. George was the keeper from Bruny Island who was holding the fort on Swan Island, wifeless and single-handed, after travelling up to fill the breach when the resident head keeper's wife died and the assistant resigned. We had brought Kenny to keep him company and help with the chores, until such time as we returned with reliefs.

These were the old head keeper and a new young cow puncher from the New South Wales outback, who, with his wife, was having his first taste of lighthouse life. The English principal keeper, ex-Indian Army and said to have a yen for talking about 'When I was in Poona', was not quite his type and the new man did not jump at the suggestion that they share the chief's house until their own was done up. I hope they hit it off in the end. Islands are too small for incompatibles to share, but then so are islands of humanity in the vast spaces of the outback. Aussies outside the cities have to learn to be very forbearing or very self-sufficient.

Back ashore it seemed that the bullocks were being marshalled for work, but the bovine kerfuffle proved to be the arrival of Mollie, who was to accompany us to Bruny Island, with a stop off at Hobart for some green grass.

She created quite a diversion during her stay on board and became known as Sabrina — because of her waist line, or lack of it. Four or five seamen persuaded her out along the jetty into the ship's horse box, which was swung off into the pinnace by crane and winched onto "*Cape York*'s" deck. Here she was penned in a corner and consented to settle when offered hay and cake.

Mollie had the reputation of being a nice natured cow but temperamental and given to kicking at milking time or liable to hold her milk back if she felt so inclined. Only two of us on board owned up to being able to milk. After almost five years of hand milking during my wartime service in Britain's Women's Land Army, I felt fairly competent. Geordie, on the other hand, had been a farmer's boy on the outskirts of Durham only until he had run away to sea at the ripe age of sixteen. Together we took her on.

Mollie thought very little of either of us. The first afternoon we collected only clotted milk from the front teats, which were sore on the outside, and about two quarts from the back ones. This we got in spasms, Geordie squatting to milk and me holding the can and swinging it clear each time the bony black leg lifted.

She beat me to it once and we finished with little more than a mugful. This Chiefy, who was cheering us on throughout, took to the galley, strained and put out on deck to cool in the breeze — a special reward for me, who complained the loudest about the powdered substitute. It was the real thing, but pathetically thin.

Geordie achieved nothing in the evening, so we changed places from then on and I stowed a couple of quarts in the smoke room fridge for future use. Had there not always been about ten crew members round the pen, giving spurious support and dubious advice, we might more easily have lulled our charge into a sense of security, but we gradually developed an understanding.

I was to see Swan Island lighthouse — second oldest tower under the control of the Department of Transport — twice more. This was the earliest Australian lighthouse still intact, together with its original lantern, and is now regarded as a building of national importance. Lanterns of this calibre were replaced in all other lights in the 1890s.

The tower itself is a modified Tuscan Doric column with plain base and expertly worked freestone capital. Attractive ruins round about consist of the original oil store and the convict light-keepers' quarters, both roofless. The original superintendent's quarters, abandoned around 1953, came to be used as a drinking water catchment. Shown in the accompanying sketch are the subsequent oil store and wireless room.

We returned in due course with the old, bereaved, keeper and the new, betrothed, cow hand, accompanied by an eight-week-old cocker spaniel. Gough's wife and baby had travelled overland from Hobart to join *"Cape York"* at Eddystone Point, rather than face the part of the journey from Bruny Island between. George joined them on board and the family headed for some well-earned leave in Melbourne before flying back to Bruny, where life was spiced with mutton bird poaching and sheep rustling. The exchange was effected in heavy rain and I elected not to go ashore.

My third sighting of Swan Island was more than thirty-six years later, from among the saltbush and tea-tree bordering Musselroe Bay on the mainland. The island drowsed in springtime green beyond sapphire shallows.

Seven pelicans fished offshore, ducking heads below the surface, then throwing great beaks skywards to swallow. Were these birds from the Swan Island colony, I wondered. Probably not. The main concentrations of nesting pelicans in Tasmania are in the north-east, but on Foster Island, a little to the west of Swan, and on the Low Islets just east of Clarke Island in the Furneaux Group.

Oystercatchers spurted, pied and piping, from tidal pools and the rare kelp or dominican gulls stood out among the two common kinds. This is the species of New Zealand and sub-antarctic islands and was a relative newcomer to Tasmania in the 1950s. It had become increasingly common since then, spreading north from Bruny Island and Hobart.

Another recent immigrant from New Zealand is the white-fronted tern — an elegant sea swallow depicted on the cover of my 1965 *"A Naturalist in New Zealand"*, as illustrative of my adventures there. This species moved into the Furneaux Group in the late 1970s, the first breeding colony in Australia being discovered there in 1979. This was a fitting entry point for a new tern, as the largest Tasmanian colony of crested terns had been recorded on these islands a few years before and the group holds the largest number of breeding fairy terns in Tasmania — this a species which is declining throughout its Australian range.

A lone hawk and a bevy of swallows swept over bull okes and Banksia and starlings foraged among golden guinea flower. The years between slipped away. Those days on board with Mollie seemed but yesterday!

* * * * *

During our first milking session in 1959 the anchor chain came rattling up and we headed south, away from the sun, to our next port of call, the Cape Eddystone lighthouse.

Water whipped up by storm winds meeting the flood tide head on had produced what is known to local seamen as "a high-topping sea, dangerous for small craft", but merely uncomfortable for craft the size of *"Cape York"*.

More than ten per cent of the Tasmanian crayfish catch comes from waters around Swan Island and accurate information about sea conditions issued by lighthouse personnel on the spot is vital to the fishermen. Automated stations issue weather reports — when all the automated parts are in working order — but nothing on the state of the sea locally. An incomplete automatic forecast in late 1982 led to the tragic loss of three lives in an unpredicted Banks Strait storm.

Heavy surf, symbolic of the sea's contempt for lightkeepers and mariners, was breaking on the rocks round Eddystone Point, but somehow the boat managed to get to the further side of the headland. Cargo would be delivered on the return voyage, and the engineers attempted only essential repairs this time. Keeper Williams and mechanic Bob came off to join us.

I went ashore neither on this occasion nor eight days later when we stood once more off the headland before breakfast — in mist and rain. No mutton birds nested and I was not tempted, spending the time in the smoke room instead, peering out through the porthole at intervals to see what was afoot. The boats were rocketing around on the sullen but significant swell, although things were calmer at the landing cove, where the lighthouse family from Tasman Island went ashore with their stores.

I remedied my omission thirty-six years later. It was springtime then, 4th November, and I was on tour with two old friends from my spell with the Australian Antarctic Division, Hope and Ian Black, one an expert in sea shells, the other a meteorologist. We were headed north up the east coast from St Helens, where the shoreline dips back in the Bay of Fires, to curve seaward again at Eddystone Point.

The bay was so named because of the fiery *Gasparinnia murorum* lichen that I was soon to become more familiar with on Flinders Island: a splendid sight on the wind-smoothed granite tumps. There were black swans and coot offshore, where looping fronds of Durvillea kelp broke surface at low water: black cockatoos and kookaburras onshore, where climbing lignum scrambled over paperbarks and beard heath.

Just south of Eddystone Point we came to the great lagoon of Ansons Bay, the restricting sand bar breached to allow the beery brown waters of the River Anson their freedom. The low acid heath which we crossed to the lighthouse was alight with the massed white flowers of wedding bush *(Ricinocarpos pinifolius)*, sprinkled with the blue of spotted sun orchids *(Thelymitra ixioides)*, *Dampiera stricta*, slender speedwell and ivy-leaved violet.

With such easy road access now, the notion of bringing stores in from the tossing lighthouse ship seemed ludricous. Servicing from the sea was symptomatic of earlier times, when few roads had been cut through the bush and heavy goods must perforce go by sea. The ocean supplied yesterday's highways, the sky tomorrow's, but today's were comfortably catered for by Mother Earth.

Currently two roads led to Eddystone Point lighthouse — now a tourist attraction in the southern part of the Mount William National Park, which stretched north up the coast to beyond Cape Naturaliste.

Wedding bush and kunzea spread white blossoms across boobialla and honey myrtle, with flowering blackboys standing out like exclamation marks. We walked the broad path to the tower, built between 1887 and 1889. A green rosella chortled its way from the cover of woolly heath *(Epacris lanuginosa)* and an echidna emerged from the sun-polished leaves of a patch of New Zealand mirror plant, on the prowl for ants. (In a wilder setting, earlier in the day, we thought we had spotted a Tasmanian devil disappearing into the undergrowth.)

Hope Black, too, then Hope MacPherson, had travelled on *"Cape York"* during her marine studies, and we aired nostalgic memories when we met up with a 1990's lighthouse official on the tourist track. He told us that diving petrels and storm petrels often flew into the light, ending up as sad little corpses on the ground below: mutton birds too, although these no longer nested on the point. A lively colony of blue penguins bred on George Island just offshore, these kicking up a shindy at night with their ear-shattering trumpeting.

There was no coast road for us to follow through the Mount William National Park, but we came to the sea again at Musselroe Bay to renew our acquaintance with Swan Island, before moving on to Cape Portland, Ringarooma Bay and the caravan park at Tomahawk.

* * * * *

But, back to *"Cape York"* on that rumbustious autumn day of long ago. Our next port of call was Cape Forestier, an automatic light on a great granite mound which was nearly but not quite an island. A deep rift, almost to sea level, separated it from the spectacular rocky cape which stretches south to form the western outlier of the Freycinet National Park. Behind us were the untrammelled waters of the Tasman Sea. Across the narrows and lagoon between Wineglass Bay and Promise Bay were the spreading waters of Great Oyster Bay, beyond which lay the sandy shores of Swansea on the Tasman Highway.

The landscape was dominated by the sparkling pinky-red peaks of the Hazards, darkly streaked with manganese and highlighted by brilliant sunshine. The red rock crumbled into gritty sand, pink at first but bleaching to a pristine white further from the cliffs. Where had all the colour gone? It transpired that the rosy hue was imparted by mineral feldspars, which were progressively leached by the sea to leave beds of shining white crystals. These were so insoluble that no particles took off into the overlying water, leaving this immaculately transparent, as crystal clear as the crystals themselves.

Once again I elected not to go ashore. There were no sea bird colonies and plants seemed to be restricted to stunted specimens in crevices. When I saw the steep landing and the metal stanchions by which boarders hauled themselves up the next lap, I was not unduly sorry, settling for a day of typing and an evening of cards.

I was to come again to Swansea in 1989, to learn something of the inland with forester John Cunningham. This time I viewed the dominating outline of the Hazards from sands where penguins and mutton birds burrowed. The darkly forested range continued south to the tip of the Freycinet Peninsula to crop out again as Schouten Island, suspended like the dot of an exclamation mark off its end.

Schouten had a chequered human history. First it had housed convicts, then a nineteenth century whaling station followed by an unsuccessful vineyard. Chinese miners had come to extract alluvial tin and then coal, to fuel a brickworks and cement factory on Maria Island away to the south, itself now reverted to a state of Nature and designated as a national park.

On our later visit at the end of 1995, we booked a boat trip to Maria Island from Triabunna, but two inches of rain fell in the night and the day was little better. The countryside was awash, with water surging across fields to tumble into swollen creeks and pour over new weirs. Yesterday's stream was a muddy torrent, the ducks in clover but the sheep languishing on isolated mounds.

In lieu of the island visit we splashed north, past fifty black swans idling off the marine culture operations of Little Swanport Bay, through Swansea and round the north end of Moulting Lagoon, where there were more shellfish beds and black swans which could be numbered in thousands. This body of water is separated from the great inlet of Oyster Bay, with its Oyster Bay pines and Tasmanian mud oysters, by the Nine Mile Beach, which boasted a road, but there was no way across at the end.

Swansea to Coles Bay, nestling under the Hazards, was ten km as the crow flies but forty km by road. Beyond, shrouded in mist and drizzle, lay the Freycinet National Park and Cape Forestier, accessible only to walkers and the wallabies and other wildlings which infiltrated the car parks to sneak the best of that other world beyond their inviolate sanctuary.

The moderns had given up on the Cape Forestier lighthouse, which was deemed too hazardous to service, even though automated. It had been replaced by an automatic light on Cape Tourville about five km further north, at the southern end of the Friendly Beaches and a highlight on the tourist trail. This we followed through woolly tea-tree *(Leptospermum lanigerum)* and blanket bush *(Bedfordia salicina)*, with attractive herbs like the equally downy winged spyridium *(Spyridium vexilliferum)*. Somehow a lighthouse viewed thus, just like another dwelling house, held little of the romance of the old days, being rather a hallmark of the easier lifestyle that we all enjoy. Now that life would be so much more comfortable for the keepers, there are no keepers. Their function has been taken over by robots, which cannot be expected to care.

147 Swan Island Lighthouse

148 Wedding Bush *Ricinocarpos pinifolia*

149 Spotted Sun Orchid *Thelymitra ixioides* and Blue *Dampiera stricta*

2. TASMAN ISLAND AND THE SOUTH

During the night *"Cape York"* steamed south past Maria Island and fetched up in the morning off Tasman Island. The view when I emerged on deck was quite breathtaking, the ship dwarfed by towering columns of dolerite, welded side by side and rising to both port and starboard. This was the greatest geological spectacle yet on a not unspectacular voyage.

Organ pipe columns, as of a mammoth Giant's Causeway, rose sheer to 800 feet (246 metres) on the flanks of Tasman Island, the grassy top sloping on beyond to the lighthouse at a thousand feet. On our opposite beam the equivalent rocks of Cape Pillar on the mainland rose even higher, forming an attractively castellated outline against the wan sky. Ahead to the west, barely discernible in the sea mist, was the equally splendid and not dissimilar Cape Raoul.

The two capes marked the southern extremities of the much dissected Tasman Peninsula, which stretches seaward to protect the state capital of Hobart from the worst onslaughts of the Tasman Sea. Most people know of the area because of the infamous convict settlement at Port Arthur, set well back on an inlet between the two capes.

It was to be thirty-six years before I was able to explore the peninsula to glean something of its geological and human history, but today I was to enjoy the rare privilege of setting foot on the precipitous lighthouse island.

Expert boat handling was essential here, as it was a flying fox landing. The seaward end of the cable was attached to an offshore rock round which the waves surged with surprising force, even on such a calm day as this. Ex-captain Bob Lines directed the boat work with a confidence and nicety of judgement which two other mates had a job to emulate on our return trip after he left us.

I went ashore in the first load, stepping into the canvas-lined passenger basket with Charles and Brian when it was lowered into the tossing pinnace, to be whisked aloft and hauled up along the cable. The sensation as we swung over the dark turbulence was like being in a communal breeches buoy. Once above the eighty feet (25 metre) jetty — or perhaps platform would be a better term this high above the waves — we were lowered as from an air balloon, but with more creakings and groanings. These were obliterated by mechanic Bob Flute doing the rounds of the moving parts with his grease gun before the next run.

The remaining 800 feet of the ascent was accomplished on a wheeled wooden trolley along a track carved at an angle of forty-five degrees across the near vertical cliff face — one wondered by what sort of intrepid workmen. There were no sides to the timber platform, just a twelve-inch board across what would be the lower end when we started, to brace the feet against.

It was a matter of luck for newcomers as to which way they settled on the level boards before these tilted. Brian got it wrong, but hung grimly on without being tilted off. At least he didn't travel feet upwards as Mac, fourth engineer, had done once, to his acute discomfort. I was luckier and the forty-five degree 'stand' was sufficiently comfortable for me to snatch a few plants in passing and scribble down the odd names.

Leaving the work parties to their chores, I went off exploring the fascinating rockscape. Recent collapses had left a series of vertical funnels, thirty to 100 feet deep, where a group of columns, presumable undermined by infiltrating waves, had subsided. Some were only a few feet across, with marginal plants encroaching over the edges, so I kept a careful lookout.

Sheep should have been more wary or more agile, but the occasional one came a cropper. Later I found an article entitled "The loneliest sheep in the world". It concerned two animals which had fallen over the cliff here onto a sloping grass platform 400 feet from both top and bottom. They survived there without water for several years, but had finally to be shot because their unshorn wool got so thick that they could scarcely drag themselves around when it got wet.

Some of the older established gulches were veritable fern gullies providing havens from both the ferocious elements and the hungry livestock, like massive grykes between the clints of a limestone pavement. Here were tree ferns, ground ferns and herbs in profusion, with marine ferns and shrubs coming in again in notches of a 900 feet high brink further on.

Most of the island summit was clad in coarse grass and sedge, broken by clumps of she-okes, banksias and other woody plants, most spectacular of which was the metre-high thicket of coast pink-berry *(Cyathodes acerosa, now abietina)*, putting out massed pink fruits in a fine show of bravado on those wind-blasted heights. They were large and closely packed — moreso than those of juniper-leaved pink-berry *(Cyathodes juniperina)* that I came across on parts of the mainland coast.

As well as the few sheep and cattle, the vegetation supported Whistler, a light draught horse of ingenuity, able to open gates and doors and turn on taps when he wanted a drink. Unfortunately he had no incentive to turn them off again but, so far, no amount of barbed wire entanglements had stopped him satisfying his thirst in this way. Water was a precious commodity in as lofty and isolated a site as this and such persistence did not endear him to the keepers.

I joined a group at morning tea, hosted by a keeper's wife, Mrs Nichols, her adopted ten-year-old son, Lance, and small daughter Susan. Lance volunteered as my guide, leading me off to the old stables where house sparrows and European starlings nested, as in many a more run-of-the-mill site elsewhere. Geared as these are to the domestic urban and suburban scene, it was singularly incongruous to come up against them in such a wild setting. Man and his livestock are evidently a strong draw, however remote they be.

From the Yate's house a keeper took me to the nearby rookery. We scrambled down below the lighthouse to a broad grassy ledge where many thousands of mutton birds nested. A hail from above took him back to work and I pottered among Poa and spinach, densely riddled with burrows. Another tier of rookery sloped away from the lower edge. With nine hundred feet of fresh air below, there would be no take-off problems for the inhabitants. Their problem was feral cats, which had taken a harvest as surely as birding families did on other islands, and of adults as well as young.

Pulling myself up alongside a palisade of volcanic columns, I found I was covered with bidgee-widgee burs and halted to clean them off. They needed no help in their inexorable spread. Sheep that ventured onto that spacious terrace were not so mindful of the consequences.

There was a technical hitch with the flying fox on our return. We slid neatly to the end of the run but there the mechanism seized up, so that the basket could not be lowered into the boat that was bucketing around below. Bob Flute clambered aloft to the cable with a boat hook, but there were three more of us aboard, hindering his efforts with our dead weight. Just as we decided we would have to shin down the rope into the waiting craft, he managed to dislodge the jam and all was well.

Visitors found such mishaps exciting: lighthouse personnel no doubt found them aggravating, but, sadly, their future occurrence was limited. By the 1980s the keepers were evacuated and the beacon automated — with loss of the many services the men had afforded the seafaring community, necessary to both their safety and their welfare.

John Whinray, writing in "*The Mercury*" of 26th April 1982, in relation to the de-manning of lighthouses in general and of Deal Island's in particular, stated: "The miserable record of the automatic weather station at the unmanned Tasman Island light station shows that such equipment cannot supply even limited information regularly."

Much of the cost of keeping the lighthouses functional is borne by major shipping companies, which are unwilling to pay up now that their craft are fitted with radar. De-manning saves money, but ignores the plight of fishermen and yachtsmen who are likely to be less well equipped. The greater efficacy of a manned light as a community service in search and rescue work and coastal surveillance, not to mention that of wardening wildlife and maintaining buildings and equipment, is widely recognised, but has carried insufficient weight to prevent de-manning of most of the lights.

The Tasman Island landing was sheltered from the lively gale which thundered across the summit but, as we drew away from the island under leaden skies, we found ourselves at its mercy. Everything was made as fast as possible, tablecloths were wetted to prevent the crockery from sliding and the captain forewent his favourite chair at coffee to help hold things steady.

After three hours in my bunk, I emerged to find that we were almost out of Storm Bay and entering the mouth of the Derwent. As we drew towards Hobart Dock the telephone became viable and the pilot came aboard accompanied by radio and press reporters seeking news of the female who was not part of the normal lighthouse personnel. I was kept busy filling slots for the seven and nine p.m. news bulletins and supplying copy to others, photographs deferred till the morrow.

Then I hit town, or, more accurately, the office of the Tasmanian Fauna Board, which august body was largely responsible for getting me to all the exciting places that the media men had been asking about. As I joined the Fauna Board's queen bee, Alison Cox, I failed at first to recognise the little man on the wharf in the dark trilby as the captain. It is remarkable what a uniform with lavish gold braid can do for a man.

During our two days in Hobart, I was able to visit bird colonies on Fulham Island, the Iron Pot and the bigger island of Bruny, as well as Dunally and the heights of Mount Wellington — a tourist must.

When we got back to Tasman Island on the return leg of the journey to Melbourne, I had an invitation to lunch in the lighthouse but was unable to accept. The sunlit sky was kept free of clouds by a wind sweeping all before it and the captain said NO!

"*Cape York*" was anchored on an undersea platform between the island and Cape Pillar, with deep water both sides. A fraction more wind and sea, he assured us, and she would drag her anchor. The idea of me being a thousand feet up on the other side of the island when he wanted to move out in a hurry did not appeal. Those who went ashore reported a gale on top. I had had a job to stand against the wind last time but that, apparently, was nothing as compared with this.

It got steadily worse after the first load of stores, which was swapped for the pregnant wife and the children of the keeper with whom I had enjoyed smoko the week before. Hopefully when the mother returned, there would be one extra in the family.

The new second mate's inexperience resulted in him getting water in the engine of his boat, putting it out of action, so that Hughie, the new first mate, had to do most of the dangerous job alone. 'Chiefy' was very scathing the next time 'second' got in a pickle, putting the others at risk.

"He won't stay long: the work's too dangerous. There's no other ship on the sea has to do this sort of job. Not many can cope. Needs bags of confidence." In fact various of the little cargo ships like "*Sheerwater*," "*Naracoupa*" and "*Prion*" achieved equally dangerous landings in the course of their everyday work.

Don, the third engineer, who rejoiced in the nickname of 'Orrible', did what he could with the boat in the water, his spare parts sent down in a bucket by rope, but she was heaving too much and had to be hauled up eventually to be made seaworthy.

A large consignment of coal and all the stores had to be got ashore, this being one of the lights victualled from Hobart. Hughie, doing his best in the watery turmoil, had three misses for every hit when it came to grabbing the flying fox as his boat gyrated past. His back-up, when he finally got back into the water, did even less well, circling repeatedly.

Several times Captain Herriot was on the point of calling the whole operation off, but he knew the weather was breaking up. If he didn't manage now, he might be waiting around for several days, so he let his men continue while they conceded it possible. By the time they had finished, the roast duck and ham in the oven had dried to a frazzle and the disgruntled 'third', who had been checking the cargo in at the landward end, went off muttering to his bunk with a plateful of cold meat and bread.

Tasman had never been serviced in worse weather, they said. There was relief and exhaustion on all faces as we steamed away north, the sun glinting silver on the heaving bosom of the deep and the land rising, starkly menacing, to the west.

On our 1995 visit to the adjacent mainland both Cape Pillar and Cape Raoul were accessible by foot track, but we obtained fine views of them from the smaller peninsula of West Arthur Head between the two. This is due south of Port Arthur, with the delightful declivity of Remarkable Cave insinuated into the cove on the west.

The cliff top was remarkable for the purple everlasting bushes *(Helichrysum purpurascens)*, exploding into golf ball sized rosettes of pinkish-purple buds. By December these would open into more mundane white flower heads: a few precocious sprouts already had, but the purple button-bush stage was much more attractive.

Nevertheless, it was the rock sculpting around the cave which had led to the name of Remarkable. I trundled down the flights of steps to just above sea level, passing a team of men cutting back encroaching tea-tree and constructing a new stairway, of treated timber above and galvanised steel lower down. Dark tongues of sea water licked into the narrow gulch below and the vista revealed through the arch of crumbling yellow rock to the dancing blue seascape outside was exquisite.

From the cliff above and, later, from the elevated, flower-embellished viewpoint of Palmer's Lookout, we had splendid views of both the mightier capes. Away to the east Tasman Island lay a little apart from the towering basalt of Cape Pillar, its white (now automated) lighthouse clearly visible on the summit. If anything, it looked even more remote and inaccessible from here, reaching to greater heights than the darker columns of Black Head in the foreground.

Cape Raoul, off in the opposite direction, had the same unmistakable bone structure of vertical prisms, their tops eroded unevenly to give a more rugged outline dropping less precipitously to the sea.

It was good to see this country again after so long and I also enjoyed glimpses of other old haunts — Wedge Island on the nearer side of Storm Bay and Betsy Island on its further shore, near the oldest lighthouse in Australia off South Arm. From near Gwandalan, close to the historic convict coal mine, I was able to identify Sloping Island and Spectacle Island, with Fulham Island off to the east. These, too, I had landed on all those years ago, from a motley selection of craft, all a great deal smaller than *"Cape York"*.

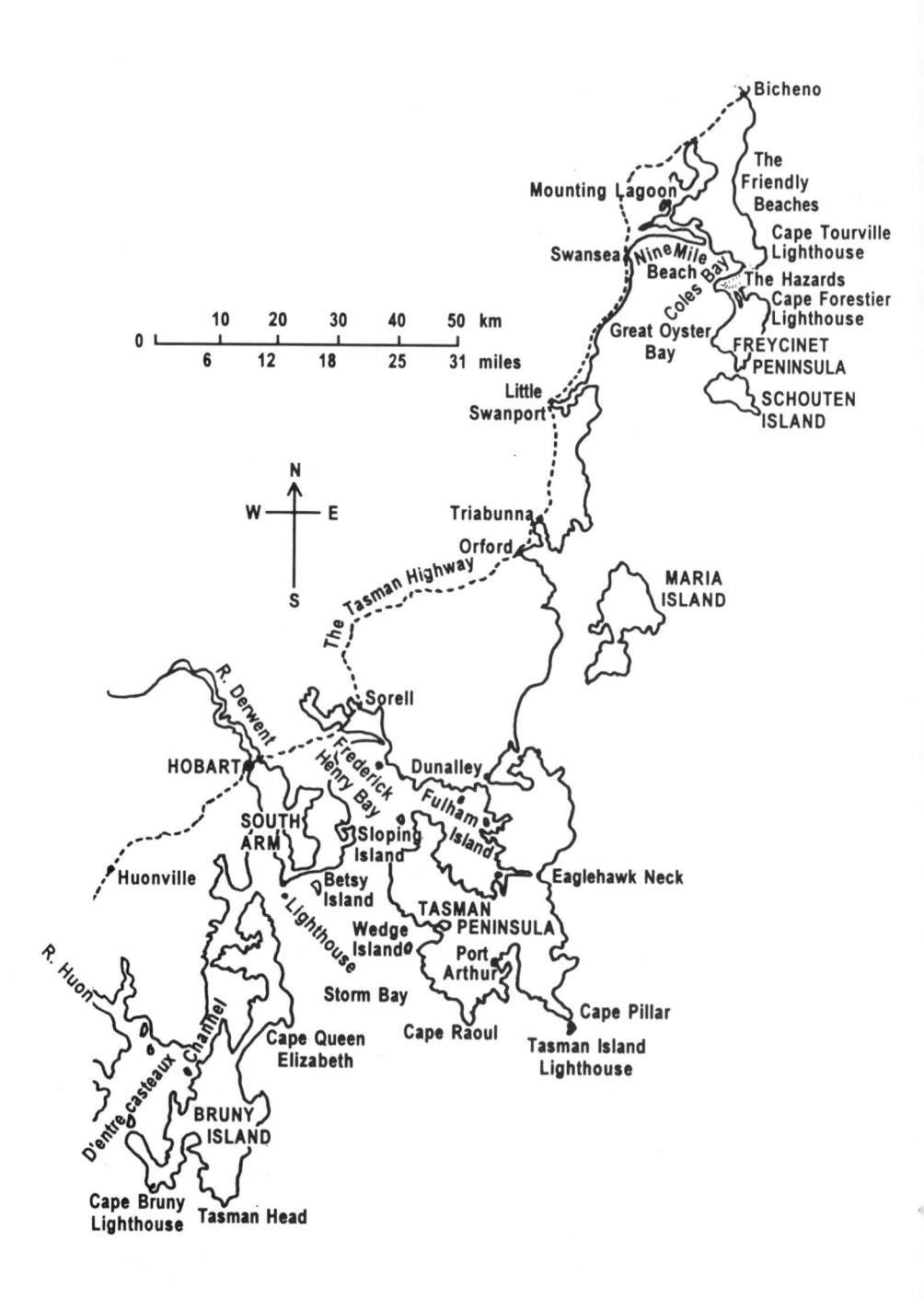

150 Map of South-east Tasmania

151 Winged Spyridium *Spyridium vexilliferum* and
Swampweed *Selliera radicans*

152 White Correa *Correa alba* and Coast Pink Berry *Cyathodes abietina*

3. LOADING AND OFF-LOADING LIVESTOCK: BRUNY ISLAND

It was four in the afternoon when I got back to *"Cape York"* after a visit to the penguins of Fulham Island — just one of many delightful inshore islands occupied by sea birds that I was able to visit on my various visits to Hobart.

The crew were loading twenty-two sheep for a keeper-grazier, not without incident. The first batch of animals had been transferred from the truck to the grey horsebox, to be hoisted on deck but, when nicely out of reach of all hands, the door swung open. A bewildered sheep was shouldered out by its indifferent fellows and dropped down between ship and open plan wharf.

The third officer and half a dozen able seamen dropped down after it, scrambling among the slippery beams under the decking for twenty minutes — with an agility exemplified only by sailors and our early primate relatives. Anxious faces peering down the crack from above could see little, but the game of hide-and-seek ended when the animal was spied swimming purposefully between the dark obstacles, buoyed up by the air in its ample fleece.

A rope was passed around its neck and the animal threaded back between the wooden piles. The rope's end was thrown onto the deck and the 'lost sheep' hauled up without being throttled. (There was no way the rope could have been got around its body without a man going into the water, and there were no volunteers.) Even the well wrapped sheep was shivering as hands reached out to receive it. The rescuers shinned up after it to wring quarts of water out of the thick coat, warming their hands in the lanolin-protected under-fleece the while.

The mate in charge opted for a different method for the rest. Each side of the gangway was walled with canvas and the sheep driven along a ramp direct from truck to boat. The little flock scampered down with only muted complaints. They were shepherded to an appropriate corner of the afterdeck and penned in with the offending horsebox and a set of hurdles. Soon after all, including the errant swimmer, were contentedly munching hay from each other's backs.

Close on their heels came Mollie the cow, satisfyingly topped up with green grass for the second part of her voyage. She was slung aboard and tethered in a new spot, the sheep having appropriated her old corner, but she settled immediately, quite the old hand by now, and ready to show those foolish lesser creatures how to behave.

Last, and least, came a little ginger suckling pig with a long nose, a Tamworth. This became an immediate pet and was almost killed with kindness. After eating more of the men's tea than was good for it, the excited squeals for 'more, more' tailed off and it burrowed into the heap of hay provided, to sleep off the effects. Mollie was bound for Bruny Island, the lesser livestock for Maatsuyker.

A pleasant young journalist and part timer for ABC came aboard to record another chat in my cabin before supper, returning later to play the tape back. He divulged that he had wanted for a long time to travel on *Cape York* and he left with the firm resolve that he would return ere long to do a major project recording lighthouse keepers' views on their life and work. I hope he made it before all the keepers were pronounced redundant.

Captain Herriot's drive to get the ship into port before the Easter holiday put a stop to operations proved successful and early on Good Friday we slipped our moorings and disappeared into the mist. There were no public holidays for the crew when in transit. My last few days on smaller boats had been flawlessly sunny, but the clammy atmosphere had sucked all light from the sky by now. This climate was as fickle as the one I lived with in Britain.

The leafy shores of Derwent Mouth slid by in sombre mood as we chugged by at our usual sedate ten miles per hour. Opposite Cape Direction we slipped through the narrows into the D'Entrecasteaux Channel and moved south, with the strawey paddocks of Bruny Island to port and the apple orchard country towards the Huon Valley to starboard.

We dropped anchor in the Bay of Islands south-west of Bruny. The lighthouse was three miles away on the ocean coast at Cape Bruny, but the small chances of being able to land on that side had necessitated the jetty being built into the comparatively calm waters of this sandy bay to the north. My captain had chosen the same anchorage for overnighting when I had travelled the channel some months before with Keith Meldrum on his luxury yacht, *"Pegasus"*, in company with police sergeant, George Hanlon.

Mutton birds nested on Courts Island below the lighthouse, which could be reached at low tide by wading, and I hopped onto a land rover for the lighthouse to explore the chances of getting there. Strangely, everyone I asked seemed a little hazy about tides. They knew that the tidal range in the Derwent at Hobart was only six feet, as opposed to fifteen feet in the Tamar at Launceston, and that a tide gauge had been installed on Maatsuyker Island, but that didn't help much. Nobody seemed to have surveyed this particular stretch of overwhelmingly complicated coastline, with its conflicting currents swirling round the islands in opposing directions.

The mutton bird harvest had just opened, although some deemed Good Friday an unpropitious day for the initial takes. There were huge rookeries elsewhere on Bruny Island, as at Cape Queen Elizabeth, and I had already looked at some of these, with more visits to come. The 1959 birders exploiting the southern rookeries favoured the same landing place as *"Cape York"* and some half dozen birders' camps had been set up onshore where our stores were to be landed.

Some of their inmates would be collecting in the Pineapples Rookery, but others would be on Courts Island, so I had only to observe their movements to avoid being cut off. At least, that was the idea. In the event I got involved in getting the cow ashore instead.

* * * * *

Because of the shallow sea bed, "*Cape York*" lay many cables from the shore, 'cable' being a term still used by my colleagues on board, as was 'league'. A cable equals 100 fathoms or 200 yards, a league approximately three miles. It looked like a marathon swim for a cow that had been idling on a short tether with little exercise for so long, but it was decided to tow her in behind the dinghy at a slow speed which would enable her to paddle dutifully along astern. The dinghy was chosen ostensibly to spare her the noise and exhaust fumes of one of the three-ton motorboats, but more realistically because the powerboats would be pressed into service landing stores.

Chick from Scotland manned the oars, Geordie from Northumberland was to manoeuvre Mollie out of the dangling horsebox and board the dinghy with her lead rope. I was allowed along to make soothing feminine noises and take photos. I thought I might be *de trop* but, as things turned out, it was as well I was there.

Ensconced in the stern, I fired the first camera shot as horsebox and cow were swung out from the deck on the mini crane. That was my first and last photo. The offshore current had drifted us well away from the ship and it was clear that Geordie, balanced unsurely atop the swaying horsebox, was loosening the fastenings prematurely.

As the contraption was lowered into the sea, Mollie panicked, bursting through the ineffectually restraining door and heading out to sea at a rate of knots. The rope was wrenched from Geordie's grip, leaving him swaying dangerously and finally toppling into the sea. Fortunately Mollie's course took her close enough for me to grab the trailing end of the rope, the only bit not deeply submerged when the frail craft had recovered from the surge of her determined bow wave.

It was a very long rope. By the time I had reefed in the slack she had dragged us far out to sea. I managed to turn her head and tie some girl guide knots to secure her to the ring on the stern seat, with just enough freeway for comfort. Some manful heaves on the oars by Chick and we had veered around to head for the now distant shore.

At this stage Mollie's momentum was greater than ours and she kept coming alongside and fouling the starboard oar until I reefed her in, but this burst of energy was short-lived. She soon lost her equilibrium, rolling over onto her side, though still kicking out gamely with inadequately thin legs, and snorting in terror as waves washed over her face.

I was fascinated to observe, however, that she was able to close her nostrils, seal-like, when under water, opening them momentarily on surfacing. This is a useful attribute, which we have lost, having to use fingers to pinch the nose closed when rash enough to jump in.

It soon became obvious that we would never make it to the sandy beach, as intended, so we turned instead towards the nearest, boulder-strewn, part of the shore. Very soon Mollie gave up, rolling over onto her back, her body bouyed up by the flatulent belly, but head trailing well below the surface. From then on I struggled to keep her nostrils above water, finding out just how heavy a cow's head can be when held at arm's-length beyond an uncomfortably twisted body.

Mostly she was a dead weight, but a few violent, thrashing spasms racked her body, partly swamping the boat, and on one of her upward heaves she must have spotted the shore, as her struggles returned in a final bid to survive. Chick was pulling with the last ounce of his strength against a combination of offshore wind and falling tide, with the cow acting as a restraining sea anchor. We had all just about had it when we heard the welcome scrunch of granite under the keel.

As her hooves came in contact with rock, Mollie lunged forward in one final heave, almost landing in the dinghy beside me. As Chick jumped out and jerked the boat up, I toppled back and we narrowly missed changing places. For the next half hour we all relaxed, Mollie up to her neck in water, but with chin and feet resting on solid rock: Chick and I trying to work out the next move.

When we were all duly rested, we managed to get her onto terra not-so-firma, Chick hauling on the rope in front and me pulling her head round with one hand and shoving on almost immovable buttocks with the other. She slithered alarmingly on the boulders and we feared for broken legs, but reached the narrow pebble beach without mishap and let her stay next time she went down. One of the motorboats brought a sea-soaked Geordie alongside and I took the dinghy out to meet him, to avoid another wetting, while Chick made our charge fast to a tree,

It was not that she was going anywhere of her own volition, but we had ideas of hauling her up the rugged slope using tree trunks as pulleys. We cleared a semblance of a path and managed to get her up a few yards by brute force, but this was obviously not going to work. On steep bits she jibbed, sliding onto her back with legs in the air and eyeballs rolling back in their sockets in an alarming fashion. My eleven stone braced below could only hold her bulk for so long. How many stones does an inert cow weigh, even with two men taking the strain ahead? We were forced to desist and let gravity have its way.

Chick scrambled up through the bush to bring the lighthouse horse to the rescue, the terrain being quite unsuitable for land rovers. He left us wearing dungarees torn at the knees and was delivered back, by boat, in borrowed shorts, his original coverings a write-off.

"That bush is completely no go, for horse or cow. Fallen trees, thorny scrub, boulders, the lot."

Mollie would have to take to the sea again. For the moment we settled her down with some hay, which she was tucking into with apparent relish when a boat came to take us to tea. We returned in the gathering twilight, with a powerboat and eight men. The idea was to get a canvas sling under her belly and lash her to the side, but that meant getting her back into the water and Mollie wasn't game for another swim yet.

There was no need for her to struggle, she just lay down, and we discovered that eight men are insufficient to lift a cow bodily if that cow has other ideas under her bovine brow — even when goaded by the volatile little Yugoslav sailor issuing excited orders to all and sundry.

The suggestion of returning for more men was rejected in favour of the bosun's decision that we retire into the bush and let her get up on her own. This she did, no problem, and finally allowed herself to be cajoled to the water's edge, where she panicked and plunged into the sea, straight out of the canvas sling. When the Yugoslav failed to lasso her from the boat the bosun thundered: "In after her Bugs."

Bugs was the junior crew member, likely to land such tasks and so-called because his teeth were said to resemble those of the TV rabbit which went by that name.

The sling was reinstated, order was restored and two men held Mollie's head out of the water as she lay quiescent on her side, legs trailing under the boat and making no attempt to swim. Did she, at last, feel she was in safe hands, or had she given up? It would be good to get into an animal's mind on these occasions.

We chugged slowly past the mutton birders' cooking fires to where a light-keeper swung a lantern on the jetty. As we closed, Bugs was sent into the water again to walk her ashore. Her hooves grazed the sand and she righted herself to walk cautiously ashore, and stand, dripping and trembling, while her small cuts were examined by torchlight.

Offered a bucket of fresh water as a change from salt, she kicked it over. Enough was enough! We left her munching hay at the top of the beach — heartily glad to be rid of us.

"Extra rum ration for you tonight Bugs."

This from the bosun; but Bugs was not yet twenty-one, the legal minimum age for such rewards. Hard luck!

Geordie and the first mate met me at the top of the Jacob's ladder to enquire anxiously about our charge. I assured them that all was well — but all was not well with my back until another three days had passed.

153 Cape Bruny Lighthouse

154 Flame Robin *Petroica phoenicea* and Seaberry Saltbush *Rhagodia candolleana*

155 Potoroo or Long-nosed Kangaroo Rat *Potorous tridactylus*

Chapter Eighteen

LANDINGS BY SEA AND AIR ON SOME WESTERN ISLES

1. MAATSUYKER IN THE DE WITT GROUP

Maatsuyker Island off Tasmania's rugged South-west, at latitude 43° 40' S and longitude 146° 19' E, is Australia's last bastion of land towards Antarctica. Beyond is the Southern Ocean, where frigid gales evolve into those Southerly Busters that cast a chill on many a summer picnic along the Southern coast of the continent. Sometimes *"Cape York"* would be laid up for days before she could attempt relief of the lighthouse, but this time she was lucky.

When I emerged on deck next morning, we were lying under the rugged land mass of our destination — which towered to 300 metres and occupied 200 hectares. Several loads of cargo had already been manhandled ashore, including the twenty-two sheep and ginger piglet.

Landing the sheep had been achieved with little trouble, but one was to die in transit. The animals had been hobbled, by tying three legs together, and they sprawled inert, allowing themselves to be handled like inanimate parcels. When I got ashore they were lying on the squarish wharf, trying to ignore the men tramping back and forth alongside.

The one which died was suffocated by the ones on top when the rail trolley in which they were loaded tilted to take the one-in-one section on the ascent of the cliff. A lighthouse child ran for a knife and the sheep's throat was slit to release unwanted blood. The animals were imported as mutton-on-the-hoof, so death was inevitable, but might have been kinder.

Later in the day I saw the rest of the flock grazing in one of two fenced paddocks, revelling in the spaciousness of their new surroundings. Left on free range in strange territory, they could all too easily have slipped into trouble on the precipitous cliffs or got entangled in the patches of temperate rainforest which persisted in parts. The dominant trees were dwarfed by bludgeoning winds, but the aspidistra-like rosettes and robust ferns of the understorey were as daunting as anywhere along these rainy coasts.

After a brief survey of the shearwater burrows penetrating lush green succulents just above the landing, I perched on top of a load of luggage to be hauled up the cliff. The gradient was neither as steep nor as long as that of Tasman Island's railway, but I felt less secure as the piled miscellany jiggled beneath me.

The knowledge that the last truck going up had been derailed was not conducive to a sense of security. It had continued its ascent, those below in the know unable to communicate with those above who were not. A party of ABs had been sent up to gather the scattered parcels and stores and manhandle the truck back onto the rails.

My fellow passenger was 'Gran'pop', an ex-lighthouse keeper visiting his lighthouse keeper son, the youngest of eleven which he had produced in his busy life. Most of the island population awaited his arrival at the upper platform.

There seemed to be a lot of women and children for such a lonely spot but, except for the lady who had come on "*Cape York*" for the birding season, they all belonged to the three lighthouse families. I joined some of them in a land rover for the journey to the light tower around a mile away.

The lighthouse was built in 1889-90, two and a half centuries after Abel Tasman had first sighted the island in November 1642. The name is said by some to mean 'Mate's sugar', by others, more credibly, to be named after Maatsuyker, then Governor of the Dutch East Indies. The light beams out from 118 metres above sea level, well below the island summit, and is the most southerly light in Australia.

At the time of my visit it was the only habitation along a 240 km stretch of coastline, so it was vital to the local fishermen and yachtsmen that it stayed manned. There was no other help at hand, either to guide them out of trouble or to succour them when in it. Controversy raged more fiercely over the automation of Maatsuyker lighthouse than over any of the others.

Next up the coast was Low Rocky Point, fifty-five km north by the shortest sea route, and beyond that was Cape Sorrell at the mouth of the great natural inlet of Macquarie Harbour, another fifty-five km to the north as the cormorant flies. A battery-powered light was installed at Low Rocky Point in 1963 and Cape Sorrell, likewise, was fully automated in 1971.

In the early days Maatsuyker light burned a wick soaking up liquid kerosene, this progressing to a mantle lamp burning vaporised kerosene. Later it was to be made electric. With a range of forty km on a clear night, the lenses revolved every 180 seconds, powered by a clockwork mechanism which had to be wound up every hour by the keeper on duty. Keepers also relayed a three-hourly weather report to Cape Bruny lighthouse by radio.

In the 1930s, before radio was installed, urgent messages were despatched to Hobart by carrier pigeons. These needed to be fit and good homers, whether they flew over those rugged mountains or along the equally rugged coast, and several were despatched together, lest some fall by the way. Radio telephone was installed in 1974, but that was not yet, and, by the end of the 1970s, stores were coming in by helicopter instead of ship.

On my visit in 1959 the keepers were a vital lifeline to mountain backpackers tackling the little-used tracks through the uninhabited hinterland, and they could also locate and report bush fires. From the top of the island the whole of the South Tasmanian coast, from nearby South West Cape to distant South East Cape, was visible when the weather was right. It couldn't have been better when I was there and the sunlit vistas were quite magical, framed sometimes by an equally magical foreground of rainforest greenery, laced with ferns and looped with creepers.

Two of the lighthouse children volunteered to guide me around. One was quiet, intelligent thirteen-year-old Wendy Harrison, who had a natural affinity for her environment. The other was freckled, curly-haired Bobby, aged ten, impatient to be up and away.

Wendy was a Lone Guide. I had been both guide and guider in my time and it was an experience for both of us to swap our widely differing views of the great international sisterhood that meant so much to so many in their formative years in those unsophisticated days.

We moved up the grassy slope behind the lighthouse, passing the time of day with Brownie, the docile draught horse. The view, as I turned back, took my breath away and I have a treasured photograph to remember it by. Brownie grazed peacefully in the foreground, with the lighthouse shining white in the middle distance, and beyond that the Needles — a line of rugged stacks, less white than the better known chalk Needles of England's Isle-of-Wight, but similarly aligned.

I learned that these were the haunt of Tasmanian fur seals, although we were too far away to see any. This was a breeding colony and on the up and up since the bad old days of sealing. By the late 1970s the colony had reached the thousand mark and its progress was being monitored.

At the other end of the mammalian scale were the Tasmanian marsupial mice *(Antechinus minimus)*, which led a snake-free life in this island sanctuary, where there was no need to progress noisily or to beat the grass ahead to walk safely. The only reptiles were skinks, little ones, not the hefty blue-tongues. We disturbed one and I learned later that there were two kinds here, both of them familiar on the Furneaux Group: the three-lined and spotted skinks *(Leiolopisma trilineata* and *L. ocellata)*.

Wendy and Bobby led me up and along the island crest to a huge short-tailed shearwater rookery in vegetation as lush as the smaller colony by the landing place. Another Wendy — Morrah — aged fifteen, whom I met later, on *"Cape York"*, told me of dove or blue petrels which flew in nightly, many coming to grief around the light. She also spoke of petrels smaller than mutton birds, with brown backs and mottled buff breasts, which dropped down through the branches at night and scuttled into their holes underneath. She knew of twelve pairs which nested on an unburrowable ledge, in the cover of the plants alone.

'Gran'pop' reckoned that 25,000 pairs was a conservative estimate of the number of short-tailed shearwaters on Maatsuyker. He and the younger keepers also maintained that there were about fifty 'king mutton birds', with white fronts, like those of New Zealand, presumably sooty shearwaters *(Puffinus griseus)*, and that a similar number were present on Tasman Island.

None had any explanation for the fact that only half as many mutton birds had come ashore in this 1958-59 season as in the years immediately before. Nevertheless, 12,500 would be spectacle enough. How I wished I could spend a night on the island to savour the commotion of their coming and going.

Rocks shouldering from the mantle of green were shaly and contorted, blackish or rust-coloured and veined with quartz, the surrounding soil a dark, damp loam. In parts of the summit rookery birds tunnelled among metre-high bower spinach, seaberry saltbush and sea celery: another colony was in almost pure variable groundsel. Where birds dug beneath the twisted trunks of coast pink-berry and coast everlasting the bushes looked rather the worse for wear.

Other woody plants withdrawing as the birds advanced were prickly tea-tree and lacquered daisy bush, whose flat-topped flower clusters protruded above the darkly shining leaves. These and tree broom heath survived better on the white sand alongside the picnic site, and the birds there had an easier time, because they were able to scrabble out onto the bordering land rover track to get a good runway for take-off.

Where undisturbed, the west coast peppermint gums *(Eucalyptus nitida)* grew seven to ten metres high, with coast banksia and jagged westringia. Clusters of hairy white florets on the cherry rice flower *(Pimelea drupacea)* were swelling into berry-like fruits, which changed from green through red to black.

Two plants with rather similar oval fruits were quite unrelated. One, the turqoise-berry *(Drymophila cyanocarpa)* belongs to the lily family; the other, the purple apple-berry *(Billardiera longiflora)* to the Pittosporum family and grows here with the related banyalla or cheesewood, sometimes rooted, like that, in a shaggy tree fern base. Bush birds relish the red seeds exposed by the splitting banyalla capsules, but the only one I saw was a long-tailed blue wren. In the ground flora were trigger plants, violets, flax lilies and smooth nettle *(Australina muelleri)*, with the splaying rosettes of pandani *(Richea scoparia)* pushing up between,

During a lunch break with the Harrisons, Wendy proudly displayed some of her father's handiwork. There were cleverly carved wooden animals, a model lighthouse working off a battery and a series of rings fashioned from a light aluminium alloy salvaged from the aircraft industry and inlaid with polished fragments of coloured stones or mutton fish shells — a favourite with New Zealand jewellers.

I left with a present of a fine *Haliotus* shell and was able to reciprocate later with a nature book — as great a rarity in an environment lacking shops, libraries and schools as the opalescent shell was in mine. The youngsters, like so many in wilderness Australia, were served by 'The School of the Air', relying on the spoken rather than the written word, as their successors a few decades later would be working with computer screens rather than books.

Bobby had better things to do in the afternoon, when Wendy led me off to the island picnic ground and down through a woody area to a sequestered ferny creek. The generous rainfall and prevalence of sea mists kept Maatsuyker greener than most islands I had visited and ferns grew in abundance.

They included bat's wing ferns *(Histiopteris incisa)*, their soft bluish fronds contrasting with the associated ruddy ground fern *(Hypolepis rugosula)*. On the tip of each frond of mother shield fern a tiny plantlet was awaiting the opportunity to launch out on its own, when it had weighed the supporting leaf down to ground level. Blunt spleenwort covered patches several metres across, while other spleenworts, water ferns and kangaroo fern *(Microsorium diversifolium)* did not have to be sought in crevices as on wind-shorn Tasman Island.

We made our way down to the landing in good time for the returning boats. Penguins nested hereabouts, to save the long slog up the cliffs, and the tracks along which they trudged were clearly marked through the ground cover of plants, which was notable for the elevation reached by the salt-demanding glasswort. This did not lack for salty splashings when heavy seas flung themselves onto the unprotected shore.

It was dead low water by now and the shallows had become a shimmering kelp field as the *Durvillea* and *Macrocarpa* fronds swished to and fro at the surface, deflecting the late afternoon light. Even beneath "*Cape York*'s" keel the weed seemed perilously close. The mooring rope, with its wooden bollards, was well and truly fouled and the boat's screws became entangled as we edged alongside. The boatman guided us through with an oar.

"*Cape York*" needed more water before she could move out and we lay off the landing stage, drinking in the views until 6.30 p.m., when the anchor was hauled up and the chain cleared with sheath knives. This was the furthest point of our voyage, so the Maatsuyker families could not look forward to a return visit as the other lighthouse inmates could. We turned our backs on the sunset and steamed away through the ethereal light reflected off the eastern sea. Once again the spectacular coastline would be lost to view under cover of darkness.

I was, however, to be favoured with one more visit to this wilderness corner of Australia's smallest state, but that was to be thirty years hence — in February 1989. By that time a small tourist enterprise had started up, air-lifting backpackers in to the roadless South-west from Cambridge Airport at Hobart.

The Cessna planes were six seaters but I was the only passenger going out on the one which went to bring back a party of campers. Rex, the sun-tanned, hairy-armed pilot, sat me beside him and furnished me with a pair of earphones, which mellowed the screeching noise of the engines to an ominous and unrelenting rumble. He gave me a running commentary on the peaks as we passed, much of which I failed to unravel from the background noise, but I was completely mesmerised by the panoramas of geologically new knife edges passing very close beneath and sometimes even alongside, and managed to record some of them on film.

At first there were the Pittwater Creeks, all dammed now, making freshwater ponds for water storage and private duck shooting, where before it had been a free for all on the salty flats. There was the Derwent, with the new Hobart Bridge looking even smaller than from the summit of Mount Wellington, and the Huon Valley, with its partially flooded wooded islets.

As the D'Entrecasteaux Channel faded into the distance, we zoomed over the Harz National Park with its ice-flattened summit and scattered tarns. The unsightly blemishes of cleared areas gullied by rust-coloured, dendritic creeks, in otherwise unsullied green, gradually lessened, until we were over the precipitous peaks and ridges of dolerite with quartz intrusions and wooded slopes.

Black storm clouds were massing behind Federation Peak as we moved into the high rainfall area and a parallel-sided rainstorm marked the end for me of the long heat wave prevailing in the South-east. Our skimming progress over the wonderland of uninhabited mountains and gullies opened out all too soon. There ahead was a spread of silver sea, studded with the De Witt Group of islands, with Maatsuyker lying as she had so often lain, a bright emerald in an aquamarine sea.

We circled low over Cox's Bight, Rex aligning the plane to utilise the col before turning into the wind and touching down on the long strip of white sand bordering the Southern Ocean. After taking the waiting group back to Hobart, he was returning for another, including me, to be lifted inland to Melaleuca Creek in dense bush bordering peaty button-grass moor.

The low peat bank backing the sands was topped by a narrow mossy greensward fringed with button-grass and bidgee-widgee — the dinkum native and invasive alien. The bush behind was a nigh impenetrable thicket of paperbarks and tea-trees, laced with fruiting juniper-leaved pink-berry and hazel pomaderris, whose supple, hazel-like twigs were in demand for weaving cray pots before the influx of synthetics.

All too soon our pilot was back and we were piling in among rucksacks and bedding. We seemed to be heading straight for the western cliff, but veered right and got airborne at the crucial moment, missing it by a whisker. As we tilted to the turn, the wing tip almost brushed the grassy crest of the dune: a hairy experience for us first-timers, but all in the day's work for these intrepid bush pilots.

I gazed my last on Maatsuyker, and soon we were landing on the little Melaleuca Creek airstrip, with its peaty pools speckled with the mauve flowers of the charmingly named fairy aprons, an insectivorous bladderwort.

Back in 1959, as darkness closed down, *"Cape York"* chugged her lonely way along that uninhabited coast. The virgin hills were enveloped in almost total blackness, the twinkling of the myriad stars insufficient to elucidate their mysteries. I ducked into the smoke room for a cribbage session with the third mate and third engineer, who had lost their cobber, Hughie Fisher, when he was promoted to first mate and a different watch.

Seldom have I indulged in card games, before or since, but this was a different existence from the norm. The life of a seaman is a mixture of hard graft and killing time. Watches could be strenuous, cold and wet, or deadly boring. Whichever way, men looked for relaxation when off duty and there was nowhere to go for it except the smoke room. Filling the breach with alcohol consumption was inhibited by shipboard discipline. Or should have been. Roy, our highly popular third steward, found a way around the restrictions, which left him under a cloud.

A few days from the home port on the return voyage, he imbibed eleven cans of beer from the officers' fridge and spent the night in the rain on a canvas hatch cover. Being under twenty-one, he was disallowed beer anyway, especially officers' beer. A nicer-mannered, merrier lad, would have been hard to find and the entire crew, officers included, were sad that discipline would necessitate his dismissal.

But Roy had no intention of spending the rest of his life as a ship's steward, like one of his brothers. He would bounce back unscathed, having other strings to his bow, such as timber-getting and sheep-droving, which activities relied heavily on casual labour passing, like ships in the night. He proposed to return to tin-smithing, a trade in which he had already served an apprenticeship.

Life had never been easy. He was the middle one of thirteen children, begat by a ne'er do well father and a steadfast, much appreciated mother, who had held the brood together, the older boys working to keep the younger ones in food and schooling. Roy's cheery personality would see him through — so long as he kept off the beer.

He epitomised for me those happy-go-lucky seafarers, few of whom, officers excepted, stayed at sea for long. The rough, tough life was often a sowing of wild oats — a satisfying of the craving for adventure that assails young males. There was a whole world out there, where they moved from one job to another, amassing more know-how than the average white-collar worker gleans in a lifetime, if usually not a fortune.

This had been an exceptional voyage for good weather and quick turn-around and *"Cape York"* steamed back into Melbourne eight days before expected. Boss man, Barrett, had to return a week early from leave to receive us. It had been a great trip and I left them all with regret, but not empty-handed. From the bosun I received six frozen mutton birds and from Mac, fourth engineer from Belfast, two monster crayfish; all much enjoyed.

156 Brush-tail Possum *Trichosurus vulpecula*

157 Red-bellied Pademelon *Thylogale billardierii* and Austral Seablite *Suaeda australis*

158 Marsupial Mouse *Antechinus minimus* and Subterranean Clover *Trifolium subterraneum*

2. BY TIGER MOTH TO TREFOIL ISLAND IN THE HUNTER GROUP

A few weeks before my epic voyage on "*Cape York*", I had been working my way along Tasmania's north coast visiting as many of the inshore sea-bird islands as possible. To get to the more far-flung islands of the Hunter Group, I needed more sophisticated transport than I had been using around Devonport, and not many days in which to rustle it up. Having a few names to contact in Wynyard, I left the bus there and was directed by the bus driver to the Federal Hotel, where I booked in.

None of my contacts were available until evening and the day was still young, so I set off to explore a silver gull colony at the mouth of the Flowerdale River, having to hitch a lift across to the further side. On my return there was only one boat in sight — a leaky tub manned by four urchins, from six years old up. I shouted at them and they agreed to take me across, adding the proviso: "The boat's full of water, lady."

Indicating my willingness to put up with such small inconveniences, I watched them flounder to the beach and leap into the water to drag the boat ashore, wetting everything that wasn't already awash.

"The lady doesn't want to wade."

I stepped in and sat on the stern gunwhale, as the two seats were in use as paddles. Not having changed into slacks for this minor jaunt to a town bird colony, my skirt draped in the bilge water and the best of balancing tricks failed to keep my haversack dry.

The youngsters were bursting with confidence, but confessed to not having been in a boat before. The little one rowed with little strokes on the port side, the big one with big strokes on the starboard side. The two lads in the bow, which was being temporarily used as the stern, were wielding the two plank seats as paddles.

We progressed like an inebriated frog experimenting with breaststroke. Their lunges were seldom synchronised and they often converged as they applied navigational science to right the erratic passage. We travelled in a number of directions and leaned at a variety of angles, covering a deal more than the minimum distance before bumping into the sea wall, but a good time was had by all. I commended their efforts and gave them the wherewithal for four ice creams. A little voice followed me. "Your dress is a bit wet lady, but we got you over."

Then, with a note of triumph, the overworked Aussie encouragement: "You'll be right!"

Back at the Federal Hotel, I enquired for the barrister I had been referred to and found that he was the barman. He passed me onto a mutton-birder, deep in a pint of the best, who, like everybody else, said I had little chance of getting to the north-west islands in the little time at my disposal.

"Your only hope is Karl Jaeger's plane. He's at Smithton."

They told of a bus leaving for Smithton in half an hour. Someone phoned, to ask it to stop and pick me up. I tumbled my things together, tried to make the towel look as though it hadn't been used, swallowed some tea and ran. The bus driver who picked me up proved to be the same who had put me down five hours earlier.

"I thought you'd booked in here for the night!"

"So did I. Things change!"

Part of the lovely ride west through Stanley to Smithton was lost in the dark and I was thoroughly chilled by the time we got there. A chap at the bus station gave me a lift to the town's only lodging, the Ryan's Bridge Hotel. There followed a chaotic session of phone calls and conversations which produced three results.

First and most important, Karl Jaeger promised me the use of his little plane on the morrow. Second, Pat Harrison, farmer's daughter and pre-medical student, offered me hospitality for the rest of my stay in Smithton and thirdly, a carpetbagger with a singsong voice (he called himself a traveller in carpets) took me off in his car for coffee and what proved an entertaining evening.

The next day, third of March 1959, was one to remember, island-hopping in a two-seater Tiger Moth biplane. Karl Jaeger arrived at Ryan's Hotel early, at the same moment as Pat Harrison's parents, who had come to take my luggage to their farmhouse on the Bass Highway. Karl went off to the town airport to refuel and his wife, Joan, scooped me up a quarter of an hour later to drive me to the plane. Karl had a corner of the airport and a hangar to himself — also a key to the gate.

"I expect you've flown before. I'll put the dual control on."

I hastened to assure him that my only experience in Tiger Moths was as a passenger, and clambered into the front cockpit, where I was secured with waist and shoulder straps. These machines were controlled by back-seat drivers, it seemed. Had I known all the stories about my daredevil pilot then that I heard during the next twenty-four hours, I might not have felt so secure. My philosophy when islanding, however, is always to have faith in the captain of my craft, who has more to lose than me if we founder.

We taxied into position and rose smoothly after a few preliminary lollops. Karl said we would go and look at Trefoil Island, the most promising one from my point of view, but he didn't think we'd be able to land there in the current force five easterly.

As we headed west along the coast I experienced his rather disconcerting habit of stalling the engine every time he wanted to say something. His voice would have been lost in the roar without this proviso, but he failed to get my undivided attention, as I waited for the plane to drop out of the air. Then I saw a metal plaque on the dashboard which read "Cruising speed 94 mph, stalling speed forty-five mph". Evidently it was the done thing to stall and still keep going, albeit at a speed that most motorists now regard as slow.

Another of Karl's disconcerting habits was to point something out below and follow up by tilting the plane on edge without warning and circling on one ear, so that the exhibit became more visible.

Trefoil Island was five hours out by boat, twenty minutes by plane! Between it and the mainland is a tremendous tide rip, attaining velocities of up to nine knots on spring tides. Rocks and sandbanks send the water swirling all ways, and with it swaying entanglements of bull kelp. I felt lucky to be airborne.

We swooped over the precipitous cliffs to examine the landing, almost touching down but not quite. This preliminary run gave Karl the confidence that he could make it. We circled and came down into the teeth of the wind. Two landing strips had been cut diagonally across each other, two years before, in 1957, but there were still a few tussocks and burrows to add to the excitement and the debris scraped from the runways had been dumped too close for comfort so that the plane had to be kept dead centre. Karl had said several times that he didn't like landing on Trefoil, so I considered myself fortunate to be safely down.

On one occasion he had been becalmed here with insufficient wind for take-off, like a stranded mutton bird on a windless night. He had narrowly escaped ditching in the sea, despite the height of the island. Another time mechanical damage had forced him down here in a Gypsy Major, with a punctured cylinder, but he had managed to find enough tools in the island house to make temporary repairs sufficient for take-off.

Pauline Buckley, in her book *"Around Circular Head"*, published in 1984, states that the first airstrip on Trefoil had been cleared after James Luck took over the island from Bob Luck in 1961. That was two years later and must have been in a different place, because she reports that it took three months to grub out the tussocks and fill in the holes, and that the expelled birds created havoc on the newly-cleared strip, so that it had to be covered with wire netting. This was part of a scheme to export mutton bird carcases fresh from the newly-installed freezer, the boatman charging threepence per bird for sea transport. It looked as though our "St Andrew's cross" airstrip was discounted as a viable proposition.

South-westerlies can bring fifty foot waves crashing onto the south coast of the island. While not of this order today, there was quite a stiff breeze blowing. Karl left me holding onto the tail of the plane and hared off to the summit mutton-birders' hut to get a stake and a rope to peg her down, lest she take-off on her own.

There were two quarter-cast Aboriginal birders here from Cape Barren Island, building new birding huts. One of these, followed by a shaggy old English sheepdog, came to the plane to collect the newspapers that casual visitors usually brought to keep the beleaguered islanders in touch, but Karl had forgotten this civic duty.

Trefoil Island is quite small, just 275 acres of dirty grey sand with a superficial layer of peat in parts. Generally acid, with a pH around 5.5, and poor in calcium, guano from the big mutton bird population boosted the usually deficient phosphate and nitrogen.

Most was covered with silver tussock grass and about three-quarters was burrowed by birds, these particularly dense south-west of our landing place and in the north-west, where nest holes averaged about two per square metre. Capeweed from South Africa and grasses from Europe romped everywhere, with stinking pennywort one of the few natives.

Capeweed gives good forage in winter and spring, its leaf rosettes starred with golden daisy flowers, but it dies off at the beginning of summer, just when it would be most valuable. It came in from the Cape in the old sailing ship days, when vessels bringing livestock out from the old country put into Capetown to stock up with hay.

There were thistles, docks and sorrels, dove's-foot cranesbill and the related British storksbill among the perennial ryegrass and subterranean clover planted for pasturage. Trees, too, had been planted — for shelter belts and firewood — pines, macrocarpas and South African boxthorn. Now, at the tail end of a dusty summer, short-lived ephemerals like allseed and chickweed had come into their own.

Bracken was rife along the north coast, as good at standing the periodic fires as was the tussock, but we saw no signs of recent burning except to the south-east of sheds west of the house, where burrows were seriously eroded.

"No need to fire the rookeries here, where it's all tussock and knobby club-rush. It's different on Three Hummock, where it's tea-tree and boobialla scrub." This from the birders.

Here on Trefoil Island farm livestock and birds seemed to be quite well integrated on the humpy slope above the house, where the soil was deep and the burrows went almost as far down as those by the blowhole, where the chicks were safe from reaching hands.

The ground was the right consistency for both birders and graziers — not so friable as to cave in, yet not so easily consolidated as to hinder tunnelling. Some of the burrows actually penetrated beneath much-trodden sheep tracks. Others went into the flaky yellow-orange rock which broke down to sandy gravel and patches of silver sand to form mini dunes, an area favoured by blue penguins.

Penguins were better able than shearwaters to excavate in the more compacted soils and thousands nested in the paddock behind the house. Unusually, a number of these were outside their burrows in full daylight, adults moulting their breeding plumage or youngsters shedding the last of their baby down. Fortunately for them, penguins were not regarded as edible. Burrow density ranged from one to three per square metre, and penguins in occupation when the mutton birds arrive in spring were said to be well able to fight for their rights of ownership. Silver gulls were picking over some shearwater corpses along the beaches, the cause of death not apparent.

159 Masked Lapwing or Spur-winged Plover *(Vanellus miles)*

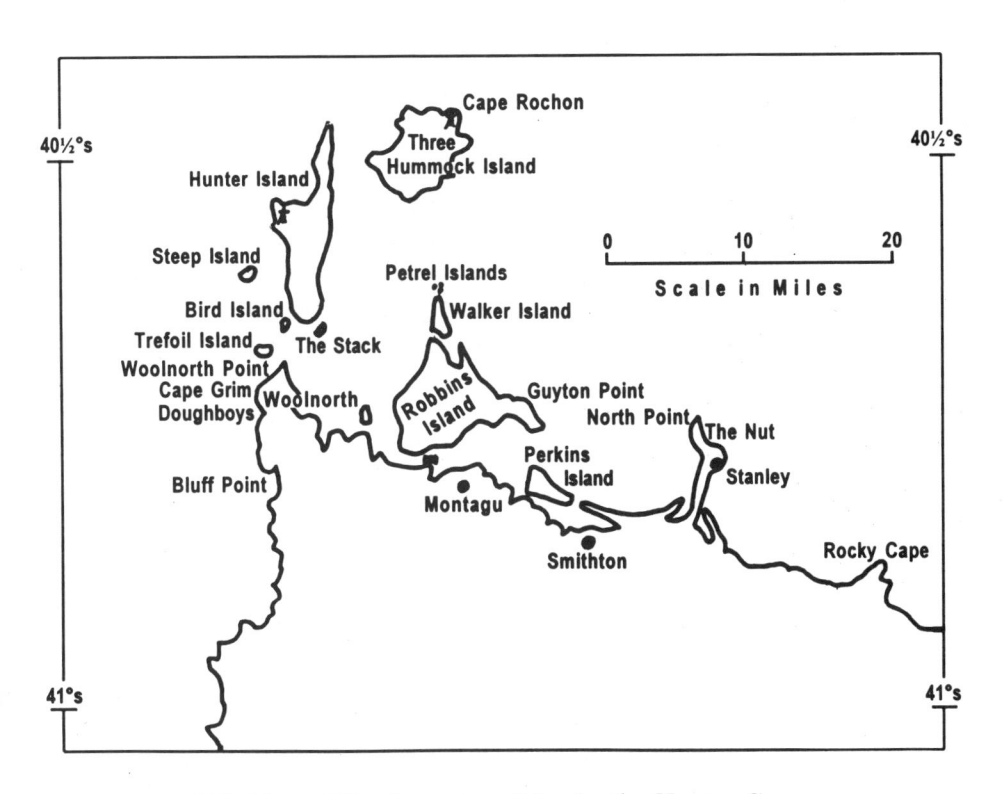

160 Map of North-western Islands: the Hunter Group

161 Mutton Bird *Puffinus tenuirostris* and
Swamp Paperbark *Melaleuca ericifolia*

3. TREFOIL ISLAND'S MUTTON-BIRDERS AND STEEP ISLAND

After doing the rounds of Trefoil Island's mutton bird rookeries, I joined the three men in the house near sea level for smoko, in a typical bachelors' kitchen, with a minimum of crockery and saucepans and a maximum of magazine pin-ups adorning the walls. We swigged from large enamel mugs of billy tea with condensed milk and ate leaden home-made scones and fruit cake, despite no newspapers to swap for the hospitality.

Over the mugs we learned that the harvest this year was intended to bring in around 120,000 birds. Only a quarter of the island had been covered by the birders the previous year, with a take of 84,000.

Even this was more than the best harvests around 1920, when 80,000 was remembered as the biggest take, 20,000 of these going to New Zealand, salted, to supplement the local harvest of sooty shearwaters. The price then was £1 per 100 birds, plus the proceeds of the oil and fat and feathers at two and sixpence per pound.

The quarter of the 275 acre, mile long island not burrowed was the shallow soil of the airstrip and the fields where the owner, who was farmer as well as birder, ran his sheep and two carthorses. His full grazing capacity was 750 sheep, but only 450 had been on the pasture through the latter part of the summer and 150 of these had just been taken ashore — not without problems.

The birders told us that sheep were first put onto the island around 1890, this early livestock rearing contemporary with the earliest mutton bird harvests taken by Europeans. In 1920 the island carried only 500 sheep, but these were said to have grown to prodigious sizes, of 98-100 pounds weight, and carried heavy fleeces.

Shearwater numbers were increasing, despite the considerable annual harvest, and a lot of new burrows had been opened in the north-west of the island, with birds coming back into the sandy paddocks that they had occupied before these were ploughed. A later informant reckoned numbers to be in the region of a quarter of a million birds. By 1995 the official figure was over half a million — more than on all the other islands of the Hunter Group put together.

For some reason not understood, the Trefoil Island shearwaters, like the sheep, were fatter than most. Four hundred Trefoil birds in the late 1950s, were claimed to be of equivalent weight to 600 birds from Hunter Island, where they nested mostly among scrub. This was more likely attributable to better food gathering at sea than the quality of nesting site, but there was still a lot to learn about mutton bird ecology.

Farmers who allowed the sea-going hosts to nest on their land were well rewarded. Sheep had to be fed from the land if they were to yield profit: whereas all the energy input to the crop of mutton birds came from the sea, with no effort on the farmer's part. Properly harvested, there was no danger of numbers dwindling — so long as there was sufficient krill in the sea to feed the thousands of mouths. With a likely life span of twenty to thirty years and an increment of one chick per pair per year after the first nine or so years, there should be plenty of chicks to spare for the pot.

Dr Dominic Serventy, who had no axes to grind regarding profits from harvests, reckoned that Trefoil Island could produce 200,000 harvestable chicks per year with no deleterious effect on numbers, this rather more than the 171,362 birds recorded as having been killed in 1790.

When Serventy ringed 300 birds here only a third of these turned up in the processing plant. This may have been "rigged" by birders wishing to justify their activities in relation to conservation of the population, but, if it was a genuine random sample in the part of the rookery known to be harvested, it suggested that two-thirds of the youngsters might be evading capture. The 1971 take was of 192,500 birds, very close to the recommended maximum.

The 1995 annual report on mutton birds, compiled by the Tasmanian Parks and Wildlife Service (successor of the old Tasmanian Fauna Board) recorded the commercial harvest on Trefoil Island that year to be 106,400 of the estimated 520,000 available chicks — assuming only half the burrows to be occupied.

Figures for other islands of the Hunter Group in 1995 showed takes of 21,000 from 98,100 on Walker Island, 18,000 from 155,250 on Steep Island and 11,578 of 118,000 on Three Hummock Island. None of the 93,500 on Hunter Island were collected that season, suggesting that they might still be regarded as of inferior quality.

More likely this was just part of the gradual diminution in markets. There was no harvest on Babel Island, either, in 1995, where the number of chicks ripe for the taking was reckoned to be 1,430,000 — almost three times the population on Trefoil Island. The only commercial harvest in the Furneaux Group that year was on Great Dog Island — 46,447 or 12% of the 375,000 chicks fledged. This amounted to little more than 2.5% of the total available from just these two islands, ignoring the rest. Taking both groups together, the commercial toll was just 7%, with perhaps another 3% taken non-commercially, the total falling well within the annual sustainable yield of 27%.

The dwindling of harvests is fuelling the steady increase of bird numbers in the Hunter Group, where commercial colonies on Walker, Robbin and Three Hummock Islands were non-existent or very small until the turn of the century.

Irynej Skira's detailed background information for the mutton bird management programme suggests that the population, formerly in equilibrium with the available resources, was given a boost by the unprecedented slaughter of whales, seals and fish in the nineteenth century, disrupting the food chain and releasing more food for their use.

Nevertheless, without the conservation of birds for the annual harvest, all the islands might have been turned over to grazing and many of the rookeries destroyed. Meat and oil are still saleable, despite the shrinking markets, but the outlet for feathers closed in 1994. The three tons produced annually represented only one week's stock for Kimpton's Feather Mill in Melbourne, which had bought them since the 1930s, and they were regarded as inferior to duck and goose down, which involved smaller freight costs.

The Commonwealth Government acquired Trefoil Island in 1980 for traditional use by the Aboriginals, to ensure the continuation of birding, but no increase is envisaged.

Our part-Aboriginal hosts in the late 1950s, the 'farm labourers' who brought in the harvest, were ill satisfied with the current system of collection. Each load of birds had to be carried back to one of three large huts instead of to six smaller ones more strategically placed around the island. Small sheds could each be worked by four men, whereas large sheds needed twelve to fourteen men, as so much time and effort went into carrying birds long distances from the burrows, with no vehicular help.

But this was not all. Birds carried for a quarter of a mile arrived at the treatment huts cold, having lost their body heat, and this made the plucking more difficult. Usually the parts of the rookery furthest from the huts were never worked.

Disgruntled they might be — like many other labourers gathering harvests from land or sea — but they believed in their product, and had miracle cure stories to tell of the medicinal properties of mutton bird oil, particularly in relation to chest complaints.

By 1971, twelve years after my visit, there were four collecting sheds for plucking, scalding and gutting, and tractors collecting tins, each containing 100 carcases, every evening and taking them to the processing 'factory' alongside the new airstrip. Here birds were subjected to a jet of salt water under pressure and then passed between foam rollers to squeeze out the excess liquid. Sorted for size, the bigger ones destined for New Zealand, they were packed twelve in a box and conveyed to the freezer, for eventual export by air. The smallest ones were rubbed with salt, in the traditional manner and packed in four pound, plastic-lined tins.

By this time, fresh frozen birds were being cooked in vast ovens, in Hobart or Launceston, to be sold as ready-cooked convenience food, to a public not brought up in the tradition of preparing their own. Twelve hundred birds were cooked daily in each oven, taking one and a quarter hours to pass through on a conveyor belt. How very different from the late 1950s!

The normal method of killing the chicks was a swift breaking of the neck. These half-castes believed this method to cause blood to accumulate in the chest and they preferred to smash the heads, when the meat was "White and a pleasure to look at". A gruesome business, whatever way it was achieved, but one could only hope the end to these small lives scarcely begun was swift.

When the harvest was under way there would be 13 x 4 or 52 birders from the Trefoil rookeries alone, taking their 'leave' in Smithton, intent on imbibing their pay in liquid form. No wonder my erstwhile policeman friend from the West Coast had singled Smithton out as the place where pubs overran their licencing hours by the widest margin.

We were told that 300 feet high Trefoil Island had been named from the sea by the mariner, Flinders, who thought it looked as though it was covered with trefoil. (Could he have been a homesick Irishman?) Later landings were said to have proved that it was, though the botanist in me wondered what native trefoil this could be, as all the clovers were introduced during subsequent settlement, the only one at all common even now being subterranean clover.

There were no indigenous snakes on Trefoil Island to bother the birders except for odd ones brought in with the firewood, but these could not be trifled with. We learned of a man who had had his ear bitten when carrying wood to fuel the bird scalding fires and had died.

Our hosts were in no hurry to return to their hut building and regaled us with stories of their earlier rough, tough lives in the whaling industry and experiences with antarctic shrimps and many more. They were still taking goodies from the sea, having got twenty-two crayfish in their pots the day before — rather many for just two of them to cope with. So are the poor rich when bounteous Nature smiles. When we left, we were each carrying a large newspaper parcel of crayfish — worth a great deal more on the mainland than the forgotten newsprint replacement that we might have given in return.

* * * * *

We took off from Trefoil Island into the wind and were soon circling over the magnificently formed Steep Island or Steep Head Island, with its clear sea water lagoon in a circular crater. This was delimited by knife-edge cliffs, 200 feet high, dropping almost vertically to the sea on both sides in places. The enclosed water lay translucently calm, aquamarine, with cobalt patches over the kelp and sea-grass beds and overshadowed by steep grassed slopes, burned brown by the sun.

Steep Island was riddled with burrows, in soil said to be only twelve to eighteen inches deep, and was believed to have a potential harvest of 45,000 birds in the days before erosion had set in, although only 32,000 shearwaters burrowed in the 1920s. There were some 30,000 there now and thought to be no room for more, but this prediction was belied by the 1995 census of 155,250 burrows.

The steep little island had not been worked for twenty years now and was said to be going downhill as a money-making enterprise, although one of the first to be exploited. Along with Trefoil Island, it was purported to be the only one harvested in the 1890s, before the general spread of birds throughout the area had begun.

Steep Island occupies thirty to fifty acres, depending on how one assesses precipitous slopes of considerable extent, yet little more than a fine line on a two dimensional map. The soil is pebbly, with not much sand, making digging difficult, so that burrows are shallow. A birder met later said that a lot of loose pebbles usually had to be cleared from the burrow before they could haul the chick out. Despite the almost perpendicular nature of much of the terrain, penguins were said to nest right to the summit.

Poa tussock covered most, with greenswards of leafy peppercress, which was referred to as goose-weed by the birders. Clumps of red pigface in the south-east concealed a large number of white-faced storm petrel burrows.

There was no question of landing here, in the absence of suitable beaches, and to make an airstrip would ruin half the island and remove the reason for needing to visit. After circling low enough for me to conduct my first aerial plant survey, we headed off for nearby Hunter Island.

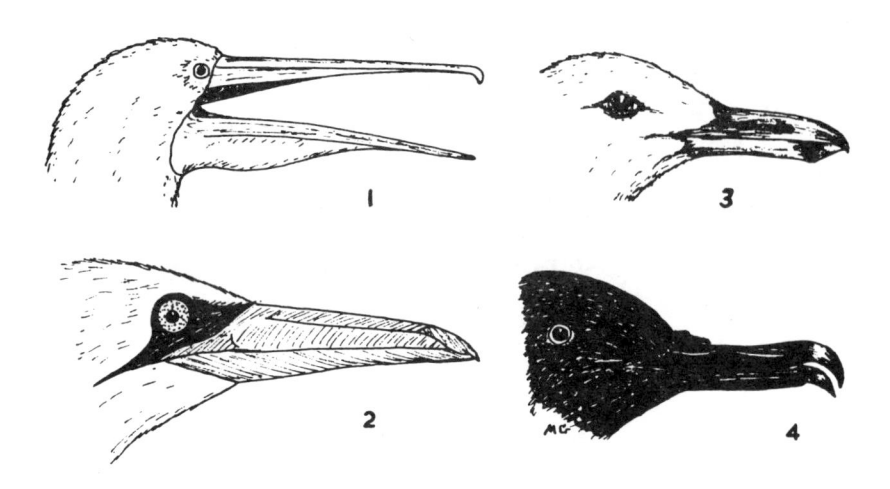

162 Sea Bird Beaks: Pelican, Gannet, Gull, Shearwater

163 Black or Grey Duck *Anas superciliosa*

164 Ross's Noonflower or Karkalla *Carpobrotus rossii*

Chapter Nineteen

AIRBORNE VISITS TO MORE NORTH-WESTERN ISLES

1. HUNTER ISLAND AND THE STACK

Karl Jaeger headed the little Tiger Moth plane into the south-east corner of Hunter Island for a beach landing. We skimmed over the tumble of rocks at the near end of the beach, with what could have been little more than a few inches clearance, but rolled to a smooth halt on firm, tide-washed sands. Again the craft had to be pegged down against the wind, before we retreated to the shelter of some boulders for our lunch.

The southern shearwater rookery spreading up the slope behind us was the main one on the 30,000 acres of Hunter Island, and included an outlier offshore, the Stack. In the late 1950s it was yielding an annual harvest of 12,000 chicks, workers taking an average of 400 a day during a six day working week. With numbers at this high level, it was comforting to know that a substantial proportion of the population was fairly safe from exploitation among spiky bushes.

Two thousand of the harvested birds came from Stack Island beyond the Hunter Passage. Sixty years before, at the end of the nineteenth century, birders claimed that there were 25,000 burrows on this rocky tump, from which 7,000 — 8,000 chicks were taken annually.

There were also rabbits, however, and the combined digging, scuffing and grazing had initiated a general collapse, followed by severe sand blowing. The octogenarian birder, Mr Samson, claimed that the whole island apart from the rock itself had blown away. Another birder, Mr Burnell, reported that the tussock grass recovered sufficiently well in the next quarter century to have attracted back a hundred pairs of nesters by the mid-1920s, and that there had been a steady rise since, as drifting dust and sand were trapped between the clumps. No doubt many of the birds nested in rock crevices, not relying on the fragile skin of soil for cover.

The rabbit population was kept in check by the limited amount of forage, only a small patch of grass on the summit being available to sustain them. When this was used up they gnawed the bark off the tea-trees, then many died of starvation, giving the grass a chance to regenerate, so the rabbit population went in cycles.

The only other island thought to have any rabbits at that time was Penguin Island off the east side of Hunter Island, although Hunter Island itself had had some warrens in the past.

* * * * *

Hunter Island is elongated from north to south, with twenty-four km between the southern Stack and Cape Keraudren in the north. Amidships the strip of land broadened to six km, with a lighthouse on a west-facing headland.

The shearwater rookery which we explored after lunch occupied the southern tip of the island, from coast to coast. Although commercial birding was carried out here, many of the burrows were in dense dune scrub, well out of reach of the harvesters.

Karl thought the law should be changed, to enable birding to be carried out by night as well as by day, when the youngsters might be out of the burrows and easier to pick up. The main difficulty with this was that more adult birds were abroad than young ones during the hours of darkness — either swooping in from the sea with crops full of half-digested krill or released from brooding duties underground and off to get a well-earned feed. Although less and less time was spent brooding as the nestlings got bigger, the intensity of the unearthly crooning was proof enough that plenty of foragers were still plumping earthward through most of the harvesting season.

Grabbing birds in the dark would be quite unselective. Not only are adult birds too tough to eat, no breeders being less than five years old, but this would be culling the geese that laid the golden eggs. Inroads into the capital as well as the interest — much of which would be lost by later mortality at sea anyway — would jeopardise future harvests.

Not until the end of the breeding season did the adults stop coming ashore, leaving the chicks once they had attained a weight greater than their own, to make their own way to the sea when they got hungry enough. For only the few nights before they left would the youngsters be out in the open on their own, exercising their long, unmanageable wings in preparation for their final departure.

While the law remained as it was, those birds clever enough to nest in the scrub without getting tangled up, were likely to rear their full quota of offspring, at least as far as the fledging stage.

As both birders and scientists were fond of telling us, the short-tailed shearwater still vies with the Wilson's storm petrel as Australia's most numerous bird, despite the magnitude of the annual harvests. The short-tailed, too, is the only shearwater to nest exclusively in Australia.

It was here, off Three Hummock Island, that Matthew Flinders wrote in 1798:- "There was a stream (of birds) from fifty to eighty yards in depth and 300 yards or more in breadth. The birds were not scattered, but flying as compactly as free movement of their wings seemed to allow, and during a full hour and a half this stream of petrels continued to pass without interruption. On the lowest computation I think the number could not have been less than a hundred million."

Later workers regarded this as a considerable underestimate!

The birds were thriving then and were thriving still, despite the huge commercial harvests taken over the years since there were men here to take them. Where the substrate is right, there can be 2,500 burrows to the acre (zero point four hectares), all containing a pair of breeding birds.

The years of bird banding in the Eastern Bass Strait Islands has established that an individual bird returning to the same burrow to breed thirty-six years in succession has a life almost twice as long as that of a horse and nearly three times that of a cat or dog, although longevity is so often related to size.

The yellow rocks of Hunter's southern foreshore changed to white on the south-east corner, while the rest was characterised by extensive sand blows. The rookery by the south-eastern huts was in almost pure beach sand, very collapsible and stabilised mainly by sword-grass and silver tussock. Purple swainsonia, Ross's noon flower and knobby club-rush helped to bind the soil, and there were a few bushes of white correa, coast wattle and coast tea-tree.

Further afield the colony looked less vulnerable to wind blow, stabilised by coast beard heath and boobialla bearing purple fruits to tempt passerines. Small nettles and large mullein mingled with slender thistles which swarmed around the huts.

The rookery followed a narrow valley, its flanks bushy with coast banksia and tree broom heath. Burrow density was about two per square metre, despite heavy trampling by cattle and fouling with their dung.

Hunter Island was government owned, the grazing leased to McGuire, who ran 600-700 head of cattle here. Although there was reckoned to be not overmuch feed, shelter was good and the cattle did well. On Three Hummock Island across Hope Channel, (also government-leased) the animals could only be classed as stores when growth ceased and they had to be shipped elsewhere for fattening.

The valley head merged into woodland with bracken understorey, where the burrows faded right out, reappearing in grassy clearings where shiny cassinia was disappearing under wiry tangles of climbing lignum.

In my wanderings I came across a few penguins, a brush-tail possum and a whip snake, part, I learned subsequently, of a considerable snake population.

Mr Sampson told me later that this southern rookery was non-existent in 1900, although birds probably started to colonise soon after. At that time there were two shearwater nesting areas on bluffs of the west coast and a generous scatter of smaller ones were now extending south from these. The western outliers were purported to hold no less than 100,000 young birds, these having never been harvested.

In 1925 a new rookery was opened up on the east coast, half a mile to the north, twenty to thirty burrows appearing in high dunes, but the modest collection of burrows in the north was occupied by penguins.

Hunter Island was too big to walk across in the time at our disposal, so we took off from the beach to make another landing on the airstrip, to allow me to get a look at scrub vegetation unaffected by birds.

We circled over the inland lagoons on the south-west of the island where black swans sailed the waters among the flotillas of ducks that attracted wildfowlers to the island.

"I won't circle the house to say 'how do'" bawled Karl (we were too low to risk stalling the engine). "I've been in and out during the past two days delivering and collecting shooting parties."

Landing here was no problem. The landing field was dominated by a smooth sward of native danthonia grass with bog club moss and sedge-like tufts of

Hypolaena fastigiata. Round about were eucalypts, silky tea-trees and heath tea-trees, big scented paperbarks and two-styled she-okes.

Heath plants were exemplified by heath proper, Victoria's national flower, broom spurge, spreading guinea flower *(Hibbertia procumbens)* and a fine-leaved parrot pea. I made a rapid list of the plants and we were aloft again within the hour.

A small fishing boat lay at anchor on the west side of the island.

"They're asleep" exulted Karl. "They've been putting their cray pots down and they're having a siesta while the crays drop into them. Let's beat 'em up." Suiting action to words, he zoomed down from the peace of the heavens, skimming so low that his wing nearly brushed the deck. I began to wonder whether it was me or them that was being beaten up. The crew crawled up through the hatch, rubbing sleepy eyes, and we left to the shaking of fists.

165 Silver Banksia *Banksia marginata*

166 Variable Groundsel *Senecio pinnatifolius* and
Rough Fireweed *Senecio hispidulus*

167 Nankeen Kestrel Falco *cenchroides* and
Shiny Cassinia *Cassinia longifolia*

2. THREE HUMMOCK ISLAND, SANDY AND STONY PETREL ISLANDS AND WALKER ISLAND

Three Hummock Island was our next port of call. As before, we headed in to a point just below the clifftop. When I expressed alarm (later), I was reminded of the up-currents of air that lift planes as well as gulls to the level of the land above.

"Come in at what you think looks the right height and you get lifted up and over and off the island on the other side before you can get your wheels down!"

We turned in over a lagoon, where cattle were standing up to their withers in water, to get away from the flies, and touched down on a hummocky paddock in the west. This had been ploughed at some time in the past, but was not a recognised airstrip.

A small new rookery had recently been started here by an overspill of shearwaters from elsewhere. Karl had only visited it once before — in the dark — and it took him a while to find it. We walked over a mile, back and forth before homing in on it. Ten years before there had been no birds nesting here.

Another rookery in the west had suffered a general collapse ten to twelve years before, in the 1940s, burying the young birds, whose bones were spread through the surface sand. Breeders had returned to open up new burrows since, but there was little or no harvesting here. A rookery existed near the automatic lighthouse at Cape Rochon in the North-east and a much older one in the South-east, established in 1900. The Mermaid Rookery was unusual in that the birds burrowed in quite clayey soil, instead of the usual looser sand. I was assured that these birds had not taken over ready-made burrows from rabbits.

Sheep and cattle were run on Three Hummock Island, although the soil was very deficient in cobalt and, to a lesser extent, magnesium. Their pastures had been sown with perennial ryegrass and subterranean clover. The one examined contained another thirty plant species, more than half of them the same that invade ryegrass pastures in the UK.

These weeds also ran amok in the disturbed soil of the bird colonies, where cat's-ear, rough hawkbit, buck's-horn plantain, sheep sorrel, Yorkshire fog and silvery hair-grass gave an almost perfect illusion of a Manx shearwater colony off the coast of Wales.

There were some natives among the indigenous grasses and sedges: — smooth grey domes of button-bush, the elegant spiky wattle known as prickly Moses and untidy swamp paperbarks, pushing from gritty sand and white quartz chippings. Angled lobelia and kidney-weed filled some of the gaps, while tiny feathery mounds of *Centrolepis* peeped out beneath aromatic sticky boronia.

While I was fossicking through the rookeries, the pilot went off to rout out Commander Allison, owner of the nearby house, who had offered me accommodation — way back — had he been in residence. He wasn't. We spotted him later on, off Robbins Island, in his fine yacht, speeding south, with all sails set.

But that was on the flight after next. First we took to the air again for a short hop to the other side of Three Hummock. This was too far away for us to reach on foot with such a tight schedule if schedule it could be called. Our progress was savouring more and more of maximum use of an all-day ticket on the local buses!

It was a beach landing again this time, on the south-east corner. We had another shearwater colony to view before taking off for the next of these intriguingly different fragments of Mother Earth, dropped like pearls in the turbulent waters of Bass Strait, for the sole use, it seemed, of these so pelagic sea birds, which could do everything they had to do at sea, except rear their chicks.

Backing the pristine golden sands, on which our wheel tracks formed the only blemish, were two contrasting rock types. To the eye not versed in geology, these looked like a black basaltic conglomerate or pudding stone, and a coarse, crystalline granite.

To the west, rolling dunes extended well inland with the fresh mauve flowers of sea rocket following the blow outs towards more stable scrub, as on temperate beaches the world over.

To the east the sand was firmer, accommodating the astonishing number of three to four burrow mouths per square metre. These tunnels must surely run into each other below the surface unless some of the holes might represent breaks in the roofs. It was scarcely conceivable that each denoted a separate nesting pair.

Although so bountifully blessed, this rookery had not been harvested since the taking of a limited number of birds a few years back. Livestock was excluded by the density of the surrounding scrub of sticky-leaved daisy bush, but this was open-based and birds were able to creep in below without getting tangled up. Roots tapping the depths for moisture would give stability as well as hindering easy digging. As in most natural situations, a compromise had to be reached.

Apart from the shrubs encountered already, sea box and Tasmanian coast everlasting contributed to the thicket. Blue penguins, at the peak of their moult, found shelter here, as well as the shearwaters.

* * * *

Staggering back to the plane, clutching a growing sheaf of notes and lists, I detected a slight wilting of the inner woman, physically, mentally and emotionally. There were no such signs in my pilot and he regaled me with a (stalled) commentary on the rookeries of Sandy and Stony Petrel Islands as we flew over them, unable to touchdown.

These two lay off the north end of Walker Island, which itself lay off the northern point of Robbins Island. There were actually four islands, harbouring a lot of mutton birds in tussock grass, the largest quite flat and supporting some scrub.

A band of slate reaches right across Walker and Robbins Islands and out through the Petrel Islands, its worn surface covered by sand on Sandy Petrel until the big sand blow in 1890 which had destroyed the rookery there.

Coast wattle had grown up subsequently, serving to hold the sand together, and birds began to move back, building up to about 500 pairs by the late 1920s. Their guano had deleterious effects on the wattle but boosted the succulent pigface, which clambered over its low branches as these died and sagged. Shearwaters continued to increase, notwithstanding harvesting. Samson put the late 1959 numbers at 6,000 — 7,000 pairs: Burnell, more optimistically, at 10,000.

Little soil covered the rock of Stony Petrel Island, but the tussock bases had built up on the three acres to accommodate about 1,000 burrows. The devastating fire here, which had burned off the strawey mat, was in 1926, followed by at least one year of no birds at all. Build up in the next thirty years had brought the population to 500 — 600. Now the birders were back, an added bonus being the absence of snakes likely to be coiled in the burrows, enjoying the body warmth emanating from the fat chicks.

* * * * *

We landed on a sandy beach at the west of Walker Island. Karl was worried that the sand might prove too soft: he had been bogged down here once before.

"If I feel the wheels sinking I'll rev up and we'll take off again, without losing way." He kept close to the sea where the sand was firmer, his wing tip overlapping the sucking wavelets. All was well and we taxied along this long straight beach and round the corner to a shorter one, nearer the rookery and firmer under wheel.

Time was short and the tide making, and time and tide wait for no man. The beach was almost horizontal: it would go under as a unit in less time than it took to tell. It looked a bit rash to me but Karl seemed to be happy — so long as we were quick. We were. I raced off to do my stuff, working against the clock, as so often on islands.

Walker provided conditions more suited to birds than birders. Its 4,000 acres had apparently held no birds in 1870, 1,000 pairs by the 1890s and 3,000 by the late 1920s. Now there were reputed to be between 25,000 and 50,000, about 20,000 of these taken for the pot. The widely fluctuating estimates came from different sources, a population of such magnitude being impossible to count and any assessment highly subjective. Samson believed there to have been a tenfold increase in the island archipelago as a whole during the last sixty years.

Hundreds of acres of Walker Island were covered by scrub, which "not even a dog could get through", but somehow the birds managed to nest in it, quite immune from human molestation. A few acres were burned allowing tussock to take over, but the shearwaters were slow to move back.

Harvesters claimed that youngsters growing up in scrub or fern were smaller than those from tussock country. They were also slower to mature, possibly because of the high infestation by bracken ticks. Harvest season used to open on 19th March, but the date had been put back to the 27th recently, as the pin feathers were so much harder to extract from chicks which were not fully developed — quite apart from the inferior weights.

Two birders' huts stood at the north end of Walker Island opposite the Petrel Group, on an oasis of tussock in a sea of scrub. Our landing was at the other end, on the edge of Mosquito Sound, the sandy channel separating Walker from Robbins Island.

An unexpected find at the back of the rippled sands was mudwort, an unassuming little rosette plant of wet, muddy hollows, native to but very rare in Britain. With it were a moisture loving sedge, *Scirpus inundatus*, and sea rush, grading up to dune pepper cress.

Penetrating the western scrub, which included white elderberry and fringe beard heath, I encountered a bandicoot and some small wallabies — an unexpected bonus for so brief a visit. There were snakes here, too, but I did not linger long enough to find out which kinds.

Burrows were quite sparse at first, penetrating pure white sand at a density of about one per three square metres, but they increased where bracken afforded more stability and reached to one per square metre in pockets of tussock and sedge, which was the preferred vegetation in all localities, both Tasmanian and Victorian.

Further north there had been some controlled burning, possibly to help birds and birders, possibly livestock and graziers. I saw neither sheep nor cattle, but the area had been grazed recently. A stream trickled seaward, nurturing slender pennywort and sea celery, with a backing of native nettle.

The rookery extended up a sandy valley behind a bushed ridge, half in tussock, half in bracken. My plant list numbered twenty-nine species by the time Karl's urgent shouts summoned me pell-mell back to the landing beach.

He went ahead, saying he'd get the engine started. I was not far behind but found the plane was surrounded by water, on a slight elevation less than its own diameter and diminishing apace. The sea had sneaked into the end of the headland that we had rounded, effectively cutting us off from the long landing beach.

We had to wade through a hollow to landward of the beleaguered aircraft before tumbling aboard. Karl steered the plane between outcropping rocks to the point. Here he had to hop out and lift the tail round to face about, so that we headed into the wind, as there was no room to taxi. Meanwhile I struggled with straps and crossed my fingers.

With no chance of reaching the long beach, we had to make the best of the short one. The plane raced madly through the shallows, raising fountains of spume and narrowly missing the rock platform near where we had parked. It veered seawards the moment it became airborne, just in time, to swing out across the end of the bounding headland instead of running into it. I let out the long breath that I discovered I had been holding. This day was not short of thrills.

The grim lines on Karl's face relaxed, the Aussie nonchalance returned as he pretended that such little problems were all in the day's work, and conversation was resumed.

168 Green Rosella *Platycercus caledonicus* and
Sweet Wattle *Acacia suaveolens*

169 Grey Fantail *Rhipidura fuliginosa* and
Common Heath *Epacris impressa*

170 Beautiful Firetail Finch *Emblema bella* and
Juniper Wattle *Acacia ulicifolia*

3. ROBBINS ISLAND

I thought we must be on the way home by now, but no, there was still Robbins Island to visit. We sped across Mosquito Sound and on over extensive mobile dunes bordering the northern lagoons.

A neat homestead, with yards full of idling cattle had been cut from the eucalyptus scrub of the island centre, the bulk of which remained rough, but some paddocks had been cleared in the south-east. It was on one of these, by the old abandoned school house, that we landed — to the consternation of the carthorses whose reverie we shattered. I nipped a bit off one of the eucalypts, and this was later identified at the National Museum of Victoria as manna gum.

The unexpected presence of the school house pointed to a once more thriving population than at present. Robbins is one of the largest islands and is closest to the mainland, so it is natural that it should have become settled in the early days, when everyone travelled by boat. It is, in addition, accessible from the mainland on foot, or with horse and cart at very low tide, the crossing of Robbins Passage lying a little to the west of Montagu Island.

It has been occupied since before 1850 — many of the original ditches dug by convicts — and paddocks were already delimited by 1900. These exploited the patches of good soil among much which was poorer, the sites identified by the natural vegetation which they carried.

Like Trefoil Island, which is not much further from the mainland, but more difficult of access, it changed hands many times. One of the major difficulties, that of getting livestock on and off, might be thought to have been eased by the low tide land connection, but this failed to help. Having livestock at large on the mud flats could be a nightmare and animals were transported by barge on a fuller tide when the Van Diemen's Land Company had charge of the island.

Trefoil Island, too, was settled early, being leased for £25 a year in 1874, when the fortunes of the owning Van Diemen's Land Company were low. Because of the quantity of mutton bird guano sprinkled across most of that island during the birds' breeding season, Trefoil Island's grazing was always regarded as superior to that of the mainland.

Tea-trees in the north-east of Robbins Island formerly harboured wallabies, as well as affording good sheep shelter, but this site had suffered some severe sand blows and was now badly eroded. Mutton birds started to invade the paddocks and burrow under the buildings between 1910 and 1920.

The rookery where we landed was between Guyton Point and Cape Elie in the south-east and was known as the Bluff. Another, the Little Bluff, in the north, is now much bigger, although no birds were recorded there either sixty or ninety years before. Today's birders suspected that they had been over exploited by the Aboriginals, but this seems unlikely, with a nomadic people only too well versed in the art of conserving their resources for another year. We shall never know.

Bird numbers began to build up from the Little Bluff and spread along the east coast, with 200 burrows counted in 1898. They peaked at 7,000 — 8,000 in 1950, since when there had been a drop to less than 2,000, which was out of keeping with growth in the rest of the archipelago, and not satisfactorily explained. Maybe birds were moving from one site to another and not fluctuating in numbers.

The locals put the exodus down to the march of the bracken, the strong underground rhizomes obstructing the nesting tunnels. It is unlikely that the light cover of the fronds above ground would prove too much of a hindrance, although making burrow recognition from the air difficult and necessitating an exit afoot before an opportunity to get airborne was found.

Robbin's 26,000 acres was an amalgam of open-floored sclerophyll woodland, tangled scrub, windy heath and mobile dunes, with a few cleared fields. Birds burrowed deeply in the dark sand of the cart horse paddock, where 35% of the ground was bare and 50% covered by ryegrass and barley grass, in contrast to 90% of ryegrass in their absence. The eighteen other species seen in the rookery were all English farm weeds, with not a single native.

I was told later that horses dislike the smell of mutton birds and seldom venture into rookeries. This could be to avoid stepping through into unseen burrows and breaking a leg, these the weightiest of the farm livestock and likely to injure themselves — as well as the burrow occupants.

This was an inland bulge of a clifftop rookery beyond the fence, which dropped to what appeared to be a raised beach of black cobbles. Of eleven other species here, only the knobby club-rush and bracken were indigenous. Further along birds were living in a 70% cover of native spiny mat-rush, co-habiting with small, mound-building black ants, thousands of which were just setting off on their nuptial flight.

Sand was firmer here, allowing incipient colonisation of manna gum and coast paperbark seedlings, Conversely, the rookery on the steeper section of cliff was very mobile, the sand precariously held by Yorkshire fog and barley grass with slender thistle.

Silty soil was hard and unburrowed. This ground was steep and terraced by parallel sheep tracks following the contours, and probably never ventured onto by cattle. It seemed that the slaty rocks yielded an unsuitable burrowing medium until ameliorated by blown beach sand.

While I did my brief survey of the rookeries, Karl picked a fine bunch of hydrangea flowers from the overgrown school garden for his wife. Dusk was not far away when we took off — after chasing the carthorses from our line of progress.

Crossing the low lying southern paddocks, we spotted 'the Yank', who had recently bought the island from Holman, and dipped in salute — then headed out across the shallow strait, which came above water at low tide.

Back along the coast Karl described a tight circle and a turn over his house, to notify wife Joan that we were back and would like to be collected, and then landed for the eighth time. Nine islands had been viewed, five of them not landed on but two landed on twice. I had come to enjoy the gentle approach to earth at slow speed — so much more circumspectly than the tremendous roar of a big plane landing at speed. It seemed cosy somehow, as a little touring car is to an express train.

As I extricated myself from the safety straps, I noticed that the fuel gauge was sitting perilously near zero. I had seen Karl keeping his eye on it during the last few laps. We had used almost every drop of the nineteen gallons put in when we left, nineteen gallons that had made possible a memorable day — for me if not for him.

Joan was astonished to learn where we had been. Her comments on three of our destinations were: "But he's never landed there before." "So he's started landing there, has he?" "He hates having to land there, he must have been feeling particularly daring today." Then the admission. "I've only flown with him once — over Smithton — never again!"

In 1972, despite the fine new landing strip on Trefoil Island, the Department of Civil Aviation was concerned at the grim record of eight light plane accidents off the north coast and islands in eighteen months, and it was feared that the island airstrips would be closed until upgraded. It was the beginning of the five week mutton bird season in early April and the annual turnover from Trefoil Island alone was 80,000 dollars at that time, so any such closure would have spelled disaster.

Fortunately the airstrips were passed as safe and extra planes were hired to replace those lost, the most recent being the third accident in twenty-six days. Perhaps people were right about the hazards of flying, but fortunately I knew none of this until after the event.

Pat Harrison drove up as we unpacked the gear and I refused the Jaeger's kind invitation to dinner as she was expecting to take me back. A welcome shower, a change of garments, hot roast chicken and we settled to a cosy evening round a blazing log fire, helping the middle range of the five children with their French homework.

171 Blackwood *Acacia melanoxylon*

172 White-faced Herons *Ardea novaehollandiae*

173 Silver Gulls *Larus novaehollandiae*

Chapter Twenty

KING ISLAND IN MIDWINTER

1. LAND SETTLEMENT SCHEME AND NORTHERN MUTTON BIRDS

King Island, reaching northwards across the western portals of Bass Strait, is part of the old land bridge from Tasmania to Cape Otway in Victoria and the counterpart of the Furneaux Group in the east. Forty miles long and sixteen broad, it lies in mid-channel, some fifty miles from both Tasmania and Victoria. Unlike the Furneaux, it is not a complex archipelago but a single island with a few minor islets close inshore.

It lies athwart the entrance to Bass Strait as far as the prevailing south-westerlies are concerned and has been responsible for as many, if not more shipwrecks than the Furneaux Group. *"Echoes of the Past: The Story of Shipping Disasters on King Island,"* by W. D. Keating, relates the tragic tales of fifty-seven wrecks occurring around the island.

Many of these were in the early 1850s, when the gold rush in Victoria brought large ships pouring into these little-known waters from Europe and America. The erection of Wickham lighthouse in 1861 warned seamen of their whereabouts and lessened the scale of the losses, the decline boosted by three other lighthouses built subsequently.

The airstream which nurtures the 'Roaring Forties' travels unhindered across the Southern Ocean, the nearest land in the direction of its origin being South America. The climate is temperate, with few frosts and few temperatures above twenty degrees Celsius, with a comfortable annual rainfall of thirty-three inches, so wind is the paramount feature.

It is reflected in the 'lean' of trees away from it, this only an apparent lean suggested by a killing of the buds on the windward side, leaving most growth pushing out to leeward. Climatologists tell us that gale force winds of thirty-four knots or more occur on average for 20% of the year, or seventy-three days, with slightly more days than this having 'strong winds'. I must have experienced quite a lot of these during my first visit in late July, 1959. At least, once ashore, I did not need to put to sea and worry about the risk of another wreck.

My King Island plane left Melbourne early on that winter's morning, affording the passengers an expansive view of the partially flooded city and Altona Salt Works, before breaking through the ceiling of cloud to the sunlit firmament above. A rift in the rolling grey mass during breakfast, revealed the long arm of the Mornington Peninsula stretching out to The Heads as we reached the open ocean, and what a breakfast that was. The fresh pineapple, two lamb chops, sausages and tomatoes put the 'plastic' food served up in modern airlines to shame.

I had been put in touch with King Island's ornithologist, Max McGarvie, and he and his wife Helen met me at Currie Airport. They had intended taking me to a shearwater colony at Seal Rocks in the south, but the weather was so foul that they headed north instead — for a hot lunch at their farm and a more local excursion by tractor in the afternoon.

Being farmer as well as naturalist, Max was the perfect guide and the story of the landscape unfolded as we went along, the background theory illustrated by vistas of the rural economy in action. Almost everyone on King Island, Max and his family included, was a relative newcomer at that time and Max was in process of seeking out the whereabouts of the shearwaters and other birds. I was fortunate, indeed, that he was happy to let me tag along — in between the necessary farm chores. Helen, an experienced gardener, was able to chip in with titbits about the plants.

Until the beginning of the 1950s, much of King Island was unbroken and unfarmed. The indigenous forest had been destroyed long before, soon after settlement, and the land had regenerated to a wilderness of tea-tree scrub.

Then "the Bank" stepped in, under the auspices of the Ex-servicemen's Land Resettlement Scheme — clearing the forgotten acres and parcelling them out to returning soldiers who looked set to get them into good heart as productive farmland. My visit coincided with the early days of this process. When I returned in the 1990s, it was to find a very different King Island, supporting a bigger population and beginning to attract tourists.

A dairy farmer, Max had fought in the 1939-45 war and moved in a year earlier to his allocated plot — as others were doing during this period on Flinders Island. As a young man he had been a stockman on a northern cattle station, later tending his own sheep and cattle at Colac in Victoria, so he had the necessary farming know-how. His Colac farm had been flooded when the new lake was constructed there, so he had a strong case to be one of the lucky ones selected to hold land here.

Buildings, livestock and equipment were supplied by the Bank, the farmer paying back over a period of thirty years with interest at three and three-quarters per cent. There were more applicants than there were farms and the successful ones were selected on their potential suitability and pioneering spirit rather than the possession of an adequate amount of capital — as was required in Victoria.

The McGarvie patch was the one furthest from Currie, the island's hub — out on the north-east corner at Martha Lavinia, a location named after the wreck of that name in 1871. The captain and crew had been miraculously saved and returned to Tasmania in the schooner "*Helen*", which was sheltering from the same storm behind New Year Island. Parts of the broken hull were visible for many years afterwards. The McGarvies' outlying location meant that the three blond sons, aged five, seven and nine, had to leave for school every day at 7.30 a.m. to catch the school bus, the oldest, who went to Currie, travelling by devious routes eighty miles each day.

The official target in 1953 was to make 140 farms of from 220 to 250 acres, but sights were set lower at first. On the poor land in the south 200 acres was designated as a "living area": on the better land of the north, 120 acres was regarded as sufficient. This was supposed to carry forty-five dairy cows and their followers but the farmers had found it inadequate. They were hoping to get another 100 acres each when the Cape Wickham lighthouse reserve in the north was divided up shortly. This would be used for the dry stock and would entail Max getting a pony for rounding up his animals. At present, to save having to feed an extra mouth, he had only a dog for this.

It was the Bank which cleared the land initially, bulldozing out the tea-tree scrub and pushing it up in heaps to eliminate the back-breaking sawing, chopping and burning carried out by settlers in the last century. The original plant cover was tall eucalyptus forest with blackwood *(Acacia melanoxylon)*. Almost totally destroyed by fire, these had been partially replaced elsewhere on the island by alien pines. Here only the burned stumps of the big original trees remained, with just a few medium sized ones surviving near Sea Elephant on the east coast.

Where the piles of scrub were burned the grass grew better than elsewhere, the ash correcting the inherent acidity and adding nutrients. This effect lasted for five years. Everywhere the tea-trees — first stage of the succession to regenerated forest — tried to return and subsequent management was geared to repress them. Growth was fast and they soon took over any land that was let go.

Two methods of attack were followed. One was cutting with a rotary slasher, which might have a swathe as wide as eight feet, this repeated at intervals to weaken the plants. The other was to roll, allow the crushed saplings to dry out and then burn them.

The acid soil lacked the macro-nutrients of calcium and phosphorus and the micro-nutrients of copper and cobalt. It is deficiency of these last that causes the nefarious "coast disease", limiting the grazing of livestock to little more than four months a year. Max was giving his cattle and sheep cobalt pellets to compensate — having nowhere else to graze them on his limited acres.

Nitrogen was not normally added as a fertiliser, this being supplied by the natural activities of the clover root nodules, so the ryegrass was poor for the first year or so until the benefits of this were felt. Indeed, much of the seed lay dormant at first and that which did germinate had to be supplemented by another sowing. The standard mixture was perennial ryegrass with white and subterranean clovers, sown in autumn — March or April. Possible additions were cocksfoot grass, strawberry clover and lucerne. Sometimes red-legged earth mites completely eliminated the clover and this land had to be re-sown too, but Max had now 'cleaned out' the mites with a 25% solution of DDT — one of today's banned chemicals.

His initial treatment of newly broken heathland and scrub was to add two tons per acre of lime, followed by annual dressings of one and two-thirds hundredweights of superphosphate per acre with copper and cobalt added, for four years.

In contrast to the beef-producing Furneaux Group, dairying was the island's main industry, with a big export of butter, and formerly of cheese. There was smaller production of fat cattle, wool, mutton, pigs (which included a high proportion of ginger Tamworths) and crayfish. Three crayboats fished from Currie, one of their owners living part time on New Year Island off the west coast.

Land clearance was proceeding apace in the late 1950s and the population was rising steadily from 2,100 in 1953 to nearly 3,000 souls in 1957. Resettlement was scheduled to be complete by 1959, when births were greatly exceeding deaths as a result of the youth of the settlers. The problems of isolation during the 150 years of its development, had slowed down progress, but air transport was helping to minimise this disadvantage. By 1990 farming was prospering, catering for the gourmet market as well as ordinary mortals, with tourists helping to consume the bounteous cray harvest.

Donning all the winter woollies we could lay hands on after that first welcome lunch, Max and I set off on the tractor for the Martha Lavinia rookery. I perched on the mudguard, one foot for'ard on the tool box and the other aft on the hitching bar, swaying drunkenly as we lurched over the rough heathland.

It was typical sedgy, heathery style heath, with twiggy shrublets as we chugged past Lake Martha Lavinia to the sand dunes approximately nine miles short of Cape Wickham, with its 157 feet (48 m) high lighthouse, said to be the tallest in the Southern Hemisphere.

Brush bronze-wing pigeons seemed to be everywhere, defying the weather. There were charming flame robins and rufous fantails and a few marsh harriers swooped across the windy sky. Aliens were best represented by the familiar blackbird, but there were also greenfinches and goldfinches, English pheasants and Californian quails, and the ever present house sparrows and European starlings.

As we approached the mutton bird rookery a sizable Bennet's wallaby went bounding off along the cliff — these the Tasmanian counterpart of Victoria's red-necked wallabies. Max's last sheep dog, Bluey, had had a penchant for wallabies, rounding them up as he rounded up the livestock, but making heavier weather of it. The problem was to know what to do with them when he'd got them. He would chase an animal, quite literally, for hours, herding it back to where Max was working.

Here pursuer and pursued would lie down, looking each other in the eye, too exhausted to go further. Finding that the dog meant it no permanent harm, the wallaby thought it easier to stay beside it than to move off and be chased again. Once they had lain thus for two hours before Max put an end to the stalemate by shooting the 'roo for the pot, but not all Bluey's prizes were betrayed thus by his master.

Later on our rookery jaunt, we flushed a blue-grey possum from its hidey-hole in a tangle of bower spinach. Max nearly trod on it before it emerged, sleepy and slow, wakened from a sort of semi-hibernation. It ambled off into the scrub, well wrapped in thick grey fur with bushy black tail, but pausing to glare at us in disgust at having to turn out in the bitter cold. The bower which had sheltered it was of seaberry saltbush and bower spinach looping over low beach wattle damaged by shearwaters burrowing among the roots.

The older part of the rookery was being choked by these and the birds were moving out. The newest section, an outlier, was in tall wattle and tea-tree scrub, where bird pressure had not yet had time to kill this back. The giveaway rookery plant which led us to it was the seaberry saltbush, straggling up through the dying trees to their very tops.

A delightful floriferous touch was the host of small winter orchids sprouting from the calcareous sand. Quite a few others were flowering, the chill being in the wind, rather than as plant inhibiting frosts.

Young shearwaters had matured earlier than usual this season, but were smaller than the norm, because of shortage of food in the sea, this applying to almost all the rookeries hereabouts.

A recent press report in *"The Burnie Advocate"* stated that the young birds had not gone far out to sea when they left the rookeries but that large mobs were milling around Circular Head at Stanley, when they should have been well on their way to their Arctic wintering grounds in the Bering Sea.

Not all had made it to hatching. I picked up the skeletal remains of an adult that had died while pregnant and disintegrated around the contained egg, which was chalky white, as when newly laid. Small wogs had cleaned up inside the shell, like the one I had found only the previous day in the Cape Woolamai Rookery on Phillip Island in Victoria.

Max told of mutton birds that he had seen flying seven miles from the sea at dawn, when he was fetching the cows, swooping and soaring like swifts. Normally they fly overland only at night. These flew inland in the half light and back out again after full sun-up.

All would be well away now on their great trans-equatorial flight around the North and South Pacific. One of their larger relatives, an unidentified albatross, swept low over the waves beyond the dunes and a pack of gannets was diving for fish. A magnificent white-bellied sea eagle shot past under the impetus of a following wind.

How we wished we could have wound up the windows to keep out that wind as we bumped back on the tractor, but those were the days of the basic Fordson, with none of the weather-proof cabs enjoyed by today's farmers. A cuppa with home-made biscuits by the kitchen fire soon put matters to rights. Then it was outside again, taking hay to the dry cows in the paddock and bringing in the others for milking, escorted through the yard by a gaggle of ducks and hens.

Milking was done in a six cow milking bail, with rather natty leg chains and a few gadgets that were new to me and had been to Max when he arrived. Everything was quite up to date, with the milk pulsating along an overhead pipe to a drum in the dairy. From here it was passed through a separator, the only exportable product being the cream, which went to the local butter factory. The separated milk was fed to the black and Tamworth pigs which lived among a year's regeneration of tea-tree in the calf paddock.

I helped to chain up a few batches of cows but left before the arrival of the two flightiest, which might well have taken to their heels at the sight of a stranger. The wood fire which burned under the dairy sterilising copper, coaxed into being by kerosene, tempted me to linger. When I emerged, Helen was feeding the fowls and collecting the eggs from among the straw bales in the Dutch barn. She would take over the milking when Max had to be away.

We returned to the house, gathering up the pet lamb as we went. He scampered excitedly through the downstairs rooms while his milk was heating on the stove. Once stuck in, his little hooves kept skidding on the kitchen lino as he tried to coax milk through the rubber teat faster than it wanted to come. He need not have bothered. Unlike that in the ewe, this was not likely to move off when he was only halfway through. He was a puny, 'tucked-up' creature, but not lacking in either voice or spirit.

The three boys came in on the school bus, ten hours after they had left in the morning, and were bathed and fed before spreading themselves over the lounge floor in pyjamas, with books. Tough old mallee roots ripped from the new paddocks burned in the big fireplace, sponsoring a drowsiness well suited to story time.

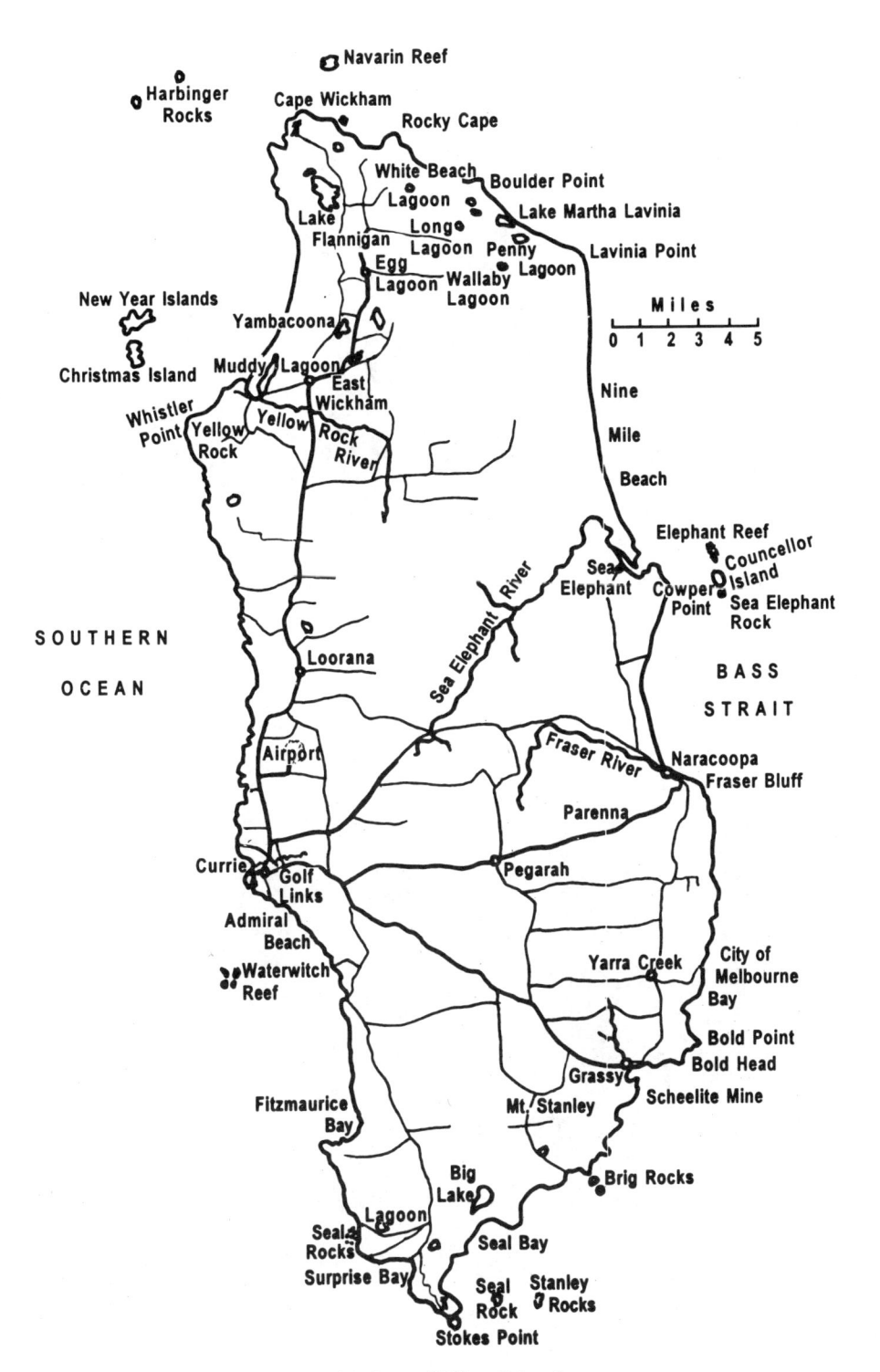

174 Map of King Island

175 Large Black and Black-faced Cormorants
Phalacrocorax carbo and *Leucoarbo fuscescens*

176 Coast Wattle *Acacia longifolia var. sophorae*

2. SKINNER'S GRAVEYARD AND YELLOW ROCK LAGOON

After rising early next day for the morning milking and farm chores, Max, Helen and I were away in the car in search of more mutton birds. We set off north-west, towards Cape Wickham and then cut across the paddocks to intercept the coast on the south-west side of Disappointment Bay. It was my job to open and close gates, whippy affairs of four light poles attached by wires which, with a bit of luck, could be looped over a gatepost, but some had wills of their own.

By the time the going became impracticable for four-wheel drive vehicles, we were already in a shearwater rookery. This land was different from yesterday's, having been subjected to cattle grazing since an earlier resettlement scheme after the 1914-18 war. While most of the bird burrows were on sand hills overlying the granite shore, with its shaggy brown cover of knobby club-rush, a good many penetrated the deep brown loam of the paddock — a surprisingly solid soil for burrows to have persisted through forty years of trampling by cattle.

With no rabbits on King Island, the shearwaters had to dig their own burrows. These were marked by well established patches of Yorkshire fog grass and thistles, with black nightshade, lesser nettle, dove's-foot cranesbill and buck's-horn plantain. The entire sward, weeds and all, was of alien Britishers. Burrows went deep, below the level consolidated by hooves, and greatly enlarged by renovations in successive years.

A bitter wind blew across the island — from the Southern Ocean or the Tasmanian Mountains or both, but it was reasonably sheltered on the seaward side of the north facing dunes. Max found a suitable niche among the rocks and lighted a driftwood fire to heat soup and boil the billy for coffee.

There was no shortage of driftwood here in the path of the Roaring Forties. Earlier in the day Max had been looking longingly at some fine specimens of Oregon pine lying on the beach, but had decided against carrying them to the car — we already had some shorter lengths stacked on its floor. There was a glut of this material on the island as American ships often lashed their deck cargoes with balks of Oregon pine, but were required by law to jettison these before entering Tasmanian ports and jeopardising the home timber crop.

The American timber was likely to be infested with the young stages of a wood-boring wasp, which would be well and truly plasmolysed (it was hoped) by the salt water before the timbers eventually drifted ashore under their own volition. What Max did fall for, to add to his collection of island treasures, was a pair of fine glass flagons which had washed into the mouth of a little creek, probably from some foundered vessel.

Before the building of the two lighthouses at Cape Wilson and Currie in the mid-nineteenth century, many ships and hundreds of lives had come to grief on the surrounding reefs. King Island had earned for itself the unenviable title of 'The Graveyard of Bass Strait'. A recent sinking off the coast in 1934 had triggered the building of a third lighthouse in 1952 at Stoke's Point in the far south.

The timbers which fed Max's billy fire were off ships rather than of ships and they blazed merrily with a salty sputtering, outliving the two short sharp rain squalls which sent us running for the shelter of the car. We stayed inside it to eat, marvelling at the colossal waves breaking over the Navarin Reef a couple of miles offshore, then gathering their forces again to pound the rocks near at hand.

The sandy beach was strewn with granite boulders, the rock platform behind with succulent, saltworthy rock plants. Behind this again was a peaty quagmire, dominated by the sedge, *Carex appressa*, and much trodden by cattle, which went in to graze and drink. Only inland of this did the land rise to the sand hills of the bird colony.

Duly refreshed, we set out on foot for Rocky Cape rookery a few miles along the coast. The track continued, plunging through standing bracken, but was unsuitable for motors. We left it quite soon and took to the rocks, where Max found a simple-fronded polypody fern new to his collection.

Emerging through the silvery spinifex dune grass, onto the long, wave-smoothed stretch of sand, we disturbed seven hooded dotterels, which trotted along in front of us until they reached the end of their beat, then doubled back in flight to resume feeding on their chosen patch. During the last few laps they were joined by a party of smaller, red-capped dotterels which led the posse, their little legs twinkling over the sand at unbelievable speed.

Several dozen swallows skimmed the beach and rested on low outcrops. Cold though we were this midwinter day at latitude forty degrees south, the swallows remained all winter and the bracken stood, wintergreen, although brown-tipped, by the gales. Even Southern Britain, blessed though she is by the warm Gulf Stream, lies some 700 miles further from the Equator, at latitude fifty degrees north.

A small flock of white-fronted chats was busy at the eastern end of the beach and gannets soared offshore on the wings of the wind. Washed up with the flotsam was the sorry corpse of an albatross and we found a few cowrie shells among the run-of-the mill cockles and mussels.

I recognised the big sand blow beyond this end of the beach as the great yellow scar across the base of Rocky Cape that I had seen from the plane as we flew in, the sand ridges running transversely across the cape.

We walked into the blow out and found ourselves among hundreds, possibly thousands of mammal skeletons of various shapes and sizes, among calcified roots which had been exposed by drifting sand many feet below a former land surface.

My questioning comment of "Abo middens?" was met by the information that there had been no Abos on King Island. History tells us that the first men set foot here in 1798 — these being Captain Reed and the crew of the thirty-ton schooner, *"Martha"*. The name of King Island (in honour of Governor King of New South Wales) was not given until three years later, when Captain

Black visited in the brig *"Harbinger"* in 1801. Formal possession for the British Crown was taken by Lieutenant Robbins of the sloop *"Cumberland"* on 14th December 1802.

We decided we must have found our way into a skinner's graveyard, where a fur trapper had abandoned the grisly remains of his toil. I later described the site to Mr Brazenor, director and mammologist at the State Museum of Victoria, and he confirmed our diagnosis. He also identified the two skulls which I took back and passed to him surreptitiously under the table at the formal dinner following a lecture by Professor Hill the next week. (Opportunities come but once.)

The short, broad skull with a full complement of teeth, including canines, had belonged to a silver possum. Although mainly vegetarian, these are actually omnivorous and will eat meat, dead or alive, kill chickens and even attack cats. The long, narrower skull was that of a rufous-bellied wallaby or pademelon. A true herbivore, this had a gap between incisors and molars.

It would have been more exciting if some of these northern relics could have been fossil remains of less everyday creatures, such as were found by J. Bowling at Stokes Point in the South. One of his fossil finds was of the Tasmanian wombat, known to have existed also on Cape Barren, Clarke and Deal Islands, but surviving now only on Flinders Island.

Other fossil finds were of two quolls or native cats, *Dasyurus bowlingii*, named after Bowling, and the spotted *Dasyurus maculatus*: also two kangaroos, *Macropus anak* and the red-necked *Macropus ruficollis*. Perhaps most special was the dwarf or King Island emu, *Dromaeus minor*, known to have been present until at least 1802, but now extinct.

History records that there was much coming and going of game hunters, trappers and sealers to King Island before the area was finally settled around 1855. The main carnage was among the sea elephants and seals, now virtually extinct and remembered only in a few place names.

Thus Sea Elephant Bay was the place where two French ships, *"Le Geographe"* and *"Le Naturaliste"*, were anchored in 1802 when the island was being claimed for Britain — the French, under Commander Baudin, being unable to produce the proofs of occupation that they said they had put at four points on the island to claim it for France.

King Island had a worldwide reputation for sea elephants in the first two decades of the nineteenth century and ships came from all over to exploit them and supply the growing market for the skins in China. Captain Campbell of the *"Snow Harrington"* records the killing of 600 sea elephants and no less than 4,300 seals, mostly on New Year Island, during one short spell.

The first settlers tried to make a living from farming rather than trapping, but their cattle and horses were decimated by a poisonous plant known as the Darling pea or tare *(Swainsonia greyana)*. The sheep tried later fared little better. One settler failed to exercise the option on his lease and sub-let his area for hunting. So often in new countries settlers must live off the wild game until they can clear enough land to start generating their own income.

It is small wonder that so many creatures are on the verge of extinction or were pushed over the brink by early exploitation.

Climbing out of the animal graveyard, only recently exposed by vagaries of sand movement, we had no difficulty in recognising the shearwater rookery on Rocky Cape by the sudden change in vegetation. Massed bower spinach loomed low and green where burrows penetrated, contrasting with the overall community of tussock grass and silvery mounds of cushion bush regenerating after fire.

Cattle had access, but seemed not to venture far into the rookery to get at the succulent herbage. Noon flower is poisonous and spinach, only occasionally nibbled by cattle. Possibly the risk of a broken leg when the soil collapsed underfoot letting them down into an unseen burrow under the trailing shoots deterred them, as it certainly will a horse.

The suggestion had been made in Flynn's rookery on Phillip Island that cattle were afraid of the cooing and gurgling noises arising from the burrows. But this was winter and the birds were not in residence, yet the cattle still fought shy of entering, a reticence seldom shown by sheep.

Plants here included Olearia and Correa bushes permeated by the spear leaves and prickly fruits of sword grass with little clumps of yellow and purple ragwort.

Specimens examined and lists compiled, we made our way back to a sumptuous tea of locally caught sea salmon. On the way we spotted a number of pheasants which, in my limited experience, were more a part of the New Zealand scene than the Australian. As the native targets for the gun-happy residents disappeared, new ones were being substituted. There were still plenty of wild duck and other waterfowl and these were extensively shot, along with what remained of the native game, while mutton birds were there for the taking in season, legally or illegally.

Then there was the fishing, the streams and lagoons full of trout and the coastal waters of fish and crayfish — the latter providing a lucrative living for professional fishermen, both then in the fifties and now in the nineties.

Max told me of a sizable flock of the rare orange-bellied grass parrots *(Neophema chrysogaster)* that had passed through this very place a short while ago. He had notified the Bird Observers' Club in Melbourne and had received instructions to keep quiet about them — agriculturalists often liking to supplement their income by catching such attractive creatures to sell as cage birds.

At that time I had not seen these birds but I have been lucky on two subsequent visits to Australia. In 1982 I was taken by ornithologist Richard Loyn to watch them feeding on the seeds of saltbushes at Point Wilson in Port Phillip Bay, Melbourne — one of their few wintering sites. In 1988 I was fortunate to see a pair in their nesting territory in South-west Tasmania, near Melaleuca Creek. Their fluctuating fortunes are being closely followed by researchers,

Our destination the next day was Yellow Rock rookery on the northern part of the west coast. It was Saturday and the three boys were able to join us. Some of the delightful long-tailed blue wrens flipped around the garden as we prepared to leave and we saw hosts of black swans grazing on the improved pastures as we headed on our way. These were highly unpopular with the farmers, who were not bothered here by Cape Barren geese, as were their counterparts on Flinders Island. This was strange, as these distinctive *Cereopsis* geese extend from Eastern Bass Strait to South Australia, but Max had seen not a single goose on the island since his arrival.

Having been busy during this, their first year, erecting buildings and fences and clearing land, the McGarvies had visited none of the mutton bird rookeries apart from those on their own land and the paddock tracks which we followed from the South Yellow Rock road led us nowhere. Spotting a Dutchman driving a tractor along the crest of a hill, we bumped across to meet him, to be told in perfect Australian with a Dutch accent "No, there ain't no mutton birds ere". He directed us the way he thought we should go and we finished up some distance to the south of our goal.

This was a delightful spot, however, apart from the biting wind, and it proved a fine haven for sea birds. Max was thrilled and resolved to come again. We were on a low rocky coast, where cattle grazing the marshes behind wandered down the beaches to pick at the brown wracks and potter among the rocks, as at home in this environment as cattle in Western Scotland or Ireland. (Fortuitously, some of these brown seaweeds might in due course find their way to join those others in the Hebridean kelp industry.)

Offshore lay the notorious New Year Island and Christmas Island and a series of low rocky reefs broke the force of the waves, with thousands of waterfowl riding the calm waters within. Most of these were black duck and grey teal, seemingly an inexhaustible quarry for the hunters, but there was a good scattering of musk duck and black swans. Little pied cormorants were the most numerous of this group of sinuous necked fishers, but there were a few black-faced cormorants as well.

Sixteen sooty oystercatchers (the first that Max had seen on the island) flitted round the rocks, with fewer pieds, and we were to see more on the morrow on the opposite coast. The flock of white-faced herons was at least seventy-five strong — an astonishing sight, when one is used to seeing these birds in ones and twos. There were fairy terns and spur-winged plovers, alias masked lapwings, both in good numbers, also silver and Pacific gulls.

Marsh harriers quartered the sky and a nankeen kestrel searched diligently with its hawk eyes for land-bound prey. Welcome swallows were enjoying the wind while white-fronted chats were trying to keep out of it, skulking among tussocks. The singing magpies were the white-backed kind, intruders introduced from Victoria in 1910 and now more abundant here than in mainland Tasmania. The British intruders were greenfinches, skylarks and the seemingly inevitable sparrows and starlings.

Some 62,000 pairs of shearwaters were based here on Whistler Point. A much greater concentration was to be found on the two offshore islands — 120,000 on New Year Island and 48,000 on Christmas Island, but these were very much out of bounds for landlubbers.

177 Stinkwood *Ziera arborescens*

178 Black Currawong *Strepera fuliginosus* and Box *Alyxia buxifolia*

179 Coast Tea-tree *Leptospermum laevigatum*

3. ERODING DUNES AND LIMEY CONCRETIONS

Max went off to seek out the shearwaters while I pottered in the silver gull colony, where nests were scattered along verdant lines of ferny sea celery in crevices. The little swamp-weed *(Selliera radicans)* was the only other dinkum native; the rest were from seeds coughed up by the gulls. We met again by the wood fire, where Helen was warming soup and boiling the billy, then swapped areas, Max going to the bird lagoons and me to the shearwaters.

As I approached through wind-battered cushion-bush, I disturbed a large feral cat. He no doubt waxed fat on mutton birds during the summer but didn't seem to be doing too badly now — even without that general stand-by of rabbits.

I was among sand hills here and much of the surface had gone with the winter winds, to expose some spectacular 'forests' of petrified calcareous concretions: calcified plants turned to stone under a blanket of limey shell sand and now exposed again to view as the blanket was lifted.

There were horizontal shelves of consolidated sand projecting over depressions and resisting the undercutting of a wind armed with an abrasive load of mobile sand grains. Similar material rose as walls. This was travertine or aeolianite (aeolian implies wind-borne) — limey sand half changed to sandstone and resisting the test of exposure as the original sand could never have done.

Such intricate fantasies are likely to turn up wherever ground lime and rain water mix to form natural cement, that moulds around or insinuates within other material. Particularly fine specimens occur on the southern islands of Western Australia and at The Pinnacles north of Perth, now a national park. Others are scattered along the south coast to the fine columns and solution pipes of Victorian cliffs where erodible limestones alternate with harder volcanic basalts.

Cattle had access to this area and may have triggered off some of the erosion, but were using the rookery very little at present. Their attentions were centred on the shiny leaves of the boobialla bushes, with slight inroads into the spinach.

Many burrows had been trodden in, to be reopened when the birds returned in spring from their great migration. They were more than on Rocky Cape, where cattle seemed to avoid them, and the whole system was more stable, especially on the steep, fully vegetated slopes which the bovines did not attempt to climb.

The 'petrified forest' had been largely abandoned as a shearwater nest site — deserted burrows collapsed under the onslaught of the erosive forces. There were a few left but a long calm spell would be needed to allow plants to creep back and stabilise things enough for burrowing to re-start. The fairy-tale dunescape had been created by a combination of mutton birds, cattle and wind.

Some scudding rain squalls came in with the unrelenting wind, hastening our return to the evening milking and a supper of home killed roast lamb — not Junior. We picked him up en route. He needed feeding at three-hourly intervals, so he had to be parked out while the family was away. He snuggled up with the boys on the back seat, content to be comfortably warm and headed for the next meal.

Sunday was another cold grey day with intermittent showers. We travelled *en famille* to Sea Elephant on the east coast. This was little more than eight miles away as the crow flies, but forty miles by road. We had to go almost to Naracoopa, which shares its name with the Furneaux Islands' trading ship, a name said to be Aboriginal for something like "Well Met". From here we drove north, with Councellor Island on our right.

Sea Elephant River mouth in pre-settlement days was the site of a thriving sealing enterprise, preying on the great seals which lumbered out of the sea onto the salt marsh south of the river. The exploiters succeeded in exterminating them and the nearest breeding colony of sea elephants at present was probably the one on MacQuarie Island in the Sub-Antarctic. The broad sandy estuary cut through a scrub of banksia, paperbark and tea-tree, floored in part by bog club moss.

Bird-wise it did not come up to Max's expectations, just a few black swans and gulls and skimming swallows. High bracken-clad sand ridges ran parallel to the coast, reaching probably 150 feet high at the seaward end.

While the rest of us ambled around in the wet scrub, Max prospected to see if the continuation of the track was suitable for the car. When he failed to return, I set off in pursuit, armed with a bag of sandwiches and oranges. The track veered away from the marshy river bank, separated from the sea by several lofty ridges. I finally cut across to intercept him on the highest point opposite Councellor Island.

He had found no signs of shearwaters, though this small promontory seemed the most likely spot. He returned while I continued, scrambling up and down where tough bracken impeded progress but provided useful handholds. The broad wooded flat between sand dunes and estuary ahead looked unpromising, so I turned back, and came unheralded on the rookery in the very spot where Max said it wasn't but we both thought it ought to be. Burrows were too sparse to have caused any significant change in the heathy undershrubs.

The nesting area occupied several shallow valleys at right angles to the sea, but not the rising ground between, though continuing over the valley heads and down the seaward slope beyond. This summit furnished a take-off point where birds could get sufficient lift from sea winds to become airborne. Bird tracks converged on it from all directions, baring the final runway, which was bordered by austral stonecrop, noon flower and English fumitory. A few corpses told of birds which had failed to make it. Shrubby fireweed mingled with sedge and grass under bushes of Westringia, coast beard heath, olearia and correa, with spider orchids *(Caladenia patersonii)* and inconspicuous little *Acianthus* orchids.

To landward four Bennet's wallabies were hopping languidly between food items, untroubled by my prying. To seaward a number of skeleton trees lay naked but still rooted on the beach, testifying to a progressive swallowing of the land by the sea. This was further evidenced by the collapsing face of the yellow dune, which appeared to be receding inland and swallowing up some of the shearwater burrows in the process. I found a sheltered nook in which to record my findings, then rejoined the others. Max had stumbled upon the rookery on his way back and was wondering where to hide if I had missed it through misinformation.

We called in at Naracoopa to view the new jetty. This was in the nature of an experiment, to open up the island in all weathers — because Currie was on the west, and often stormbound. Not that the east coast was a sinecure. The first attempt at Naracoopa had been swept out to sea just before completion, but the second still stood. Lagoons lay behind the beach, their wind-ruffled surface providing sustenance for more hawking swallows, with sooty oystercatchers pottering at the water's edge.

We visited the cairn marking the spot where Captain Robbins took possession of the island for the British crown in 1802 — some years after the sealers had taken possession for themselves.

Leaving the white-fronted chats of the coast, we moved into unbroken, heath where black cockatoos chortled raucously from the tops of mighty eucalypts, such as once dominated the whole. (The choicer celery-top pine and sassafras had been eliminated by burning and clearing long since.) Brush bronze-wings foraged along the verges and an echidna appeared at the roadside, delaying its crossing until we had passed. Then we were back on the cleared land with its cattle, Tamworth pigs and free-range turkeys.

Next day I was catching a plane to the mainland, but not until late afternoon. The morning milking completed, we drove to Seal Point in the south-west corner, lingering en route in some delightful rocky bays. We found ourselves in pleasantly undulating dune country, climatically wetter and agriculturally poorer than the north and only partially cleared.

Starlings foraging along the dunes fed on the fleshy fruits of seaberry saltbush and spinach, carrying the seeds back to the boxthorn hedges where they roosted. These germinated, so these rookery dominants had made a partial takeover of the hedges — to feed more starlings and spread yet further.

The metalled road deteriorated into something less than a track and petered out some distance from where we were heading. We continued afoot, along low sand hills and beach, enjoying a beautiful stretch of coast, with dark precambrian rocks pushing from the sand and forming offshore reefs.

Well over fifty black currawongs thronged the beach — far more than I had seen together before. They were very tame, continuing to poke among the stranded seaweed for succulent morsels of animal life as we approached, but keeping a wary eye cocked for anything resembling a gun. On the driftline their sooty plumage merged perfectly with the dark weed and we failed to see many until they rose just ahead of us. The cawing throng escorted us on the first part of our walk — a few paces ahead as we displaced those in the rear. Some breaking away to perch awhile on a boxthorn bush or a wire fence.

When the currawongs dropped behind their place was taken by almost as many white-fronted chats, which are sand hill foragers throughout southern Australia. Again, at something over thirty-five, the flock was larger than I was used to seeing. Other birds were pied oystercatchers, pied shags, silver and Pacific gulls and swallows.

I came upon the first signs of life underground when, head bent to a sudden squall, I raced for cover behind a bush. There were several hundred burrows tucked in among the roots of the introduced marram grass, but they were too small for any bird bigger than a storm petrel — none more than two inches in diameter. I enlisted Max's help.

He excavated some, finding each to contain a nest of yellow grass, chopped into three inch lengths. In among the nest material were tapered, oval dung pellets, which had to be mammalian rather than avian. I produced some of these for Mr Brazenor between courses at the dinner party, with the wallaby and possum skulls, and he had no hesitation in naming them. 'Dark Kangaroo Rats', quoth he, the diagnostic feature being the little tapered beak at the end.

Soon after this find the weather changed for the better, the sun dispelling the icy chill of the morning. I began to lag behind, encumbered by too many clothes. To avoid getting my corduroys sodden, I had donned thin slacks over pyjama trousers, topped off with waterproof over-trousers and a generous helping of jumpers! The lean, more soberly clad and tireless Max pressed on ahead and returned to report a shearwater rookery, so I staggered on.

This colony was most rewarding, with a wide range of soils, plants and degrees of erosion — the whole accessible to cattle and sheep. The scrub was of dusty and club moss daisy bush, with swamp paperbark and common fringe myrtle *(Calytrix tetragona)*.

Part of the rookery on peaty loam had been ploughed, so that returning shearwaters would need to dig out new burrows. This they would do readily, the ploughing loosening things up nicely, and leading to easier digging.

Natural systems are never static, however, and over-population at Seal Point (about one burrow per square yard in the most crowded parts) leads to slums as surely in the world of birds as in the world of man. Spinach and noon flower moved in as the bushes and tussocks died out, finally choking the burrows and causing the birds to move. It was the less palatable of the two, the noon flower, that stood the greatest cattle pressure, being seldom if ever grazed, and much of this, the ultimate survivor, had been torn apart in the recent ploughing.

Chalky concretions from past floras had been exposed by sand-blow in places, but erosion was no longer occurring and much of the land between was covered by noon flower — the first in on new ground as well as the last out on old; maltreatment bringing the vegetation round full circle, back to its starting point. Lesser plants catching the eye included blue Lobelia, hairy and shining pennyworts and South African capeweed. But I had a plane to catch.

The walk back was long and hard and I was bathed in sweat when I rejoined the others at the car — only two minutes behind schedule. Then began a mechanised marathon, with Max at the wheel and Helen plying me with the wherewithal to slake a mighty thirst and quell the pangs of hunger. I scrambled out of one lot of garments and into another for the flight (no-one would have bothered in these enlightened days, thirty years on). Swapping of the nether garments was achieved in Currie High Street while Max went on an errand for a neighbour, lest he see things he shouldn't.

We spotted the plane overhead and timed our arrival at the airport to coincide. There, almost as dishevelled as before the change, and regarded askance by fellow travellers, I bade my kind hosts farewell. As we lifted off I was able to trace through gaps in the clouds the metalled roads we had followed and recognise the skinner's graveyard as we passed out over Bass Strait.

180 Brush Bronzewing Pigeon *Phaps elegans* and
Running Postman *Kennedya prostrata*

181 Hoary-headed Grebe *Poliocephalus poliocephalus*

182 Red-capped Plover or Dotterel *Charadrius ruficapillus* and
Slender Twine-rush *Leptocarpus tenax*

Chapter Twenty-one

KING ISLAND IN MIDSUMMER

1. NORTHERN FARMLANDS

It was 17th January 1990 and, along with a friend from Wales, I had arrived in Launceston after completing the standard coach tour of Tasmania with "Australian Pacific Tours". We were now heading off on our own for some less formal viewing on King Island, away from the tourist trail.

It was unlikely that Max and Helen McGarvie would still be there, after more than thirty years, but it was worth a try. I had sent a letter off into the blue before leaving the UK and had received a warmly welcoming reply.

We flew out of Launceston at lunch time, touching down at Wynyard to pick up a few locals before speeding on west along the coast. Sea water lapping into sandy inlets was as turquoise as any in the Caribbean, but changed abruptly to a more sinister slate grey as it deepened.

The most unforgettable feature of this coastline was the protruberance of the Stanley Nut, with its spacious lagoons cutting in along both sides of the narrow connecting strip of land. The north-western islands were spaced out like a living map, straw coloured in the blinding sun, but King Island lay under cloud.

Max was helping a neighbour with shearing, but Helen came to meet us at Currie Airport with two granddaughters, of much the same age as her three oldest sons had been on my last visit. Her four sons had produced nine grandchildren to date — most now part of the mining communities of Western Australia. Thus had the King Island settlers increased and multiplied and dispersed back to the mainland.

Time had mellowed the two original settlers physically, but their cheerful optimism and love of life remained unchanged. Helen had matured to a more comfortable figure: Max, when he appeared later, was stringier and more sinewy than ever, all spare flesh dissipated by hard work.

The little airport bus trundled us into Currie township between close-clipped boxthorn hedges and we settled in at the new motel, which commanded a fine vista of blue sea beyond a scrub of sticky daisy bush and coast beard heath. Max scooped us up for dinner just after six.

He had been working as a roustabout, rolling fleeces for a fellow settler, whose shearing took three weeks.

"He's just gone out of cattle into sheep. A mug's game unless he's got a big purse to carry him over."

This comment was not from Max but from Mick Bennett who ran a rising business conducting minibus or taxi tours around the island for the likes of us.

Max had added to his original holding and held a thousand acres when he retired as a full-time farmer in the late 1970s. His oldest son, Rod, then working the next block, had taken over the family lands and more beyond and was currently farming three thousand acres — a far cry from those modest plots envisaged by the creators of the Land Settlement Scheme in the 1950s.

Many more animals were needed now to supply a living wage, whether the farmer was 'in' sheep or cattle. Rod was a cow cockie, milking in an eighteen-a-side herring bone milking parlour, but milch cows had not always supplied a livelihood and the years had had their ups and downs for Max. He had moved out of dairying into beef production when the bottom fell out of the milk market and then into sheep. When all markets dwindled and farming no longer paid, he had worked as a builder's labourer. After passing the reins to Rod he had moved to Currie and worked for ten years in a shop. Constantly busy, he could turn his hand to almost anything and still have time for ornithology.

Most farms were now amalgamating into larger, more viable units — as in Britain. An exception was the eight hundred acre dairy farm at Storton, which was divided into smaller blocks when the elderly owner retired, leaving only two daughters, who had married and gone away. Steaks from the ranches and Brie cheese from the dairies were still among the home products advertised to tempt visitors, along with 'bakehouse bread' (where else, one asks?). Many of the local specialities were from the sea, like 'fresh-caught crayfish, smoked eel paté and sea elephant oysters'.

"Good cattle land up here in the north, the stocking rate one beast per acre, but it gets very wet in winter. It would grow vegetables too, but there's no market. Someone tried it and they went bust. The island supermarket wants a continuous supply, not the brief harvest that a local could produce, and cost of air freight mitigates against export. There might still be a good opening for a Dutchman or a Chinaman."

An interesting observation that. I did not enquire why them particularly.

Land had been drained, but rushes sprang up as inexorably here as on the Welsh Hills at home. Mowing helped to keep them down but the herbicide, "Round-up", which we had used during the war, had proved the best deterrent.

It was hay time now, in mid-January, with cylindrical hay bales commoner than oblong ones. Clumps of these were covered with black polythene, held down by ropes anchored to rocks or sandbags — as in equally windy Orkney. Roadside grass was sometimes mown and baled, partly because it could be a fire hazard, and we saw the odd bull using it fresh.

Year by year, as more land was opened up for livestock farming, remnants of the once extensive eucalyptus: Blackwood forest had dwindled. Earlier settlers had made inroads into the wet sclerophyll forest of the south-east and, as long ago as 1888, Campbell referred to another skeleton forest in the island centre, "indicated by blanched naked tree barrels". By 1903 he wrote: "It is difficult to get enough (wood) for fencing and the only large tracts along the east coast have been decimated by fire."

This eastern scrub woodland occupies the poorest soil, so has been the least sought-after by farmers and supports the most natural vegetation. As on Flinders Island, ring-tailed possum numbers had diminished with the woodland, the brush-tailed possums adapting better to open country. Echidnas and the same three snakes, tigers, copperheads and whip snakes, were satisfied with minimal ground cover.

The address of Max's farm was Egg Lagoon, but the lagoon was no more, having been converted to flat pasture land by drainage.

"Once it was full of swans, geese and ducks; now there's just a ditch through the middle. Mind you, they could be back. It's only a couple of feet above sea level and would flood if the sea broke through the dunes."

Penny Lagoon nearby was in little better shape, but boasted a wealth of butterflies on the rayless heads of rough fireweed. Sometimes things went the other way. Just beyond the fine sticky hop bush, red with flowers and fruits, at Max's farm gate, was a sandpit from which material had been taken for road-making. This was now flooded to form a decent pond.

Despite the drainage projects, there were still natural wetlands in the north. Freshwater fish included spotted mountain trout, Cox's mountain trout, common jollytails and pigmy perch, and line fishing was one of the baits dangled to attract tourists.

On our first brush with Egg Lagoon Farm, Rod was out catching yabbies, the local freshwater crayfish, slowly drawing a piece of meat towards him through the water on the end of a line. Catches were good at first, yabbies always homing in readily to bait of this sort, but they suddenly stopped coming. A very satisfied musk duck popped to the surface several times before Rod twigged that the bird was swimming underwater and methodically tweaking the assembled titbits off the line!

Some of the lagoons were brackish or saline, intermittently connected with the sea, depending on the state of the separating sand bars. This made little difference to the bird life — waterfowl, waders, terns and swallows — but affected the fish and lesser life more closely.

Although the coast is predominantly rocky, three-quarters of King Island is bordered by sand dunes, the more essentially rocky section being the southern half of the eastern shore. Frank Ellis of the Queen Victoria Museum in Launceston has studied these in relation to changing sea levels (Museum Papers no. 11, 1959). His map shows a discontinuous line of older, vegetated dunes, from which much of the lime has been leached, inland of the current broader and more mobile dunes to seaward.

Some of the northern lakes lie at the junction of old and new dunes, squeezed off from the sea when active build-up of sand recommenced. North of Penny Lagoon are Lake Martha Lavinia, Long and White Beach Lagoons, with Wickham Lake, Cask Lagoon and the bigger Lake Flannigan along the north-western line of demarcation. Reedy Lagoon, now drained, occurs in the centre, where old dunes extend almost across from the west to meet those of the east.

The wind-moulded new dunes, often parabolic or U-shaped, do not merge gradually into the landscape behind, as might be expected, but retain an almost continuous steep slope on the inner side where they have overridden or are still overriding the older sand country behind. Those down the west coast and across the south are mainly of creamy-yellow shell sand, rich in lime and full of the skeletal concretions that I found so fascinating. On the McGarvie Farm at Martha Lavinia, the dunes were mostly of quartz sand, slightly reddish in colour and without the crusty inclusions.

On our first full day, when Max went off to the shearing sheds, we joined Mick Bennett of "Top Tours, King Island" and another visitor for a tour of the North. As we headed out from Currie on the one main road, we experienced at close quarters the chequer-board of hedgerows which had dominated the landscape as first viewed from the air.

The planted components were macrocarpa and African boxthorn, the latter tolerated because its effectiveness as a deterrent against straying stock outweighed the abominable task of keeping it in trim. Paperbarks sprang up spontaneously to add to their effectiveness, particularly after bush fires had released their seeds from the imprisoning woody capsules.

Out beyond the old airstrip and the cheese factory, which made only Cheddar, Camembert and Brie these days, we were in cattle country. The rushy fields held mobs of the traditional Friesians, Herefords and Aberdeen Angus, with an infiltration of sleekly fat, yellow, European beefers at Yellow Rock River and Penny Wickham. The sheep were Merinos, as in most of Australia.

The words HOWS TRIX stood out blatantly on a dark hillside of the Cooper property, like a white horse on an English chalk down. The letters were made from lines of discarded tyres, whitewashed on one side. Unwanted tyres were upturned, their dark forms invisible against the ground, but ready for use when the message was changed to a longer one. The perpetrator of this bit of fun was the owner's sister.

Another interesting artefact was the Bottle House, already mentioned on Flinders Island, where the owner formerly lived. That one had been dismantled, but his current effort on King Island — a fantasy of bottle-studded walls, arches and pillars — must have taken years to construct and many hundredweights of cement. We were assured that he had not achieved the formidable feat of emptying all the bottles unaided! It was a Jack Russell terrier which trotted out to show us round.

A troupe of peacocks with chicks followed a skyline in orderly procession, these escapees as numerous here as on Flinders Island. Nick said the cocks formed stag parties numbering forty to fifty — a splendid sight if all the tails were spread at once, but, with no pea-hens to impress, that would have been a wasted exercise.

Turkeys, too, are feral here and referred to as scrub turkeys. We saw flocks of up to thirty, on the sort of free range that might be envied by the thousands of battery birds that serve the Christmas and Thanksgiving markets of the Western World — except that there was no food laid on. One, scavenging in the forecourt of an old village hall, had a brood of pure white chicks at heel. The hay crops would provide rich pickings of seeds if not cut too young, but the only other crops seen were lucerne and turnips.

We passed the Aero Club, its members farmers who hired the planes to spread superphosphate on their fields. Another landmark was the Ricara Primary School, built as part of the post-World War II land settlement scheme, but now in danger of closure, with pupils having to go to Curry or Grassy. The education of eleven to sixteen-year-olds was catered for in Currie, but sixth formers had to go to mainland Tasmania to complete their schooling.

We crossed to Martha Lavinia Beach, the site of my first island skirmish by tractor, for morning tea. A wallaby bounced across to the sea's edge, for no obvious reason, certainly not to drink. It was not the only one, to judge by the tracks and oval dung pellets leading down from the marram-covered foredunes.

The fly in the ointment on my first sortie had been the bitter wind: today it was flies without the restraining ointment: not only the little ones that are the scourge of Australia, but larger, more vicious, but mercifully rarer March flies.

Mooching inland from the Spinifex:button bush fringe, we discovered why boobialla is sometimes called the blueberry tree, its branches hung with globular blue fruits. Leaving the wide expanse of sand to two longshore line fishermen, we moved off to Penny Lagoon, its waters crystal clear and fringed with the needle-leaved tassel cord rush *(Restio tetraphyllus)* as well as common rushes. Two white-backed magpies shot up the face of some banksia scrub, causing a passing brown hawk to veer aside.

Back only briefly on the bitumen, we passed Lake Flannigan. This had been stocked with fish, but anglers were worried by the unstoppable spread of a brown pondweed with floating leaves. They had tried cutting and herbicides but, so far, the plants were winning.

A few more minutes and we were on the pre-Cambrian schists alongside the Cape Wickham lighthouse. Nick pointed out the Navarin Reef, where the *"Neva"*, a convict ship of 837 tons, foundered at 4.0 a.m. on 14th May 1835. Of the 241 persons aboard, 150 were female prisoners, nine free women, thirty-three children and the remainder officers and crew. After suffering the rigours of the long passage from Cork in Southern Ireland, all but twenty-two were drowned and seven of the survivors died of starvation after getting ashore.

The fifteen survivors met up with the crew of another vessel, the *"Tartar"*, wrecked on Boulder Point, further east. Miraculously the group was located only a fortnight later by Captain Friend of the *"Sarah"*, come to search for the missing *"Tartar"*; a friend indeed. Bones of some of the deceased were exposed by a bush fire long after.

"The dead were the lucky ones" quoth Nick.

The *"Neva"* had been bound for Sydney, where life for female convicts was likely to be something well avoided. It was just a pity their release could not have happened before they had suffered the privations of the long voyage below decks under sail.

The most notorious place for wrecks was New Year Island, a little to the south of our viewpoint. Cape Wickham lighthouse, built twenty-five years after the *"Neva"* broke up, was automated in 1941. A telecom tower now relayed messages between Tasmania and Victoria.

Once upon a time there had been a village here, this now marked by a bicentennial monument with a map of the settlement and a list of wrecked seafarers helped by the lighthouse keepers. The shouting and the tumult had died and we were the only persons present on the rolling dunescape, its wispy coating of hare's-tail and fog grass interrupted by spherical boxthorn bushes interlaced with spinach and seaberry saltbush. Fat cattle grazing contentedly below the trilling larks, were the product, no doubt, of the four big bulls at the local AI centre.

We detoured on our return to Yellow Rock River, now home to a fine Charolet stud from Europe, a breed unheard of here on my last visit and a quite recent addition to British herds, fattening faster than the traditional breeds.

The local Penny Wickham Farm was a dairying concern in the late 1950s, with cheese made in the farmhouse. Only the land bore signs of husbandry now: the house had been fitted out as a hostel, having several rooms with bunk beds and cook-your-own facilities alongside a 'shop', where one selected the required item and put the appropriate money in the container provided. Our driver barbecued steaks on a Calor Gas stove on the verandah and served them up with salad, wine and coffee.

Yellow Rock River was named after the anomalous yellow rocks on what is predominantly a granite coast. It meanders past Muddy Lagoon, its mouth deflected away from Whistler Point by the sandy arm of Yellow Rock Foreland, where several hundred crested terns had gathered among old nest hollows along the inland face, to rest and preen. Little sea water penetrated the estuary, which was thronged with black swans and duck. Only the green weed, *Enteromorpha* told of brackishness, sea spurge and spurrey the most salt-tolerant of other plants.

The pleasant sea breeze failed to dispel the flies, which congregated to pester the cattle. We moved on south, past an abandoned Kraft cheese factory for which no use could be found this far from the centre of population.

In its heyday, the dairy industry had sent a regular 850 tons of cheese and 350 tons of butter to the mainland. During the Second World War cheese production tailed off in favour of butter. Both were durable enough to be exported by sea, along with animal skins, fleeces and meat, but most of the fish products go out by air.

A licensed grocer had set up shop in the old Kraft factory for a while but few customers materialised this far north of Currie and he went broke. Life on sea-girt islands has a universal appeal in theory but is hard going in practice.

A new cheese 'factory' had come into being nearer the town. We had hoped for a tour, but it proved to be only a shop — not much help as we were not self-catering. The day ended on an interesting note with a crescent moon seemingly the wrong way up as Max ferried us back from another convivial evening.

183 Flax Lily *Dianella revoluta*, Coast Swainson Pea *Swainsonia lessertifolia* and Spotted Sun Orchid *Thelymitra ixioides*

184 Brown Quail *Coternix ypsilophorus* and Tassel Rope-rush *Hypolaena fastigiata*

185 Wickham Lighthouse, King Island

2. EAST COAST, MAMMALS, MINERALS AND PENGUIN PARADE

Eastwards along the north coast past Rocky Cape to Martha Lavinia, the precambrian schists change to granite and the limey dunes to siliceous ones. The acidity of soil derived from granite and unmellowed by the lime from shell sand has little potential for agriculture, but the farmer's 'wasteland' can be the conservationists' opportunity. This is not just a matter of taking what is left, because poor soils are often the richest in wild flowers, which compete poorly with the lusher grasses and shrubs of more fertile areas.

Near the northern end of the fine Nine Mile Beach a notice informed us that we were in the Sea Elephant:Lavinia Nature Reserve, said to occupy some 3,800 hectares of a 7,000 hectare national park. Bennets or red-necked wallabies *(Wallabia rufogrisea)* were not persecuted here as on the farmlands and some took a lively interest in our movements in the hope of a few leftovers.

"A plague. They breed all the year round and we have to thin them out. There are no kangaroos. Kangaroo rats yes, but we don't often see them; only where they've been scuffling and digging."

Despite culling by farmers and clearance of scrub, the Bennets wallabies were thriving, although an alternative name of brush wallaby denotes their preference for brush country.

"Often see thirty or forty in the paddock at one time. They're easy to snare because they always use the same tracks and they're unafraid of a man shooting from a tractor. Why, they even stay around when one of their number has been killed."

Spotlighting for 'roos was as popular a pastime as shooting pheasants and one of Max's neighbours had been determined to stop this practice on his property. When he drove into the scene of slaughter, the poachers drove out, so he decided to lie in wait for the miscreants in a patch of scrub with his dog. When the marksmen's light reflected back from the dog's eyes, they shot it dead beside its master — who never lay in wait in the scrub again.

Max filled us in on the other fauna. The Tasmanian or red-bellied pademelons *(Thylogale billardierii)* were based in tea-tree thickets, making sorties into the grasslands. A few potoroos or long-nosed rat kangaroos *(Potorous tridactylus)*, smaller and browner than the Tasmanian form, were holding on in the densest scrub, but had suffered badly from land clearance.

The story was the same for the Tasmanian ring-tail possum *(Pseudocheirus convolutor)*, which was common until about 1960 but dwindled with the rise of the brush-tail possum *(Trichosurus vulpecula)*, as on the Furneaux Group. Pigmy possums *(Cercartetus nanus)* were occasional residents around Egg Lagoon during my first visit and one was found drowned in a water drum in 1967.

Brush-tail possums, deprived of their traditional lairs in big old trees, tended to lie up by day in rock crevices, even haystacks, or on platforms of sticks and litter among tree branches. A couple had been found in old nests of night herons. Only the grey phase occurs on King Island (as on Flinders) and the animals were considered rare until 1945, since when the population has flourished.

No spotted tiger cats *(Dasyurops maculatus)* have been seen since 1923. Formerly common, they were destroyed in the early days of settlement because they killed poultry and damaged the pelts of animals caught in the trap lines. Bush fires also contributed to their extinction, but echidnas and platypus survive.

Domestic cats are a menace, as always, one bringing in four marsupial mice *(Antechinus minimus)* from the edge of a pine plantation. Bats seem to be scarce, with a very few records of the grey-headed fruit bat *(Pteropus poliocephalus)* and of the lesser long-eared bat *(Nyctophilus geoffroyi)*. Max had come across bats roosting in the church tower when he was doing some building repairs there.

The eastern swamp rat *(Rattus lutreolus)* — a vegetarian and not to be confused with the eastern water rat *(Hydromys chrysogaster)*, which is a carnivore — is locally common in tall fescue grass. Interlopers from Europe, black rats and house mice, are unfortunately equally common. Luckily the main island is clear of rabbits, foxes and dingoes. There are heavy penalties, fines or prison sentences, for anyone attempting to introduce rabbits — assuming the farmers allow the culprit to live long enough to receive sentence!

Six species of frog and six of lizard have been recorded, as well as the three common poisonous snakes, which are most prevalent on New Year Island, where Max had counted fifty-eight in four hours. He found that only the larger tiger snakes were black, smaller ones showing the striping of mainland animals more clearly. Storm petrels as well as mutton birds nest there, as an extra source of snake food.

A good road took us to Sea Elephant River at the southern end of the Nine Mile Beach, where a rock-hopper penguin *(Eudyptes chrysocome)* had come ashore to moult — a wanderer from one of the sub-antarctic island colonies. Local bird-watchers had been weighing it every day during its enforced abstinence and had recorded a marked weight loss — apparent in the inward sagging of the once plumped out white waistcoat.

We deployed ourselves alongside a small watercourse, a tributary of the Sea Elephant River, thinking of those other breeders on sub-antarctic islands, 850 miles south of Tasmania, the sea elephants. Formerly known as *Macrorhinus proboscideus*, indicative of the proboscis developed in the old bulls, these are now *Mirounga leonina*. They are true seals, not sea lions like the fur seals, so the leonine component of the name seems singularly inappropriate.

In the early days of exploration it was the sea elephants and fur seals that attracted ships from many parts of the world, these converging on the main concentration on New Year Island. Although permanent settlement of King

Island did not begin until around 1885, sealers had been coming and going for many years prior to this.

Wetlands with tassel cord rush and narrow sword grass at Sea Elephant attracted migrant waders and waterfowl and there was a rich shrub layer of river wattle and swamp bull-oke under the manna gums. Some supported parasitic native 'mistletoe' *(Cassytha pubescens)*; not a true mistletoe but a relative of the smaller native dodder *(Cuscuta tasmanica)* which romped across the ground layer of common swamp and pink beard heaths, parrot pea and guinea flower.

Frank Ellis has identified a parallel series of old shorelines to as much as two miles inland of Cowper Point opposite Councellor Island. Narrow bodies of water are trapped between and there is a broad swampy flat, scarcely above sea level, between the older and newer series of strands, with the seaward, later formed dunes, rising to a hundred feet. These terminate abruptly in a cliff, which is retreating under the onslaught of the waves. Some of the displaced sand is being washed north to form an encroaching spit diverting the mouth of the Sea Elephant River.

South of the river mouth is the only coastal outcrop of Tertiary limestone, as seen around the blowhole and further inland in a line of sink holes.

The trapped wetlands are a magnet for passing migrants. King Island itself, as part of the old Pleistocene land bridge between Victoria and Tasmania, is a stepping stone on the north-to-south flyway and many birds follow the coasts. Max McGarvie's bird count in 1959, after only a year of residence, amounted to seventy species, excluding waders and including seven of the twelve species which are confined to Tasmania. By 1990 the number was up to a hundred and sixty-four, with at least eighty-one species breeding, these including nine aliens.

Some of the more interesting were the raptors. Swamp harriers *(Circus approximans)* flew south in August and returned north in February. Max had had a few sightings of whistling eagles or whistling kites *(Milvus sphenurus)* feeding on wallaby carcases, these uncommon in Tasmania as a whole, but wedge-tailed eagles *(Aquila audax)*, so common in Australia's dry country, are seldom seen. A much likelier sighting is of the non-migratory white-bellied sea eagle *(Haliaeetus leucogaster)*, and a nesting pair high in a eucalyptus was pointed out to us by Mick.

Masked and banded plovers have increased with the spread of grassland, the typical skylark habitat, but Californian quails *(Lophortyx californicus)*, introduced around 1920, have gone the other way, probably as a result of shooting.

"We used to see coveys of twelve or so as a regular thing: now there's usually only two or three."

Goldfinches have a bonanza with the seeds of thistles and other farm weeds and swallows enjoy the flies attracted by livestock.

The Sea Elephant mutton bird rookery is one of the smallest of the twenty-three identified around the coast of King Island. Burrows number around five hundred, a mere offshoot of the twenty thousand or so pairs nesting on Councellor Island off Cowper Point, where a further seven thousand seven hundred are domiciled on the mainland.

The curve of Sea Elephant Bay terminates southwards in Naracoopa, which made a bid to become an important settlement when the, at first ill-fated, jetty was constructed off Fraser Bluff, but this did not divert shipping from Currie as hoped and the town remained small when Grassy burgeoned further south as the centre of the mining.

Inland and between the two is Pegarah, a forest reserve of 2,470 acres, maintained and harvested for fence posts and other timber needs. Two hundred acres was planted with pines and 734 acres with introduced messmate stringybark *(Eucalyptus obliqua)*. There is, however, natural regeneration of Tasmanian blue gums, manna or white gums and swamp gums, along with prickly Moses and river wattle, coast banksias, lancewood and the usual tea-trees and heaths.

The island's industrial mainstay has been the mining enterprise at Grassy. As so often, it started with the search for gold, in 1861, but this came to nought. Tin and gold leases were worked near the Sea Elephant River for a while after 1905 and then silver and lead south of the Fraser River, which flows to the sea at Naracoopa. In 1919 an attempt to export slates from deposits at City of Melbourne Bay between Naracoopa and Grassy, failed because it proved impossible to cleave slates of the size required by commerce.

Scheelite, which saved the day, was discovered at Grassy by Thomas Farrell and grew into a world famous industry. It is used for hardening steel and is in greatest demand during wartime. The mine had been closed down just before my first visit, but a boost was given by the Korean war. When the needs of this fell off there was little demand, nor, it seemed, for the King Island wolfram from which rutile and zircon were produced. One of Max's sons had worked in the rutile mine, excavating a special quality of sand used in paint manufacture, but was now earning more money elsewhere. Unfortunately there are always wars somewhere and the scheelite workings opened up again and have had a chequered existence during the past few decades. Most of the men laid off found jobs in the Burnie Paper Mills on the nearby Tasmanian coast.

Our visit to Grassy Mine in 1990 was ostensibly for viewing penguins — a jaunt made possible by the building of a mining causeway connecting the penguins' nesting island to the shore. Helen and the grandchildren had been at the local horseraces in the afternoon, while Max was showing us some of the more natural sites. He returned to our motel in the late afternoon looking slightly fraught.

"Brakes have gone: I'll drive on the hand brake. Wouldn't do this anywhere else."

He proceeded with care, particularly on the down grades. Four in the back and two in the front was quite a load, but he rose to the challenge — as islanders must — and still managed a running commentary on properties and people.

We detoured along the coast north of Naracoopa to Helen's dream house, semi-castellated and backed by a wooded hill. This was not to be hers, but the couple had been lent a house further north and she had enjoyed a holiday there with some grandchildren, Max joining them at the weekends.

"A super beach of sand and rock pools — on the sheltered side — and almost to ourselves. Oh we did have fun."

Many might envy the temperament that got such a kick from simple pleasures close to home — and not by one who was untravelled. When younger Helen had worked in many parts of Australia as a wartime WREN and she and Max now flew annually to Western Australia to visit the part of the family that had emigrated back. They always stayed for several months since Max had handed over the responsibility of the farm: not a cheap trip, particularly the previous year when they had paid over a thousand dollars to a bus company which went broke, so that they had to pay out again.

"But I wouldn't live anywhere else but here," quoth Helen, indicating the knife-edged reefs of smooth black rock curving elegantly out across the sands. It certainly had its points. Nobody locked doors and crime was difficult to pull off where everybody knew everybody.

We stopped in a grassy embayment to view the modest stone monument where the British had managed to run their flag up a short hop ahead of the French. A little further on we homed in on a delectable picnic site. A brush-tailed possum dived for cover and a fan-tailed cuckoo *(Chrysococcyx flabelliformis)*, a summer visitor from north of Bass Strait, sat it out on a roadside wire.

Settling the 'eski' of food, three blankets and two canvas chairs in a corner of the beach backed by a scrub full of New Holland honey-eaters, we set off beachcombing. Seaweeds ranged from Sargasso weed and Neptune's necklace to large and small sea grasses.

The red algae were quite beautiful when their feathery filaments or lobed branches floated freely in the sea, but they collapsed into sad little heaps when lifted out. I showed the girls how to float them onto mounting paper in a bowl of water and cover them with butter muslin to prevent them sticking to the press.

"No butter muslin now, but plenty of cheese cloth" exulted Helen, with novel home-made Christmas cards in mind.

One of the outsize cuttlebones had some polished goose barnacles attached and there were a lot of sponges, including some uncommon open-meshed wineglass shapes. The children gathered humbug-striped winkles, purple and grey tops and big green turban shells.

Sarah produced the membranous skeleton of a by-the-wind-sailor, asking if it was an outsize fish scale. It seemed these often washed up in company with Portuguese men-of-war, as in the Northern Hemisphere. Picking up a fine abalone shell, Helen tried to persuade me how delicious these were if properly cooked.

"Boil them and they're inedible, slice finely and fry in butter: lovely."

I had had several tries, but made no impression on their rubbery substance and extracted no flavour from the unyielding flesh. She wasn't persuading me.

There was an important abalone industry on King Island, the shells gathered by divers, who might have to go so deep that they risked the bends if surfacing too fast. They said it was scary, but kept at it because the so-called mutton fish fetched good prices and they became wealthy, despite the hefty cost of a licence to fish. During recent years the shells have been sent to the Far East for sale as ornaments and jewellery.

We reassembled for a sumptuous picnic, glad to don the woolly caps brought for the night-time penguin watch, as the cool of the evening swallowed up the heat of the day. Then we were away to the deserted scheelite workings, where penguins continued to nest in the tumble of overgrown boulders on Green Island, even though the industrial causeway had destroyed its island status.

Mick arrived soon after us with two visitors and a powerful spotlight. He had dreams of developing a Phillip Island style 'penguin parade' for tourists, but my recent sightings of droves of camera-clasping Japanese being disgorged from coaches for the nightly celebration of incoming penguins on Phillip Island was a far cry from this remote corner. Our spot had the added bonus of seclusion. Bring the crowds and most of the magic would be lost.

While daylight lasted we explored the guano-fouled tracks leading to hidden burrows and it was 9.30 p.m. when we spotted two circular clusters of birds on the water, fifty or sixty in each, drifting imperceptibly into the bay with no apparent effort, their progress measured against a tall offshore stack. As the gentle swell rose and fell, the living stains appeared and disappeared, black smudges against the silvered waters, until birds reared up in the shallows to expose white breasts.

Mutton birds swooped back and forth over the floating groups. If these had rafted, they had done so further out to sea. Two big shearwater rookeries lay close by. 26,000 pairs nested at Grassy and 68,000 pairs on Bold Head projecting into the sea just to the north. The last was surpassed on King Island only by two rookeries in the south, where recent estimates were 85,400 pairs at the Red Hut and 82,650 at Seal Rocks.

Early settlers had recorded no rookeries on King Island proper, only on Christmas and New Year Islands. Numbers there were expanding rapidly and the overspill was taking up residence around the coast of the main island. Licences for commercial mutton bird harvests here in North-western Bass Strait were confined to islands of the Hunter Group: Hunter, Steep, Trefoil, Walker and Three Hummock. Only non-commercial harvests were allowed on King Island, for family consumption with sale illegal. Permitted daily bags were halved from fifty to twenty-five in 1991.

As darkness settled over the Grassy penguin colony, expectant calls drifted up from the burrows, quietly at first, then as a rising crescendo. The crooning of the shearwaters remained muted, but the squawling, chattering, booming roars of the penguins rose to laughable decibels — whether from youngsters demanding food or adults demanding relief.

A third raft of penguins floated in around 10.30 and, as darkness descended sufficiently to give decent cover, the rush began. This was the time of day that we had watched the influx of the herbivorous wallabies and possums and carnivorous devils and marsupial cats to the bounty supplied by The Lodge at Cradle Mountain in Central Tasmania the week before. The dark that hampers our own movements is the signal for 'all go' with more secretive creatures.

As their feet touched bottom, the penguins reared half erect and scuttled through the shallows, each leaving a trail of phosphorescence in its wake. Once ashore they held their bodies well forward by penguin standards, as though over anxious to arrive, but halted at intervals to reach up and look around for trouble, although showing no discomfort at the spotlight which followed them in. Assured that all was well, they would scuttle on.

Once in among the scrub, they threw caution to the wind and paused to preen, though the shadowy paths seemed too foul to receive such pristine incomers from the sea. Birds coming off duty would be in greater need of a tidy up. We counted about 150 and they were still coming when we left, although most of the shearwaters had passed on. Without the spotlight we would have seen little and, strangely, we saw no mammals on the road during the drive back.

186 Sea Elephant Bull *Mirounga leonina*

187 Diving Petrels *Pelecanoides urinatrix* and
Hairy Pennywort *Hydrocotyle hirta*

188 Little Blue Penguin *Eudyptula minor* moulting among
Pigface *Disphyma crassifolium*

3. SOUTHERN CALCIFIED FOREST AND KELP HARVEST AT CURRIE

When the scheelite company pulled out it left a valuable infrastructure behind and a public meeting on the future use of these assets had taken place the night before our penguin visit. It was decided that the electricity and the swimming pool be left for the use of the residents, but there was no indication as to who might buy up the vacated houses, keep the roads and sewage system in order and patronise the chemist and other shops. Perhaps tourism will be the answer, but it will all need to happen at once, with hotels, cafes, shops and other amenities, backed by vigorous marketing.

It was ironic that the meeting should be held on the day another highly mechanised war broke out in the Middle East. The mines had not been sealed. Maybe they would be opened up again. For tourists Currie was not too far off on the opposite coast and there was a superb tourist attraction in the form of the Calcified Forest.

Memories of those bizarre formations had stayed with me over thirty years and I asked Max if we could visit them again. He confessed to not having been since he went with me in 1959, but readily agreed. In the doing he was so thrilled by the skeleton landscape that he vowed to take the grandchildren on his next free day. How often the high spots close to home are neglected. Only when on holiday do we make time to visit all features of interest.

Our route south from Currie to Seal Bay seemed to be across an endless succession of gently rolling sand hills, grasslands freckled with the furry bobbles of hare's-foot grass and crumpled velvet mats of Yorkshire fog. I commented on the absence of livestock. "This is winter country. Warm and dry. Used when the rest is cold and wet."

"Not very windproof though. Not a tree in sight. Just wire fences."

"Granted. Boxthorn's the only tree able to withstand the wind and this has been ripped out because of the trouble of keeping it within bounds. Birds scatter the seeds everywhere."

Wintering cattle might have dry feet but had to suffer chilly hides, also, at first, ailing metabolisms.

"Animals have to be treated at least once a year with injections of copper and bullets of cobalt, pushed far down their throats into the rumen."

When we finally moved into paperbark and tea-tree scrub, we were in pademelon habitat. I had lost count of the number of Bennet's wallaby carcases by the road through the open country, some quite fresh. Here the corpses were smaller.

"Wallabies — Bennets — so thick on the ground that a cobber of mine selling them for cray bait caught forty-eight in one spot on the first night and fifty-seven in the same place the next night!"

There had been a penetrating smell of cooking meat and bone meal on my arrival at the airport, prompting the question: "Is waste from the abattoir used as bait?"

It seemed not.

"The usual bait now is European carp; big fish which have invaded many Australian waters and fouled them for other fish."

Max indicated a blackbird singing its heart out from a Banksia bough. "Aliens. Lovely song, but they play havoc with the fruit in the garden. I caught and killed thirty-one a few days ago."

It seemed there were problems sharing a limited environment. Even ornithologists had to draw the line somewhere; like our suburban householders feeding garden birds with one hand and pampering pussy cats with the other. Always there is compromise to get our bread buttered on both sides.

Lagoons hereabouts looked very English with their marginal greater birds-foot trefoil and willow-herb. One showed a green raft of lesser duckweed threaded with red lines of *Azolla* water fern and harbouring only a few black duck. Another supported a hundred black swans and two hoary-headed grebes, along with black duck and musk duck, all of which are at home on sea water as well as fresh, although not venturing far from the shore. We had fine views of the grebes *(Poliocephalus poliocephalus)*, which Max had first recorded breeding here in 1971. They are nomadic and irregular, although sometimes numerous.

A long-legged native hen *(Gallinula mortierii)* stalked across the road like a moorhen on stilts. Although flightless, this water-loving, land-living gallinule seems to have got everywhere and is another that can be a pest on farmland. Less threatening was the grey shrike thrush *(Colluricincla harmonica)*, which trilled evocatively from a she-oke, well in tune with its name. Originally there had been no crows on King Island; these had moved in with the onset of sheep farming.

We drew into a parking area showing two finger posts: "Scenic Walk" and "Calcified Forest". Max fingered the peeling rind of a swamp paperbark. "Only this one, *Melaleuca ericifolia*, is called paperbark here. The others are lumped with the tea-trees." As on Flinders Island.

A female Bennets wallaby hopped across, soliciting food. She could not know that Max was a farmer, just that she was well away from farmland where her kind were persecuted. Here she was greeted as one of the local attractions. The joey in her pouch was not so sure, peering out timidly at intervals but popping back in when the cameras appeared.

We followed the "Calcified Forest" sign through a low scrub of sticky daisy bush and coast beard heath laden with white berries like Christmas mistletoe. Yellow heads of fireweed sprouted everywhere, while scarlet pimpernel, yellow bartsia and pink centaury decorated the path.

Welcome swallows were lined up along overhead wires, their twitterings mingling with those of the white-eyes in the scrub. Dusky robins gave way to brush bronze-wing pigeons as we moved onto the huge spread of sand —

almost bare of today's vegetation but covered with the petrified remains of yesterday's.

Erosion had revealed a complex of ramifying root systems as well as tall splaying shoot systems. Some of the old trunks were hollow and a few had been infiltrated so gently by the limey solution that the old concentric growth rings were still distinguishable on broken ends. Many had toppled and there were shattered fragments everywhere.

Such a graveyard of plants was more incongruous than a graveyard of animals, where the calcified skeletons are ready made. Plants so readily rot to humus or, under sufficient pressure, to coal, that the bleached ogre-like forms clawing skywards seemed wholly bizarre.

My 1959 photographs were mostly of chalky white branches, still erect and mostly less than seven cm diameter. Today's remains were chunkier and included tree boles and root balls changed to a creamy yellow as from organic staining over a longer period at greater depth.

Presumably erosion was continuing, or the brittle exposures would have fragmented and dispersed while new plants would have colonised the more stable sand. The elements seem to have scoured to the very base of the ancient eucalyptus:Blackwood forest of pre-settlement days, when trees were left to die in situ and not felled or burned. On both occasions we found plenty of thin crusts of travertine, simulating slivers of bedrock.

* * * * *

Currie was an unpretentious but homely little town, similar to but larger than Whitemark on Flinders Island, with little need for the locks and bolts of more populous places. Wandering along a stony track used by trucks laden with building materials, we found ourselves by a new harbour wall, south of the shipping haven — an extension to protect the cray fleet. Currie was a working port, with few pleasure craft prepared to brave the turbulent water outside. A formidable line of white was stretched across the narrow harbour mouth on even such a gentle summer day as this.

The port could accommodate only ships of fairly shallow draft, but was not dogged by a big tidal rise and fall. Tides were, indeed, negligible, with a range of only five feet at springs and three at neaps — very different from the forty-five to fifty feet vertical difference we were used to at home in Cardiff.

Cormorants rested on sodden piles here as there and twelve to fifteen turnstones were flipping seaweed and stones aside in their ongoing search for food. Swallows skimmed, oystercatchers shrieked, silver gulls squawled and musk ducks slept on the water, pulling their misshapen heads from the shoulder feathers at intervals to glance around and ascertain that all was well.

The white automatic lighthouse, unlike most, had the cylindrical iron lamp-housing elevated on a narrower cylinder stabilised by a slightly splaying meshwork of girders. Wickham lighthouse was of solid stone, like most of those visited on the *"Cape York"* voyage.

We enjoyed some good beach fossicking at the foot of the new breakwater, where a variety of drifting seaweeds and seashells had come to rest, with the inevitable cuttlebones. Banks of boobialla and buckthorn growing out of flowering drifts of the other sort of periwinkles were topped by a scramble of Cape ivy, while white mignonette, wild radish and golden melilot contributed to a largely alien ground flora.

There were few people about, this was a race day and even the café closed at one o'clock. We only just made it for our fish and chips. Quite a number of racehorses were bred on the island, although the racing season only lasted for about six weeks around January. Colts were exported and a lot of horses were brought over from Tasmania for the events.

The museum was closed, but we had a fascinating insight into one of Currie's more interesting exports on another day. This was the kelp industry, started here in 1975 by a partnership between Kelco/AIL International Ltd. of London and Webster Ltd. of Hobart.

Raw material in the form of the big brown oarweeds *(Durvillea pototorum)* was brought in by islanders on a variety of trucks, trailers and utilities, to be processed here and exported to Scotland. The fronds were not cut, as at some of the North-west European sources, but selected from plants cast ashore in storms.

A forest of iron poles was strung with wires some four metres up, but the mighty fronds attached to these by S-shaped meat hooks almost touched the ground. The whole contraption resembled oversized, overstocked fish drying racks, except that fish were never that long. Suppliers draped their wares over racks of more convenient height, to be lifted up mechanically. Here the weed hung for around two weeks to evaporate the bulk of the moisture.

Rubbery fronds blackened and corkscrewed into untidy spirals, some crisping to such frilly-edged banners as to appear another species. The whole array had a sinister feel, reminiscent of a mob of shrunken prehistoric bog men lifted from the embalming peat onto a multipe gallows. The final drying, in a wood-fuelled oven, drove off sufficient residual water to prevent rotting and render the plant material sufficiently brittle for milling.

The resulting granules were put into bags holding 1.5 tonnes apiece, each supplier having his quota weighed separately, as payment was made on the weight of the dried product, which was transferred to standard steel containers for export to Scotland.

The first stage of their two-month journey was by truck to the deep water port of Grassy, for sea passage to Melbourne, where the containers were loaded onto specialised carrying vessels of the OCL Fleet, bound for Tilbury Docks in London. A rail journey came next, to Coatebridge at Glasgow, and then once more by truck on the last leg of the journey to Girvan or Barcaldine on the West Scottish coast. Here the containers were opened and the contents transferred to hoppers, now the sole property of Kelco International Ltd., the world's largest producer of alginate supplying about a third of world demand.

Alginic acid, from which the versatile alginate is extracted, is produced only by a limited range of brown seaweeds. A note at the foot of the leaflet produced by the King Island processors read as follows: "The purchaser of our King Island product makes over 380 types of alginate for more than a thousand uses around the world. In one form or another, we think that you eat, drink, wear or in some manner enjoy the benefits of our King Island bull kelp every day! (And in the most unlikely event that you don't — isn't it high time that you started?)"

They could be right. When we were botany students in West Wales in the 1940s our professor was Britain's seaweed queen, Lily Newton, who delighted in enumerating the vast number of commercial uses for this, her favourite plant group.

Being edible and harmless to human skin, alginates are used as thickeners in sauces and syrups, cosmetic creams and lotions. The foam of detergents and shampoos is stabilised by it and it is easily washed from textile printing pastes. It controls the penetration into fabrics and paper of rubber and synthetic latices and some adhesives. Two unexpected uses are to thicken water for fire fighting, where it proves non-corrosive, and in root dips for crop and garden plants, because of it moisture retention.

Alginate colloids prevent the formation of ice crystals in ice cream and hinder dripping in water ices, as well as giving body to imitation cream, fruit drinks and tooth paste. On the non-culinary front the colloidal properties are utilised in ceramic glazes, emulsion paints, wallpaper printing, creamed rubber latex and welding electrode fluxes.

The gelling properties are employed in table jellies and blancmanges, pet food, semi-solid pharmaceuticals, material for dental impressions and the grouting of tiles. Its propensity for creating a surface film makes it useful in sizing paper, textile warps and pills and for glazing over porous surfaces.

How many of us know that kelp may be used in sausage skins and temporary threads (as calcium alginate yarns), as a hardening gelatine in photography, for flocculating impurities in water treatment and sugar processing and for many medical uses?

Visits over the years to Atlantic Islands off Scotland and Ireland had given us brief insights into the collecting phase of the kelp trade and three years earlier we had experienced the sea harvest in faraway Orkney. Tractors with broad frontal scoops (like the graders which level Australia's outback roads) scraped sand and driftweed from broad level beaches and piled them in heaps to rot for use as fertiliser — the shell sand particularly valuable in the peaty soils, although an impurity in the kelp trade.

That industry, functioning alongside, was more selective, requiring only the big oarweeds or *Laminaria* species. Merely the basal stipes or stalks went to the Scottish processing factories from Orkney, these drying into tough rods which took too long to rot down to useful manure, so the land was not robbed of its traditional input from the sea.

In mid-June the wharves of the Outer Isles were busy with shunting tractors and trucks, unloading bundles of unruly bent stipes tied with orange binder twine, to be transferred to the little boats for the first stage of their journey.

Norwegians, the other nationals most closely involved, used special dredges to slice through the fronds just above the holdfast so that almost the whole plant is exported from their shores.

In the old days, when industrial chemistry was less sophisticated, the Scottish seaweed was burned on the beaches and exported as ash, for glass making, iodine extraction and the making of explosives — this last a good money-spinner for the lairds and factors and less lavish pocket money for the crofters during the Napoleonic wars.

The King Island industry, starting in 1975, knew none of the drudgery of men wading in icy seas with scythes to cut and women toiling up beaches under dripping bundles of sea ware. In June the hay-cock like heaps were melted to a gelatinous sludge in stone troughs by the heat of wood fires. The molten mass cooled to become rock-hard, when it was smashed into pellets and crumbled to powder, to be exported in sacks.

We tend to use the word kelp for all oarweeds as they grow, but the Orkney folk reserve the term for the final granules, referring to the living weed as tangle. As the kelp industry has been practised in Orkney since the early seventeen hundreds, we should defer to them for the correct terminology, stretching the term kelp to include granules produced by different means but not the growing plants.

It was marine matters which occupied my attention during our final morning in Currie, before flying out to Melbourne. Beyond the motel's daisy and everlasting bushes were the golf links and beyond these the delectable shoreline of Admiral Beach.

Wave action had left little sand on this west facing coast, but the sun blazed down on a strand of beach cobbles, gravel and shingle — as pleasing a seascape as any holiday-maker could wish. Flat black rocks extending into the sea were streaked with lighter veins. These were ancient pre-cambrian schists and quartzites, as along the South-east coast and briefly at Naracoopa on the opposite side of the island, although granite formed the coasts roundabout.

A splendid variety of sea ware had been ripped from the ocean floor and cast ashore. Sponges won the day, hands down, with at least nine different kinds among the uppermost flotsam — keeping my camera clicking busily. With them were the almost equally weightless tests of sea urchins. The porous but weightier cuttlebones and spongy but sodden *Codium* weed had settled further downshore.

Scattered at all levels were disintegrating seed pellets of New Zealand mirror plants coughed up by silver gulls. (Pacific gulls were almost as rare here as Dominicans.) Masked lapwings probed the shingle and the odd shrike thrush fraternised with the bickering mobs of starlings.

Out across the gleaming waters the fishing fleet was making for home, boats straggling in from nine until eleven. They headed from the spread of the Southern Ocean into the warm northern breeze — a breeze so gentle that I learned its direction only by observing the heading of the hovering nankeen kestrel. It was not always thus.

Admiral Beach was named after the wreck of the *"British Admiral"*, a ship of 1781 tons on her second voyage from Liverpool in 1874. She struck in the small hours of a May night and, of eighty-eight persons on board, only nine lived to tell the tale. The vessel was balanced atop a reef about a mile from the shore for half an hour before sliding off into seven fathoms. Ten people scrambled into the only boat that got away, but were tipped out on the shore where four, including the chief officer, were drowned. A few days later three more survivors appeared, after being tossed ashore clinging to a spar. One of these, whose grasping finger had penetrated a thimble hole in the spar, had to cut the sea-bloated digit off to free himself.

The nine survivors were taken to Melbourne in the six ton fishing boat *"Kangaroo"*, while the few hunters then resident buried bodies and salvaged what they could use of the cargo.

Later the wreck was purchased by a Melbourne businessman and drays, horses and bullocks were brought from Tasmania to haul up enough cargo to keep four Melbourne schooners busy plying to and fro for over twelve months. A small steamer was chartered to tow sailing vessels to a platform moored above the wreck when it was calm enough to dive. A marble tablet on site commemorates William Dalzell Nicholson, aged twenty-five, who perished along with seventy-eight others. — "To live in the hearts we leave behind is not to die."

This is the end of my tale of those irresistible but untameable islands around Tasmania. It is those that I leave behind, but they will live on in my heart and mind for as long as I have consciousness to savour their lure and beauty.

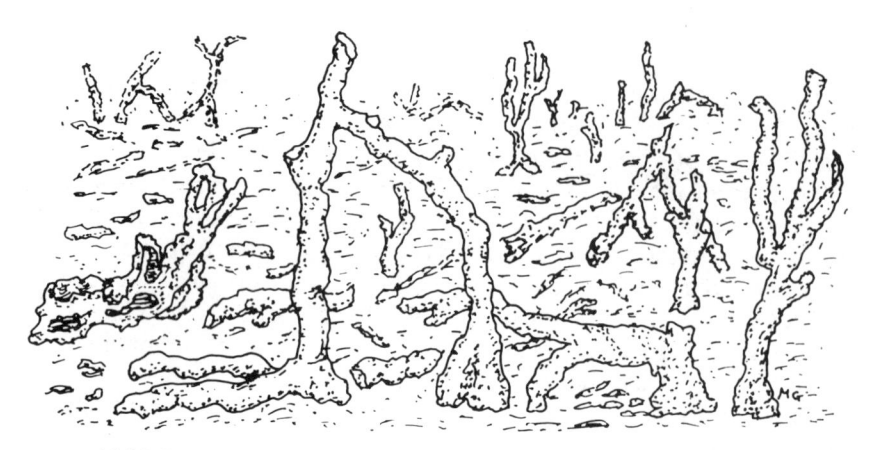

189 Metre-high Calcified Concretions on King Island Dunes

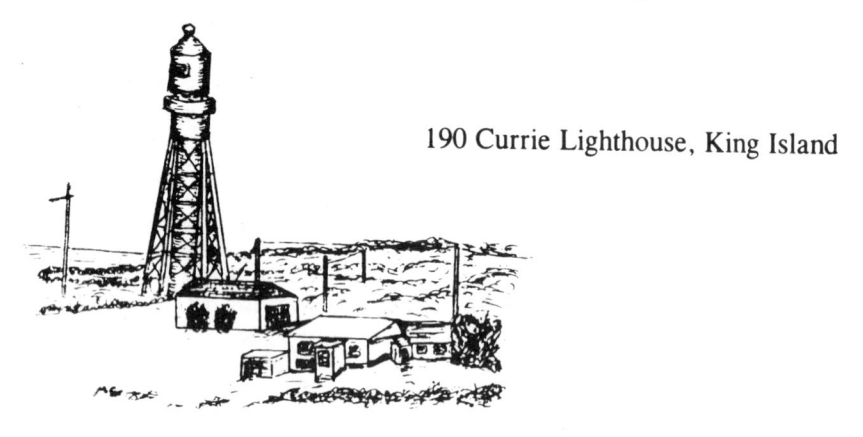

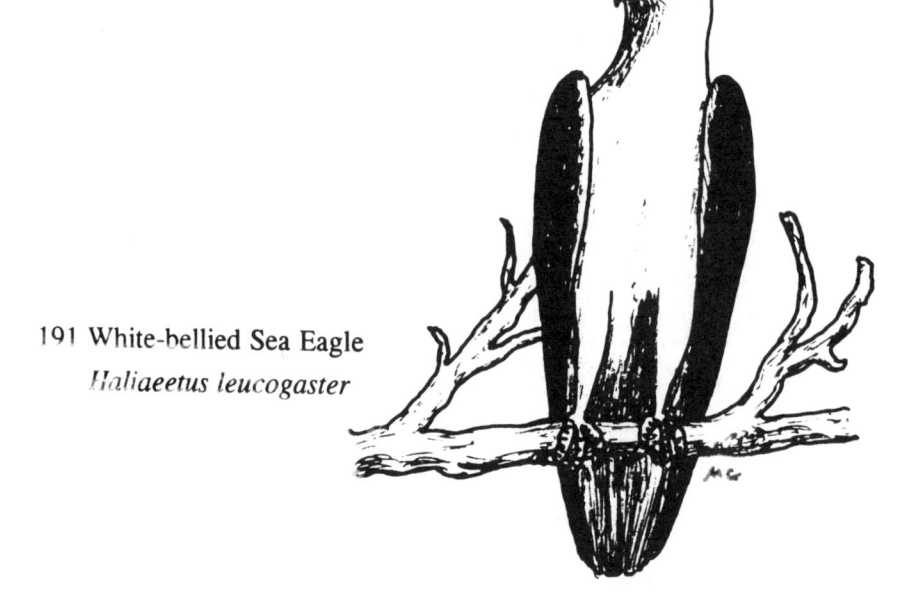

190 Currie Lighthouse, King Island

191 White-bellied Sea Eagle
Haliaeetus leucogaster

PLANTS REFERRED TO IN THE TEXT

ALPHABETICALLY UNDER THE VERNACULAR

Albizzia	- *Paraserianthes lophantha*
Allseed	- *Polycarpon tetraphyllum*
Apple berry, purple	- *Billardieri longiflora*
Arrow grass, streaked	- *Triglochin striatum*
Austral bluebell	- *Wahlenbergia gracilis*
Austral brooklime	- *Gratiola peruviana*
Austral hollyhock	- *Lavatera plebeia*
Australian salt grass	- *Distichlis distichophylla*
Austral seablite	- *Suaeda australis*
Austral stonecrop	- *Crassula sieberiana*
Austral storksbill	- *Pelargonium australe*
Banksia, coast	- *Banksia marginata*
saw	- *B. integrifolia*
silver	- *B. serrata*
Banyalla or cheesewood	- *Pittosporum bicolor*
Barilla or coast saltbush	- *Atriplex cinerea*
Barley grass, meadow	- *Critesion murinum ssp. leporinum*
wall	- *C. murinum*
Bat's wing fern	- *Histiopteris incisa*
Bauera, wiry or dog rose	- *Bauera rubioides*
Beard heath, coast	- *Leucopogon parviflorus*
pink	- *L. ericoides*
Beech, southern	- *Nothofagus cunninghamii*
Belladonna lily	- *Amaryllis belladonna*
Bidgee-widgee or piripiri	- *Acaena novae-zelandiae*
Bindweed, pink	- *Convolvulus erubescens*
Black anther flax lily	- *Dianella revoluta*
Blackberry	- *Rubus fruticosus agg.*
Blackboy, grass tree	- *Xanthorrhoea australis*
Black eyed Susan	- *Tetratheca pilosa*
Black nightshade	- *Solanum nigrum*
Blackwood	- *Acacia melanoxylon*
Bladder pea	- *Gompholobium hugelii*
Blanket bush	- *Bedfordia arborescens*
Boobialla	- *Myoporum insulare*
Boronia, sticky	- *Boronia anemonifolia*
Bottle brush, lemon	- *Callistemon pallidus*

or see Banksia	
Bougainvillea	- *Bougainvillea spectabilis*
Bower spinach	- *Tetragonia implexicoma*
Box or sea box	- *Alyxia buxifolia*
Boxthorn, South African	- *Lycium ferrocissimum*
Bracken	- *Pteridium esculentum*
Brome grass	- *Bromus catharticus*
	- *B. diandrus*
	- *B. hordeacus ssp. hordeacus*
Brookweed, creeping	- *Samolus repens*
Broom heath, glaucous	- *Monotoca glauca*
prickly	- *M. scoparia*
Broom spurge, leafless	- *Amperea xiphoclada*
Buck's horn plantain	- *Plantago coronopus*
Buffalo grass	- *Stenotaphrum secundatum*
Bulbine lily, large	- *Bulbine bulbosa*
leek	- *B. semibarbata*
Bulloke, swamp	- *Allocasuarina monilifera*
Bursaria, sweet	- *Bursaria spinosa*
Bush pea	- *Pultenaea daphnoides*
Butterfly iris or white flag	- *Diplarrena moraea*
Button bush	- *Leucophyta (Calocephalus) brownii*
Button grass, Tasmanian	- *Gymnoschoenus sphaerocephalus*
Candles, coastal	- *Stackhousia spathulata*
common	- *S. monogyna*
Cape gooseberry or Chinese lantern	- *Physalis peruviana*
Cape ivy	- *Senecio mikanioides*
Capeweed	- *Arctotheca calendula*
Cassinia, shiny	- *Cassinia longifolia*
Catchfly	- *Silene gallica*
Cats ear	- *Hypochoeris radicata*
Celery, coarse, eastern	- *Apium insulare*
fine-leaved	- *A. prostratum var. filiforme*
sea	- *A. prostratum*
Celery top pine	- *Phyllocladus aspleniifolius*
Centrolepis, hairy	- *Centrolepis strigosa*
Cheesewood or banyalla	- *Pittosporum bicolor*
Cherry ballart	- *Exocarpus cupressiforme*
Chickweed	- *Stellaria media*
Clematis, Austral	- *Clematis aristata*
small-leaved	- *C. microphylla*

Clover, clustered	- *Trifolium glomeratum*
Dutch or white	- *T. repens*
hare's foot	- *T. arvense*
red	- *T. pratense*
star	- *T. stellatum*
strawberry	- *T. fragiferum*
subterranean	- *T. subterraneum*
suffocated	- *T. suffocatum*
white or Dutch	- *T. repens*
yellow	- *T. dubium*
Club moss, bog	- *Selaginella uliginosa*
Club-rush, knobby	- *Isolepis nodosa*
Coast beard heath	- *Leucopogon parviflorus*
Coast daisy, small	- *Brachycome parvula*
tall	- *B. diversifolia v. maritima*
Coast pink-berry or cheeseberry	- *Cyathodes abietina*
Coast saltbush or barilla	- *Atriplex cinerea*
Coast spear grass	- *Austrostipa stipoides*
Coast spinifex grass	- *Spinifex sericeus*
Coast wattle	- *Acacia longiflora v. sophorae*
Cocksfoot grass	- *Dactylis glomerata*
Coral fern, scrambling	- *Gleichenia microphylla*
Correa, reflexed or wild fuchsia	- *Correa reflexa*
white	- *C. alba*
Cotula, common white-flowered	- *Cotula australis*
large creeping	- *Leptinella longipes*
slender	- *C. vulgaris*
water buttons	- *C. coronopifolia*
Cranberry heath	- *Astroloma humifusum*
Cranesbill, dove's-foot	- *Geranium molle*
Crantzia	- *Lilaeopsis polyantha*
Cudweed, common	- *Euchiton involucratus*
cottony	- *Vellereophyton dealbatum*
cushion	- *Gamochaeta purpurea*
Jersey	- *Pseudognaphalium luteo-album*
Curved sea hard-grass	- *Parapholis incurva*
Cypress pine	- *Callitris rhomboides*
Dagger Hakea	- *Hakea teretifolia*
Daisy bush, club moss	- *Olearia lepidophylla*
coast	- *O. axillaris*
dusty	- *O. phlogopappa*

lacquered	- *O. persoonioides*
moss	- *O. lepidophylla*
starry	- *O. stellulata*
sticky	- *O. glutinosa*
twiggy	- *O. ramulosa*
Dampiera, blue	- *Dampiera stricta*
Danthonia grass	- *Danthonia caespitosa*
Darling pea	- *Swainsonia greyana*
Dock	- *Rumex brownii*
Dodder laurel	- *Cassytha glabella*
Dodder, native	- *Cuscuta tasmanica*
Dog rose	- *Bauera rubioides*
Dogwood, common	- *Cassinia aculeata*
yellow	- *Pomaderris elliptica*
Duckweed, lesser	- *Lemna minor*
Dune thistle	- *Actites megalocarpus*
Dusky coral-pea	- *Kennedya rubicunda*
Eel grass	- *Zostera muelleri* and *Heterozostera tasmanica*
Elderberry, white	- *Sambucus gaudichaudiana*
Everlasting, golden	- *Helichrysum ?*
satin	- *H. leucopsideum*
silver	- *Argentipallium dealbatum*
Tasmanian coastal	- *H. gunnii*
tree	- *Ozothamnus ferrugineus*
Fairy aprons	- *Utricularia dichotoma*
Fan flower, blue	- *Dampiera stricta*
Fennel = fireweed	- *Senecio capillifolius*
Fig, edible	- *Ficus carica*
Filmy fern, austral	- *Hymenophyllum australe*
bristle	- *Polyphlebium venosum*
Fireweed, Bass Strait	- *Senecio capillifolius*
rough	- *S. hispidulus*
shrubby	- *S. minimus*
Flag, white or butterfly iris	- *Diplarrena moraea*
Flat pea	- *Platylobium obtusangulum*
Flax lily	- *Dianella revoluta*
Fog grass	- *Holcus lanatus*
Fringe myrtle	- *Calytrix tetragona*
Fuchsia, native	- *Correa reflexa*
Glasswort or samphire, beaded	- *Sarcocornia (Salicornia) quinqueflora*

black	- *S. blackiana*
shrubby	- *Sclerostegia (Arthrocnemum) arbusculum*
Goosefoot, glaucous	- *Chenopodium glaucum*
Gorse bitter pea	- *Daviesia ulicifolia*
Grass tree or blackboy	- *Xanthorrhoea australis*
Groundsel, purple	- *Senecio elegans*
variable	- *S. pinnatifolius*
Guinea flowers	- *Hibbertia species*
King Isld.	- *H. fasciculata*
spreading	- *H. procumbens*
Guitar plant	- *Lomatia tinctoria*
Gum - manna or white	- *Eucalyptus viminalis*
messmate, stringy bark	- *E. obliqua*
silver peppermint	- *E. tenuiramis*
swamp	- *E. ovata*
Tasmanian blue	- *E. globulus*
West Coast peppermint	- *E. nitida*
Hair-grass, silvery	- *Aira caryophyllea*
Hakea, dagger	- *Hakea teretifolia*
rare	- *H. epiglottis*
Hawkbit, rough	- *Leontodon taraxacoides*
Hazel pomaderris	- *Pomaderris apetala*
Heath, blunt-leaved	- *Epacris obtusifolia*
common or Victorian	- *E. impressa*
swamp	- *E. paludosa*
woolly	- *E. lanuginosa*
Honey myrtle	- *Melaleuca squamea*
Hop bush, sticky	- *Dodonaea viscosa*
Horny cone bush	- *Isopogon ceratophyllus*
Hypolaena	- *Hypolaena fastigiata*
Ice plant, South African	- *Disphyma crystallinum*
Iris, small purple	- *Pattersonia fragilis*
Isotome, swamp	- *Isotome fluviatile*
Kangaroo apple	- *Solanum aviculare*
Kangaroo fern	- *Microsorium pustulatum* and *M. diversifolium*
Karkalla, Ross's noon-flower	- *Carpobrotus rossii*
Kidney weed	- *Dichondra repens*
Kikuyu grass	- *Pennisetum clandestinum*
Knawel	- *Scleranthus biflorus*

Knob sedge	- *Carex inversa*
Knobby club-rush	- *Isolepis nodosa*
Kunzea, white	- *Kunzea ambigua*
Lancewood	- *Phebalium squameum*
Large-leaf bush pea	- *Pultenaea daphnoides*
Leafy peppercress	- *Lepidium foliosum*
Leek lily	- *Bulbine semibarbata*
Lepidosperma sedge or sword grass	- *Lepidosperma gladiatum*
Lignum, climbing	- *Muehlenbeckia adpressa*
Lilac bells or pink bells	- *Tetratheca pilosa*
Lobelia, angled	- *Lobelia alata*
Love creeper	- *Comesperma volubile*
Macrocarpa	- *Cupressus macrocarpa*
Mallee	- bushy Eucalyptus species
Mallow, small-flowered	- *Malva parviflora*
Manna gum	- *Eucalyptus viminalis*
Manuka or tea-tree	- *Leptospermum scoparium*
Marram grass	- *Ammophila arenaria*
Mazus, swamp	- *Mazus pumilio*
Melilot	- *Melilotus spp.*
Messmate	- *Eucalyptus obliqua*
Mignonette, white	- *Reseda alba*
Mint, native	- *Mentha diemenica*
spiked	- *M. spicata*
Mirror plant, NZ or taupata	- *Coprosma repens*
Mistletoe, native	- *Cassytha pubescens*
Monkey flower	- *Mimulus repens*
Mountain pepper	- *Tasmannia lanceolata*
Mudwort	- *Limosella australis*
Nablonium	- *Ammobium calyceroides*
Native Daphne or bush pea	- *Pultenaea daphnoides*
Needlewood or striped hakea	- *Hakea tephrosperma*
Nettle, common	- *Urtica dioica*
scrub	- *U. incisa*
small	- *U. urens*
smooth	- *Australina pusilla ssp. muelleri*
Noon-flower, angled	- *Carpobrotus aequilaterale*
Ross's	- *C. rossii*
Norfolk Island pine	- *Araucaria excelsa* or *heterophylla*
Old man's beard	- *Clematis aristata*
Olive berry, blue	- *Elaeocarpus reticulatus*

Orache, halberd-leaved	- *Atriplex prostrata*
Orchid, Acianthus	- *Acianthus spp.*
onion	- *Microtis unifolia*
spider	- *Caladenia pattersonii*
spotted sun	- *Thelymitra ixioides*
striated rock	- *Dendrobium striolatum*
Oyster Bay pine	- *Callitris rhomboidea*
Pampas grass	- *Cortaderia*
Pandani	- *Richea scoparia*
Paperbark, coastal or swamp	- *Melaleuca ericifolia*
mauve or swamp honey myrtle	- *M. squamea*
scented	- *M. squarrosa*
Parrot pea	- *Dillwynia glaberrima* and *D. floribunda*
Paspalum grass	- *Paspalum dilatatum*
Pennywort, hairy	- *Hydrocotyle hirta*
mossy	- *H. muscosa*
shining	- *H. sibthorpioides*
slender	- *H. tripartita*
stinking	- *H. laxiflora*
Pepper cress, dune	- *Lepidium praetervisum*
leafy	- *L. foliosum*
Peppermint gums	- *Eucalyptus species*
west coast	- *E. willisii* and *E. nitida*
Periwinkle	- *Vinca spp.*
Pigface	- *Disphyma crassifolium (australe) ssp clavellatum*
Pink bells or lilac bells	- *Tetratheca pilosa* or *T. labillardieri*
Pink berry, coastal	- *Cyathodes abietina*
juniper-leaved	- *C. juniperina*
Piripiri or bidgee-widgee	- *Acaena novae-zelandiae*
Poranthera, small	- *Poranthera microphylla*
Poverty raspwort	- *Gonocarpus tetragynus*
Pratia	- *Pratia irrigua*
Prickfoot or sea holly	- *Eryngium vesiculosus*
Prickly currant bush	- *Coprosma quadrifida*
Prickly geebung	- *Persoonia juniperina*
Prickly Moses	- *Acacia verticillata*
Purslane, pink	- *Calandrinia calyptrata*
Quaking grass, large	- *Briza maxima*
Radish, wild	- *Raphanus raphanistrum*

Reed, common	- *Phragmites australis*
Rice flowers	- *Pimelea species*
cherry	- *P. drupacea*
Ruddy ground fern	- *Hypolepis rugosula*
Rufous stonecrop	- *Crassula decumbens*
Running postman	- *Kennedya prostrata*
Rush, pale	- *Juncus pallidus*
sea	- *J. kraussii ssp. australiensis*
Ryegrass, Italian	- *Lolium multiflorum*
perennial	- *L. perenne*
Saltbush, coast or grey or barilla	- *Atriplex cinerea*
glistening	- *A. billardieri*
samphires	- see Glasswort
Saltmarsh creeper	- *Selliera radicans*
Samphires	- see Glasswort
Sassafras	- *Atherospermum moschatum*
Scarlet pimpernel	- *Anagallis arvensis*
Screw fern	- *Lindsaea linearis*
Seaberry saltbush	- *Rhagodia candolleana*
Sea box	- *Alyxia buxifolia*
Sea celery, common	- *Apium prostratum*
fine-leaved	- *A. prostratum var. filiforme*
Sea fescue	- *Austrofestuca littoralis*
Sea-grass, strapweed	- *Posidonia australis*
turtle grass or sea nymph	- *Amphibolis antarctica*
(oval-leaved)	- *Halophila australis*
Sea holly or prickfoot	- *Eryngium vesiculosus*
Sea rocket	- *Cakile edentula*
Sea spurge	- *Euphorbia paralias*
Sedge	- Family *Cyperaceae*, mostly *Lepidosperma gladiatum* also *Scirpus, Carex* &c
Selliera	- *Selliera radicans*
Sheep sorrel	- *Acetosella vulgaris*
Sheep trefoil	- *Trifolium dubium*
She-oke, she-oak, black	- *Allocasuarina littoralis*
drooping	- *A. stricta*
Tasmanian	- *A. monilifera*
two-styled	- *A. distyla*
Shield fern, leather	- *Rumohra adiantiformis*
mother	- *Polystichum proliferum*

Silver tussock grass	- *Poa poiformis*
Slender twine-rush	- *Leptocarpus tenax*
South African boxthorn	- *Lycium ferocissimum*
South African Capeweed	- *Arctotheca calendula*
South African iceplant	- *Disphyma crystallinum*
Sow thistle, common	- *Sonchus oleraceus*
prickly	- *S. asper*
Spanish broom	- *Spartium junceum*
Spear grass, coastal	- *Austrostipa stipoides*
Spear thistle	- *Cirsium vulgare*
Speedwell, slender	- *Veronica gracilis*
Spike rush	- *Eleocharis spp.*
Spinifex dune grass	- *Spinifex sericeus*
Spiny mat-rush	- *Lomandra longifolia*
Spleenwort, shore or blunt	- *Asplenium obtusatum*
Spotted sun orchid	- *Thelymitra ixioides*
Stinkwood	- *Zieria arborescens*
Storksbill, Austral	- *Pelargonium australe*
British	- *Erodium cicutarium*
Sundew, broad-leaved	- *Drosera peltata ssp. auriculata*
dwarf	- *D. pygmaea*
Swainson's pea	- *Swainsonia lessertifolia*
Swamp heath	- *Sprengelia incarnata*
Swamp honey myrtle	- *Melaleuca squamea*
Swamp mazus	- *Mazus pumilio*
Swampweed	- *Selliera radicans*
Sweet bursaria	- *Bursaria spinosa*
Sword grass, common	- *Lepidosperma gladiatum*
narrow	- *L. elatior*
Tassel rope-rush	- *Hypolaena fastigiata*
Taupata or N Z mirror plant	- *Coprosma repens*
Tea-tree, broom or manuka	- *Leptospermum scoparium*
coast	- *L. laevigatum*
prickly	- *L. continentale*
silky	- *L. myrsinoides*
woolly	- *L. lanigerum*
Thistles	- *Carduus, Cirsium* and *Sonchus spp.*
Tree broom heath	- *Monotoca elliptica*
Tree mallow	- *Lavatera arborea*
Tree fern, man	- *Dicksonia antarctica-*
rough	- *Cyathea australis*

Trigger plant, grass-leaved	- *Stylidium graminifolium*
Turquoise berry	- *Drymophila cyanocarpa*
Turtle-grass	- *Amphibolis antarctica*
Tussock, silver	- *Poa poiformis*
Twin leaf, coastal	- *Zygophyllum billardieri*
Victorian heath	- *Epacris impressa*
Violet, ivy-leaved	- *Viola hederacea*
Water buttons	- *Cotula coronopifolia*
Watercress	- *Rorippa nasturtium-aquaticum*
Water fern, hard	- *Blechnum wattsii*
Water milfoil	- *Myriophyllum salsugineum*
Wattle, blackwood	- *Acacia melanoxylon*
coastal	- *A. longifolia var. sophorae*
juniper	- *A. ulicifolia*
prickly Moses	- *A. verticillata*
river	- *A. mucronata*
straight	- *A. stricta*
sweet	- *A. suaveolens*
Wedding bush	- *Ricinocarpos pinifolia*
Westringia, jagged	- *Westringia angustifolia*
Willowherb	- *Epilobium spp.*
Wilsonia	- *Wilsonia rotundifolia* and *W. backhousei*
Winged Spyridium	- *Spyridium vexilliferum*
Wood sorrel, yellow or creeping	- *Oxalis corniculata*
Yellow bartsia	- *Parentucellia viscosa*
Yorkshire fog grass	- *Holcus lanatus*